WHAT
THE
BIBLE
TEACHES

Contributor
NORMAN CRAWFORD

Norman Crawford was born in Canada of Irish immigrant parents. His love for the Lord and for perishing souls led to his commendation to preach the gospel in the USA and Canada in 1946. Since then his ministry of teaching and preaching has widened to include the British Isles.

For ten years he has edited the monthly magazine *Truth and Tidings*. He compiled and contributed to a volume on *The Person of Christ* and recently another book from his pen, *Gathering Unto His Name*, was published and well received on both sides of the Atlantic.

WHAT THE BIBLE TEACHES

with
Authorised Version
of
The Bible

IN ELEVEN VOLUMES
COVERING THE NEW TESTAMENT

VOLUME 7

JOHN RITCHIE LTD
KILMARNOCK, SCOTLAND

ISBN-13: 978 1 904064 44 2
ISBN-10: 1 904064 44 2

WHAT THE BIBLE TEACHES
Copyright © 2000 by John Ritchie Ltd.
40 Beansburn, Kilmarnock, Scotland

www.ritchiechristianmedia.co.uk

Re-typeset and printed 2007

Typeset at John Ritchie Ltd., 40 Beansburn, Kilmarnock.
Printed by Bell and Bain, Glasgow.

CONTENTS

Page

ABBREVIATIONS

AV	Authorised Version of King James Version 1611
JND	New Translation by J.N. Darby 1939
LXX	Septuagint Version of Old Testament
Mft	New Translation by James Moffat 1922
NASB	New American Standard Bible 1960
NEB	New English Bible 1961
Nestle	Nestle (ed.) Novum Testamentum Graece
NIV	New International Version 1973
NT	New Testament
OT	Old Testament
Phps	New Testament in Modern English by J.B. Philips 1962
RSV	Revised Standard Version 1952
RV	Revised Version 1881
TR	Textus Receptus or Received Text
Wey	New Testament in Modern Speech by R.E. Weymouth 1929

PREFACE

They follow the noblest example who seek to open the Scriptures to others, for our Lord Himself did so for those two dejected disciples of Emmaus (Luke 24:32). Whether it is the evangelist "opening and alleging that Christ must needs have suffered and risen from the dead" (Acts 17:3) or the pastor-teacher "expounding ... in all the scriptures the things concerning himself" (Luke 24:27) or stimulating our hope "through the patience and comfort of the scriptures" (Rom 15:4), he serves well in thus giving attendance to the reading of the Scriptures (1 Tim 4:13).

It is of course of equal moment to recognise in the exercise of able men, the continued faithfulness of the risen Head in giving gifts to the Church, in spite of her unfaithfulness. How good to recognise that "the perfecting of the saints ... the work of the ministry...the edifying of the body of Christ" need not be neglected. Every provision has been made to ensure the well-being of the people of God. And every opportunity should be taken by the minister of Christ and those to whom he ministers to ensure that the saints "grow up into him in all things which is the head, even Christ" (Eph 4:15).

At various times in the post-apostolic period, certain teachers have come to prominence, sometimes because they succumbed to error, sometimes because in faithfulness they paid the ultimate price for the truth they had bought and would not sell. Some generations had Calvin and Luther, others Darby and Kelly, but in every generation God's voice is heard. It is important that we hear His voice today and recognise that He does speak through His servants. The contributors to this series of commentaries are all highly-respected expositors among the churches of God. They labour in the Word in the English-speaking world and have been of blessing to many throughout their years of service.

The doctrinal standpoint of the commentaries is based upon the acceptance of the verbal and plenary inspiration of the Scriptures so that their inerrant and infallible teachings are the only rule of conscience. The impeccability of Christ, His virgin birth, vicarious death and bodily resurrection are indeed precious truths worthy of the Christian's defence, and throughout the volumes of this series will be defended. Equally the Rapture will be presented as the hope of the Church. Before the great Tribulation she will be raptured and God's prophetic programme will continue with Jacob's trouble, the public manifestation of Christ and the Millennium of blessing to a restored Israel and the innumerable Gentile multitude in a creation released from the bondage of corruption.

May the sound teaching of these commentaries be used by our God to the blessing of His people. May the searching of the Scriptures characterise all who read them.

The diligence of Mr. J.W. Ferguson and the late Professor J. Heading in proof-reading is gratefully acknowledged. Without such co-operation, the production of this commentary would not have been expedited so readily.

T. WILSON
K. STAPLEY

LUKE

N. Crawford

LUKE
Introduction

1. The Author

The evidence for the authorship of the Gospel according to Luke is closely linked to the book of Acts. They are both letters, addressed to the same Theophilus, about whom we know nothing except that the form of address in Luke suggests a man of dignity and official rank. The name of Luke is not found in either book, but from post-apostolic days until the present time, Luke, the beloved physician (Col 4:14), has been almost universally acknowledged as the author.

Irenaeus ascribes both the Gospel and the Acts to Luke in AD 180. Earlier, external evidence for Luke's authorship may be found in the fact that Marcion, who was excommunicated for his merging of christian and gnostic teachings about AD 144, attributes the Gospel to Luke and identifies him as Paul's companion. In the Anti-Marcionite Prologue to the Third Gospel, written between AD 160 and 180, he is described as coming from Antioch in Syria, having never married, that he might serve the Lord without distraction, and having died in Boeotia at the age of 84. This material is interesting, but does not carry the authority of inspired writings.

Luke was self-effacing and allows us to see very little of himself in the two books of the NT that he wrote. It is inferred that he was a Gentile from the fact that he is not counted in Col 4:7 -11 among the list of names that are said to be '(of the circumcision". Luke wrote a longer Gospel than the other three evangelists and his two books make up a larger portion of the NT than the work of any other

3

NT writer. If he was a Gentile, as we believe, then he was uniquely honoured, for he might well be the only Gentile writer of any portion of Scripture.

His writing is of high literary quality, suggesting that he was well-educated. James H. Moulton, in his *Grammar of New Testament Greek*, describes Luke as a Greek who was superb in both his style and structure, varying his style to give the most graphic expression to each scene. Many language scholars point to his classical and polished preface as evidence of his skill in the Greek language, but it is also evident throughout his writings. He uses almost three hundred words that are found only in Luke (see Appendix 2), many of which only occur once. Some of these are compounds of well known words, but the use of them shows the extent of his vocabulary. In the first chapter, no less than twenty-six unique words occur. In Acts 27, there are about seventy words that are only used by him.

Paul, who tells us that Luke was a physician, had a particular love for him, and found in him a worthy companion. Much has been written about Luke's medical language, but the question remains if any special technical medical language even existed in Luke's day. However, there is ample proof of his interest in medical things. Evidence of this is seen in the way the birth accounts are given, as well as in his descriptions of sickness such as "a great fever" (4:38); a man "full of leprosy" (5:12), and a woman whose eighteen years of sickness had left her "bowed together, and could in no wise lift up herself" (13:11).

As a historian, he is deeply respected for his exact accounts, his geographical accuracy and his care in giving correct titles to political figures. Sir Wm. Ramsay, in a lifetime of archaeological studies, moved from a position of being extremely sceptical of Luke's reliability to an acceptance of Luke's geography and history as being amazingly accurate. This does not surprise those who accept the Scriptures as being inerrant.

2. Luke and Paul

There are four passages in the book of Acts where the third person narrative form is replaced by the first person plural. From these passages (16:10-17; 20:5-21:8; 27:1- 28:16), we learn that Luke joined Paul, Silas and Timothy at Troas and travelled with them to Philippi. Following the change back to the third person plural at the time Paul and Silas were arrested and thrust into the inner dungeon, it is evident that Luke did not share their imprisonment, nor did he travel with them to Thessalonica (Acts 17:1). We cannot state dogmatically that he lived at Philippi during this period, but it may be true. Seven years later, he sailed with Paul from Philippi on the journey that took them to Troas, Miletus and Jerusalem. We do not know how Luke spent the two years when Paul was a prisoner in Caesarea, but we know that he accompanied Paul on the voyage to Rome, and gives us graphic descriptions of the voyage, storm and shipwreck (Acts 27). At the very close of his life, Paul wrote tenderly, "Only Luke is with me" (2 Tim 4:11).

Paul's reference to Luke as the beloved physician in Col 4:14 indicates an appreciation of personal, tender care from his hands, probably during his journeys as well as during his imprisonments. Although Luke must have exhibited loving care and skill as a physician, his service was much wider than medical assistance; he was also a fellow-labourer with Paul (Philem 24), and as an evangelist, he writes a Gospel that is full of evangelistic appeal. Many have drawn attention to the difference between the subject matter of Luke and Paul's letters, but this is accounted for by the difference in purpose. However, in the examples we have of Paul's preaching, there seems very little similarity to Luke's material, so he was not dependent on Paul, but must have been most familiar with the way Paul preached the gospel to Gentiles. Some of this surely is reflected in Luke's treatment of gospel material.

As an evangelist for over forty years, the present writer has taken an account of his preaching, and has discovered that he has preached more often from Luke than from any other book in the Bible.

3. The Date of Writing

We know that the book of Acts was written later than the Gospel of Luke; the earlier writing is mentioned in the later one (Acts 1: 1,2). We can also be certain that, when Luke wrote, the destruction of Jerusalem and its temple in AD 70 had not yet taken place. Also, there is no suggestion in either book that it had yet become a crime to be a christian. Luke describes bitter persecution from the Jerusalem Sanhedrin and Jewish communities in the various places in which the gospel was preached, but Gentile officials often dismissed the charges that were made against the christian missionaries. This appears, in the eyes of many scholars, to date Luke's writings prior to Nero's anti- christian policy that followed the great fire in Rome in AD 64.

Acts closes with Paul as a prisoner in Rome, yet allowed to live in his own rented house under the guard of a soldier. The writing of the Acts took place before Paul's release and his final arrest and imprisonment. No event is described that took place after AD 62. These considerations indicate that the Gospel was likely written about AD 6 1. There seems to be no valid reasons for accepting a later date. It is an interesting suggestion that it was written during the two years of Paul's imprisonment at Caesarea.

4. The Synoptics

Matthew, Mark and Luke are called the Synoptic Gospels because they share much of the material that makes up gospel truth; yet there is no evidence of dependence of one writer on the others. It can be shown that a major part of Mark appears in Luke. Luke contains 1149 verses, and up to 250 of these are shared in some degree with Matthew, though they are not found in Mark. There are about 520 verses in Luke that are not found in Matthew or Mark. Much more could be written on this subject, but more important to us is the fact that each Gospel is unique, having its own distinct emphasis and handling even the material that is shared with the other Gospels in a manner that suits the Holy Spirit's purpose for each one.

Luke plainly tells us that he had at his disposal both written and oral accounts of the material that he was to write (1:1-4). Many had recorded the events that make up the gospel story. This is not a denial of the Holy Spirit's inspiration or His superintendency of all that Luke wrote. He is saying that he was acquainted with the accounts given by eyewitnesses and ministers of the Word, yet he " had perfect understanding of all things from the very first" (1:3), or "having investigated all things carefully from the beginning" (NASB). The Greek word *anōthen*, which the AV here translates, " from the beginning", is used by Luke to indicate that first, he searched the material to its source, and second, he wrote an account from the very beginning rather than one that was fragmentary.

5. The Purpose of Writing

Few of the penmen of the Holy Scriptures state their purpose for writing with greater clarity than Luke. He begins by telling Theophilus, " that thou mightest know the certainty of those things, wherein thou hast been instructed" (1:4). Luke is stating his purpose to give an historically accurate account of the birth, life, death and resurrection of the Lord Jesus. In both his books, he is giving a defence of the faith, first, "of all that Jesus began both to do and to teach, until the day in which he was taken up" (Acts 1: 1,2), and then, a further defence of the Holy Spirit's activities during the early days of testimony. Luke's purpose is apologetic, in the sense of vindicating and defending divine revelation in the Person of the Son of man and in the activities of the Holy Spirit.

We cannot read the mind of Luke and describe all the thoughts that he had as he so ably wrote this wonderful Gospel of the tender, sympathising Saviour of lost sinners, but we can say from the finished product what has been accomplished. His gospel message is complete and full, true to every gospel doctrine.

6. Major Themes

Under this title, we want to look at the unique character of this Gospel. Luke shares with the other evangelists the one blessed theme of the Person of Christ, but according to the divine plan, he traces the pathway of the perfect Man on earth, from the manger of Bethlehem until He ascended up to the mansions from which He came.

Every careful reader of the four Gospels is aware that each has a distinctive character. According to our own measure, we have appreciated the glory of the

Sovereign in Matthew's account of the Son of David; the glory of the unfailing Servant in Mark's account of the Son of toil and John's majestic presentation of the glory of the perfect Saviour, the Son of God. Luke presents to us in unparalleled beauty, the Son of man, the tender Sympathiser.

In a unique way, Luke displays the grace of the Person of Christ (2:40). Luke agrees with John, "the law was given ... but grace and truth came by Jesus Christ" (John 1:17). The evangelists do not describe grace, because grace came, and they describe Him. Luke occupies our hearts with the gentleness of a glorious Man, a Man whose inmost being was full of joy, and yet was truly the One who bore "our griefs, and carried our sorrows" (Isa 53:4), and earned, as none other ever has, or could, the unique title, "the Man of sorrows".

Therefore, we want briefly to outline the major themes of the Gospel of Luke.

i. The Saviour of Lost Sinners. Luke uses "save", "Saviour" and "salvation" twenty-one times, more often than appears in any other Gospel (1:47, 69, 71, 77; 2:11, 30; 3:6; 6:9; 7:50; 8:12; 9:24,56; 13:23; 17:33; 18:26; 18:42; 19:9,10; 23:35,37,39). He proclaims that this salvation is for the lost, the poor, the outcast, the sinner who is at a guilty distance from God, in fact, " afar off", so Luke is the gospel of the far country, and has a special meaning for sinners of the Gentiles. "The Son of man is come to seek and to save that which was lost" (19:10), would make a fitting title to this Gospel.

Although this salvation is universal in its offer, embracing a Gentile world (2:32; 4:25-27; 7:2-10; 13:29; 24:47), yet it is very personal and must be received by personal faith (1:45; 7:9; 7:50; 8:48; 17:19; 18:42).

ii. The Lordship of Christ. In all four Gospels, Jesus Christ is Lord, but He is given the title of Lord one hundred times in Luke, seventy-two times in Matthew, seventeen times in Mark and forty-four times in John. It is significant, then, that when the angel announced His birth to the shepherds, He is proclaimed as "a Saviour, which is Christ the Lord" (2:11), and after His resurrection, when the women came to the tomb, Luke records, "they ... found not the body of the Lord Jesus" (24:3).

iii. The Day of Salvation. Luke frequently uses the words "now" and "today" to emphasise the necessity of receiving God's salvation during "the acceptable year of the Lord" (4: 19) before "the day of vengeance of our God" (Isa 61:2) falls on sinners. The nearness of God's judgment on sin and sinners is often described (3:9,17; 10:9,11; 21:28).

iv. The Joy of Salvation. Gladness, joy and rejoicing are major themes throughout this Gospel (twenty-four times). From the joy at the birth of John the Baptist (1: 14), Luke moves to the "good tidings of great joy" at the birth of the Saviour (1:19,47; 2:10). He then writes of joy in persecution (6:23); the joy of believers in knowing that their names are written in heaven (10:20); the joy of the Lord in His own (10:21), and the special joy relating to the lost being found (15:5,6,7,9,10,32), and finishes with the great joy of the witnesses to the resurrection and ascension of their Lord. In keeping with this theme of joy is Luke's account of the song of Mary (1:46-55), the song of Zacharias (1:67-79), the song of the angels (2:14) and the song of Simeon (2:29-32).

Luke wrote a Gospel of joy. Even though he traces the pathway of the Man of sorrows that led Him to the cross, he never once describes the Lord as being sorrowful, not even in the garden with all its agony. This is in contrast to Matt 26:3 7, " He began to be sorrowful and very heavy", and Mark 14:34, "My soul is exceeding sorrowful". Matthew emphasises the royal majesty of the Lion of Judah's tribe; Mark portrays the patient, steady service of the ox; John gives us the lofty heights of the eagle, but it is left to Luke to give us the face of a Man (see Ezek 1:10). There is a face, which only to behold is an eternity of joy and bliss, even though it is the blessed face of "the Man of sorrows".

Three creatures from the animal kingdom illustrate the themes of the other Gospels, but the theme of Luke is illustrated by a Man. However, the OT does not leave us without an illustration from the animal kingdom for Luke. It is the Gospel of the Dove, the gentle mourning dove of Lev 1: 14-16. It is impossible to read Luke's account and not be moved by the gentleness and meekness of the true, impeccable humanity of Christ.

v. The Journeys of the Son of Man.
Luke describes the journeys of the Son of man from Nazareth, where He was brought up, to every town and village of Galilee to which He carried the gospel. It is worthy of note that He did not send His disciples to Galilee as His witnesses (Acts 1:8), for He had already covered it on foot (Luke 8:1).

Luke takes a major part of his Gospel, from 9:51 to 19:41, to tell of the journey toward Jerusalem, where He would be put to shame and nailed to the tree. With great care he describes the short journey from Pilate's judgment hall, until "they were come to the place, which is called Calvary, where they crucified him" (23:27,33).

Luke then gives us a longer journey to Emmaus as the risen Christ expounded all the Scriptures concerning Himself to two disciples with burning hearts that walked with Him.

Finally, he describes the journey that took Him back to the glories of heaven, from which in grace He had descended (see 19:12). When He led the little company out as far as Bethany, "it came to pass, while he blessed them, he was parted from them, and carried up into heaven" (24:51).

In addition to these historical journeys, there are other journeys that appear in the parables such as the journey of the Samaritan (10:33); the Shepherd going "after that which is lost, until he find it" (15:4); the "certain nobleman (who) went into a far country" (19:12), who "when he was returned, having received the kingdom" (19:15), called his servants to account.

vi. **The Prayers of the Perfect Man.** Luke's descriptions of the praying Christ suit well his theme of the perfect manhood of our Lord. The Lord Jesus prayed often, but only Luke tells us that He was praying at His baptism when the Holy Spirit descended on Him (3:21). When great multitudes were drawn to Him because of His healing power, Luke says, "he withdrew himself into the wilderness and prayed" (5:16). He prayed before making choice of the twelve disciples (6:12), and even when the disciples were with Him, Luke says, "he was alone praying" (9:18), for He communed with His Father in secret, unhindered by their presence. Only Luke tells us that He prayed on the Mount of Transfiguration (9:29) before "the fashion of his countenance was altered". The disciples were well aware of His prayer habits, for they waited until He had ceased praying before they asked Him to teach them how to pray (11:1). Luke 11 contains His special instructions to His own about prayer and ch.18 begins with two parables about prayer. Luke's unique description of the earnest prayer of Christ in the garden when "his sweat was as it were great drops of blood falling down to the ground" is the most vivid and graphic in the Gospel records.

vii. **The power of the Holy Spirit.** Luke's second book has well been called "the Acts of the Holy Spirit". In his Gospel, the Holy Spirit is the power displayed in the events of the birth and life of the Lord Jesus. The promise to Zacharias was that John would be "filled with the Holy Ghost, even from his mother's womb" (1:15). He attributes the miraculous conception of Mary to the overshadowing Holy Spirit (1:35). Elisabeth was filled with the Spirit when Mary came to visit her (1:41). The Spirit revealed to Simeon that he would "not see death, before he had seen the Lord's Christ" (2:26), and it was by the Spirit that he came into the temple at the time when Joseph and Mary brought in the child Jesus" (2:27).

John's witness to Christ was, "He shall baptize with the Holy Ghost" (3:16). Full of the Holy Spirit, the Lord Jesus "returned from Jordan, and was led by the Spirit into the wilderness" (4:1). When He stood up in the synagogue in Nazareth, He found the place where it was written in Isaiah, "The Spirit of the Lord is upon me, because he hath anointed me to preach the gospel to the poor" (4:18). After telling the disciples that they should rejoice because their names were written in heaven, "In that hour Jesus rejoiced in spirit. . ." (10:21). This joy in His own spirit is a result of being filled with the Holy Spirit. He promised that the Spirit would be given to the one who asked (11:13), and foretold that the Spirit would endue His own "with power from on high" (24:49) on the day of Pentecost.

viii. **The Use of Contrasts.** There are frequent warnings against trusting in riches (12:21), and it is to the poor that the gospel is preached (7:22). Many contrasts are drawn between the rich and the poor (1:52,53; 6:20-24; 7:22; 8:14; 12:15-21; 14:12-24; 16:19-31; 18:18-30; 19:1-10; 21:1-4). His frequent use of pairs is illustrated in his comparison between Christ and John, but he more often contrasted the one with the other as in the case of Mary and Martha, the Pharisees and publicans, the rich man and Lazarus, Peter and Judas and the thieves on either side of the cross.

ix. The Gentle Service of Women. Luke mentions widows twelve times in contrast to only four mentions in Matthew and Mark, and none in John. He wrote of the widowhood of Anna (2:37), and when writing of the feeding of Elijah in the famine, he said, "she was a woman that was a widow" (4:26). Only Luke records the raising of the young man at Nain, and tells us that he was " the only son of his mother, and she was a widow" (7:12). It was a widow who petitioned the unjust judge (18:1-6), and a widow that the Lord commended as He saw her casting two mites into the temple treasury (21:2).

Luke gives detailed accounts of the devotion of women. Elisabeth (1:5), Mary, His mother (1:26), Anna (2:36), the grateful woman who wept at His feet (7:37-50), Martha and Mary of Bethany (10:38-42), the women from Galilee who ministered unto Him of their substance (8:1-3), those who wept as He went out to Calvary (23:27-31) and the witnesses to the empty tomb (24:1-10) are all part of Luke's careful record of the activity of women. In keeping with the other Gospels, Luke never records an abuse against Christ by a woman.

x. The Praise and Glory of God. Throughout this Gospel, the praise of God and ascribing glory to Him take a prominent place. Mary began her praise with the words "My soul doth magnify the Lord" (1:46). Zacharias began his praise by saying, "Blessed be the Lord God of Israel" (1:68). The language of the heavenly host was, "Glory to God in the highest" (2:14). When the shepherds had seen the infant Saviour, they returned, "glorifying and praising God for all the things that they had heard and seen" (2:20). Simeon "blessed God" (2:28) when he received the child Christ in his arms. When the Lord healed the palsied man, the people "were all amazed and glorified God" (5:25,26; see comment). The people of Nain, when they saw the widow's son raised to life, "glorified God" (7:16). The woman bowed down for eighteen years "glorified God" (13:13) when she was made straight. It was with a loud voice that the Samaritan leper (17:15-19) glorified God when he was healed. The blind man near Jericho "received his sight, and followed him, glorifying God: and all the people, when they saw it, gave praise unto God" (18:43). In 19:37, "the whole multitude of the disciples began to rejoice and praise God with a loud voice". They blessed the King and gave glory to God. Therefore, it is in keeping with this theme that Luke closes his Gospel with the disciples returning to Jerusalem from the mount from which Christ had ascended "with great joy: And (they) were continually in the temple, praising and blessing God" (24:52,53).

7. Bibliography

Alford, Henry. *The Greek New Testament,* Moody Press, 1958.

Barnes, Albert. *Notes on the New Testament,* Baker, Grand Rapids, MI 1953.

Bellett, J.G. *The Evangelists, Meditations on the Four Gospels,* W.H. Broom, London, 1882.

Bellett, J.G. *Notes of Meditations on the Gospel of Luke,* Bible Truth Publishers, Oak Park, IL.

Blaiklock, E.M. *Bible Study Books, Luke,* Wm. Eerdmans, 1966.

Boice, J.M. *The Parable of Jesus,* Moody Press, 1983.

Bruce, F.F. *The Hard Sayings of Jesus,* Hodder and Stoughton, London, 1983.

Burton, Henry. *The Gospel of Luke,* Hodder and Stoughton, NY.

Creed, J.M. *The Gospel of Luke,* MacMillan and Co. London, 1930.

Edersheim, Alfred. *Jesus the Messiah,* Wm. Eerdmans, 1889.

Ellicott, C.J. *Historical Lectures on the Life of Our Lord Jesus Christ,* John W. Parker and Son, London, 1860.

Erdman, C.R. *The Gospel of Luke,* Baker, Grand Rapids, 1966.

Garvie, A.E. *The Joy of Finding, An Exposition of Luke 15:11-32,* T.&T. Clark, 1914.

Gideon, V.E. *Luke, A Study Guide Commentary,* Zondervan, Grand Rapids, 1967.

Godet, F.L. *Commentary on the Gospel of Luke,* Zondervan, Grand Rapids, Classic Library.

Gooding, David. *Windows on Paradise, 14 Studies in the Gospel of Luke,* Everyday Publications, 1976.

Gooding, David. *According to Luke,* Inter-Varsity Press, Leicester, Wm. B. Eerdmans, 1987.

Gunn, James. *Christ, The Fulness of the Godhead,* Loizeaux, Neptune, NJ 1982.

Guthrie, Donald. *New Testament Introduction,* IVP, The Tyndale Press, 1965.

Harlow, R.E. *The Perfect Man, Studies in Luke,* Everyday Publications, 1976.

Heading, John. *Luke's Life of Christ,* Everyday Publications, 1981.

Heading, J.; Paisley, H. *What the Bible Teaches,* volume 2, General Editors Wilson, T.; Stapley, K., J. Ritchie Ltd, Kilmarnock, 1984.

Hendricksen, Wm. *New Testament Commentary, Gospel According to Luke,* Baker, Grand Rapids, 1978.

Howley, G.C.D. *A New Testament Commentary,* Howley, Bruce, Ellison, Zondervan Pub. Grand Rapids, 1973.

Ironside, H.A. *Addresses on the Gospel of Luke,* Loizeaux, Neptune, NJ 1982.

Jukes, Andrew. *Characteristic Differences in the Four Gospels,* James Nisbet, London, 1988.

Kelly, William. *An Exposition of the Gospel of Luke,* Pickering and Inglis, London.

Kittel and Friedrich, *Theological Dictionary of the New Testament,* Translator and Editor, Geoffrey W. Bromiley, Eerdmans, 1969.

Liefeld, Walter L. *The Expositor's Bible Commentary,* General Editor, Frank E. Gaebelein, Vol.8, Zondervan, Grand Rapids, 1984.

Littleproud, J.R. *Gospel Pictures from Luke's Pen,* Gospel Folio Press, Grand Rapids, 1938.

Luck, G.C. *Luke, The Gospel of the Son of Man,* Moody Press, 1960.

Machen, J. Gresham, *The Virgin Birth of Christ,* Baker, 1965.

Manson, Wm. *The Gospel of Luke,* Hodder and Stoughton, 1948.

Marshall, I.H. *Luke, Historian and Theologian,* Zondervan, Grand Rapids, 1971.

Miller, D.G. *The Layman's Bible Commentary, Luke,* John Knox Press, 1971.

Morgan, G. Campbell, *The Gospel According to Luke,* Revell, Westwood, NJ, 1928.

Morgan, G. Campbell, *The Parable of the Father's Heart,* Baker, Grand Rapids, 1981.

Morris, Leon, *Tyndale New Testament Commentaries,* Eerdmans, 1984.

Pentecost, J. Dwight, *A Harmony of the Words and Works of Jesus Christ,* Zondervan, Grand Rapids, 1981.

Pentecost, J. Dwight, *The Words and Works of Jesus Christ,* Zondervan, 1982.

Plumtre, E.H. *The Commentary for Schools, Luke,* Cassell, Petter, Galpin and Co. London, 1876.

Plummer, Alfred. *Gospel According to Luke,* T. and T. Clark, Edinburgh, 1986.

Ramsay, W.M. *Luke, The Physician,* Hodder and Stoughton, London, 1908.

Ramsay, W.M. *Was Christ Born at Bethlehem?* Hodder and Stoughton, London, 1898.

Ridout, Samuel. *The Four Gospels,* Bible Truth Library, NY.

Robertson, A.T. *Word Pictures in the New Testament, Luke,* Broadman Press, 1930.

Robertson, A.T. A *Translation of Luke's Gospel,* George H. Doran Co. NY 1923.

Robinson, J. Armitage, *Study of the Gospels,* Longmans, Green and Co. London, 1903.

Ross, J.M.E. *The Gospel According to Luke, A Devotional Commentary,* The Religious Tract Society, London.

Ryle, J.C. *Expository Thoughts on the Gospels, St. Luke,* Vol.2, R. Carter, NY 1976.

Schofield, A.T. *The Journeys of Jesus Christ, the Son of God,* Pickering and Inglis, London.

Scroggie, W. Graham. *Luke and John,* Ark Pub. PA 1984.

Scroggie, W. Graham. *A Guide to the Gospels,* Revell, Westwood, NJ 1962.

Thomas, W.H. Griffith. *Outline Studies in Luke,* Kregel Publications, Grand Rapids, 1984.

Stuart, C.E. *From Advent to Advent, An Outline of the Gospel According to Luke,* E. Marlborough and Co. London.

Stonehouse, Ned B. *Origins of the Synoptic Gospels,* Eerdmans, 1963.

Stonehouse, Ned B. *The Witness of the Synoptic Gospels to Christ,* Baker, 1979.

Tinsley, E.J. *The Cambridge Bible Commentary, Luke,* University Press, 1965.

Trench, R.C. *Studies in the Gospels,* Baker, 1979.

Tyndale, *The Illustrated Bible Dictionary.* 3 volumes, IVP 1980.

Van Doren, Wm. H. *The Gospel of Luke,* two volumes in one, Kregel Pub. Grand Rapids, 1981.

Vincent, Marvin R. *Word Studies in the New Testament,* Vol.2, The Gospels, Eerdmans.

Walvoord, John F. and Zuck, Roy B. *The Bible Knowledge Commentary,* Books, Wheaton, IL 1983.

Walvoord, John F. *Jesus Christ, Our Lord,* Moody Press, 1969.

Wilcock, Michael. *Saviour of the World, The Message of Luke's Gospel,* IVP, Downer's Grove, IL 1979.

Zahn, Theodor. *Introduction to the New Testament,* Kregel, Grand Rapids, 1953.

8. Outline

I. *The Birth Narratives*   1:1-2:52
    Chapter 1:
    1. Preface and the Purpose of the Book   1:1-4
    2. The Birth of John the Baptist Foretold   1:5-25
    3. The Promise of the Birth of the Lord Jesus   1:26-38
    4. The Visit of Mary to Elizabeth and Mary's Praise   1:39-56
    5. The Birth of John   1:57-66
    6. The Song of Zacharias   1:67-80
    Chapter 2:
    7. The Birth of the Lord Jesus   2:1-7
    8. The Message of the Angels to the Shepherds   2:8-20
    9. The Circumcision and Naming of the Lord   2:21-24
    10. The Godly Simeon and His Prophesy   2:25-35
    11. Anna, "She Spake of Him"   2:36-38
    12. The Silent Years at Nazareth   2:39-40
    13. The Boy of Twelve in the Temple   2:41-52

II. *The Preparation for Public Ministry*   3:1-4:13
    Chapter 3:
    1. The Ministry of John the Baptist   3:1-20
    2. The Baptism of the Lord Jesus   3:21-22
    3. The Genealogy of the Lord Jesus   3:23-28
    Chapter 4:
    4. The Temptation in the Wilderness   4:1-13

III. *The Ministry of the Lord Jesus in Galilee*   4:14-9:50
    1. The Ministry at Nazareth   4:14-30
    2. The Ministry at Capernaum   4:31-37
    3. The Healing of Peter's Wife's Mother   4:38-44

Text and Exposition

I. The Birth Narratives (1:1-2:52)

1. *Preface and the Purpose of the Book*
1:1-4

v.1 "Forasmuch as many have taken in hand to set forth in order a declaration of those things which are most surely believed among us,

v.2 Even as they delivered them unto us, which from the beginning were eyewitnesses, and ministers of the word;

v.3 It seemed good to me also, having had perfect understanding of all things from the very first, to write unto thee in order, most excellent Theophilus,

v.4 That thou mightest know the certainty of those things, wherein thou hast been instructed."

Luke's preface is made up of one long sentence, written in the accepted classical Greek style which reflects Luke's education and tells us a little of Theophilus to whom he addressed his two-volume work. The formal nature of this introduction preserves us from thinking that Luke is writing a personal letter. He is well aware that he is writing a true Gospel.

1 Luke wants his reader, Theophilus, to know that the carefully composed account that he is writing is drawn from original sources, but that he is not the only one who drew up such a record, "many have taken in hand to set forth in order a declaration of those things which are most surely believed among us". Although we cannot exclude from these "many" accounts the written records that preceded the writing of this Gospel, such as Matthew and Mark as well as other accounts which, although accurate, were not intended to be preserved for us, we should note the fact that the words "to set forth in order" refer to the gathering up of the material, rather than the writing down of it, which is the meaning of the words of v.3, "to write unto thee in order".

The word translated "declaration" is *diēgēsis* and is only found here in the NT. W.E. Vine points out that it means "narrative" (RV) rather than "declaration". It is a description of the narrative form in which Luke will write the story that follows. What a story it is! The gospel story, unparalleled in all of speech or literature.

"The things that are received with full assurance among us" (Weymouth) refers not to a subjective acceptance of the truth of the narrative by Luke and his companions, although this is involved in the statement, but to a fulfilling of all events as they were foretold, or in accordance with the highest hopes of those who had traced the story from its beginning. This narrative was totally unlike the Greek tragedies that ended disastrously because of fate or a tragic flaw in the leading character, for this story led on to triumph and joy. Its chief character is proven to be all that He claimed and much more worthy than tongue can ever tell, and best of all, it is true.

2 Those who drew up in order the gospel material were original eyewitnesses and servants of the Word. Of the five or more synonyms that could have been used for "servant", Luke uses *hupēretēs*, which means one who acts under the direction of a superior, waiting on the command from above. These were servants who attended on the word of their Lord and when they had received it, they declared it accurately, in order and in keeping with its spiritual meaning.

The word *archē* ("from the beginning") is used in such familiar passages as: "The beginning of the gospel" (Mark 1:1); "In the beginning was the Word" (John 1:1); "Now ye Philippians know also, that in the beginning of the gospel..." (Phil 4:15); " who is the beginning, the firstborn from the dead..." (Col 1:18). These references use "beginning" in four different ways. Mark uses it for the beginning of the public ministry of the Lord; John uses it to apply to the eternity of the Word; to the Philippians, Paul uses it for the time the gospel came to them; to the Colossians, he uses it to describe the beginning of the new creation in the resurrected Christ. The word is the same, but the context dictates its meaning. Luke uses it here to express the fact that his account begins not with the public ministry of Christ, as in Mark's Gospel, but his record goes back to the birth accounts of John the Baptist and then of the Lord Himself. So Luke's " from the beginning" should be understood as the beginning of the events as he writes them. He was privileged to have eyewitness accounts of the wonderful events from the birth narratives to the empty tomb and the sight of the risen Lord, all the material that makes up his Gospel. *Autoptēs* ("eyewitness") is found only here in the NT and means just what our English word implies, to see with one's own eyes.

Some may have difficulty in understanding the relationship of previous records to inspired Scriptures. Their question is usually phrased like this, "Why would the Holy Spirit allow an inspired writer to research sources and gather material when every word of Scripture is from God? " The difficulty is in the mind of the questioner, for he is confusing the instrument with the product. God used many different methods to disclose His truth (Heb 1: 1), but the doctrine of inspiration applies to the writing of Scripture. The Holy Spirit superintended the entire operation so that what was produced was the word of God written, without error (2 Pet 1:21).

3 "Also" informs us that Luke's account will agree with the former accounts in their orderly presentation and their content. There is no suggestion that Luke will be correcting or purging his sources, for he is not referring to unreliable records. The witnesses had first hand experience of the facts that they narrated.

The opening phrase of this verse is the explanation of the purpose of the writer. " Many have taken in hand" (v. 1) should be linked with " it seemed good to me also" (v.3). J. Heading comments, " this being a divinely-given motivation to write". Luke's desire to write was spiritual, so that with the result before us we can confidently affirm that the Holy Spirit begat the desire and superintended all. that he wrote. However, there are those who see in the immediate context nothing more than that Luke is saying that he desired to write a complete and orderly account. Without doubt, he accomplished this purpose, but there seems to be evidence here that Luke was aware that he was only an instrument under the control of the Holy Spirit. Of course this was true, whether Luke is stating it here or not.

In the phrase "having had perfect understanding of all things", the thought conveyed is of tracing events, or as A.T. Robertson has expressed it, "following along by the side of the events". The word *akribōs* ("perfect") means to be "accurate" (JND). The entire sentence, including the two expressions "all things" and "perfect", expresses the thought of the fulness of his account. *Akribōs* is from *akron*-the highest point. It is used only five times in the NT. Luke uses it in Acts 18:25 to describe how Apollos "taught diligently the things of the Lord". The AV translates it "diligently" in Matt 2:8; " circumspectly" in Eph 5:15, and "perfectly" in 1 Thess 5:2.

Anōthen ("from the very first") is found thirteen times in the NT. Matthew and Mark use it for the rending of the veil in the temple, where it is rendered "from the top" (Matt 27:5 1; Mark 15:38). In John, it is translated "again" (3:3; 3:7) and "from above" (3:31; 19:11). James used it three times (James 1:17; 3:15,17) in the sense of John 3:31, "from above". The only other time Luke used it was to record Paul's words before King Agrippa, "The Jews, which knew me from the beginning" (Acts 26:5). It is likely that he used it in this same sense in his Gospel preface. The subject here is the beginning of the gospel records. A.T. Robertson and many others link this beginning to the birth narratives and Luke's unique accounts of the infancy of Christ. Luke had "perfect understanding of all things from the very first".

Kathexēs ("in order") has generated much discussion and varying opinions. Some understand it to be a moral order, others see in this expression a thematic order. However, Luke generally follows a chronological order, even though at times a topical one can be traced in the section 9:51 to 18:10, much of which is unique to this Gospel.

Theophilus' name means "loved of God" or "friend of God", and the term "most excellent Theophilus", as Sir Wm. Ramsay suggests, is a title of high office, such as "Your Excellency". In Acts 23:26, Claudius Lysias, in a letter to Felix, uses this same form of address to "the most excellent governor" (see also Acts 24:3; 26:25). This title, missing from the preface to the Acts, has caused some to conjecture that he may have lost his office because of his faith in Christ. There are those who believe that the phrase "most excellent Theophilus" may mean nothing more than that he was a middle class Roman citizen who was esteemed by Luke.

4 "That thou mightest know" is not to suggest that Theophilus had no knowledge of the gospel. The close of this verse makes it clear that he had already been instructed. The aorist, subjunctive, active verb *ginōskō* ("to know") is prefixed by epi, which means that Luke desired him to have full knowledge in addition to what he already had.

Tēn asphaleian ("the certainty") comes from *sphallō* ("to slip, totter or fall"). The *logos* ("things") are words he is receiving from Luke that will make him know that this truth is based on "an impregnable historical foundation" (A. Plummer). The "things most surely believed" (v.1) begin with the virgin birth and are revealed in the amazing events of the life and ministry of Christ, climaxing in the uplifted cross, the empty tomb, the resurrected Lord and His ascension to heaven (ch.24). In contrast to the uncertainty that accompanies the best products of human reasoning, here is a solid foundation of divine truth on which we can plant our feet with the blessed assurance that this rock will never shake.

In the phrase " wherein thou hast been instructed", *katēcheō* ("instructed") is a word that has been anglicised into catechise and catechism, so commonly used in many religious systems.

The high literary quality of these four verses has been noted by many scholars: "This preface by Luke is in splendid literary Koine and is not surpassed by those in any Greek writer" (A.T. Robertson).

2.   *The Birth of John the Baptist Foretold*
   1:5-25

v.5   "There was in the days of Herod, the king of Judaea, a certain priest named Zacharias, of the course of Abia: and his wife *was* of the daughters of Aaron, and her name *was* Elisabeth.

v.6   And they were both righteous before God, walking in all the commandments and ordinances of the Lord blameless.

v.7   And they had no child, because that Elisabeth was barren, and they both were *now* well stricken in years.

V.8   And it came to pass, that while he executed the priest's office before God in the order of his course,

V.9   According to the custom of the priest's office, his lot was to burn incense when he went into the temple of the Lord.

V.10 And the whole multitude of the people were praying without at the time of incense.

V.11 And there appeared unto him an angel of the Lord standing on the right side of the altar of incense.

v.12 And when Zacharias saw *him*, he was troubled, and fear fell upon him.

v.13 But the angel said unto him, Fear not, Zacharias: for thy prayer is heard; and thy wife Elisabeth shall bear thee a son, and thou shalt call his name John.

v.14 And thou shalt have joy and gladness; and many shall rejoice at his birth.

v.15 For he shall be great in the sight of the Lord, and shall drink neither wine nor strong drink; and he shall be filled with the Holy Ghost, even from his mother's womb.

v.16 And many of the children of Israel shall he turn to the Lord their God.

v.17 And he shall go before him in the spirit and power of Elias, to turn the hearts of the fathers to the children, and the disobedient to the wisdom of the just; to make ready a people prepared for the Lord.

v.18 And Zacharias said unto the angel, Whereby shall I know this? for I am an old man, and my wife well stricken in years.

V.19 And the angel answering said unto him, I am Gabriel, that stand in the presence of God; and am sent to speak unto thee, and to shew thee these glad tidings.

v.20 And, behold, thou shalt be dumb, and not able to speak, until the day that these things shall be performed, because thou believest not my words, which shall be fulfilled in their season.

v.21 And the people waited for Zacharias, and marvelled that he tarried so long in the temple.

v.22 And when he came out, he could not speak unto them: and they perceived that he had seen a vision in the temple: for he beckoned unto them, and remained speechless.

v.23 And it came to pass, that, as soon as the days of his ministration were accomplished, he departed to his own house.

v.24 And after those days his wife Elisabeth conceived, and hid herself five months, saying,

v.25 Thus hath the Lord dealt with me in the days wherein he looked on *me*, to take away my reproach among men."

5   Herod the Great was the king of the Jews from 40-4 BC. His father, Antipater, a Jew of Idumaean descent was appointed procurator of Judaea by Julius Caesar in 47 BC. Herod, after three years of conflict with Antigonus, a Hasmonaean, "was able to make his title effective, and for thirty-three years governed Judaea as a friend and ally of Rome" (F.F. Bruce). He was not well loved by his Jewish subjects. Although he professed to be a Jew by religion, and rebuilt the temple in Jerusalem at great cost, he also built temples to pagan gods in other parts of his domain and was not trusted by priest or Pharisee. His destruction of the Hasmonaean priestly family, the Maccabees, great heroes of Israel in the days of Antiochus Epiphanes, the Syrian ruler, one of Israel's cruellest oppressors, was never forgiven by loyal Jews. His destruction of the children, from two years old and younger, in Bethlehem and all the region around it (Matt 2:16) was very much in keeping with his character.

Zacharias was of the priestly course of Abijah. The multiplication of the priestly line made it necessary to divide the priests into twenty-four divisions.

This happened in the days of David (1 Chron 24:1-6), and was confirmed later by Solomon (2 Chron 8:14). Only four divisions came back from Babylon with Zerubbabel (Ezra 2:36-39), but they were divided again into twenty-four divisions and given the old names. Abia was not one of the four that returned from Babylon, nevertheless one of the new division of twenty-four orders was given the original name.

6   It was in a day of general departure from God among His professed people, in contrast to the conditions of the day, that there were a man and woman who are described as righteous and blameless, "walking in all the commandments and ordinances of the Lord" (v.6). These same words were written about Abraham (Gen 26:5) and Jehoshaphat (2 Chron 17:4, LXX). The presence of a tiny, faithful remnant, made up of such people as Zacharias and Elisabeth, Mary and Joseph, Anna and Simeon reminds us of the closing words of OT revelation, "Then they that feared the Lord spake often one to another: and the Lord hearkened, and heard it, and a book of remembrance was written before him for them that feared the Lord, and that thought upon his name" (Mal 3:16).

7   Both Zacharias and Elisabeth were "well stricken in years", and Elisabeth was barren. The desire for children among the women of Israel was so strong that Rachel said to Jacob, "Give me children, or else I die" (Gen 30:1). Hannah shed bitter tears when Peninnah, her rival, constantly reminded her of her barrenness (1 Sam 1:6). It had been the prayer of this righteous couple for years that God would give them a son (v.13). It is not mere speculation to say that they desired a son that he might serve in the priest's office. Both Zacharias and Elisabeth were descendants of Aaron. It was not required that a priest marry within the priestly line, but only that his wife should be a virgin of his own people (Lev 21:13-15); however, it was considered an added blessing to be born of the priestly line on both sides. A parallel to this godly couple can be seen in the parents of Moses, "And there went a man of the house of Levi, and took to wife a daughter of Levi" (Exod 2:1).

God's way, so unlike man's way, waits until nature is in the place of death. How often we have seen God working when all hope in human ability was gone! And yet, God is never late. He works "all things after the counsel of his own will" (Eph 1:11). This is beautifully illustrated in the events that led up to the birth of John.

8-11   The appearance of the angel, Gabriel, to Zacharias in the temple, promising the birth of John, marked the first word from the Lord since the clays of Malachi, 400 years before. Stirring events were about to happen. We are indebted to Alfred Edersheim for the information that although each course of the priests served twice a year, the privilege of burning incense before the golden altar occurred only once in a priest's lifetime. It was on this long-awaited day in the life of Zacharias, when he went into the temple to burn incense, and the people prayed without, that the angel Gabriel appeared to him, standing on the right side of the golden altar. "He executed the priest's office" is a translation of one word (*hierateuō*), found only here in the NT, but used frequently in the LXX for official priestly service. This was the most memorable day of his life and was made even more wonderful by the appearance of the angel of God.

The word "appeared" (*ōphthē*, v. 11) is used four times by Paul in 1 Cor 15:5 -8 in the same form to describe the appearances of the Lord to the witnesses of the resurrection. Zacharias saw Gabriel who appeared to him in a physical form.

Angels are spirits, but in communicating with man, they are given the ability to appear in a form that can be seen and identified.

Our minds reel when we consider the staggering number of events, of marriages, births and deaths that all took place in God's appointed time, so that on this day, Zacharias the priest stood in the temple of the Lord and had announced to him by the angel the events that would lead up to the birth of the Lord of all.

12-13   The fear that fell on Zacharias was relieved by the first words of the angel, "Fear not". The first four messages from heaven after the long interval between Malachi and Matthew are almost identical. To Joseph, the words were spoken, "fear not to take unto thee Mary thy wife" (Matt 1:20); to the troubled Mary, Gabriel said, "Fear not, Mary: for thou hast found favour with God" (1:30); and to the shepherds who were "sore afraid", the message was, "Fear not: for, behold, I bring you good tidings of great joy" (2:10). What a wonderful dawning for the new day when the "dayspring" (1:78) stepped into a dark world of sin!

As soon as the angel had calmed the fears of the shaken priest, he informed him that his prayer "is heard". This is called a sort of timeless aorist (A.T. Robertson). The tense of the verb informs us that this was the lifelong prayer of Zacharias and his wife. It is generally agreed that his prayer in the sanctuary (v.9) Zacharias and His wife. It is generally agreed that his prayer in the sanctuary was "an entreaty for the advent of Messiah" (Godet). The personal prayer for a son had gone up to God for many years. It was heard when it was uttered, and it "is heard" now, that is, it was ever before God. What an encouragement for us as we pray!

God would give them a son whose name would be called "John" which in its Hebrew form combines the name of God with the word that means "be gracious". Many believe that John should be understood as meaning "the gift and favour of God". The name applies not only to John personally, but to the grace of God that was displayed in the entire epoch of which his birth was the introduction. The Lord Jesus later said of him, "Among those that are born of women there is not a greater prophet than John the Baptist" (7:28).

14   This is the first mention of joy in this Gospel. The gloomy and dark "silent years", as they have been called, have at last come to an end, and joy is proclaimed by a heavenly messenger. There are three words in this verse that run through this Gospel and form one of its major themes (see the introduction). *Chara* ("joy") is found in this verse and in 2:10; 8:13; 10: 17; 15:7,10; 24:41 and 52. W.E. Vine literally translates 2:10, "I announce to you a great joy". *Chara* is used in 1: 14 and 2: 10, by metonymy, of the occasion or cause of great joy. In Greek literature *agalliasis* ("gladness") is found only "in the LXX and the NT, so far as is known" (A.T. Robertson). It is a word for the highest exultation, used by Peter, " ye rejoice with joy unspeakable" (1 Pet 1:8) or " with exceeding joy" (1 Pet 4:13). Luke uses it twice in this chapter, here and in v.44, where the unborn infant, John, leaped "for gladness" at the voice of Mary, the mother of the Lord. Luke used it also in Acts 2:46 to describe the "gladness" of the believers as they met together after the Day of Pentecost. The third word is *chairō* ("rejoice"), and is found twelve times in this Gospel, so it is the Gospel of joy, gladness and rejoicing.

The words of the angel take on a metrical form when turned into Hebrew, and in Greek it is a prose poem (J.T. Sanders). Four typical Hebrew hymns or poems are preserved in the following verses of these first two chapters of Luke. They have been called the *Magnificat*, uttered by Mary (1:46-55); the *Benedictus*, which are the words of Zacharias (1:68-79); the *Nunc Dimittis*, which is Latin for Simeon's first four words, " now lettest thou depart" (2:29-32), and the *Gloria*, the wonderful song of the heavenly host (2:14). These poems are in the style of OT psalms, majestic in their language, and constructed on the pattern of verbal parallelism that made up Hebrew poetry.

15   He was to be a Nazarite from his birth (Num 6:1-21), dedicated to the Lord in a life of separation and service. Many have struggled over the words of the angel, "he shall be filled with the Holy Ghost, even from his mother's womb". Some have gone so far as to claim that John had a spiritual birth before he had a natural birth. All such human speculation is unnecessary. There is an obvious contrast being drawn between being filled with the Spirit and the words, he "shall drink neither wine nor strong drink". This is the contrast drawn by Paul in Eph 5:18. To be filled with the Spirit is to be under His control for service and is quite distinct from the NT truth of " indwelling", which was contingent on the resurrection and ascension of the Lord Jesus (John 14:12-17). This is Luke's first mention of the Holy Spirit, a major theme of his two books.

16   We do well to see John as the greatest of a long line of prophets who pointed forward to the coming Saviour and King. He was truly unique, for his entire service was foretold before he was born (Isa 40:3-5), but as all others, except the Lord Jesus, he was born a sinner and needed the Lamb of God to be his sin-bearer too. His mission was to prepare hearts for the coming of the Lord and the burden of his ministry was, "Repent for the kingdom of heaven is at hand" (Matt 3:2). John was well aware of the greatness of his mission, yet he ever lived by the principle which he declared at the end of his public life, "He must increase, but 1 must decrease" (John 3:30). John had a humble and sensible view of himself and his own abilities, not thinking so little of himself that he attempted nothing for the Lord, but serving all his days with all his heart (v.15), yet conscious of his own limitations.

17   In the coming of John, as the forerunner, in the spirit and power of Elijah, we are taken back to the closing promise of the OT (see Mal 4:5,6). A threefold effect of his preaching is described. Turning "the hearts of the fathers to the children" should be taken as meaning that true repentance would be toward God (v.16), but some of the first effects of it would be seen in the home life. Any thought of pleasing or displeasing the long departed patriarchs, as some have suggested, is very fanciful. The two statements in vv.16 and 17 about the need to "turn" show that Israel had departed far from God and that this departure had affected every aspect of their lives as Malachi had so solemnly warned (2:11,14). Mixed marriages, divorce and remarriage and a deplorable moral condition had affected the nation. The turning of " the disobedient to the wisdom of the just" reminds us of the words spoken to Israel so long before, "O that there were such an heart in them, that they would fear me, and keep all my commandments always, that it might be well with them, and with their children for ever" (Deut 5:29). It is in this sense of preparing hearts that John's preaching would "make ready a people prepared for the Lord".

In the phrase "a people prepared", *kataskeuazō* ("prepared") is a perfect passive participle, describing a state of readiness for Christ. This is an amazing description of the character of John's ministry. *Laos* ("people") is found thirty-five times in this Gospel and only fourteen times in the other synoptic Gospels. It is frequently used of Israel as God's chosen people (1:68; 2:32; 7:16; 22:66), which is its meaning in this verse, but Luke also uses it in a wider sense to comprehend all the people who hear the word of God (2:3 1; 7: 1; 19:48; 20:45). This latter use is in keeping with the character of this Gospel, written, as we believe, by a Gentile believer.

In the quotation from Mal 3:1, "he shall go before him", Malachi's words were "he shall prepare the way before me". In agreement with the OT prophet, Luke uses "him" as a relative pronoun, going back to the precedent noun, " the Lord their God" (v.16). In both Malachi and Luke "the Messiah is no other than Jehovah Himself" (Godet).

18 Zacharias responded to the words of the angel with unbelief. It is strange how we have come to use the word "doubt" for sheer unbelief. We speak of "doubting Thomas" even though he said, "I will not believe" (John 20:25). We often speak of the doubts of Zacharias, even though Gabriel said, "thou believest not my words". Knowing our own hearts, we have no difficulty in understanding his lack of faith, but we should call unbelief by its correct name. His unbelief seems incongruous with the appearance of the angel, the appeal to the fulfilment of the words of Isaiah and Malachi, and the joyous character of the glad tidings (v.19). We have often been like Zacharias who through his unbelief lost much of the joy that could have been his. He also lost his power of speech (v.20), and we have no problem in applying this to our own experiences, for the lack of faith leads to loss of joy and power to witness. There is evidence that he also lost his hearing (1:62).

19 "I am Gabriel, that stand in the presence of God" must be carefully considered. Gabriel means "God is mighty", "mighty one of God" or "man of God". He was the angel who had given to Daniel the great prophecy of the seventy weeks (Dan 8:16; 9:21-27), and in the following verses would give to Mary the wonderful promise of the birth of the Son of God. He stood "in the presence of God" - the same words that are written of the seven angels in Rev 8:2. This position is not so much the one from which he has just come, as the position he constantly holds, that is, standing to minister, ever ready to be God's messenger, for the perfect participle in the active voice carries in it the thought of what is presently true. Perhaps at this moment Zacharias ceased to be an unbeliever, for we need to remember the true character of this righteous man. It is noteworthy that the unbelief of Zacharias did not rob either the message or the messenger of its gladness.

Euangelizō ("glad tidings") is used in the sense of declaring the glad tidings and is used ten times in this Gospel (1:19; 2:10; 3:18; 4:18,43; 7:22; 8:1; 9:6; 16:16; 20:1) and is found only once elsewhere in the four Gospels (Matt 11:5). This is significant for it shows Luke's deep interest in the declaration of the gospel message. He also uses *kērussō* ("to preach as a herald") nine times and in 4:18; 4:43-44; 8:1; 9:2-6 both words occur. Luke's association with Paul is evident in his strong conviction of the need for the preached word (Titus 1:3).

20-25 The words of the angel were confirmed. The conception of John was fulfilled in its season. The miracle of the birth of John is not lessened because God used natural agencies to cause His word to be fulfilled. This should be instructive to us. There are times when supernatural power moves outside of the channels of nature, and there are other occasions when God is pleased to move within these channels, but nonetheless controlling them to fulfil His word.

"After those days Elisabeth conceived". *Sullambanō* ("conceived") is used only by Luke for conceiving offspring (1:24,31,36; 2:21). In his *Medical Language of Luke,* Hobart writes that Luke used almost as many different words for bearing a child and barrenness as Hippocrates. In speaking of her "reproach" as a barren woman, Elizabeth is including her own mother's longing for a child, her desire for an heir for her husband, and also the hope of the Messiah that burned in the breast of every godly women in Israel.

Elisabeth had no questions in her mind that what had happened was by divine plan and intervention in the natural course of nature. "The Lord did this for me" is the sense of her words in v.25. How many times we have been caused to confess to His goodness in the same language!

In these verses there are three of Luke's unique words. *Dianeuō* (v.22, "beckoned") is used in the LXX in Ps 35:19, "wink" (W.E. Vine). It means to nod or to signal by moving the head. *Perikruptō* (v.24. "hid") means to hide by placing something around oneself and to keep hidden, in this case, for five months. The word "reproach" (*oneidos*) also is only here in the NT. W.E. Vine points out that in the Jewish mind it was not merely a misfortune to have no children, but was a shame and disgrace and implied divine punishment for some secret sin. This explains the envy of Rachel against her sister Leah (Gen 30:1), and the grief of Hannah over her barrenness (1 Sam 1:8). Throughout the long history of mankind up to the birth of the Saviour there lived in many a mother's heart the longing to be the instrument of the coming of "the Seed of the woman".

3. The Promise of the Birth of the Lord Jesus 1:26-38

v.26 "And in the sixth month the angel Gabriel was sent from God unto a city of Galilee, named Nazareth,

v.27 To a virgin espoused to a man whose name was Joseph, of the house of David; and the virgin's name *was* Mary.

v.28 And the angel came in unto her, and said, Hail, *thou that art* highly favoured, the Lord *is* with thee: blessed *art* thou among women.

v.29 And when she saw *him*, she was troubled at his saying, and cast in her mind what manner of salutation this should be.

v.30 And the angel said unto her, Fear not, Mary: for thou hast found favour with God.

v.31 And, behold, thou shalt conceive in thy womb, and bring forth a son, and shalt call his name JESUS.

v.32 He shall be great, and shall be called the Son of the Highest: and the Lord God shall give unto him the throne of his father David:

v.33 And he shall reign over the house of Jacob for ever; and of his kingdom there shall be no end.

v.34 Then said Mary unto the angel, How shall this be, seeing I know not a man?

v.35 And the angel answered and said unto her, The Holy Ghost shall come upon thee, and the power of the Highest shall overshadow thee: therefore also that holy thing which shall be born of thee shall be called the Son of God.

v.36 And, behold, thy cousin Elisabeth, she hath also conceived a son in her old age: and this is the sixth month with her, who was called barren.

v.37 For with God nothing shall be impossible.

v.38 And Mary said, Behold the handmaid of the Lord; be it unto me according to thy word. And the angel departed from her."

It would be difficult to find in all the fields of literature a more beautiful story than the one that is now unfolding in this lovely Gospel. More wonderful than its beauty is its truth. These are actual events in what Graham Scroggie has called, "God's great unfolding drama of redemption". The prophecies that culminate in this great birth-event go back to the very dawn of human history. The hope awakened by that first promise never died, even though through thousands of years it was kept alive only in the hearts of a faithful remnant. It is quite staggering to consider that this young virgin of Nazareth was in that first promise. Speaking to Satan in Eden, God said, "I will put enmity between thee and the woman, and between thy seed and her seed; it shall bruise thy head, and thou shalt bruise his heel" (Gen 3:15). The words of Paul in Gal 4:4 help us to understand the significance of this promise as it relates to Mary, "but when the fulness of the time was come, God sent forth his Son, made of a woman, made under the law".

He was born of a woman, but was uniquely the Seed of a woman, without earthly father, truly virgin born.

26   When Gabriel was sent to Zacharias with the glad tidings of the birth of John, his message was met with unbelief. In comparison, the message to Mary was far more difficult to believe, yet Gabriel did not hesitate to obey God. In communicating the message to Mary, there is no evidence of his disappointment with Zacharias, in fact he clearly entered into the joy of the message that he was privileged to carry. There are some solemn lessons in this for us. We too carry a blessed message, but we are often discouraged by the unbelief which we meet, and lose our joy in declaring the glad tidings. We may even be guilty of delivering our message with a tone that says plainly, "I know you won't believe this, but it is true". Gabriel can teach us how to carry a message.

The little town of Nazareth is located in southern Galilee, at the place where the southernmost slopes of the Lebanon mountains level out into the fertile Plain of Esdraelon. It lay almost equally distant between the southern tip of the Sea of Galilee to the east and the Mediterranean Sea to the west. This region of Galilee remained outside the mainstream of Israelite life and was held in scorn by strict Jews (John 1:46). It was a place of deep poverty. The Lord Jesus was to be known throughout His years of ministry as "Jesus of Nazareth", a title of dishonour.

27   It is very likely that Mary was not yet twenty years of age when Gabriel came to her. This young virgin of Nazareth who was promised in marriage to the village carpenter, Joseph, was not only a part of the first promise ever given of the coming Saviour (Gen 3:15), but she was a sign to the whole house of David (Isa 7:14). "Espoused" is "betrothed", and the betrothal period usually lasted a year. Unfaithfulness on the part of the bride was punished with death (Deut 23:24).

28-29   She was one of the most humble servants whom God ever used. When Gabriel called her highly favoured and blessed, " she was troubled at his saying". It was not fright at the appearance of the angel that alarmed and disturbed her, but the manner of his salutation. Her lowliness of mind and willingness to be used by God is evident in the description that she gives of herself as the bondslave of the Lord (vv.38,48). *Diatarassō* ("troubled"), another of Luke's unique words, conveys the thought of being troubled throughout her entire being. Dialogizomai "cast in her mind" is used in v.29 and in 3:15 "all men mused in their hearts". To be so honoured by the heavenly messenger was staggering to the mind of this lowly young woman.

30-33   She was given a most difficult service to do for God, perhaps as difficult as has ever been asked of any servant of the Lord. Virgins do not give birth. Who would believe her? Even Joseph, a righteous man, thought that he should hide her so that she would not be an object of shame (Matt 1:19-21). The Lord Jesus bore this stigma from unbelievers all the days of His life on earth (John 8:41). In humility, Mary accepted her task (v.38).

The first words to Mary about the birth were simply that she would "conceive in thy womb, and bring forth a son". As she listened to the angel's words disclosing His name, His greatness, His deity, His royalty and His eternal kingdom, her heart must have been filled with wonder. The fact that she, a virgin, would become a mother was staggering, but to learn of the greatness of the One she would bear must have been even more staggering. In a flash her mind was taken back to the first promise of the Seed of the woman at the dawn of human history and then moved forward to the very end of time when her Son would sit upon the throne of David and "reign over the house of Jacob forever". The entire programme of the Messiah was flashed before her in a few words, and she was to be the mother of the long desired Deliverer of her people.

34   Her simple question, "How shall this be, seeing I know not a man?" is a marvel of restraint and faith. She has just been told that her Son "shall reign over the house of Jacob for ever, and of his kingdom there shall be no end" and she expresses no doubt, but only asks about the conception. And well might she ask!

35   This conception is to take place in the womb of a virgin, a one-time-only event that has never happened before and will never happen again, a miraculous conception that is to be brought about by the Holy Spirit of God coming upon her and the power of the Highest overshadowing her as the cloud overshadowed the mercy-seat in the tabernacle.

It has been argued that there is a synonymous parallelism in the two statements, so that "The Holy Ghost" and "the power of the Highest" both refer to the same Holy Spirit, and the "coming upon" and the " overshadowing" refer to the same action. This may be correct, but I believe that the two statements are better understood as being distinct. The "coming upon" caused the miracle of the conception; the "overshadowing" was a time of special guardianship while Mary carried in her womb the Son of God.

There is a third fact to be considered in the great event of the virgin birth. It has been said that the Lord Jesus had a miraculous conception, but a natural birth. This is not a true statement. The birth itself was unique. Prophetically, the Lord Jesus said, in speaking to God, " thou art he that took me out of the womb; thou didst make me hope when I was upon my mother's breasts. I was cast upon thee from the womb; thou art my God from my mother's belly " (Ps 22:9, 10). Mary, the lowly virgin from Nazareth bore and nursed the Son of God.

The statement, "that holy thing" has been a problem to some. It has been suggested that this is the only time in Scripture that a neuter adjective is used for the Person of the Lord Jesus. This is not strictly true, for Acts 4:27 uses a neuter adjective for the Christ who stood before Pilate. No one would suggest that it was not a true Man against whom Herod, Pilate, the Gentiles and the people of Israel arrayed themselves. This statement in 1:35 is best read as many have translated it, "Wherefore also the holy (One) which shall be born shall be called Son of God".

He "shall be called the Son of God" has been interpreted by some as implying that He became the Son of God at His birth, thus denying His eternal Sonship. The Scriptures teach that He was the Son before He was sent; not only was one of the persons of the Godhead sent, but the One sent was the beloved Son of the eternal Father: " the Father sent the Son" (1 John 4:14). Many other such verses teach that it was the eternal Son who came: John 1:18; 3:16,31-36; 4:34; 5:24,30; 17:24; Heb 1:1-3; 7:1-3; 1 John 4:9-10.

36   Mary was given a task to perform that would leave her open to false charges. It was grace on God's part that she was informed of the one person who would understand what God was doing. She was told that her cousin, Elisabeth, had conceived in her old age, and was spiritually intelligent about these great events.

37   What had happened to Elisabeth was an extra assurance to Mary that all the words spoken to her would be fulfilled in their time. Our Father in heaven knows our frame and remembers our frailty; He is never slow in giving full assurance, even when we are "slow of heart to believe" (Luke 24:25); so Mary was assured that "with God nothing shall be impossible". *Pan rhēma* ("every word") is used with *ouk* ("will not") and is translated "nothing". It means that every single item will be fulfilled, not merely the general content of the promise.

38   Mary's submission to the message is most touching. Even though the angel said that she was highly favoured and blessed among women, she said that she was the "bond maiden of the Lord", in His hand to do with her according to His will. A right appreciation of the Lord leads to a correct assessment of self.

4.   *The Visit of Mary to Elisabeth and Mary's Praise*
       1:39-56

v.39 "And Mary arose in those days, and went into the hill country with haste, into a city of Juda;
v.40 And entered into the house of Zacharias, and saluted Elisabeth.
v.41 And it came to pass, that, when Elisabeth heard the salutation of Mary, the babe leaped in her womb; and Elisabeth was filled with the Holy Ghost:
v.42 And she spake out with a loud voice, and said, Blessed *art* thou among women, and blessed *is* the fruit of thy womb.
v.43 And whence *is* this to me, that the mother of my Lord should come to me?
v.44 For, lo, as soon as the voice of thy salutation sounded in mine ears, the babe leaped in my womb for joy.
v.45 And blessed *is* she that believed: for there shall be a performance of those things which were told her from the Lord.

v.46 And Mary said, My soul doth magnify the Lord,
v.47 And my spirit hath rejoiced in God my Saviour.
v.48 For he hath regarded the low estate of his handmaiden: for, behold, from henceforth all generations shall call me blessed.
v.49 For he that is mighty hath done to me great things; and holy *is* his name.
v.50 And his mercy *is* on them that fear him from generation to generation,
v.51 He hath shewed strength with his arm; he hath scattered the proud in the imagination of their hearts.
v.52 He hath put down the mighty from *their* seats, and exalted them of low degree.
v.53 He hath filled the hungry with good things; and the rich he hath sent empty away.
v.54 He hath holpen his servant Israel, in remembrance of *his* mercy;
v.55 As he spake to our fathers, to Abraham, and to his seed for ever.
v.56 And Mary abode with her about three months, and returned to her own house,"

39-41 Mary's need for understanding may have been the cause of the haste with which she took the journey to the hill country of Judaea. *Oreinos* is found only here and in 1:65 in the NT and means mountainous terrain, suggesting a difficult journey. Her need for comfort was very great, for she had to bear, at least for a time, the misunderstanding of Joseph. J. Heading points out that the distance would have been about 100 miles if she travelled directly through Samaria and Jerusalem. Upon her arrival at the home of Zacharias and Elisabeth, the babe in the womb of Elisabeth leaped, and filled with the Holy Spirit, she greeted Mary with a loud cry (*kraugē*), calling her the most blessed of women. The word "leaped" (*skirtaō*), a word used three times and only by Luke (1:41,44; 6:23), is used in the LXX for the struggle of Jacob and Esau in the womb of Rebekah (Gen 25:22). Elisabeth is the only woman in Scripture about whom it is recorded that she "was filled with the Holy Ghost".

42 "She spake out" is the translation of one word *anaphōneō*, and is found only here in the NT; it means to lift up one's voice, in this case, "with a great cry". This was the immediate result of being "filled with the Holy Ghost" (v.41). Perhaps our familiarity with the language of the AV allows us to read of this great cry without being aware of the feeling that accompanied it. The heart of Mary must have been deeply moved by such a greeting.

43 "Whence is this to me?" is an expression of wonder. Elisabeth, filled with the Spirit, said, "Why am I so honoured to be thus visited?" The cause of her wonder was that "the mother of my Lord should come to me". "My Lord" is a most significant expression, spoken by Joshua (Josh 5:14), David (Ps 110:1), Mary of Magdala (John 20:13), Thomas (John 20:28) and by Paul when he allowed the Philippians to look into his devoted heart, "I count all things but loss for the excellency of the knowledge of Christ Jesus my Lord" (Phil 3:8). Elisabeth acknowledged an unborn babe as her Lord. At the moment that she spoke the words, they were true. It is hoped that none will weaken this statement by saying that she is speaking of a fact that would be true some day. Within the womb of Mary was resident the Lord of all. In a day when many attempt to tell us that a foetus is merely a collection of cells that can be destroyed at will, this is a solemn reminder that an unborn babe is a person.

44   Elisabeth, under the power of the Holy Spirit, recognised that a holy Person was present in her humble home that day, though unseen by human eye. Also, with Spirit-given intelligence, she interpreted the movement of her own babe as a leap of joy. It is impossible to ascribe joy to a non-person, so both the forerunner and his Lord were present. Such a holy scene bows our hearts in worship, for He of whom Solomon said, "the heaven and the heaven of heavens cannot contain" (1 Kings 8:27), inhabited the womb of the virgin of Nazareth. It has been touchingly stated that He left that womb, as He later left the tomb, undefiled.

45   Elisabeth was a woman whom the Holy Spirit describes as being righteous and blameless. She was also a humble, spiritual person who, although she acknowledged the blessing that had come from God to her, was quick to recognise that Mary's blessings were far greater. Not a tinge of jealousy appears in her words, "blessed is she that believed: for there shall be a performance... from the Lord".

46-48   It is usual to divide the song of Mary into four stanzas:

1.   God's grace in using a handmaiden of lowly birth (vv.46-48)

2.   Praise to the holy God for His mercy (vv.49,50)

3.   The goodness and severity of God contrasted (vv.51-53)

4.   The covenant-keeping faithfulness of God (vv.54,55).

In her expressions of worship we are shown what can cause our hearts to well up with praise: it is a consciousness of God's greatness, His holiness, His righteous acts, His mighty power and His faithfulness, coupled with a heart appreciation of what He has done for us.

The song of Mary is often compared with the song of the godly Hannah in 1 Sam 2:1-10. If two columns are made of the two songs, there is a unique parallelism. We can learn that, contrary to the belief of the Pharisees about women, the spiritual understanding of these women was of the very highest level. It is impossible to read the magnificent song of praise that ascended to God from the soul of Mary and not be deeply impressed by her knowledge of Scripture, her spiritual intelligence and the depth of worship that flowed out from a full heart.

The Saviour God is a theme of the Pastoral Letters, but in all of Scripture only

Mary ever uttered the words, "God my Saviour". It is not wrong to understand her words as meaning that she had learned her need of a Saviour and that God was known to her as her personal Saviour. Any understanding that is less than this will not do justice to this gospel of salvation. Far from being without sin, as the great Roman system claims for her, she acknowledges her own lowliness, but because of the work of God in her, all generations to come will deem her to have been blessed of God.

49-50   In her deep thanksgiving to "the Mighty one" (JND), she has a great sense of His holy character, on the one hand, and His tender mercy on the other; a mercy which, she says, rests from generation to generation on them that fear Him, and from which she has not been excluded. She had learned the meaning of the words of one of her greatest forebears, "The fear of the Lord is the beginning of knowledge" (Prov 1:7). The fear of the Lord involves a right attitude toward God in view of His holiness and His mercy.

51-53   The six aorist tenses that Mary uses in this stanza may refer not so much to events in the past, as to that which God does in keeping with His unchanging nature. She uses a form of speech that is characteristic of prophetic utterances. The mighty deeds of God are manifest in keeping with His holiness and mercy in the second stanza, and in His goodness and severity in this third stanza. Her description of God's goodness toward the unworthy, and His severity toward the proud reminds us of the words of Paul, "Behold therefore the goodness and severity of God" (Rom 11:22). This led him on to the anthem of praise, "O the depth of the riches both of the wisdom and knowledge of God! how unsearchable are his judgments, and his ways past finding out!" (v.33). Mary's praise was similar and finds an echo in every redeemed heart, for God has truly "exalted them of low degree".

54-56   The unconditional covenant made to Abraham (Gen 12:3) is not forgotten by the faithful God. Mary is able to grasp the fact that, after so long a time, God is about to bring into the world the promised Seed, through whom all the nations of the world shall be blessed. This understanding of the dealings of God with her and His people, Israel, made the supernatural conception and the promise of Messiah's birth fill her heart with joy and praise. During the three months that she spent with Elisabeth, before returning home to Nazareth, the communications between the two women must have been full of the wonder of the deeds of the Almighty.

5.   *The Birth of John*
   1:57-66

v.57   "Now Elisabeth's full time came that she should be delivered; and she brought forth a son.

> v.58 And her neighbours and her cousins heard how the Lord had shewed great
> mercy upon her; and they rejoiced with her.
> v.59 And it came to pass, that on the eighth day they came to circumcise the child;
> and they called him Zacharias, after the name of his father.
> v.60 And his mother answered and said, Not *so*; but he shall be called John.
> v.61 And they said unto her, There is none of thy kindred that is called by this name.
> v.62 And they made signs to his father, how he would have him called.
> v.63 And he asked for a writing table, and wrote, saying, His name is John. And they
> marvelled all.
> v.64 And his mouth was opened immediately, and his tongue *loosed*, and he spake,
> and praised God.
> v.65 And fear came on all that dwelt round about them: and all these sayings were
> noised abroad throughout all the hill country of Judaea.
> v.66 And all that heard *them* laid *them* up in their hearts, saying, What manner of
> child shall this be! And the hand of the Lord was with him."

57-58 As the angel had foretold, Elisabeth's son is born, causing great rejoicing among relatives and neighbours. They saw this event as a display of divine mercy.

59 The circumcising of a male child on the eighth day was in obedience to the law (Gen 17:12; Lev 12:3). The eighth day is linked in typical Scriptures with a new beginning (see Lev 23:6,11,15,16). The birth of John was truly a new beginning, the dawn of a blessed day.

The OT does not link the naming of a child with the ceremony of circumcision, but there were special reasons for the naming being linked with this day. The custom may have arisen from the fact that Abraham and Sarah received their new names when circumcision was first commanded by God. The naming by friends seems an unusual event, but Ruth 4:17 records, "And the women her neighbours gave it a name, saying, There is a son born to Naomi; and they called his name Obed". These friends took it for granted that the child would be named Zacharias after his father.

60-64 Elisabeth was aware of all that had happened in the temple on the day when Gabriel had appeared to Zacharias. Her words, "Not *so*; but he shall be called John", are emphatic. The friends argued that this name was unknown among the relations and appealed to Zacharias to settle the matter. Surely he would agree that this child of his old age should be called after him. Zacharias answered, "His name is John". He was literally saying, "My son is already named and I have no say in it". He asked for a "writing table" (*pinakidion*) which means a small writing tablet and is the only time this word is used in Scripture.

We know that Zacharias' unbelief in the temple meant that he was unable to speak. The word *kōphos* which is used in v.22 to describe his affliction can mean " deaf and dumb". This seems to have been the case, for they had to make signs to him. Immediately, he was able to speak, and he used his first words to praise God.

65,66 A deep reverence fell upon all who knew of these events in the hill country of Judaea. It was not merely a subject of gossip, for all that heard these things " laid them up in their hearts". Later, almost identical words are recorded of Mary (Luke 2:5 1). God was not only preparing His servant John for a unique ministry, but was also preparing hearts in Israel to receive the Messiah. Two of Luke's unique words are found in v.65. *Perioikeō* is a compound word meaning "to dwell around", or simply" all the neighbours around". Laleo is the common word "to speak", used very frequently in the NT, but *dialaleō* ("were noised abroad") means to discuss the subject until every facet of it has been considered.

6.   The Song of Zacharias
1:67-80

v.67 "And his father Zacharias was filled with the Holy Ghost, and prophesied, saying,
v.68 Blessed *be* the Lord God of Israel; for he hath visited and redeemed his people,
v.69 And hath raised up an horn of salvation for us in the house of his servant David;
v.70 As he spake by the mouth of his holy prophets, which have been since the world began:
v.71 That we should be saved from our enemies, and from the hand of all that hate us;
v.72 To perform the mercy *promised* to our fathers, and to remember his holy covenant;
v.73 The oath which he sware to our father Abraham,
v.74 That he would grant unto us, that we being delivered out of the hand of our enemies might serve him without fear,
v.75 In holiness and righteousness before him, all the days of our life.
v.76 And thou, child, shalt be called the prophet of the Highest: for thou shalt go before the face of the Lord to prepare his ways;
v.77 To give knowledge of salvation unto his people by the remission of their sins,
v.78 Through the tender mercy of our God; whereby the dayspring from on high hath visited us,
v.79 To give light to them that sit in darkness and *in* the shadow of death, to guide our feet into the way of peace.
v.80 And the child grew, and waxed strong in spirit, and was in the deserts till the day of his shewing unto Israel."

There are five songs in the early chapters of Luke. The words of Elisabeth when Mary came to visit her were a poetic utterance, a song about God's blessing (1:42-45). We have already looked at Mary's song of faith (1:46-55), and we now have the song of Zacharias (1:68-79) which is full of hope. In ch.2, we will yet look at the song of the angels (2:14) which is full of adoration and will then examine the song of Simeon (2:29-30). Luke is writing a Gospel of joy, and it is fitting that he should begin with these songs of praise.

67 The filling with the Holy Spirit which has been used to describe John, Elisabeth and now Zacharias emphasises for us one of Luke's major themes. The Holy Spirit is the divine Mover in these events. Luke's two books follow this theme throughout. The words of Zacharias are said to be a prophecy. The song is made up of four stanzas: thanksgiving for the coming of Messiah (vv.68-70), the great deliverance that He will bring (vv.71-75), the unique ministry of John (vv.76,77), and praise to God for His tender mercy (vv.78,79).

68   God is blessed for visiting His people and redeeming them, in keeping with the words of Exod 3:8, "I am come down to deliver them". This redemption is a loosing away from bondage that involves the paying of a great price.

69-70   The "horn of salvation" is a reminder of Jer 50:34, "Their Redeemer is strong; the Lord of hosts is his name: he shall throughly plead their cause", and many similar OT statements that describe God's almighty power in salvation. "The house of his servant David" indicates that Zacharias understood that Mary was of the house of David. It would be unnatural to suppose that he is linking her to David through Joseph to whom she was not yet joined in marriage. His reference to the promise of "holy prophets ... since the world began" shows his understanding of the link that existed from the first promise (Gen 3:15) through the Davidic covenant (2 Sam 7:4-17; 1 Chron 17:4-15), extending to all the prophets that foretold the coming of the Saviour. Some may question whether Zacharias understood all that he said. We have no criteria by which we can judge what he understood, nor is this necessary; however, it is better to give him full credit for spiritual intelligence.

71-75   Some have limited the words of Zacharias to a political sense, but we should understand that he was speaking by the Spirit, and saw far beyond the immediate Roman domination of the land. His words have spiritual meaning and tell of the blessing brought to Israel and all the true " sons of Abraham" (Gal 3:7 RV) through the coming of Messiah. However, it is to an ultimate victory over all the enemies of God that he points, when the "holiness and righteousness" of perfect service to God will be fulfilled in a redeemed earth, " for the earth shall be full of the knowledge of the Lord, as the waters cover the sea" (Isa 11:9).

76   It was not until Zacharias gave preeminence to the coming Saviour that he spoke of his newborn son, "the prophet of the Highest", who will "go before the face of the Lord to prepare his ways". Even then, he fully understands the subordinate nature of John's work, preparing the way for the coming of the "Lord"; yet John will be a true prophet of God, the first that has been sent to Israel for four long centuries.

77   Only God Himself can forgive sins and give the knowledge of salvation, but John would be the sign post pointing to the Saviour who would accomplish this salvation.

78   Two of the words normally used in the NT to express mercy are used here, *eleos* and *splanchnon*, so that the phrase, "the tender mercy of our God" is best understood as being the mercy into which He has put His whole heart. It is loving kindness and tender love from God's heart, expressed to needy men in the misery of their fallen state. This mercy is as high as the heavens, for "so great is his mercy" (Ps 103:11).

"The dayspring from on high" is a title of the Lord Jesus in keeping with all that has been said about Him in these days that preceded His birth. As the "dayspring", He is the sunrising, bringing in the dawn of a new day. The gospel that has Him as its centre and theme is the light of it. The AV "dayspring" has captured the thought of a moment of brilliant light breaking on a dark world, a moment that has been anticipated, eagerly awaited, restrained until this very moment when "the fulness of time" has dawned. However, the dawning holds the promise of an eternal day that will never know a nightfall.

The Lord Jesus is also the "daysman" (Job 9:33) who was able to bridge the great chasm that separated guilty mankind from a holy God. As God, with a right to place His hand on the eternal throne, and yet, " himself man" (1 Tim 2:5 RV), able to reach to us in all our need, He is the true Mediator between God and men.

The Lord Jesus is also the "day star" (2 Pet 1:19) who as the "morning star" will appear for His church, the first event of the glorious future which will lead on to the eternal day.

79   Light dawning on them that "sit in darkness and in the shadow of death" is an OT description of the coming of the Saviour into a fallen scene where sin and death reigned over the affairs of men. To "sit in darkness" suggests willing ignorance, an unawakened state even though in such danger. Ps 107:10 adds to this description that men are "bound in affliction and iron". The valley of the shadow (Ps 23:4) is not death itself, it is the world where death reigns by sin. The OT description of salvation is, "He brought them out of darkness and the shadow of death, and break their bands in sunder" (Ps 107:14).

The peace into which He guides the feet of His own is all the rich blessing that comes to those whose sins are forgiven. A former enmity on our part is removed; thus there is peace with God in the sense of Rom 5:1. Yet there is also here the sense of Phil 4:6-9, for He guides our feet into the way of peace, so that we not only enjoy peace with God, but now, knowing the God of peace, we have the peace of God guarding our hearts.

80   John was born in the semi-arid hill country of Judaea. The "wilderness of Judaea", the eastern slopes of the hills that run down to the Dead Sea, was the place of his first preaching (Matt 3:1). This was likely the area of his upbringing. His aged parents may not have lived to see him raised, but he had many relatives in the region around. The one thing that we do know is that he was unnoticed by the mainstream of Jewish society until the day of his showing to Israel. *Anadeixis* ("shewing") is found only here in the NT and means "to show forth" or literally "the day of his public appearance" (NASB).

1.   The Birth of the Lord Jesus
2:1-7

v.1 "And it came to pass in those days, that there went out a decree from Caesar Augustus, that all the world should be taxed.

v.2 (*And* this taxing was first made when Cyrenius was governor of Syria.)

v.3 And all went to be taxed, every one into his own city.

v.4 And Joseph also went up from Galilee, out of the city of Nazareth, into Judaea, unto the city of David, which is called Bethlehem; (because he was of the house and lineage of David:)

v.5 To be taxed with Mary his espoused wife, being great with child.

v.6 And so it was, that, while they were there, the days were accomplished that she should be delivered.

v.7 And she brought forth her firstborn son, and wrapped him in swaddling clothes, and laid him in a manger; because there was no room for them in the inn."

1 The "decree from Caesar Augustus" was the working out of the divine plan that would cause the Saviour of the world to be born in Bethlehem in accordance with the prophecy of Mic 5:2. Caesar Augustus, whose name was Gaius Octavius and more familiar to us as Octavian, was the Roman emperor from BC 2 7 until AD 14. His sister was married to Antony, who left his wife for Cleopatra. In the naval battle of Actium, Antony was defeated by Octavian, and shortly afterward, both Antony and Cleopatra committed suicide (BC 31). Octavian's great-uncle, Julius Caesar, had named him as his heir, so the imperial throne was guaranteed to him at the murder of Caesar in BC 44, but he was unable to make his claim good until BC 27. In that year, the Roman senate conferred on him the title of Augustus, with the meaning of "his august majesty". Though often cruel, he became a wise ruler and is given credit for good administration of his vast empire. The bibliography should be consulted for sources for these historical facts and much more that concerns this period.

"The decree" was not the gathering of tax money, for that was the work of the publicans, but was rather an enrolment, a census that made it possible for the authorities to make certain that all paid their legal taxes. Only Luke notes this imperial decree and this is in keeping with his carefulness in relating NT events to historical data of the secular world. Although secular history does not record a special census that was commanded by Augustus, it gives much evidence that such census taking was a common practice throughout the empire, and as Wm. Barclay has carefully chronicled, took place about every fourteen years, but not necessarily at the same time in each country.

2 Quirinius was governor of Syria between AD 6 to 9, and at the beginning of his governorship organised a census in Judaea. This is about nine years too late for the census of Luke 2. However, Sir Wm. Ramsay in his book *Was Christ Born at Bethlehem?* has pointed out that Luke carefully tells us that this was a first census. Luke was acquainted with a second census and writes about it in Acts 5:37, when "Judas of Galilee" rose up "in the days of the taxing (census)". From inscriptions, Ramsay believed there was evidence of a former term when Quirinius served as the Syrian imperial legate, during a time which would fit the date of Luke's statement here. It was Luke's extreme accuracy in all his historical notations that made Ramsay such a defender of Luke's accounts. There are many occasions when scholars have questioned Bible history, only to be put to shame by later discoveries that verified its accuracy.

3　It is believed that the hand of Herod the Great is seen in this regulation that all families must return to their ancestral homes for the registration. Being Rome's faithful puppet, "It would be quite like Herod's skill in governing Jews to disguise the foreign nature of the command by an appeal to tribal patriotism" (B.S. Easton). A Roman census would likely have required only registration in the closest city to a family's residence.

4-5　There is no NT word for "town" so even though Nazareth was not very large and Bethlehem was little more than a village, both are called cities. Joseph "was of the house and lineage of David". It is a measure of the low ebb of Israel's fortunes that the royal house was so lowly, represented by a carpenter from Nazareth.

The journey of about seventy miles, if the direct route was taken, and at least ninety miles, if they went the roundabout way through Trans-Jordan, must have been difficult for the expectant mother. Luke says that Mary was Joseph's betrothed wife, which is his way of expressing the truth of Matt 1:24,25 that they were married, but that he "knew her not till she had brought forth her firstborn son". Only Luke says that Mary was *enkuos* ("great with child"). It is another evidence of the interests of a physician. The word means to have conceived and be carrying a child.

We do not know that the regulations required both husband and wife to be present for the census, but Joseph would have been reluctant to leave her behind in Nazareth considering the circumstances of the miraculous conception and the slanderous tongues of their neighbours. They travelled on the long and lonely road together, but the power of the Highest overshadowed the young woman and the precious burden that she bore. Divine counsels brought them on the journey, being plans that had been made before the world began and will outlive all of this physical universe. Sometimes people have been heard to say, "If we had been present to see it, we would believe it all". No they would not. If we had seen the humble travellers on the road, how difficult it would have been to believe that time and eternity were to be radically changed as a result of their journey.

Bethlehem was the place of David's birth, and it was in the area of Bethlehem that he "delighted himself among the flock" (1 Sam 16:11, Young's Literal Trans.). He often returned there for a family yearly sacrifice (1 Sam 20:6), and it is probable that the family records were kept there. Many years before David, another son was born there. The first mention of Bethlehem is at the birth of Benjamin. The dying Rachel called him Ben-oni, "son of my sorrow", but Jacob called him "the son of my right hand" (Gen 35:18-19). The law of first mention certainly applies here, for the sufferings of the Man of sorrows and the glory to follow were illustrated in the birth of Benjamin.

6 The simple words "And so it was" in our beloved AV are so eloquently expressive. God came down to visit us; the Lord of eternity stepped into time; the Creator took the likeness of His creatures, apart from sin; the Lord of history became part of an event of history; Immanuel came to dwell with us; He who inhabited eternity became a babe in the arms of an earthly mother.

> "No less almighty at His birth,
> Than on His throne supreme,
> His shoulders held up heaven and earth,
> While Mary held up Him."

7 One of the OT comments on the birth is found in the Psalm of the suffering Saviour, "thou art he that took me out of the womb" (Ps 22:9). Yet this tremendous event takes place amid poverty, obscurity and rejection. It has often been taught, preached and sung that the Lord was born in a stable, but the only authority for this is the statement in our verse that she "wrapped him in swaddling clothes, and laid him in a manger". It is possible that the manger was located in a stable. *Phatnē* ("manger") is found three times in this chapter, vv. 7, 12 and 16. Its only other use in the NT is 13:15 where the AV translates it "stall". The LXX has *phatnē* for "stall" in 2 Chron 32:28. A manger might be located in a corner of a field, but it has been traditionally believed that the manger in which the infant Christ was laid was a building to stall and feed animals connected to the inn. Many believe the manger was in a cave, but we have no evidence other than that given in these few verses.

We are told that there was no room in the *kataluma* ("guest-chamber" in 22:11) (see Mark 14:14). The more common word for inn is *pandocheion* (10:34), which is made up of the two words *pas* ("all") and *dechomai* ("to receive"). The inn in Bethlehem was crowded with guests because of the census, so that even at His birth the Lord Jesus was excluded from the shelter that others enjoyed. Perhaps none of the guests knew anything of the tremendous event that took place that night. If they had known about the needs of the young mother, would they have been willing to give up their place for her? We do not know. Surely, we will never be able fully to appreciate that manger until we have seen the mansions that He left in His down-stooping from glory.

The new mother wrapped her infant Son with loving hands in long strips of cloth that she may have prepared months before in Nazareth. We have no information that any other than Joseph attended the birth. H.S. Paisley believes that they may have been clothes of blue, purple and scarlet, befitting His Person and the work He had come to do, and he may well be right. Although Mary was unable to provide for Him the surroundings she would have desired, it is unlikely that any mother has ever looked with greater wonder on her newborn son. She knew Him, though at that moment not another person on earth did.

2.   *The Message of the Angels to the Shepherds*
2:8-20

v.8   "And there were in the same country shepherds abiding in the field, keeping watch over their flock by night.

v.9   And, lo, the angel of the Lord came upon them, and the glory of the Lord shone round about them: and they were sore afraid.

v.10 And the angel said unto them, Fear not: for, behold, I bring you good tidings of great joy, which shall be to all people.

v.11 For unto you is born this day in the city of David a Saviour, which is Christ the Lord.

v.12 And this *shall be* a sign unto you; Ye shall find the babe wrapped in swaddling clothes, lying in a manger.

v.13 And suddenly there was with the angel a multitude of the heavenly host praising God, and saying,

v.14 Glory to God in the highest, and on earth peace, good will toward men.

v.15 And it came to pass, as the angels were gone away from them into heaven, the shepherds said one to another, Let us now go even unto Bethlehem, and see this thing which is come to pass, which the Lord hath made known unto us.

v.16 And they came with haste, and found Mary, and Joseph, and the babe lying in a manger.

v.17 And when they had seen *it*, they made known abroad the saying which was told them concerning this child.

v.18 And all they that heard *it* wondered at those things which were told them by the shepherds.

v.19 But Mary kept all these things, and pondered *them* in her heart.

v.20 And the shepherds returned, glorifying and praising God for all the things that they had heard and seen, as it was told unto them."

The description of the watching shepherds, by night guarding their precious flock, is very suggestive to us of NT exhortations to spiritual shepherds (1 Pet 5:1-4), but the immediate lesson about the shepherds is that the great of earth remained in ignorance while humble shepherds were visited by a heavenly messenger, "a multitude of the heavenly host" then informing them of the great event that had taken place in Bethlehem. This is in keeping with the lowly birth and life of our Lord.

8 Leon Morris, quoting from rabbinical sources, tells us, "Shepherds were generally forbidden to give testimony before the Sanhedrin". Their reputation was not very high in the eyes of the religious leaders of Israel, for their work made it difficult for them to observe the ceremonial laws, and they were not known for the strictest honesty as they moved from place to place with their flocks. However, these lowly shepherds, known to God, were chosen by Him to give testimony to the birth of His Son.

It has been stated that a winter birth-date for the Lord is incorrect because shepherds would not be in the fields in the winter, but this is not true. In that land, it was not unusual for shepherds to be with their flocks all the year round. This does not prove anything, for we do not know the date of the Saviour's birth. *Agrauleō* ("abiding in the field") is found only in Luke in the NT. It literally means that they lived in a sheepfold in the open field being made up of the words for "fold" and "field".

9-10 The appearance of the angel was sudden. "The splendour of the Lord blazed round them" (Phps), lighting up the dark night, and they were seized with fear. The first words of the angel were to calm their fears and assure them that he came not as "a destroyer", but as a bearer of "good tidings of great joy". The literal translation of his words are, "I declare to you a great joy". It was a gospel declaration, for he uses the word that means to evangelise. This helps us to understand Paul's words to the Galatians, "But though we, or an angel from heaven, preach any other gospel unto you" (Gal 1:9), the very same language that Luke uses to describe the message from the angel. However, an angel was not the first gospel preacher, for God "preached before the gospel unto Abraham" in Gen 12:3 (see Gal 3:8).

11 "To all the people" (RV) in this immediate context indicates that it is the people of Israel to whom the tidings are given, not only to the shepherds. "To you is born a Saviour who is the Messiah, the Lord" (NEB) is addressed to the shepherds, but not exclusively to them. Once in the Gospel of John, Christ is called "the Saviour of the world" (John 4:42) by the men of Samaria. Luke 2:11 is the only time in the Synoptic Gospels that He is called Saviour. There are times when a great word or name used only once enhances its beauty, and this is true of "Saviour".

It is good to take note that the Lordship of Christ is declared in His resurrection from the dead in a unique way (Acts 2:36), but He was not less than "the Lord" when He lay in the manger. His Lordship is from eternity. Isaiah saw "the Lord ... high and lifted up" (Isa 6:1). John refers to that event by saying, "These things said Esaias, when he saw his glory, and spake of him" (John 12:41), and the context clearly shows that John is writing about the pre-incarnate glory of Christ. He is Lord in the realm of creation as is shown clearly in Luke 8:22-25 as He arose amid the storm and stilled wind and waves. He is Lord in the moral realm as He made clear in His spotless life and holy teaching (Matt 5:31-39). He is Lord in the realm of history, for He said, "I am Alpha and Omega, the beginning and the end, the first and the last" (Rev 22:13). He is Lord in the realm of death, and in resurrection and exalted glory (Phil 2:9-11), and this Lord of glory is Lord in His birth. This subject is included here so as to attempt to overcome the danger, so common in the religious world, of becoming so occupied with the sentimental aspects of the young mother and her babe that it is almost forgotten that He is the Lord of all, and she was but an instrument in His hand.

12 The "sign" to the shepherds was unmistakable; surely there was only one babe in Bethlehem that night that was "wrapped in swaddling clothes, lying in a manger". The virgin was to be a sign to the whole house of Israel and had the shepherds any knowledge at all of prophetic Scripture, they would have linked the sign with Immanuel (Isa 7:14).

13-14 The song of the heavenly host, an army of angels, is about the glory of God and His pleasure in men and their peace as a result of the birth of the Saviour. It has often been suggested that the angels were "saying", not singing. Many of US, including the writer, have taught that angels sang at the creation of the world (Job 38:4-7), but when sin entered the world it stilled the song of angels and they will not sing again until sin is obliterated from the universe and the eternal day dawns. Many believe the singing "stars" of Job are literal stars and not angels. If this be so, we have no Scripture for angels singing, for the language here is that they were "praising God and saying". As we have already pointed out (1:13-14), this is poetic language and may be sung, but we are told that the heavenly host "spoke" the words of this beautiful hymn.

"Peace, good will toward men" is a statement that is familiar even to the godless. It is a part of the pageant of Christmas and should scarcely require explanation; however, there has been much misunderstanding of this benediction. In his introduction to his *New Translation* of the NT, Mr. Darby shows how Westcott and Hort erred in following a reading that may have been the result of a scribal error. The RV translation reflects this disputed Greek text in its reading, "peace among men in whom he is well pleased". As Mr. Darby says, "The Revisers ... have placed the better text in the margin". The AV reflects the Textus Receptus reading of "good will toward men", or as Mr. Darby translates, "Glory to God in the highest, and on earth peace, good pleasure in men". The poor reading of the RV suggests that there are men on earth who are well pleasing to God. This must be rejected on doctrinal grounds. Nor is Luke saying that men find their pleasure in God, but that God, because of His sovereign grace, has bestowed His pleasure on men. The OT counterpart to this statement is found in Prov 8:3 1, "and my delights were with the sons of men". The heavenly host rejoiced that the sons of men should be the objects of God's "so great salvation". They showed no envy that, although salvation had not been provided for fallen angels, God, in the riches of His grace, had sent the Saviour to redeem the fallen sons of Adam. The peace is the bridging of the separation that sin caused-sin that placed men at a guilty distance from God, but the good pleasure of God is that reconciling grace should bring us nigh (Eph 2:13).

15-18   The angel from heaven was truly "sent" to these particular shepherds who went to Bethlehem, found Mary and Joseph, and the babe lying in a manger, and then made known in a wide sphere the proclamation of the angel to them that this child was none less than Christ the Lord, the Saviour. They were good communicators, for their words created in the hearts of those who heard them the same wonder that the angels' words had created in their hearts. God chose His messengers well; they spoke from their experience and from their hearts, the key to all effective testimony.

19   In contrast to the shepherds who told all who would listen, "Mary kept all these things", as a person would gather and guard a very costly treasure. A similar statement is found in 2:51, "his mother kept all these sayings in her heart". It was a mother's heart, we can be sure, but it was a believing heart, and therefore she pondered all that she had heard and seen. If this had been in view of pouring out her heart in public teaching some day, these statements would be far more understandable to people of our day. Mary was present in the upper room in Acts 1:14, as well as when the Spirit was poured out (Acts 2:1), but there is no suggestion that she ever taught publicly at all. What was the point of treasuring up truth then? There is a higher and holier occupation than public declaration: it is communion with God. All of us, including our sisters, should learn the value of storing up a treasury of truth and pondering it in our hearts that we might be able to communicate with our Father about His Son. No occupation is greater.

20   The shepherds returned to their flocks, but they were changed men. E.V. Rieu, in his translation of *The Four Gospels*, renders this verse, "Meanwhile the shepherds went back to their flock, glorifying and praising God for the news they had heard and the sight which confirmed it".

9.   *The Circumcision and Naming of the Lord*
2:21-24

v.21 "And when eight days were accomplished for the circumcising of the child, his name was called JESUS, which was so named of the angel before he was conceived in the womb.

v.22 And when the days of her purification according to the law of Moses were accomplished, they brought him to Jerusalem, to present *him* to the Lord;

v.23 (As it is written in the law of the Lord, Every male that openeth the womb shall be called holy to the Lord;)

v.24 And to offer a sacrifice according to that which is said in the law of the Lord, A pair of turtledoves, or two young pigeons."

21   In accordance with the sign of the covenant given to Abraham (Gen 17:1

-14), the Lord Jesus was circumcised on the eighth day. Paul, by the Spirit, followed the very order of these events in his great gospel statement in Gal 4:4, "but when the fulness of the time was come, God sent forth his Son, made of a woman, made under the law, to redeem them that were under the law". Although He was the Author of that law, He voluntarily was made under the law and was therefore subject to it. In all of His life He fulfilled the law flawlessly. This is the meaning of Isa 42:21, "The Lord is well pleased for his righteousness' sake; he will magnify the law, and make it honourable". In his comment on this verse, W.E. Vine links it with the words of Ps 40:8, "I delight to do thy will, O my God; yea, thy law is within my heart". There was never a point in time when this desire was not in His heart, so that He could say, "I do always those things that please him" (John 8:29). To "magnify the law, and make it honourable" was one of the results of the life of the perfect Man, who never failed in one point of it, thus proving that it can be lived.

Mary had not forgotten the initial message of Gabriel to her (1:31), so the child was called Jesus. This lovely, precious name, meaning, "the Lord is Saviour" (see Matt 1:21), containing in itself the very purpose of His coming into the world, should be used by us with great reverence in accordance with its use by the Holy Spirit. The name "Jesus" is found in Luke over one hundred times, but He is never called "Jesus" by the disciples. The Holy Spirit, through Luke, in His sovereign rights as a divine Person, may well speak of "Jesus", but the disciples, who we may judge had often been slow to learn, very carefully called Him Lord and Master and were commended by the Lord for so doing (John 13:13).

The name of the "Lord" is also found one hundred times in the Gospel of Luke. The record begins by giving Him His titles, "a Saviour ... Christ the Lord" (2: 11), and it closes by telling us that when the women came to the tomb, they ... found not the body of the Lord Jesus" (24:3).

The habit that has been linked to the modern "Jesus Movement" of calling Him "Jesus", and praying "in the name of Jesus", is a result of ignorance. A proper attitude toward untaught believers will make us treat them with love and grace, but, "Jesus is the Lord" (1 Cor 12:3), and even a young believer will soon learn this truth. It is of interest that the Lord only twice called Himself "Jesus"; both occasions were from heaven (Acts 9:5; Rev 22:16), and each time the response from earth was to call Him "Lord"; "Lord, what wilt thou have me to do?", and "Even so, come, Lord Jesus". Whenever the name "Jesus" stands alone, throughout the Acts and the Epistles, there are clear reasons for it in the context.

The reasons that we have just given will help to explain why He is called Lord throughout this commentary.

22-23 Being devout children of Israel, Mary and Joseph carefully carried out the law in relation to the presentation of the child before the Lord and the rites of purification for the mother. The presentation of the firstborn son of a mother was taught in Exod 13:11-16. Its significance was that the firstborn son " shall be the Lord's", and the reason given is that God had slain all the firstborn in Egypt, but Israel's sons were redeemed by the blood of the lamb. Is it not amazing that He who was the only true Israelite should submit to these regulations?, but when we consider that He, Himself was the true Lamb of God, it bows our hearts in worship.

Num 18:15,16 also required the payment of five shekels of silver. Luke says nothing about the silver, but 2:39 tells us that they did "all things according to the law of the Lord", so they must have paid the shekels too.

24 When a mother in Israel gave birth to a son, seven days of ceremonial uncleanness were observed up to the eighth day when the child was circumcised (Lev 12:1-8). During the next thirty-three days, the mother was to "touch no hallowed thing, nor come into the sanctuary" (v.4). At the close of the days of purification, she was to "bring a lamb of the first year for a burnt offering, and a young pigeon, or a turtledove, for a sin offering" (v.6). The closing verse of these instructions make a special allowance for the poor, " And if she be not able to bring a lamb, then she shall bring two turtles, or two young pigeons; the one for the burnt offering, and the other for a sin offering: and the priest shall make an atonement for her, and she shall be clean" (v.8).

Mary was one of the poor in Israel, unable to bring a lamb, so she came before the Lord with her two little birds. We need to take note that she was well aware that the one bird was for a sin offering. Mary never professed what others have said about her. She knew her need as a sinner and humbly brought the little bird that it might die for her ceremonial cleansing, a feeble picture at best of the Substitute who would bleed and die on the cross for sinners. *Nossos* ("young"), used in the phrase "two young pigeons", actually means "two nestlings of doves", two birds from the nest, likely well fed, but not yet having flown.

10.   *The Godly Simeon and His Prophecy*
        2:25-35

v.25 "And, behold, there was a man in Jerusalem, whose name *was* Simeon; and the same man *was* just and devout, waiting for the consolation of Israel: and the Holy Ghost was upon him.
v.26 And it was revealed unto him by the Holy Ghost, that he should not see death, before he had seen the Lord's Christ.
v.27 And he came by the Spirit into the temple: and when the parents brought in the child Jesus, to do for him after the custom of the law,
v.28 Then took he him up in his arms, and blessed God, and said,
v.29 Lord, now lettest thou thy servant depart in peace, according to thy word:
v.30 For mine eyes have seen thy salvation,
v.31 Which thou hast prepared before the face of all people;
v.32 A light to lighten the Gentiles, and the glory of thy people Israel.
v.33 And Joseph and his mother marvelled at those things which were spoken of him.
v.34 And Simeon blessed them, and said unto Mary his mother, Behold, this *child* is set for the fall and rising again of many in Israel; and for a sign which shall be spoken against;

v.35 (Yea, a sword shall pierce through thy own soul also,) that the thoughts of many
hearts may be revealed."

25   At the time of Mary's purification, when she brought the Lord Jesus to
Jerusalem (v.22), the prophecy of Simeon was given. "The same man was just
and devout, waiting for the consolation of Israel: and the Holy Ghost was upon
him", are four statements that describe a person who belonged to a small, godly
remnant in Israel, such as Malachi had described four hundred years earlier (Mal
3:16). Before men he was righteous; before God, he was truly reverent and careful
to keep the word of God in its demands on personal and public life. He waited
for the Messiah to appear, the Hope of Israel, the first Comforter (John 14:16-18),
a truth that had long lived in his heart, and the Holy Spirit was upon him.

26   "And it was divinely communicated to him by the Holy Spirit" (JND), not by
a sign in the sky, but by a communication to his heart. The same word used in
relation to Cornelius in Acts 10:22 is translated "warned from God". JND translates
this latter expression by the words, "has been divinely instructed", and this is the
sense in Luke 2. It is interesting to us that Cornelius is also described as being
devout (Acts 10:1).

He was assured that he would not die until he had seen the Lord's Christ. This
communication to Simeon had been made at some time in the past, for the verb
is a perfect tense, which denotes a past action with present, continuing results.
The truth that had been communicated to him by the Holy Spirit lived in him in
power. It is in this same sense that the truth of the second coming should live in
our hearts. The Lord promised to the overcomer, "I will give him the morning
star" (Rev 2:28). We are not assured that we will not die before He returns, but
the imminent reality of His coming should live in our hearts every day. This was
the case with Paul; he said, "we which are alive and remain" (1 Thess 4:17),
including himself among the living, and was he not writing by the Spirit?

27   Simeon had already arrived at the temple and was waiting there when Mary
and Joseph brought in the holy Child. It was divine timing. God's time is very
different from our reckoning. It is likely that Simeon had waited long, but hope
did not die. What a lesson to us while we wait God's time! The word for "custom"
is a participle of *ethizō* and is only found here in the NT. It "is equivalent to a
noun" (W.E. Vine). It means that which was prescribed by law and shows the
carefulness of Joseph and Mary to obey all that God had commanded.

28   Gentle arms cradled the Son of God. How tenderly and reverently he handled
the One he knew to be the "Lord's Christ"! In this connection, Dr. Heading has
drawn attention to the hands of evil men stretched out against the Lord. The
Lord Jesus said, "the Son of man is betrayed into the hands of sinners" (Matt
26:45); Matthew further records, "Then came they, and laid hands on Jesus, and

took him" (26:50). Luke tells us that the angel at the tomb said, "The Son of man must be delivered into the hands of sinful men" (24:7). Luke writes again, "him, being delivered ... ye have taken, and by wicked hands have crucified and slain" (Acts 2:23). In contrast, John tells us, " we have seen with our eyes, which we have looked upon, and our hands have handled, of the Word of life" (1 John 1:1).

29-30 Simeon addressed God as *despotēs* and called himself *ton doulon sou*, His bondslave. *Despotēs* is found ten times in the NT; three times it is a title of God and twice a title of the Lord Jesus. It means" A master, lord, one who possesses supreme authority" (W.E. Vine). It is closely related to the control of behaviour. Speaking of the apostates, Peter writes, "even denying the Lord that bought them" (2 Pet 2: 1). In a similar context, Jude writes, " ungodly men, who pervert the grace of God into immorality and disown Jesus Christ, our only Sovereign (*despotēs*) and Lord" (Jude 4, Wey). Simeon spoke of God as the sovereign Lord over all his conduct. He was truly a godly man.

"This day, Master, thou givest thy servant his discharge in peace; now thy promise is fulfilled" (NEB) is good gospel material and God has used it many times. It is a good thing when using a verse like this to apply the gospel in a personal way, stating clearly what it means in its context before applying it. Simeon was one of those who waited for salvation in Israel; he is certain that it has come; God has fulfilled His Word to His people. With his heart full, Simeon is ready now to have the moorings loosed that hold him to time. With his own eyes, he has looked upon the salvation of God.

31 A salvation which "thou hast made ready in full view of all the nations" is the NEB reading here, but "peoples" is a better rendering than "nations". This is very likely a comprehensive display before all, whereas v.32 divides "all peoples" into all nations and God's people. The Holy Spirit seldom uses *ethnos* to refer to Israel. There are some exceptions, as when the men who were sent by Cornelius to Peter spoke of "the nation of the Jews" (Acts 10:22), but the distinction between *ethnos*, a nation, and *laos*, a people, is carefully guarded. The reason is that Israel "shall not be reckoned among the nations" (Num 23:9). We do well to observe distinctions that God makes. In the melting pot of modern society, it is good for believers to remember that it is God who has "put a difference between holy and unholy, and between unclean and clean" (Lev 10:10). In Exod 11:7, the Lord put " a difference between the Egyptians and Israel", and this difference pertains to the present day. Simeon was speaking by the Holy Spirit and was intelligent about the difference.

32 There are two distinct statements in this verse. The fact that this salvation was "a light to lighten the Gentiles" did not by any means detract from the "glory of... Israel". God is not diminished by giving. What a pity that the enemies of the gospel among the Jews did not know this! A man standing for the first time on the Pacific Coast of America, and who had spent his life in poverty and deprivation, was heard to say, as the Pacific breeze wafted from the mighty ocean, "At last, here comes something there is enough of". Perhaps this expresses the thought of Simeon.

The statement of Isa 42:6,7 is quoted by Paul and Barnabas in Pisidian Antioch. When the Jews rejected their message, they turned to the Gentiles and said, "For so hath the Lord commanded us, saying, I have set thee to be a light of the Gentiles, that thou shouldest be for salvation unto the ends of the earth" (Acts 13:47). The messengers were not speaking of themselves as the light, but of their Lord.

"The glory of ... Israel" is another divine title of the Lord Jesus. Perhaps this is the place to set the titles in order that are found in the preceding verses:

1.	"The Son of the Highest"	-His nobility (1:32)
2.	"The Son of David"	-His royalty (1:32)
3.	"The Holy One"	-His purity (1:35)
4.	"The Son of God"	-His deity (1:35)
5.	"My Lord"	-His priority (1:43)
6.	"The "horn of salvation"	-His omnipotency (1:69)
7.	"The dayspring"	-His refulgency (1:78)
8.	"A Saviour"	-His mercy (2:11)
9.	"Christ the Lord"	-His supremacy (2:11)
10.	"The consolation of Israel"	-His monarchy (2:25)
11.	"A Light of the Gentiles"	-His universality (2:32)
12.	"The glory of ... Israel"	-His majesty (2:32).

All the glories that ever were related to the promises to Abraham, Isaac, Jacob and David are centred in this blessed Deliverer who has been for all ages the hope of mankind.

33 It is not amazing, then, that the hearts of this righteous couple were filled with wonder at all that they had seen and heard. So little is said or known of Joseph, but all that is said is good, and a heart that is full of wonder at such things will also be full of worship. Puritans used to say, "When we cease to wonder, we cease to worship".

34 "Simeon blessed them" and the antecedent to the pronoun "them" seems clearly to be Joseph and Mary. The song of Simeon (vv.29-32) was a public declaration to all who were present, but that which followed was spoken to the couple and then there was a private communication to Mary alone. The blessings that have been described are not to come easily or without tremendous cost. "This child is set," or as E.J. Goodspeed has translated, ('This child is destined to cause the fall and rise of many in Israel". Some take this to mean that many will fall before Him in repentance and rise to be blessed. No doubt, at times, this has been a gospel application of this text, but the word for "fall" means " an irretrievable fall" (W.E. Vine, *Expository Dictionary*, p.73). The word "again" in the AV suggests that the same ones who fall will rise again in resurrection, but Vine and many others believe that *ptōsis* ("to fall") is a description of the lost, and the "rising again" (*anastasis*, "resurrection") is a description of the saved. If this be true, it is not necessary to consider this resurrection to be figurative, but it can be understood in the sense of the Lord's promise to those who believe on Him, "I will raise him up at the last day" (John 6:40,44,54).

"For a sign which men will reject" or "spoken against" (JND) seems to be the sense of the last clause of this verse. This sign is a mark or token of a message or warning from God. Even though He is an infant, the fact must be known that He will be "despised, and rejected of men; a man of sorrows, and acquainted with grief: and as one from whom men hide their face he was despised, and we esteemed him not" (Isa 53:3 RV).

35   The two statements of this verse are distinct and yet truly belong together. This Child by whom the many of Israel were to be divided, some receiving Him to be eternally blessed, and some rejecting him to be irretrievably lost, would also be the cause of the piercing of Mary's heart. John says, "Now there stood by the cross of Jesus his mother... " (John 19:25). The sword that pierced her heart that day was sharp and deep. The word "sword" is *rhomphaia*, a Thracian weapon of large size (Moulton and Milligan), larger than a *machaira* which was a short sword or dagger.

The next statement surely is related to that day of suffering at the cross as well. The closing clause of v.35 also relates back to the "sign which shall be spoken against" of v.34, but none will deny that it was at the cross that the thoughts of many were laid bare. They were thoughts of envy, unjust hatred, scorn and fear. The sinful hearts of men were brought to the light by their attitude toward the Lord Jesus. By way of contrast, the heart of God was revealed there as well in the yielding up of His beloved Son and the pouring out on the sinless Sufferer the judgment that our sins deserved.

11.   *Anna, "She Spake of Him"*
   2:36-38

> v.36 "And there was one Anna, a prophetess, the daughter of Phanuel, of the tribe of Aser: she was of a great age, and had lived with an husband seven years from her virginity;
> v.37 And she *was* a widow of about fourscore and four years, which departed not from the temple, but served *God* with fastings and prayers night and day.
> v.38 And she coming in that instant gave thanks likewise unto the Lord, and spake of him to all them that looked for redemption in Jerusalem."

36-37 The Talmud, the book of Jewish law and tradition, records the name of only seven women who were prophetesses, so it was most unusual that at this time there was a prophetess in Israel. Added to this must be the consideration that Israel had heard no prophet for many hundreds of years. It is unlikely that the godly Anna was accorded much attention during the long years of her faithfulness to God.

Anna was truly old, just how old will not be decided here. Some believe that after seven years of married life, the young woman was left a widow, and the length of her widowhood was 84 years, making her as much as 110. The NASB renders this part of the verse that she was "a widow to the age of eighty- four", meaning that she was eighty-four at this time. JND seems to allow for this in his translation, but others support the thought that her widowhood had lasted eighty-four years. Her constant attendance at the temple may mean that she lived within its precincts, but it is more likely that it means that she fasted and prayed, not only at the accustomed hours of prayer, at 9 am and 3 pm, or on the ordinary fast days, but without ceasing in the sense of Paul's words to the Thessalonians, "Pray without ceasing" (1 Thess 5:17). God had preserved her alive for so long a time that she might be present on that day when the Lord Jesus as a child was brought into the temple.

Anna knew her tribal ancestry. This is more unusual than Paul being able to identify himself as being of the tribe of Benjamin, for Benjamin was closely linked with Judah, but not so the tribe of Asher. It is usually referred to as one of "the lost tribes", but we seriously wonder if this expression is not more misleading than helpful. When the Babylonian captivity ended, and the remnant under Zerubbabel returned to Judah and Jerusalem, they are called "all Israel" (Ezra 2:70); they built the "altar of the God of Israel" (3:2), and thirty-seven more times in Ezra, the remnant is called "Israel". Their enemies called them "these Jews", but God called them "all Israel". In BC 721, prior to the fall of Samaria to the newly-crowned Assyrian king, Sargon 11, and the exile of some 27 000 captives, many from the northern kingdom came down to Judaea because of the temple, the priesthood and David's royal line. In the days of Hezekiah's great passover, "posts went with the letters ... throughout all Israel and Judah" (2 Chron 30:6), and "divers of Asher and Manasseh and of Zebulun ... came to Jerusalem" (v.11). This also happened during the revival under Josiah, and throughout the years when the kingdom of Israel was divided. Enough of these people stayed in Judaea to perpetuate their families, and to ensure that there were representatives of all the tribes in the return from Babylon. Seven hundred years later a woman in Jerusalem can still identify herself as being of the tribe of Asher. It is this author's conviction that the expression "lost tribes" is inaccurate.

Her name, Anna or Hannah, was carried by another great woman of God in OT days (1 Sam 1:1-2:11). It is interesting to compare how both of them were marked by fasting and prayer and by a longing for a man child. Godly Hannah wanted a son to present to the Lord; godly Anna longed to see the Son that God was to send to His people, and the prayers of both of these women were answered in God's time.

38 "And she coming in that instant", that is, at the hour when Simeon blessed Joseph and Mary and spoke of the Child, she gave God praise for His Son and spoke "of him to all them that looked for redemption in Jerusalem". It is suggested that she was acquainted with all the remnant in the city who had kept faith and still waited with glad anticipation for the coming of the Saviour. *Anthomologeomai* ("give thanks") is only used here in the NT, even though it is often used in the LXX. The imperfect tenses of this verb and the next one, *laleo* ("to speak"), tell us that she continued to give thanks and continued to speak "of him". These two things are evidences of true godliness. It is tragic if our conversation is filled either with high praise of self or harsh criticism of others. How blessed to be continually thankful and to speak of Him always!

12.   *The Silent Years at Nazareth*
         2:39-40

> v.39 "And when they had performed all things according to the law of the Lord, they returned into Galilee, to their own city Nazareth.
> v.40 And the child grew, and waxed strong in spirit, filled with wisdom: and the grace of God was upon him."

39   This is the place in Luke's narrative to understand that the flight into Egypt took place. When Joseph was returning from Egypt, Matthew tells us, "he arose, and took the young child and his mother, and came into the land of Israel ... he turned aside into the parts of Galilee: and he came and dwelt in a city called Nazareth" (Matt 2:21-23). Luke's account agrees, "they returned into Galilee, to their own city Nazareth", but gives no account of the journey into Egypt.

In Isa 11:1, the word used for "Branch" is *netser*, to which the name of the town of Nazareth may be connected. This helps us to understand the words of Matt 2:23, "that it might be fulfilled which was spoken by the prophets, He shall be called a Nazarene". Mr. Darby has an excellent note in his translation at this verse, showing that this particular grammatical construction implies "an event which was within the scope and intention of the prophecy". No other OT prophecy mentions the Nazarene, so Matthew may well be referring to Isa 11. Dean Alford points out that the word "Branch" that is used of Messiah in five other passages is the Hebrew *tsemach*, a sprout, which is a synonym of *netser* which means a shoot. Nothing in the life of the Lord Jesus was without significance, and Nazareth reminds us of the fruitful Branch of the Lord that was of such sweet fragrance, beauty and great fruitfulness.

1.   The Branch of David (Jer 23:5; 33:15; Isa 11:1) which corresponds to the Son of David in Matthew.

2.   "My servant the Branch" (Zech 3:8) corresponding to the Son of Toil in Mark.

3.   "The man whose name is The Branch" (Zech 6:12) corresponding to the character of the Lord Jesus as Luke portrays the Son of man.

4.   "The Branch of the Lord" (Isa 4:2), the glorious Son of God, as John's Gospel describes Him.

Nazareth, the despised and poverty-stricken town of southern Galilee, was the home of the Lord on earth for almost thirty years.

40   The difficulties that we see in this verse may be of our own making. We thank God for this teaching, for it reminds us that He was the fulness of deity and the perfection of manhood in one Person, but the mystery of the hypostatic union of two natures in one blessed Person will always be beyond our comprehension. In these holy matters, we do well to use the Holy Spirit's own language about Him. He is never called "the Godman" which suggests that He was part God and part Man, and was some kind of a blending of the two. He was not a mixture, but as H. Champney has said, "Verily God, yet become truly human". This should never be a rock on which we break our meagre, limited intelligence regarding divine things. "Human thought is here confounded, 'Tis too vast to comprehend", and we bow our hearts in worship. His growth was natural, yet at the same time all the attributes of deity resided undiminished in His Person. We need to guard particularly against the kind of reasoning that suggests that at some time in His bodily development, He became aware of His mission. He left heaven with the Father's will in His heart: "I delight to do thy will, O my God" (Ps 40:8) is a timeless truth, unrestricted by circumstances.

"The grace of God was upon him" is one of the most touching statements in all the Gospel records. *Charis* "Grace" is mentioned only twice in Luke (2:40; 4:22), and this is amazing when we consider the fact that this is the Gospel of the grace of God. But see also Luke 1:30; 5:52; 4:22, 6:32,33,34 and 17:9 for other translations, e.g. favour, gracious and thank. The only other place where grace is mentioned in the Gospels is John 1:17, "the law was given by Moses, but grace and truth came by Jesus Christ" and v.14 and v.16. Notice the verbs in this verse, "the law was given", is an aorist passive, but "grace and truth came" is the aorist middle indicative of *ginomai* (to become). He acted Himself to become "grace and truth", and that action reflects back upon Him who is both Grace and Truth. The reason that the doctrine of grace is not found in the Gospel accounts is because He who is Grace was here; grace was personified in a blessed Person. The grace of God is not expressed in words because it was expressed in a living Reality.

13.   *The Boy of Twelve in the Temple*
     2:41-52

v.41 "Now his parents went to Jerusalem every year at the feast of the passover.
v.42 And when he was twelve years old, they went up to Jerusalem after the custom of the feast.
v.43 And when they had fulfilled the days, as they returned, the child Jesus tarried behind in Jerusalem; and Joseph and his mother knew not *of it*.
v.44 But they, supposing him to have been in the company, went a day's journey; and they sought him among *their* kinsfolk and acquaintance.
v.45 And when they found him not, they turned back again to Jerusalem, seeking him.
v.46 And it came to pass, that after three days they found him in the temple, sitting in the midst of the doctors, both hearing them, and asking them questions.
v.47 And all that heard him were astonished at his understanding and answers.
v.48 And when they saw him, they were amazed: and his mother said unto him, Son why hast thou thus dealt with us? behold, thy father and I have sought thee sorrowing.
v.49 And he said unto them, How is it that ye sought me? wist ye not that I must be about my Father's business?
v.50 And they understood not the saying which he spake unto them.
v.51 And he went down with them, and came to Nazareth, and was subject unto them: but his mother kept all these sayings in her heart.
v.52 And Jesus increased in wisdom and stature, and in favour with God and man."

41-42 It was customary for a Jewish boy of twelve years of age to go up to the temple at Jerusalem. From twelve and onward, the males of Israel were to appear before the Lord three times in the year, at Passover, at the Feast of Pentecost and at the Feast of Tabernacles (Exod 23:14-17; Deut 16:16). Although we are not specifically told that He did so, we can be assured that He who would " magnify the law, and made it honourable" fulfilled this requirement as well; this episode, when He was twelve, may have been the first time that He was present in Jerusalem since the days of His infancy, but He must have been present every year afterward until His death at the Passover time.

43 The days that were fulfilled refer to the seven days of Unleavened Bread that followed the Passover. Luke tells us that the entire festival was called " the Passover" (22:1). After this holy observance, Joseph and Mary were returning to Nazareth in the company of a number of their family and friends. Unknown to them, the Lord was not with them. In v.40 He is called to *paidion* ("the child"), but here He is called *ho pais* ("the boy"), for the diminutive no longer applied to Him. This is a tender touch from the beloved physician; it pictures to us a growing boy, developing in wisdom and grace.

44-45 They journeyed for an entire day before discovering that He was not in their company, and when they did not find Him among their relatives and friends, they turned back to Jerusalem, seeking for Him.
There are serious spiritual lessons in this incident. Their supposition that He

was with them, when He was absent, can be used to illustrate to unsaved people the mistake of supposing all is well with them on the journey of life when the great tragedy of their lives is that they do not have Him.

There is also rich teaching here for believers. The transcendent truth of omnipresence is unrelated to the restrictions of time, condition or events (Ps 139:7 -10; Jer 23:23,24). We are assured that He is never absent, yet there is in Scripture clear teaching that His presence can be realised and enjoyed subjectively, or lacking and missed, much to our sorrow (Ps 23:4; Isa 43:2). In days of service and of sorrow, His personal, known presence is often the subject of our prayers. God promised His presence with Moses even before he said, " If thy presence go not with me, carry us not up hence" (Exod 33:14,15). This distinction in omnipresence and realised presence will help us to apply the lessons that are before us.

Joseph and Mary failed because of presumption; they supposed that He was present when He was absent. In John 20:11-18, Mary Magdalene made a mistake in perception; she supposed that He was absent when He was present. Both of these failures are commonly known in our experiences. We should never presume that He is with us. Presumption is not faith (Heb 11:29).

The first step in recovery is to miss His presence, the second step is to seek for Him. It is a tragic thing for any believer when He cannot be found among friends; if this is true of us, we have the wrong kind of friends (v.45). The third step is to retrace our steps, to turn about. There are many Scriptures that tell of the blessing that comes to those who turn (Ps 80:3,7,19; Rev 1:12). It was on the third day that they found Him (v.46). Philip said to Nathaniel, "We have found him, of whom Moses in the law, and the prophets, did write" (John 1:45).

A contrast to the above can be found in John 20. Mary continued to stand at the sepulchre weeping, dazzled by the sight of two brilliant angels, one at the head and the other at the feet where the body of Jesus had lain, with the empty grave clothes lying between them. Yet she was turned from such a glorious sight to a greater glory. The Lord stood behind her, but "She, supposing him to be the gardener, saith unto him, Sir, if thou have borne him hence, tell me where thou hast laid him, and I will take him away" (v.15). The failure on Mary's part was to suppose that He was absent when He was truly present. How many times have we made the same mistake. Amid pain, sorrow and loneliness, we have supposed that He was absent; when in the trial, He had not forsaken us and we learned our mistake, and then have said like Mary that she "had seen the Lord, and that he had spoken ... unto her" (v.18).

46-47   When Joseph and Mary found Him, He was "sitting among the teachers, now listening to them, now asking them questions" (*Twentieth Cent. NT*). We should note that He was not teaching them, although they might have learned much from His questions, for "All were amazed at His powers of comprehension". It has been suggested that this conversation probably took place on the terrace where the rabbis, sitting on benches in a circle, gave public instruction on sabbaths and feast-days. As Paul sat at the feet of Gamaliel (Acts 22:3), "this eager boy, alive with interest" (A.T. Robertson) listened and asked questions. The verb *existēmi* ("were amazed") is the imperfect indicative in the middle voice and means literally, "they stood out of themselves", and tells us that their astonishment was repeated again and again as they heard the questions and answers that came from the lips of this twelve year old boy.

Young people and children can learn a lesson from the Lord's choice of company. White they need the companionship of their own peer group, we should not think that they must always find their company among those of their own age, or that it is boring for them to be in the company of those who are older. Wise young people will, at times, seek the company of those who are wiser than themselves, who have learned lessons in the school of experience. The example of the Lord is very valuable.

48   The statement of His mother was spoken in haste and in amazement at what she had discovered. Who could know better than she that Joseph was not physically His father? "Why hast thou thus dealt with us?" has often been the bewildered question of believers under difficult circumstances.

49-50   His answer exhibits the truth of the comments that have been made about v.48. He was calm and undisturbed. "How is it that ye sought me?" was likely linked to the sorrow that she said had accompanied their search. She seemed to have forgotten the overshadowing presence of the Almighty. "Wist ye not that I must be in the affairs of my Father?" (literally) as a gentle reminder that His Father was in heaven. Mary had spoken of "thy father", meaning Joseph, the Lord said, "my Father's business" making His claim to deity. Only He had the eternal right to use such intimate language about the Father. To Mary Magdalene He said, "I ascend unto my Father, and your Father "(John 20:17). He was Mary's Father by redemptive grace, but His Father by eternal relationship. These first words of the Lord about His Father should be compared with His last words on the cross, "Father, into thy hands I commend my spirit" (23:46), so His first recorded words and His last expressed His relationship to the Father. The Father's business which occupied Him throughout His life was culminated by His death, and was the subject of the cry, "It is finished" (John 19:30).

51   The gentle grace of His Person was displayed in His subjection. Obviously, as any dutiful son of the day, he learned the business of Joseph. Mark records that the people said of Him, "Is not this the carpenter, the son of Mary? " (Mark 6:3). H.S. Paisley, in his commentary on Mark, writes, "What grace that the great Creator should wear the garb of a village carpenter!" We are truly amazed to think that He who formed the swirling galaxies of space, formed the door and window frames of Nazareth, and was a truly obedient son to

Joseph and Mary. He is the perfect example to every son and daughter who profess to know Him as Saviour and Lord: "Children, obey your parents in the Lord: for this is right" (Eph 6:1). If it was right for Him, then it is right for our homes as well.

H.A. Ironside has told of an incident when he and his wife visited Palestine in 1936. On a journey from Damascus to Jerusalem, having passed through many places, hallowed once by the Lord's presence, they came to Nazareth. Poverty and need were apparent everywhere; an open drain carrying raw sewage ran beside the road. Mrs. Ironside stood in the street as her husband went to look at a sight in which he had interest. Turning back, he found his wife weeping and asked the cause of her tears, to which she responded, "Can it really be that the Lord of all was here?" Yes, He was, and for almost thirty years He lived in Nazareth.

52   This verse is akin to the statement of v.40 and should be understood in the same way. His deity in no way lessened His sinless humanity, and His humanity could never lessen His deity.

> "As Man he walked, as God He talked,
> His words were oracles, His works were miracles;
> Of man, the highest specimen; of God, the true expression;
> Full-orbed deity, clothed with humanity,
> Veiled in flesh, the Godhead see,
> Hail the incarnate deity!"

The increase in wisdom, stature and favour (grace) that creates such wonder in our hearts, has been well expressed in the words. "At each stage (of life), He was perfect for that stage" (A. Plummer). The apocryphal gospels have pictured the child Jesus constantly displaying unusual powers and performing meaningless miracles with bits of stick and clay. The inspired records contain nothing like this. He was a normal child and youth, but perfectly so, "foregoing the use of His divine powers" (W. Liefeld), waiting in grace and patience for the day of His manifestation to Israel. So little is revealed of these silent years that the window provided by vv.51-52 takes on great significance.

II. The Preparation for Public Ministry (3:1-4:13)

1.   *The Ministry of John the Baptist*
3:1-20

> v.1   "Now in the fifteenth year of the reign of Tiberius Caesar, Pontius Pilate being governor of Judaea, and Herod being tetrarch of Galilee, and his brother Philip tetrarch of Ituraea and of the region of Trachonitis, and Lysanias the tetrarch of Abilene,

v.2   Annas and Caiaphas being the high priests, the word of God came unto John the son of Zacharias in the wilderness.

v.3   And he came into all the country about Jordan, preaching the baptism of repentance for the remission of sins;

v.4   As it is written in the book of the words of Esaias the prophet, saying, The voice of one crying in the wilderness, Prepare ye the way of the Lord, make his paths straight.

v.5   Every valley shall be filled, and every mountain and hill shall be brought low; and the crooked shall be made straight, and the rough ways *shall be* made smooth;

v.6   And all flesh shall see the salvation of God.

v.7   Then said he to the multitude that came forth to be baptized of him, O generation of vipers, who hath warned you to flee from the wrath to come?

v.8   Bring forth therefore fruits worthy of repentance, and begin not to say within yourselves, We have Abraham to *our* father: for I say unto you, That God is able of these stones to raise up children unto Abraham.

v.9   And now also the axe is laid unto the root of the trees: every tree therefore which bringeth not forth good fruit is hewn down, and cast into the fire.

v.10   And the people asked him, saying, What shall we do then?

v.11   He answereth and saith unto them, He that hath two coats, let him impart to him that hath none; and he that hath meat, let him do likewise.

v.12   Then came also publicans to be baptized, and said unto him, Master, what shall we do?

v.13   And he said unto them, Exact no more than that which is appointed you.

v.14   And the soldiers likewise demanded of him, saying, And what shall we do? And he said unto them, Do violence to no man, neither accuse *any* falsely; and be content with your wages.

v.15   And as the people were in expectation, and all men mused in their hearts of John, whether he were the Christ, or not;

v.16   John answered, saying unto *them* all, I indeed baptize you with water; but one mightier than I cometh, the latchet of whose shoes I am not worthy to unloose: he shall baptize you with the Holy Ghost and with fire:

v.17   Whose fan *is* in his hand, and he will throughly purge his floor, and will gather the wheat into his garner; but the chaff he will burn with fire unquenchable.

v.18   And many other things in his exhortation preached he unto the people.

v.19   But Herod the tetrarch, being reproved by him for Herodias his brother Philip's wife, and for all the evils which Herod had done,

v.20   Added yet this above all, that he shut up John in prison."

As this third chapter begins, the silent years in Nazareth are coming to a close. Only eternity will disclose the story of those thirty years of silence and submission. We can be certain that they were necessary, and filled with joy for the One who was truly ever in His Father's business.

In giving us the ministry of John the Baptist, Luke begins with the word of God coming to him in the wilderness, describes his preaching of repentance in the Jordan valley, reaches back into the OT to tell us that John is the voice that Isaiah had foretold would prepare the way for the coming of the Lord, and describes the solemn warnings of this faithful prophet who brought upon himself the enmity of priests and Pharisees. His reproof of king Herod for his wickedness cost him his liberty and eventually his life.

We are indebted to many sources for the following historical data. An interested reader should consult the bibliography.

1   Tiberius Caesar succeeded his stepfather, Augustus, to the imperial throne in August, AD 14. At that time, he was already fifty-six years of age with a lifetime of government experience behind him. For twenty-three years he loyally carried out the policies of Augustus throughout the empire. Whenever Caesar is mentioned in the four Gospels, it is Tiberius Caesar.

Luke's carefulness in dating the beginning of John's public ministry should leave no doubt about the date of these events; yet some degree of doubt exists, so a short explanation might be helpful. All are aware that AD, Anno Domini, from the year of our Lord, dates from His birth. In the 6th century, Dionysius Exiguus assumed that AD 1 was the year 754 from the building of Rome, but most modern chronologists believe that he was mistaken by as much as four years, so that our Lord may have been born four years prior to our reckoning of AD 1. The Gospel records are undated, but Luke is careful to anchor events to a particular time. However, the best that most scholars are willing to say about "the fifteenth year of the reign of Tiberius Caesar" is that it was approximately AD 26 or 27.

Pontius Pilate was governor of Judaea from AD 26-36, so he appeared on the scene shortly before John began to preach. How little Pilate could have known about the part that he would play in the greatest events the world has known!

Herod, the tetrarch of Galilee, is Herod Antipas, the son of Herod the Great. He ruled over Galilee and Peraea from BC 4 until AD 39. Herod the tetrarch, which means a ruler of a fourth part, is the man who beheaded John the Baptist, made mock of Christ and, finally deposed by the emperor Caligula, died in exile. He was a cruel and cunning man. The Lord Jesus called him "that fox" (Luke 13:32).

Philip, the tetrarch of Ituraea and the region of Trachonitis, was the brother of Herod Antipas. He ruled a region that is north-east of the Sea of Galilee for thirty-seven years, from BC 4 until AD 33, and was noted for moderation and justice, most unusual traits for anyone of the Herodian family. He rebuilt Panias and called it Caesarea Philippi, the city where the Lord Jesus spoke the notable words of Matt 16:18, "I will build my church". There were two Philips among the sons of Herod the Great.

"Lysanias the tetrarch of Abilene" is mentioned only here in Scripture. No mention is made of him in extra- biblical literature, but a man with the same name is mentioned by Josephus (Antiquities xv.92) as having been executed by Antony in BC 36, so it was said by many scholars that Luke was mistaken. F.F. Bruce, in his note on Lysanias in the *Tyndale Illustrated Bible Dictionary*, and M.F. Unger in *Archaeology of the New Testament* verify from inscriptions that there were two men of this name and one of them was truly the tetrarch of Abilene at this time. By the time that Luke wrote, the region ruled by Philip and that ruled by Lysanias were combined under Herod Agrippa, but Luke is very careful not to confuse the time at which he writes with the time about which he is writing. This is a small example of the Holy Spirit's control over the accuracy of all Scripture.

2 "Annas and Caiaphas being the high priests" has often caused confusion in the minds of readers of the NT. The high priest was the ultimate civil, political and religious authority recognised by the most of the Jews. Throughout the Gospel records, Annas appears as man of great influence and authority, and yet the official high priest was Caiaphas (Matt 26:3,5 7; John 18:12-14,24). "Annas was high priest AD 6-15, when the Roman Governor Gratus deposed him" (L. Morris). Five of his sons were appointed by the Roman authorities to be high priest after him, but were quickly deposed until Caiaphas, Annas' son-in-law, was appointed in AD 18. This arrangement suited the Roman authorities well, for Caiaphas held the office for eighteen years, but it did not suit many of the Jews. They believed that a high priest was ordained of God for life, and still recognised Annas, though deposed, as being the high priest. He wielded great influence, so John tells us that the Lord Jesus was brought first to stand before Annas, and only afterward was he taken before Caiaphas (John 18:12,13). Luke's accuracy is again apparent. He uses the singular when speaking of the high priest, for there was only one high priest officially, even though Annas had great influence.

There is great importance to the clause, "the word of God came unto John". "The word of God came" is a very common expression in the prophetic books of the OT, and it is intended here in just that sense. To this servant of God who ranked as great as any of the prophets of old, *rhēma* ("a word") from God came. *Rhēma theou* ("a word of God") indicates a particular word, addressed to a specific need, whereas *ton logon tou theou* ("the word of God", 5:1) is used for the word of God generally. *Rhēma theou* is used in the NT in John 3:34; 8:47; Acts 11:16; Rom 10:17; Eph 6:17; Heb 6:5; 11:3; 1 Pet 1:25 and Rev 17:17, and is common in the LXX. Only Luke records "the word of God came unto John". This is the tenth time that Luke has used *rhēma*, and he uses it nine more times in the remainder of his Gospel. The two other synoptic Gospels use it only eight times between them. The significance of this may be that Luke is stressing the importance of a specific word from God to meet the immediate need of lost sinners, which is a theme of this Gospel.

3 John preached, in the Jordan valley, a message of repentance and forgiveness of sins, and baptised those who gave evidence of repentance. The parallel account in the other Gospels, and vv.7-18 of this chapter, show that he did not baptise all who came as candidates. True repentance was necessary before there could be a public testimony of it in baptism. There are many times in the NT when repentance stands as a covering term that includes faith in Christ (Acts 11:18; 17:30; Rom 2:4; 2 Tim 2:25; 2 Pet 3:9). The washing away of sins in baptism is twice mentioned in the Acts. In both cases (Acts 2:38; 22:16) the baptism is an outward witness of the turning away from sin in heart and practice. After the resurrection, the particular sins that were cleansed in public baptism were the sins of the nation in the rejection of Messiah. Those who were baptised were cutting themselves off from Israel, disowning any part in the crimes associated with the rejection of Christ.

4   John said, when asked if he were the Christ, "I am the voice of one crying in the wilderness" (John 1:23). He identified himself in Isaiah's prophecy; it was a lowly claim, only a "voice ... in the wilderness" that would not be heard by anyone, but John was heard (Matt 3:5) and the people came from the towns and villages to hear this strange preacher who was so plain in his dress, diet and delivery (Matt 3:4). His preaching was a preparation for the coming of the Lord, that is, a preparation of the hearts of men to receive Him.

5-6   Seeing that John aimed at hearts, we must interpret Isaiah's prophecy in this way. It was not a physical road-bed in the desert for a highway, but his preaching did prepare hearts, and we are told exactly the preparation that was necessary. John's preaching about the coming King and his baptism unto repentance were a distinct ministry, but repentance is the same in whatever context it is viewed, and John's preaching was "unto repentance".

John's preaching was addressed to a nation that owned God with their lips, but whose hearts were far from Him. The call to repentance was national. There were times when cities, such as Nineveh were called to repentance (Jonah 3), but this was a call to an entire nation; yet repentance had to be a work of the Holy Spirit in individuals who made up the nation of Israel, so it must be very personal. John therefore preached to bring about personal conviction, and his preaching was effective in the case of a small remnant. This has ever been the experience of those who preach repentance.

"Every valley shall be exalted" requires that the dark lives of the people must be brought to the light and exposed. "Every mountain and hill shall be made low" is a bringing down, a humbling before the Lord. Zacchaeus was such a hill (19:1-10); the proud Pharisee who did not come down was a mountain (18:9-14). "The crooked shall be made straight" is indicative of the honesty that is necessary toward God before the heart is prepared for the Lord. It was said that the good-ground hearers are they, "which in an honest and good heart, having heard the word, keep it" (8:15). All hearts are "deceitful... and desperately wicked" (Jer 17:9), so this honesty is toward God in acknowledging what He says about our sins to be true. "The rough places plain" involves the removal of every obstacle, every hindrance before the "salvation of God" would be revealed. Every preacher of the gospel will see how closely this parallels our preaching today.

7   The crowds went out to him from "Jerusalem, and all Judaea, and all the region round about Jordan" (Matt 3:5). Scant comment has ever been made about what drew the crowds. Dr. Heading, in his commentary on Matthew in this series, outlines three possible motives, mentioned by the Lord in Matt 11:7-15, that drew the crowds. To see " a weak and uncertain man", to see " a man of pomp, luxury and authority", or to see "a prophet". The first two questions had an obvious negative answer, while the response to the third was positive, but the Lord added, " yea. . . and more than a prophet" (v.9). He was the Lord's messenger that went before His face-His forerunner. "Among them that are born of women there hath not risen a greater than John the Baptist" (vv. 10,11). It was a visitation from God in Israel that drew the crowds, and all the people were "persuaded that John was a prophet" (Luke 20:6).

It was certainly not smooth preaching or pleasing words that drew them. "0 generation of vipers" is literally "a brood of poisonous snakes". He preached that God's wrath was awaiting them and on its way to overwhelm them. "The wrath to come" is closely linked to Jerusalem's destruction in AD 70, but not limited to it. The coming wrath of God that will fall like a pent-up storm upon Israel and the nations in the coming day of the Lord is truly the wrath to come.

8   Many of the people reacted to John's preaching by claiming that they were sons of Abraham. The teaching of the Lord Jesus in John 8:33 -40, and of Paul in Gal 3:6-9, is that Abraham's true children are the genuine children of faith and will do the works of Abraham. The Lord told those who claimed to be the children of Abraham, "Ye are of your father the devil, and the lusts of your father ye will do" (John 8:44). So John tells his hearers that their claim to be the children of Abraham will not save them in the day of wrath. God could destroy them and raise up from the very stones children to Abraham in whom He would fulfil His covenant.

9   Already, the axe lay at the root of the tree, ready for the blow that would cut them down. Bringing "forth good fruit" is called in the previous verse "fruits consistent with your professed repentance" (Goodspeed). He said, "Let your lives prove your repentance" (TCNT). The only other alternative was to be cut down and cast into the fire. The axe at "the root of the trees" is a figurative way of saying that God's judgment has already been determined, and will be carried out in due time, when the sinner least expects it. There are other expressions of impending judgment in the NT, such as "it is near, even at the doors" (Matt 24:33); "behold the judge standeth before the door" (James 5:9). The Lord spoke of the person who observed the sky and was warned of rain, or the south wind and knew that heat would come (Luke 12:54-56). So the axe laid to the root of the trees is the warning that judgment is imminent.

10   The people were disturbed, and well they might be. There was power in John's preaching. The Holy Spirit was upon him and his preaching was in the spirit and power of the ancient prophet Elijah (Luke 1:15-17). John's preaching reached their consciences and condemned their ways, so they asked, "What shall we do then?". This question takes full knowledge of the serious warnings in John's preaching and can be paraphrased, "Since this is true, then (*oun*) what shall we do?". Again Luke uses the imperfect tense to indicate that it was not a passing notion, for they continued to say, "What then shall we do?". Their acceptance of John's preaching is the strongest evidence that the people regarded him as a prophet.

11   John cannot be charged with being impractical. He did not tell them to give one coat, if that was all they had, but if they had two coats and another had none, they should share with them, and likewise, they should share their food. John's teaching harmonised with the Lord's own teaching (Matt 5:42).

12-13   The Romans had developed a tax system throughout the empire that involved bids for tax collecting. A publican paid to the government the cost of the tax bid and then collected the taxes and the extra to cover expenses and profit. They often exacted more than was fair. Publicans are linked with sinners throughout the Gospels, and were mistrusted and hated. Many of the Jews thought that publicans were traitors to their nation. John's teaching to them was "Collect no more than you have been ordered" (NASB), indicating that the government had set a limit to what could be called the cost of collection.

14   The soldiers were very likely Jewish, for John was sent to Israel. There were soldiers of the governor in Jerusalem (Matt 27:27), but these men who were doing military service may have been the enforcers of the tax laws and therefore were the strong arm of the publicans. They were characterised by maliciously reporting against rich people so that by fear they could extort money. John's words to them covered all the excesses of their profession. His teaching was that they should stop their extortion and false accusations and be content with what they could honestly earn.

The expression, "Do violence to no man" contains another of the unique words employed by Luke. This is the only time when this word *diaseiō* ("violence") is used in the NT, but it is found in the LXX (Job 4:14). It means to thoroughly shake a victim until he gives up his possessions rather than submit to further terror. "Neither accuse any falsely" is another graphic word picture. *Sukophanteō* ("accuse falsely") is only found here and in 19:8, but is frequent in the LXX. It means to make false accusations with the intention of exacting money from the accused by threat or force.

15   Listening to John put the people "on the tiptoe of expectation" (NEB). The expression does not imply a looking for judgment, but, as the rest of the verse indicates, an expectation of Messiah. The first recorded words of John were concerning the coming Deliverer, and all of his preaching had Christ as its theme. Lessons are to be learned here. It is wrong to preach judgment apart from the Spirit's power, or without tenderness, or without preaching the blessed Remedy.

16   To those who were asking in their hearts if John were the Messiah, he had a twofold answer, "I indeed baptize you with water ... he shall baptize you with the Holy Ghost and with fire", and "one mightier than I cometh, the latchet of whose shoes I am not worthy to unloose". This was a permanent characteristic of John, "He must increase, but I must decrease" (John 3:30,31). "None knew better than John, himself, his own inferiority to Christ. He was the voice, Jesus was the Word. He was a lamp, Jesus was the light. He was a herald, Jesus was the King. He was the axeman, Christ was the landowner" (E.W. Rodgers, *Jesus the Christ*). John was a sign post who ever sought to point people to his Lord and to keep self as much out of sight as possible. He is a worthy example for all servants of the Lord.

The baptism "with the Holy Spirit" should be understood as a foretelling of Pentecost, but individually it is synonymous with salvation. "With" is en ("in"), but is instrumental, so the AV, RV, RSV, NASB, Phps, NEB, JND and many other translations, retain "with". The "baptism with fire" is coming judgment and should never be imagined to be the cloven tongues of fire that were seen on the day of Pentecost. To be immersed in fire for eternity is a tragedy beyond our feeble comprehension.

17-18   Winnowing was a tossing of the grain into the wind, after it had been trod upon by oxen. The wind carried away the chaff, leaving only the winnowed grain on the threshing floor. The winnowing fan or fork was the instrument used for this separation of wheat and chaff. Every word of this solemn text, that describes the eternal separation of the saved from the lost, is significant. The word "gather" has been called a word of *congregation*. There is a present gathering out of the nations, but there will be a future gathering of the people of God out of the world of the ungodly at the rapture (2 Thess 2: 1). It also applies, and more accurately, to the day when the sheep will be separated from the goats (Matt 25:32). "The wheat" is a word of *designation*. In Matthew, it is called "his wheat" (Matt 3:2). The Lord Jesus said to Peter, "Satan hath desired to have you, that he may sift you as wheat: but I have prayed for thee" (Luke 22:31,32). It should be noticed that "you" in this statement is plural, referring to all the disciples (Judas had already gone out), but "thee" is singular, referring to Peter. "Into his garner" is a word of *destination*, and the solemn "but" is a word of *separation*. This is the message of this solemn warning; the day will come when the real will be separated from the false.

"Will throughly purge" is a translation of *diakathairō*, another of Luke's words that are only found once in the NT. It means a thorough cleansing with no traces of the chaff left behind.

The examples of John's preaching that are given are but a few of the many exhortations that he gave to the people. The word *euangelizō* ("preached") is the declaration of the good news, but it also refers to the content of what is preached. It is used ten times in this Gospel (see comments, 1:19) and only once in the other synoptic Gospels (Matt 11:5). The verb *kērusso* ("to preach"), used sixty-one times in the NT, always is used for the act of preaching as a herald. The noun kerugma ("preaching"), found eight times in the NT, refers to the content of what is preached; but *euangelizō* is frequently used to emphasise both the act of the herald and the good news that he proclaims.

19-20 Philip, who is here called the brother of Herod the tetrarch, is not Philip, the tetrarch of v.1. Herod the Great had two sons named Philip. The Philip who was married to Herodias was a private citizen. His father had once named him as his chief heir, but in a later will, he excluded him. On a visit to Philip and Herodias, Herod Antipas became infatuated with his brother's wife. They agreed together to forsake their marriage partners and to marry each other. The language of our verse says that John continued to reprove (a present participle) Herod for this wickedness and for all the evils that he had done. Herodias was Herod's niece and his half-brother's wife; their marriage, therefore, was both adulterous and incestuous. For his honesty and faithfulness, John lost his liberty and eventually his head. It was Salome, the daughter of Herodias, who so pleased Herod with her dancing that she was promised whatever she would ask. Prompted by her evil mother, she asked for the head of John Baptist, and although the king was sorry, he had John beheaded in the prison, so Herodias had her evil revenge. But this happened many months after the beginning of the ministry of the Lord. The death of John is recorded here to complete the story of John's ministry.

2.   *The Baptism of the Lord Jesus*
   3:21-22

> v.21 "Now when all the people were baptized, it came to pass, that Jesus also being baptized, and praying, the heaven was opened,
> v.22 And the Holy Ghost descended in a bodily shape like a dove upon him, and a voice came from heaven, which said, Thou art my beloved Son; in thee I am well pleased."

21 The first part of this verse is merely stating that it was at the time that all the people were baptised that the Lord Jesus was also baptised by John. Although Luke does not say that John performed it, we know that he did (Matt 3:13-17; Mark 1:9-11).

Why was the Lord Jesus baptised? We know from Matt 3:14 that this question perplexed the Baptist. The answer of the Lord to John is the answer to our question, but in that answer what is the meaning of the words, "thus it becometh us to fulfil all righteousness" (Matt 3:15)?

Many have attempted to answer this question. Those who believe that baptism is a cleansing from sin, usually explain it by saying that although He was without sin, He identified Himself with the sins of a lost world that He would one day bear on the cross. But baptism does not wash away sins from before God's face and judgment throne. It cannot be more than an outward sign of a work that has already been done in the soul. Baptism is always primarily linked to death, not to the receiving of life (Rom 6:3). The washing away of sins in baptism, as already stated in the comment on v.3 of this chapter, was a public disassociation with the sins of Israel in their rejection of their Messiah (Acts 2:38). This identification with the sins that He would bear is also taught by some who are very clear on salvation. They claim that as baptism is a symbol of death, burial and resurrection, so He is symbolising His own work.

Others have taught that the Lord was showing His submission to the law of Moses, but how John's baptism, a new work to announce the coming of the Lord, can be identified with the law of Moses is a puzzle. Lewis Sperry Chafer taught, "The baptism is related to the priestly office and the voice that spoke is the attestation of Christ's appointment as a Priest" (*Systematic Theology*, 5:62). We believe that on earth the Lord Jesus manifested priestly character, but that He did not enter into priestly office until His resurrection and ascension (Heb 5:9,10).

There are those who teach that it was a Messianic anointing, thus identifying Himself with the preaching of John, attesting that He was the Lord whom John came to announce. This is much closer, but we believe it still fails to explain the meaning of His baptism.

In the Matthew passage, the Lord told John, "it becometh us", that is, the Lord and John, so the baptism displayed a righteousness that could be seen in both John and his Lord. This clearly limits its meaning. We cannot make it a unique righteousness of the Lord if John shared it, so many explanations, such as those mentioned above are disqualified. All are agreed that the Lord had no sins of which to repent or that needed cleansing, whereas all others baptised by John had this need. In this respect, the baptism of the Lord was unique, but we still need to understand the fulfilling of all righteousness, which was the Lord's reason for being baptised.

Baptism is an outward sign. If the inner reality is absent, the baptism is a mere pretence and has no more value than to make the candidate wet. There was a false righteousness among the Jews, and the Lord often condemned it, but there was also a genuine righteousness that was seen in such people as Zacharias and Elisabeth, Mary and Joseph, Simeon, Anna and John. These people and others were a godly few, comprising something that God has always had in this world, a godly remnant. In His baptism, the Lord showed His approval of this godly remnant by identifying Himself with it. Many false candidates came to be baptised by John, and being baptised did not make them real, but he did baptise the truly righteous remnant, forming a company of baptised people who were waiting for the kingdom of God, like Joseph of Arimathaea (Luke 23:51). "They shall be mine, saith the Lord" (Mal 3:17). This generally is the view of J.N. Darby, W. Kelly, A.T. Robertson, A.C. Gaebelein, G.C. Morgan, C.L. Feinberg, A. Plummer and many others.

"Being baptised, and praying" is a characteristic statement of Luke. He traced the prayer life of the Lord Jesus with great care (3:21; 5:16; 6:12; 9:28; 11:1; 18:1-8; 22:32,40-46; 23:46). Not only did the Lord teach His disciples the need to pray, but He was the great example to them of a life of prayer and thanksgiving. It is often difficult for us to grasp the fact that the Lord lived the life of faith, as a dependent Man (Heb 12:2).

22   The previous verse closes with the opened heavens (Ezek 1:1), and now, out of that opened heaven, "the Holy Ghost descended in a bodily shape like a dove upon him". Many have referred to the meekness, gentleness and purity of the dove. Perhaps just as important is that it is a symbol of a single eye. Singleness of purpose marked the life of the Lord, "I do always those things that please him" (John 8:29). The oil of the meal offering is typical of the life that was ever and always under the control of the Holy Spirit; the frankincense typifies that all was done for the glory of God.

But did He not have the Holy Spirit in full measure prior to His baptism? The answer to this is an assured yes, "God giveth not the Spirit by measure unto him" (John 3:34), but at His baptism, we have the truth of Isa 42:1, " Behold my servant ... I have put my spirit upon him". On the distinction between the Spirit being always in Him and coming upon Him by public manifestation in His perfect service, Dr. Heading ably explains, "The Lord always possessed the Spirit in Himself, but here the Spirit comes upon Him. The difference is seen in connection with the oil of the meal offering, 'upon it' and 'mingled with oil' (Lev 2:1-5). Internal oil speaks of essential and absolute possession, external oil speaks of anointing for specific service" (*Luke's Life of Christ*, p.44).

The voice of the Father from heaven said (literally), " my son, the beloved, in thee I am well pleased". Immediately our minds are carried to the secret recesses of eternal relationship where the Son ever was the object of the Father's everlasting pleasure, "thou lovest me before the foundation of the world" (John 17:24). Luke 3:22 is one of the many verses that include all the Trinity. How wrong it is to think of God as the eternal Father without also thinking of the eternal Son and Holy Spirit. God did not call an "it" His Beloved. "In thee I am well pleased" has been called "an excellent example of the timeless aorist" (W. Hendriksen). There was no time when this was not true. It is quite staggering to consider that the Spirit also says to us, " beloved" (Rom 1: 7; Eph 5:1). There was every reason that He should call His own Son " my beloved", but no reason in us.

So far as we know from the Gospel records, John the Baptist came face to face with the Lord Jesus only on this one occasion, but it was the greatest moment in his life (John 1:31); in fact, it was the very purpose of his life and ministry (3:4-6). When Christ stooped to be baptised by John and demonstrated His submission to the will of God, it was the opportune time for heaven's approval of Him to be expressed. There is a principle in Scripture that whenever Christ and sin are linked, His absolute purity is declared (2 Cor 5:23; 1 Pet 2:22-25), for no sin could ever taint His holy person. At the commencement of His public ministry, the Father spoke from heaven to express His love and delight in His Son, and at the close of it a voice is heard again from heaven (John 12:28). The dove resting on the ark was a beautiful type of the descent of the Spirit as a dove upon Christ, for just as the dove found nowhere to rest its feet in the scene of death that followed the flood, so the Spirit here found a true resting place only on Christ.

This is the end of Luke's story about John, and is a good place to demonstrate how Luke has kept the two persons of John and the Lord Jesus before us in a parallel way. This can be seen in the following comparisons.

John	Jesus
Gabriel announced his birth, 1:13.	Gabriel announced his birth, 1:31.
"Whereby shall I know?", 1:18.	Mary, "How shall this be?", 1:34.
Name given before birth, 1:13.	Name given before birth, 1:31.
"He shall be great", 1:15.	"He shall be great", 1:32.
Elisabeth hidden five months, 1:24.	Mary away from home three months, 1:56.
The child is born, 1:57.	The child is born, 2:7.
The song of Zacharias, 1:68-79.	The song of Mary, 1:47-55.
The growth of John, 1:80.	The growth of Jesus, 2:40.
John baptising, 3:3.	Jesus baptising, 3:21.
His work described by Isaiah, 3:4.	His work described by Isaiah, 4:18.

3.   *The Genealogy of the Lord Jesus*
      3:23-38

v.23 "And Jesus himself began to be about thirty years of age, being (as was supposed) the son of Joseph, which was *the son* of Heli,

v.24 Which was *the son* of Matthat, which was *the son* of Levi, which was *the son* of Melchi, which was *the son* of Janna, which was *the son* of Joseph,

v.25 Which was *the son* of Mattathias, which was *the son* of Amos, which was *the son* of Naum, which was *the son* of Esli, which was the son of Nagge,

v.26 Which was *the son* of Maath, which was *the son* of Mattathias, which was *the son* of Semei, which was *the son* of Joseph, which was the son of Juda,

v.27 Which was *the son* of Joanna, which was *the son* of Rhesa, which was *the son* of Zorobabel, which was *the son* of Salathiel, which was *the son* of Neri,

v.28 Which was *the son* of Melchi, which was *the son* of Addi, which was *the son* of Cosam, which was *the son* of Elmodam, which was the son of Er

v.29 Which was *the son* of Jose, which was *the son* of Eliezer, which was *the son* of Jorim, which was *the son* of Matthat, which was *the son* of Levi,

v.30 Which was *the son* of Simeon, which was *the son* of Juda, which was *the son* of Joseph, which was *the son* of Jonan, which was *the son* of Eliakim,

v.31 Which was *the son* of Melea, which was *the son* of Menan, which was *the son* of Mattatha, which was *the son* of Nathan, which was *the son* of David,

v.32 Which was *the son* of Jesse, which was *the son* of Obed, which was *the son* of Booz, which was *the son* of Salmon, which was *the son* of Naasson,

v.33 Which was *the son* of Aminadab, which was *the son* of Aram, which was *the son* of Esrom, which was *the son* of Phares, which was *the son* of Juda,

v.34 Which was *the son* of Jacob, which was *the son* of Isaac, which was *the son* of Abraham, which was *the son* of Thara, which was *the son* of Nachor,

v.35 Which was *the son* of Saruch, which was *the son* of Ragau, which was *the son* of Phalec, which was *the son* of Heber, which was *the son* of Sala,

v.36 Which was *the son* of Cainan, which was *the son* of Arphaxad, which was *the son* of Sem, which was *the son* of Noe, which was *the son* of Lamech,

v.37 Which was *the son* of Mathusala, which was *the son* of Enoch, which was *the son* of Jared, which was *the son* of Maleleel, which was *the son* of Cainan,

v.38 Which was *the son* of Enos, which was *the son* of Seth, which was *the son* of Adam, which was *the son* of God."

23   The age of thirty was linked in the OT to the time when the public service of the Levites began (Num 4:3,23,30,35,39,43,47). It is most touching to think of the Lord spending thirty silent years in Nazareth that He might never give cause for anyone to find a flaw in His fitness to serve.

24-38   It is not possible to consider the genealogy of Luke in isolation from the comparable record in Matthew. There are some similarities, in the time from Abraham to David, the same fourteen names appear in both, and Shealtiel and Zerubbabel appear in both, but in all other aspects, except the name of Joseph and of the Lord Jesus, they are different. The reader should be aware that this problem has engaged the best of minds for centuries, so what is written here will be a summary of what others have discovered.

Including the name of the Lord Jesus and God, Luke's list contains seventyseven names (11x7) and this may be the result of design, for Matthew also follows a system of sevens. Both genealogies omit names, Matthew's more than Luke's and this was a usual manner of making a genealogy easier to follow, and giving it a pattern, such as Matthew's fourteen generation system. Several differences are obvious to all of us. Matthew follows a descending system from father to son, whereas Luke gives an ascending list, from son to father, and Matthew emphasises that the Lord is the Son of Abraham, but Luke goes back to Adam and the eternal God.

The problem in identifying the genealogies lies in the fact that both mention Joseph; Matthew says, "Jacob begat Joseph the husband of Mary, of whom was born Jesus, who is called Christ" (Matt 1:16), Luke says that Joseph was the son of Heli. Luke actually wrote, "Being son as was supposed of Joseph, of Eli". This follows to the end, so that Adam is "of God". The only time that "son" is used in the entire list is at the beginning as quoted above. Joseph could not be both begotten of Jacob and yet be "of Heli". In fact, the name of Joseph in Luke's list is the only one that is not preceded by the Greek genitive article *tou*, and some scholars believe the statement should be translated, "Being a son (as was supposed of Joseph) of Heli" (Lenski), which would literally mean a grandson of Heli. Others deny this on the ground that it is unlikely that the same word can mean both son and grandson in the same context.

The purpose of the genealogy in Matthew is to show the royal credentials of the King, so His royal line is traced through David to Abraham. In Luke, the genealogy of the Son of man is traced through David and Abraham to Adam. In both cases, though the genealogies are followed through different sons of David, and have different purposes, yet the Davidic line is important. Both Joseph (Luke 1:27) and Mary (Luke 1:32,69) could trace their lineage through David, so the Lord Jesus was officially registered as the son of Joseph, but Joseph was not in any physical way the father of our Lord. Legally, Christ could trace His lineage through Joseph, but literally, He was the virgin-born child of Mary. Luke, then, is actually tracing the genealogy of Mary; Matthew traces the official, royal genealogy of Joseph and this can account for all the differences, but the reader should be advised that he will find other conclusions in various writings.

The majestic royalty that has been seen and will be seen in our Lord did not come from David's house. In fact, any royalty that David or his sons ever displayed came from the One who is the Root of David, as well as the Offspring.

4.   *The Temptation in the Wilderness*
        4:1-13

v. 1   "And Jesus being full of the Holy Ghost returned from Jordan, and was led by the Spirit into the wilderness,
v.2   Being forty days tempted of the devil. And in those days he did eat nothing: and when they were ended, he afterward hungered.
v.3   And the devil said unto him, If thou be the Son of God, command this stone that it be made bread.
v.4   And Jesus answered him, saying, It is written, That man shall not live by bread alone, but by every word of God.
v.5   And the devil, taking him up into an high mountain, shewed unto him all the kingdoms of the world in a moment of time.
v.6   And the devil said unto him, All this power will I give thee, and the glory of them: for that is delivered unto me; and to whomsoever I will I give it.
v.7   If thou therefore wilt worship me, all shall be thine.
v.8   And Jesus answered and said unto him, Get thee behind me, Satan: for it is written, Thou shalt worship the Lord thy God, and him only shalt thou serve.
v.9   And he brought him to Jerusalem, and set him on a pinnacle of the temple, and said unto him, If thou be the Son of God, cast thyself down from hence:
v.10   For it is written, He shall give his angels charge over thee, to keep thee:
v.11   And in *their* hands they shall bear thee up, lest at any time thou dash thy foot against a stone.
v.12   And Jesus answering said unto him, It is said, Thou shalt not tempt the Lord thy God.
v.13   And when the devil had ended all the temptation, he departed from him for a season."

Before looking at this section verse by verse, there must be some explanation of the nature, scope and meaning of the temptation. As to its nature, it was genuine. The absolute impeccability of the sinless Man is the subject of the second, third and fourth chapters of Luke. His sinlessness has been demonstrated by His virgin birth, totally apart from man's ruin in sin (ch.2); the supreme pleasure that He has ever brought to the Father, ever delighting in His will (ch.3), and now in the face of the onslaught of Satan with all wiles and craftiness, the Man Christ Jesus is proven to be impeccable.

There are those who believe strongly that Christ did not sin, but they claim that He was peccable, that He could have sinned. They have humanly reasoned that He could never have known true temptation had there been no possibility of a fall. Such teachers and preachers say that it is more honouring to Christ to say that He was able not to sin than to say that He was not able to sin. Even worse, they reason that His divine nature would not allow His human nature to sin. Seeing that this is the position of many evangelicals, there is ever a need to state clearly the NT teaching about impeccability. If God incarnate could sin, then our salvation and security are both in serious doubt; see *The Person of Christ,* pages 79-89, Gospel Tract Publications.

The temptation was genuine. Temptation is not sin, and suffering in temptation is linked to victory rather than defeat. "He himself hath suffered being tempted" (Heb 2:18). If you suggest to a murderer that he can receive great profit by committing murder, his mind immediately begins to plan how he can do it undetected; he does not suffer as a result of the suggestion. If you suggest murder to a truly righteous person, he is instantly shocked and repelled and suffers at such a suggestion. The offers of the devil to One who is intrinsically holy caused suffering to Him that we, in our sinful condition with such a feeble grasp of divine holiness, can never comprehend. The very fact that Satan's suggestions were so contrary to His holy nature made His suffering most intense.

He took human nature in wondrous grace, but it was not fallen nature, or even flawed nature. His humanity was more than innocent; it was holy and perfect (Heb 7:26), so that there was nothing in Him to respond to the evil suggestions of the master tempter. He said, "the prince of this world cometh, and hath nothing in me" (John 14:30).

The temptation covered every aspect of human dependence on the one hand, and every hope of honour on the other. In its scope it encompassed heaven and earth. The meaning of the temptation has already been stated. It was not to bring out weakness or failure in the perfect Man, but to manifest His flawless perfections.

1   The Lord Jesus ever had the Spirit of God in full measure, but He has just come from the baptism at the Jordan, where the Holy Spirit descended upon Him and He is moving in the fulness of the Holy Spirit's power. We should be aware that it was the Holy Spirit who led Him into the wilderness where He was to be tempted by the devil. There is a most practical lesson in this. Baptism was never intended to be only a past experience. It should ever be a living reality in our lives. We have died to this world and are alive unto God.

The Lord's temptation followed immediately after the Father had opened the heaven and expressed His delight in His beloved Son. This is a lesson to us, for frequently the greatest temptations follow a time of greatest blessing. In fact when God expressed His delight in Adam and His fair creation (Gen 1:27-31), or in Job and his righteousness (Job 1:8), or Paul expressed his delight in the Thessalonians (1 Thess 1:6-10), Satan immediately made these objects of God's pleasure the target of his attacks. He still makes a special target of any person or thing that brings glory to God.

Satan's arrogance and daring are evident in the temptation. We are amazed to think that he would dare to attempt to overthrow the Son of God. Only the one who has overcome an enemy can know the extent of his power. Our Lord never underestimated the power of Satan.

2   Adam was tempted amid the riches of the garden of God, where its fruitfulness bore no trace of death or decay. The Lord Jesus was tempted in a scene where death held sway and the marks of the curse were all around Him, where there was nothing on which to feed, where all was barrenness. Amid a scene of death, He was the "plant of renown" (Ezek 34:29) known for His fragrance, beauty and fruitfulness.

The Lord had not eaten anything for forty days, and during all this time He was "tempted of the devil". Those days are shrouded in mystery and nothing is told us about them. The temptation of which we have any knowledge began only after the forty days were finished.

It was by the power of the Holy Spirit that the Lord met the tempter, thus leaving us an example. We too must meet the enemy in the power of the Spirit if we are to overcome. The Lord Jesus is the great pattern for us. He was not only a perfect man, but He was a dependent man, trusting God to meet His every need. We must always know our dependence and habitually know the Spirit's leading in our lives if we are to know it in times of testing and temptation.

The word *peirazō* ("tempt", v.2) is used three times by Luke in his Gospel and four times in the Acts. It originally meant to test or try, but it is frequently used in the NT in the sense of tempting to sin. A very different use is made of it in John 6:6 where the Lord Jesus questioned Philip about how they would feed the 5000, "And this he said to prove him". Another such case is Heb 11:17, "By faith Abraham, when he was tried, offered up Isaac". These were the tests of faith and not temptations to sin; however, when Satan tempts us, it always has an evil purpose, and in our sinful flesh he finds a ready ally. In the Lord Jesus, he found nothing to answer to his evil suggestions (John 14:30).

3   It was a very natural temptation that was presented. God had always provided food for the hungry (Ps 107:9), and it was only right that He should not be exempt from the provision made by God for the most humble of His creatures. It was not a meaningless expenditure of power that Satan suggested. It could be called lawful and expedient, but the Lord Jesus resisted it. He who healed the lame, gave sight to the blind, cleansed the leper, loosed the tongue of the dumb, opened deaf ears, delivered the demon-possessed and raised the dead, never once used His power for His own needs. He became Man and as such was subject, voluntarily, to all human need, sin apart. He would not use His power to escape from human circumstances. This is a marvel of restraint that enhances the glories of the perfect Man.

4   Man is a spirit-being. He is more than flesh, more than soul. He is spirit, in the image of Him that created him. Man, that is, man as a spirit, cannot exist by mere fleshly nourishment. He must have spiritual nourishment, refreshment and fellowship. What a lesson for us to learn! When Satan said, "Indulge yourself", the Lord of all said, " man doth not live by bread only, but by every word that proceedeth out of the mouth of the Lord doth man live" (Deut 8:3).

5   This was a vision of the kingdoms of the world in all their glory as it appealed to Satan and fallen mankind. No natural mountain would be high enough to get a clear view of such a panorama. This was a satanic delusion, but the devil is very limited and even he could not make all the glories that men so highly prize to last more than a moment. The word *stigmē* (" a moment") is only here in the NT and is literally a pin-point or a dot of time. As the god of this age, perhaps Satan is the only created being who could have drawn such a comprehensive picture in a moment and throw into that moment everything that men prize in the world system. John wrote, "the whole world lieth in the power of the evil one" (1 John 5:19, Wey).

6   With respect to those who see this as a false claim, they say that Satan did not have the kingdoms and therefore could not rightly offer them, I suggest that the offer was genuine and the kingdoms were truly in his realm. When Adam was given dominion, it was universal; every creature in heaven and earth and sea came under it. When he fell prey to the devices of the devil, man forfeited his dominion. He turned over the dominion to a usurper and from that day onward Satan has truly been "the prince of this world" (John 14:30). At the present time, he is also "the god of this age" (2 Cor 4:4 RV marg). It is difficult to believe in a genuine temptation that caused the Lord suffering, and then deny that this was a genuine offer. Satan literally said, "Exalt yourself; the cross of shame and agony is unnecessary. Go to the throne and bypass the cross". When Peter said similar words, the Lord immediately recognised the voice and said, "Get thee behind me, Satan: thou art an offence unto me" (Matt 16:23). This statement explains the sense in which the Lord suffered. He was not leaning toward the suggestion, but it was an offence to Him, and it wounded His tender spirit.

7   This lust for worship has ever been in the mind of Satan. The language of Ezek 28:12-19, ascribed to the king of Tyre, is very definitely the language of the exalted being who in his pride fell from his high place (1 Tim 3:6). The religions of the world are his particular sphere of activity, and under many guises he is worshipped there, and his ministers pay him homage (2 Cor 11:13-15).

8   The appeal of the Lord Jesus to the word of God is a tremendous lesson to us. In each of these temptations, He lifted a stone of the brook out of his bag and, like David, flung it at the head of Goliath. Each answer of the Lord was from Deuteronomy. He could have silenced Satan by personal power and authority. He chose to do it from Scripture, thus giving us the pattern of using Scripture against every fiery dart of the wicked one (Eph 6:16,17). As in v.4, so here in v.8, the word *graphō* ("it is written") is a perfect passive indicative which A.T. Robertson translates "it stands written". In John 19:30, "it is finished" is also a perfect passive indicative and rightly means "it stands finished". The eternal value of the word of God and the work of Christ are beautifully expressed in these two statements.

9-11 The first temptation was to indulge Himself, the second was to exalt Himself and this third temptation was in Jerusalem, and to be effective must be performed in the presence of witnesses, for the devil was saying, "Display thyself'. Surely Satan recognised the Lord of all; even demons did not fail to recognise Him (Mark 1:34), so the "if" is not expressing doubt, but "Seeing thou art the Son of God, cast thyself down from hence". Such a display of power cannot help but convince the people was the argument, and on this occasion Satan even quoted Ps 91:11,12 as the authority for such an act. However, it was a wrong use of Scripture as the answer of the Lord indicated. The Lord knew that displays of power do not win genuine converts (John 2:23-25), and we can be certain that Satan knew it too. Otherwise, there seems to be no point to the temptation, unless it was to have the Son of God perform that which Satan suggested, no matter how trivial. Luke uses a strengthened form of *phulassō* ("to keep"), the word is *diaphulassō* and this is its only occurrence in the NT.

The chronological order of the temptations has long been debated, for as a comparison of Matthew and Luke will show, the first Gospel puts the offer of the kingdoms last while Luke puts it second. Mark 1:12-13 gives a brief mention of the temptation without details. The only eyewitness to the temptation was the Lord Himself and it is likely that the disciples heard it from the lips of Christ. Many believe that Matthew follows a chronological order that also suits the theme of his Gospel and Luke follows a thematic order. Matthew's account makes the offer of the kingdoms of the world the climax of the temptation, and this is in keeping with his portrayal of the King. Luke, as the Gospel of the perfect Man, has as its climax display before others. In Luke's order, we have the moral order of 1 John 2:16:

1.   "the lust of the flesh" - "stones made bread";

2.   "the lust of the eyes" - "showed into him all the kingdoms";

3.   "the pride of life" - "cast thyself down from hence".

12 Again the Lord answered from Scripture (Deut 6:16), and again it was from the book that describes the obedience of a wilderness people. How sadly Israel failed in their obedience in contrast to our Lord who was obedient to God up to and into death itself (Phil 2:8). After we have looked at his answer with great care, and have seen the possible meaning to be that if He were to cast Himself down from a pinnacle of the temple, He would be unduly tempting God, there seems still to be more truth that has been untouched. Dealing with the spirit world, the Lord dealt directly, using very plain language. "Thou" (vv.8,12) may be taken as a direct address to the devil. "Thou shalt not tempt the Lord thy God", means, "Thou shalt not tempt me". Dr. Heading (*Luke's Life of Christ*) writes, " 'The Lord thy God' refers to Himself, proving His deity".

13   When the devil had exhausted every form of temptation, he departed from Him. That which follows is a revelation about satanic tactics. The RV margin says "until a season". Other readings are: "biding his time" (NEB); "until another time" (Goodspeed); "until an opportune time" (RSV); "until a fresh season should present itself" (E.V. Rieu). It is likely that the opportunity presented itself through Peter (Matt 16:23) and through Judas (John 13:27). On these occasions, we know that it was Satan, but on the cross, the drugged vinegar may have been another act of Satan. We learn a solemn lesson. Satan is ever waiting an opportunity, and the word of God is ever available to us. The Lord Jesus has taught us to say, "It is written".

III. The Ministry of the Lord Jesus in Galilee (4:14-9:50)

1.   *The Ministry at Nazareth*
   4:14-30

v.14 "And Jesus returned in the power of the Spirit into Galilee: and there went out a fame of him through all the region round about.
v.15 And he taught in their synagogues, being glorified of all.
v.16 And he came to Nazareth, where he had been brought up: and, as his custom was, he went into the synagogue on the sabbath day, and stood up for to read.
v.17 And there was delivered unto him the book of the prophet Esaias. And when he had opened the book, he found the place where it was written,
v.18 The Spirit of the Lord *is* upon me, because he hath anointed me to preach the gospel to the poor; he hath sent me to heal the brokenhearted, to preach deliverance to the captives, and recovering of sight to the blind, to set at liberty them that are bruised,
v.19 To preach the acceptable year of the Lord.
v.20 And he closed the book, and he gave *it* again to the minister, and sat down. And the eyes of all them that were in the synagogue were fastened on him.
v.21 And he began to say unto them, This day is this scripture fulfilled in your ears.
v.22 And all bare him witness, and wondered at the gracious words which proceeded out of his mouth. And they said, Is not this Joseph's son?
v.23 And he said unto them, Ye will surely say unto me this proverb, Physician, heal thyself: whatsoever we have heard done in Capernaum, do also here in thy country.
v.24 And he said, Verily I say unto you, No prophet is accepted in his own country.
v.25 But I tell you of a truth, many widows were in Israel in the days of Elias, when the heaven was shut up three years and six months, when great famine was throughout all the land;
v.26 But unto none of them was Elias sent, save unto Sarepta, *a city* of Sidon, unto a woman *that was* a widow.
v.27 And many lepers were in Israel in the time of Eliseus the prophet; and none of them was cleansed, saving Naaman the Syrian.
v.28 And all they in the synagogue, when they heard these things, were filled with wrath,
v.29 And rose up, and thrust him out of the city, and led him unto the brow of the hill whereon their city was built, that they might cast him down headlong.
v.30 But he passing through the midst of them went his way,"

The ministry of the Lord Jesus throughout Galilee takes up the next five chapters in Luke. The feet of the Messenger of Peace traversed every road and entered every city and village of this humble region of the land (8:1; 23:5). After His resurrection, He sent His disciples to be "witnesses ... in Jerusalem, and in all Judaea, and in Samaria, and unto the uttermost part of the earth" (Acts 1:8), but Galilee is missing. Two reasons can be given for this. The first is that He had fully evangelised it, and the second is very solemn: they already had had their opportunity.

14-15   Isaiah spoke of "the land ... by the way of the sea, beyond Jordan, in Galilee of the nations. The people that walked in darkness have seen a great light: they that dwell in the land of the shadow of death, upon them hath the light shined" (9:1,2). Commenting on this passage, W.E. Vine says, "The prophecy passes from the immediately subsequent calamities of invasion to the shining light of the incarnate Christ amidst the people and especially in Galilee". The region of Zebulun and Naphtali suffered the most in the invasion described by Isaiah in ch.8. In the latter time the same people would see a great light. Luke does not record that the Lord Jesus had done any mighty deeds to make His fame go through all the region, but this event at Nazareth happened after the miracles of John 2:1-12; 4:46-54, and from Cana and Capernaum the stories had quickly spread throughout Galilee.

16   He stood up in the synagogue of Nazareth, the city where He had been brought up and was known as the son of Joseph, the carpenter. It was His custom to go into the synagogue on a Sabbath day, and in such synagogues it was the custom to read the Scriptures. His honour to the word of God is seen in His standing up to read and sitting down to teach (v.20). It was the custom to begin a service with prayer, then to read from the books of Moses, before there was any reading from the historical or prophetic books (Acts 13:14). "The Lord desired on the present occasion to undertake the office of Maphtir, or reader of the lesson from the prophets" (C.J. Ellicott). In the synagogue of Pisidian Antioch, after the reading of the law and the prophets, the leaders of the synagogue invited Paul, or any of his companions to speak (v. 15). This also was a custom.

17   The scroll of the prophet Isaiah was put into the hand of the Lord by the ruler of the synagogue. There is no evidence that He asked for it, and we have no real authority to be able to say that there was a particular passage read in all synagogues on any given Sabbath. This practice was common in later days, and is common in synagogues today. Yet we are certain that the Lord arrived at the synagogue at exactly the right day, and His standing up to read from Isaiah was in the divine plan. He unrolled the scroll until He came to the place that we know as Isa 61:1,2.

18   "The Spirit of the Lord is upon me" must have been evident to many
(v.14). "Anointed ... to preach the gospel to the poor" was His divine mission
and He fulfilled it. Later, when He gave to the messengers from John the
assurance of His Messiahship, one of the signs was "to the poor the gospel is
preached" (7:22). But He became poor Himself that this gospel might meet
the need of the poor: "For ye know the grace of our Lord Jesus Christ, that,
though he was rich, yet for your sakes he became poor, that ye through his
poverty might be rich" (2 Cor 8:9). He was never rich on earth, but in pre-
incarnate glory, He was rich beyond human conception, and for our sakes He
became poor beyond human ability to measure. In Him extremes meet, the
highest became the lowest, the richest became the poorest, the lofty One
became the lowly One.

He personally experienced the need of every statement that He read from
Isaiah. The great Physician from heaven, who came "to heal the brokenhearted",
had His own heart broken in grief upon the tree. "Reproach hath broken my
heart; and I am full of heaviness: and I looked for some to take pity, but there
was none; and for comforters, but I found none" (Ps 69:20). As the tender Man
of sorrows, He could fully enter into the pain of the heart-broken.

The great Emancipator who proclaimed "liberty to the captives" was Himself
arrested and led away. "He was taken from prison and from judgment ... for he
was cut off out of the land of the living" (Isa 53:8). As a captive of cruel men to
whom He willingly yielded Himself, He could enter into the feelings of the
captives.

There was a day when they led Him into the high priest's palace and "when
they had blindfolded him, they struck him on the face, and asked him, saying,
Prophesy, who is it that smote thee?" (Luke 22:64). In view of the treatment that
He would so willingly endure, He had deep compassion for those who were
physically blind, and also for those whose eyes Satan had spiritually blinded (2
Cor 4:4). All who know and love Him can thank God for the moment when
"Grace the sightless eyes received, His loveliness to see".

He who came to set free "them that are bruised" knew well that He would be
"bruised for our iniquities" (Isa 53:5). Millions of the broken victims of sin and
Satan have been set free by the great Liberator. In giving us this scene in the
synagogue at Nazareth, the Holy Spirit is introducing us to the ministry of the
tender Sympathiser.

> "That tender heart that felt for all,
> For all its life blood gave;
> Which found on earth no resting place,
> Save only in the grave".

19-21   "To preach the acceptable year of the Lord" should be understood as
the time when great favour is shown to men, when a welcome for sinners is

offered, the time when men can find acceptance with God. "He closed the book" without completing the statement about "the day of vengeance of our God" (Isa 61:2). There immediately follows, in the prophecy, a glorious description of millennial comfort and rest, but He had read as far as He desired. It was the year of favour, not the day of vengeance, and for this we thank God from our hearts. As He gave the scroll back to the synagogue attendant, every eye was riveted on Him as He said, "This very day this Scripture has been fulfilled, while you have been listening to it" (Phps).

22 The words of grace that fell from His lips caused all that heard Him to wonder. *Thaumazō* (wonder) usually means astonishment, not admiration, but there may have been a mingling of reactions. All were impressed with the power with which He spoke, and were stirred by His gracious words. They were also amazed, and, as the events unfold, full of unbelief, that one of their own, Joseph's son as they thought of Him, should make the claim that these OT Scriptures were fulfilled in Him. Also, they heard Him say that "this day" these promises were coming to pass, instead of in a future kingdom.

23 Although Luke gives us this incident first, the Lord had already turned the water into wine in Cana (John 2:1-12), and healed the nobleman's son at Capernaum (John 4:46-54). We can be certain of this from John 4:54. There are clear reasons why Luke records the events at Nazareth first. Not only had the Lord spent so many years there, but the rejection of His claims was typical of the Galilean ministry. The parable that He used, "Physician, heal thyself" is interpreted by the Lord as meaning, "Do here in your home town whatsoever we have heard done in Capernaum" (NASB). They are not saying that they believe that He performed a miracle at Capernaum, merely that the stories have been told in Nazareth. Now they want to see His miracles themselves.

24-27 The people of His own home town were demanding proof of His claims through miracles. He responded by reminding them that it had been the experience of two of God's mightiest prophets that "No prophet is accepted in his own country". Elijah had been raised up of God in one of the darkest days of Israel's history, when the worship of Baal threatened to destroy the faith of the people. The drought and the famine that followed were evidences of the judgment of God upon the nation. It was a time of great need. There were many widows in Israel, but only a Gentile widow of Zarephath believed the words of the prophet and saw the mighty power of God working through him fully to meet her need.

In the days of Elisha, Israel had many lepers, but the words and works of God's prophet were rejected, so none of them was healed. Only Naaman, the Syrian, a Gentile, was healed of leprosy, and he belonged to a nation that was traditionally regarded as an enemy of Israel.

28   There was no mistaking the Lord's words. All in the synagogue became enraged. He had compared them to apostate Israel who had turned from the worship of the Lord to Baal, and as the nation then had rejected God's prophets and their message, so they were rejecting Him. God's blessings had been withheld from Israel in those dark days, so He would perform no mighty work among them now. Luke does not tell us of the Lord's second visit to the synagogue of Nazareth (Matt 13:54-58; Mark 6:1-6), but on that occasion as well, though He had performed miracles elsewhere, "he could there do no mighty work" (Mark 6:5). His own Nazareth utterly rejected Him.

29   The power of His words had struck home. They could find no way to refute the message, so they determined to destroy the Messenger. Little did they realise how much they were like Israel in the days of Elijah. Rising up in great anger, they thrust Him out of their synagogue, out of their city, and led Him to the brow of the hill on which Nazareth was built, intending to hurl Him over the cliff. The spade of the archaeologist has unearthed evidence that the Nazareth of the first century was built higher up the hill, slightly to the north of the present site, which is lower in the valley. *Katakrēmnizō* ("to cast down") is only found here in the NT. It means to throw over a precipice (*krēmnos*), to cast down headlong. It expresses intense violence and gives strong evidence of the depth of anger.

In this faithful preaching by the Lord in His own city of Nazareth, there is a solemn lesson for all who preach or teach the word of God. If the Lord had not directly applied His teaching to the wilful blindness of His hearers, He would have been hailed as the most gracious minister ever present in the synagogue. When the message was applied, they manifested their true character. The tragedy of our day is that sublime ministry is given without any practical application. Thus ears are tickled, but lives are not changed. In this first sermon in this Gospel, there is a foreview of the final utter rejection of Christ and His teaching. The enmity shown here would eventually lead to the cry to take His life, but not until God's time.

30   "His hour was not yet come" (John 7:30), and it was never to be that He should so die, so He walked straight through the very midst of them and went His way. What must have been in His tender heart at that moment of utter rejection! We do not know the nature of the miracle that preserved the Lord Jesus at this time, but that His escape was miraculous, we cannot doubt. A similar event happened in John 8:59 where the Jews took up stones to cast at Him, "but Jesus hid himself, and went out of the temple, going through the midst of them, and so passed by". Luke 24:16 speaks of the two travellers to Emmaus whose eyes "were holden that they should not know him". The Lord makes Himself known when He so desires and holds eyes from seeing when this is His will, but we suggest the blindness is in the eyes of the beholder rather than any change of form in Him.

2.   The Ministry at Capernaum
   4:31-37

v.31 "And came down to Capernaum, a city of Galilee, and taught them on the sabbath days.

v.32 And they were astonished at his doctrine: for his word was with power.

v.33 And in the synagogue there was a man, which had a spirit of an unclean devil, and cried out with a loud voice,

v.34 Saying, Let *us* alone; what have we to do with thee, *thou* Jesus of Nazareth? art thou come to destroy us? I know thee who thou art; the Holy One of God.

v.35 And Jesus rebuked him, saying, Hold thy peace, and come out of him. And when the devil had thrown him in the midst, he came out of him, and hurt him not.

v.36 And they were all amazed, and spake among themselves, saying, What a word *is* this! for with authority and power he commandeth the unclean spirits, and they come out.

v.37 And the fame of him went out into every place of the country round about."

31-32   Luke merely says that He came to Capernaum, but we know from Matt 4:13-16 that He left Nazareth and settled in Capernaum. It was located on the border between Zebulun and Naphtali on the shore of the Sea of Galilee; no wonder that Matthew quoted Isa 9:1,2 as being fulfilled in this event. Capernaum was in the midst of a populous, thriving area, where main roads converged. Josephus, not a totally reliable witness, wrote, "The very numerous villages are so full of people because of the fertility of the land ... the very smallest of them contains above 15 000 inhabitants".

It was the custom in the synagogues to allow any qualified man to read the Scriptures and comment on them. In Capernaum, the Lord availed Himself of this opportunity and amazed the people with His doctrine and the authority with which He spoke. They were accustomed to the scribes quoting from the ancient rabbinical teaching, but this Man taught as one who had ability and authority to interpret the Scriptures Himself.

33-35   There were very likely present in the synagogue those who questioned the authority of Jesus of Nazareth to take upon Himself the interpretation of the holy Writings, but opportunity was given for Him to display His authority. A man was there who was possessed of an unclean spirit. It is serious error to think that the Lord was not able to distinguish between a physical or mental disease and demon possession. Any modern day denial of this phenomenon flies in the face of reality. Satan works in the way that he finds most effective at the particular place or time in history. It is much easier to recognise Satan in his "roaring lion" character (1 Pet 5:8) than when he appears as an angel of light (2 Cor 11:13-15). There are places in our modern world where demon possession is obvious, and there are other places where this possession is carefully disguised; but do not doubt that Satan's power is growing, rather than diminishing.

This man was possessed by a demon that recognised that "Jesus of Nazareth" was the "Holy One of God' , a title of the Lord used thirty times by Isaiah in such passages as "the Lord, your redeemer, the Holy One of Israel" (43:14). Ps 16:10 describes Christ as "thine (God's) Holy One", an expression used by Peter in John 6:69 (JND). Knowing Him as the final Judge of all, the demon feared Him. The Lord would not receive witness from the realms of darkness and immediately rebuked the spirit, commanding it to speak no more and to come out of the man. The result was immediate: the demon hurled the man to the ground before the synagogue crowd, a final act of defiance, but meaninglessly, for the man was uninjured by the fall. Unable to resist the authority of the word of the Lord, the demon departed from him.

36-37 "And astonishment came upon all, and they spoke to one another, saying, What word is this?" (JND). Two results were seen in the synagogue: the people recognised the authority of the Person of Christ, and the power of the words with which He spoke. His authority over the unseen world convinced many of them of the authority of His teaching so that "the fame of him" or "a rumour" of Him (Marshall, JND) went into all the country around.

3. The Healing of Peter's Wife's Mother
   4:38-44

v.38 "And he arose out of the synagogue, and entered into Simon's house. And Simon's wife's mother was taken with a great fever; and they besought him for her.

v.39 And he stood over her, and rebuked the fever; and it left her: and immediately she arose and ministered unto them.

v.40 Now when the sun was setting, all they that had any sick with divers diseases brought them unto him; and he laid his hands on every one of them, and healed them.

v.41 And devils also came out of many, crying out, and saying, Thou art Christ the Son of God. And he rebuking *them* suffered them not to speak: for they knew that he was Christ.

v.42 And when it was day, he departed and went into a desert place: and the people sought him, and came unto him, and stayed him, that he should not depart from them.

v.43 And he said unto them, I must preach the kingdom of God to other cities also: for therefore am I sent.

v.44 And he preached in the synagogues of Galilee."

38-39 This healing is also recorded in Matt 8:14-17 and Mark 1:29-34. The Lord Jesus has just displayed His authority over the unseen world in the synagogue at Capernaum. He now displays His authority in the physical realm by healing a woman "taken with a great fever". Luke shows his interest in the treatment of sickness by accurately portraying her condition as "seized with a great fever". Mark, giving us the movements of the Servant, says, "he came and took her by the hand, and lifted her up". Matthew, giving us the portrait of the King, says, "he touched her hand", but Luke, giving us the tenderness of the perfect Man, says, "He went to her, and bending over her, commanded the fever to leave" (W.F. Beck). In His act of bending down over the stricken woman, we are reminded of the tremendous down-stooping that brought Him from His place in glory to a world in sin and under the curse.

How unlike many professed healings of our time! Some claim to have been healed while they totter on the very brink of their grave. " And immediately she arose" and with full health restored, with not a trace of lingering weakness, "She began to wait on them" (NASB). Such loving deacon service is characteristic of those who have come into living contact with the Lord Jesus. Her service was rendered to the Lord first, and to all in the house, which gives us a beautiful picture of the true motives for service to the Lord and His own.

Peter's wife's mother was "taken with a great fever" which illustrates in three ways the power of sin. Just like a great fever, sin is a restless, controlling and consuming thing that leaves its victim helpless and totally in its power. The hapless sinner has no rest in time, and will have no rest for ever (Rev 14:11). The fever takes many forms such as a restless seeking for pleasure, popularity or possessions, but the result is always the same; its victim eventually comes under its control, sapped of all strength and usefulness, with no rest or satisfaction in anything. Life ceases to have meaning, and, if we correctly judge this symptom of the fever of sin, there is a universal epidemic today, for to many worldlings, this is a world without meaning. There is a link between the woman "taken with a great fever" and the people of Gadara, "taken with great fear" (Luke 8:37). James wrote, "The judge standeth before the door" (5:9). When He opens it and steps into this feverish scene, men's hearts will fail them with fear.

40-41 It was at the close of a long day, when many would be thinking of home and rest, that the blessed Lord stood and healed all that were sick with various diseases that were brought to Him. Many who were possessed of demons were delivered from their cruel bondage, and He rebuked the demons, for they knew Him and shouted, "Thou art Christ the Son of God". The people of Nazareth had thought that He was making false claims, but the veil of flesh did not hide from demons the supreme authority of the Son of God. The Lord Jesus would not receive approbation from demons. Paul learned this by the Spirit and rebuked the demon-possessed woman in Philippi (Acts 16:17,18). The testimony of these demons was true, but "what concord hath Christ with Belial?" (2 Cor 6:15). We can learn a lesson here. Many evangelicals have accepted support from apostate men and systems that deny many of the cardinal truths of Scripture in the name of christian unity, and a united gospel appeal. The Lord and His apostles refused such support.

Again the scene that is described here is being enacted. The day of grace is closing, the sun is setting, the patient Lord stands ready to receive all who will come to Him in faith. Well can sinners cry in the language of the ancient prophet, "Woe unto us! for the day goeth away" (Jer 6:4).

> "Day is declining, and the sun is low,
> The shadows lengthen, light makes haste to go,
> Room, room, still room! Oh enter, enter now."

42-43   It is usually Luke that tells us of the Lord praying, but on this occasion it is Mark that tells us that He went to a solitary place to pray (Mark 1:35). Luke tells us "The people flocked out to find Him" (Wey), giving Him little time for either prayer or rest. They "tried to prevent Him from leaving them" (Phps), but He informed them that He "must preach the kingdom of God to other cities also: for therefore am I sent", which is the aorist passive of *apostellō*, meaning to be sent as a special representative. He was truly the sent One of God.

44   The TR is represented by the AV reading, "He preached in the synagogues of Galilee", but many texts support the reading, "in the synagogues of Judaea". Nowhere else in the Synoptic Gospels is there any support for a journey to Judaea at this time. The TR may be correct, but conservative scholars with a background to evaluate manuscripts tell us that the original was likely "Judaea" rather than "Galilee". However, there does seem to be an explanation for the problem. A. Plummer states, "The analytical tense (He was preaching) indicates that what is stated continued for some time". This was not a brief visit to another place, but an extended preaching tour that took Him to many places within Galilee and beyond its boundaries (Peraea, Decapolis and Gaulanitis or Ituraea). Luke uses Judaea as a comprehensive term meaning the whole country of the Jews in 23:5, "He stirreth up the people, teaching throughout all Jewry (Judaea), beginning from Galilee to this place". Other illustrations of this use of Judaea in Luke's writings can be found in Acts 2:9; 10:37; 26:20.

4.   *The Miracle of the Great Number of Fish*
         5:1-11

v.1   "And it came to pass, that, as the people pressed upon him to hear the word of God, he stood by the lake of Gennesaret,

v.2   And saw two ships standing by the lake: but the fishermen were gone out of them, and were washing *their* nets.

v.3   And he entered into one of the ships, which was Simon's, and prayed him that he would thrust out a little from the land. And he sat down, and taught the people out of the ship.

v.4   Now when he had left speaking, he said unto Simon, Launch out into the deep, and let down your nets for a draught.

> v.5 And Simon answering said unto him, Master, we have toiled all the night, and have taken nothing: nevertheless at thy word I will let down the net.
> v.6 And when they had this done, they inclosed a great multitude of fishes: and their net brake.
> v.7 And they beckoned unto *their* partners, which were in the other ship, that they should come and help them. And they came, and filled both the ships, so that they began to sink.
> v.8 When Simon Peter saw *it*, he fell down at Jesus' knees, saying, Depart from me; for I am a sinful man, O Lord.
> v.9 For he was astonished, and all that were with him, at the draught of the fishes which they had taken:
> v.10 And so *was* also James, and John, the sons of Zebedee, which were partners with Simon. And Jesus said unto Simon, Fear not; from henceforth thou shalt catch men.
> v.11 And when they had brought their ships to land, they forsook all, and followed him."

1-3 The fame of the Lord Jesus had spread throughout the entire country, and at this stage in His Galilean ministry great numbers of people came to hear Him. On this day, as He stood on the shore of the Lake of Gennesaret (Galilee), the people crowded close around Him to hear the word of God. Two ships were there, the fishermen busy washing their nets. The Lord stepped into Simon's boat and requested that He would row out a little from the land, and sitting down He taught the people from the boat.

It was no coincidence that this was the boat that belonged to Simon Peter. "The waters of the lake were ploughed by four thousand vessels of every description, from the war-vessel of the Romans to the rough fisher-boats of Bethsaida, and the gilded pinnaces from Herod's palace" (F.W. Farrar). Simon had already been brought to Christ in Judaea by his brother Andrew (John 1:40-42), and had returned to his fishing. The two corresponding passages in Matt 4:18 -20 and Mark 1:16-20 are far less detailed than Luke's account.

4-5 When the Lord finished speaking to the crowd, He said to Simon, "Push out into the deep and let down your nets for a catch" (RSV). Calling Him Master, Simon told Him that he and his companions had laboured through the whole night and had taken nothing, " nevertheless, at thy word I will let down the net". This is significant. Simon could have concluded that a carpenter from Nazareth could know nothing about fishing. Having spent his lifetime on the lake, Simon's experience would surely have given him superior knowledge. He could have told the Lord that daytime fishing on the lake was almost useless, especially net fishing, for the fish only came near the surface to feed during the dark of the night, but he used none of this kind of human reasoning, or perhaps he did and then discarded it as worthless, in the face of the fact that the Master had told him to let down his net.

6-8 A great number of fish were caught, so great that the net could not hold them, and then both the boats were not large enough to contain the catch.

Immediately Simon realised that what had happened could not be explained naturally; this was an act of the Creator. "He fell down at Jesus' knees, saying, Depart from me; for I am a sinful man, O Lord", - not only Teacher now, but Lord. There are those who suggest that the name "Jesus" should be taken here as in the dative case, giving the reading, "he fell on his knees before Jesus" (Phps).

It is only here in Luke that the double name Simon Peter is used. Before this verse, Luke called him Simon, but after the choosing of the twelve (6:14), he calls him Peter, the name given to him by the Lord.

Peter's reaction was neither joy nor praise, but a fearful sense of holiness that produced self- knowledge. There is only one way to understand his actions and words; Peter realised that before the eyes of the One who saw the fish in the lake, he was exposed in all his sinfulness. He was in the presence of divine holiness and knew that he was totally unfit; in fact, he was full of sin. "Depart from me" was not his wish that the Lord would leave, but was wrung from his soul as the sense of his own sinfulness overwhelmed him. The only place where human sin can be seen in its true character is before the eyes of a holy God. Although this can well be used as an illustration of salvation, this was not Peter's salvation, but it was his fitness for service. Like Isaiah, he had a true sense of the sinfulness of self first of all. An honest estimate of self is always a prelude to a right estimate of the Lord.

From what has been already written, it will be seen that this was not Peter's first experience with the Lord, nor was it his conversion, but it was his call to service. All servants of God must learn their own sinfulness in the presence of God, must obey the Lord even when it is against human reasoning, and must leave all that they value to follow Him. Peter left when the boats were full. He never forgot what it cost him to follow the Lord, but he never regretted it.

9-10   Peter was overcome with amazement at the miracle that he had seen as were his fishing partners, James and John, the two sons of Zebedee. But it was to Peter that the Lord spoke words of comfort and the blessed promise, "from henceforth thou shalt catch men". What a great catch of men Peter gathered in when he preached his great message on the day of Pentecost!

"He was astonished" (*thambos*) is an expression only used by Luke in the NT, twice in this Gospel (4:36; 5:9) and once in Acts 3: 10. W.E. Vine suggests that it is likely taken from a root that signifies to render immoveable. In this case, thambos is used with *periechō* ("to seize around"). A.T. Robertson translates literally, "for a wonder held him round". In the promise, "from henceforth thou shalt catch men", Luke carefully uses the verb *zōgreō* ("to catch alive"). It has been translated, "catching men that they may live" (J.B. Rotherham). The same word is used in a negative sense in 2 Tim 2:26, where it is said that the power of Satan leads men astray.

11   The ships did not sink as was feared. They were so full of fish that they began to sink, but the Lord who gave them the great catch saw to it that the vessels reached land safely. "They forsook all, and followed him". The Lord had need of Peter's boat and it was given, but then He also had need of Peter, James and John, and they gave their all. The Lord called twelve men to follow Him, but these three were the nearest to Him, and most often with Him in times of glory, as on the mount; and in times of grief, as in the garden.

5. *The Healing of a Leper*
5:12-16

v.12 "And it came to pass, when he was in a certain city, behold a man full of leprosy: who seeing Jesus fell on *his* face, and besought him, saying, Lord, if thou wilt, thou canst make me clean.

v.13 And he put forth *his* hand, and touched him, saying, I will: be thou clean. And immediately the leprosy departed from him.

v.14 And he charged him to tell no man: but go, and shew thyself to the priest, and offer for thy cleansing, according as Moses commanded, for a testimony unto them.

v.15 But so much the more went there a fame abroad of him: and great multitudes came together to hear, and to be healed by him of their infirmities.

v.16 And he withdrew himself into the wilderness, and prayed."

For many centuries, the word leprosy has had the effect of striking terror to the hearts of men. In its worst form, it was loathsome, disfiguring and terminal. Moses wrote, "And the leper in whom the plague is, his clothes shall be rent, and his head bare, and he shall put a covering upon his upper lip, and shall cry, Unclean, unclean ... he shall dwell alone; without the camp shall his habitation be" (Lev 13:45,46). Yet, such a leper must live as a beggar, for there was no government support for this tragic outcast; he was dependent on any who would take pity on him.

No wonder that this unclean, defiling disease that brought a dreadful death was used by the Holy Spirit as an illustration of sin and its consequences. Isaiah vividly describes Israel's spiritual condition as being like a leper, "From the sole of the foot even unto the head there is no soundness in it; but wounds, and bruises, and putrifying sores: they have not been closed, neither bound up, neither mollified with ointment" (Isa 1:6). It is most significant that when Isaiah tells of the suffering Servant of Jehovah whose soul is made an offering for sin, he writes about the wounds and bruises that He bore as the Substitute, but omits the putrifying sores (Isa 53:5). These are the outward signs of inward, moral corruptness, and this Substitute, who " was brought as a lamb to the slaughter", was God's perfect Servant (42:1-4). He is the one exception, for the charge of being spiritual lepers includes all others, " we are all as an unclean thing, and all our righteousnesses are as filthy rags" (64:6). This may well be a reference to the polluted, filthy rags of a leper.

12   Luke says that the Lord was "in a certain city" when this leper came to Him. It may have been his desperate need that compelled him to enter the city, contrary to the law. Luke, with his interest in matters of disease and sickness, alone of the Synoptists, tells us that the man was "full of leprosy". There is a remarkable account given in Lev 13:12,13 "if... the leprosy cover all the skin of him that hath the plague from his head even to his foot, wheresoever the priest looketh . . . he shall pronounce him clean". Here was a man who was full of leprosy like the example in Lev 13, and he too is ready for cleansing. The spiritual application is clear. It is only when a sinner has been awakened to his utter sinfulness, when he is aware that sin has defiled him in every part of his being, "from the sole of the foot to the head", when he has learned that "the whole head is sick, and the whole heart faint" (Isa 1:5), that his sin is "exceeding sinful" (Rom 7:13), that he is truly ready for cleansing.

The leper threw himself on his face, and addressing Jesus as "Lord", said, " if thou wilt, thou canst make me clean". His faith was simple and true, directed toward the one Person who could truly cleanse him. It may have been a sense of his own unworthiness that caused him to question the Lord's willingness, but whatever the reason for his doubt, it was instantly removed.

13   The Lord Jesus "put forth his hand"; He reached out to the leper who may have remained at a distance, perhaps because he had the experience of Peter, "Depart from me; for I am a sinful man". The Lord Jesus touched him, and remained undefiled. For all the days of his leprosy, he was untouched by human hands, except by defiled lepers like himself; but now he is touched by a hand that heals, and that cannot be defiled. In addition to the touch, he hears the blessed words, "I will: be thou clean. And immediately the leprosy departed from him". In the touch and the spoken word there are clear gospel pictures. Our defilement in sin puts us at a guilty distance from God, but He has reached out to us in the Person of His Son. Only a vital link with the Saviour can heal our sin-sick souls and only His Word can assure us that "with his stripes we are healed" (Isa 53:5).

14   Charging the leper to be silent, the Lord sent him to the priest to fulfil the requirements of the law for a testimony to the fact that neither the Lord not those who were blessed by Him denied the authority of the law. The priest had the right to pronounce the leper as having been cleansed. No more powerful evidence of the cure could have been produced.

The leper has often been blamed for reporting his healing, but even if he had never spoken, the change wrought in his body was so apparent to all who knew him that to keep his secret was impossible. It is wonderful when the change in the lives of sinners is so great after their conversion that it is known by all who see them, even without the telling of it. Peter speaks of the husbands who " may, apart from a word, be won over by the daily lives of their wives" (1 Pet 3:1, Wey).

15-16   The report of the mighty power of Christ to heal spread ever further through every town of Galilee and as far as Judaea and Jerusalem (v.17). Mark tells us that the cleansed leper blazed abroad the matter (Mark 1:45). Great crowds gathered from many parts to be healed, and the Lord, knowing well the hearts of men, drew apart into a desert place to pray. Only Luke uses *hupochōreō*("withdrew"), and only twice, here and in 9:10, where it is translated, "went aside". The present participle *proseuchomenos* ("prayed") expresses continued or repeated action. This sentence has been variously translated, "But He Himself would often slip away" (NASB); "From time to time he withdrew to lonely places for prayer" (NEB), and "He habitually withdrew" (Berkely). What a pattern He has left us!

6.   *The Healing of a Paralytic*
     5:17-26

> v.17 "And it came to pass on a certain day, as he was teaching, that there were Pharisees and doctors of the law sitting by, which were come out of every town of Galilee, and Judaea, and Jerusalem: and the power of the Lord was *present* to heal them.
> v.18 And, behold, men brought in a bed a man which was taken with a palsy: and they sought *means* to bring him in, and to lay *him* before him.
> v.19 And when they could not find by what *way* they might bring him in because of the multitude, they went upon the housetop, and let him down through the tiling with *his* couch into the midst before Jesus.
> v.20 And when he saw their faith, he said unto him, Man, thy sins are forgiven thee.
> v.21 And the scribes and the Pharisees began to reason, saying, Who is this which speaketh blasphemies? Who can forgive sins, but God alone?
> v.22 But when Jesus perceived their thoughts, he answering said unto them, What reason ye in your hearts?
> v.23 Whether is easier, to say, Thy sins be forgiven thee; or to say, Rise up and walk?
> v.24 But that ye may know that the Son of man hath power upon earth to forgive sins, (he said unto the sick of the palsy,) I say unto thee, Arise, and take up thy couch, and go into thine house.
> v.25 And immediately he rose up before them, and took up that whereon he lay, and departed to his own house, glorifying God.
> v.26 And they were all amazed, and they glorified God, and were filled with fear, saying, We have seen strange things to day."

17   Matthew tells us that the healing of the paralytic man took place in "his own city" (9:1-8). Mark confirms that it was in Capernaum (2:1-12). After returning from His itinerant ministry throughout Galilee, great crowds gathered in Capernaum to hear the Lord. As he taught in a house, "They flocked to Him in such numbers, there was no longer any room for them, no, not even about the door" (Mark 2:2, Rieu). Among the crowd were Pharisees and doctors of the law, some from Galilee, but others from as far away as Judaea and Jerusalem. The presence of such critical men did not restrict the power of God on this occasion, for many were healed. This is the first mention of Pharisees in Luke, but we have already met the doctors of the law in 2:46.

18-19   Mark says that it was four men who brought the paralysed man to be healed. Luke says, they "sought means to bring him in" but were frustrated by the large crowd. Not to be easily turned aside, they carried him to the roof, likely by stairs on the outside of the house, and having made an opening in the thin slabs of limestone that covered the roof, they lowered him down into the middle of the crowd, immediately in front of the Lord Jesus.

20   Many comments have been made about the statement, "when he saw their faith". To limit this to the four who carried the man makes the man not only a paralytic, but a person without voice or will. Surely his faith was at least as strong as the four friends! The Lord Jesus could very easily have told him to take up his bed and walk and thus avoided the confrontation with the scribes and Pharisees. Knowing their thoughts, He said, "Man, thy sins are forgiven thee".

We can learn an excellent lesson from this story of a helpless man who received such timely help from the four who were able to carry him. Most people who are saved in our day, who are not related to believers, are brought to hear the gospel through the influence of saved people who have concern for them. Like the four men, who would not be deterred in their efforts to help the poor man, we can also labour to bring sinners to hear the message and in confidence trust in God to bring them to know their sins forgiven. These men could neither forgive sins nor heal the man, but they could bring him to One who could do both.

21   The Rabbis ascribed all physical sickness to the judgment of God for particular sin. According to their teaching, this man was under judgment from God, and only God could forgive and recover him. This great fact is obscured in the minds of many by the teaching of religious systems where men profess to forgive sins. The authority to forgive can only be the prerogative of the One who has been wronged. If you attempted to forgive a person who had wronged someone else, the response from the person who received the wrong would be, "How can you claim to forgive him? You have not been sinned against". All sin is ultimately against God, therefore the Pharisees were correct; only God, the One wronged, can forgive, and in this act the Lord Jesus was making the highest claim to deity.

22   The next three verses contain some of the highest teaching about the forgiveness of sins that can be found in all of Scripture. The authority to forgive resides in God. The act of forgiveness must be on terms that are in harmony with His character. The assurance of forgiveness is the result of believing His Word. There will be, in the forgiven one, clear evidence of it, and the acceptable time of forgiveness is set by the Lord Himself.

He "perceived their thoughts" is one of Luke's many statements that indicate that all the attributes of deity were fully resident in the gentle Man of this Gospel.

These Pharisees and scribes, as experts in the Law, surely knew that in Num 16 Korah, Dathan and Abiram are described as being sinners against Moses and Aaron, their fellow men (v.3), and against their own souls (v.38), but the ultimate tragedy of their sin and of all sin is that it is against God (v.11). God's charge to Israel was, ("behold, ye have sinned against the Lord: and be sure your sin will find you out" (Num 32:23).

23   To forgive sins can never be a matter of mere words, any more than healing a paralytic can come about by merely uttering words. Particularly in Luke, the Lord described sin as being a vast debt, while He described sinners as being destitute, with nothing to pay (7:42). When sin is a debt, the thought of an easy, free forgiveness is impossible. The price must be paid in full. If you forgive a person a debt, it is not free. The act of forgiveness will cost you the amount of the debt. At this early point in the ministry of the Lord, there is the teaching of His redemptive work and the ransom that He was so willing to pay.

24   A mighty act of power accompanied the gracious act of forgiveness. His authority to forgive was displayed in visible results. The people could not see a forgiven heart, but they could see a paralysed man arising and taking up his couch and departing to his own house. The Jewish teaching was here put to the test. If sickness is the result of particular sin, and a man cannot be raised up until he is forgiven, then here was the evidence of healing and forgiveness.

"The Son of man hath power (authority) upon earth to forgive sins" is the highest claim to deity. It is also a statement about the place and limitations of that forgiveness. Here, on earth, where He was to bleed and die for sinners, is the very place where His forgiveness can be known. Once beyond the boundary of time, all hope of forgiveness is eternally past.

25   The man who was instantly healed went away giving glory to God. We must also believe that he was forgiven and was in no doubt about the source of that forgiveness. God had healed him and God had forgiven him.

The result of obeying the command of the Lord was "immediately he rose up". *Parachrēma* ("immediately") is found ten times in this Gospel (1:64; 4:39; 5:25; 8:44,47,55; 13:13; 18:43; 19:11; 22:60) and is found seven times in the Acts (3:7; 5: 10; 9:18; 12:23; 13:11; 16:26,33), but is found only in one other place in the NT: in Matthew's account of the fig tree, where it is used twice and translated in the AV as "presently" and "soon" (21:19-20). Immediate healings and immediate conversions are characteristic of Luke's two books.

He "departed to his own house glorifying God" and all the people, "glorified God" (v.26), remind us that the giving of glory to God is a main purpose of this Gospel. This expression is used nine times by Luke (2:20; 4:15; 5:25,26; 7:16; 13:13; 17:15; 18:43; 23:47) and only half as often by Matthew and Mark combined.

Glorifying the Father and the Son is a main theme in the fourth Gospel, but
there is a distinction in the way that Luke and John use it. Luke's emphasis is on
giving glory to God in heaven, John stresses the glory of the Son of God on earth
in nineteen of the twenty-two times he uses it.

26   The language of "they were all amazed" is stronger than our AV suggests.
J.B. Phillips says, "Sheer amazement gripped every man", but the word is really
"awe" and suggests something of what Peter felt in the boat when he realised
that what he had witnessed was an act of God. Their expression was, " We have
seen strange (unaccountable, incredible or marvellous) things today". This is
the only use of *paradoxos* ("strange things") in the NT, but its English derivative
is fairly common. Para ("beside") and *doxa* ("opinion") go together to make
paradox or paradoxical.

Notes

1.   There were five major sects in the Jews' religious life: Pharisees, Sadducees, Essenes, Herodians
and Zealots. A good Bible dictionary will give much fuller explanations.

i.   The Pharisees are often mentioned in the four Gospels (twenty-eight times in Luke). Their
name can be traced to the inter-testamental period when the Maccabean ruler-priests held
sway in the land. A group of men, zealous for the law, separated themselves from the leaders.
They were known as separatists or Pharisees. The leaders had lost their zeal for the law and
were much more interested in maintaining their own political power. By the time of our
Lord's public ministry, these separated men, or Pharisees, were by far the most influential
religious party among the Jews. According to Josephus, their ranks never numbered more
than six thousand, but they had captured the loyalty of the common people in their opposition
to the chief priests and rulers, most of whom belonged to the sect of the Sadducees.

The Pharisees' zeal had degenerated into mere form and ceremony. Their interpretation
of the law became a complex system that governed the smallest detail of public and private
life and displaced the Scriptures (Mark 7:9). The Lord Jesus met with their opposition because
His holy life and teaching condemned their empty formalism and self-righteousness (Luke
7:36-50).

Often linked to the Pharisees were "doctors of the law" (Luke 2:46; 5:17). In Luke's Gospel,
they are called "lawyers" six times and "scribes" fifteen times. The scribes were trained from
early youth in the application of the complicated teaching of the oral law and a vast amount
of written regulations that had been handed down from former generations, but not written
in the law of Moses. The *Halakkah* was "The Way in which the Fathers Walked", and the
Haggadah were "The Sayings of the Scribes". Much that was good was contained in these
writings, as well as much that was trivial, but the method was wrong. The Pharisees and their
scribes began with a meticulous outward observance of these regulations with the intention
that eventually it would gradually, by long process, produce a true righteousness within. The
teaching of the Lord Jesus was the very opposite. He taught that the heart of man was utterly
sinful and only regeneration could produce the inner transformation that would result in

right outward observance. The Pharisees' teaching was, "Do good and you will be good", so it had much in common with all who trust to self and good works for salvation.

ii.   The Sadducees were the wealthy, influential political leaders of Israel, with little genuine interest in religion except as it provided the cement that held the nation of Israel together. The chief priests belonged to the sect of the Sadducees. The Pharisees were orthodox, but the Sadducees did not believe in angels, spirits or resurrection (Luke 20:27; Acts 23:6-8). It is doubtful if they believed in any coming kingdom of God or even in an after-life. Their numbers were smaller than the Pharisees, but they held the presidency of the Sanhedrin, giving them a large degree of civil, religious and political rule under the Romans. Their opposition to the Lord was politically motivated.

iii.   The sect of the Essenes scarcely comes into the Gospel record. They lived in communities west of the Dead Sea, above Engedi. They revered the Scriptures, and paid their tribute to the temple, but did not go to it. They were opposed to animal sacrifice and had rites of purification and a reverence for the sun that came from pagan sources. A document from the ancient Qumran caves has been published by the Israelis in 1986 which compares the teachings of the Essenes Community with the more orthodox teaching of the Pharisees.

iv.   The Herodians were more political than religious. They supported the rule of the Herods, even though they were Idumaeans and not true Jews. Religiously, they were orthodox like the Pharisees.

v.   The Zealots were also in the tradition of Pharisees, but believed in the violent overthrow of the Roman authorities. They never were large, but the sentiments that moved them eventually affected the entire nation and led to the uprising against Rome that brought about the destruction of Jerusalem under Titus in AD 70. We know at least one former zealot by name, "Simon called Zelotes" (Luke 6:15).

2.   In the five mighty miracles that are given to us from 4:31 to 5:26, there are vivid pictures of the condition of all sinners.

i.   The demon possessed man of Capernaum was under the power of Satan.

ii.   The woman taken with a great fever is a picture of being under the power of sin.

iii.   Peter's realisation of his own sinfulness reminds us of being under the eye of God.

iv.   The leper pictures sinners under the law of death.

v.   The paralytic is illustrative of sinners under the helplessness of a lost condition.

7.   The Call of Matthew
5:27-32

v.27 "And after these things he went forth, and saw a publican, named Levi, sitting at the receipt of custom: and he said unto him, Follow me.

v.28 And he left all, rose up, and followed him.

v.29 And Levi made him a great feast in his own house: and there was a great company of publicans and of others that sat down with them.

v.30 But their scribes and Pharisees murmured against his disciples, saying, Why do ye eat and drink with publicans and sinners?

v.31 And Jesus answering said unto them, They that are whole need not a physician; but they that are sick.

v.32 I came not to call the righteous, but sinners to repentance."

27-28 The Lord "went forth" either from the house or from the town of Capernaum. The latter is the likely meaning, for it is improbable that the tax office was inside the town. Levi, or Matthew, as he is called in Matthew and Mark (see Luke 6:15), was sitting at the place where taxes were collected. These taxes from the region of Galilee were paid to Herod Antipas, if Josephus is accurate on this point. The tax collectors were reckoned to be the lowest stratum of Jewish society, traitors against their own nation. The amounts demanded by the Roman authorities were far from excessive, but the dishonesty of the tax-collectors and their methods of extorting more than was required made them a hated class.

We are told nothing that would make us think that Matthew was an exception to the general rule, and, if he was like his fellow-publicans, he was a wealthy man. It is difficult not to speculate about the dealings of God with this man prior to the call of the Lord Jesus. We are certain from the tenor of Scripture that he was not a stranger to the Person of Christ, or His claims. There was a preparation in his heart, for when he heard the call of the Lord Jesus, "Follow me", he "abandoned everything" (Rieu), giving up all his opportunities for further gain, and his right to collect taxes for which he had paid a large sum of money. Tax-collectors were chosen by the Roman authorities by the lucrative method of giving the right to the highest bidder.

29 Matthew paid a high price to follow the Lord Jesus, but he counted it as a great privilege and longed that his fellow tax-collectors should meet his Lord. The feast that he made in his own house for the Lord Jesus, when such a large company sat down together, verifies the wealth to which he had attained, unlike the Galilean fishermen who came from a background of poverty.

Luke often describes feasts to which the Lord was invited (7:36-50; 10:38-42; 11:37-41; 14:1-6; 19:1-10; 24:28-32). It is Matthew and Luke that picture the gospel call as an invitation to a great supper (Matt 22:1-14; Luke 14:16-24). There is no doubt that Luke speaks much of the Lord sitting at a feast with sinners to show the truth of the charge that the Pharisees levelled against Him, "This man receiveth sinners, and eateth with them" (15:2).

30   "But their scribes and Pharisees" is a clear indication that some of the scribes belonged to the Pharisees and others may have belonged to the chief priests and were Sadducees. Luke links the scribes with the Pharisees on five occasions, and seven times he links scribes with the chief priests. When the Lord sat down with the great company of publicans, the Pharisees spoke indignantly against it to the disciples. Their charge linked the publicans with sinners, company in which they would never be found.

31-32   The Lord did not deny the Pharisees' description of the assembled company; in fact, He used the occasion to tell them of the reason for His coming into the world. Did He mean that the Pharisees were "whole" and not in need of healing by the great Physician? If so, this would fly in the face of all that the Lord ever said elsewhere about them. No, they were not "whole", but they thought they were. As on other such occasions, the Lord took people on their own ground. They claimed that they were not numbered among sinners, so He made them aware that His coming was not for them, but for sinners. This line of teaching was fully developed by the Lord Himself in John 9:39-41, after He had opened the eyes of the blind man. He said that He had "come into this world, that they which see not might see; and that they which see might be made blind" (v.39). His words went home, for the Pharisees responded, "Are we blind also?" V.41 of this chapter makes it clear that they were blind, but did not know it. Those who do not see their own need put themselves outside of the healing power of the great Physician. This is a great theme of Luke and Paul; all are guilty, lost and perishing, but only those who acknowledge their need are saved. A reader of Paul's letter to the Romans will have no problem in understanding that He "came not to call the righteous" because "There is none righteous, no, not one" (Rom 3:10).

8.   Fasting and Things New and Old
   5:33-39

v.33 "And they said unto him, Why do the disciples of John fast often, and make prayers, and likewise *the disciples* of the Pharisees; but thine eat and drink?
v.34 And he said unto them, Can ye make the children of the bridechamber fast, while the bridegroom is with them?
v.35 But the days will come, when the bridegroom shall be taken away from them, and then shall they fast in those days.
v.36 And he spake also a parable unto them; No man putteth a piece of a new garment upon an old; if otherwise, then both the new maketh a rent, and the piece that was *taken* out of the new agreeth not with the old.
v.37 And no man putteth new wine into old bottles; else the new wine will burst the bottles, and be spilled, and the bottles shall perish.
v.38 But new wine must be put into new bottles; and both are preserved.
v.39 No man also having drunk old *wine* straightway desireth new: for he saith, The old is better."

33   The question about fasting and prayers seems to be related to a formal time set aside for fasting and a preset schedule of prayers at particular hours. This was the custom of the Pharisees, and their fasting was accompanied by every outward evidence that they were depriving themselves (Matt 6:16). One of Luke's great themes is the many secret prayers of the Lord and His disciples, but they were not public displays of prayer (Matt 6:5-8). As was usual for the Pharisees, they were occupied with exterior evidences of religion.

34-35   While the Lord was present with His own, they were in a state of continual rejoicing, as if they were guests at a wedding. The word that the Lord uses for being "taken away" suggests a violent snatching from their midst. It is a clear reference to the violence that those who rejected Him would show when they would take Him "by wicked hands" and crucify Him. The Lord is teaching that true fasting is linked to a loss of desire to eat or rejoice as a result of the grief of the parting from their Lord. This was the disciples' actual experience between the cross and their full understanding of His resurrection after the descent of the Holy Spirit at Pentecost. There were many times when the apostles gave themselves to fasting and prayer, but it was not for display.

36   A wise person would never patch an old garment by tearing a piece from a new one, for it would have two bad results. The new would be ruined by the tearing and the old would not be helped by a mis-matched piece added to it. Luke does not say why the application of the new to the old is unacceptable, but Mark adds that the greater strength of the new fabric would so strain the old that it would make a greater tear than was there at the beginning.

The force of this parable is that the Lord Jesus is not merely putting a new patch on the old system of law and ceremony, but the old is being set aside completely. Paul faced this problem with the Judaisers. They clung to the old garment, determined to patch up Judaism with gospel truth. The Galatian epistle is the Spirit's answer to such error.

We often meet religious people who would like to add salvation to their religion. They believe they are basically good, but just have a spot or two of sin that the work of Christ will remove. This mistake is aggravated by much that passes as gospel preaching among evangelicals today. They preach and teach that a sinner should confess his sins and ask God to forgive him. Very often, this confession of sins is not accompanied by a sense of utter sinfulness. It is possible to confess to certain sins and at the same time be full of self-righteousness. Naaman thought that the prophet would come out and strike his hand over the spot and he would be recovered of his leprosy, but the disease was not just a spot, it had affected the total man and he must dip seven times in Jordan to be cleansed (2 Kings 5:11). Such people want the Lord Jesus to forgive their minor failures. It is a new patch on an old garment, but Luke's Gospel makes it clear that only utterly lost sinners get to Christ for salvation.

37-38   The second form of this parable not only strengthens the first, but adds the fact that the old cannot be used; the old wineskins will burst. They are incapable of holding the new wine. The old empty wineskins, dried and withered, are a graphic illustration of the Jews' religion, particularly that form of it that made up the teachings of the Pharisees, that man at the core was good and could do good. The new wine is the joy of the coming of Christ, bringing salvation to the lost sons of Adam's fallen race. The day of grace is a totally new beginning, not a mere adjunct to the Jewish religious system.

39   However, the Jews were so content with the old wine that they did not desire the new. They said, "The old is better", or "The old is good enough" (NASB). They preferred their old religion to the new teaching of the Lord Jesus. Their good works and external religion suited them well and they desired nothing else.

9.   *Lord of the Sabbath*
   6:1-5

v.1   "And it came to pass on the second sabbath after the first, that he went through the corn fields; and his disciples plucked the ears of corn, and did eat, rubbing *them* in *their* hands.
v.2   And certain of the Pharisees said unto them, Why do ye that which is not lawful to do on the sabbath days?
v.3   And Jesus answering them said, Have ye not read so much as this, what David did, when himself was an hungered, and they which were with him;
v.4   How he went into the house of God, and did take and eat the shewbread, and gave also to them that were with him; which it is not lawful to eat but for the priests alone?
v.5   And he said unto them, That the Son of man is Lord also of the sabbath."

1   Sabbath-keeping was a major part of the external religion of the Jews. The sabbath regulations were so detailed that the rabbis gave a large part of the Mishnah to it and scribes spent long periods of their lives studying every minute detail of its restrictions. The Mishnah was a six part collection of traditions written in Hebrew about the end of the second century, but containing material from a much earlier period. In it, the Scripture, "Remember the sabbath day, to keep it holy" (Exod 20:8) was not a simple statement about setting aside this day for holy things. For law-keeping Jews, there was a frantic need to know a mountain of traditional regulations concerning it and a constant dread lest some minor infraction of an unknown rule might bring divine disfavour on their heads. It was unlawful to harvest or thresh grain on the sabbath day, but the rabbis had extended this to mean that even plucking grain and rubbing it in the hands to get rid of the chaff so it could be eaten was harvesting and threshing. They had even prescribed the amount that could be plucked and eaten on the Sabbath; it need be no larger than the size of a dried fig to convict a sabbath-breaker.

This was a law of the rabbis, not a law of Moses. God through Moses had made allowance for hungry travellers, "When thou comest into the standing corn of thy neighbour, then thou mayest pluck the ears with thine hand; but thou shalt not move a sickle unto thy neighbour's standing corn" (Deut 23:25).

The RV translation "Now it came to pass on a sabbath" is regarded by some scholars as being a poorer reading than the one the Revisers have placed in their margin, "Now it came to pass on the second-first sabbath". Mr. Darby believed that the strange expression, " second-first", was omitted by scribes who did not understand it (Introduction to the *New Translation*). Following the TR text, the AV reads, "And it came to pass on the second sabbath after the first". Explanations of the second sabbath include the three that follow: the first sabbath of the second year in a sabbatical cycle of seven years; the first sabbath of the second month of the year, or the difference between the Jewish civil year and the religious year making the reading to be, "the second first sabbath" because there were two first sabbaths and this would be the second one of the two (See *International Critical Commentary*, Alfred Plummer).

2   The Pharisees did not charge the disciples with stealing grain, but with breaking the Sabbath. But they did not break the Sabbath, for the simple preparation of a meat was not unlawful. At the institution of the feast of unleavened bread, Moses was told by God regarding Sabbaths, "no manner of work shalt be done in them, save that which every man shall eat, that only may be done" (Exod 12:16).

3-4   The answer of the Lord Jesus linked sabbath-keeping with showing grace and mercy to the needy, rather than with the rigid, authoritarian rules of the Pharisees. Only the priests could eat the bread that had been placed in two rows on the golden table in the holy place before the Lord. Fresh loaves were placed every Sabbath on the table and the priests were allowed to eat the loaves that had been removed (Lev 24:8,9). David and his hungry men ate the loaves from the hand of Ahimelech, the priest at Nob. These loaves had already been replaced with fresh ones on the table (1 Sam 21:6), yet they were food for the priests alone, so in their need David and his men ate food that was unlawful. Is the Lord Jesus saying that it is all right to flout the laws of God? Not at all, for Isaiah said, "he will magnify the law, and make it honourable" (42:21). He is saying that ceremonial law, distinct from moral law, should never be allowed to violate principles of compassion and mercy. In this very Gospel, the Lord said, "woe unto you, Pharisees! for ye tithe mint and rue and all manner of herbs, and pass over judgment and the love of God: these ought ye to have done, and not to leave the other undone" (11:42). We should not overlook the Lord's words, (these ought ye to have done", for it is possible for us to minimise His emphasis that the law was from God and must be obeyed, whereas the many traditions of the rabbis were human. The confrontation between the Lord and the Pharisees was almost always linked to their concern for rigid, external regulations that were man-made, while they ignored love and mercy.

It is important to notice how the Lord linked His disciples with the followers of David. If David had not been rejected, his followers would never have needed the shew-bread, and had Christ not been rejected as Israel's Messiah, His followers would not have been hungry.

5   In claiming to be "the Lord also of the sabbath", He is not merely comparing His authority as a teacher with the scribes and Pharisees. He is making the highest claim to deity. "And God blessed the seventh day, and sanctified it: because that in it he had rested from all his work" (Gen 2:3). First of all, the Sabbath was the creation rest of God, long before it was given to Israel as an institution (Exod 12:16), and later as a law (Exod 20:8). The Lord Jesus is saying that He is the Lord of God's rest and of Israel's day of rest which is typical of the rest of redemption (Heb 4:9-11). What a claim! It ranks with such words as, "the Son of man hath power upon earth to forgive sins" (Luke 5:24), and "Heaven and earth shall pass away, but my words shall not pass away" (Matt 24:35). He is truly the Lord of all.

10.   *The Withered Hand Healed on the Sabbath*
     6:6-11

> v.6   "And it came to pass also on another sabbath, that he entered into the synagogue and taught: and there was a man whose right hand was withered.
> v.7   And the scribes and Pharisees watched him, whether he would heal on the sabbath day; that they might find an accusation against him.
> v.8   But he knew their thoughts, and said to the man which had the withered hand, Rise up, and stand forth in the midst. And he arose and stood forth.
> v.9   Then said Jesus unto them, I will ask you one thing; Is it lawful on the sabbath days to do good, or to do evil? to save life, or to destroy *it*?
> v.10 And looking round about upon them all, he said unto the man, Stretch forth thy hand. And he did so: and his hand was restored whole as the other.
> v.11 And they were filled with madness; and communed one with another what they might do to Jesus."

6   The written traditions of the rabbis allowed healing on the Sabbath day, but only to save a life, and they rigidly held to this principle. If an Israelite was injured on a Sabbath day, but no threat to life was apparent, they could do no work to treat the injury until the sun had set. The case of the healing of the man with the withered hand is introduced by Luke at this point to illustrate the teaching about the Sabbath that has just been given. It happened on another Sabbath day when the Lord was teaching in a synagogue, and Luke, the beloved physician, with his care to detail, tells us that it was the man's right hand.

7   The man with the withered hand must have attracted the attention of the Lord in some way, because the scribes and Pharisees watched Him closely to see if He would heal him. The hand was " withered" (a word used for dried fruit), so it was not functional and constituted a major disability. The Lord's enemies were hoping for a new opportunity to accuse Him of sabbath-breaking.

8   The Lord knew their thoughts, not merely by observing their faces, as we would attempt to do, but because He knew the innermost thoughts of all that were around Him. It was the sense of this omniscience that had made Peter say in the boat, "Depart from me; for I am a sinful man, O Lord" (5:8). Luke is very aware that he is portraying a gentle, gracious Man with all the attributes of deity. The Lord invited the man to stand up in the midst of the whole congregation. Every eye was now fixed on him, and a silence of expectation among the people, or of suspicion and enmity on the part of the Lord's foes, filled the synagogue.

9   In the question asked by the Lord, we cannot escape the conclusion that He was willing to do good, but much that was done by the religious leaders was neither good nor merciful. They had truly neglected mercy, and the Lord Jesus was exposing them. The Lord's question went unanswered for the obvious reason that they would have condemned themselves by a positive or a negative response. This impotence fed their rage.

10   The penetrating eyes of the Lord of all looked "round about upon them all". We are reminded of a day when men will meet Him in judgment and John says, "his eyes are a flame of fire" (Rev 19:21 JND). In simple language, yet in words of almighty power, he said to the man, "Stretch forth thy hand". Luke records no struggle, or any evidence of unbelief; he stretched out his hand and it was restored to health and strength.

11   Unimpressed by the power of the miracle, the authority of His words, or the compassion of His heart, "they were filled with madness". This is a strong expression. The NASB translates it, "They were filled with rage". Wild fury at an act of mercy must be fed by fear, fear of what? Was is a genuine fear that the people would be misled and deceived and eventually damned as a result of following this "Jesus of Nazareth"? Or was it a fear of losing their own prestige and influence? Subsequent developments answer these questions. In the case of many of these proud men, self-interest, greed and a lust for power motivated them. Their discussion afterward likely centred on how they could combat such opposition to their teachings.

11.   *The Calling of the Twelve*
   ### 6:12-16

v.12   "And it came to pass in those days, that he went out into a mountain to pray, and continued all night in prayer to God.

v.13   And when it was day, he called *unto him* his disciples: and of them he chose twelve, whom also he named apostles;

v.14   Simon, (whom he also named Peter,) and Andrew his brother, James and John, Philip and Bartholomew,

v. 15   Matthew and Thomas, James the *son* of Alphaeus, and Simon called Zelotes,

v.16   And Judas *the brother* of James, and Judas Iscariot, which also was the traitor."

12   The Lord departed from the crowds and the scene of controversy to a mountain, far removed from the din of earth, to pray to the Father. Luke portrays a dependent Man who does only the Father's will and desires communion with Him, a communion into which no others can be allowed to intrude. The Lord Jesus is often found in "the secret place", and on this occasion, Luke records that He "continued all night in prayer". We may never know what He said on such occasions. There were times when He did reveal the burden of His prayers, as when He said to Peter, "but I have prayed for thee" (22:32). The burden of His heart on this occasion is usually taken to have been regarding the choice of His disciples, although we are not told that this is so. Only He and the Father are able to understand the vital importance of the choice. He is our great example for a life of prayer, and if He knew His need of communion with the Father, how much greater is our need!

13   As the day was breaking, "he called unto him his disciples". A larger number gathered to Him, and from their ranks, "he chose twelve, whom also he named apostles". The figure twelve is significant and relates to the twelve tribes of Israel to whom they were sent, which is the meaning of the new name "apostles". Luke used this term six times in his Gospel and thirty times more in the Acts. The other Gospels use it only once each. An apostle was a messenger who was sent directly by the Lord Himself to preach (Mark 3:14; Acts 1:21). Luke's association with "the apostle to the Gentiles" gave him an eyewitness view of the work and authority of an apostle.

It should never cease to amaze us that these humble men from Galilee, their hearts won, their lives transformed, should become the men to whom was committed "the apostles' doctrine", and who laid the foundation of church truth and testimony. Their love to Christ cost them everything in this world, " we have left all, and followed thee" (18:28), but they received "manifold more in this present time, and in the world to come life everlasting" (18:30). As apostles (*apo*, "from"; *stellō*, "to send") they were sent by the Lord personally. They were with Him from the baptism of John and were "ordained to be witnesses of his resurrection" (Acts 1:22). These are the three requirements of apostleship laid down in Acts 1:21,22. Of them the Lord said, "Ye have not chosen me, but I have chosen you, and ordained (appointed) you, that ye should go and bring forth fruit, and that your fruit should remain" (John 15:16).

14-16   The lists of the names of disciples found here and in Matt 10:2-4; Mark 3:16-19 and Acts 1:13, all have the same groupings, but differ only in the form of some of the names. Each list is divided into three groups of four, or tetrads. Peter always heads the first group. Simon was his domestic, intimate, personal name. Simeon was his Aramaic and official name and it is used only twice (Acts 15:14; 2 Pet 1:1). Peter is his new name, given by the Lord to him. It has great significance as an indication of his character. Once Luke has told us that Simon's name was changed by the Lord to Peter (v.13), he never afterward calls him anything else in his Gospel.

Three men, Peter, James and John, were often chosen by the Lord from among the twelve to be nearer to Him at times of special revelation, as on the mount (9:27-36), or at times of deep grief, as in the garden (Matt 26:36-46). Along with Andrew they are the first four in every list. Philip is the fifth in every list and heads the second group that includes Bartholomew, Matthew and Thomas. Bartholomew means the son of Talmai and may be a last name. The other name of this disciple may well be Nathaniel of Cana (John 1:45-51; 21:2), who was found and brought to the Lord by Philip. This may explain the close link between Philip and Bartholomew.

James, the son of Alphaeus, heads the third list of four which includes Thaddaeus (Lebbaeus, Matt 10:3) whom Luke calls Judas, the brother of James (two or three names were as common then as now); Simon, the Zealot (zelotes) whom Matthew calls "the Canaanite" (*Cananaean*, "zealot", 10:4), and last in every list, Judas Iscariot; only Luke adds, "which also was the traitor". He may have been the only non-Galilean among the disciples (L. Morris). The derivation of Iscariot has long been a subject of debate. Some link it with *sikarios* ("an assassin", Acts 21:38, O. Cullmann), but it possibly means "a man of Kerioth", a town in Judea, south of Hebron. This is made more likely by the fact that John 6:71 and 13:26 should probably be translated as "Judas, the son of Simon Iscariot" (JND, RV), making Kerioth the family home.

Judas was not a traitor when the Lord called him, but none who believe in the deity of our Lord can deny that He knew who would betray Him. Our problem here is of our own making. As finite creatures, we find it impossible properly to understand infinite foreknowledge in relation to choices made about events in time. In our present state, any attempt to rationalise divine prerogatives and temporal choice is doomed to failure. We may never be in a condition when we will fully understand this relationship, even in a glorified state. We can be confident that God will reveal to us all that we are able to understand, but we will never have the infinite wisdom and knowledge that belongs only to God. A little humility of mind in the present will keep us from stumbling over revealed truth that transcends our thought.

Two names appear in this list that teach, in a unique way, the profound influence of the Lord over the hearts and minds of men. They are Matthew the publican, and Simon the Zealot. These two men were at the two extremes of Jewish life. One was an employee of Rome before the Lord called him; the other belonged to a radical group among the Jews who were fanatically opposed to Rome and had taken a blood oath never to bow to her authority, and never to countenance those who did. Around the Lord Jesus these two extremes met. We never read of a clash between them. The Lord Jesus so radically changed them both that there was perfect calm in His presence. What a lesson for us when believers of various backgrounds are brought together in an assembly! "Let the peace of Christ preside in your hearts, to which also ye have been called in one body, and be thankful" (Col 3:15 JND).

12.   *The Lord's Instruction to His Disciples*
   6:17-49

v.17 "And he came down with them, and stood in the plain, and the company of his disciples, and a great multitude of people out of all Judaea and Jerusalem, and from the sea coast of Tyre and Sidon, which came to hear him, and to be healed of their diseases;

v.18 And they that were vexed with unclean spirits: and they were healed.

v.19 And the whole multitude sought to touch him: for there went virtue out of him, and healed *them* all.

v.20 And he lifted up his eyes on his disciples, and said, Blessed *be ye* poor: for yours is the kingdom of God.

v.21 Blessed *are ye* that hunger now: for ye shall be filled. Blessed *are ye* that weep now: for ye shall laugh.

v.22 Blessed are ye, when men shall hate you, and when they shall separate you *from their company*, and shall reproach *you*, and cast out your name as evil, for the Son of man's sake.

v.23 Rejoice ye in that day, and leap for joy: for, behold, your reward *is* great in heaven: for in the like manner did their fathers unto the prophets.

v.24 But woe unto you that are rich! for ye have received your consolation.

v.25 Woe unto you that are full! for ye shall hunger. Woe unto you that laugh now! for ye shall mourn and weep.

v.26 Woe unto you, when all men shall speak well of you! for so did their fathers to the false prophets.

v.27 But I say unto you which hear, Love your enemies, do good to them which hate you,

v.28 Bless them that curse you, and pray for them which despitefully use you.

v.29 And unto him that smiteth thee on the *one* cheek offer also the other; and him that taketh away thy cloak forbid not *to take thy* coat also.

v.30 Give to every man that asketh of thee; and of him that taketh away thy goods ask *them* not again.

v.31 And as ye would that men should do to you, do ye also to them likewise.
v.32 For if ye love them which love you, what thank have ye? for sinners also love those that love them.
v.33 And if ye do good to them which do good to you, what thank have ye? for sinners also do even the same.
v.34 And if ye lend *to them* of whom ye hope to receive, what thank have ye? for sinners also lend to sinners, to receive as much again.
v.35 But love ye your enemies, and do good, and tend, hoping for nothing again; and your reward shall be great, and ye shall be the children of the Highest: for he is kind unto the unthankful and to the evil.
v.36 Be ye therefore merciful, as your Father also is merciful.
v.37 Judge not, and ye shall not be judged: condemn not, and ye shall not be condemned: forgive, and ye shall be forgiven:
v.38 Give, and it shall be given unto you; good measure, pressed down, and shaken together, and running over, shall men give into your bosom. For with the same measure that ye mete withal it shall be measured to you again.
v.39 And he spake a parable unto them, Can the blind lead the blind? shall they not both fall into the ditch?
v.40 The disciple is not above his master: but every one that is perfect shall be as his master.
v.41 And why beholdest thou the mote that is in thy brother's eye, but perceivest not the beam that is in thine own eye?
v.42 Either how canst thou say to thy brother, Brother, let me pull out the mote that is in thine eye, when thou thyself beholdest not the beam that is in thine own eye? Thou hypocrite, cast out first the beam out of thine own eye, and then shalt thou see clearly to pull out the mote that is in thy brother's eye.
v.43 For a good tree bringeth not forth corrupt fruit; neither doth a corrupt tree bring forth good fruit.
v.44 For every tree is known by his own fruit. For of thorns men do not gather figs, nor of a bramble bush gather they grapes.
v.45 A good man out of the good treasure of his heart bringeth forth that which is good; and an evil man out of the evil treasure of his heart bringeth forth that which is evil: for of the abundance of the heart his mouth speaketh.
v.46 And why call ye me, Lord, Lord, and do not the things which I say?
v.47 Whosoever cometh to me, and heareth my sayings, and doeth them, 1 will shew you to whom he is like:
v.48 He is like a man which built an house, and digged deep, and laid the foundation on a rock: and when the flood arose, the stream beat vehemently upon that house, and could not shake it: for it was founded upon a rock.
v.49 But he that heareth, and doeth not, is like a man that without a foundation built an house upon the earth; against which the stream did beat vehemently, and immediately it fell; and the ruin of that house was great."

17 The Lord Jesus never spoke one redundant word, yet He did repeat Himself, as the Gospel records will show even to a casual reader. The teaching given by the Lord on the level plain has many parallels to Matthew's longer "Sermon on the Mount", but the time and circumstances are distinct from it. There are those who believe that Matthew gathered other material and put it together in his three chapters 5-7. Such a compilation of teaching would in no way weaken what was produced, the written word of God, but as all of us who preach know, it is often necessary, under varying needs and circumstances, to repeat material, often in an altered form that suits the context or the different audience. To deny this to the Lord does not make a man a great literary critic or Bible exegete, even though such a profession is made for him or by him. The gospel material used by each writer has value in fulfilling his purpose, and is handled in such a way that each portrait of the Lord Jesus is unique.

An alternative view is that the sermon in Matt 5-7 is the same as here and that the Lord went up the mount, spent the night in prayer, and having spoken to the twelve, descended to a level place. *Pedinos* ("plain") is only here in the NT, and refers to a level place which may well have been on the side of the mountain instead of being "a plain" at the base of it. Those who equate this sermon with the sermon on the mount believe that the brief account, given by Luke, was all that he felt necessary for his purpose. Those who give this explanation think it is most unlikely that two sermons so alike would have been preached by Christ on different occasions.

The teaching that followed was not only on a level place, but in the presence of "a crowd of his disciples" (JND), so there were more disciples than the twelve apostles, as we have already seen in v.13. Also present were "a great multitude of people" from distant places, as far away as Jerusalem to the south and Tyre and Sidon to the northwest. Among the crowd were many who had come to be healed of various diseases.

18   The intolerable bondage imposed on people by Satan is vividly described. Mr. Darby renders, "those that were beset by unclean spirits", which closely parallels the AV translation, "vexed with unclean spirits". We treat this matter too lightly. Satan uses whatever means are available to him to enslave people. To claim that such enslavement is a thing of the past is to be both blind and deaf to the conditions of our day. The drug cult and many similar enslaving devices of Satan are all too real to be ignored. Satanic power is more evident than ever and, if there is a change in tactics, then the present methods are more effective than the past, or Satan would not have made the change.

19   It is an interesting statement, "there went virtue out of him, and healed them all" (AV), or "power went out from him and healed all" (JND). The question arises, Was His power at all diminished as this virtue flowed out? John tells us, cc of his fulness (His full store) have all we received, and grace for grace" (John 1: 16). Was the fulness any less? Certainly not. He is not impoverished by giving. He knew when virtue went out of Him, as in the case of the woman who touched Him amid the jostling crowd (8:43-48), but the flow came from an inexhaustible supply that was ever resident in Him.

20   Before looking at the particulars of the Lord's teaching on this occasion, it is valuable to summarise its contents. Like all other sermons in Scripture, it has a pattern of teaching, thoughtfully developed. It is divided into three main parts:

1.   The blessings given to the subjects of the kingdom   vv.20-26.

2.   The law of love toward others   vv.27-38.

3.   Three parables that test reality   vv39-49.

The subjects of the kingdom, even though they are tried, are richly blessed, while those who seem to be rich will have eternal poverty. The tried who are blessed have three motives to strengthen then:

a.   they are suffering for the Son of man's sake;

b.   they have a reward in heaven;

c.   they have a place in the kingdom.

In the first part, the apostles are linked with the prophets of the old economy and must expect to be treated as they were. In the next part, the motivating power is love because they are the sons of the Highest and of their Father who is love. In the closing section, the true disciple knows where he is going, bears fruit because of his nature and can endure the tests of coming storms.

The words of the discourse that followed were spoken to the twelve and the many other disciples who were present, as He looked steadily on them. Many dear believers have said how much they would have loved to have been present in such a company, to hear His own words. Such a privilege would indeed be very great, but it would also be very solemn and searching. Luke has been careful to let us know that when He looked on anyone, He truly saw their innermost thoughts.

"How happy are you who own nothing" is J. B. Phillips' rendering of this clause. The blessing of their poverty is not that they are poor, but that they have a Father in heaven who is able to meet their every need. Their poverty casts them on God and makes them blessedly independent of human resources. Although there are those who say there is freedom in poverty that stands in contrast to all the enslavement of a materialistic society, we may well wonder if people who really are poor would think so. It must be a terrible thing to be poor and hungry. There is no virtue in being poor, and those who know it best would have great difficulty in describing it as a blessed existence, but this is not what the Lord is saying. These poor disciples are in the kingdom of God at the very time that He addresses them. Many of the rich of this world will never be in it.

"But thou art rich" (Rev 2:9) was spoken by the Lord to the impoverished, persecuted saints of Smyrna and could be equally applied to these disciples. James, who in his epistle so closely parallels the teachings of the Lord, says,

"Hath not God chosen the poor of this world rich in faith, and heirs of the kingdom which he hath promised to them that love him?" (James 2:5). This is the context in which we should understand the happiness of the poor. It is not to be poor that is the desirable thing, but it is better to be poor and be an heir of the kingdom of God than to be rich and miss it altogether.

21   Luke calls happy those who hunger and weep now. Matthew tells us that it is a hungering or thirsting after righteousness. This seems to be the context implied in Luke as well, although Luke is emphasising the physical hunger as illustrative of something deeper. He is contrasting present need with future kingdom blessing, and is speaking of something more than physical appetites. Even the tears are not because of personal trials or pain, but for the desperate plight of fallen humanity and the long night of darkness that has held the world in the thraldom of sin and Satan. The laugh is not scornful or vindictive in any degree, but a joyous laugh at the triumph of righteousness and truth. These conclusions are necessary when we consider that the time for the wrongs to be set right will be when the Lord returns in the glory of His kingdom.

22   Persecution for the sake of the Son of man will be the portion of these disciples in the meantime. The storm clouds are already on the horizon. Even at this early stage in His ministry, opposition to the Lord is growing in intensity. Luke describes needy, inquisitive and curious crowds in these early chapters, who come to the Lord for heating, but already the opposition of the Pharisees and scribes is arising as an ever increasing storm of hatred and malignity. The Lord knows it well. The fury that was aimed at Him after the heating of the man with the withered hand was a harbinger of much worse to come. The servant was not greater than his Lord (John 15:20), and could expect no better treatment from a hostile world.

   We need to understand that this is ever the lot of the believer as he lives in the world. Instead of expecting acceptance by it and approval from it, must we not ever remember that "the friendship of the world is enmity with God? and whosoever therefore will be a friend of the world is (literally, makes himself) the enemy of God" (James 4:4).

23   This was a day of tears for His disciples, but the day of joy and reward would surely come. The disciples had the great honour of being part of a long line of those who were a suffering remnant for God amid general unbelief and blindness. The prophets before them had also suffered like things from their own contemporaries. There is no thought here of seeking for persecution. It would surely come, and the disciples would be lifted above it by the prospect of the day of reward, but to be hated, ostracised, reproached and to have your name cast out as evil is indeed a most bitter experience.

24-26   Luke is the only one of the Synoptic Gospels that records the "woes". The English word "woe" does not fully convey the thought of the Greek word *ouai*. It is not a threat, nor is it only a pronouncement of doom. It does include the thought of displeasure and coming judgment, but it is also a cry of compassion, and an expression of regret and grief. The gentleness of the tender Man of sorrows is behind these words.

The four woes must be understood in the light of Luke's frequent contrasts between "here" and "hereafter", between time and eternity (see 12:15-21; 16:14-31). The things upon which the Lord pronounces woe are "highly esteemed among men" (16:15). To be rich, full, joyful and spoken well of by all men are things that are prized and avidly sought after, but in the light of eternity, they are empty and meaningless. This description should be carefully compared with the language of the rich men in chs.12 and 16. It is possible to have everything for time and nothing for eternity.

27-28   The expression, "you which hear" should be compared with "ye poor"; and "ye that hunger"; "ye that weep"; "ye, when men shall hate you" should be contrasted with "you that are rich"; "you that are full"; "you that laugh now"; "you, when all men shall speak well of". These contrasting statements that are all in the second person have made many think that the company who heard the Lord were divided into radically contrasting groups. It may well be that the use of the second person pronoun for the second group was rhetorical, and is simply stating that such people were part of the society of the time. This seems to be the preferable view after a careful consideration of all the teaching of the Lord on this occasion. This view is taken in the light of the fact that we are told that the Lord spoke these words to His disciples (v.20).

The love (*agapē*) that the true disciple shows is not based on merit or worthiness in the object of love. A believer loves as God loves, not to the same measure, but of the same kind; that is, it is an unselfish love for those who do not or cannot draw love to themselves. God so loved us when we were unlovely and unlovable, so we are to love even those who hate, curse and despitefully use us.

This is the first time that the verb *agapaō* ("to love"), is used in this Gospel. It occurs thirteen times in all: 6:27,32 (four times), 35; 7:5,42,47 (twice); 10:27; 11:43; 16:13. The noun *agapē* ("love") is found only in 11:42, where it is used of the love of God. The other word for love (*phileō*) is used twice: for "those who love greetings in the markets" (20:46); for the kiss of Judas (Matt 26:48; Mark 14:14 and Luke 22:47), because that false kiss was a profession of tender affection.

The response to abusive conduct toward us is not merely to ignore it stoically, or endure it as a martyr, but actively to love, bless and pray for those who so treat us. The Lord's teaching was contrary to human reasoning even when He spoke of material things, but now that He is speaking about love, the contrast is even greater. In fact, these commands go far beyond human ability, but if the disciple is to have the spirit of his Master, he will manifest this kind of love. For the believer today, likeness to Christ, produced in us by the indwelling Holy Spirit, will enable us to love our enemies. Revenge, retaliation, or "getting even" is far removed from this teaching of our Lord.

29   The word for "cheek" is really the jaw, so the Lord is speaking of a painful blow from a fist, rather than an insulting slap of the hand. Either injury would not be easy to accept without immediate retaliation. Behind this teaching is the great Example, "when he was reviled, reviled not again; when he suffered, he threatened not; but committed himself to him that judgeth righteously" (1 Pet 2:23). There has been a tendency on the part of some to pass this teaching on to the remnant in tribulation days, or in some other way to vitiate its plain demands. In the light of the Lord's own conduct under the cruel hands of sinners, it is impossible not to accept this teaching as being for us. We may not have this kind of thing in mind when we pray to be more like Him, but such a likeness involves this example as well as all the other blessed moral features of His walk among men. The standard is very high, but let us be careful that we do not reason it away.

Turning the other cheek does not mean seeking for injury. It does mean that there will be no retaliation and there will be a willingness to suffer for Christ's sake whatever is necessary. The taking away of the coat suggests a violent seizure, so the subject is still the action of persecutors. Once again, the great Example comes to our minds. Luke says, "they parted his raiment, and cast lots" (23:34). Mark says, "they parted his garments, casting lots upon them, what every man should take" (15:24). It is Matthew that tells us that, in the common hall the soldiers of the governor "stripped him" (27:28). They took away all His garments. After they had crucified Him, His garments were divided into four parts, to each soldier a part, while the unseamed garment went to the winner of the lots that were cast. Seeing that "no ungentle, murmuring word escaped His silent tongue", we surely cannot deny the literalness of giving the tunic to the one who snatches the coat.

30   The present, continuous force of the verb "Give" should be emphasised here. The Lord is not speaking of an occasional spurt of generosity that may move us at times, but rather, a continuous willingness to give. It is giving that is motivated by an unselfish love that desires the very best for its object. It may not be a kindness to give to everyone who asks. There is a kind of giving that is forbidden by Paul, "If any will not work, neither let him eat" (2 Thess 3:10 RV). Such a person should not be encouraged in his bad conduct, but should be made to feel ashamed (v.14). Paul was not contradicting the Lord Jesus, so we must understand the Lord's words in their own context of need or persecution, and not allow them to be used to encourage laziness.

The first part of this verse is dealing with need. It seems clear that the second part returns again to the subject of persecution that has been in the context from v.22. The meekness and gentleness of Christ is the background against which we should understand "taketh away" and "ask... not again".

31   The Lord Jesus gave this blessed rule of life as a pivotal point of His moral teaching regarding the behaviour of man toward his fellows. "Thou shalt love ... thy neighbour as thyself" (see Luke 10:27) is the heart from which the doing must come. The rabbis wrote, "Do not do to your neighbour that which would be hateful if done to you". It should be recognised that much rabbinical writing had as its background the revelations of Jehovah to Israel, so much that had been written was good. In contrast to the negativeness of the rabbis, the Lord Jesus uniquely taught, in an active sense, the doing of good to all men.

32-34   The love of genuine disciples is like God's love to us and extends even to our enemies. We must do good to those who are undeserving and lend to those who cannot repay, and in so doing show a goodness that exceeds that which sinners show, or we cannot claim that we are like the Father who is revealed in the Lord Jesus. The Lord is teaching that there is a human level of goodness, but the love and righteousness which He is describing far surpass it. We make a mistake to suppose that He did not recognise a "godless goodness", for He often referred to it. There are those who do not believe in God or Christ who maintain a moral standard that is most acceptable on the human level. Let us understand that the goodness that was seen in the Lord Jesus and heard in His teaching was of a far higher nature. He said to the disciples, "except your righteousness shall exceed the righteousness of the scribes and Pharisees, ye shall in no case enter into the kingdom of heaven" (Matt 5:20). The NT does allow for a righteousness that is produced by sinful self. The OT and NT agree that this self- righteousness is only as filthy rags in the sight of God (Isa 64:6; Rom 3:9-12). We should never be content with mere human goodness.

35-36   The order is significant here. True goodness that marks the children of God comes from love and mercy in the heart. The motives are known to the Father, so the teachings of the Son reach far deeper than external actions, and they examine the spring from which the actions arise. This was in strict contrast to the righteousness taught by the Pharisees and scribes. Only in this verse is the Father mentioned, but He is frequently named in the Matthew sermon.

The phrase "hoping for nothing again" is a translation of one word, *apelpizō* It is not found elsewhere in the NT, so we cannot get help from other NT uses. W.E. Vine has shown that it is made up of *apo* ("away from") and *elpizō* ("to hope"), so it literally means, not to give up in despair or "never despairing" (RV). The RV margin suggests "despairing of no man", but this is rejected by many. The disciple should love his "enemies, and do good and lend" even though the returns from men are utterly lacking, for he is not motivated by a reward from men, but by devotion to his Lord. The last half of the verse assures him that God takes note of all that is done, and a full recompense from God will be given in a coming day. Human nature is tempted to think that if a recipient of kindness is unappreciative, he deserves nothing more, but this is not a question of deserving at all. Paul preached on Mars' Hill, "he giveth to all life, and breath, and all things" (Acts 17:25). This is the standard for Christ-like kindness. How poorly we have fulfilled it!

37 The three terms, "judge not... condemn not... forgive", belong together. The difference between *krinō* ("judge") and *katadikazō* ("condemn") may be described as declaring guilt and passing sentence, while *apoluō* ("forgive") means to release. The Lord is not using these terms in a legal sense, yet we cannot escape from the fact that He is describing a judgment throne. It is very unbecoming for us who have stood condemned before the bar of God, and been fully forgiven, now to sit upon a judgment throne judging others. If we do this kind of judging and condemning, the very reality of our own forgiveness is in question. "Ye shall not be judged" refers to God's future judgment of men. In this context; it is a future day of reckoning that is involved. We cannot be in the enjoyment of forgiveness while entertaining a hypocritical condemnation of others. There are many passages of Scripture that make it clear that sin must be judged in ourselves and in the world system, fruits must be inspected (vv.43,44), but persons should not be brought under our condemnation. We must leave that to the true "Throne-Sitter".

38 The exhortation is to keep giving; it is a way of life that is described. It means more than the giving of material things, although it includes them; it also involves the giving of ourselves, our time and our efforts. The return is "good measure, pressed down, and shaken together, and running over". The AV translators have supplied the word "men" because of the impersonal construction of this clause, but, as stated above, the One who will reward present deeds is the Lord Himself (v.35). It is a principle that "The liberal soul shall be made fat" (Prov 11:25), and without doubt, there is recompense in this life for kindness and mercy that is shown to others. However, the Lord Jesus is describing a future reward. "The bosom" is literally "a fold of a garment overhanging a girdle" (see Ruth 3:15). The generous measure of return, pressed down by the hand, shaken to and fro to receive the maximum amount, and then more poured in until it overflows is a vivid description of the fulness of God's repayment of all that is given in love to Christ in the present time. The last sentence of this verse should not be understood as meaning that an equal return will be made for what is given. It means that we should give in full measure as God in His grace and love will deal a full measure to us. Although the Lord is gracious and even His rewards will be given in grace, the motive for devoted service is not reward, but to bring joy to the heart of our "beloved".

39   This verse marks a new section which does have links with the teaching that has preceded it, but contains very particular instructions for the disciples which are distinct from that which has gone before. *Parabolē* is the usual word used for a parable and is found eighteen times in Luke, yet it is also used in 4:23 as a wise word or proverb. So it is here, "Can the blind lead the blind? shall they not both fall into the ditch?". We see many examples of this in religion, but the saying is applied to the disciples in this case. They cannot lead others unless their own eyes have been opened to understand the Lord's teaching. Untaught teachers are unreliable guides. This is a solemn warning to all who would profess to teach (James 3:1).

40   The meaning that we have given to v.39 is necessary in view of this statement of the Lord. To be "perfect" is to be "fully taught", and is used in such verses as Heb 11:3 with the thought of being completely made. "The disciple is not above his master (the Lord)", that is, his understanding or insight cannot be greater than his Teacher's. "Every disciple who is fully trained will be like his Teacher". He will teach the same things by life and lip. The school of God is for all believers and the teaching process goes on through the christian life; however, we must understand this, in its context, as being special instruction for those who engage in the ministry of teaching. Being "like his Teacher" is in relation to understanding, but we must also impress on our hearts that effective teaching will be manifest by a teacher who is morally like his Lord.

41-42   A "mote" is a mere speck, while "a beam" is a log or a tree trunk. Again, this is in relation to the teacher as in the two previous verses. It is easier to see a speck in the eye of a brother and attempt its removal than to see a log in one's own eye, but a man with a log in his own eye is seriously handicapped in seeing anything that is needed. The small piece of chaff, straw or wood may be a real problem to the brother, but I cannot help him until I can see clearly. Also, the brother with the speck in his eye will find it very difficult to be corrected by the man with a log sticking out of his own eye. This teaching of the blind leading the blind and the removal of a speck from the eye of a brother should not be relegated to Pharisees and scribes, as it so often is. This was spoken to the disciples and shows that the teaching of the Lord produced self-judgment in all who were fitted by Him to teach others. The moral nature of His teaching makes it impossible to be a teacher of it unless it has power in the life of the teacher. This is a great principle of all spiritual truth. It can never be held as mere doctrine and never can be made to apply to others unless it has first had its full application to self.

43-44   The Lord contrasts a good and a bad tree and then contrasts figs and grapes with a thorn plant or bramble bush. The emphasis is on fruit-bearing and the nature of the fruit. Those who have been taught by Him and have fully applied His teaching to themselves are good trees that produce good fruit. This is linked to what has just preceded it. There is no good tree that bears "rotten" fruit, which can be the meaning of sapros, but more generally, it means bad in the sense of not being good for food. " Every tree is known by his own fruit" should be taken very literally. A pear tree produces pears, not apples or peaches. The production of the tree is the evidence of its nature. This discerning of fruit parallels the teaching of Matt 7. In that passage, as here, it is preceded by a warning about judging unrighteously as in the case of the mote and beam, yet it does require a judgment to determine the fruit and through it to judge the nature of the tree that produces it. Matthew deals particularly with the subject of false prophets, but Luke's parallel passage is more general and involves the judgment of fruit in the lives of all who profess to be good men and to teach righteousness .

45   In moving from the subject of good fruit to treasure out of the heart, the Lord is enlarging and developing the same subject. The good tree and the good man are synonymous, and the good fruit should be compared to the good treasure. The word *thēsauros* (treasure or treasure chest) is very interesting. It is not the place where the treasure is kept that is good, but the treasure itself. The remainder of the verse makes it clear that the treasure is made up of good works. We use thesaurus in this very way, having transposed the Greek word into our own language. It is necessary to see that "the good man" has treasured up these good things in his heart. He did not produce them, they were given to him, and knowing their value, he guarded them in his heart. Again the Lord is describing the servant who hears his Lord's words and does them and becomes a teacher of others, having been fully taught himself. Then out "of the abundance of his heart his mouth speaketh". What a blessed pattern for all who attempt to speak to men from God! The Lord Jesus fulfilled this perfectly. It is also an indication of what is in the heart when it overflows with bitterness and unrighteous accusations of others.

46   The double vocative, "Lord, Lord", is being used by the Lord as a reference to high profession. The verse is a contrast between what the lips say and what the heart, hands and feet do. There is a most valuable lesson here that is amplified by Paul in 1 Cor 12:3. The use of His title as Lord is a confession of allegiance. We should never call Him Lord when we are not willing to bow to His claims over us. There is a second lesson. The disciples did not call Him Jesus; they never did so as far as we can tell from the text. The Holy Spirit called Him Jesus, but the disciples called Him Lord. Let us call Him Lord and fully own His claims!

47-49   We preach the gospel from the parable of the two builders and rightly so, for the difference between the house that stood and the one that fell is eternal salvation or damnation. There is a very obvious link to what has gone before.

Hearing His words and applying them to heart and conscience has resulted in judging self, producing good fruit and treasuring His teaching in the heart to be brought forth at a needed time for the enrichment of others. The preceding verse has dealt more specifically with not having a mere lip profession, which is always a false profession, but giving evidence of reality by doing. Now the eternal result of coming to Him and hearing His words and doing them is to be saved or lost.

All are building for eternity. Both of the builders had some sense of need, for a house is a place of shelter and rest. It should also he a place of love and joy, so it is a very vivid description of preparation for eternity. So far as we know, the design of one house was not superior to that of the other, and did not show greater skill or craftsmanship. The entire difference was in the foundations. This was such a plain condemnation of the teaching of the Pharisees which was occupied with mere external observance which they believed would eventually change the inner man. It is only Luke who tells us that one man " digged deep" to lay his foundation "upon a rock", an apt illustration of the word of God, going deep into the heart and conscience, producing genuine repentance. Both men felt safe in their houses, as many do even though their hope is not based on Scripture. The difference between them was unknown until the storm came and the raging torrent (rampaging river) struck the houses. Of the house on the rock, the Lord Jesus says that the flood was unable to shake it, for its strength was the rock on which it rested. Of the other, He says, "It collapsed and its destruction was complete" (NIV). The gospel preacher can draw searching and solemn material from this parable. It is possible to have every outward aspect of christian profession and yet to lack the true foundation. A foundation cannot be damaged by examination, and these verses are a solemn warning to search well the foundation because this is for eternity.

13.   *The Centurion's Servant Healed*
   7:1-10

v.1   "Now when he had ended all his sayings in the audience of the people, he entered into Capernaum.
v.2   And a certain centurion's servant, who was dear unto him, was sick, and ready to die.
v.3   And when he heard of Jesus, he sent unto him the elders of the Jews, beseeching him that he would come and heal his servant.
v.4   And when they came to Jesus, they besought him instantly, saying, That he was worthy for whom he should do this:
v.5   For he loveth our nation, and he hath built us a synagogue.
v.6   Then Jesus went with them. And when he was now not far from the house, the centurion sent friends to him, saying unto him, Lord, trouble not thyself: for I am not worthy that thou shouldest enter under my roof:
v.7   Wherefore neither thought I myself worthy to come unto thee: but say in a word, and my servant shall be healed.

> v.8 For I also am a man set under authority, having under me soldiers, and I say unto one, Go, and he goeth; and to another, Come, and he cometh; and to my servant, Do this, and he doeth *it*.
> v.9 When Jesus heard these things, he marvelled at him, and turned him about, and said unto the people that followed him, I say unto you, I have not found so great faith, no, not in Israel.
> v.10 And they that were sent, returning to the house, found the servant whole that had been sick."

It would be difficult to find a gospel passage that portrays the power and grace of the Saviour more fully than this section of Luke. From 4:14 to 9:50, the power of Christ is seen in raising up the sick and dying, and even the dead; in fact, the entire Gospel has been outlined with this fact in mind.

1:1-4:13	Growing up-The virgin birth	
4:14-9:50	Raising up	-The visible power
9:51-19:48	Going up	-The virtuous life
20:1-23:56	Lifted up	-The vicarious death
24:1-48	Raised up	-The victorious resurrection
24:49-53	Taken up	-The Victor ascended.

1   The Lord had finished all that He had intended to say to the people on this occasion. "All he wished to say" (Rieu) is the sense of the statement, "he had ended all his sayings". He had spoken "in the audience (literally, into the ears) of the people", not only to His disciples, even though they were the intended objects of much of His teaching. Luke tells us "he entered into Capernaum" without any information about the distance He had been away from it.

2   The healing of the centurion's servant marks a significant point in this Gospel. We must keep in mind that the penman was a companion of Paul, the apostle to the Gentiles, therefore Gentiles who fear God, and, as in this case, manifest greater faith than the Jews (v.9) are indicative of the gospel going out to the world, far beyond the confines of Israel. A centurion was originally the captain of a hundred soldiers, but the number under such a command varied (Josephus). The first word in the sentence (in Greek) is "centurion" because he is the main personality of the story that follows. Something of the character of the centurion is seen in his deep concern for the slave whom he held as *entimos*. This word has the same root as the name of Timothy and means honoured or respected, and yet also implies that he loved him. The servant was so sick that he was at the very point of death.

3   The approach of the centurion to the Lord Jesus was not direct. He went to the elders of the Jews that they might act as intermediaries, no doubt believing that they would have a greater influence on the Healer than he, a Gentile, would have. In this healing, there is an illustration of how the message of the gospel would reach to Gentiles and many of them would receive Christ even though the Jewish nation to whom He came would reject Him. A second characteristic of our day is illustrated. All who are saved now "have not seen, and yet have believed" (John 20:29). So it was in this case, the servant never saw the One who healed him. Peter has this in mind in writing, "Whom having not seen, ye love; in whom, though now ye see him not, yet believing, ye rejoice with joy unspeakable and full of glory" (1 Pet 1:8).

4-5   The intense interest of the elders in this healing was in contrast to their resistance to the healing of the man with the withered hand (6:6-11). They begged Him that He would come and save this slave from death. Their contention was that the centurion was deserving of help, for he loved the people and in Capernaum stood "the synagogue" that he had built at his own expense. These facts are enlightening. It is no wonder that the Jews had such an interest, or that the centurion went to the elders to get help for his servant. He may have been a genuine "God-fearer". Every centurion mentioned in the NT showed integrity in his attitude and actions (Matt 27:54; Acts 10:22; 22:26; 23:17; 27:43).

6   The Lord willingly went with them, not because the elders had influence upon Him, but because, as is so often implied in Luke, the omniscience of the Lord enabled Him to see behind the events and allowed Him to move unerringly. Not one step of the gracious Man who moved for God in this scene was taken without foreknowledge of what awaited Him. When He was not far from the house, friends came with a message. The Lord had already taken more trouble than the centurion believed that he deserved. The elders said that he was worthy, but in contradiction he said, "I am not worthy that thou shouldest enter under my roof". Matt 8:5-13 abbreviates the account and does not describe the mediation of the elders or friends. Luke's record emphasises the humility of the centurion.

"Trouble not thyself" is from an old Greek verb, *skullō*, found in Matt 9:36 ("were distressed" RV), which originally meant "to skin, to mangle" in a physical sense and then was used metaphorically for "extreme annoyance". The centurion's choice of this word indicates that as yet he had no understanding of the tender heart of the Saviour. *Hikanos* ("worthy") is an expression very common in Luke and Acts, being found twenty-nine times in these two books, and only twelve other times in all the NT. It means to be "sufficient, adequate, large enough", or simply "much" or "many". The centurion used a negative with it, so he was literally saying that he was insufficient cause for the Lord to come. The word he used in the next verse, *axioō* ("worthy"), is a stronger word than the adjective *hikanos*, and is used only seven times in the NT: three times by Luke (7:7; Acts 15:38, "thought not good"; 28:22, "desire to hear"); it means "to count worthy" or "to esteem". Again, he denied that he possessed it.

7   The words of the centurion should not be construed as being merely those of politeness. The important factor to remember is that the One who knows the hearts of men (John 2:24,25) accepted his words as genuine. He acknowledged that it would be presumptuous for him even to approach the Lord. His knowledge of Christ caused him to have an attitude like Peter in the boat, "Depart from me; for I am a sinful man, O Lord" (5:8). He did have some knowledge of the power of the words of Christ, for he said, "say in a word", or literally, "say only in a word and my servant shall be healed".

8   He illustrated from his own position exactly how he believed that the word of Christ, even from a distance, could accomplish the saving from death of his servant. He could have used the illustration very differently by saying that he was a man with authority to command, but instead, he describes himself as a man under the authority of his superiors. Even as such he is able to give commands to his soldiers and slaves that are carried out in his absence; how much more He who has sovereign control over the very forces of nature can command them and be obeyed. He really said, "I am given orders that I obey, and those under me are given orders that they obey". He believed that if the Lord commanded, disease and even the approach of death would be controlled. The authority over all created things was resident in a Man. How thoroughly the centurion grasped this we cannot say, but we do know that whatever rays of light had penetrated his heart were from God. In a great doctrinal statement Paul tells us that creation existed in the Lord Jesus, was created by Him and came into being for Him as its goal (Col 1:16 RV).

9-10   The foregoing description of the faith of the centurion has been written with these verses in mind. The Lord Jesus marvelled at it. Only twice in His ministry did the Lord speak of great faith. The other occasion was in Matt 15:21-28 when the woman of Canaan took the place of a little dog waiting for crumbs from the table of its master. She took the lowest place and the Lord said, "O woman, great is thy faith". The centurion gave to the Lord Jesus the highest place, and the Lord called it, "so great faith". These contrasting circumstances give to us as clear a definition of great faith as can be found in Scripture: great faith is to take the lowest place and give to the Lord Jesus the highest place. The healing of the servant took place just as the faith of the centurion anticipated it, by a word from the Lord.

We can learn much from this account. We too sense our unworthiness that the Lord should come near and bless us. How often we take the words of this man on our lips, and pray that the Lord will speak "the word only". A word from the Lord brings life out of death, fruitfulness out of barrenness and joy out of grief.

14.   *The Raising of a Widow's Son*
7:11-17

> v.11 "And it came to pass the day after, that he went into a city called Nain; and many of his disciples went with him, and much people.
> v.12 Now when he came nigh to the gate of the city, behold, there was a dead man carried out, the only son of his mother, and she was a widow: and much people of the city was with her.
> v.13 And when the Lord saw her, he had compassion on her, and said unto her, Weep not.
> v.14 And he came and touched the bier: and they that bare *him* stood still. And he said, Young man, I say unto thee, Arise.
> v.15 And he that was dead sat up, and began to speak. And he delivered him to his mother.
> v.16 And there came a fear on all: and they glorified God, saying, That a great prophet is risen up among us; and, That God hath visited his people.
> v.17 And this rumour of him went forth throughout all Judaea, and throughout all the region round about."

11   The AV has translated "in the subsequent time" as "the day after". This is not accurate. All that Luke states is that this event happened soon after the healing of the centurion's servant. Nain was a village about six miles south-east of Nazareth. It was a day's journey from Capernaum and the Lord was accompanied by his disciples and a great crowd of people.

12   The events along the way are not mentioned, but as the large company approached the gate of Nain, they met another company leaving the village. Luke gives careful details. The dead man was the only son of a widowed mother, and the funeral procession was large because the people were deeply sympathetic. Luke refers to widows nine times in his Gospel and three times in the Acts. In contrast, Matthew mentions widows once, Mark three times and John not at all (see Introduction ix).

13   It was toward the weeping mother that the Lord directed His sympathy. She was left alone in the world, without support and comfort and, possibly, very limited as to how her material needs would be supplied. The compassionate heart of the tender Son of man went out to her and He said, "Weep no more" (Rieu). How impotent these words would be if they were spoken by mortal lips! We often bid people to cease their weeping without any ability to alleviate the cause of their tears. It is characteristic of God that He is able to wipe away tears. It is interesting that the last statement in the Bible about tears links them with death, " And God shall wipe away all tears from their eyes; and there shall be no more death" (Rev 21:4). Had this widow known that her son would be raised and never buried, she could not have wept if she tried. We can learn from this that many tears are shed simply because we do not know the full facts. If Mary Magdalene at the tomb of Christ (John 20:11) had understood the meaning of the missing body of her Lord, she would have cried out for joy instead of weeping in sorrow and bewilderment.

14   In the order of the funeral procession, the lone mother would have been walking in front of the bier. Luke describes the Lord speaking to the mother first; then, approaching the bier on which the body lay in full sight of the mourners and the large number of witnesses, He touched it and the bearers stopped. It was most unusual to touch the bier, for ceremonial defilement was the result for any Israelite, but no defilement could ever touch His holy Person (Heb 7:26). Ignoring the bearers, the Lord spoke directly to the corpse, "Young man, I say unto thee, Arise".

15   The man who had been dead sat up, began to speak and was delivered to his mother by the Lord. The command to arise was obeyed. The Lord never gives a command without giving the power to obey it. This is a good thing for us to remember in our obedience to His Word. The verb "sat up" is used only here and in Acts 9:40. The intransitive use of the verb is rare "except in medical writings" (A. Plummer). Luke is showing his medical interest again. The young man began to speak but, as in the case of Lazarus (John 12:2), none of his words are recorded.

   For the first time in this Gospel in a narrative section, Luke calls Jesus "the Lord" (v.13). It is significant that he ascribes this great miracle to the Lord. Death could not exist in His presence. It is recorded that the Lord attended a wedding (John 2:1-11), but it is not recorded that he attended a funeral, or at least when He did, He raised the dead to life. If He had been in Bethany when Lazarus was dying, there would have been no death. This is the plain meaning of His words in John 11:14,15, "Then said Jesus unto them plainly, Lazarus is dead. And I am glad for your sakes that I was not there, to the intent ye may believe". The presence of the Lord would have forbidden the presence of death. This was true at Calvary. The death of the Lord Jesus preceded the death of the two thieves. They could not have died in the presence of a living Lord.

   The gospel preacher rightly applies this ability of the Lord to impart life as an illustration of a sinner receiving eternal life, for this is the way the Lord Himself applied it. This is the significance of His words, "For as the Father hath life in himself; so hath he given to the Son to have life in himself" (John 5:26). John 5:25 links this statement with giving eternal life to those who are spiritually dead, but vv.27,28 link it to His authority to raise the dead in the resurrection of life and the resurrection of damnation. In the case of the young man lying dead on the bier, we have a plain picture of the utter helplessness of a sinner to save himself. In the life-giving word that reached his ears, we have an illustration of the power of the preached word of the Lord. In the joy and thankfulness that followed the miracle, we have a beautiful picture of the joy that accompanies salvation. Many a mother, who has wept bitter tears over a son who was dead in his sins, has had the great joy of seeing her son raised to life.

16 A holy awe fell upon the people who saw the miracle. They realised that they had seen a mighty work of God and rightly they gave glory to Him, acknowledging, "God hath visited his people". They also honoured the Lord Jesus, "a great prophet is risen up among us". It was not the full appreciation of His Person, but it was the highest thought of which they seemed capable. Their knowledge of Scripture would have brought to their minds the miracles of Elijah and Elisha in raising the dead.

Their language also reminds us of the words of Ruth 1:6, "the Lord had visited his people". *Episkeptomai* ("visited") is a very interesting word. It was used in the praise of Zacharias, "Blessed be the Lord God of Israel; for he hath visited and redeemed his people" (1:68). Commenting on this earlier verse, W. Liefeld writes, "In secular Greek it means simply 'to look at' or 'reflect on' (often in a charitable way, such as a doctor visiting the sick, Matt 25:36,43; James 1:27). The element of special concern is deepened to the spiritual level in the LXX use of the word. A particular example is that of God 'visiting' people in grace or judgment (Exod 4:31; Zech 10:3)" (*The Expositor's Bible Commentary*, Vol. 8).

We have drawn special attention to this word because Luke has used it in Acts 15:14 to record the memorable words of James that sum up for us the purpose of God in this age, "how God at the first did visit ('showed his concern for' NIV) the Gentiles, to take out of them a people for his name". This visitation is a major theme of Luke's Gospel, so that the rejection of the visit of God in grace is lamented by the Lord, "thou knewest not the time of thy visitation" (19:44).

17 The report of the miracle "went forth throughout all Judaea". It took place in Nain of Galilee, so the reference to "all Judaea" is best understood as being "all Jewry", that is, throughout all the land of the Jews. "All the region round about" means that these tidings spread to Gentile lands adjacent to Palestine. Such a deed could not be hidden.

15. *The Question of John the Baptist*
       7:18-35

v.18 "And the disciples of John shewed him of all these things.
v.19 And John calling *unto him* two of his disciples sent *them* to Jesus, saying, Art thou he that should come? or look we for another?
v.20 When the men were come unto him, they said, John Baptist hath sent us unto thee, saying, Art thou he that should come? or look we for another?

v.21 And in that same hour he cured many of *their* infirmities and plagues, and of evil spirits; and unto many *that were* blind he gave sight.

v.22 Then Jesus answering said unto them, Go your way, and tell John what things ye have seen and heard; how that the blind see, the lame walk, the lepers are cleansed, the deaf hear, the dead are raised, to the poor the gospel is preached.

v.23 And blessed is *he*, whosoever shall not be offended in me.

v.24 And when the messengers of John were departed, he began to speak unto the people concerning John, What went ye out into the wilderness for to see? A reed shaken with the wind?

v.25 But what went ye out for to see? A man clothed in soft raiment? Behold, they which are gorgeously apparelled, and live delicately, are in kings' courts.

v.26 But what went ye out for to see? A prophet? Yea, I say unto you, and much more than a prophet.

v.27 This is *he*, of whom it is written, Behold, I send my messenger before thy face, which shall prepare thy way before thee.

v.28 For I say unto you, Among those that are born of women there is not a greater prophet than John the Baptist: but he that is least in the kingdom of God is greater than he.

v.29 And all the people that heard *him*, and the publicans, justified God, being baptized with the baptism of John.

v.30 But the Pharisees and lawyers rejected the counsel of God against themselves, being not baptized of him.

v.31 And the Lord said, Whereunto then shall I liken the men of this generation? and to what are they like?

v.32 They are like unto children sitting in the marketplace, and calling one to another, and saying, We have piped unto you, and ye have not danced; we have mourned to you, and ye have not wept.

v.33 For John the Baptist came neither eating bread nor drinking wine; and ye say, He hath a devil.

v.34 The Son of man is come eating and drinking; and ye say, Behold a gluttonous man, and a winebibber, a friend of publicans and sinners!

v.35 But wisdom is justified of all her children."

18-20 The tidings about Christ and His miracles had been told throughout the land and reached John in the prison. He sent two of his disciples to the Lord with the question, "Art thou he that should come? or look we for another?" Most of the speculations about why John asked the question are unsatisfactory. To suggest that John was uncertain of the identity of the Christ is a contradiction of the account that Luke has already given (3:1-22). To say that he had been certain, but was now doubting seems out of keeping with the Lord's statements about him (vv.24-28). Others have suggested that John was certain about Christ, but wanted his disciples to get first-hand evidence, so the question was asked for their sake. This seems to be in keeping with the Gospel of John where John pointed his disciples away from himself to Christ (John 1:35-42), so this explanation has corroborating evidence to support it. However, another factor needs to be considered. The genuine remnant "that looked for redemption in Jerusalem," (2:38), as well as the majority of the nation, expected a deliverance that would fulfil the great OT predictions of a day of glory that would exceed the golden age of David. The coming of Jesus of Nazareth had as yet given no evidence of such a kingdom. John's recognition was not faulty, but his eschatology was based on the promises of the coming of the true Son of David, to judge wickedness and set up a glorious kingdom of righteousness (Matt 3:10-12). Therefore the rejection and crucifixion of the Lord were serious problems in the minds of the disciples until after the resurrection. Their hope was right, but their timing was wrong. Being in the line of the great prophets of old, and greater than them all, John was not exempt from this thinking. In fact, regarding God's great timetable of events, none was enlightened. Even after His resurrection, the Lord said, "It is not for you to know the times or the seasons, which the Father hath put in his own power" (Acts 1:7). So John was looking for the coming of the Lord in glory and power, and did not fully grasp His coming to suffer shame and be crucified.

   John had introduced the King to the nation and fully expected that the kingdom would be inaugurated in all the promised glory of the prophets. This did not happen, but not only did the kingdom not appear, but he, the forerunner was cast into prison without any intervention of the King on his behalf. This was a shattering blow. John knew he was not mistaken about the Person of the King, but he knew he must be mistaken about the plan for the kingdom. The suffering remnant of Israel in the future will have the same problem. Their faith will be sorely tried as they experience a time of unparalleled trouble (Dan 12:1). Their deliverance will come after much affliction and in the darkest hour of their trial (Zech 14:2-4).

21   It has been suggested that the Lord Jesus merely told John's disciples of His own messianic works, but "in that same hour" indicates that they witnessed the miracles. The two aorist verbs in this verse emphasise that the healing was done in the very presence of John's disciples. Incurable sicknesses were healed, demons obeyed His commands and He bestowed (*charizomai*) on the blind a gracious gift of sight.

22   John was looking for the coming of the righteous judge who would establish a kingdom of peace and righteousness (Isa 11:1-5), but the Lord directed him to other prophecies that describe the tender mercy and grace of the coming Saviour (Isa 35:5,6; 61:1). The Lord sent the messengers back with a testimony of what they had "seen and heard". It is very possible to be an eyewitness to events that are not understood, therefore the Lord made certain that they would be able to interpret intelligently what they had seen. The Lord graciously gave John an answer from Isaiah, the book that referred to him as "The voice of him that crieth in the wilderness" (Isa 40:3).

23   Rather then being a rebuke to John, the blessing of this verse belonged in full measure to him. He was able to interpret rightly the works and words of Christ. He was not repelled or stumbled by the meekness, gentleness and grace of the Saviour. The Lord makes this clear by describing John as the greatest of men. However, there were many others who were present that day who did not rightly interpret His works and words and did stumble. The verb *scandalizō* (to take offence) is the word from which we get our English word scandal. It means to shock or offend moral feelings and to bring disgrace by shameful actions. This is the word that Paul uses about the attitude of unbelieving Jews toward the cross; it was an offence to them (1 Cor 1:23). Believers bore reproach and persecution because of "the offence of the cross" (Gal 5:11). In a day when a cross is a symbol of religious veneration, we can scarcely grasp what a scandal it presented to the minds of unbelieving Jews, "Cursed is every one that hangeth on a tree" (Deut 21:23; Gal 3:13). The Lord Jesus ever had the cross before Him, and we do not go beyond the meaning of the text when we suggest that the Lord is describing those who would stumble at Him, reject him and eventually crucify Him. We should never accuse John of taking such offence.

24   The Lord's questions to the people were used as a means by which they would be compelled to face the testimony of John to Christ. "A reed shaken with the wind" suggests a feeble, unresisting plant that is moved in whatever direction the wind blows. Paul used similar language about untaught children who were like waves of the sea, "carried about with every wind of doctrine" (Eph 4:14). John's powerful preaching about Israel's sins, his rebuke of leaders and Pharisees and his announcement of impending doom (3:7-9) set him as a great contrast to a wind-shaken reed.

25   John's plain food, dress and words were also a great contrast to kingly courtiers who were professionals at fawning on their lords, cringing before them and servilely approving all that they said and did. John was the very opposite of such men, so a resounding no is the answer to the first two questions.

26-27   The third question must be faced by all who heard John. They were "persuaded that John was a prophet" (20:1-8; Matt 21:23-27) and therefore he must have spoken words from God. In giving John the place of being more than a prophet, the Lord Jesus confirms that he was the forerunner before the face of Messiah that had been foretold in Mal 3:1. This was testimony that verified John's ministry, but it also gave to Jesus the credentials of Messiahship. To accept John's message was to accept Christ, and to reject Christ was to reject John's message.

28   The greatness of John was his calling as the forerunner before the face of the Lord. This was a greatness that none shared. John was unique in his task, but in looking forward to the coming Saviour, his greatness could not be compared with the many who would believe the message about the Saviour who came, died and rose again. The key to the understanding of this difficult verse is to see the measure by which greatness is measured. John belonged to a day of promised redemption, while we belong to a day of accomplished redemption, so there is no thought here of personal worth. Greatness is entirely dependent on our place in God's great programme of redemption. It is infinitely greater to look back on a work done than to anticipate a work that is still future. To this writer, this seems to be the best way to interpret these words rather than attempting to differentiate between various aspects of the kingdom. In fact, this verse strikes a discordant note against any attempt to draw a sharp contrast between the kingdom of God and the kingdom of heaven.

29   The purpose of the Lord's words about John the Baptist was to show the inconsistency of accepting John as a prophet and yet not accepting his testimony to Christ. Those who accepted John's preaching justified God, that is, they declared that God is righteous in His condemnation of their sin, and they responded to the call to repentance. Their baptism was an outward expression of this repentance. John rejected as candidates for baptism those who did not show "fruits worthy of repentance" (3:7,8). Sufficient numbers of the hated tax-collectors came to be baptised to cause Luke to name them separately. The Lord Jesus had said that He "came not to call the righteous, but sinners to repentance" (5:32).

30   This is a key verse in understanding the unbelief of the human heart. John's preaching is called "the counsel of God", which fully agrees with the words of the Lord Jesus that John was His messenger to prepare His way in the hearts of men. The Pharisees and lawyers saw that this preaching was "against themselves"; it condemned them, found them out as guilty. Refusing to own their guilt and justify God in their own condemnation, they rejected it. This can be said to be the reason behind all rejection of the word of God. By this rejection, sinners put themselves in opposition to the purpose of God in their salvation. God's counsel is truly "against us" in condemning us, but those who accept it are justifying God when He passes sentence on them (Ps 51:4; Rom 3:4). Then, in the full declaration of the gospel, God, in the riches of His grace, is able to be just and yet be "the justifier of him which believeth in Jesus" (Rom 3:26).

31-34   The enigma of accepting John as a great prophet and yet rejecting his testimony to Christ is further pressed home to the hearts of His hearers. The men of that day were like children sitting in the market place, calling one to another to join in their play, but no matter what was proposed, whether dancing or mourning, there was refusal. The men of that generation responded neither to John's message of judgment and repentance nor to Christ's message of joy and forgiveness. Both messages made them uncomfortable, but if they had accepted John's preaching of repentance, they would have been prepared for Christ's message of forgiveness. This is the sense in which John prepared the way of the Lord (see v.27). They said that John had a demon and that Christ was a friend of publicans and sinners because such people gladly heard His words of forgiveness.

Some have understood this illustration very differently and interpret it that the people were blaming John for not joining in their mirth and blaming Christ for not joining in their austerities, but this is unlikely to be the import of the story.

35 The wise are not the Pharisees and lawyers. The wise of this verse are those who repent and believe the message of forgiveness. The need of forgiveness is unappreciated by those who assume that they have no sin of which they must repent, but those who are truly wise will accept the teaching both of John and the Lord Jesus. They will acknowledge their sin and mourn with John; they will accept their forgiveness and rejoice with Christ. Luke is now going to give an illustration, in Simon the Pharisee and the sinful woman, of the great contrast between the wise who are brought to repentance and those who lack this wisdom.

16. The Forgiveness and Gratitude of a True Believer
7:36-50

v.36 "And one of the Pharisees desired him that he would eat with him. And he went into the Pharisee's house, and sat down to meat.

v.37 And, behold, a woman in the city, which was a sinner, when she knew that *Jesus* sat at meat in the Pharisee's house, brought an alabaster box of ointment,

v.38 And stood at his feet behind *him* weeping, and began to wash his feet with tears, and did wipe *them* with the hairs of her head, and kissed his feet, and anointed *them* with the ointment.

v.39 Now when the Pharisee which had bidden him saw *it*, he spake within himself, saying, This man, if he were a prophet, would have known who and what manner of woman *this is* that toucheth him: for she is a sinner.

v.40 And Jesus answering said unto him, Simon, I have somewhat to say unto thee. And he saith, Master, say on.

v.41 There was a certain creditor which had two debtors: the one owed five hundred pence, and the other fifty.

v.42 And when they had nothing to pay, he frankly forgave them both. Tell me therefore, which of them will love him most?

v.43 Simon answered and said, I suppose that he, to whom he forgave most. And he said unto him, Thou hast rightly judged.

v.44 And he turned to the woman, and said unto Simon, Seest thou this woman? I entered into thine house, thou gavest me no water for my feet: but she hath washed my feet with tears, and wiped *them* with the hairs of her head.

v.45 Thou gavest me no kiss: but this woman since the time I came in hath not ceased to kiss my feet.

v.46 My head with oil thou didst not anoint: but this woman hath anointed my feet with ointment.

v.47 Wherefore I say unto thee, Her sins, which are many, are forgiven; for she loved much: but to whom little is forgiven, *the same* loveth little.

v.48 And he said unto her, Thy sins are forgiven.

v.49 And they that sat at meat with him began to say within themselves, Who is this that forgiveth sins also?

v.50 And he said to the woman, Thy faith hath saved thee; go in peace."

A simple outline of this story may help in grasping its significance:

1. The great difference between a proud Pharisee and a sinful woman.

2. The great dilemma in which Simon found himself regarding Christ.

3. The great debt of sin and the terms of its forgiveness.

4. The great devotion of a forgiven sinner.

36 Luke frequently records the act of eating and tells of at least seven feasts to which the Lord was invited (see comment at 5:29). The Pharisees and scribes murmured against Him, "This man receiveth sinners, and eateth with them" (15:2). One of the sweetest gospel illustrations in the Scriptures is Luke's likening of salvation to a great supper. The events that follow give some credence to the suggestion that Simon may have invited the Lord Jesus to his house that he might find some way of accusing Him (see 11:54).

37-38 Each Gospel records an anointing of the Lord Jesus by a woman. It is likely that Matt 26:6-13; Mark 14:3 -9 and John 12:1-8 describe the same event, an anointing by Mary of Bethany. The event in Luke is very different from this other occasion, and took place at a much earlier time in the ministry of Christ. The only similarity is that both anointings were in the house of a man called Simon, a very common name.

Sitting at the table was not with the feet under the table as we would normally assume. The usual mode was to recline on a low couch, with the head toward the table and the feet extending away from it. The sandals were removed. This explains how the woman could come in and approach the feet of the Lord Jesus without disturbing those who dined.

The woman was known in the city as a sinner. The "alabaster box of ointment" brought by her with the purpose of anointing the feet of the Lord was a rounded container with a long neck, made of white stone. The best of these containers were made of alabaster, which has the ability to retain the full fragrance of the contents for very long time periods. To use the contents, the neck was broken and the perfume poured out. It was not a solid, as we think of ointment, but a free-flowing, perfumed oil, which was very costly.

As she "stood at his feet behind him", her emotions welled up and tears began to fall on His feet. She promptly wiped them with her hair, which she must have loosened for this purpose. It was not customary for Jewish woman to allow their hair to be unbound in public unless they were in mourning (see v.32). The washing of feet was the work of the lowest level of household slaves (*The Illustrated Bible Dictionary,* Tyndale, vol. 1, page 519). It is significant that this courtesy had not been provided by the Pharisee (v.44). She proceeded to kiss His feet and to anoint them with the ointment. Mr. Darby translates *muron* as myrrh, and this is a possibility, for the name comes from *murra*, meaning myrrh-oil, but Moulton and Milligan give evidence that the word was used for a perfumed oil which need not contain myrrh. However, Darby may well be right, as the myrrh has deep spiritual significance which belongs to the context of this anointing. In myrrh, there is the mingling of bitter and sweet. It was a most fitting tribute to the Man of sorrows. Myrrh is linked with His birth, His death and His burial (Matt 2:11; 27:34; John 19:39).

39   The thoughts of the Pharisee were known to the Lord. This is yet another occasion when Luke gives evidence of the omniscience of Christ. The reasoning of Simon's unbelieving mind brought him to the conclusion that this man, Jesus, was not a prophet, or if He was, He was not a righteous man. If He were a prophet, He would know the character of the woman who was washing His feet. It was unlikely that He was a prophet, but even if this were so, He was not a holy man, for He was allowing a sinful woman to touch Him. He thought that he had incontrovertible evidence to reject Christ. We have already suggested that the invitation to the feast might have had as its purpose the exposing of the false claims of Jesus, as he perceived them. In his mind, events over which he had no control have worked to fulfil his purpose. It moves our own hearts to think that the gracious Lord Jesus knew his every thought, as He knows the thoughts of all men.

40   When the Lord Jesus told Simon that He had something to say to him, the response He received was polite, but no more than that. The words "Teacher, speak" were terse, revealing very little interest in what He might have to say. For Simon, the matter was already settled; this Jesus of Nazareth was an impostor. Some in our day have come to just such a faulty conclusion. Probably one of the most foolish things a person can say about Jesus is that He was a good man and His teaching contains the highest morality known to man, but His claims to deity must be rejected. How could He be good and yet make such claims, if they are not true? What are these claims? Christ said that the Father and He are One (in substance, equality and authority, John 10:30); He existed before the worlds were made (John 8:58); His words will exist when time is no more (Matt 24:35); He can forgive sins (Luke 5:24); He will be the final judge of all intelligent beings (John 5:22), and will reign supreme over the universe of God (Matt 25:31). It has often been pointed out that a good man could not make such claims; he would not be good, he would be either insane or the most evil of men. So the Lord Jesus is as much an enigma to unbelieving minds today as He was to Simon the Pharisee.

41-42   This mini-parable is sweet, simple and most appropriate to the need of the moment, but it contains truth that many miss. It is not the great difference between the two debtors to which the Lord is drawing Simon's attention, but rather the likeness. Simon was occupied with the vast difference between his own supposed goodness and the sin of this woman of the city. This kind of thinking is common to almost all religious minds. The Lord is impressing on him that although one debtor owed ten times the debt of the other, both were alike, for they were destitute, utterly bankrupt, with nothing to pay. Even the fifty denarii was a very great debt for a destitute man. A labourer would need to work for six weeks to earn enough to meet such a debt, and then it would cost every denarius that he earned.

The phrase, "And when they had nothing to pay", needs to be set beside such expressions as "the lost" (19:10) and "without strength" (Rom 5:6). These descriptions of sinners are different aspects of our inability to save ourselves, but the Lord's teaching of sin as a debt and God as the Creditor is most important in our understanding of divine forgiveness. For instance, we can learn from this parable that there is no such thing as "free forgiveness". Wise men have argued that if God is good and He is merciful, loving and kind and desires to forgive His erring creatures, then He has the prerogative just to speak our forgiveness and the entire question of sin would be settled. There would be no need for the sacrifice of the Saviour, no need for the blood of His cross. Such reasoning is extremely faulty. When a debt is forgiven, there is always a cost. The gospel preacher rightly emphasises that sin is the most costly thing in the universe, and the price paid at Calvary to cancel the debt is infinite. When the creditor forgives the debtor for all his debt, the cost to him is exactly the amount that has been forgiven. In the language of Paul, the Lord Jesus could say to God about our sins, "If he hath wronged thee, or oweth thee ought, put that on my account... I will repay it" (Philem 18,19).

There is a very interesting word in this verse, *charizomai*, the word used in v.21, "unto many that were blind he *gave* sight". He bestowed sight on them as a gracious act of His mercy. The same word is used in this verse for forgiveness, although it is not the word used for forgiveness in the rest of the chapter. The AV translates, "he frankly forgave". Alfred Plummer translates it, "he made them a present of what they owed". It conveys the thought of an unconditional act of mercy. It is the word Paul used in such passages as Rom 8:32, God who "spared not his own Son, but delivered him up for us all, how shall he not with him also freely give us all things", and Col 2:13, "*having forgiven* you all trespasses". Coming back to the woman, we read that the Lord Jesus asked Simon the question, "which of them will love him most?"

43   The grudging answer of the Pharisee has not been missed in our AV. "I suppose" or "I imagine" was spoken with the caution of one wanting to leave a way out for himself, perhaps even suggesting that he saw that he was not going to escape easily. The Lord ignored his attitude and said, "Thou hast rightly judged".

44-46   The woman had been a silent listener to a conversation that so deeply involved her; the Lord Jesus now pointed Simon to her, "Seest thou this woman?". There is a suggestion here that Simon did not see her as she is now; in fact, he did not see himself. She was forgiven, he was unforgiven; she was wise, he was foolish (v.35). No unrepentant sinner has ever seen himself and cannot appreciate the forgiveness enjoyed by others. Simon had not provided water to wash the feet of his Guest, nor a kiss of welcome, not even common olive oil to anoint His head. In contrast, the woman has washed His feet with tears and wiped them with her hair. She has kissed His feet and anointed them with costly ointment. These were acts of devotion and worship from the heart of a forgiven sinner, who like the five-hundred-pence debtor was forgiven much and loved much.

47   The measure of love is directly related to the measure of forgiveness. She was not forgiven because of her acts of devotion; her devotion was the result of enjoying forgiveness. A warning here is not amiss. Roman Catholic theologians have interpreted this verse as meaning that her love had earned forgiveness for her, and have built on it a doctrine of forgiveness through contrition, giving a basis for penance. In fact, the Lord said, "Her sins (yes, her many sins) have been forgiven", or "She has received forgiveness for her sins" (A. Plummer). This woman is already in the enjoyment of forgiveness, hence her gratitude. There is a story behind these words which we are not told, but they suggest a prior meeting with the Lord.

48   Now for the first time the Lord addresses the woman. He has no more to say to the Pharisee. Alfred Plummer translates these words, "Your sins have been and remain forgiven". The use of the perfect tense of the verb *aphiēmi* adds confirmation to the view that has been taken on this subject. The words spoken to her were for assurance of her forgiveness as well as being a public declaration of the reason why He had accepted her devotion.

49   The words of the Lord to the woman were not only for her ears, but were intended to be heard by the company that was gathered at the meal. Instead of "to say among themselves" (RV marg), we probably should read, "to say within themselves" (A. Plummer). Just as the Lord knew the thoughts of Simon and of the woman, so He knew the thoughts of the rest of the company. Their thoughts were contemptuous, "Who is this who even forgives sins?" (A Plummer).

50   Ignoring the objection of the seated company, the Lord continued His words to the woman, "Depart into peace" (A. Plummer), that is, into a lasting condition of peace, which is a stronger expression than "in peace" (Acts 16:36). It is also possible that the salvation of which He assures her needs to be understood in full scope; not only a salvation from sin's penalty, her great debt paid, but the power of salvation seen in a changed life.

Note

In rightly interpreting the conversation that took place between the Lord and Simon, it seems necessary to this writer to conclude that the woman who is called a sinner of the city had previously met with the Lord and been forgiven all her sins. A harmonisation of the Gospels will show that it was just prior to this time that the Lord Jesus had spoken the lovely words of invitation that are recorded in Matt 11: 28, "Come unto me, all ye that labour and are heavy laden, and I will give you rest". It is very possible that this poor, sinful woman had heard the invitation and had come to the Saviour. The event described in these verses is not a conversion, but the gratitude of a forgiven sinner. There is excellent material in this incident to use in gospel preaching, applying it as her experience of conversion but the evidence seems to indicate that the tears she shed were tears of thankfulness and worship, rather than tears of repentance.

17.   *Journeys Throughout Galilee*
8:1-3

v.1   "And it came to pass afterward, that he went throughout every city and village, preaching and shewing the glad tidings of the kingdom of God: and the twelve *were* with him,

v.2   And certain women, which had been healed of evil spirits and infirmities, Mary called Magdalene, out of whom went seven devils,

v.3   And Joanna the wife of Chuza Herod's steward, and Susanna, and many others, which ministered unto him of their substance."

1   The closing words of ch.4 must be contrasted with the beginning of ch.8. At the beginning of the ministry of the Lord in Galilee the synagogues were open to Him, but as opposition grew and the jealousy of the Jewish leaders became more evident, the streets, lanes and market places became the locale of His preaching. His home at Capernaum had been His headquarters for some time, but at this point, the Lord's ministry has taken a turn in that He is travelling throughout Galilee in a more extensive manner. The verb *diodeuō* ("went throughout") indicates the thorough way in which every road was traversed. The only other use of this word in the NT is Acts 17:1: "when they had passed through Amphipolis and Apollonia, they came to Thessalonica". F.F. Bruce points out that Paul and his company travelled the "Via Egnatia, which ran from Neapolis to Dyrrhachium through Philippi and the three towns mentioned in this verse". *Diodeuō* indicates that the messengers in Acts 17, and the Lord here, searched for interested hearers "every foot of the way".

Throughout this chapter, Luke tells of the common people gathering in crowds to hear Him: "much people were gathered together" (v.4); they " could not come at him for the press" (v.19); "the people gladly received him: for they were all waiting for him" (v.40), and "the multitude throng thee and press thee" (v.45). In the tender grace and mercy of His heart, the Son of man traversed the highways and byways of Galilee and fulfilled the words of Isaiah, written eight centuries earlier: "to the poor the gospel is preached" (7:22; cf. 4:18; Isa 61:1), and the twelve were with Him, learning lessons from the master Soulwinner.

2-3   The first three verses of this chapter form one long sentence that can be summarised: He went throughout every (single) city and village ... preaching ... and the twelve were with Him ... and some women ... which ministered unto Him. Luke has painted a graphic picture of lowly grace, displayed in a gentle Man. The acceptance of the ministry of these women of Galilee, by the Lord of all, is one of the most tender areas of the many facts related to His incarnation. Probably more than at any time in history, the role of women has been demeaned in our society. Striving for equality in the work-place and for leadership in the political and business worlds, much has been gained by women, for they have manifested great ability, but there has been lost something of the uniqueness of the woman's true sphere which was divinely given (Titus 2:3-5). Far from treating them as inferior, the Lord gave to women a place of high honour. The rabbis regarded women as being incapable of receiving religious instruction and made laws which forbade a man to address a woman, even his own wife, in a public place (Edersheim). The Lord taught women: "Mary, which also (including Martha) sat at Jesus' feet, and heard his word" (10:39), and He accepted the sacrifice of their service to Him. There is not a hint in the four Gospels that a woman ever opposed or abused Him.

In His more extensive travels, the Lord and His disciples are in need of daily supplies. It is interesting to trace how these needs were met from His infancy to His burial. The wise men brought enough to pay His expenses in Egypt; the material needs in Nazareth were met by the labour of His own hands; invitations to homes provided meals during His public ministry; when He needed an ass, it was lent to Him; an upper room was provided, and a new tomb for His body in death. These women must have been no small comfort to Him in His pilgrimage.

Three women are named in these verses, Mary Magdalene, Joanna and Susanna, but there were "many others, which ministered unto him of their substance". We need not suppose them to have been wealthy. Joanna, whose husband held high office under Herod Antipas, may have been an exception; the others were likely poor women, in keeping with their Galilean background. It is not what a person possesses, but what he is willing to part with for the Lord's sake that makes his ministry of such value (21:1-4).

Mary Magdalene has been portrayed by artists and described by writers with vivid imaginations. They see her as a very beautiful, immoral woman that the Lord had saved and changed. There is no reason for thinking that she is the sinful woman of the city in ch.7, nor does the fact that seven demons once indwelt her mean that she was unchaste. She must have been cruelly tormented by the evil spirits, and her deliverance produced great gratitude to her Saviour. As Peter is mentioned first in every list of the twelve, she is first in every list of women who served the Lord.

18.   *The Parable of the Sower*
8:4-15

v.4   "And when much people were gathered together, and were come to him out of
      every city, he spake by a parable:

v.5   A sower went out to sow his seed: and as he sowed, some fell by the way side;
      and it was trodden down, and the fowls of the air devoured it.

v.6   And some fell upon a rock; and as soon as it was sprung up, it withered away,
      because it lacked moisture.

v.7   And some fell among thorns; and the thorns sprang up with it, and choked it.

v.8   And other fell on good ground, and sprang up, and bare fruit an hundredfold.
      And when he had said these things, he cried, He that hath ears to hear, let him
      hear.

v.9   And his disciples asked him, saying, What might this parable be?

v.10 And he said, Unto you it is given to know the mysteries of the kingdom of God:
      but to others in parables; that seeing they might not see, and hearing they
      might not understand.

v.11 Now the parable is this: The seed is the word of God.

v.12 Those by the way side are they that hear; then cometh the devil, and taketh
      away the word out of their hearts, lest they should believe and be saved.

v.13 They on the rock *are they*, which, when they hear, receive the word with joy;
      and these have no root, which for a while believe, and in time of temptation fall
      away.

v.14 And that which fell among thorns are they, which, when they have heard, go
      forth, and are choked with cares and riches and pleasures of *this* life, and bring
      no fruit to perfection.

v.15 But that on the good ground are they, which in an honest and good heart, having
      heard the word, keep *it*, and bring forth fruit with patience."

The parable of the sower is simple to outline, seeing that the Lord interpreted it, leaving us in no doubt about its meaning.

The Sower   - "He that soweth ... is the Son of man" (Matt 13:37).

The Seed   - "The seed is the word of God" (Luke 8:11).

The Soils   - "they that hear" (Luke 8:12-15).

The Summer - "bring forth fruit with patience" (Luke 8:15).

4   Matthew tells us that when this parable was spoken, the Lord sat by the sea side and "great multitudes were gathered together unto him" (Matt 13:1,2). These crowds caused the Lord Jesus to go into a ship while "the whole multitude stood on the shore". Luke writes about "much people ... gathered together, and were come to him out of every city". Luke uses two words in this sentence that are found only here in the NT: *sunerchomai* (" gathered together") may convey the thought of an agreement to gather together (G. Friedrich); *epiporeuomai* ("were come", "restored unto him" RV) which suggests further the thought that they agreed together to travel to the place where they could hear the Lord's teaching. There was an attentive crowd present to hear this great parable.

This will be a good place in the study of Luke to examine the Lord's use of parables. Our English word parable comes from the Greek word *parabolē* which literally means "putting things side by side". Spiritual things are put beside earthly things to illustrate the meaning of the spiritual. We do well to remember that a parable is usually a short descriptive story, intended to illustrate a single truth or answer a single question. There are parables in Luke that give a vivid picture of a number of related truths, but it is a mistake to think that a parable can be interpreted as a type, with precise meaning given to every aspect of it. At the very least, we must understand the main purpose of it before we attempt to draw other lessons from it, and each related lesson must be in full harmony with the main one.

Luke has recorded at least five previous parables from the lips of the Lord Jesus (5:36-39; 6:39, 41-44, 47-49; 7:41-42), but the parable of the sower is much more detailed, and marks a change in His way of teaching. A parable enlightens willing minds and hearts, but veils the truth from those who are opposed (v.10). As the tide of opposition increased, the Lord used parables more often. They instructed His disciples but did not give unnecessary opportunity to His enemies. They separated the sincere seeker from the careless hearer. A failure in the understanding of this parable was an evidence of spiritual darkness about the meaning of all the parables. The Lord Jesus said, "Know ye not this parable? and how then will ye know all parables?" (Mark 4:13). Some believe that the Lord is saying that this is the easiest parable to understand, but it is more likely that He gave it as a key to the understanding of the others (Matt 13:1-9). This is one of the three parables recorded in all the Synoptic Gospels; the others are the mustard seed and the wicked husbandmen.

5 We have stated above that the Sower is primarily the Lord Jesus (Matt 13:37), but in a lower sense it includes all who have been sent by Him: apostles, evangelists and every believer who carries the message of salvation to others, all whose business it is to sow.

The seed is the word of God. In speaking of the children of the kingdom, the Lord spoke of "good seed" (Matt 13:24); the writer of Ps 126 calls it "precious seed" (v.6), and Peter says that it is "incorruptible ... the word of God, which liveth and abideth for ever" (1 Pet 1:23). In the proclamation of the gospel, the word of God should never be superseded by anything else, never be diluted and nothing should ever be subtracted from it. With perfect confidence in the living power of the seed, we should seek to sow it in every heart, "For as the rain cometh down, and the snow from heaven, and returneth not thither, but watereth the earth, and maketh it bring forth and bud, that it may give seed to the sower, and bread to the eater: so shall my word be that goeth forth out of my mouth: it shall not return unto me void, but it shall accomplish that which I please, and it

shall prosper in the thing whereto I sent it" (Isa 55:10-11). A primary principle of
the great evangel is that "faith cometh by hearing, and hearing by the word of
God" (Rom 10:17). God grant to us a revival of confidence in the power of the
preached word (1 Thess 1:5,6)!

The four kinds of soil-the wayside, the rock, that overgrown with thorns and
the good ground-are interpreted by the Lord as four kinds of hearers (vv. 12-15).
The sower did not sow seed on the road where people walked, but rather by the
side of the way; because it was so near the road, it was trampled. Two reasons are
given for the failure of the wayside to produce fruit, the trampling of feet and the
voracity of the birds. A third reason was the hardness of the soil. It took the
passage of time and the trampling of many feet to make it so hard. It may have
been once soft and receptive. There are hearts that were once soft, tender, easily
moved and receptive to the word of God, but the passing of the years in sin and
rejection have caused them to become hard. We should be careful about the use
of the common expression "gospel-hardened" for the gospel melts hearts; it is
sin in its deceitful effect that hardens them (Heb 3:13).

6-8   We have looked particularly at v.5 because of its importance to all of the
parable, but it will be better to look at vv.6-8 in the light of the Lord's interpretation
of them in vv.11-15. However, there is a word used in v.6, *katapiptō* ("fell") that is
only found here and twice in Acts: of Paul "falling down" on the Damascus road
(26:14); and of the expectation that he would "fall down" dead when the viper
out of the heat fastened on Paul's hand (28:6). In vv. 5,7,8 and 14, the verb *piptō*
("fell") is used without prefix. It is not easy to make any distinction between the
fall of the seed "by the wayside", "upon a rock" and "among thorns", except that
the wayside and the thorns were obviously poor places for growth, while the
rock gave indication of something better, for it was covered with soil, but it lacked
depth. Perhaps Luke is suggesting this distinction by his choice of words. Many
who hear the word are shallow in their conviction, like the seed on the rock. It
"sprang up" (*phuō* passive voice) because of the shallow soil that heated quickly.
Sumphuō ("sprang up with it") is used in v.7 and *phuō* is again used in v.8. The
only other place in the NT that this word is found is Heb 12:15, "lest any root of
bitterness springing up trouble you", where it is in the active voice. There was
no evil in the seed, but active evil was present in the "root of bitterness".

9   To the question raised in this verse as to the meaning of the parable, Matthew
adds that the disciples asked why the Lord spoke to the multitude in parables.
Luke's account gives one question, but both answers (vv. 10-15). It is interesting
in Luke that the Lord often used questions to give instruction that included far
more than the question involved. We should remember that the term disciples,
as used by Luke, often included more men than twelve.

10   It is only in connection with this parable that the synoptic Gospels speak of a mystery. A mystery is a truth, known to God, but not formerly revealed to man (Eph 3:5). The "mysteries of the kingdom of God" are to characterise this entire age; through the sowing of the seed of the word of God, fruit will be produced for God's glory. Why did the Lord address Himself to the multitude at all, seeing that He knew they would not hear or understand? The answer is threefold: firstly, there were individuals who were willing to hear; secondly what the careless ear hears is remembered and there may be a time when it will sink in and its meaning will open up to them; thirdly, an even more solemn reason, the word that is refused will be used in the judgment of the rejecters (John 12:48). For the same reasons we preach the gospel to an unbelieving world. Let us take courage from our Lord's example. He knew who were willing to hear, we do not; yet He preached to all men and so must we.

This quotation from Isa 6:9,10, abbreviated by Luke but quoted fully by Matthew (13:14,15), is the OT passage most often quoted in the NT. Israel had eyes and ears but they were wilfully closed. The Lord said to His own, "blessed are your eyes, for they see: and your ears, for they hear" (Matt 13:16). It was not the ability to see and hear, but the willingness that made the difference. There can be no doubt that, as in the case of Pharaoh, those who blind their own eyes are eventually blinded, but we need to be careful that in dealing with Gentile sinners we make it clear that their present blindness is wilful, not a judgment from God. It is Satan, not God, who today is blinding minds (2 Cor 4:4). The day when God blinds them will be after the day of grace is ended (2 Thess 2:11,12). With Israel the situation is different; since the nation's rejection of their Messiah their present blindness is a judgment from God, but one day soon the veil will be taken from their eyes (2 Cor 3:13-16). This is one of the many reasons why we must distinguish between God's dealing with Jews and Gentiles.

11-12   The Lord's own explanation of the parable is an example to us of the way to handle parables that are not interpreted. He identifies the seed sown by the side of the way as being the same as the seed that was sown in all the various kinds of soil. The Lord interpreted the birds as being the arch-enemy of souls, a personal devil. The difference between the plural birds and the singular devil may well be that Satan has many allies in sinful flesh and the world, used by him in the taking away of the word. Satan's punctuality should be noted, "(then cometh the devil... ". As soon as the word is sown Satan is on hand with power that is able to take away the word out of the heart. Not only are Satan's punctuality and power displayed, but also his purpose, "lest they should believe and be saved". There is a positive way to view this negative statement: those who believe the word are saved, and the devil knows it, and exerts all his power to take it away before it can do its blessed work.

13   In looking back at v.6, the seed that fell upon the rock found some soil and some moisture. The thin soil heated quickly and the seed sprang up. This agrees with Matthew's two statements, " had not much earth" and " had no deepness of earth" (13:5). When Luke records the parable of the man who built on the rock, he writes, "and digged deep". There is a difference between building a house and sowing seed; nevertheless, there is the same comparison made between what was deep and what was shallow. A proper ploughing up would have exposed the rock and the shallow soil. The Lord Himself experienced hearers of this kind and no one who preaches the gospel is exempt. Sad to say, many make a light profession of receiving the word, but there has been no deep ploughing, no breaking up, no true awakening. They give assent to gospel truth, exhibit immediate joy, give instant evidence of rapid growth, but "these have no root, which for a while believe, and in time of temptation fall away". We need not think that the stony-ground hearers were ever saved. The words, "which for a while believe", have caused a problem to some minds, but a look at John 2:23-25 will settle the problem. There were many who "believed in his name" (v.23), but "Jesus himself did not trust himself to them, because he knew all men… " (v.24 JND). A genuine believer never believes for a time; he continues to believe in Christ.

A solemn warning is needed today when there are so many quick methods of producing converts. Salvation is very simple, and a child can be saved; in fact, all must become as children to be saved (Matt 18:3); but it can never be shallow, or light (Rom 10:9-10). Salvation is heart-business with God.

14 The springing up of the seed is not the evidence of "good ground", for in the cases of the rock and the thorns the seed sprang up (vv.6,7). The evidence of a genuine work of God is fruit, and there was none on the rock or among the thorns. The Lord draws from two extremes of life to interpret the thorns. "Cares" tell of the responsibilities, burdens, troubles, grief and heartbreak that afflict so many people. "Riches and pleasures" describe the other side of life, in which materialism and pleasure are the thorns that grow up with the seed to choke its effect on the hearers. The evangelist sees this in almost every gospel effort. Although riches and pleasure are a common cause of the failure to see souls saved, we are seeing more and more of the other hindrances, the cares that choke the life and so occupy the mind and heart that the word does not bear fruit. *Telesphoreō* ("bring (no) fruit to perfection") is only found here in the NT. Perfection in growth is full maturity, so Luke uses this word to describe the fruit that was potentially in the seed, but never developed in the thorny ground hearer.

15 No heart is by nature "honest and good". The words of the Lord do not contradict His own teaching about the heart (Matt 15:19,20), that it is full of evil instead of goodness. Paul certainly did not find goodness in the human heart when he wrote the indictment of all men in Rom 3:1-23. It is quite clear that both the Lord Jesus and Paul, by the Spirit, accepted without question the teaching of the OT: "The heart is deceitful above all things, and desperately wicked: who can know it?" (Jer 17:9). What, then, is the meaning of an honest and good or true heart? Some have answered this question by teaching that this description is not of the sinner when he hears the word, but after he has received it. They link it with the "patience", or better the "endurance", displayed in the life after salvation. It is the mind of this writer that we should equate "good ground" with an "honest heart", because the soil has been prepared to receive the seed. Only God can make this preparation by the gracious work of His Holy Spirit. The honesty is that characteristic of a heart made to be honest before God. It is in contrast to the three kinds of soil where there was failure. The "honest and good heart" has been broken and softened, ploughed deeply, the choking weeds have been removed and it is ready for the seed. Into this ground, the seed entered, went down and grew up to produce lasting fruit.

We should not miss the truth that the whole period of sowing should be related to a harvest time. We believe that in the present day we are coming to the very end of the harvest. "Behold, now is the accepted time; behold, now is the day of salvation" (2 Cor 6:2).

19.   *The Parable of the Lamp*
     8:16-18

> v.16 "No man, when he hath lighted a candle, covereth it with a vessel, or putteth *it* under a bed; but setteth *it* on a candlestick, that they which enter in may see the light.
> v.17 For nothing is secret, that shall not be made manifest; neither *any thing* hid, that shall not be known and come abroad.
> v.18 Take heed therefore how ye hear: for whosoever hath, to him shall be given; and whosoever hath not, from him shall be taken even that which he seemeth to have."

16   There is a link between the sowing of seed in the previous parable and the lighting of a candle ("lamp" RV, JND) in this brief one. Seed and light are both familiar pictures of the word of God (Isa 55:10,11; Ps 119:105). To put a lighted lamp under a vessel or under a bed would totally hinder its usefulness as a source of light. The Lord Himself is the source of the light possessed by the disciples. He said of John, "He was a burning and a shining light" (John 5:35). To His disciples He said, "Let your loins be girded about, and your lights burning" (Luke 12:35), and "Let your light so shine before men, that they may see your good works, and glorify your Father which is in heaven" (Matt 5:16). So the lighting of a lamp is not only preaching, but primarily living in such a way that the light shines clearly, giving opportunity for others to come into spiritual light and blessing. Many believe that the expression "they which enter" refers to Gentile blessing.

The witness could hide his light with a vessel, which is likely an emblem of commerce. Materialism in the life of believers has been the hiding of many a light, causing seeking souls to stumble in the dark. The light under a bed speaks of lethargy and indifference toward the need of sinners who are still groping in the darkness of sin.

17   The link between this verse and the previous one seems to be that even the light of a lamp exposes that which is hidden or secret, and it was never the divine intention that the truths of the kingdom should be kept secret. The mystery religions contained many secrets which were only for the initiates, but "light is come into the world" (John 3:19) and the Lord is pointing out that the light is so clear that it cannot be hid, so this is the light "which coming into the world enlightens every man" (John 1:9 NASB).

An alternative interpretation of this verse is that whatever now is hidden, because of human failure in testimony, will be fully made known in the day when the servants are called to account (12:2). Both this interpretation and the one in the previous paragraph are true to Scripture, but the first seems to better fit the meaning of v. 16. However, if the second view is taken, the practical lesson is that the light bearer should not hide his light, but let it shine brightly in the darkness.

18   The Lord links the hearing of the word with the shining of the light of testimony. Precious truth from the Lord has been given. "Whosoever hath" is he that has the word that has been spoken. If he truly has it, if it has taken possession of his heart and life and he has made full use of it, he will be given "more abundance" (Matt 13:12). The problem here is whether he will be given more truth in the present or more reward in the future; we know from other passages of Scripture that both are true. If he treats lightly what he has heard there will be taken from him "even that which he seemeth to have".

20.   *Natural and Spiritual Relationships*
8:19-21

> v.19 "Then came to him *his* mother and his brethren, and could not come at him for the press.
> v.20 And it was told him *by certain* which said, Thy mother and thy brethren stand without, desiring to see thee.
> v.21 And he answered and said unto them, My mother and my brethren are these which hear the word of God, and do it."

19-21   Matthew and Mark give more details than Luke of this incident and they place it before the parables of the sower and the lamp, but it is not difficult to see why Luke places it here. Both parables have dealt with two ways of hearing the word of God, and here is an illustration of them. There are those who, like Mary, receive it gladly and personally and make it their own, bringing forth fruit. There are those who, like the brethren of our Lord, do not hear with faith, "For neither did his brethren believe in him" (John 7:5).

A crowd of people thronged around the Lord Jesus so that His mother and His brethren could not come near. There is no reason other than the Catholic tradition of perpetual virginity to deny that Mary had other children. The word used for "brethren" is the normal *adelphoi* and simply means brothers. Matthew says, "he stretched forth his hand toward his disciples, and said, Behold my mother and my brethren" (Matt 12:49). But Luke records what is so much in keeping with the theme of this passage, "these which hear the word of God, and do it". The Lord is not rejecting either His mother or His brethren; He is setting the priority that God and His word are more important than any human tie. This event needs to be balanced with the account by John of the tender care of His mother by the Lord even when He hung suffering on the cross (John 19:25-27).

The lesson for us in this passage is that there is a stronger, more tender bond between the Lord and His own than any other tie. The bond between parent and child is strong; the bond between husband and wife is stronger, for they have become one flesh, but the bond between the Lord and those He has purchased with His blood is even stronger, "he that is joined unto the Lord is one spirit" (1 Cor 6:17).

21.   *The Miracle of the Storm Calmed*
8:22-25

> v.22 "Now it came to pass on a certain day, that he went into a ship with his disciples: and he said unto them, Let us go over unto the other side of the lake. And they launched forth.
> v.23 But as they sailed he fell asleep: and there came down a storm of wind on the lake; and they were filled *with* water, and were in jeopardy.
> v.24 And they came to him, and awoke him, saying, Master, master, we perish. Then he arose, and rebuked the wind and the raging of the water: and they ceased, and there was a calm.
> v.25 And he said unto them, Where is your faith? And they being afraid wondered, saying one to another, What manner of man is this! for he commandeth even the winds and water, and they obey him."

The four mighty miracles described in vv.22-56 display the authority of Christ over the forces of nature, the unseen world of spirits, disease and even death itself. He controlled the uncontrollable, cured the incurable, and conquered the unconquerable. The gentle Man of sorrows of this beautiful Gospel is shown to be, as Paul Gerhardt wrote:

> "The Lord of all transcendent,
> The life creating Sun,
> To worlds on Him dependent,
> Yet bruised and spit upon."

The calming of the storm on the lake was a miracle of such magnitude that it displayed the authority of the Creator God. It has often been said, "Everyone complains about the weather, but no none does anything about it". This ironic saying is a confession of human impotence. The Lord Jesus commanded the elements of sea and sky. He controlled forces that modern man has never been able to influence in the smallest degree. The disciples witnessed omnipotence in a Man. It produced in them fear and wonder, as well it might.

22   Luke tells us that this voyage on the lake took place "on a certain day". Mark says it was the very evening of the long day of teaching when the Lord told the parable of the sower (Mark 4:35), and adds, "And when they had sent away the multitude, they took him even as he was in the ship". This may mean no more than that the Lord had taught from the boat, having pushed out a short distance from the land because of the crowds on the shore; but "as he was" seems also to imply a condition of weariness. This is the background against which is set Luke's statement of the next verse, "he fell asleep".

23   This is the only time in Scripture that we read of a sleeping Christ. His humanity was real, and it was not different humanity. It was unique in that He was sinless. Dr. John Heading rightly speaks of "the weariness and sleep of perfect manhood", yet there is a deep mystery in the simple fact of His sleep. He was no less the Lord of all when He slept "on a pillow" (Mark 4:38) than when He arose to command the winds and the waves. It is in keeping with a unique account of the sleeping Christ that Luke uses a word found nowhere else in the NT, *aphupnoō* ("to fall asleep"), but it would be a mistake to think this sleep was anything unnatural. As a man on earth, Jesus, even though the Lord of all, must have slept many times.

The storm "came down" on the lake. This vivid and graphic description suits the Sea of Galilee exactly. It is approximately 700 feet below sea level. The surrounding heights are "furrowed with ravines like funnels down which winds rush with great velocity" (A. Plummer). In a few minutes a calm sea can be whipped into a mighty tempest. It is good for us to keep in mind that the storm was never out of His control. In the case of Job satanic power was in the storm, but even that power was by divine permission. To state that the Lord sent this storm is to go beyond what is written, but there were occasions when a storm was sent from God to fulfil His purpose (Ps 107:25-28; Jonah 1:4).

The RV says the boat was "filling with water", and this is accurate for it is a verb in the imperfect tense. The storm had great fury. Mark says, "The waves beat into the ship, so that it was now filling" (4:37 RV). Matthew describes the ship "covered with the waves" (8:24), so that the veteran sailors who knew the Galilean Sea so well believed that they were about to perish. Luke's terse statement, they " were in jeopardy" removes any doubt about the seriousness of the danger. The word Luke uses for the filling of the boat, *sumplēroō*, is the same word used in 9:51, "when the time was come (fulfilled) that he should be received up". Its only other occurrence in the NT is Acts 2:1: "when the day of Pentecost *was fully come*". The filling up of the boat gives a graphic picture of the filling up of time in the other two passages.

24   The disciples are to be commended that they went to the Lord in their distress. Would to God that all who are believers would turn to the Lord as quickly when trouble strikes! Luke omits Mark's "carest thou not", which was spoken as a rebuke to the Lord. It was many years later that one of these same disciples, the leading one, knowing his error, wrote, "Casting all your care upon him; for he careth for you" (1 Pet 5:7).

Matthew tells us that they addressed Him as *kurie* ("Lord") Mark says that they called Him *didaskale* ("teacher"); but Luke says they addressed Him as *epistata* which is translated as "Master" in the AV, but can also mean commander or overseer. Some will be puzzled and ask, If all the synoptic Gospels are describing the same event, and they are, what was the actual word of address? How can all three forms be correct? It was "they", the disciples who came to Him, and all three forms were used, each one addressing the Lord according to their own appreciation of Him and their need. Luke is describing the perfect Man who was the tender sympathiser and could meet the need of every troubled heart. It is most appropriate that Luke says that some addressed the Lord as the great Overseer of the storm and of every contingency of life. The double cry, "Master, master", is an indication of the depth of their distress. Only in Luke is the Lord Jesus so addressed (5:5; 8:45; 9:33,49; 17:13).

The Lord Jesus arose from the place where He had slept and standing amidst the howling tempest, He spoke, " Peace, be still" (Mark 4:39). Did He raise His voice in a great cry to be heard above the noise of the fierce storm? We do not know, but there is no intimation of it in the records. However, He did speak to the forces of nature, and they heard and recognised the voice of the Creator. It is stirring to compare the voice of the Lord Jesus as it was heard over Galilee's lake; at the grave of Lazarus; from the cross when the rocks rent, and in the hearts of sinners as He calls in the gospel. Inanimate nature cannot resist the power of that voice, not even death can resist it, but guilty sinners can wilfully refuse to hear. No wonder that He said to the disciples, "blessed are ... your ears, for they hear" (Matt 13:16).

A double miracle took place at that very moment, the winds and the waves instantly ceased. This is most important and alone can explain the amazement of the disciples in the next verse. Storms struck with great suddenness on the Sea of Galilee and almost as suddenly they would die out. These veterans of the sea had seen many a wind rapidly decline, but the sea would roll on and only gradually would its force be spent. That day, the sea went from raging tempest, that caused them terror, to a perfect calm in an instant.

Every believer who has ever faced trials can learn a lesson from the experience of the disciples on the lake. It was in obedience to the Lord's command that they had entered into the ship "to go over unto the other side". Many point out that faith in the Lord's command should have assured them of arriving safely. However, it must have surprised them that difficulties so great would arise when they were obeying His command. Jonah encountered a fearful storm when he was disobedient, which is not difficult to understand, but it is quite another matter to understand such an obstacle in a path of obedience. Surely all will be calm when we do what is right. The answer is that it was in the storm that the disciples learned the almighty power of their Master and at the same time the wretchedness of their own unbelief. Do not our own unexpected and bitter experiences teach us the same two lessons?

There is also a dispensational lesson in the story of the storm. It vividly pictures the godly remnant of Israel in the Great Tribulation who likewise will feel that they are going to be swamped by the enemy. He who arose and rebuked the wind will arise and calm the storms of this troubled world. As on this occasion, the Lord was met by a man full of demons (v.27), so when the Lord appears, He will be confronted with the Devil's masterpiece and with the dreadful evidence of the helplessness of man to master it.

25   So mighty was this miracle that unbelieving minds have tried to take away the wonder of it by saying that the Lord calmed the disciples, not the waves. To a true believer who accepts the fact that this Man is God incarnate who made earth and sea and sky, the miracle is perfectly in keeping with who He is. This was the very lesson impressed on the witnesses as with holy awe and wonder they exclaimed, "Who then is this?" (JND). On the sea He calmed the storm, but when He drew near to the cross and His disciples were deeply troubled He calmed their hearts (John 14:2), but He endured the storm.

The question "Where is your faith?" needs to be seen in the light of v.22. He had said to them, "Let us go over unto the other side of the lake". Their unbelief was against His words. When He said they were going to the other side, He did not mean that they were going to the bottom of the sea. Faith is always simple trust in what He has said and a lack of faith is a failure to believe the word.

In the AV translation, "What manner of man is this!" we have an excellent reproduction of the Greek text. A comparison of the use of this expression in the NT is enlightening. It was used of the woman in Luke 7; Simon the Pharisee said, "This man, if he were a prophet, would have known who and what manner of woman this is that toucheth him: for she is a sinner" (7:39). The expression literally means, "of what country?" The Pharisee was saying, "She is foreign, alien", or more literally, "She is not one of us". This helps us to understand what the disciples were saying about the nature-miracle, yet in a good sense, "He is not one of us". He was truly from another country, a heavenly one, for He was heaven's gentle Nobleman. This is also the way in which to understand the language of 1 John 3:1, "Behold, what manner of love the Father hath bestowed upon us". It was not an earthly love, but heavenly in character. No wonder that in Matt 14:33, when He stilled another storm, they "worshipped him, saying, Of a truth thou art the Son of God".

22.   *The Demon-Possessed Man of Gadara Healed*
8:26-39

v.26 "And they arrived at the country of the Gadarenes, which is over against Galilee.
v.27 And when he went forth to land, there met him out of the city a certain man, which had devils long time, and ware no clothes, neither abode in *any* house, but in the tombs.
v.28 When he saw Jesus, he cried out, and fell down before him, and with a loud voice said, What have I to do with thee, Jesus, *thou* Son of God most high? I beseech thee, torment me not.
v.29 (For he had commanded the unclean spirit to come out of the man. For oftentimes it had caught him: and he was kept bound with chains and in fetters; and he brake the bands, and was driven of the devil into the wilderness.)
v.30 And Jesus asked him, saying, What is thy name? And he said, Legion: because many devils were entered into him.
v.31 And they besought him that he would not command them to go out into the deep.
v.32 And there was there an herd of many swine feeding on the mountain: and they besought him that he would suffer them to enter into them. And he suffered them.
v.33 Then went the devils out of the man, and entered into the swine: and the herd ran violently down a steep place into the lake, and were choked.
v.34 When they that fed *them* saw what was done, they fled, and went and told *it* in the city and in the country.
v.35 Then they went out to see what was done; and came to Jesus, and found the man, out of whom the devils were departed, sitting at the feet of Jesus, clothed, and in his right mind: and they were afraid.
v.36 They also which saw *it* told them by what means he that was possessed of the devils was healed.
v.37 Then the whole multitude of the country of the Gadarenes round about besought him to depart from them; for they were taken with great fear: and he went up into the ship, and returned back again.
v.38 Now the man out of whom the devils were departed besought him that he might be with him: but Jesus sent him away, saying,
v.39 Return to thine own house, and shew how great things God hath done unto thee. And he went his way, and published throughout the whole city how great things Jesus had done unto him."

26 The careful student will find some difficulty in correctly naming the country where the demoniac was healed. Three names have vied for acceptance through the centuries: Gadara, Gerasa and Gergesa. The town of Gadara was about six miles from the lake, but may have controlled a tract of land that came down to the water. Considering the commerce that plied its waters and the fish that was taken from it, it would have been very desirable for a town to have access to the water. The text of Matthew, " the land of the Gadarenes", confirms this suggestion. However, archaeologists (Thomson, *The Land and the Book*) have found the ruins of a town on the steep eastern shore that was called Gersa (*Kersa*), so the alternative Greek word found in Mark and Luke, "the land of the Gerasenes", is also correct. It may be that two towns, Gadara and Gersa, used this section of the eastern shore of the lake and that it bore two names. The word Gergasene was inserted in the text by Origen and has little to support it. Darby and the AV have adhered to the name Gadara, so we will use this name to avoid confusion.

"Over against Galilee" is an interesting phrase. *Antipera* ("over against"), used only here in the NT, is an adverb, but is used as an adjective with a following genitive. It affords a good illustration of at least one of the meanings of the important preposition *anti* in the NT. In the classic Greek, *anti* had the primary meaning of "over against". It is not the only preposition for substitution in the NT (*huper*, Rom 5:6; 1 Pet 3:18), but it is very important. Its use in Matt 20:28 and Mark 10:45 is good proof of its substitutionary meaning.

27   When the Lord Jesus stepped on the shore, a demon-possessed man, without clothing, came out from the town to meet Him. However, the Lord Jesus had crossed the lake to meet him. His tragic condition was of long standing, and he was well known in the community where his violence had caused serious problems. Luke says that he lived not in a house but in the tombs where, Matthew tells us (8:28), he had a companion who was also demon possessed.

28   Upon seeing the Lord Jesus, the man, or the demons within him, cried out and the man fell down before Him. This was strange conduct for a man who Matthew says was "exceedingly dangerous" (JND). When the Lord Jesus came to His own people, Israel, they failed to recognise Him, for their eyes were blind, but His identity was not veiled to demons. This contrast between the way He was seen by men and by the world of spirits can be traced in several Gospel passages (Matt 8:29; Mark 1:24,34). There was terror in the demons at His presence and they besought Him that He would not torment them, but they did not acknowledge Him as Lord. To demons, He is "Jesus, thou Son of God most high ". Matthew adds, "art thou come hither to torment us before the time?" This is important. It reminds us of the words of James 2:19: "the demons also believe, and tremble". Judgment has been pronounced and the demons know who will wield the sword against them. This recognition of the Lord of judgment by demons is a terrible rebuke to unbelieving men. Many who acknowledge the high moral perfection of the teachings of Christ deny His deity. Demons are not so foolish. The torment they speak of is the authority to cast Satan and all his hordes into the abyss (v.31).

29   The people who feared the demoniac had kept a guard upon him and bound his hands and feet with chains and fetters to restrain him. Considering the tremendous strength that he showed, this must have been the work of many men. From the expression about the spirit, "oftentimes it had caught him", there were times when he was quiescent and at such times men could bind him, but when he was under the power of the indwelling demons, he went berserk and displayed superhuman strength.

Many a poor sinner today is as completely under the power of sin and Satan as the man of Gadara. His nakedness before others illustrates the shame of sin which is often so obvious to all but its victims. If the bondage takes the form of alcoholism or drug addiction or any vice or compulsion that controls lives and destroys them, is it any less tragic? The words "caught" and "driven" tell the sad story of many a life.

Sunarpazō ("caught") is another of those words unique to Luke in the NT. It is also found in Acts 6:12; 19:29; 27:15. The AV "caught" expresses well its meaning of being "violently seized". Its uses help us greatly to understand its force. The Jewish elders in Acts 6, first stirred up the people and "coming on (Stephen), they seized him". The whole city of Ephesus was "full of wrath" when they violently seized Gaius and Aristarchus. But the use Luke makes of this word in Acts 27 is the most descriptive. The "tempestuous wind, Euroclydon" (v.14) has gripped the small vessel with mighty power, and "the ship was *caught* (violently seized)" (v.15). So the man of Gadara was "caught".

Elaunō ("was driven") is an imperfect passive verb that describes a continuous, or oft repeated driving of this poor man "into the wilderness". This verb is only found five times in the NT. James writes of "ships ... driven of fierce winds" (James 14), and Peter writes of "clouds that are carried (driven Mft) with a tempest" (2 Pet 2:17). These word pictures help us in viewing the powers that were at work in the man of Gadara. "Caught" in a vice-like grip and "driven" with irresistible force.

30   The question about the name of the man of Gadara was not to provide the Lord with any knowledge that He lacked. What then was the purpose of the words, "What is thy name?". In Jacob's case, the Lord's similar question was to produce a confession, "Jacob", the supplanter (Gen 32:27). By the question to the demoniac, the Lord is identifying the power that stands opposed to him; not a mere wild man from the tombs, but a legion of demons under their cruel master. In the answer, "Legion", there was still an attempt to hide their personal identity, to do what men do, hide in the anonymous crowd. It is not too great a claim to make for the omniscient Lord that He knew the history of every one of the demons that made up the legion. It may be too much to suggest that their number could have been as many as in a Roman legion- up to 6 000. Luke gives the reason for the name, "because many devils were entered into him", and this is as much as we can say.

31-33   It has been said that the Lord did not command the demons to leave the man, but this cannot be maintained in the light of the imperfect tense verb of v.29, " he was commanding the unclean spirits". However, it is true that He did hearken to the plea of the demons that they should not be sent, at that moment, into the abyss, the place of their future punishment. *Abussos* is always an adjective and should be translated as "bottomless", so the usual translation is "the bottomless pit" (Rom 10:7; Rev 9:1, 11:7,17:8). The last use of the word in Scripture makes it clear that this abyss is an actual location, the abode in which Satan will be bound during the thousand years (Rev 20:1-3). *Tartarus*, in 2 Pet 2:4, is translated by J.N. Darby, "the deepest pit of gloom". If *tartarus* is not the abyss, at least it seems to be a similar place of punishment for spirits, because it is the place where the angels, whose sin is described by Peter, are confined until the day of their final judgment.

Several questions have frequently been asked about the herd of swine. How many were in this great herd? Matthew and Luke say that there were many, Mark says it was "a great herd", but at the end of his narrative, Mark who is so careful about details says "they were about two thousand" (Mark 5:13). This is not an extremely large herd for modern times, but it represented a vast investment even for a group of businessmen of the region of Galilee.

The next question is closely related. Unbelievers have asked it for centuries, "What right did the Lord have to destroy so many animals that belonged to someone else?". Many answers have been given. The person who asks this question would also raise a question about the right of God to allow natural disasters such as storms, earthquakes or floods to kill large numbers of people. Believers who know that they deserve eternal judgment and have in grace been saved from it do not ask such an arrogant question.

It was not the Lord's expressed will that the pigs should die. He gave permission to the unclean spirits to go into the herd of swine. It was the demons, who are so desirous of inhabiting a body, in this case even an animal's body, yet constantly work for the destruction of the body that they inhabit (Mark 1:26; 5:5), who destroyed the swine.

The keepers of these swine may have been Jews; if so, they were guilty of breaking the law (Lev 11:7; Deut 14:8). In allowing them to be destroyed, the Lord Jesus was putting His finger on their guilt and, through the demons, allowing judgment to fall on them righteously. It is also true that the curing of the man far outweighed the value of the swine, and the unusual events that surrounded the miracle would never be forgotten by the Gadarenes.

34   The fleeing of the herdsmen had an element of fear in it. It may also have been motivated by a desire to tell their story first, to save themselves from blame in the loss of the herd. The phrase "saw what was done" is only found in Luke's account. It seems to include all the events up to the drowning of the pigs, but stands as incomplete in the light of what the investigators found when they came out of the city (v.35).

35   Upon hearing the story of what had happened at the shore, the people of the town and the surrounding countryside came to see for themselves. When they came to the Lord Jesus, they saw a strange sight. The formerly demon possessed man of the tombs, who had been such a terror in all that region, sat at the feet of the Lord, "clothed, and in his right mind". This is a beautiful illustration of the change that is wrought by the Lord Jesus in the life of a person who is saved by His grace. A man freed from the cruel slavery of sin and Satan is clothed in garments of salvation, having a right mind about self and God and His Son, and as a worshipper and learner, sitting at the feet of the Lord Jesus. Darby translates these words as "sitting, clothed and sensible". We do not know the source of the clothing that the man now wore, but we do know who provides the perfect garment of righteousness (Rom 3:22; Luke 15:22).

36   The story of the healing is told again by the eyewitnesses who are still on the scene. The destruction of the swine must have occupied the central place in the story, for they told what they had seen. The healed man sat before them and little needed to be said to add to the sight. This was the man who had caused such terror to the people of the city, so that to see him healed, restored and clothed must have made them wonder if he could be the same person. The clothing of the man has been emphasised, for it is no small part of the story. The craze for nakedness in the world in our day seems to have a satanic origin. Satan wants man to forget the fall, but innocence can be enjoyed only by the innocent. One of the chief symptoms of moral decay is the nakedness portrayed by films, magazines, books and even newspapers.

37   The rejection that is described in this tragic verse has been often repeated. The cause of the great fear that laid hold of the people must have been more than the destruction of animals. The authority and power of the Lord struck terror to them. This adds to what has been said already about their sin in keeping and eating the flesh of swine. It is guilt that strikes terror to the heart in the presence of divine authority. The healed demoniac welcomed that power, the guilty people were seized with great fear. They begged Him to leave their coasts. If they had a choice they would take their pigs and reject the Lord Jesus. Whether the problem was the further loss of material gain, fleshly appetite, or rebellion against the law of God, sin makes the presence of the Lord Jesus very uncomfortable to sinners. It was a general rejection by all the people (see John 12:48). So far as we know they were not given such an opportunity again and missed their day of salvation (2 Cor 6:2).

38-39   In contrast to the general rejection of the Lord Jesus, the healed man begged to be allowed to go with Him. It is most touching that, although the Lord was rejected by the Gadarenes and He left their coast never to return, He did not leave them without witness. The healed man is sent back among them that by changed life and words he might be a testimony to them of the power of the Saviour of men. We do not read of any of his converts, but without doubt, when the saved of "every kindred, and tongue, and people, and nation" are gathered around the Lamb in heaven, there will be Gadarenes there.

There is significance to the change in language in v.39. "Show how great things

God hath done unto thee" were the final words of the Lord Jesus to him. The healed man "published throughout the whole city how great things Jesus had done unto him". I am suggesting that the change from "God" to "Jesus" indicates that, as with Thomas in the upper room, this man took Jesus as his Lord and God.

23. *The Incurable Woman Healed and Jairus' Daughter Raised*
8:40-56

v.40 "And it came to pass, that, when Jesus was returned, the people *gladly* received him: for they were all waiting for him.

v.41 And, behold, there came a man named Jairus, and he was a ruler of the synagogue: and he fell down at Jesus' feet, and besought him that he would come into his house:

v.42 For he had one only daughter, about twelve years of age, and she lay a dying. But as he went the people thronged him.

v.43 And a woman having an issue of blood twelve years, which had spent all her living upon physicians, neither could be healed of any,

v.44 Came behind *him*, and touched the border of his garment: and immediately her issue of blood stanched.

v.45 And Jesus said, Who touched me? When all denied, Peter and they that were with him said, Master, the multitude throng thee and press *thee*, and sayest thou, Who touched me?

v.46 And Jesus said, Somebody hath touched me: for 1 perceive that virtue is gone out of me.

v.47 And when the woman saw that she was not hid, she came trembling, and failing down before him, she declared unto him before all the people for what cause she had touched him, and how she was healed immediately.

v.48 And he said unto her, Daughter, be of good comfort: thy faith hath made thee whole; go in peace.

v.49 While he yet spake, there cometh one from the ruler of the synagogue's *house*, saying to him, Thy daughter is dead; trouble not the Master.

v.50 But when Jesus heard *it*, he answered him, saying, Fear not: believe only, and she shall be made whole.

v.51 And when he came into the house, he suffered no man to go in, save Peter, and James, and John, and the father and the mother of the maiden.

v.52 And all wept, and bewailed her: but he said, Weep not; she is not dead, but sleepeth.

v.53 And they laughed him to scorn, knowing that she was dead.

v.54 And he put them all out, and took her by the hand, and called, saying, Maid, arise.

v.55 And her spirit came again, and she arose straightway: and he commanded to give her meat.

v.56 And her parents were astonished: but he charged them that they should tell no man what was done."

It is important to note that this is the only occasion in the life of Christ when two miracles are intertwined. There is a reason for this. In the woman healed, we see salvation illustrated from the human standpoint in that all the efforts were her own. In the girl raised up, we see salvation from the Lord's standpoint, for in her case all depended on Him. The woman's hand stretched out and laid hold on His garment. In the house, His hand stretched out and laid hold of the girl.

The gospel preacher must remember that combined in salvation there is human responsibility and, at the same time, there is divine power. Once men try to divorce these two facts and push one beyond the other, they go wrong. It has been said, "We pray as if all depended on God (and it does); we preach as if all depended on the sinner (equally true)".

40 Returning from the eastern side of the lake, the Lord Jesus found a multitude of people who received Him gladly (see 4:42). It is tempting to contrast them with the Gadarenes who had so bluntly rejected Him. The problem in doing so is that these people of Galilee also joined in rejecting Him, but in the meantime His miracles had created much curiosity, and they were looking for signs (11:29). Yet, in describing this reception of Christ, Luke uses the beautiful word *apodechomai* ("gladly received him"), unique to Luke's writings in the NT. It is used in this Gospel once more in 9:11, where the Lord, weary with constant labour, drew aside with His own to a desert place, to which the people followed Him, but "he (gladly) received them" or "he welcomed them (NIV). It is the word of Acts 2:41: "Then they that gladly received his word"; of Paul's company being "received gladly" at Jerusalem (Acts 21:17); and finally of Paul's receiving to the hired house all who came to him to hear the word of God (Acts 28:30). It occurs in two other places in the Acts (18:27; 24:3).

41 Jairus was one of the rulers of the synagogue, men whom Edersheim describes as officials who arranged who should lead in prayer, read the Scriptures and preach. Jairus is the name Jair of Jud 10:3, which means, "he will give light". He prostrated himself in the attitude of worship at the feet of the Lord. This homage was not refused as it was by Peter in Acts 10: 26 and the angel in Rev 19: 10. Luke does not say, at this point, that the ruler made any request other than that the Lord should come into his house. Mark wrote that he asked the Lord to lay hands on his daughter and heal her. Matthew shortens the entire story, not recording the original request at all. He tells of the ruler requesting that the Lord would raise her up after she had died (Matt 9:18). The faith of this man was in great contrast to the general unbelief of the leaders of the Jews.

42 Only Luke tells us that she was an only child, although Mark also tells us that she was twelve years old. Luke had a tender interest in the needs of others. He recorded personal facts such as this, or that the young man of Nain was the only son of his widowed mother (Luke 7:12). In the narrow streets of the town, the people jostled and pushed for positions of advantage where they could see all that happened.

43 It is more than a coincidence that the only daughter was twelve years old and the woman who came behind the Lord in the crowd had suffered from her illness for the same twelve years. The sickness of the woman and the death of the maiden give a vivid picture of the spiritual condition of Israel's twelve tribes. As in this case the coming of the Lord brought healing and life, so it will be when Israel recognises her true Messiah in the day when He comes as her Deliverer.

Jairus had enjoyed twelve years of his child's life and the woman had suffered twelve years of misery. Both alike were now desperate; both helpless in their tragedies. The woman had an illness which was weakening, uncomfortable, embarrassing and rendered her unfit for temple worship. Under Levitical law, her very touch was defiling, and she must have been very aware of her ceremonial uncleanness (Lev 15:27).

To compound her problem, she had spent all her "living" (see note) on physicians from whom she had received no help. Mark was not so careful of the reputation of the physicians as Luke, who was a physician himself, for Mark says, she "was nothing bettered, but rather grew worse" (5:26). J.B. Lightfoot gives a vivid description of some of the cruel and ridiculous treatments attempted by Greek physicians in such cases.

The effort to depict the helplessness of her condition is fully intentional, for she is a picture of helpless sinners who have turned everywhere for help and have found none in religion, none in reformation, and none in self.

44 We need not look far to discover the cause of the woman's stealth. The very nature of her sickness, the fact that her touch was defiling, the size of the crowd before whom she would be most reluctant to state her need, as well as the difficulty of coming face to face with the Lord Jesus, caused her to devise a plan to come secretly. Mark says that she reasoned, "If I may touch but his clothes, I shall be whole" (5:28). It takes very little imagination to see her creeping forward and stooping down, reaching out a trembling hand, fearful of discovery, and just touching the fringe of the tallith, a square outer garment with four corners, two that hung down in front and two at the back (Edersheim). "Immediately" the blood ceased to flow. The term "stanched" in the AV is accurate and translates a medical word, *histēmi*, used only here in the NT in this sense. Although Mark and Matthew use two different words, they also are medical terms for the staying of a haemorrhage. Mark tells us that the woman "felt in her body that she was healed of that plague" (5:29).

Her condition pictures the helpless state of all sinners before God. Her instantaneous healing pictures instant salvation. It was obtained by a touch, but that touch involved a link between a sinner and the Saviour. The touch is a beautiful illustration of the personal link of faith that is so necessary in a conversion experience. The throng can crowd and jostle and press, but she touched Him. This is the great difference, and has been the experience of all who have come in desperate need as sinners to the Saviour. There were times when the Lord Jesus touched the sinner (Matt 20:34) and others, as in the case of this woman, when the sinner touched the Saviour, but the vital necessity is that there must be a personal link. The difference in these two touches can be traced in personal experiences.

45   We are not guilty of inserting an anachronism into the passage when we claim that the Lord Jesus knew both the woman's whole story and all that she had done and that she had been healed, without ever bringing her before the crowd. He was either all that He claimed to be or the greatest impostor the world has ever known. There can be no middle ground when we speak of the attributes of Deity in a Man. If He had them at all, He had them in all their fulness (Col 1:19; 2:9); therefore He knew all about her.

The question, "Who touched me?" seemed meaningless to Peter and the other disciples. The Lord was the very centre of the jostling crowd, and He least of all needed to be informed about the thronging and pressing. One purpose of the question was to show the crowd that this woman was not only healed, but that she was now fit for ceremonial cleansing; but a far greater purpose was that He might further bless her. There is much gospel truth here, and the evangelist is not wrong to stress, particularly for Jewish converts, the importance of confessing (see Rom 10:9).

46   The Lord perceived that "virtue", that is "power", had gone forth from Him. His power was not merely something from Him that might be snatched by anyone fortunate enough to be in the right location. It was used only at His bidding, as a choice of His will. He had healed the woman in as active a sense as if He had audibly proclaimed it to her in the hearing of the throng. The power that went out of Him left Him undiminished. "Out of His full store have all we received" (John 1:16 lit.), but the full store was the same afterward as before. Yet, and we are in a very deep subject, it would be wrong to say that such acts cost Him nothing. He who came to preach the gospel to the poor and to heal the brokenhearted must in grace become poor and have His own heart broken to reach such needy sinners.

47   The trembling woman who had stooped to touch His garment now bowed before His face. The throng drew back, perhaps less with the intent of giving her room than with the purpose of being able to see her. From her trembling lips tumbled the whole story of her sickness, helplessness and healing.

48   "Daughter" was used only this once by the Lord in addressing anyone. His words of grace and comfort stilled her fears. The sickness would not return; the healing was genuine and lasting and she was to enter into peace (see comments at 7:50). *Thugatēr* (" daughter") is used frequently in the Synoptics, almost always of the natural relationship, but Matt 21:5 (also John 12:15) uses it in quoting Zech 9:9 "daughter of Zion" as a synonym for Jerusalem. Its only other spiritual use in the NT is 2 Cor 6:18: " ye shall be my sons and daughters, saith the Lord Almighty".

49   The delay caused by the woman who touched the garment of the Lord has been very costly to jairus. No recorded word was spoken by him at the delay, but now the news is carried from his house that his daughter has died. The messenger was very sure that all hope was now gone. It must have been at this point in the story that Jairus requested that even yet the Lord would come into the house and raise her from the dead (Matt 9:18).

50   The answer of the Lord was likely addressed to Jairus, not to the messenger who had come with the tidings of death. His words have been correctly translated, " Cease to fear, only make an act of faith" (A. Plummer following an amended text). In Mark the tense of the verb is as the TR of Luke, "only continue to believe" (5:36). There is a moment when initial faith is placed in the Lord Jesus, but those who believe Him continue to do so. "She shall be made whole" involves a total salvation.

51   The parents were in the house and the Lord allows Peter, James and John to enter with Him; all others are excluded. This is the first time that the Lord chose these three disciples to be with Him as special witnesses. The most notable occasions are recorded in 9:28, when the Lord took them with Him into the mount of transfiguration, and Matt 26:37, when He took them with Him further into Gethsemane.

52   We have already seen that only five were in the house with the Lord Jesus. This leaves us with the problem of identifying those who were weeping and wailing. The other Gospels help us, for Mark says that at the house there was a "tumult" which would be heard both inside and outside its walls. Neighbours had gathered and Matthew speaks about minstrels playing, so the professional mourners were already at work. The Lord's words, "Weep not", are a command to cease an action already in progress. The words "wept, and bewailed" do not describe a quiet weeping, but loud and noisy wailing. It was to all of this that the Lord commanded a halt.

   "She is not dead, but sleepeth" is a metaphorical use of the word that is often used for normal sleep. In 1 Thess 5:10 it is used of those who die prior to the rapture. Its use here relates to the fact that the Lord can awaken her, so it is sleep, not death. All whom the Lord will raise in the first resurrection are spoken of not as having died, but are "fallen asleep ones" (1 Thess 4:13), though a different word for sleep is used.

53   Only on this one occasion does the NT speak of people actually laughing, and the same verb is used in the three synoptic Gospels. The laughter took place in the presence of death and was scornful and derisive. This says some very bad things about the laughter of this world. The statement "knowing that she was dead" is very emphatic.

54-55 Entering the death chamber the Lord, according to Mark, used the Aramaic words that the girl's mother would have used when calling her to awaken on an ordinary morning: "*Talitha cumi*". He took her by the hand and "her spirit came again". This leaves no doubt about the reality of her death.

There are at least three things in this account that tell of the kindness and gentleness of the Lord Jesus. Rather than raising the maid to open her eyes on a gaping throng, they had all been excluded. There is a parallel that we can draw here to illustrate what it must be like to close our eyes to earth and open them in the Lord's presence. She saw Him first. He also showed His gentleness in the way He awakened her, by His hand and His gentle words, and then by the very practical command to give her something to eat.

As in the case of the man of Gadara, the evidence for the miracle was verifiable to all in the district. Here was a living girl, walking about, who was known to have been dead a short time earlier. Evidence of life was that she could eat and it is significant that this simple matter of eating was powerful evidence for the resurrection of the Lord (24:43). As in the physical realm, so in the spiritual, those who have life have an appetite for spiritual food.

56 The healed man of Gadara was to return to his own house and give testimony to the great things that God had done for him, but Jairus, a ruler of the synagogue, and his wife are charged "that they should tell no man what was done". Various explanations have been given in an attempt to explain why one should tell about the blessing experienced and the others should not. It is not any difference in those who received the healing that will explain the difference, but rather in those to whom they would testify. The man of Gadara was the only witness to his own house. The Lord Himself had spent about three years in Galilee, witnessing in every village and town, and the days of His ministry there were almost ended. Despised and rejected He was about to leave them. The testimony of Jairus would not have brought them to repentance.

Notes

43 The expression all her "living" is a translation of *bios*; the synonym is *zōē*. In classical Greek, the word *bios* has a higher meaning involving the higher life of man; *zōē* is generally used as the common life which is shared by all living things. It is of great interest to us that in the NT the Holy Spirit has chosen the lesser word and used it more than a hundred times to describe "the life that is life indeed". Thirty-six times in his Gospel John uses *zōē* for a present, enjoyed life that is eternal. The word *bios* is used seldom in the NT, but Luke uses it four times: "had spent all her living" (v.43); "pleasures of this life" (8:14); "he divided unto them his living" (15:12,30); and in reference to the poor widow who cast into the treasure "all the living that she had" (21:4). From these occurrences as well as 1 Tim 22; 2 Tim 24; 1 John 2:16; 3:17 we learn that the Holy Spirit has used it with the restricted meaning of temporal life or that which maintains it.

45 It is of interest that the word *sunechō* ("press"), used by Peter and the other disciples is the word used by Paul in 2 Cor 5:14: "the love of Christ constraineth us", that is, it presses upon us, compelling us. Luke uses this word in such passages as 4:38 and 8:3 7 where it is translated " taken with". He also uses it of Paul in Acts 18:5, "Paul was pressed in the spirit". Paul himself uses it in Phil 1:23, "For I am in a strait betwixt two".

52   In the clause, " she is not dead, but sleepeth" , the Lord used *katheudō* (" to sleep"), that is normally used for natural sleep, but in the case of Jairus' daughter, the Lord used it for death (Matt 9:24; Mark 5:39 and here in Luke 8:42). It is used by Paul for natural sleep in 1 Thess 5:7, but it is also used of the tragic condition of believers who are capable of manifesting a carnal attitude toward spiritual things (Eph 5:14; 1 Thess 5:6,10). *Koimaomai* is a synonym of *katheudō* and is also used for natural sleep (Matt 28:13; Luke 22:45; John 11:12; Acts 12:6), but more frequently for the death of the body of believers. It is used of the bodies of the saints that arose (Matt 27:52); Lazarus (John 11:11); Stephen (Acts 7:60); David (Acts 13:36); of a saved husband who has died (1 Cor 7:39); Corinthian believers (1 Cor 11:30); witnesses to the resurrection (1 Cor 15:6); believers in general (1 Cor 15:18,20); "we shall not all sleep" of those who are alive when the Lord comes (1 Cor 15:51); of the fallen asleep ones (1 Thess 4:13,14,15); and of the fathers (2 Pet 14). It is important to note that three times in 1 Thess 4 believers "fall asleep" at death, but "we believe that Jesus died" (v.14). He did not fall asleep. His death was a stark reality and involved all that death can ever mean.

24.   *The Sending Out of the Twelve*
9:1-9

v.1   "Then he called his twelve disciples together, and gave them power and authority over all devils, and to cure diseases.

v.2   And he sent them to preach the kingdom of God, and to heal the sick.

v.3   And he said unto them, Take nothing for *your* journey, neither staves, nor scrip, neither bread, neither money; neither have two coats apiece.

v.4   And whatsoever house ye enter into, there abide, and thence depart.

v.5   And whosoever will not receive you, when ye go out of that city, shake off the very dust from your feet for a testimony against them.

v.6   And they departed, and went through the towns, preaching the gospel, and healing every where.

v.7   Now Herod the tetrarch heard of all that was done by him: and he was perplexed, because that it was said of some, that John was risen from the dead;

v.8   And of some, that Elias had appeared; and of others, that one of the old prophets was risen again.

v.9   And Herod said, John have I beheaded: but who is this, of whom I hear such things? And he desired to see him."

The days of the public ministry of the Lord were short; His Galilean ministry was coming to a close. In the calling together and sending out of the twelve there was a great sense of urgency. Time was of the essence and when this passage is compared with the sending out of the seventy (10:1-11), the need for haste is even more apparent. If this important element is missed there is a grave danger of misunderstanding this mission.

The details that are given in the Matthew account, but missing from Mark and Luke, help to enhance the unique quality of each Gospel. Luke includes in the sending of the seventy some of the facts that Matthew mentions in relation the twelve. It is Matthew, in keeping with his message of the King, who tells us that the sending was not to the Gentiles at all, nor even to the Samaritans, but it was a very restricted and specific mission to "the lost sheep of the house of Israel" (Matt 10:5-7). Mark tells us that they preached repentance (Mark 6:12), linking their purpose with that of John the Baptist, to prepare hearts for the reception of Israel's long-promised Messiah. This view is greatly strengthened when we consider Luke's words about the sending of the seventy. He "sent them two and two before his face into every city and place, whither he himself would come" (10:1). Far from being general commissions to the world, these sendings both of the twelve and of the seventy were temporary sendings for specific needs, and those sent must go with great haste, for the days of the Lord's public ministry were drawing to a close. It must be obvious that to interpret the conditions and restrictions of this mission as being for today is a great mistake. The strongest evidence for this is that the sending described here was superseded by the Lord Himself in the great commission (Matt 28:18-20; Mark 16:15-18; Acts 1:8).

1 The Lord Jesus called the twelve to meet with Him. There is a lesson here about preparation for service. No true fitness to serve can be gained anywhere but in His presence and at His feet. Matthew and Mark tell us that He gave them authority, but Luke says that He gave them power and authority. The difference in the two words is that *dunamis* refers to the power or strength to perform and *exousia* refers to authority rightly to use the power. The Lord never sends a servant who is unsuited to the need or unfitted for it.

2 In this case the ministry was twofold, both spiritual and physical. The preaching was concerning the kingdom of God and therefore is connected with the hope of Israel. This interim sending of the twelve was that they might represent their Lord in places where He was absent; therefore their works were His works, and were done by His power and authority. It was a mission not only to preach, but to perform miracles, so that messengers were equipped to do work similar to their Master because they would continue to do in His absence the work He had already begun. They had the perfect pattern of the Lord who had perfectly balanced physical and spiritual needs.

A balanced ministry has always been very difficult for the evangelist to maintain. We have not been sent to heal and perform miracles in the physical realm, but we are given many exhortations and examples of being sensitive, compassionate and liberal toward temporal need (Luke 14:13; 18:22; Gal 2:10; James 2:2-6). It has always been a snare to human messengers that when physical aspects of the work become prominent, a philosophy of social uplift takes control and the preaching suffers; in many cases it has completely replaced the spiritual work. The gospel changes lives and affects every department of life, but the work of evangelists is not to improve the age, but to rescue perishing souls from a world that is ripe for judgment.

3   God would meet their need wherever their service took them. The restrictions can be summed up as follows, "Go as you are, do not make material preparations". They had one business and they were to attend to it without distraction. Taking no staff, bag for personal belongings, bread, or money were clearly restrictions imposed on them for this specific mission, because later they were told to do the opposite (22:35-38).

4   When they entered a house they were to stay in it for the entire duration of their time in that place. This restricted the length of their stay. There were many towns and villages to cover and the need was very urgent. It also preserved them from offending a host, for if they moved from house to house, the first host might have reason to think his hospitality was not sufficient for them. Inns were scarce and most towns and villages would afford no public accommodation. The practice of love expressed in hospitality runs throughout the NT (Acts 16:15,34; 18:3, 26; Rom 12:13; 15:17; 1 Cor 16:6; Heb 13:2; 3 John 6-8). The warning against false teachers getting into the home in 2 John was because this practice of entertaining travellers was continued and is still true of saints.

5   The verb *apotinassō* ("shake off") is found only here and in Acts 28:5 where Paul shook the viper off his hand. The use of this word in the Acts passage helps us to understand its meaning here. The shaking off of the dust of their feet as a testimony against those who refused the messengers and their message was to signify that the messengers would have nothing in common with rejectors of their Lord (Acts 13:51). They would take nothing from them, not even the dust of their city. Although we do not find here our call to go to a lost world with the gospel, there are certain principles which help us greatly. How good it would be if all who profess to carry the glad evangel had nothing in common with Christ-rejectors and would take nothing from them! Preachers begging for funds on the communications media have brought much dishonour on the gospel, and have given cause to the enemies of the Lord to blaspheme the name of the Lord Jesus.

6   This was a mission completed and fulfilled by the messengers who were sent. Our mission is not fulfilled. A lost world is in greater need of the gospel than ever. The world is our mission field, but many who can become very concerned about distant lands, and they should be concerned, have never even begun with their own neighbours.

7-8   Mark calls Herod "king", a title of courtesy; Luke gives him his accurate title of "tetrarch". For further material on this evil man, the reader is referred to the comments on Luke 3:1.
   The disturbing news that came to Herod's ears may well be related to the sending of the twelve throughout the region over which he held authority. It is

more likely that Herod was moved by fear than a bad conscience. However, his conscience may have fuelled his superstitious fears about John whom he had beheaded (v.9). The verb *diaporeō* ("was perplexed") indicates that precise events came to his ears, and he continued to be "utterly at a loss". This is the only time this word is found in Luke, but it is used three times in Acts (2:12; 5:24; 10:17) and is translated "in doubt" each time. Some were saying that John was risen from the dead, others that Elijah had appeared in fulfilment of Mal 4:5. Luke carefully uses the word "risen" of John and "appeared" not "risen" of Elijah for he had never died (Matt 16:14; see 2 Kings 2:11).

9   Herod had thought that he had rid himself of this kind of trouble when he had beheaded John, but now he feared that he had failed. John did no miracle in his life (John 10:41), but it is supposed that a resurrected John might well be a worker of miracles. Herod continued seeking to see the Lord Jesus until the day when his new friend Pilate sent the bound Christ to him (23:6-12). On that day, "Herod with his men of war set him at nought, and mocked him".

25.   *Feeding of the Five Thousand*
   9:10-17

v.10 "And the apostles, when they were returned, told him all that they had done. And he took them, and went aside privately into a desert place belonging to the city called Bethsaida.
v.11 And the people, when they knew *it*, followed him: and he received them, and spake unto them of the kingdom of God, and healed them that had need of healing.
v.12 And when the day began to wear away, then came the twelve, and said unto him, Send the multitude away, that they may go into the towns and country round about, and lodge, and get victuals: for we are here in a desert place.
v.13 But he said unto them, Give ye them to eat. And they said, We have no more but five loaves and two fishes; except we should go and buy meat for all this people.
v.14 For they were about five thousand men. And he said to his disciples, Make them sit down by fifties in a company.
v.15 And they did so, and made them all sit down.
v.16 Then he took the five loaves and the two fishes, and looking up to heaven, he blessed them, and brake, and gave to the disciples to set before the multitude.
v.17 And they did eat, and were all filled: and there was taken up of fragments that remained to them twelve baskets."

There are only two miracles that are found in all the four Gospels, this one and the greatest miracle of all, the resurrection. The miraculous feeding came at the close of the Galilean ministry and was the climax to it. John says, "the passover, a feast of the Jews, was nigh" (6:4). Each account agrees with the others, yet each is distinct. Gospel writers wrote under the complete control of the Holy Spirit and were not dependent on each other. The accounts of this miracle are good illustrations of this diversity that was not contradictory. Students of the language can enumerate many points of Luke's unique style here.

10   The twelve have returned from their mission, but Luke says nothing about how long they were gone. He calls them "the apostles", the sent ones. They had fulfilled their ministry, were weary (Mark 6:31) and needed spiritual refreshment, so the Lord withdrew with them to a place of privacy. Matthew and Mark tell us that they travelled by ship to a desert place. Luke says that it was near the city of Bethsaida. As there are no archaeological remains of this town there are several theories about its location. A. Plummer and others believe that Bethsaida Julius was at the north-east end of the lake of Galilee, close to the place where the Jordan enters it.

11   Great crowds of people followed by land. It is a strong mark of the tenderness of the Lord Jesus that He welcomed them and spoke to them "of the kingdom of God". His compassion on the multitude was too great to allow any annoyance at their intrusion into His privacy. It is no wonder that Paul wrote to Timothy, "Preach the word; be instant in season, out of season" (2 Tim 4:2), for this was the example left by his Lord. It was need that ever moved the heart of the tender Saviour and Healer. He met their spiritual need by preaching the kingdom of God, and their physical need by healing them. The hymn we frequently sing says: "All the fitness He requires is to know our need of Him". Many profess to be bringing Him their lives or their hearts without ever knowing their own deep need as lost and perishing sinners.

12   The teaching and healing lasted throughout the day. As the evening descended, the twelve became alarmed at the great throng of people who had nothing to eat. This desert region could provide no food for such a company, so the disciples suggested that the Lord send them to the surrounding villages to get food. "The day began to wear away" is translated in the AV in 24:29, "the day is far spent". The vast crowd of needy people, the day far spent, and the impotence of the disciples to meet the need are so like our own circumstances at the close of the day of grace that we cannot help but make the application. The words of the Lord to the disciples, "Give ye them to eat" (v.13), would only emphasise their inability. The composite word *episitismos* ("victuals") is only here in the NT. It means to nourish people by placing food in their hands. "It was a desert place", and the disciples did not have food for their own mouths. What a picture of a world without God, "a dry place...and a weary land" (Isa 32:2)! "But this was not a desert when He was there" (J. Heading).

13   When the Lord said to the twelve, "Give ye them to eat", "ye" is emphatic. They responded that they had only five loaves and two fishes. John tells us that they were barley loaves, common among the poor, and that Andrew had received them from a little lad (John 6:8, 9). This was so little, and enough food for such a multitude would take more than "two hundred pennyworth" (Mark 6:37; John 6:7).

14-15   Luke says there were "about five thousand men". The word he uses for "men" is *anēr*, not *anthrōpos*, indicating that there were five thousand males. The background of the times would suggest that there were not many women and children present. The whole multitude was invited to sit down in companies of fifty. Mark, who gives such vivid, graphic accounts, writes that they sat down on the "green grass". The division of the crowd was the Lord's arrangement and showed His care for the needs of all who serve Him, for the companies of fifty made the serving of food so much easier. The word that is translated "companies" is *klisia*, one of Luke's unique words. It comes from a root that means to recline and is used to indicate that to recline at a meal was the normal position for eating.

16   Taking the meagre portions into His own hands, the Lord Jesus looked up to the Father and "blessed them", that is, He gave thanks, then divided them, gave them to His disciples who, in turn, set them before the multitude. In comparing the other Gospel records, it is interesting that Matt 14:19 and Mark 6:41 use the same word *eulogeō* ("to bless") as Luke, which refers to blessing the food, not necessarily giving thanks for it, but John uses *eucharisteō* (6:11, 23, "gave thanks"). However, the synoptic Gospels each say that first of all, "he looked up to heaven", which corresponds to John's "he gave thanks". He first directed His thanks to the Father and then blessed the loaves and fishes, such a meagre supply, yet infinite in His hands. "It appears...as if the miracle consisted of breaking off new pieces from the existing bread, and giving these new pieces to the disciples, rather than a vast amount of food suddenly appearing from nowhere. This is therefore similar to the one barrel of meal and the one cruse of oil failing not in Elijah's time" (J. Heading, *Luke's Life of Christ*, page 113).

17   When all had eaten and were satisfied, enough remained of the broken pieces to fill twelve baskets. The basket by which Saul of Tarsus was let down from the city of Damascus was a *spuris*, it was large enough to hold a man. The word used here is *kophinos*, a much smaller vessel, normally used to carry food when on a journey. The Lord, who could multiply food at His command, enough to feed more than five thousand from five loaves and two fish, gave direction that none of the fragments should be wasted. There is much to learn here. The Lord of heaven and earth, with wealth beyond compare, is also the lowly Jesus of Nazareth who grew up in poverty, and knew that among the crowd were many who had often been hungry. The wasting of food was a crime. Once again, in keeping with His theme of the perfect Man, Luke illustrates that He was not only holy, but *akakos* ("harmless"), giving insult or injury to none.

The twelve baskets that remained were a powerful proof that the miracle was real. What was left was the same kind of food as that which was eaten. It was what remained of the five loaves and two fishes. Those who feasted were not mesmerised so that they imagined they were eating, but they ate real bread and fish. It is also obvious from John's account that the Lord saw in the bread a symbol of His flesh, "the bread that I will give is my flesh, which I will give for the life of the world" (John 6:51).

This was a mighty miracle. It is no wonder that unbelievers have made so many attempts to explain it by some natural means. We must always be on guard against any naturalistic explanations that lessen the wonder of the power of God. Many miracles are performed through natural means, but they are none the less far beyond nature. The Lord did not need to begin with the lad's provision. He could have fed the multitude without the boy's offered lunch, but He chose to use it and to multiply it so that all were filled and satisfied. If we offer to Him what we have, even though it is small, He is "able to do exceeding abundantly" with it.

26.   *Peter's Testimony to Christ*
   9:18-21

v.18 "And it came to pass, as he was alone praying, his disciples were with him: and he asked them, saying, Whom say the people that I am?

v.19 They answering said, John the Baptist; but some *say*, Elias; and others *say*, that one of the old prophets is risen again.

v.20 He said unto them, But whom say ye that I am? Peter answering said, The Christ of God.

v.21 And he straitly charged them, and commanded *them* to tell no man that thing;"

A large section of material that is found in Matt 14:22 to 16:12 and Mark 6:45 to 8:26 is not mentioned by Luke. It includes the story of the storm when the Lord walked on the water; the teaching about the bread of life that is so prominent in John; the healing of the Syrophenician's daughter; the healing of a man who was deaf and dumb; the feeding of 4 000, and the opening of the eyes of a blind man. However, Luke's order is spiritual and what is omitted allows him to weave together some of the most vital teaching in the Gospels about the identity of Jesus of Nazareth. On the sea, after the great calm, the disciples had asked with amazement, "Who then is this?" (8:25 JND). The question of Herod displayed his consternation, "but who is this?" (9:9). To these questions, Luke appends the Lord's own question, "Whom say the people that I am?". This is a divine setting for the precious gem of Peter's confession.

18   The Lord was praying alone. The disciples were near at hand, but He was engaged in private communion with His Father. We know from Matthew and Mark that the Lord had withdrawn with His disciples from the crowds in Galilee to the Gentile region near Caesarea Philippi at the foot of Mount Hermon. Turning to the twelve, the Lord asked what the people said of Him.

The question arises in our minds why Luke with his interest in the gospel going to a Gentile world does not name Caesarea Philippi, for it was a Gentile city and for the people of Galilee was the threshold of a Gentile world. Several solutions have been suggested, but the one that seems best to suit the context is that Luke desired to disassociate Peter's confession from place or time so that the whole focus of attention will centre on the identity of Jesus, the Son of God. This is seen in the way he links Peter's answer

1.   to the questions asked about the identity of Jesus (8:25; 9:9),

2.   to Christ, the Messiah who fed the 5 000 men, and

3.   to the intimate fellowship that existed between the Son on earth and the Father in heaven.

19   Herod's fear that John the Baptist had risen was not merely his own thought (v.7). The people were saying this quite generally, but others said that He was Elijah and still others that He was one of the old prophets who had returned. Each speculation was far short of the reality, yet each one indicates a sense of need and a spirit of expectancy, as we still sometimes hear people comment, "Isn't it time for God to do something?" Those who said Elijah had returned were referring to the prophecy of Malachi that Elijah would come first before the long expected "day of the Lord". This air of expectancy has often been the forerunner of great movements of God among men.

20   In the question, "But whom say ye that I am?" the word "ye" is emphatic in all the records (Matt 16:15; Mark 8:29). This fact indicates a contrast between the crowd and the disciples that is deeper than appearance. Peter's answer was the result of divine revelation, not human deduction. Luke leaves this as an implied fact, but Matthew records the Lord's words, "flesh and blood hath not revealed it unto thee, but my Father which is in heaven" (16:17). Many give assent to the fact that Jesus is the Christ who are not born of God (1 John 5:1). Personal conviction is the result of a work of God in the soul.

Peter's confession is that He is the Anointed, the Sent One from God, the promised Messiah and therefore Immanuel. How much all of this was grasped by Peter at that moment we cannot say, but we do know that this confession was the result of divine revelation. Yet, it is not likely that this truth was revealed for the first time to Peter when the Lord asked the question. His confession is the expression of the settled conviction of all the disciples even in the face of "the defection of the Galilean masses and the hostility of the Jerusalem authorities" (A.T. Robertson). It must have greatly cheered the heart of the rejected Lord to hear such loyalty expressed by Peter and His other disciples, for we believe that Peter was but the spokesman for them all.

21 The command to tell no man His identity has resulted in many speculations. John tells us that the aftermath of the feeding of the five thousand was that the people planned to take Him by force and make Him a king. He withdrew from the crowd and departed alone into a mountain (John 6:15). This was reason enough for the Lord's strong command that His disciples should not tell the people that He was the Christ. An insurrection in Galilee was not the purpose of His being sent from heaven, and this is relevant to the discussion at this point, for He immediately announced the real purpose of His coming.

27.   *The First Prediction of Death and Resurrection*
   9:22

> v.22 "Saying, The Son of man must suffer many things, and be rejected of the elders
> and chief priests and scribes, and be slain, and be raised the third day."

22 The title "Son of man", so often used by the Lord in the Gospels, is not inferior to the title "Son of God". For a true understanding of the meaning of "Son of man" a careful reading of Dan 7 is necessary. It is the title of the Last Adam, the Man who will yet wield the sceptre of universal and eternal dominion. The disciples thought of the Christ in this way, and this announcement of suffering, rejection, cruel death and then resurrection stunned them into unbelief and misunderstanding.

The rejection is prominent here among the "many things" that He must suffer. It is a technical term, used for the rejection of the evidence. The Lord is speaking of the rulers of the Jews, divided into elders, chief priests and scribes. The higher the office, the greater was the responsibility in the national rejection of Messiah (John 19:11). The timing of this statement about His rejection must have had tremendous impact on the disciples. Peter had just confessed Christ as Messiah and revealed the belief of his mind and the other disciples when the rejection and death of this One in whom all their hopes were centred was announced. From our side of the cross and the resurrection, now that it is all over, we cannot imagine the shock that such a disclosure brought to the hearts of the little band around the Lord.

The suffering and death of Christ are the very heart of the gospel, but are not all the gospel, for without the resurrection it would not have been a victory over sin and death and Satan. Some believe that in Paul's great gospel statement in 1 Cor 15:3 it is this very verse that is referred to as "the scriptures", and this is very possible. The OT did predict His resurrection (Ps 16:8-11; Isa 53:10-12) but is difficult to find a prediction about "the third day" unless we can find it in Lev 23:11, in the description of the Feast of Firstfruits. The words of the Lord Jesus clearly stated that it would be on "the third day" that He would rise again.

28.   The Call to True Discipleship
   9:23-26

v.23 "And he said to *them* all, If any *man* will come after me, let him deny himself, and take up his cross daily, and follow me.

v.24 For whosoever will save his life shall lose it: but whosoever will lose his life for my sake, the same shall save it.

v.25 For what is a man advantaged, if he gain the whole world, and lose himself, or be cast away?

v.26 For whosoever shall be ashamed of me and of my words, of him shall the Son of man be ashamed, when he shall come in his own glory, and *in his* Father's, and of the holy angels."

23   The word "will" in "will come after me" is strong and should be given an English equivalent such as "is determined to". The same translation is necessary for the same word in the phrase "For whosoever will save his life", which means "is determined to save" it. These phrases do not describe a passing interest, but a lifelong commitment. The denial of self is an absolute necessity in following Him. This is the first mention of the cross in the recorded words of the Lord. The men from Galilee knew well the implications of a cross. The historian Josephus wrote that hundreds of insurrectionists against the Romans had been crucified in Galilee. To these men a cross conveyed not only the thought of a burden; it was an instrument of death.

Self-denial was at the very heart of the Lord's teaching about discipleship. To follow the Lord Jesus means not to please self. In a day of radical self-indulgence this needs to be emphasised more than ever before. A major concept of modern psychology is "love yourself", and some professed teachers of Scripture echo the same cry. The four major characteristics of true discipleship are to love the Lord, deny self, bear the cross and be obedient.

The disciples had been allowed to share some of the Lord's power as they fulfilled their mission. They had confessed Him as the Christ, had learned of His rejection, now they must learn that sharing with Him will involve their rejection too and in their measure, even the bearing of the cross. But just as His glory will follow His sufferings, so too will they share in His coming glory. Therefore, in order to give them a foretaste of this, they are taken up to behold His glory on the mount. The sight of glory is always a great incentive to bear His cross. This sharing of both shame and glory with a rejected and then a glorified Lord is the theme of such passages as: "If so be that we suffer with him, that we may be also glorified together" (Rom 8:17); and "If we suffer, we shall also reign with him" (2 Tim 2:12).

24   The Greek word *thelō* is often translated "will" in the AV, but this is too weak. It is the word that is used in 1 Tim 2:4, "who will have all men to be saved", and portrays the heart-wish of the Almighty for the salvation of all men. If a man is bent on saving his own life, he will lose it. It is the man who loses his life for the

sake of the Lord Jesus who truly saves it. This self-sacrifice is the teaching of
Paul in Rom 12:1, where he calls it a "holy" sacrifice, the yielding of all that
we are and have for His sake. Jim Elliot, one of the Ecuadorian martyrs, wrote,
"He is no fool who gives up that which he cannot keep to gain that which he
can never lose".

25   These words of the Lord in Luke sound weaker than the corresponding
language of Matthew and Mark. Actually, as in almost all words that are quoted
from the Lord Jesus, the language is identical. The AV translators have substituted
"advantaged" for "profit" and "cast away" for "lose". As in the other Gospels the
subject in Luke is eternal gain or loss. For a man to lose himself means eternally
to lose his soul. There is no thought in these verses that a man can gain eternal
life by his own efforts at self-denial, but Luke is teaching that it is characteristic of
all who genuinely love the Lord Jesus that they will be like their Lord, for "even
Christ pleased not himself" (Rom 15:3).

26   This is the first mention by Luke of the promise of the Lord Jesus to come
back in glory. The glory of that day will be displayed in the Son; it will be the
glory of the Father, and the holy angels will also be seen in their own unique
glory. Our feeble senses are helped by remembering that glory is intrinsic worth. The
day of glory will be when that incomparable worth is displayed. The Lord Jesus ever
had been and ever will be the outshining of the glory of God (Heb 1:3).

   To be ashamed of the Lord and His words in this present time means that in the
day of glory He will be ashamed of us. This can be applied to a loss of reward for true
believers and looked at in the light of Paul's words to Timothy, "Be not thou therefore
ashamed of the testimony of our Lord, nor of me his prisoner" (2 Tim 1:8). However,
the context of this statement, particularly the eternal gain and loss in v.25, sets these
words alongside Dan 12:2, "many of them that sleep in the dust of the earth shall
awake, some to everlasting life, and some to shame and everlasting contempt". This
is a test of the genuine against the false, real believers against mere professors, so
this is the shame of those who reject the cross as well as cross-bearing. The
loss is eternal. However, let us remember the solemn warning about
"becoming like them that go down to the pit" (Ps 28:1)! A world of
self-indulgence and indolence, characterised by a desire to be amused and
entertained, does have a deceptive influence on us. The call of our Lord is
unchanged, "If any man will come after me, let him deny himself, and take up
his cross daily, and follow me" (v.23).

29.   *The Mount of Transfiguration*
9:27-36

> v.27 "But I tell you of a truth, there be some standing here, which shall not taste of
> death, till they see the kingdom of God.

v.28 And it came to pass about an eight days after these sayings, he took Peter and John and James, and went up into a mountain to pray.
v.29 And as he prayed, the fashion of his countenance was altered, and his raiment *was* white *and* glistering.
v.30 And, behold, there talked with him two men, which were Moses and Elias:
v.31 Who appeared in glory, and spake of his decease which he should accomplish at Jerusalem.
v.32 But Peter and they that were with him were heavy with sleep: and when they were awake, they saw his glory, and two men that stood with him.
v.33 And it came to pass, as they departed from him, Peter said unto Jesus, Master, it is good for us to be here: and let us make three tabernacles; one for thee, and one for Moses, and one for Elias: not knowing what he said.
v.34 While he thus spake, there came a cloud, and overshadowed them: and they feared as they entered into the cloud.
v.35 And there came a voice out of the cloud, saying, This is my beloved Son: hear him.
v.36 And when the voice was past, Jesus was found alone. And they kept *it* close, and told no man in those days any of those things which they had seen."

27   To "taste death" implies the full experience of all the bitterness of death. The Lord Jesus tasted death for every man (Heb 2:9). Rather than meaning to sample a small taste of the great reality, it means that there was not a drop in the bitter cup that He did not taste to its utmost bitterness. We need to remember at this point that almost all these disciples were to die under torture as martyrs.

The difficulty of this verse is the meaning of the words, "till they see the kingdom of God". Matthew says "till they see the Son of man coming in his kingdom" (16:28). Mark says, "till they have seen the kingdom of God come with power" (9:1). Any interpretation must satisfy all these expressions. In the many interpretations that have been given to this verse, differing views on the course of future events are evident. Amillennialists, who do not distinguish between Israel and the church, interpret the coming of the kingdom of God as the day of Pentecost or the spread of the gospel throughout the world. Others say that the Lord is referring to the destruction of Jerusalem in AD 70, and use Luke 21:5-20 to support this view. It is very difficult to see how the destruction of Jerusalem was "the Son of man coming in his kingdom". Some teach that the Lord is not referring to the actual disciples who heard Him that day, but that He is viewing them as being representative of the faithful remnant at the close of the tribulation. Still others say it refers to the resurrection and ascension of the Lord, but the problem with this latter interpretation is that He called His death, resurrection and ascension His going away, not His coming back.

In all three synoptic Gospels these words immediately precede the display of the glory of the Lord on the Mount of Transfiguration; therefore the immediate context is the glory that was seen by Peter, James and John. These three men correspond to "some standing here", but was this "the Son of man coming in his kingdom" with power? Peter believed that it was, for this is the very language he used about his experience on the mount, "we made known unto you the power and coming of our Lord Jesus Christ, but were eye-witnesses of his majesty" (2 Pet 1:16). He then describes the glory that he and the two others saw on the mount, linking it to the "power and coming of our Lord Jesus Christ", of which it was a preview.

28   It was after a period of eight days that the Lord went up into the mountain and took with Him Peter, James and John. Eight is the number of a new beginning (Lev 23:39), so it is significant, for the mountain top experience prefigured the ushering in of the new day of righteousness and peace at the return of the Lord in glory. Matthew's six days (Matt 17:1) had the same terminus, but a different starting point. Six is the number of man (Rev 13:18), so "after six days" suggests that after all human efforts have failed the true King of righteousness will gloriously triumph.

Luke stresses one of his major themes when he writes that it was "to pray" that the Lord ascended the mount (see 11:1-13). It is not possible to be dogmatic about the identity of the mountain, but there is good support for Mount Hermon in the fact that "these sayings" were spoken at Caesarea Philippi at the foot of "*the* mountain" (that is, the mountain nearby), not merely *a* mountain. The little remnant that were with Him in the mount are illustrative of remnant testimony through the ages, and particularly typical of the remnant of those who will be found faithful to Him through the time of Jacob's trouble until their hopes are all fulfilled in the descent from heaven to earth of the Lord of glory.

29   It was "as he prayed, the fashion of his countenance was altered". No change in essential being is suggested by these words. The veil of flesh was thin. It effectively hid His glory from unbelieving Jews, but at least a measure of His glory was unveiled to demons who quailed before His majesty (Mark 1:24, 34; Luke 8:28). His face is mentioned first and then His raiment. Matthew says that His face shone "as the sun" (17:2), yet even the sun is only a created light; this was the uncreated source of all light. When Moses was on the mountain with God the skin of his face shone, but we must distinguish the reflected light of God's presence in Moses' face from the personal glory of the Lord Jesus. He always possessed holy, kingly majesty in full measure, so that when in a coming day He fully enters into His kingly office, it will be that which has ever been truly His. In Israel's history, priestly or kingly position brought glory to the man on whom the office was bestowed. The garments of glory and beauty gave to Aaron that glory and beauty he never had before. Likewise, to sit upon David's throne gave glory to Solomon that he never had before, but the offices of Priest and King will add nothing to our blessed Lord. He will bring His own beauty and glory to these offices. Therefore the glory that was displayed on the mount is the manifestation not only of what He shall be, but of what He truly is.

This radiant glory shone through His very garments so that they became white and ablaze with light. *Astraptō* is the verb used in 17:24, "For as the lightning that lighteneth (which flashes and lights up the sky, NIV)" and *exastraptō* ("glistering") in this verse is a strengthened form of the same word. Luke had a companion who had once looked on that light. Quoting Paul, he wrote, "And when I could not see for the glory of that light, being led by the hand...I came into Damascus" (Acts 22:11). These words have been paraphrased, "I looked until I was blind" and Luke uses the intense word *emblepō* for the verb "I looked".

30 The silences of Scripture are full of meaning. There is no introduction to Moses and Elijah; there did not need to be. In the light of the glory of the Son of man there are no unknown persons. This is a foreview of the millennium and of the relationship of saints in the heavenly city. We shall need no introductions and there shall be no strangers.

There are lessons to learn about the appearance of Moses and Elijah regarding departed loved ones:

1.   They lived on even though they had left earth hundreds of years before.

2.   They could be identified without any formal introduction.

3.   They could speak to each other.

4.   Their intelligence was not impaired.

5.   They knew about coming events.

6.   They showed no dread in the presence of the glory of Christ.

7.   They were able to commune with Christ (Matt 17:3).

31 Moses and Elijah represent the witness of the entire OT Scriptures which were divided into the Law and the Prophets, and were united in their testimony to Christ (24:27), so their presence with Him in glory is fitting. It was also fitting that they conversed together about His exodus, which is the exact word used for "decease". As the exodus from Egypt was by the blood of the paschal lamb, so from a far greater bondage would the blood of the Saviour bring deliverance. Peter, James and John contributed nothing to the conversation; how could they? As yet, they did not understand the cross. The exodus of the Lord Jesus was not a tragedy but a triumph. He was not to be a mere "Victim, bound to the accursed tree", but a mighty Victor who would accomplish death as the culmination and antitype of all the shadows and types of the OT.

32   The sleep of Peter, James and John under such circumstances is very difficult
for us to understand. From v.37 it seems right to say that they were in the mount
for at least an entire night and only came down the next day. Flesh has severe
limitations, and we have no way of knowing how long the conversation went on
between the Lord and these two great servants of His from the past. Even our
limited understanding of the Pentateuch would lead us to believe that the penman
of these many promises, prophecies and types would have much to learn from
his Lord. The length of the conversation, so little understood by the disciples,
might well cause them to succumb to the demands of human need, and fall
asleep.

   The purpose of the statement about sleep is found here to make us
understand that they did awake. "When they were awake" is the translation
of one composite word *diagrēgoreō*, found only here in the NT, an intensified
form of *grēgoreō* ("to watch"). It was a complete awakening: "fully woke up"
(JND); "were fully awake" (RV); "when they became fully awake" (NIV). What
they saw was not a dream, nor a vision. Many years later, Peter wrote, "we
have not followed cunningly devised fables...but were eyewitnesses of his
majesty" (2 Pet 1:16), so Luke says, "they saw his glory". Some believe that
John's statement, "we beheld his glory, the glory as of the only begotten of
the Father" (John 1:14), is a reference to this very event. The glory John
"beheld" must include what he saw on the mount, but considering the many
ways His glory is portrayed in John (see 2:11) it is not correct to limit his
statement exclusively to this one experience.

33   When Moses and Elijah were departing from Him, Peter must have had
some conception of the meaning of the mountain-top experience, and desired
that it might not pass. He may have thought of the tabernacle as an incentive
to keep Moses and Elijah from going. It is at this point that we are normally
reminded of the garrulous Peter, and maybe there is some justification for
the accusations because the verse ends, "not knowing what he said". However,
we should understand that this is written in relation to his failure to give to
the Lord Jesus the place of supremacy over Moses and Elijah, not just to his
suggestion about building tabernacles. He was partly right, for he grasped
the millennial meaning of the glory of the Son of man and related it to the
seven days of the Feast of Tabernacles (Lev 23:39-43), which will be fulfilled
when the Lord Jesus will "come in his own glory, and in his Father's, and of
the holy angels" (v.26).

   The fitness of this scene as a foreview of the millennium is obvious. The
pre-eminence of the Lord Jesus in His glory is what Peter missed and is the
principal feature. Moses and Elijah represent OT saints, and Peter, James and
John NT saints around the Lord Jesus. Thus far will interpretation take us. Some
have made an application that pictures Moses as a believer who died, but in
resurrection is with the Lord Jesus. Elijah, then, is taken as a picture of saints

who will never die, but will be raptured to be with their Lord. The three disciples are then taken to be a picture of living saints on a redeemed earth during the millennium. We may enjoy these thoughts, but we cannot call them critical interpretation.

34-35 The overshadowing cloud was not merely made of fog and mist. Such a cloud would not have caused fear to the disciples, nor would it have been "a bright cloud" (Matt 17:5). The word for "bright" is used three times in Luke 11:34-36 and is translated "full of light". The voice of the Father speaking from the cloud settles the issue for us. As so often in OT history it was the glory cloud, the evidence of the divine presence; so would men familiar with the revelation of God to man have interpreted it.

Matt 17:5 and Mark 9:7 agree with the AV translation of v.35, "This is my beloved Son: hear him". Darby and the RV margin agree with this reading. The RV reflects manuscripts that read, "my Son, my chosen". If this authority is accepted, then the entire statement was, "This is my beloved Son, my chosen One: hear him". We cannot miss the rebuke to Peter in this, but also should not miss the expression of the Father's delight in Him. Dr. Heading aptly writes, "At His baptism, the commendation refers to the Lord's hidden life prior to His public ministry. Here on the mount it refers to His public life of teaching and miracles". The Father's delight in His Son is a subject that will take eternity to explore (Isa 42:1; Prov 8:30).

36 The AV translates, "And when the voice was past", but JND translates, "And as the voice was heard". As the voice spoke, they were directed to the Son and as they looked, He stood alone before them. H. Paisley points out in his commentary on Mark in this series that He is "greater in His rule than Moses and greater in His speaking than Elijah". The lesson learned is that the Father's witness to the Son will always set Him apart as the One who is incomparable, the unique One. This is the closest we can come in our language to the meaning of David's words, "my darling" (Ps 22:20); or Luke's words, "my beloved Son" (Luke 3:22), or John's phrase, "his only begotten Son" (John 3:16). We understand that what the three witnesses saw on the mount would have little effect on their unbelieving contemporaries, so they were to tell no man, but it is full of meaning to us because of His resurrection and ascension.

30.   *The Demon-Possessed Child Healed*
9:37-43

v.37 "And it came to pass, that on the next day, when they were come down from the hill, much people met him.

v.38 And, behold, a man of the company cried out, saying, Master, I beseech thee, look upon my son: for he is mine only child.

v.39 And, lo, a spirit taketh him, and he suddenly crieth out; and it teareth him that
      he foameth again, and bruising him hardly departeth from him.

v.40 And I besought thy disciples to cast him out; and they could not.

v.41 And Jesus answering said, O faithless and perverse generation, how long shall
      I be with you, and suffer you? Bring thy son hither.

v.42 And as he was yet a coming, the devil threw him down, and tare *him*. And Jesus
      rebuked the unclean spirit, and healed the child, and delivered him to his
      father.

v.43 And they were all amazed at the mighty power of God. But while they wondered
      everyone at all things which Jesus did, he said unto his disciples,"

A comparison of Matt 17:14-18 and Mark 9:14-29 will show that in the three Gospels the healing of the demon-possessed boy is linked to the Mount of Transfiguration. A great contrast is apparent between the three who were with the Lord on the mount, blinded by the light of His glory, and the nine disciples below who are battling with the forces of darkness and suffering defeat.

Dispensationally, the struggling disciples, and their helplessness at the foot of the mountain are a picture of the struggling remnant at the time of the Lord's return. When the church is in glory with Christ, the forces of Satan will be in full array against God's earthly people. They will know the meaning of "prayer and fasting" and will be delivered at the time when the enemy will be making his last frantic attack.

37 It is only Luke who records that it was the next day that the Lord and His three chosen witnesses descended from the mountain. Mark tells us that when He returned He found the scribes questioning the disciples and "a great multitude about them". Again in this verse, two words are found that are frequently used by Luke, but rarely used otherwise in the NT. *Katerchomai* ("come down") is used twice in the Gospel (4:31; 9:37) and ten times in Acts. Its only other use is in James 3:15 where it refers to "the wisdom that descendeth not from above". If the people had known what had taken place on the mount, they would have been able to appreciate far better the One who truly came from above. To Moses, God had said, "I am come down to deliver" (Exod 3:8). The descent of the Lord from the mount was a coming down into the evil world of disease, sickness, sin and unbelief. *Sunantaō* ("to meet") outside of Luke's writings is found only in Heb 7:1 in reference to the meeting between Abraham and Melchizedek. In the person of His Son, God was truly meeting with men.

38-40 Once again it is Luke who informs us of the personal fact that this was an "only child" (7:12; 8:42). The expression used is "only begotten" and expresses both uniqueness and the deep affection of the father for him (Gen 22:1,2). "Look upon my son" was an appeal to the tender heart of the Saviour, but it also may be a plea to the eye of the Physician. It is likely that the boy bore external evidence of the violent effects of the unclean spirit taking him, tearing him and bruising him. Matthew adds that he often fell "into the fire", so that to look at him was to pity him. We should never sympathise with sin or evil, but we should ever have a heart of pity toward those who are held in the grip of sin and Satan. The distraught father had begged for healing from the disciples, but because "This kind can come forth by nothing, but by prayer and fasting" (Mark 9:29), they had failed. Again, we learn the need of a fit servant in the hand of God. Self-indulgence blunts the instrument, and self-denial is a necessity for those who expect to see the power of God working through them (v.23). Matthew lays down unbelief as a first cause of the failure (Matt 17:20). Denial of self, giving ourselves to prayer and simple faith in God are prerequisites to seeing God's power displayed in our service.

41 "O faithless and perverse generation" has often been applied to the failure of the disciples, and it does have its application to them, but it is more likely that the Lord was addressing the scribes and their followers. The father's need was real enough, but this was a test case with many witnesses present, and there was an attempt to discredit the Lord through His disciples. This interpretation fits the words about the Lord's rejection in v.44. *Apistos* ("faithless") simply means to be without faith and might well apply to the disciples, for they did lack it, but *diastrephō* ("perverse") carries the thought of being twisted or torn asunder and scarcely seems to apply to disciples. It is of interest that *epistrephō* ("be converted") uses the same root, but the different prefix makes it mean "to turn" around instead of "to be twisted". Mark's account of these words of the Lord seems to address them to all who were present (9:18-19).

42 The final effort of the demon to keep the boy within his power is characteristic. In Mark 1:23-27 the man in the synagogue at Capernaum was just about to be delivered when the unclean spirit made one last, mighty effort to hold him or destroy him. Rev 12:12 refers to a coming day, but we are seeing a great display of Satan's rage in these last days because he knows that his time is short and the church is about to be delivered forever out of his reach. We have often seen Satan make a gigantic last effort to hold a sinner who is on the very threshold of salvation. We should not miss Luke's statement that the Lord did three things: He "rebuked the unclean spirit", "healed the child", and "delivered him again to his father". The healing of the child was a necessary thing for Mark says that when the spirit was commanded to come out of him, it "rent him sore...and he was as one dead". It was a complete deliverance, for He commanded the spirit never to enter into him again (Mark 9:25). The Lord does not give a partial deliverance. And the people were "amazed at the mighty power of God" (v.43).

31.   *The Second Prediction of the Lord's Death*
      9:43-45

> v.43 "And they were all amazed at the mighty power of God. But while they wondered
>   everyone at all things which Jesus did, he said unto his disciples,
> v.44 Let these sayings sink down into your ears: for the Son of man shall be delivered
>   into the hands of men.
> v.45 But they understood not this saying, and it was hid from them, that they perceived
>   it not: and they feared to ask him of that saying."

43   Half of this verse belongs to the preceding section, but the latter half of it
gives us the circumstances under which the prediction of His death was given.
Everyone in the crowd is marvelling, not only because of the complete deliverance
of the demon-possessed boy, but at all the miracles that the Lord has done. It is
a high point of acceptance by the multitude, but the Lord knew their hearts and
all the pathway of rejection and suffering that lay before Him.

44   Even if the disciples did not fully understand at this moment the meaning
of the prediction, they were to store it in memory for the time when they would
understand. This principle still has an application. The word stored in memory is
the same word that is used by the Holy Spirit and becomes a "sword of the
Spirit" at a time of particular attack, or a time of personal need. Unless the word
has been treasured it cannot be the instrument of victory. The same principle
holds true for teaching children to memorise verses even at an age when they
may not grasp their meaning, for it is good seed and will produce fruit after
many days.

"The Son of man shall be delivered into the hands of men" must have been
heard by Judas, even though the import of these words was lost on him. However,
although *paradidosthai*, the present passive infinitive of *paradidōmi*, is
translated "to betray" in a number of passages, it does not necessarily carry in it
the thought of rejection or betrayal for a price. In fact it is the verb used in Rom
8:32, "He that spared not his own Son, but delivered him up for us all"; and Eph
5:25, "Christ also loved the church, and gave himself for it"; and Gal 2:20, "the
Son of God, who loved me, and gave himself for me". This being "delivered into
the hands of men" goes far beyond the betrayal by Judas. It was God who delivered
Him up, even though Acts 2:23 uses *ekdotos* and not *paradidōmi*.

45   Matthew tells us that the disciples were "exceeding sorry" when they heard
these words. Mark tells us of their ignorance and their fear to ask Him, but only
Luke says that the meaning was veiled from them. The phrase, "it was hid from
them", is the translation of a Hebraism that is found only here in the NT. In fact,
there are two words in this sentence that are used only by Luke in this verse:
parakaluptō ("was hid from"), suggesting that they would not understand until
it was revealed to them, a revelation that still lay in the future in the purposes of

God; *aisthanomai* ("perceived"), suggesting that as yet they did not possess the faculty by which they could grasp the truth. However, they understood enough of the meaning of the prediction to be made sad by it, but did not understand enough to perceive the true meaning and importance of the delivering up of the Son of man. Whatever we may understand about the veiling of their understanding, we are certain that it was an act of grace that later they might more fully understand when the prediction became a reality.

32.   *The Reasoning about Who Would Be the Greatest* 9:46-50

v.46 "Then there arose a reasoning among them, which of them should be greatest.
v.47 And Jesus, perceiving the thought of their heart, took a child, and set him by him,
v.48 And said unto them, Whosoever shall receive this child in my name receiveth me: and whosoever shall receive me receiveth him that sent me: for he that is least among you all, the same shall be great.
v.49 And John answered and said, Master, we saw one casting out devils in thy name; and we forbad him, because he followeth not with us.
v.50 And Jesus said unto him, Forbid *him* not; for he that is not against us is for us."

46-47   A comparison of the Gospel records indicates that the dispute about who would be the greatest took place among the disciples on the way to Capernaum. It was after they had arrived at Capernaum that the Lord commented on what they had said along the way. The "reasoning" was literally a debate that arose. Much more was thought than the actual words that were spoken. We need not suppose that the disciples were insensible to the shame of uttering proud thoughts of self-exaltation, but behind whatever proud words were spoken the Lord was able to perceive the very "thought of their heart". The debate was in their hearts before it was expressed, but the motives that caused it were known to the Lord. We may suppose that we can read thoughts, and have been guilty of judging motives, but He unerringly knew the spring behind every word and act. This is omniscience.

48   There is significance in the form of words that close the previous verse. The child was made to stand beside the Lord, and He then lifted it in His arms (Mark 9:36), an object of His affection and gentle care, and an apt picture of one who believes in Him (Matt 18:6). The child is an illustration of a lowly believer, the least among His own, for all believers must become as children to be converted (Matt 18:3). This is the meaning of "receive this child in my name"; receive it as one of Mine and therefore do not be above it or look down on it. This receiving is a spiritual act toward a spiritual child that requires humility of heart and mind. It is not a natural act, such as a general showing of love and kindness to little children. This is admirable and should be true of everyone, but even the ungodly can do this. "Whosoever therefore shall humble himself as this little child, the same is greatest in the kingdom of heaven" (Matt 18:4). The little child illustrates that "meek and quiet spirit, which is in the sight of God of great price" (1 Pet 3:4; 5:5, 6; James 4:10).

49   *Epistatēs* ("Master") is a form of address to the Lord Jesus that is found only in Luke and, with the exception of its use in this chapter, was uttered under conditions of need or perplexity. Peter used it when he was telling the Lord: "Master, we have toiled all night, and have taken nothing" (5:5). The disciples used it in the storm on the sea when they cried: "Master, master, we perish" (8:24). In the crowd that thronged the Lord Jesus, Peter said: "Master, the multitude throng thee and press thee, and sayest thou, Who touched me?" (8:45). On the mount, Peter said, "Master, it is good for us to be here" (9:33). In 17:13 it was the cry of the ten lepers: "Master, have mercy on us". As W.E. Vine says, it is used "in recognition of His authority rather than His instruction". When the four Gospels use the word "Master" in a teaching context, it is a translation of *didaskalos* which is used sixteen times in Luke and less frequently in Matthew (seven times), Mark (twelve times) and John (eight times).

50   The sin of sectarianism is usually drawn from this passage, but the subject is not church truth, or the basis of fellowship between believers, much less is it a justification for denominations and divisions. Nor should it be used to justify a person claiming that he is a law to himself and answerable to no one. Such an attitude would scarcely fit with the spirit of fellowship in a local assembly or the submission of all true servants to the Lordship of Christ. Also, such an interpretation would lead to serious difficulty in understanding Matt 12:30 and Luke 11:23, and would make the Lord to contradict Himself.

What is in the passage is interference with another man's service. It corresponds very closely to the Lord's rebuke in John 21:21, 22, when Peter asked about John, "Lord, and what shall this man do?". The Lord answered, "what is that to thee? follow thou me". The difference between "he that is not against us is for us", and "He that is not with me is against me" (Luke 11:23) can be understood only in this way. The first expression (v.50) is the correct attitude to take in judging the service of others; but the latter test (11:23) is personal. It is the way a servant is to judge his own service.

IV.   The Journey Toward Jerusalem (9:51-19:27)

It is generally agreed that this is the point in Luke's Gospel when the Galilean ministry, with Capernaum as its centre, closes. All Galilee had been privileged to see and hear the gentle, lowly Jesus of Nazareth. So far as we know He did not return to the region of the Lake of Galilee until in resurrection He met His disciples at "a mountain where (He) had appointed them" (Matt 28:16). At this point in

Luke's narrative "he stedfastly set his face to go to Jerusalem", and by this statement Luke is expressing His purpose of heart, and often returns to this subject (9:53, 57; 10:1; 13:22, 33; 17:11; 18:31; 19:11, 28). However, it was not a straight line journey from Capernaum to Jerusalem. It took several months and occupies ten chapters of Luke; we also know from John that He was twice in Jerusalem during this period (John 7:10; 10:22) and at least once in Bethany to raise Lazarus (John 11:7). Also in Luke 10:38 He is in Bethany, and in 17:11 He is in a region of Galilee and Samaria; yet it is the plan of this Gospel, divinely inspired, that Luke should give us the concept of one continuous journey, which it truly was, a journey, the purpose of which was to suffer on the cross at Calvary. Although there is not a precise route that can be followed, Luke traces His steps eastward through southern Galilee, through regions of Samaria, and southward through Peraea on the eastern side of the Jordan until He came to Jericho and finally went up to Jerusalem, coming near, beholding the city and weeping over it (19:41).

Much of the detailed material found in this large section of Luke is unique to this Gospel, giving events and much precious teaching from the lips of the Lord Jesus that is found nowhere else. This unique material does not contradict the narrative of the other Gospels, and an extreme effort to make a chronological harmony is unnecessary. Luke often records teaching and events without telling us the exact location of the Lord at the time, except for the fact that He was on His way to the cross. The spiritual meaning is stressed rather than chronological order.

1. *The Departure from Galilee*
9:51

> v.51 "And it came to pass, when the time was come that he should be received up, he stedfastly set his face to go to Jerusalem,"

51 The noun *analēpsis*, ("being taken up") which is used only here, is akin to *analambanō*, the usual word for His ascension (Mark 16:19; Acts 1:2, 11, 22; 1 Tim 3:16). The fact that it is His ascension toward which He moves, after the cross has become an accomplishment, may be linked to the glory of the mount and the conversation with Moses and Elijah. The days of His sojourn on earth were being fulfilled, suggesting an exact number of days predetermined in the counsels of eternity. Knowing the time, "he stedfastly set his face to go to Jerusalem". Language scholars frequently point to the "thorough Hebrew cast" (Plummer) of this sentence. The words convey a fixed purpose in spite of great cost and intense suffering.

It has been noted at 8:23 that Luke used one of his unique words, *sumplēroō* ("to fill"), to describe the filling of the boat in the storm. He used the same word in Acts 2:1 for the fully coming of the day of Pentecost. This is the only other time he used it, and we learn from the other two instances its true meaning.

"filling up" as the boat, or a time to be fulfilled or completed as in Acts 2. Here it is the filling up of a predetermined time. Perhaps the order of the words in the sentence are best left as Luke wrote them, "in the to-be-fulfilled days of the assumption" (A. Marshall). The days were determined in eternal counsels, and when those counsels were taken, our blessed Lord was a "Counsellor" (Isa 9:6).

2.   The Rejection of the Lord in Samaria
       9:52-56

v.52 "And sent messengers before his face: and they went, and entered into a village of the Samaritans, to make ready for him.

v.53 And they did not receive him, because his face was as though he would go to Jerusalem.

v.54 And when his disciples James and John saw *this*, they said, Lord, wilt thou that we command fire to come down from heaven, and consume them, even as Elias did?

v.55 But he turned, and rebuked them, and said, Ye know not what manner of spirit ye are of.

v.56 For the Son of man is not come to destroy men's lives, but to save *them*. And they went to another village."

52-53   The bitter feelings between Jews and Samaritans is best summed up by the Samaritan woman in John 4:9, "the Jews have no dealings with the Samaritans". The feelings were shared by each side in the dispute, so with His face set toward Jerusalem and a feast of the Jews to be celebrated there, the Samaritans would not receive Him. They regarded his intention to go to Jerusalem as a rejection of Mount Gerizim and we are reminded of the Samaritan woman's words, "Our fathers worshipped in this mountain; and ye say, that in Jerusalem is the place..." (John 4:20).

54-56   James and John were well named "Boanerges...The sons of thunder" (Mark 3:17). In the mount they must have seen the supremacy of their Master even over an Elijah, so they suggest that Elijah's miracle be repeated (2 Kings 1: 10,12). The request may have been easier to make because the offenders were hated Samaritans. The Lord "turned, and rebuked them" because they manifested a spirit of Jewish bigotry, certainly not the spirit of their Lord (v.56). Some have suggested that they showed the spirit of the false prophet who brings fire down from heaven in the sight of men (Rev 13:13-18). Although he causes all who do not worship the image of the beast to be killed, it does not say that they are killed by the fire from heaven, so this analogy may not be valid. Satan is the destroyer; the Lord Jesus is the Saviour. They would destroy; He came to save.

They went to another (*heteros*) village, that is, a village of a different kind. Was the difference that this was a village that would receive Him, or was it a Jewish village, not a Samaritan one? We cannot say dogmatically, but it is unlikely that the Lord turned away from the Samaritans as a result of His rejection in one village (10:33; 17:11, 16).

3.   *True Discipleship*
   9:57-62

v.57 "And it came to pass, that, as they went in the way, a certain *man* said unto him,
Lord, I will follow thee whithersoever thou goest.
v.58 And Jesus said unto him, Foxes have holes, and birds of the air *have* nests; but
the Son of man hath not where to lay *his* head.
v.59 And he said unto another, Follow me. But he said, Lord, suffer me first to go
and bury my father.
v.60 Jesus said unto him, Let the dead bury their dead: but go thou and preach the
kingdom of God.
v.61 And another also said, Lord, I will follow thee; but let me first go bid them farewell,
which are at home at my house.
v.62 And Jesus said unto him, No man, having put his hand to the plough, and
looking back, is fit for the kingdom of God."

57   Luke does not tell us that these three incidents took place at the same time,
but in putting them together, he is giving us a composite picture of true
discipleship. Matthew puts the first two together, but omits the third one
completely (Matt 8:18-22). In Matthew, the first man is called a scribe. These
meticulous students of the law were almost without exception rejectors of the
Lord Jesus. The scribe did not begin his statement with "Lord" as in the AV.
Following the Greek text, JND places "Lord" at the end, but has a note in his
translation throwing doubt on its authority because many ancient MSS omit the
word.

58   The Lord Jesus had been despised in Nazareth, rejected in Galilee, had left
Capernaum, and the Samaritans had refused to receive Him. To follow Him meant
to share His rejection and endure the hardships of a homeless stranger. The
foxes had holes and the birds had "roosting-places" (JND), but He had no fixed
abode. The sudden enthusiasm of the scribe seems to have quickly faded. He
corresponds to the seed on the shallow soil of 8:13. The cost of discipleship was
too great for him.

59   The second man is described by Matthew as being "another disciple", one of a
different kind than the first man. One obvious difference is that the Lord called him.
When the Lord interpreted the parable of the sower, He said that the thorns that
sprang up and choked the seed were "cares...of this life" (8:14). It has been suggested
that the man is saying, "I have responsibilities at home; my father is old, and after he
dies, I will become a disciple". This is actually a very old interpretation and has found
acceptance with many who have found difficulty in thinking that the Lord would
forbid a disciple to go to his father's funeral. I suggest that the issue here is not the
father's life, death or funeral; the real issue is "me first" which is a total denial of
discipleship. Paul expresses the opposite, "Not I, but Christ" (Gal 2:20). The problem
is one of priorities and on this subject the Lord had spoken plainly, "seek ye first the
kingdom of God, and his righteousness; and all these things shall be added unto

you" (Matt 6:33). No man should treat his father with indifference, much less with cruelty, for this would be contrary to the very law which the Lord Jesus so perfectly magnified and made honourable (Exod 20:12; Isa 42:21). The care of his father was important, but he had given it pre-eminence.

60   This is not the only time that the Lord spoke of people who are spiritually dead (John 5:25). Those who are dead in sins can bury their dead, but they cannot preach the kingdom of God. Some see a difficulty in such a change in the use of *nekros* ("dead") in the same context, even the same sentence, but John 5:21,25 use the same word for those who are spiritually dead, yet in vv.28, 29 the reference is to those who have died physically, who will be raised at the resurrection. Many take the meaning here to be as we have stated, the spiritually-dead can bury the physically dead. Many a servant of Christ has been compelled to give "the things of the Lord" (1 Cor 7:32-33) priority over legitimate earthly and family ties, such as those who go far from home and loved ones to carry the gospel to the ends of the earth. At times, they have said goodbye to a beloved father and mother, never expecting to see them again in this life. What the Lord taught here belongs in this context.

61-62   In the case of the third man, the "me first" problem is also evident, but the key to understanding his case is found in the Lord's words "looking back". He was like Lot's wife. The place that had held her attention for so long, pulled at her affections at the very moment of her escape from Sodom. This man was pulled in two directions; he had half a heart for the Lord Jesus and a half for friends at home, which is a denial of discipleship. This was the attitude of the double-minded man in James 4:8. There is no middle ground, "the friendship of the world is enmity with God" (James 4:4-10). As in the other two cases, true discipleship is not merely what a man says, but a disciple is a person in whose heart the Lord Jesus has pre-eminence (1 Pet 3:15). This third man is like the wayside of Luke 8:12, where the trampling of many feet had left too many impressions. The true disciple's language is not, These many things I dabble in, but "this one thing I do" (Phil 3:13).

The Lord's view of His own pathway here should touch our hearts. He saw it as a pathway of loneliness and hardship, "not where to lay his head" (v.58); He saw it as one of special purpose, to "preach the kingdom of God" (v.60); and He saw it as a task which would absorb His entire attention, "having put his hand to the plough" (v.62). He was the true pilgrim, the true preacher, and the true ploughman with His eye fixed on His work.

4.   *The Sending of the Seventy*
10:1-12

v.1   "After these things the Lord appointed other seventy also, and sent them two and two before his face into every city and place, whither he himself would come.

> v.2 Therefore said he unto them, The harvest truly *is* great, but the labourers *are* few: pray ye therefore the Lord of the harvest, that he would send forth labourers into his harvest.
> v.3 Go your ways: behold, I send you forth as lambs among wolves.
> v.4 Carry neither purse, nor scrip, nor shoes: and salute no man by the way.
> v.5 And into whatsoever house ye enter, first say, Peace *be* to this house.
> v.6 And if the son of peace be there, your peace shall rest upon it: if not, it shall turn to you again.
> v.7 And in the same house remain, eating and drinking such things as they give: for the labourer is worthy of his hire. Go not from house to house.
> v.8 And into whatsoever city ye enter, and they receive you, eat such things as are set before you:
> v.9 And heal the sick that are therein, and say unto them, The kingdom of God is come nigh unto you.
> v.10 But into whatsoever city ye enter, and they receive you not, go your ways out into the streets of the same, and say,
> v.11 Even the very dust of your city, which cleaveth on us, we do wipe off against you: notwithstanding be ye sure of this, that the kingdom of God is come nigh unto you.
> v.12 But I say unto you, that it shall be more tolerable in that day for Sodom, than for that city."

The reader is referred back to 9:1-9 where the sending of the twelve has many parallels to the sending of the seventy.

1   Moses, by God's command, appointed seventy elders to bear with him the burden of caring for Israel (Num 11:16, 17). Considering the summary of discipleship that closes ch.9, it is interesting that it says of the elders, "the spirit rested upon them, they prophesied, and did not cease" (Num 11:25). The MSS are divided over whether the figure in Luke 10:1 should be seventy or seventy-two. Darby does not believe it merits a footnote; and the RV puts seventy-two in the margin. In Num 11:24-26 there were seventy around the tabernacle, and two prophesied in the camp. If the two were in addition to the seventy, then the total was seventy-two.

The word *anadeiknumi* ("appointed") is found only here and in Acts 1:24, where it is translated by the AV, "show", and is used in reference to the Lord showing the apostles whether Joseph or Barsabas should take the place "from which Judas by transgression fell" (v.25). The word that is translated "appoint" (Acts 6:3) and "ordain" (Titus 1:5) is *kathistēmi*, not the word that is used here. A possible reason for this is that whether it was the "appointing" of the seven men in Acts 6, or the "ordaining" of elders in Titus 1:5, they were pointed out for recognition by their fellow believers, rather than receiving a formal ecclesiastical appointment. We know from Acts 20:28 that only the Holy Spirit is able to fit and qualify men to oversee in an assembly, and the assembly recognises the divine work in so fitting them. *Kathistemi* can have this meaning of pointing out. The *Theological Dictionary of the NT* in dealing with this word says that the chief thought in it is to recognise that the fitness or condition exists, rather than to impart it (Kittel, Vol. III, pp. 444, 445). The Lord imparts; men only recognise what God has done.

The seventy disciples sent by the Lord were to prepare His way (Isa 40:3-5), so their work was similar to John the Baptist's, to prepare hearts to receive their Lord; therefore it was a preaching to produce repentance. There are many similarities between the sending of the seventy and Matthew's much fuller account of the sending of the twelve (Matt 10: 5-42). Their mission was not to the world. The scope of their ministry was limited to the places where the Lord Himself would come, and "He came unto his own (things), and his own (people) received him not" (John 1:11). Being sent "two and two" shows the tender care of the Lord for the encouragement and support of His servants and is a display of His divine wisdom, for "Two are better than one" (Eccles 4:9, 10).

2   The great harvest has a Lord and labourers, but the labourers are few, even though the need is so vast that the most courageous must receive mercy from the Lord not to faint (2 Cor 4:1). There can be a vast difference between labourers and committee members, even in their number. These workers went before the face of their Lord, recognising Him as the great Overseer of the harvest (Ruth 2:1-4). In the field of Boaz, there was another servant, unnamed, but set over the reapers (v.5); he is a beautiful illustration to us of the Holy Spirit and His work in the harvest field. The prayer is for labourers, not just that they might go, but that they might be sent. It is the prerogative of the Lord of the harvest to prepare His labourers and to send them.

3   Lambs in the midst of wolves seem so unfair. How helpless they are! What defence have they against the teeth of wolves? Lambs are gentle, but they are also weak and defenceless. In this we are reminded of an all-pervasive principle, "God hath chosen the weak things of the world to confound the things which are mighty" (1 Cor 1:27). It is not by human ingenuity, worldly wisdom, skilfully-devised methods, large finances or strength of numbers that the labourers are effective. How easy it is to forget that in God's work only God's way is fruitful for eternity! Luke uses *aren* for "lamb", and it is found only here in the NT, but *arnion*, which is a diminutive form is the common word through the rest of the NT. W.E. Vine says, "the diminutive form is not be pressed" (*Dictionary of NT Words,* p.306).

4   The subject of the first part of this verse is encumbrances and reminds us of Heb 12:1, "let us lay aside every weight". The latter part of the verse deals with distractions. If they stopped to pass the pleasantries of the day with everyone on the road, they would be using precious time that must be spent in preaching their message. The word to all His servants is "redeeming the time, because the days are evil" (Eph 5:16).

The Lord was conscious that His days of ministry on earth were drawing to a close, and the places through which He would pass would not have another opportunity to hear Him. Because of the shortness of time, He sent His messengers with haste to the towns and villages to arouse the people and make them ready for His coming. The picture He draws is that of a harvest field, ready to be reaped. The messengers were announcing a kingdom long looked for in Israel, so they were worthy of being given the necessities of life and were no burden to anyone as they were in haste to fulfil their task. The work of the seventy is a picture of the work that will be done in the nation of Israel prior to the Lord's coming and the setting up of the kingdom on earth. Then too there will be a short time to gather the harvest before the manifest kingdom will be set up.

5-12 The seventy were sent with special instructions for an interim period of testimony prior to the cross and before the great commission was given by the resurrected Lord (Matt 28:18-20; Mark 16:15, 16; Acts 1:8). It is a serious blunder to suppose that these instructions are His final word on the conduct of His messengers. There are guidelines here for the attitude of servants toward those who receive them and those who reject them and their message (Acts 13:51), and these have value for all time, but these explicit instructions belong to a day before Pentecost.

In 9:5, the dust of the city that rejects the messengers and their message is shaken off; "shaken off" is *apomasso* ("to wipe off"), a word that is only here in the NT. The city that refused the gospel was unclean. "We do wipe off against you" indicates that the charge of rejection was laid at their own doors and an account must be given in the day of judgment. The rejection described here was repeated a short time later in Jerusalem when many of these people cried, as in the parable, "We will not have this man to reign over us" (19:14). We who will never share their doom should bow our hearts in thankfulness that though we often were deaf to His voice yet in longsuffering grace and mercy He continued by His Spirit to strive with us until we were saved.

5.   *The Pronouncement of Judgment on Privileged Cities* 10:13-16

v.13 "Woe unto thee, Chorazin! woe unto thee, Bethsaida! for if the mighty works had been done in Tyre and Sidon, which have been done in you, they had a great while ago repented, sitting in sackcloth and ashes.
v.14 But it shall be more tolerable for Tyre and Sidon at the judgment, than for you.
v.15 And thou, Capernaum, which art exalted to heaven, shalt be thrust down to hell.
v.16 He that heareth you heareth me; and he that despiseth you despiseth me; and he that despiseth me despiseth him that sent me."

13-14 It is only in this verse and in the similar passage in Matt 11:21 that the town of Chorazin, which is believed to have been two miles north-east of Capernaum, is mentioned in the NT. Both it and Bethsaida were on the north coast of the Sea of Galilee, and we learn only from these two sources that the Lord had preached and performed mighty works in them. His itinerary had taken

Him to every town and village of Galilee, so He did much that no evangelist has ever recorded (John 21:25). In fact, the privileges of these two towns would have brought about complete repentance of the great cities, Tyre and Sidon, that had formed the heart of the Phoenician empire.

These verses are of great importance in that they teach that there will be degrees of punishment meted out in the day of judgment and that these degrees will be according to light and privilege (cf. 12:47-48). It would be "more tolerable for Tyre and Sidon" than for Chorazin and Bethsaida. The rejection of the gospel by privileged sinners in this day of grace will intensify their punishment, as we solemnly sing, "Deeper down than Tyre and Sidon will the Christ rejecter be".

15   Capernaum was the nearest town to the River Jordan on the north-west of the Sea of Galilee The Lord described Capernaum as being "exalted to heaven" with privilege. This language touches our hearts, for truly heaven had come down to Capernaum. It was His own city (Matt 9:1), for when He left Nazareth He made Capernaum the centre of His labours (Mark 1:21; 2:1), but He was rejected there and His solemn words have been literally fulfilled. There is strong evidence that Tell Hum is the site of the former Capernaum. Excavations began there in 1968 and continue until the present. The workings point to a town long inhabited, in a very fertile region, with an excellent supply of fresh water, on a strategic part of the coast of the Sea of Galilee; yet it ceased to exist and for many centuries its very location was undiscovered. However, being "thrust down to hell" refers to the souls of its people, not, as some contend, to its geographical site, even though parallels may be noted.

16   To reject the Lord's messengers is to reject Him and His words. It is a solemn thing to mistreat the most lowly of His messengers, for all despisers will meet the charge of despising Him. We are reminded of the words that David delivered into the hands of Asaph and his brethren, "He suffered no man to do them wrong: yea, he reproved kings for their sakes; saying, Touch not mine anointed, and do my prophets no harm" (Ps 105:14, 15).

6.   *The True Causes of Joy*
   10:17-24

v.17 "And the seventy returned again with joy, saying, Lord, even the devils are subject unto us through thy name.

v.18 And he said unto them, I beheld Satan as lightning fall from heaven.

v.19 Behold, I give unto you power to tread on serpents and scorpions, and over all the power of the enemy: and nothing shall by any means hurt you.

v.20 Notwithstanding in this rejoice not, that the spirits are subject unto you; but rather rejoice, because your names are written in heaven.

v.21 In that hour Jesus rejoiced in spirit, and said, I thank thee, O Father, Lord of heaven and earth, that thou hast hid these things from the wise and prudent, and hast revealed them unto babes: even so, Father; for so it seemed good in thy sight.

> v.22 All things are delivered to me of my Father: and no man knoweth who the Son is, but the Father; and who the Father is, but the Son, and *he* to whom the Son will reveal *him*.
> v.23 And he turned him unto *his* disciples, and said privately, Blessed *are* the eyes which see the things that ye see:
> v.24 For I tell you, that many prophets and kings have desired to see those things which ye see, and have not seen *them*; and to hear those things which ye hear, and have not heard *them*."

17 The seventy returned with joy, reporting that even the demons were subject to them through His name. This was not part of their commission and suggests to us that as they went they had met satanic opposition, which we would fully expect.

18 The critical point for interpretation here is whether the fall of Satan is something the Lord saw in the present or the past. Did the overcoming of demons in His name have the same or a similar meaning as the final fall of Satan? and was it "as lightning"? The alternative meaning is that the Lord is speaking about an event in the distant past that He had observed. The former interpretation, that is, that the Lord saw in the victory of the seventy over Satan a preview of his final judgment, is very often suggested, but seems to me to lack a proper degree of relative correspondence. The success of the seventy was not to be a cause of rejoicing to them. Would not Satan's eternal fall be a cause to rejoice? See Rev 12:9-12, where even the casting down of Satan upon the earth is a cause of great rejoicing. The verb "beheld" is in the imperfect tense and suggests a reading such as "I was beholding". "Fall" is an aorist participle, and the RV translates, "I beheld Satan fallen", and this indicates, "I beheld Satan prostrate after his fall", no doubt true, but it is the event, "as lightning" that He is describing. The simple use of "fall", as in the AV, adequately translates *pesonta* and is, to my mind, descriptive of a great event in the past when the pre-incarnate Christ witnessed the fall of the mighty Lucifer from his exalted place. The Lord Jesus is informing the disciples of an event that He saw before Adam's creation.

If the view that we have taken is correct, that the fall of Satan is an event in the past, we have to ask, Why did the Lord mention it to the seventy? Two answers have been given to this question. First, to tell them that what they had experienced in casting out demons was to be expected, for the demons' leader was already fallen. Secondly, He detected a sense of vainglory in them because of their success and tells them this fact to warn them of the danger of pride. The latter is the more likely answer and can be seen in 1 Tim 3:6; the novice, if he is given responsibility too quickly, is in danger of being lifted up with pride, and of falling "into the condemnation of the devil".

19 The power, literally "the authority…over all the power of the enemy", that they possessed was given to them when they were sent and was greater than they had supposed. They had learned when confronted with the power of Satan that they had authority over him; he was not, as they said, "subject unto us" (v.17) but subject to the authority of their Lord. The contest was between this "authority" and "the power of the enemy". The key to the understanding of the treading on "serpents and scorpions" is the phrase, "nothing shall by any means hurt you". It was not an exhibition, as some claim, but a protection. If in the course of their service they were confronted with such dangers, they had protection (Acts 28:1-6).

20 "Notwithstanding" (*plēn*) marks a strong contrast. It is translated "but" sixteen times in the NT, but it is often translated "notwithstanding" or "nevertheless" as in Luke 13:13; 18:8, and 22:42. This last reference gives an illustration of its force, "Father, if thou be willing, remove this cup from me: nevertheless not my will, but thine, be done".

The Lord Jesus knew the temporary nature of the sign gifts, and would have His own rejoice in unchanging realities. It was a vital priority that their names were written in heaven. There are books in heaven, such as a record of sin (Rev 20:12) and the book of life (vv.12-15). Heb 10:7 may well refer to a book of eternity with a title page on which it is written, "I delight to do thy will, O my God: yea, thy law is within my heart" (Ps 40:8). In a changing world, there is great joy and quiet certainty in knowing that our names are written in "the Lamb's book of life" (Phil 4:3; Heb 12:23; Rev 21:27).

> "Let such as know no second birth,
> Labour to write their names on earth,
> My joy is this, that love divine
> On heaven's scroll hath written mine."

21 Luke is the Gospel of the Man of sorrows, yet it is a Gospel of joy and praise. In the circumstances of Jesus of Nazareth there was sorrow; in His spirit there was exultation. Many manuscripts have "Holy Spirit" here, suggesting a reading, "Jesus rejoiced by the Holy Spirit". Luke often refers to the power of the Holy Spirit in the life of the perfect Man. In this prayer of thanksgiving He intimately addresses the Father, but also gives to Him the highest title of power and majesty in the universe, "Lord of (the) heaven and (the) earth". This great God hides and reveals according to His divine will and purpose. The pride of the wise and highly intelligent men of this world unfits them to receive God's revelation in His Son, but the lowly, who are mere babes, receive it. It would be utterly unlike God and a tragedy for us if God's revelation of Himself were given to a few intellectual giants in our world. Paul gives an excellent commentary on this subject in 1 Cor 1:18-25. The Lord Jesus said that it "seemed good", that is, was according to the "good pleasure" of the Father. Paul wrote that it was "in the wisdom of God". The Lord Jesus exulted in spirit in this wisdom and good pleasure of God, and we likewise rejoice.

22   The "All things" that were delivered to the Son by the Father are not enumerated here, but John who wrote so plainly of the Son that was given (3:16) tells of many things that the Father gave into His hand (3:35). Not only was the work of creation (1:3) and the work of salvation given into His hand (17:4), but all judgment was committed unto Him (5:22), and "as the Father hath life in himself, so hath he given to the Son to have life in himself" (5:26). The works that He did were given to Him by the Father (5:36) and those who believe on Him are the Father's gift to Him (6:37, 39). They are called the sheep that the Father gave to Him (10:29), and He calls them "the men which thou gavest me out of the world" (17:6). The Father gave Him the words that He gave to His own (17:8), and the very glory given to Him by the Father He gives to them, yet there is also unique glory given to Him by the Father that He prays they will be able to behold (17:24). The "All things...delivered to me of my Father" reach back to the dawn of time and extend to the everlasting ages.

Nowhere in this Gospel does Luke come so close to the emphasis of John's Gospel as in this portion. Christ is seen here, as in John 17, speaking to the Father, appreciating the babes who know His salvation, and He, Himself, being the revealer of the Father as in John 1:18.

The Son has revealed the Father, He is the way to the Father, reveals the truth about the Father, and gives life from the Father to His own (John 14:6), but there is a unique sense in which only the Father knows the Son. There are excellencies and glories in His blessed Person that only the Father can fully appreciate. When we see Him as He is (1 John 3:2), He will not hide His beauty and glory from us, but they are so far beyond our comprehension that though we learn of Him forever, there will never come a point in the vast forever when there will not be more and more of His unfading glories to behold. Here is one blessed Person about whom it is impossible to exaggerate. The highest thought we have ever had of Him and the greatest words ever spoken about Him can never exhaust the wonders of His glorious Person.

> "But the high mysteries of His name,
> An angel's grasp transcend;
> The Father only (glorious claim!)
> The Son can comprehend."

> Josiah Conder.

23-24   He now turns aside to speak privately to the very babes to whom such great wonders have been revealed. The longing in the heart of every true Israelite was to see Messiah's day. The very prophets "inquired and searched diligently" in the very words they wrote, "Unto whom it was revealed, that not unto themselves, but unto us they did minister the things, which are now reported unto you" (1 Pet 1:10, 12). Humble Galilean fishermen were the recipients of the greatest truths ever revealed. God incarnate stood among them and they had come to know Him.

7.   *A Lawyer's Question*
10:25-29

> v.25 "And, behold, a certain lawyer stood up, and tempted him, saying, Master, what shall I do to inherit eternal life?
> v.26 He said unto him, What is written in the law? how readest thou?
> v.27 And he answering said, Thou shalt love the Lord thy God with all thy heart, and with all thy soul, and with all thy strength, and with all thy mind; and thy neighbour as thyself.
> v.28 And he said unto him, Thou hast answered right: this do, and thou shalt live.
> v.29 But he, willing to justify himself, said unto Jesus, And who is my neighbour?"

25 Lawyers were experts in the Law of Moses, professed lifelong students of the first five books of the Bible, but, sad to say, they spent most of their time studying the voluminous writings of the rabbis, in which were found detailed regulations for every aspect of the moral and ceremonial law, rather than Scripture. This lawyer "stood up" as the people sat around the Lord while He taught them. The word for "tempting" is used in the Lord's quotation from the LXX in 4:12, "Thou shalt not tempt the Lord thy God". Plummer says the word indicates that the lawyer is testing the Lord's knowledge. Certainly his attitude was wrong. He was not an earnest inquirer and there are three errors in his question:

1.   Ignorance about the identity of the Lord

2.   Thinking that eternal life could be obtained by doing

3.   Thinking it could be the result of inheritance such as being of the natural seed of Abraham.

26 The Lord Jesus dealt with individuals according to their need. When Satan tried to tempt Him He rebuked him from Scripture (4:12), but when the lawyer attempted the same thing He directed him to the law, about which he professed expertise. The second question by the Lord is not merely redundant. It has been paraphrased, "What is the effect upon you as you read it?". The rabbis had a formula: "What readest thou?" The Lord Jesus reached beyond mere academic study to ask a question that touches the affections and motives of the heart, and must be answered in glad and ready obedience: "How readest thou?"

27 The lawyer's answer included the physical, emotional, intellectual and moral aspects of man's being. Love for God should be with our entire being. This summary of the law must have been an accepted formulation. The Lord used it in Mark 12:30,3 1. It is interesting that the lawyer immediately went to the very heart of true law-keeping, love for God, rather than mere observance of regulations. Many who know that love is the real test are not motivated by it.

There is reference in the answer of the lawyer to Deut 6:3; 11:13 in the first part, and to Lev 19:18 in the second part. The first part was written on the phylacteries, which were parchments containing four passages of Scripture that were bound on the forehead or the left hand of men before morning prayers. The phylacteries contained Exod 13:1-10; 13:11-16; Deut 6:4-9; 11:13-21, so Deut 6:5, "And thou shalt love the Lord thy God with all thine heart, and with all thy soul, and with all thy might", was very familiar. However, the second part, "and thy neighbour as thyself", though so familiar to us because of its use in the NT, was not familiar even to many teachers of the law. The addition of these words from Lev 19:18 in the answer of this lawyer "indicates a deep knowledge of the law" (A.T. Robertson).

28   The commendation of the Lord was for the truth of the lawyer's words, not for the motive behind the question, which He well knew. This knowledge of what is in man (John 2:25) is behind the words, "this do, and thou shalt live". There are two views of this statement. The first one is that perfect law-keeping would bring eternal life, and the second, that eternal life cannot come from a legal system but results only from divine love. In one sense, both views arrive at the same point, that no man can keep the law unless divine righteousness is imparted, and no man can love with God's love unless it is implanted divinely.

In the first case it is claimed that the Lord is saying that it is possible to do right and obtain eternal life, but it must be a perfect, flawless righteousness, of which none is capable. This means of proving human depravity may be valid, and has often been effective, but it is not the normal method of Scripture, even though Paul employs it in Rom 2:6-12. Rather, "that no man is justified by the law in the sight of God, it is evident: for, The just shall live by faith" (Gal 3:11) is the usual argument of Scripture. Paul goes on to explain, "if there had been a law given which could have given life, verily righteousness should have been by the law" (Gal 3:21). The answer to what some may see as an enigma is that the weakness of the law was not within itself but in man's fallen nature (Rom 8:3). It is not possible to believe that Paul's teaching is at variance with his Lord's.

The second view, to which this writer subscribes, is that the Lord Jesus is not teaching some better form of legalism as being a way of salvation. His coming into the world was the death knell for every legal system, "Christ is the end of the law for righteousness to every one that believeth" (Rom 10:4). The lawyer's words were correct because he had appealed to love and not to a legal system for obtaining salvation. In simple language, "this do" means "show this love", and what follows proves the utter failure of the lawyer and the entire legal system of which he formed a part to manifest this love.

29   "Who is my neighbour?" is the lawyer's question and this should be kept in mind as we read the following parable. The word for "neighbour" has a wider meaning than the person living in the next house and the lawyer seemed to be aware of this, but that "neighbour" should be exemplified by a hated Samaritan had never entered his mind or the mind of his teachers. The lawyer had already suffered a damaging exposure. He had asked a question of the Lord with the pretence of an honest seeker, but had been exposed as one whose mind was already made up as to the answer. This exchange had put him on the defensive and he wished "to justify himself. *Plēsion* ("neighbour") literally means "one who is near", but the Jews had carefully circumscribed the meaning of neighbour with the definition, "one of us who is near", thus excluding Gentiles and particularly excluding Samaritans for whom they had great contempt.

8.   *The Parable of the Good Samaritan*
   ## 10:30-37

> v.30 "And Jesus answering said, A certain *man* went down from Jerusalem to Jericho, and fell among thieves, which stripped him of his raiment, and wounded *him*, and departed, leaving *him* half dead.
> v.31 And by chance there came down a certain priest that way: and when he saw him, he passed by on the other side.
> v.32 And likewise a Levite, when he was at the place, came and looked *on him*, and passed by on the other side.
> v.33 But a certain Samaritan, as he journeyed, came where he was: and when he saw him, he had compassion *on him*,
> v.34 And went to *him*, and bound up his wounds, pouring in oil and wine, and set him on his own beast, and brought him to an inn, and took care of him.
> v.35 And on the morrow when he departed, he took out two pence, and gave *them* to the host, and said unto him, Take care of him; and whatsoever thou spendest more, when I come again, I will repay thee.
> v.36 Which now of these three, thinkest thou, was neighbour unto him that fell among the thieves?
> v.37 And he said, He that shewed mercy on him. Then said Jesus unto him, Go, and do thou likewise."

We have just noted that the Lord is not answering a question such as was asked by the Philippian jailer, "what must I do to be saved?" (Acts 16:30). However, there is much precious gospel truth in this story and it has ever been a favourite passage in preaching. The Christ of redemption is the narrator and the care of the redeemed and the claims of the Redeemer can be traced in the story. The Samaritan gave to the wounded man good cause to love him, care to keep him and comfort in waiting for him. In looking at the Samaritan as a beautiful illustration of the Saviour, we can trace the journey of love, the depth of love, the look of love, the heart of love and the supreme act of His love. In looking at the wounded man, we see an apt illustration of sinners who have been accosted, wounded, stripped, robbed and left for dead by sin and Satan. His helplessness, healing, happiness and the house to which he was brought can be easily applied.

But let us not lose sight of the great contrast between the heart of love of the Samaritan and the hypocrisy of the priest and Levite which is the major theme of the story. A simple outline would be:

1. The hated name   — "Samaritan" (v.33);

2. The heavenly blessing   — "came where he was" (v.33);

3. The holy companion   — "took care of him" (v.34);

4. The house of care   — "brought him to an inn" (v.34);

5. The hope of his return   — "when I come again" (v.35).

30   The reader is urged to read the preceding paragraph for a general outline of the story which is often called a parable, and perhaps it is, but there is no reason to suppose that the Lord is not giving a true account of an event. "A certain man" allows a very broad application. He was likely a Jew, but the Lord does not say so. The journey to Jericho was a steeply descending road, dropping 3,000 feet from Jerusalem to the River Jordan, lonely and desolate for most of its seventeen miles, providing many hiding places for robbers who infested it. A more fitting illustration of the downward course of sinners, away from God, toward Jericho the place of the curse, would be difficult to describe. The thieves who met him, stripped, robbed, wounded and left him half-dead, aptly picture the activities of sin and Satan.

This wonderful story is found only in Luke's Gospel. How much we would have missed if this teaching of the Lord had never been recorded! However, there is another feature in these verses that is of deep interest. This section is rich in expressive language, and in vv30-41 there are fourteen words that are peculiar to Luke, most of them used only here. We will draw attention to them in commenting on the verses. The first of these is in v.30: *hēmithanēs* ("half dead") which is made up of *hēmi* ("half") and *thnēskō* ("to die"). The modern, casual use of the term "half-dead", often used as a synonym merely for being tired, falls short of expressing the condition of this man who actually hovered between life and death.

31   The priest happened to come by and seeing a man lying in the road, he was not certain if he were dead or alive. If he were dead, to touch him would mean defilement (Lev 21:1-4). How unlike was our great High Priest above who is touched with the feelings of our infirmities (Heb 4:15)! Pity and compassion must give way to ceremonial exactness, so "he passed by on the other side", as far removed from the defilement as he could be. The inadequacy of the priestly system is exemplified in his attitude. *Sunkuria* ("by chance") is only here found in the NT, but rather than being a matter of chance, as we use this expression, the thought is that without any design or intent of his own, the priest arrived on the scene in time to fit in with a sequence of events that exposed his character. *Antiparerchomai* ("he passed by on the other side") with the prefix *anti* is only here and in v.32 in the NT, but *parerchomai* ("to pass by") is frequent. Luke uses it in the familiar language of 18:37, "Jesus of Nazareth passeth by", but the meaning is just the opposite. The priest and Levite intentionally remained out of reach; the passing Saviour was within reach and call.

32   The Lord seems to be painting a blacker picture of the Levite than had already been given for the priest. He "came and looked on him", so if the priest thought it was a dead body, the Levite knew it was not; yet he was not moved with pity or mercy. Turning his back, he quickly removed himself as far from the need as was possible and went on his way. The primary meaning in the story is the tender mercy of the Saviour to a helpless sinner, but a second meaning is that we should act as the Samaritan did in showing mercy to the needy. Separation from sin and unscriptural practices must never be allowed to degenerate into isolation from need or insulation from caring.

33   It is said only of the Samaritan that "he journeyed". The priest and the Levite were there by coincidence, the Samaritan was there by purpose. His was the journey of love, for there are many ways in which he illustrates the Lord Jesus. He was a stranger on the scene and bore a hated name, but in his journey, he came to where the man lay "and when he saw him, he had compassion on him".

   We have noted in the introduction that journeys take on great significance in this Gospel, both actual journeys and the journeys that are in the parables. Luke uses *hodos* ("a journey") twenty times in his Gospel and twenty times more in the Acts. In the most of these instances, the AV translates "way", but three times in the Gospel the AV translates *hodos* as "journey" (2:44; 9:3; 11:6), and once "highways" (14:23). But this is the only use of the verb *hodeuō* ("as he journeyed"). As has been already suggested, the Samaritan was "in the way" of divine leading so that at this critical moment he arrived at the place where the wounded man lay half dead by the roadside.

34   The picture is vivid and touching. The Samaritan went to him and, stooping down beside his prone form, he poured oil and wine into his wounds, binding, or bandaging the hurts. This is not very far removed from modern first aid, but we can see beautiful truth illustrated in the look of love, the stoop of mercy, the oil of healing and the wine of comfort and joy. Strong arms reached beneath the wounded man and lifted him, placing him in the very place from which the Samaritan had so recently stooped. It does not require a fanciful mind to see Ephesian truth here: a sinner lifted and seated in the heavenlies in Christ Jesus. Then, the one who has lifted him becomes his companion along the way, conducting him safely to an inn where he "took care of him". What additional care is involved in this statement, we cannot tell. It reminds us of Rom 5, "And not only so" (vv.3, 11), but "much more" (vv.9, 10, 15, 17, 20).

Four significant words that are found only in this verse in the NT add much to this carefully drawn word picture. The first one is *katadeō* ("bound up"). It is used twice in this Gospel without the prefix: to describe the woman who was "bound (*deō*), lo, these eighteen years" (13:16); and in the clause, "ye shall find a colt tied (*deō*)" (19:30), but the prefix *kata* ("down") gives the binding a very tender meaning. It literally means "to bind down", that is securely, but in our idiom means to bind up, to bandage, to dress in the sense of giving both healing and comfort.

The word for "wounds" is *trauma* (pl. *traumata*) from which we get our English word trauma, that means a bodily injury, wound, or an emotional shock. *Trauma* is only here in the NT and helps us to understand the violence with which the man had been attacked. The "pouring in oil and wine" is expressed in a unique way. *Ekcheō* means "to pour out", such as the "pouring out" of the Spirit at Pentecost (Acts 2:17, "shed forth"). *Katacheō* means "to pour down upon" such as the ointment (Mark 14:3), but *epicheō* ("pouring") is used only here in the NT and literally means "to pour upon (into)" the very wounds that lay open before the compassionate eyes of the Samaritan.

The other unique word in this verse is *pandocheion* ("inn"). It is the normal word for a place of business along the road that caters to travellers. Pan ("all") means that it was a place where all were received. There was also provision made for cattle and beasts of burden (W.E. Vine, *NT Words*, page 261). In contrast, a *kataluma* ("guest-chamber", 2:7; 22:11) was a room in a private house that was set apart for the entertaining of guests. *Kataluma* literally means "to loosen down", i.e. it was the place where travellers unburdened their beasts and "untied their packages, girdles and sandals" (W.E. Vine).

35 The Samaritan was on business and must pursue it (2:49), so on the next day he departs, but not before he makes provision for the one he has saved. The inn is a place of care, a beautiful picture of a local assembly, and at the inn is a host, for an assembly is the place where the Holy Spirit makes His residence on earth. The two pence have been used to illustrate baptism and the Lord's supper, or the word of God and prayer, the twin sustainers of the believer, or the Holy Spirit and the word of God. But in each of these applications, it is very difficult to fit in the words, "whatsoever thou spendest more". I suggest another application, and this is all it is, an application, not an interpretation. It suggests to me the two gifts of evangelist and teaching-shepherd which are such a blessing to the inn until the Lord returns.

As was the case with *pandocheion* ("inn") in v.34, so here, *pandocheus* ("the host") is a word unique to Luke. There is an application of the meaning of the "two pence" which fits with the second unique word in this verse, *prosdapanaō* ("thou spendest more") of which we can be certain. There is a large price that must be paid by those who are engaged in the care of a local assembly and all who are brought to it, as the injured man was to the inn. The Lord gives present rewards to those who do this work and when He returns, He will give them a crown for all that they have spent in His absence. This care is mentioned in 1 Tim 3:5; the crown is promised in 1 Pet 5:3-5. *Epanerchomai* ("when I come again") is also used only by Luke, here and in 19:15 ("when he was returned"). Both its uses are in relation to the Lord's return and the day of the reward of His servants.

The last words heard by the man in the inn from the lips of his saviour were, "when I come again". Every time he heard the inn door open, he must have thought, He has returned. So the last words spoken by our Lord to His own were "Surely I come quickly". "We can almost hear His footfall on the threshold of the door."

36-37   The Lord returns to the question of the lawyer. He has fully answered it. A neighbour is not the person next door, but the one who shows mercy and compassion in need. We do not know the effect on the lawyer but there is evidence of an unchanged heart, for in answering the Lord he refused to use the despised name Samaritan, but said, "He that showed mercy on him". If he had been able to see himself, it was not in the Samaritan that he was pictured, but in the poor man who was beaten, wounded, robbed and left helpless to do anything for his own salvation. All those who would try to be saved by law-keeping must be brought to this place of utter helplessness if they are ever to be saved.

9.   *Bethany, Mary and Martha*
10:38-42

v.38 "Now it came to pass, as they went, that he entered into a certain village: and a certain woman named Martha received him into her house.

v.39 And she had a sister called Mary, which also sat at Jesus' feet, and heard his word.

v.40 But Martha was cumbered about much serving, and came to him, and said, Lord, dost thou not care that my sister hath left me to serve alone? bid her therefore that she help me.

v.41 And Jesus answered and said unto her, Martha, Martha, thou art careful and troubled about many things:

v.42 But one thing is needful: and Mary hath chosen that good part, which shall not be taken away from her."

38   From 9:51, we have pointed out that in His heart and purpose the Lord is journeying toward the cross. We know from 10:38 and 17:11 and at least three passages in John that He made several trips north and south during this period, but the significant fact is the journey to Jerusalem and Calvary. Bethany, the home of Martha and Mary, was only two miles from Jerusalem. Bethany is called "a certain village" here, and "a certain woman named Martha received him into her house". This may have been His first visit to Bethany, a place that became very dear to Him and where He spent some of His last nights before the cross (Matt 21:17). It should be noted that it was Martha who received the Lord into "her house".

39 The feet of the Lord Jesus are three times linked with Mary. In this verse she "sat at Jesus' feet, and heard his word", for it was the place of learning. In John 11:32 she fell at His feet as the place of comfort in sorrow and looked up into a face that was wet with tears (v.35). In John 12:3, she "anointed the feet of Jesus, and wiped his feet with her hair"; it was a place of worship. Twenty-one times in Scripture the feet of the Lord Jesus are mentioned. At their first mention they are pierced (Ps 22:16), and at their last mention, they are planted on land and sea, claiming it all for God (Rev 10:1-3). No university on earth can ever teach the lessons that are learned at those blessed feet. *Parakathezomai* ("to sit down beside") in the passive voice, is used in good manuscripts for "sat". Some texts have *parakathizō* as an active verb in the middle voice. The meaning is unchanged whichever text is used. *Para* means "beside" His feet, and this expresses the place of her learning, comfort and worship.

40 Martha was "distracted with all her preparations" (NASB). Her words to the Lord, "dost thou not care?", and her words about her sister, she "hath left me to serve alone", indicate a wrong spirit. Before we become over-critical of Martha, we should count how many times we have served out of a compulsion that was something less than love for our Lord. Even work done out of a sense of duty can become tedious and wearying to mind and spirit. The work may be done well and even manifest affection for others, but unless it is done in love to Christ, we have lost the joy of serving Him.

41 The repetition of her name "Martha, Martha", is a mark of love and tenderness. How well the Lord understood the heart of this faithful woman! It is of note that when the Lord's love for this household is mentioned, the order is, "Now Jesus loved Martha, and her sister, and Lazarus" (John 11:5). The two words, "careful and troubled" are more accurately, "thou art anxious and troublest thyself" (Dean Alford). This is an anxiety that believers should never entertain. Paul wrote, "Be careful for nothing" (Phil 4:6). The "many things" were not wrong or forbidden, but they had been allowed to take priority and to weigh on her spirit and this made them wrong. Everyone of us has a Martha within.

42 Some have laboured hard to prove that Martha had prepared a meal with many dishes and that the Lord is saying that one dish was all that was needed. How this can be made to fit with Mary's "good part", or "good portion" (Alford) has never been explained. The one thing needful was not one dish on the table, but to give first place to communion with the Lord Jesus. How easy it is to be bustling and busy in many activities, professedly for Him, and yet to miss the "one thing that is needful", sitting at His feet and hearing His word!

The Lord's words about Mary, "that good part, that shall not be taken away from her", teach that what she is doing will be her portion forever. There are services that will end on earth, but there is a portion which will be enjoyed in communion with Christ long after time has ended. Did not Mary show something of what she had learned at His feet when she anointed Him in view of His burial?

10.   *Teaching on Prayer*
11:1-4

v.1   "And it came to pass, that, as he was praying in a certain place, when he ceased, one of his disciples said unto him, Lord, teach us to pray, as John also taught his disciples.

v.2   And he said unto them, When ye pray, say, Our Father which art in heaven, Hallowed be thy name. Thy kingdom come. Thy will be done, as in heaven, so in earth.

v.3   Give us day by day our daily bread.

v.4   And forgive us our sins; for we also forgive every one that is indebted to us. And lead us not into temptation; but deliver us from evil."

There are many precious truths, introduced in the Gospels that are developed throughout the epistles. This growth of teaching in the NT is given solid support in such verses as Acts 1: 1,2, "all that Jesus began both to do and teach, until the day in which he was taken up". Teaching about prayer is a clear example of what T. Bernard called, *The Progress of Doctrine in the New Testament*. It is very strange that so many readers of the Bible believe that what they call "The Lord's Prayer" is the final word on prayer in the NT. In Luke 11 the Lord gave the most basic principle about prayer, "Ask, and it shall be given you" (v.9). He later taught that after His departure from His own (John 16:16-22) they were to ask in His name (vv.23-28), which they had not done when He was with them (v.24). There was to be a distinct change in their prayer after His departure, "At that day ye shall ask in my name- (v.26). This is a most important fact. The disciples who walked with the Lord were taught to pray, but their prayer took on new features after He ascended to the Father.

Later in the NT, it was taught that believers draw near within the veil, into the very presence of God in prayer and worship (Heb 10:19-22). We have confidence to come "unto the throne of grace, that we may obtain mercy, and find grace to help in time of need" (Heb 4:14-16), and this privilege is ours because the Son of God "has passed through the heavens" (v.14 JND). The disciple's pattern for prayer in the Gospels was for men on earth when the Lord was with them. It is not the final word on the subject, nor does it even conform to the pattern of the Lord's own teaching in John about prayer after His departure.

The disciple's prayer is not a form to be repeated by believers in the church age. In introducing this prayer, the Lord taught, "use not vain repetitions, as the heathen do" (Matt 6:7). In Phil 4:6, Paul taught, " in every thing by prayer and supplication with thanksgiving let your requests be made known unto God". This verse contains every word for prayer that is commonly used in the NT, yet not here, or anywhere else in the epistles, are we told to repeat the words that the Lord taught His disciples.

1 The Lord Jesus is the supreme example of prayer as He is of every virtue and grace. He prayed at His baptism (121); when He chose His disciples (6:12); when He was alone (5:16; 9:18), and when others were with Him (9:28). He prayed in Gethsemane (22:41) and when He was on the cross (23:34,46), and His prayers moved others to pray. He was praying and when He had ceased, a disciple asked, "teach us to pray". The emphasis is not on a method, or on a subject, or on a form of words to be used, but on the very act of praying. It may even be possible to know how to pray and yet never have learned to be a praying man or woman. We have no other record of John having taught his disciples to pray, but this evidence is all that is needed. John was a man of prayer as all godly men and woman have ever been, and his disciples learned from his example.

2 Reasons are given in the introductory section of this chapter why we believe that this is a prayer for disciples on earth while the Lord is physically present with them. It is a model of prayer, a pattern through which they can learn approach to God, proper reverence in His presence, and what is truly meant by prayer that is "according to his will" (1 John 5:14).

A problem about textual authority is before us in the readings from the TR that are reflected in the AV. It has frequently been pointed out that copyists attempted to conform the words of the prayer in Luke to fit the longer version in Matt 6:9-15, which was the general form used in repeating the prayer in churches. Darby, along with many careful, conservative scholars, follows a shorter form in Luke than is contained in the AV. The form that is found in Matthew was spoken by the Lord at an earlier time in His ministry. The Lord gave teaching about prayer at different times.

He began the prayer with a simple, intimate, reverent address to the Father, followed by five distinct requests. The first two requests relate to the divine Essence and purpose. "Hallowed" is a reference to all that God is in His holiness and all He has revealed Himself to be, and asks for a proper reverence in His presence. We should always, in addressing God, avail ourselves of every means of showing reverence. There are good and valid reasons to retain "thou, thee, thy and thine" and not to conform to the habit of addressing God by a common you' .

The second request, "Thy kingdom come", looks forward to the future, manifest kingdom. F. Cundick in his excellent book *The Kingdom in Matthew* refers to five aspects of the kingdom: in power, patience, present possession, profession and prospect. An understanding of these aspects is a great aid in understanding the teaching of the Lord in the Gospels about the kingdom. It has already been set up in the hearts of men, but it will come in manifestation when the King returns.

3   The petition for bread is a request to have the needs of each day met. In a day of material plenty it is easy to forget that all that we need has been supplied by God's bounteous mercy to us. Believers should continue to pray for daily needs and should not forget to thank God when they are received. The witnesses in the coming day of the Great Tribulation will truly look to God for sustenance because faithfulness to their Lord will have deprived them of shelter and food (Rev 13:17).

4   This statement has been understood by many to mean that our forgiveness of others is the ground of God's forgiveness of us. The forgiveness of our sins before God's throne is a result of the propitiation of Christ at the cross, whether we are speaking of "sins that are past", that is, in a past day, or our sins in the present day of grace (Rom 3:22-26). The thought here is that if even sinful men do forgive one another, surely a merciful Father in heaven will forgive us all our sins by sovereign grace alone. Again, we point to the time when this prayer was spoken and draw a contrast between it and our circumstances. We do not ask for forgiveness as believers, but "If we confess our sins, he is faithful and just to forgive us our sins, and to cleanse us from all unrighteousness" (1 John 1:9). However, let us not forget the principle that is here, often taught by the Lord (Matt 6:14,15) and repeated in the epistles (Eph 4:32), that we cannot be in the enjoyment of the Father's forgiveness or know communion with Him while we are unforgiving toward others.

"Lead us not into temptation" has also caused many a misunderstanding. "God cannot be tempted with evil, neither tempteth he any man" (James 1:13) is a divine truth, unchanging in any age. "Temptation" (*peirasmos*) in its various forms is the basis of every word that refers to trial or temptation in the NT. We understand from the context if it is temptation to sin, which originates in our own flesh (James 1:14), or trial or testing sent from God (James 1:2-4). The very word "evil" can mean that which originates in sinful hearts and from satanic devices, or a day of testing and trouble such as calamity or sickness. The meaning of "temptation" in this request for deliverance seems to be trial, not being tempted to sin. If, as some contend, the temptation here is to sin, then the request is that as disciples they will be preserved from circumstances which will give occasion to the flesh. Again, in tribulation days this request will have great significance for those who cry to be delivered from the evil one and all his allies.

11. *The Parable of the Needy Friend*
   ### 11:5-3

v.5 "And he said unto them, Which of you shall have a friend, and shall go unto him at midnight, and say unto him, Friend, lend me three loaves;

v.6 For a friend of mine in his journey is come to me, and I have nothing to set before him?

v.7 And he from within shall answer and say, Trouble me not: the door is now shut, and my children are with me in bed; I cannot rise and give thee.

v.8 I say unto you, Though he will not rise and give him, because he is his friend, yet because of his importunity he will rise and give him as many as he needeth.

v.9 And I say unto you, Ask, and it shall be given you; seek, and ye shall find; knock, and it shall be opened unto you.

v.10 For every one that asketh receiveth; and he that seeketh findeth; and to him that knocketh it shall be opened.

v.11 If a son shall ask bread of any of you that is a father, will he give him a stone? or if *he ask* a fish, will he for a fish give him a serpent?

v.12 Or if he shall ask an egg, will he offer him a scorpion?

v.13 If ye then, being evil, know how to give good gifts unto your children: how much more shall *your* heavenly Father give the Holy Spirit to them that ask him?"

5-8 It was customary in households to bake the daily supply of bread each morning. Unexpected company has arrived late at night when there is nothing left in the house to eat. Rather than send the weary traveller to bed hungry, the host goes to the house of a friend where there is bread and asks to be lent three loaves. The friend is in bed and is loathe to rise, but pity for the need of the host moves him, so that he arises and supplies the need. However, the word "importunity" suggests another factor in the simple story. The host will not go away; he shows great persistence, his need demands it, so he continues to ask until the friend sees no way to get back to his sleep until he arises and meets the request.

The word *chraō* ("lend") is only here in the NT. W.E. Vine points out that *daneizo- (6:34-35)* means to lend on security or with the assurance of a return, but *chraō*simply means to supply what is needed. There is an application of this parable that will be appreciated by all who attempt to teach the word of God to fellow believers or even to preach the gospel. "A friend ... in his journey" represents needy saints. Going to the friend at midnight reminds us of all who know what it is to cry to God even in the midnight hour for a portion to satisfy the great need. How thankful we are when we are given three major thoughts, like the three loaves in this story. *Anaideia* ("importunity"), used only here in the NT, literally means "shamelessness". The friend was shamelessly persistent. If the friend to whom the host goes represents God, then it is good to see that His children are resting with Him when and where He rests.

9-10 The story expresses human feelings, and even suggests some of the selfishness that is inherent in us. However, with God, there is no reluctance to give; He delights in showing mercy and showering blessings on us, but halfhearted approaches to God will bring no blessing. There must be a felt sense of need and a persistence in asking; this is a true "waiting on the Lord" (Ps 37:9; Isa 40:31). In this waiting, God is teaching us utter dependence. So the three verbs, "ask", "seek" and "knock", do not describe a one-time act, but a continuous attitude. God is always willing to give, but it must be a giving that is truly for our good and in a way from which we will receive permanent blessing. We ask for what we need; we seek for that which we have not and we knock when the door of supplies is closed.

11-12   Only answers that are for God's glory can be for our good, therefore, there are delays. The context here is the asking for genuine needs. If we ask otherwise there will be denials, "Ye ask, and receive not, because ye ask amiss, that ye may consume it upon your lusts" (James 4:13). A loving father will not give to his children a thing that is harmful to them, such as a serpent or a scorpion.

13   This is a lesson every gospel preacher needs to learn, for it is sometimes wrongly stated that sinners never do any good. Every such statement needs to be qualified by explaining that men are incapable of good that will please God (Rom 8:9) or purchase them a place in heaven (Eph 2:8,9), but the Lord Jesus taught that sinners do good deeds. There is a goodness that is merely human, man at his best, but even it is as " filthy rags" (Isa 64:6) in the sight of God, if it is offered in payment for salvation. Paul refers to it in Phil 3:9: "not having mine own righteousness, which is of the law". There is also a righteousness that is done to be seen by men, a godless goodness that was practised by scribes and Pharisees (Matt 5.20) and by the elder brother (15:29). On this important subject, we should read carefully Rom 10:33: "For they being ignorant of God's righteousness, and going about to establish their own righteousness, have not submitted themselves unto the righteousness of God".

The gift of the Holy Spirit in every other passage in the Gospels refers to the giving of the Holy Spirit at Pentecost, but He was not given then for the asking. This teaching of the Lord may refer to the disciples asking for the Spirit's help as they felt the need of His power. The Holy Spirit who was to be given at Pentecost is described by the Lord as He that "dwelleth with you, and shall be in you" (John 14:17), so the disciples were not strangers to His working prior to Pentecost, but the new condition was a permanent indwelling, which would be the experience of all believers (John 14:16,17; 1 Cor 12:13; Gal 3:2; Eph 1:13). It would not be scriptural to pray for the gift of the Holy Spirit today, but it is right to pray that He will work and move in power among us.

12.   *The Kingdom of Darkness*
11:14-28

> v.14   "And he was casting out a devil, and it was dumb. And it came to pass, when the devil was gone out, the dumb spake; and the people wondered.

v.15 But some of them said, He casteth out devils through Beelzebub the chief of the devils.

v.16 And others, tempting *him*, sought of him a sign from heaven.

v.17 But he, knowing their thoughts, said unto them, Every kingdom divided against itself is brought to desolation; and a house *divided* against a house falleth.

v.18 If Satan also be divided against himself, how shall his kingdom stand? because ye say that I cast out devils through Beelzebub.

v.19 And if I by Beelzebub cast out devils, by whom do your sons cast *them* out? therefore shall they be your judges.

v.20 But if I with the finger of God cast out devils, no doubt the kingdom of God is come upon you.

v.21 When a strong man armed keepeth his palace, his goods are in peace:

v.22 But when a stronger than he shall come upon him, and overcome him, he taketh from him all his armour wherein he trusted, and divideth his spoils.

v.23 He that is not with me is against me: and he that gathereth not with me scattereth.

v.24 When the unclean spirit is gone out of a man, he walketh through dry places, seeking rest; and finding none, he saith, I will return unto my house whence I came out.

v.25 And when he cometh, he findeth *it* swept and garnished.

v.26 Then goeth he, and taketh *to him* seven other spirits more wicked than himself; and they enter in, and dwell there: and the last *state* of that man is worse than the first.

v.27 And it came to pass, as he spake these things, a certain woman of the company lifted up her voice, and said unto him, Blessed *is* the womb that bare thee, and the paps which thou hast sucked.

v.28 But he said, Yea rather, blessed *are* they that hear the word of God, and keep it."

14-15   The casting out of the demon from the man who was dumb is briefly recorded by Luke, but the reason for telling it is to explain the controversy that followed about the power used by Christ. Baal-zebub, Beelzebub, Beekeboul is found in 2 Kings 1:1-6,16, a name given to an idol worshipped by the Philistines who lived in Ekron. Although it may mean "the lord of the high place", it was commonly accepted among the Jews as Baalzebub, "the lord of the flies", or as Baalzebul, "lord of dung", which were means of heaping ridicule on a Philistine idol. It is not certain if the Jews regarded this being as Satan himself, or one of his subordinates. He is called here the prince of demons (v. 15), and the Lord Jesus linked the name with Satan (Matt 12:26; Mark 3:23; Luke 11: 18). In whatever way the Jews identified Beelzebub, the charge that the Lord cast out demons through "the prince of demons" literally meant that He received His power from Satan, either directly or indirectly.

16   The Lord answered the question about Beelzebub immediately. This second question about a sign from heaven is dealt with in vv.29-32. The ones who ask for a sign are called *heteroi* ("others"), so they are different people from the ones who laid the charge about being in league with Beelzebub. The *sēmeion* ("sign") for which they looked was something out of heaven, some spectacular evidence of power as fitted, in their minds, the claims of Messiah. "Sought" is an imperfect tense, telling us that they kept on seeking. The gentle patience of the Lord Jesus under these circumstances might well fill us with wonder.

17-18   The Lord understood what was behind the charge. Once again Luke describes the Lord Jesus as knowing men's secret thoughts. An internally divided kingdom is laid waste by its own disunity, and a divided house will fall. If Satan rules a divided kingdom, or if he is fighting against himself, his kingdom cannot go on existing. Even the accusers should know that Satan would not be using his power to destroy his own kingdom. *Dianoēma* ("thought") is found only here in the NT and hence in this context means "a stratagem in the mind" by which they hoped to catch the Lord unawares. W.E. Vine uses the word "machination".

19   Some have thought that the Lord was referring to some of His own disciples as "your sons" who have cast out demons, but this is a most unlikely interpretation. There were Jewish exorcists who used charms and incantations to cast out demons. The argument is valid whether they were successful or not, for they professed to cast them out, and if casting out demons means to be in league with Satan, then "your own people" (E.V. Rieu) are also in his camp.

20   "The finger of God" does not imply that the casting out was done with ease; rather it was a display of the mighty power of God, and the kingdom of God had come upon them. The Lord's hearers would immediately have cause to think of the judgment of God against "the gods of Egypt", when the magicians failed to produce lice by their incantations and recognised the miracle done by Moses as "This is the finger of God" (Exod 8:19). The two tables of stone at Sinai were "written with the finger of God" (Exod 31:18). But the sense of the Lord's words are best seen in the light of Dan 5:5 where the fingers wrote words of judgment on the wall of Belshazzar's house. The coming of the kingdom of God meant judgment brought to Satan and all who allied themselves with him.

21   The Lord used five descriptive terms about Satan; his strength, weapons, palace, goods and peace. It is a great mistake to underrate his power: as "the wicked one" he lulls souls to sleep in his bosom (1 John 5:19); as "the god of this age" he blinds eyes (2 Cor 4:4); and as "a strong man armed" he binds his captives in chains that they cannot break. He has an arsenal, with weapons that are deadly. The world and all that is in it are his allies, and are used as weapons to hold his captives securely. As believers we are not immune from this great arsenal of weapons, for they include the pride, possessions, pleasures and popularity of this evil age.

   Satan has a palace with a room for every taste. In Acts 16 a prison was turned into a palace for Paul and Silas, but Satan's palace becomes a cruel prison for his captives (2 Tim 2:26). The saddest note of all is struck when the Lord spoke of "his goods". Rev 18 gives a list of twenty-eight goods that have value in commerce, and the last item on the list is "the souls of men" (v.13). How tragic to be numbered among Satan's goods! Satan does give a false peace that will be shattered at the coming of the Lord in judgment. This is the context in which we have viewed the coming of the kingdom of God in v.20.

22 This short parable compares a strong man with one who is coming who is stronger than he. We may apply this strength of the Lord Jesus to the power of His love, mercy and grace, but the context convinces us that it is the final overthrow of Satan and all his forces that is the correct interpretation. Perhaps the dividing of spoils can be applied to the release of those who were once the captives of Satan, but is more likely to have the same meaning as Isa 53:12 when the Lord Jesus, in the day of His glory, divides the spoils of His victory with His own. By this interpretation, we are not denying that it was at Calvary where Satan was conquered, his power broken, and his doom sealed.

23 An explanation of this verse is given at 9:49,50. We suggest that 9:50 is the correct attitude by which the service of others is judged, but this verse is a test of our own service. No person can be neutral; the claims of the Lord Jesus demand a personal response. The metaphor is taken from caring for sheep.

24-26 There is no suggestion that this man has been delivered from the indwelling evil spirit by the power of God. Rather, the spirit goes out and the man walks in "waterless places" (RV), where there is no comfort and no rest, even though he seeks it, and decides to return to his own house. Matthew gives us a key when he closes this teaching with the words, "Even so shall it be also unto this wicked generation" (Matt 12:45). As has often been suggested, perhaps the Lord is giving a brief history of Israel and of their present attitude toward Him. Demon power, behind pagan idols, was once a snare to them, but in judgment they were taken to Babylon where they tasted idolatry to the full and were cured of it. Now the kingdom of God has drawn near with all its blessings, but their pride and unbelief has left them in a worse state than ever. Many were stirred by the preaching of John the Baptist, and may even have turned from their wicked ways, but when the Lord Jesus was presented to them, they refused Him, stumbling over the stone that was so lowly when they were looking for a high rock (20:17).

The unclean spirit had gone out of the man, and he had wandered about and found no rest, but upon returning to his house, he found it different than when he had left it. The house being "swept and garnished" is not easy to interpret. The word *saroō* ("swept") is used in 15:8 for the woman who swept the house diligently in searching for the coin. The word *kosmeō* ("garnished") is the verb form of the noun *kosmos* ("adornment"). This verb is translated "trimmed" in Matt 25:7 and "was adorned" in this Gospel, when speaking of the goodly stones of the temple (21:5). The house was not empty of furnishings; it was certainly adorned, for Israel had much of the furnishings, but from Matt 12:44, we learn that upon his return, he found the house "unoccupied" (JND). This emptiness is a graphic picture of Israel without Christ, for the rituals and forms of Judaism were empty and meaningless without the great Antitype of which they spoke. Returning to an empty house, that is, to the forms without their fulfilment, the man goes and gathers other spirits, more wicked than the first. Emptiness is a very dangerous condition. Unless God takes possession of a man he is exposed to every form of satanic evil.

27-28 God Himself, through Gabriel, had pronounced Mary as "blessed" (1:28), but Matthew tells us that it was at this moment that Mary and his brethren "stood without, desiring to speak with him" (Matt 12:46). The Lord did not deny the truth of the woman's words, but added to them that all are blessed who "hear the word of God, and keep it". The Lord Himself followed the principle of true service that He had taught in 9:57-62.

Notes

Demons: Satan has a kingdom of darkness made up of principalities, powers and rulers of the darkness (Eph 6:12). In this kingdom of spiritual wickedness are numerous demons (*daimonia*), who are unclean spirits under Satan's control. Luke uses *daimonion* twenty-three times against Matthew's ten, Mark's thirteen and John's six uses. Luke alone uses the expression "an unclean demon" (4:33), but five times in his Gospel he writes about "an unclean spirit" (4:36; 6:18; 8:29; 9:42; 11:24) and twice about "evil spirits" (7:21; 8:2). We know nothing about their origin, even though it has been the cause of much speculation. According to *The Theological Dictionary of the New Testament* the origin of *daimonion* is not clear and may come from a root that means "to rend apart". W.E. Vine suggests a root that means "to know". They are Satan's agents in idolatrous worship, for though the idol may be mere wood or stone, yet behind it is demon power (1 Cor 10:19,20), so every pagan system to some degree gives worship to Satan. Demons do seem to have the ability to afflict man physically, as many cases in the Gospel records indicate, but the NT distinguishes between sickness and demon possession; see Matt 4:24 as an example. The chief sphere of demon activity is in the spiritual realm where they are the source of evil doctrines that deceive many (Eph 4:14; 1 Tim 4:1). They know their final doom (Matt 8:29; Mark 1:24), and yet their master is the father of lies and may even deceive them about this. Nowhere do demons display anything like the power that is at the disposal of angels (2 Kings 19:35), but at their head is a mighty prince of darkness whose power is very great, yet inferior to the power of the Lord Jesus (1 John 4:4). They have a penchant for inhabiting a body, and controlling the person; however no body that has become the temple of the Holy Spirit can be indwelt by an unclean spirit. It is interesting to note that no case of demon possession is recorded in Judaea, and this may explain why John does not mention any miracle of their expulsion. Satan changes his methods from place to place and even from people to people. He knows the form of deception that will be most successful whatever the environment.

13.   *Great Examples from the Old Testament*
11:29-32

v.29 "And when the people were gathered thick together, he began to say, This is an evil generation: they seek a sign; and there shall no sign be given it, but the sign of Jonas the prophet.
v.30 For as Jonas was a sign unto the Ninevites, so shall also the Son of man be to this generation.

> v.31 The queen of the south shall rise up in the judgment with the men of this
> generation, and condemn them: for she came from the utmost parts of the
> earth to hear the wisdom of Solomon; and, behold, a greater than Solomon *is*
> here.
> v.32 The men of Nineve shall rise up in the judgment with this generation, and shall
> condemn it: for they repented at the preaching of Jonas; and, behold, a greater
> than Jonas *is* here."

29   In v.16 there were those who demanded a sign from Him. He has dealt with
the issue of the authority over demons, and now, as an even greater crowd presses
around Him, He takes up the subject of signs. All His miraculous works were
signs of His power and authority, but "This ... evil generation" desired something
more spectacular. Perhaps they had in mind the overthrow of the Roman
domination, for Israel looked for a political Messiah, or it may be that they merely
wanted some spectacular entertainment. No sign would be given but the sign of
the prophet Jonah, and this was yet future, the resurrection of the Lord Jesus.

30   The emphasis is not on Jonah preaching to the Ninevites, but being a sign
to them, for he was a man who had come through an experience that was a vivid
picture of death, burial and resurrection. He stood before the people of Nineveh
as a living man with the marks of death on him. So the Son of man would be a
sign "to this generation" of the mighty power of God by which He would be
raised from the dead. This passage and many others in the NT look upon the
resurrection of Christ as the greatest of all miracles (John 2:18-22). The sign of
Jonah was chiefly his figurative death, burial and resurrection, yet it may also
include his going to the Gentiles. This is in keeping with what follows, for the
Queen of the South was also a Gentile.

31   The Queen of Sheba had come from a great distance "to hear the wisdom
of Solomon". A careful reading of the accounts in 1 Kings 10: 1 -13 and 2 Chron
9:1-12 impresses us with her search for Israel's God. The Lord draws sharp
contrasts between this seeking woman and the unbelieving men of this
generation. She was a Gentile without God, they are the chosen nation with the
divine oracles committed to them. She came from the uttermost parts of the
earth, but the kingdom of God had come to them; as Paul later wrote about
them, "The word is nigh thee" (Rom 10:8). She came to hear Solomon's words
and her heart was won to God; they have listened to the Son of man Himself and
have closed their ears. These witnesses, such as the Queen of Sheba, who will
stand up in the day of judgment suggest that there will be present at the great
white throne those who will not be judged, but will give evidence against the
impenitent. It also makes plain to us that those who have had less light and yet
were saved will be witnesses against those with greater light who rejected it.
    There can be no question that the Lord Jesus calls Himself the Son of man,
and to Jewish ears no claim could be higher than the words, "a greater than

Solomon is here". He was greater than Abraham, Jacob and Moses, greater than the temple, Solomon and Jonah. It is not only that the dominion of the Son of man will far outreach the lands over which Solomon reigned, or that the glory of His kingdom will be far greater, or even that the extent of His reign will be forever, but He, in His Person, is greater than Solomon could ever be. Far from being a lesser title than Son of God, "Son of man" is the divine title of the One who will have universal dominion and an everlasting kingdom (Dan 7:13,14).

32   The Lord has already said that the Queen of Sheba, in the day of judgment, will be a witness against the men of this generation, and now He says that the men of Nineveh, who repented under Jonah's preaching, will also arise to condemn them. "Behold", used about the greater than Solomon in v.31, and used here of the greater than Jonah, is a word to arrest the ear and fasten the eye on a blessed Object. He is greater than Solomon in His glorious reign and greater than Jonah in His suffering, death and resurrection. Jonah suffered for his own disobedience, the Lord Jesus suffered for our sake.

14.   *The Single Eye*
11:33-36

> v.33 "No man, when he hath lighted a candle, putteth *it* in a secret place, neither under a bushel, but on a candlestick, that they which come in may see the light.
> v.34 The light of the body is the eye: therefore when thine eye is single, thy whole body also is full of light; but when *thine eye* is evil, thy body also *is* full of darkness.
> v.35 Take heed therefore that the light which is in thee be not darkness.
> v.36 If thy whole body therefore *be* full of light, having no part dark, the whole shall be full of light, as when the bright shining of a candle doth give thee light."

33-34   What is the link between what has gone before and a man lighting a candle and hiding it in a cellar or putting it under a bushel? The Lord is still speaking to those who demand some sign from Him. They were saying, If He is Messiah, why does He not display His great authority and power? with the implication that His claims were false. His answer was that the light was truly shining, but evil had blinded their eyes, leaving them in utter darkness even though the light shone all around them. The men of this generation had impaired sight because they suffered from sinful blindness that was of their own making.

35-36   The eye that fails to see is now looked at as the eye of the soul, blinded by unbelief so that no ray of divine light is able to penetrate it (Matt 13:14-16). They stood in the midst of the full light of divine revelation. He had come to reveal the Father (10:22), but though they had eyes, they saw Him not. No wonder He said to His own "But blessed are your eyes, for they see" (Matt 13:16).

15. *The Pharisees and Lawyers Denounced*
11:37-54

v.37 "And as he spake, a certain Pharisee besought him to dine with him: and he went in, and sat down to meat.

v.38 And when the Pharisee saw *it*, he marvelled that he had not first washed before dinner.

v.39 And the Lord said unto him, Now do ye Pharisees make clean the outside of the cup and the platter; but your inward part is full of ravening and wickedness.

v.40 *Ye* fools, did not he that made that which is without make that which is within also?

v.41 But rather give aims of such things as ye have; and, behold, all things are clean unto you.

v.42 But woe unto you, Pharisees! for ye tithe mint and rue and all manner of herbs, and pass over judgment and the love of God: these ought ye to have done, and not to leave the other undone.

v.43 Woe unto you, Pharisees! for ye love the uppermost seats in the synagogues, and greetings in the markets.

v.44 Woe unto you, scribes and Pharisees, hypocrites! for ye are as graves which appear not, and the men that walk over *them* are not aware of *them*.

v.45 Then answered one of the lawyers, and said unto him, Master, thus saying thou reproachest us also.

v.46 And he said, Woe unto you also, *ye* lawyers! for ye lade men with burdens grievous to be borne, and ye yourselves touch not the burdens with one of your fingers.

v.47 Woe unto you! for ye build the sepulchres of the prophets, and your fathers killed them,

v.48 Truly ye bear witness that ye allow the deeds of your fathers: for they indeed killed them, and ye build their sepulchres.

v.49 Therefore also said the wisdom of God, I will send them prophets and apostles, and *some* of them they shall slay and persecute:

v.50 That the blood of all the prophets, which was shed from the foundation of the world, may be required of this generation;

v.51 From the blood of Abel unto the blood of Zacharias, which perished between the altar and the temple: verily I say unto you, It shall be required of this generation.

v.52 Woe unto you, lawyers! for ye have taken away the key of knowledge: ye entered not in yourselves, and them that were entering in ye hindered.

v.53 And as he said these things unto them, the scribes and the Pharisees began to urge *him* vehemently, and to provoke him to speak of many things:

v.54 Laying wait for him, and seeking to catch something out of his mouth, that they might accuse him."

37-38 Luke is the Gospel of the Friend of publicans and sinners, but even an invitation to a Pharisee's house for lunch is not refused. The astonishment of the Pharisees was not merely over a matter of hygiene; the ceremonial law of washing was given in great detail in the rabbinical writings. It professed to be a cleansing from worldly defilement rather than a washing away of dirt.

39 There is no time more difficult to be faithful in pointing out wrong than when a favour is being received from the guilty person. The Lord Jesus was a perfect Man in the midst of sinners and He was truly a light shining in a dark scene of sin. It is interesting that Luke says, "the Lord said unto him", for very often, though men did not address Him as Jesus, the Holy Spirit often speaks of Him as *Jesus* (10:21,30,37,39,41), but it is *the Lord* who speaks to the Pharisee. The outside of the cup and platter is in contrast with the hearts of the Pharisees. The Lord who sees all hearts says, "your inward part is full of ravening (extortion) and wickedness".

40   "Fools" is a very strong word. He is pointing out the folly of outward cleanliness while nurturing inner wickedness. The God who made them both can see them equally; therefore all the ceremony of washing was to be seen of men, and was not done as before the eye of God. What a powerful warning against all mere external conformity when the heart is not right with God!

41   This is a difficult verse and has received numerous interpretations. The main thought is that love and kindness shown to others are more important in God's sight than ceremonies, but giving money and food can be acts of kindness apart from God, or apart from a changed heart. The giving that is of the greatest importance is the giving of the heart to God without holding anything back. The other giving will follow and will be clean. The problem in the verse is the meaning of the clause, "and behold, all things are clean unto you". It must be understood in the context of the scrupulous rituals of the Pharisees for cleansing vessels (vv.38-39). It must not be taken as a licence to practise moral uncleanness so long as we are liberal in our giving. The Lord is teaching just the opposite: that out of a pure heart, pure deeds with pure motives will flow. Such a person will not be very concerned about the ceremonial cleansings held to be so important by the Pharisees.

42   The Pharisees showed great carefulness in giving tithes of the least valuable of the herbs that flavoured their food, but passed over justice and the love of God. To all such conduct the Lord said "woe", a word of regret and grief. They were over-occupied with trivial matters of paying tithes, which was not wrong, but was of far less importance than having compassion on the poor and needy and treating them with justice. We should not miss the point that the Pharisees took great pride in these meticulous scruples that they observed so carefully.

43   They loved prominence. It is a mark of fleshly nature wherever it is found. Their anger against the Lord Jesus arose from the fear that His teaching might take away from them their prestige, influence, power and authority as the religious teachers of Israel. They loved self and therefore hated Him "without a cause".

44   Unseen graves over which men walk unaware should be compared to Paul's picture of sinners having mouths that are as an open grave, sending out the stench of death (Rom 3:13). The Lord's simile is that whoever comes near them is defiled by them, so there is a great likeness in the two pictures. There is a great contrast here between men who are defiled unaware and the Lord who was fully aware of their sin and could not be defiled when He was in their company. He is the One "who is holy, harmless, undefiled, separate from sinners" (Heb 7:26). The Pharisees who had been so concerned about cleansing "the outside of the cup and platter" (v.39) are defiling all who come in contact with them. Like walking on unseen graves, many who were defiled by them were unaware of their defilement.

45 The Lord did not turn and attack the doctors of the law, who also belonged almost exclusively to the sect of the Pharisees, although there were scribes of the Sadducees as well. Instead, He was charged by the lawyer with insulting them also; "giving them outrageous treatment" is a fair explanation of the verb used.

46 A threefold woe against the lawyers follows. They compelled others to carry a heavy burden of meticulous law-keeping, but did not obey the law themselves; as clever lawyers, they found loopholes. In Acts 15, over the issue of circumcision for Gentile converts, Peter said, "why tempt ye God, to put a yoke upon the neck of the disciples, which neither our fathers nor we were able to bear?" (v.10). In v.28 it is called a burden, but it was never God's intention that law-keeping should be a burden. However, only with a changed heart can it be a joy. It was Israel who put themselves under the burden. The purpose of the law was as a mirror to show them their guilt, not as a ladder by which they should climb up to God (Rom 3:19). *Duobastaktos* ("grievous to be borne") is used only here. Some MSS have it in Matt 23:4. Not only is the burden very heavy and difficult to carry, but it is a burden that is injurious to the person on whom it is laid (W.E. Vine, *NT Words,* p.179). How aptly this word fits the burden of which this verse speaks. Another word unique to Luke is found here: *prospsauō* ("touch") meaning to touch slightly, to merely pass a finger over the burden without making any attempt to lift it.

47-48 When the prophets were alive their teaching was rejected; they were hated and many of them were slain, but after men are gone, it is safe to honour them. If the same prophets had been among them, they would have been hated and slain, for the lawyers proved by their lives that they were no better than their fathers who killed the prophets.

49-51 The Lord Jesus is not quoting from the OT or some lost book called *The Wisdom of God.* He who came from God and heard the words of God spoke as from God. He is just saying, God in His wisdom said. In Isa 9:6 one of the divine names of the "child born" and the "son given" is Counsellor, telling us that He was a member of the divine council that planned redemption and knew every word spoken in those councils. The Lord speaks not only of the sending of prophets, but also the sending of apostles, suggesting that this is a summary of the Jews' persecution of God's messengers from Abel until the time when the apostles will be treated in like manner. There is a reason why all these murders will be required of the generation then living, for all the others who were sent were servants, "But last of all he sent unto them his son" (Matt 21:37). In rejecting the Son, who is the Beloved and the Heir (Luke 20:13,14), they committed the crowning crime; therefore all the righteous blood ever shed is required of this generation.

The murders of Abel and Zacharias are the first and last murders in the order of the books in the Hebrew OT (Chronicles being the last book). Of the first one it is written, "the voice of thy brother's blood crieth unto me from the ground" (Gen 4:10). As Zechariah, the son of Jehoiada, the priest, the last victim in OT history, died by the commandment of king Joash, "he said, The Lord look upon it, and require it" (2 Chron 24:22). It is good to see how the writer to the Hebrews handles this matter of the avenging blood that has been wrongly shed. The blood of Christ "speaketh better things than that of Abel". Abel's blood cried for vengeance, the precious blood of Christ speaks of eternal blessing in a heavenly city (Heb 12:22-24).

52   The key which opens the door to knowledge, the knowledge of God and of His word, was Christ Himself. The lawyers rejected Him and did all in their power to discredit Him to the people. They discouraged anyone from learning the Scriptures for themselves, judging them to be incapable of grasping meanings which only they, the great doctors of the law, could understand. This is not unlike many today who take the place of being spiritual guides. However, the words of the Lord, particularly "them that were entering in ye hindered", describe men who deprived others of the key of knowledge, an expression that either means the knowledge of the Scriptures that speak of Christ or Christ Himself. In John 7:45-49, the officers had returned to the chief priests and Pharisees, saying, "Never man spake like this man" (v.46). The Pharisees answered, "Are ye also deceived? Have any of the rulers or of the Pharisees believed on him? But this people who knoweth not the law are cursed" (vv.48,49).

53-54   Vehement anger was the response of the lawyers (scribes) and Pharisees. They attempted to entrap Him as they would trap a wild beast, waiting for a word from His lips that they might use to condemn Him, not merely that they might discredit Him, but that they might kill Him.

The word that is translated "to provoke" (*apostomatizō*) is another of Luke's words used only once in the NT. In classical Greek, it meant to quote from memory. It came to be used for the instruction of a pupil, particularly drawing out of the pupil the lessons that had been previously taught. The scribes and Pharisees were extremely angry, so the AV "to provoke" gives the true sense "to excite to speak". It has ever been a tactic of the enemy to try to excite his opponents so that they will be off their guard in what they say. We must ever be on our guard against this tool of Satan and remain calm and unhurried under attack. The calmness of the Lord is beautiful to behold.

The closing verse of this chapter contains two words used only by Luke: *enedreuō* ("laying wait") also found in Acts 23:21 where it is used for the more than forty men who lay in wait to kill Paul; and *thēreuō* ("to catch"), normally used for the hunting and catching of wild animals (*thērion*, a wild beast). The intention of these scribes and Pharisees was no less vicious than of those forty who lay in wait to kill Paul; they sought to kill Christ. Perhaps *thēreuō* helps us to understand better than anything else could the attitude of the religious leaders to Christ at this time.

16. *The Warning Against the Leaven of the Pharisees*
12:1-14

v.1   "In the mean time, when there were gathered together an innumerable multitude of people, insomuch that they trode one upon another, he began to say unto his disciples first of all, Beware ye of the leaven of the Pharisees, which is hypocrisy.

v.2   For there is nothing covered, that shall not be revealed; neither hid, that shall not be known.

v.3   Therefore whatsoever ye have spoken in darkness shall be heard in the light; and that which ye have spoken in the ear in closets shall be proclaimed upon the housetops.

v.4   And I say unto you my friends, Be not afraid of them that kill the body, and after that have no more that they can do.

v.5   But I will forewarn you whom ye shall fear: Fear him, which after he hath killed hath power to cast into hell; yea, I say unto you, Fear him.

v.6   Are not five sparrows sold for two farthings, and not one of them is forgotten before God?

v.7   But even the very hairs of your head are all numbered. Fear not therefore: ye are of more value than many sparrows.

v.8   Also I say unto you, Whosoever shall confess me before men, him shall the Son of man also confess before the angels of God:

v.9   But he that denieth me before men shall be denied before the angels of God.

v.10 And whosoever shall speak a word against the Son of man, it shall be forgiven him: but unto him that blasphemeth against the Holy Ghost it shall not be forgiven.

v.11 And when they bring you unto the synagogues, and *unto* magistrates, and powers, take ye no thought how or what thing ye shall answer, or what ye shall say:

v.12 For the Holy Ghost shall teach you in the same hour what ye ought to say.

v.13 And one of the company said unto him, Master, speak to my brother, that he divide the inheritance with me.

v.14 And he said unto him, Man, who made me a judge or a divider over you?"

This chapter is packed with teaching. There are at least nine main subjects in the first 21 verses:

v.1	Defilement of leaven	Leaven of the Pharisees
vv.2,3	Day of exposure	Nothing hid
vv.4,5	Destination of the lost	Body and soul in Gehenna
vv.6,7	Definition of worth	God cares for sparrows
vv.8,9	Denial of Christ	Total denial by Pharisees
v.10	Danger of blasphemy	Expressing total unbelief
vv.11,12	Disciples persecuted	Brought before magistrates
vv.13-15	Delusion of materialism	True meaning of life
vv.16-21	Damnation of a soul	The soul required.

1   The AV translates *murias* as innumerable; more literally it means "the people in their myriads", and Luke adds that they were treading on one another to find a place within sight and hearing of the Lord. The teaching about the leaven of the Pharisees is also found in Matthew and Mark, but the reference in Matthew is certainly to a different time. There is every reason to believe that the Lord repeated certain teaching with variations that suited particular occasions. In spite of the crowd who were waiting in expectancy "he began to say" a warning to the disciples "first of all", that is, before speaking to the crowd, showing the high priority He gave to instructing them. The warning was very personal, "Beware ye of the leaven of the Pharisees, which is hypocrisy". This hypocrisy was an external correctness while giving license to secret evil. It also involved making rigid rules for others that they did not obey themselves. Leaven is always a type of evil in both OT and NT, invading silently, secretly, and not stopping until the entire lump of dough is leavened. Leaven puffs up, greatly increasing size without adding weight or value, and eventually it sours all that it touches, unless it is stopped by the heat of the oven. So the teaching of the Pharisees made them appear as very great, but their practice proved that it was mere emptiness.

2-3   In the clause "For there is nothing covered", *sunkalupto* is an intensive form of the verb *kalupto* ("to cover"); it means to wholly cover, to cover completely. However, the hypocrisy of the Pharisees will be completely exposed, but the Lord's teaching goes far wider, pointing out that a day of reckoning is coming when all that is unreal will be revealed. "Man's day" (1 Cor 4:3 JND) is characterised by great unreality, but the only success a hypocrite can have is to stay hidden. Exposure is the thing that he fears the most. The context of the Lord's teaching is not an exposure by men, but a day of judgment by God, when every hidden thing shall be made known. The subject of v.2 concerns inner thoughts and motives; v.3 describes words spoken in the dark that will be heard in the light, and whispered in private rooms that will be proclaimed for all to hear; so whether it is wrong motives or wrong words or acts "the light" will expose them. Because we are all sinners a day of full revelation is very searching and solemn. The believer has assurance that his sins have already been fully exposed in God's presence and dealt with righteously at Calvary, so that the record has been blotted out (Isa 44:22) and will never have to be met in a coming day of judgment (Rom 8:33,34). How good it is to have no fear of coming judgment! It is the subject of the fear of judgment or freedom from such fear that carries through the next verses.

4   "My friends" is an intimate form of address, used only here in the synoptic Gospels but clearly defined in John 15:14, "Ye are my friends, if ye do whatsoever I command you". The Lord Jesus was a friend to publicans and sinners (7:34), but to be called His friend involved moral likeness. The opposite of being His friend is found in James 4:4, "Whoever therefore is minded to be the friend of the world is constituted enemy of God" (JND).

The disciples are not to fear those who can kill the body, "and after that" (*meta tauta*, plural; literally, "after these things") have no more that they can do. The plural suggests all the tortures that persecutors are capable of inflicting on their victims. These words were spoken to disciples who would face the death of martyrdom. They are to remember that their persecutors have "no more that they can do" after they have killed the body; the thought is that they would do more if they could. The Lord drew a sharp distinction between soul and body. A key OT verse is Gen 35:18 where we are told that Rachel's soul was departing from her body at death. Most cults deny the separation of body and soul at death.

5 "I will show you whom ye shall fear" (JND) introduces solemn teaching about the fear of God. In v.4 the Lord has told them not to fear men; v.5 tells them to fear God and v.7 tells them not to fear. This seeming contradiction requires understanding. God is identified as the God who has authority to cast body and soul into *gehenna* fire. Bodies do not go to Hades, so the Lord used instead the solemn word that describes a lake burning with eternal fire (Matt 5:22-30; 10:28; 23:33; Mark 9:43-47; James 3:6; Rev 20:11-15). The Lord is dealing with the eternal salvation or damnation of souls (vv.4-10). However, the disciples are told to fear God, not "the lake of fire". This is not a fear of coming judgment, but a reverent fear of God that is compounded of a strong sense of His holiness, righteousness and justice and an appreciation of His grace. This kind of fear is quite compatible with enjoying His love and having perfect confidence of acceptance in His sight. It is this "fear of the Lord" that is the beginning of all true knowledge (Prov 1:7) that is most lacking in our souls and our age. For believers this is a holy fear of grieving the heart that loves us best of all. At the close of this verse, He who never uttered a redundant word repeated the exhortation, "yea, I say unto you, Fear him".

6 Matthew and Luke agree on the price of sparrows. Matthew said that two could be bought for a farthing (10:29), and Luke tells us that if two farthings are spent the buyer gets five. Sixteen farthings (*assarion*) were required to make a denarius (*dēnarion*, often translated "penny", 7:41; 10:35; 20:24). Even though these sparrows have so very little market value "not one of them is forgotten before God". Matthew adds, "one of them shall not fall on the ground without your Father" (10:29).

7 "Even the very hairs of your head are all numbered", continues the blessed subject that there is nothing so small that it is beneath the notice of our heavenly Father; yet we also rejoice that nothing is beyond His power. It is a wonderful comfort to remember that the Speaker is revealing His own intimate, eternal knowledge of the Father (10:22), and He is so great that He can stoop to notice the smallest need of His own. It was this revelation of God that caused Paul to write, "in everything by prayer and supplication with thanksgiving let your requests be made known unto God" (Phil 4:6).

8-9 Many understand these verses as being degrees of faithfulness in testimony on the part of believers. True confession of Him is the test of reality, and there is very practical teaching about witnessing in v.11, but the interpretation that agrees with the context is a denial of the Lord Jesus and His claims by the Pharisees and their disciples, and a confession by life and lip on the part of His own disciples. The denial of the Lord is doctrinal error (Jude 4). The verb *arneomai* is used of Peter's denial before the cross, but is never used of believers afterward. The test of 2 Tim 2:12 is a test of the real against the false. No true believer can deny the Lord in this sense today; only apostates do this (see 1 Tim 5:8; 2 Tim 33; 1 John 2:22,23; Jude 4). This is a denial of His deity and the value of His shed blood. The denial of the Master is moral error and apostasy (2 Pet 2:1; Titus 1:16), and is seen in those who are reprobate. Although no genuine believer can be an apostate, it is possible for believers to adopt at least some of the behaviour of apostates (Heb 10:25; Jude 20-25). To "be denied before the angels of God" means that in the presence of God the Lord will deny that these belong to Him, and they will perish eternally.

10 To speak "injuriously against the Holy Spirit" (JND) is not descriptive of a form of words that is uttered. When the Lord said that a word spoken against Him would be forgiven, He did not use *arneomai* ("to deny"), but *blasphēmeō* ("to blaspheme"). As christians we almost always use blasphemy as taking the Lord's name in vain, but there is a distinct difference between the two expressions, "speak a word against the Son of man" and "blasphemeth against the Holy Ghost". The usual significance of "blasphemy" in the epistles is not the use of swear words (1 Tim 1:20; 6:1; 2 Pet 2:2) but is a denial of the faith. This blasphemy against the Holy Spirit is not idle words at all, but a denial of the Spirit's testimony to the Lord Jesus. Apart from accepting the testimony of the Spirit there can be no new birth (John 13-7), so a person who rejects His testimony "lies under the guilt of an everlasting sin" (Mark 3:29 JND).

11-12 The subject of persecution goes back to v.4. These disciples will suffer for the sake of their Lord and the truth of which they are witnesses. Under the inquisition of their persecutors they were not to rely on human ingenuity but on the Holy Spirit to teach them what to say. These verses do not apply to preaching the gospel or teaching the word of God. There is no effectual preaching or teaching without diligent prayer and study. In fact, the words "take ye no thought" are the translation of *merimnaō* (literally, to divide the mind) with a negative. The Lord is assuring them that they need not be anxious or worried. This word is used again in v.22, "Take no thought"; v.25, "taking thought" (present participle); and v.26 "why take ye thought". In each case the exhortation is that they are not to be anxious.

13-14   The request of the man who desired his brother rightly to divide the inheritance with him is very far out of context, but we can learn a solemn lesson from this. The Lord is speaking of a day when those who are faithful to Him will be delivered up to the authorities, subjected to torture and a martyr's death. Breaking into this solemn teaching a man asked a question about getting something for himself. It must have been this failure to understand His teaching that was very trying for our blessed Lord. We may get very angry with the disciples when the Lord was speaking about His approaching suffering and they disputed about who among them would be the greatest in the coming kingdom (9:44 -48), but how easy it is to have the wrong priorities and to be attempting to establish ourselves in this world when the whole will be burned with fire! It was the question of the man that was concerned about his right to an inheritance that caused the Lord to give the teaching about the rich businessman that follows.

Notes

1   Leaven:
1. The leaven of the Pharisees was their doctrine of external religion (Matt 16:12) when inner reality was missing.
2. The leaven of the Sadducees (Matt 16:6) is interpreted for us by the Lord as being their evil doctrine of unbelief and denial of the supernatural (Matt 16:12).
3. The leaven of Herod is listed with the leaven of the Pharisees in Mark 8:15, but is likely very different from it. The leaven of Herod was political intrigue and double dealing, and a compromise with Roman paganism that had spread through every stratum of Jewish society.
4. The leaven that the woman hid in three measures of meal (13:21) is the principle of evil introduced into the professing kingdom of heaven. There is much evidence of this leaven in christendom today, but the whole is not yet leavened. The full and final results of this evil will be seen in an apostate church under the scarlet woman of Rev 17:4.
5. The old leaven of 1 Cor 5:7,8 is all that characterised the lives of the Corinthians before conversion, or the deeds of the old man (Col 3:9). In the case of the Corinthians it was moral evil (v.7) that had defiled the assembly (vv. 1 -5), and must be dealt with by excommunication.
6. The leaven of malice and wickedness (1 Cor 5:8) invaded the church at Corinth, affecting their relationship one with another, causing serious injury that was capable of corrupting the whole assembly. It had to be purged out.
7. The leaven of the Judaisers in the assemblies of Galatia (Gal 5:3-10) was a turning away from Christ (1:6) and the acceptance of another gospel, which was not another, but a perversion. This was doctrinal evil that must be exposed and denied (5:9,10).

17.   *The Parable of the Rich Businessman*
   12:15-34

v.15 "And he said unto them, Take heed, and beware of covetousness: for a man's life consisteth not in the abundance of the things which he possesseth.

v.16 And he spake a parable unto them, saying, The ground of a certain rich man brought forth plentifully:

v.17 And he thought within himself, saying, What shall I do, because I have no room where to bestow my fruits?

v.18 And he said, This will I do: I will pull down my barns, and build greater; and there will I bestow all my fruits and my goods.

v.19 And I will say to my soul, Soul, thou hast much goods laid up for many years; take thine ease, eat, drink, *and* be merry.

v.20 But God said unto him, *Thou* fool, this night thy soul shall be required of thee: then whose shall those things be, which thou hast provided?

v.21 So *is* he that layeth up treasure for himself, and is not rich toward God.

v.22 And he said unto his disciples, Therefore I say unto you, Take no thought for your life, what ye shall eat; neither for the body, what ye shall put on.

v.23 The life is more than meat, and the body *is more* than raiment.

v.24 Consider the ravens: for they neither sow nor reap; which neither have storehouse nor barn; and God feedeth them: how much more are ye better than the fowls?

v.25 And which of you with taking thought can add to his stature one cubit?

v.26 If ye then be not able to do that thing which is least, why take ye thought for the rest?

v.27 Consider the lilies how they grow: they toil not, they spin not; and yet 1 say unto you, that Solomon in all his glory was not arrayed like one of these.

v.28 If then God so clothe the grass, which is to day in the field, and to morrow is cast into the oven; how much more *will he clothe* you, O ye of little faith?

v.29 And seek not ye what ye shall eat, or what ye shall drink, neither be ye of doubtful mind.

v.30 For all these things do the nations of the world seek after: and your Father knoweth that ye have need of these things.

v.31 But rather seek ye the kingdom of God; and all these things shall be added unto you.

v.32 Fear not, little flock; for it is your Father's good pleasure to give you the kingdom.

v.33 Sell that ye have, and give aims; provide yourselves bags which wax not old, a treasure in the heavens that faileth not, where no thief approacheth, neither moth corrupteth.

v.34 For where your treasure is, there will your heart be also."

15   This most important statement gets to the very root of the evil of covetousness, which is literally a "lust for things"; these things are idols that displace God in the heart and life (Col 3:5,6) and cause souls to be damned, as the following account explains. The Lord's summary of a life is most tragic or most blessed. He summed up the life of another rich man in one brief sentence (16:19). All of human history and all our personal experience teach us the truth of the Lord's words. When man, with his eternal soul, attempts to make life out of the possessions he can gain, he comes to disappointment, emptiness, despair and eternal loss. The present world, devoid of meaning for so many who live for it, gives powerful testimony to the truth of the Lord's words. Prefaced by "Take heed, and beware", the Lord makes this warning very personal and pointed. "Beware" means to stand guard against the vicious attack of a deadly foe. A similar warning is given by Paul against those who "will be rich" (1 Tim 6:9).

16-17 The parable of this wise and successful businessman has been one of the most fruitful sources of solemn, searching warnings to careless sinners who live for time and forget eternity. Those of us who have spent most of our lives preaching the gospel read the word of God with gospel messages in mind, so the reader will find some outline material for the gospel in the treatment of this portion and in a number of other such sections throughout this book. The outlines have very limited value, but from them the reader may develop his own way of handling the material.

The man in the parable is called a rich farmer, but every successful farmer is also a successful businessman, so whether he worked the fields, or was the owner of fields worked by others, the crops were so abundant that his storage was insufficient to the point of requiring new barns. The verb *euphoreo* ("brought forth plentifully") is used only here in the NT, but from it has been derived the English word euphoria which means to be in high spirits or have a feeling of great well-being.

18-20 His plans were wise and well-conceived and would have been successful for time, except for God's intervention in his affairs. The man who left God out found that God intervened without an invitation. The rich man's fatal mistake was that he laid careful plans for his eternal soul, but forgot God and eternity. It is significant that he spoke of his goods first and his soul last. God spoke of his soul first and his goods afterward. He spent his last night on earth planning for a future life of ease, plenty and pleasure which he would never live to see. All his interests were temporal; he showed total indifference to eternity, a fatal mistake that cost him his soul, for he was but a step from death.

This rich man spent his last night on earth in great plans; Belshazzar spent his last night in great pleasures (Dan 5:1-4), but Jacob and many other saints have spent their last night in great peace (Gen 48:1-4). From all we know of the story, the rich man laid his head on his pillow that night without a tremor of fear, but already the words had gone forth from the throne of God, "this night thy soul shall be required of thee" (v.20). He knew nothing of the fear of v.5. The verb *apaiteo* (require) indicates a rightful claim and reminds us of the words of Job: "In whose hand is the soul of every living thing, and the breath of all mankind" (Job 12:10). The construction of the sentence allows a translation, "they require thy soul", but this was a common way of expressing an action of God and should not be thought to mean that demons or spirits required his soul.

21 The solemn lesson is now applied. It is possible to be very wise for time but a fool for eternity, and it is possible to be a rich man in time and in poverty forever. The great contrast is between a man viewing time in the light of time and viewing time in the light of eternity. It is described as the difference between laying up treasure for self and being rich toward God. This verse must be understood in light of the Lord's teaching about priorities. It does not negate the value of the advice of Joseph to Pharaoh (Gen 41:33-36). To make provision for the need of our homes and families is required of a believer (1 Thess 4:11-12), but we must not make material possessions a primary goal in life (vv. 15,31; Matt 6:33).

22-23   We learn at this point that the parable about the rich man had been spoken to the great crowd that had assembled, for once more the Lord turns to His disciples. The teaching in vv.22-34 is closely linked with the subject of covetousness that began in v.13, but the emphasis now is not on the lust of things but on allowing the cares and legitimate needs of life to hold too prominent a place. As greed, the desire to have too much, can displace God and eternity in the life, so a fear of not having enough can do likewise. Paul wrote to the Corinthians, "I would have you without carefulness" (1 Cor 7:32), and to the Philippians, "Be careful for nothing" (4:6).

"Take no thought" is not a precise translation, nor does it agree with the teaching of the Lord in many other places, nor the Spirit's teaching in the epistles. A husband and father must take thought for the provisions needed in his household, and if he does not do so he is worse than an unbeliever (1 Tim 5:8). As in v.11, "Take (no) thought", *merimnaō* means to be anxious, worried or fretful. To be burdened down with worry over the need of food and clothing is unbecoming for those who have trusted their eternal wellbeing to God. He who is able to save the soul can surely meet the needs of the body.

24   It is significant that the Lord used ravens as an illustration of God's care of His own. They were unclean birds, unfit for the food of a redeemed people (Deut 14:14); yet they brought food to sustain Elijah in the famine (1 Kings 17:4-6), and God provides their food (Ps 147:9). Perhaps it is this latter verse that the Lord had in mind in using ravens as an illustration of the benevolence of the Creator, who provides even for unclean birds who do not lay up any stores for themselves. Surely His own are worth far more than many such birds.

25   Again the Lord uses the word for anxiety from v.22 to speak of the impossibility of adding to height or to length of days. A cubit is about eighteen inches, so the impossibility of effecting such an increase in height is obvious. The expression can also mean to add to length of life, which may be more in keeping with the context; if this rendering is adopted there is difficulty in interpreting the cubit. However, Ps 39:5 measures life as a hand breadth, so adding a cubit to it means to extend it a little. It is almost impossible to think of adding a cubit to the stature as "doing that which is least" (v.26), so the adding to length of days seems to be the better interpretation.

26 The impossibility of man being able to add to his length of days is now used to apply to day-to-day needs. There is to be no anxiety about the means by which life is maintained. The quiet confidence of the disciple in the unfailing provision from the hand of his heavenly Father should silence every fear. Sometimes older, sick or handicapped christians are kept in a constant state of worry by the fear of being unable to support themselves to the end of their days. How good it is to know that God is faithful, so we can trust Him for whatever contingency arises, and stop being anxious about it.

27 God's provision will not be niggardly. A hand-to-mouth existence is wonderful if it is God's hand and our mouth. The lilies are clothed by His hand. They do not manufacture cloth and yet are clothed by the hand of God with such glory that even Israel's most glorious monarch could not rival them. The Father has reserved the best robe for those He forgives (15:22).

28-29 It is difficult to identify the exact flowers that the AV calls "lilies" in v.27, but evidently it was a common flower of the field. How often, when we have stooped to examine closely the most ordinary of them, have we been amazed at their intricate design and delicate beauty.

The expression "O ye of little faith" is literally "little-faiths", a plural descriptive term. When we consider the goodness and mercy of God to us, we bow our hearts with shame that the name "little-faiths" still applies, for we are often anxious and at times our joy and even our usefulness are seriously hindered by our worries. The expression "doubtful mind" again uses the word for anxiety. An anxious mind is a burdened mind, a distracted mind, that is too full of worry to be receptive to the Holy Spirit and the word.

30 The believer is not to see time as does a worldling, nor is he to seek the things on which a worldling sets his heart. He is not to be anxious about temporal needs because the Father knows all his needs. How good it is to be assured that He knows, even if not a person beside knows or understands!

31 As in Matt 6:24-34 the kingdoms of the world are set in contrast to the kingdom of God. Whether it is a matter of serving a master, securing possessions or seeking a kingdom, there is a principle of first things. This priority is stated in Matt 6:33 and clearly implied in this verse. To "seek the kingdom of God" obviously does not mean to seek to enter it, for this is a gift from the Father (v.32). It means to give it priority, making it our goal in life, the very purpose of our being; to seek its righteousness, its growth and its full manifestation as expressed in the prayer (11:2). This verse is very similar to Matt 6:33, but Luke does not have "first", "his righteousness" nor "all". However, these principles of priority, true righteousness and full supply can be found in vv.24-30.

32   It takes honesty to admit our fears or even that we fear at all, but the Lord who knows our inmost needs knows that we are creatures who are prone to fear. The blessed "fear not's" of this chapter are precious to us, for it begins with the light of His presence, but God has removed the fear from what His light has revealed. The first four messages from heaven in the NT are four "fear not's", and all but one are in Luke (Matt 1: 20; Luke 1:13,30; 2:10).

"Little flock" suggests a beautiful picture of a loving shepherd taking care of a little flock. This "little flock" comprised the company of disciples, but the diminutive word for flock that is used here is found four times in the NT as a descriptive term for an assembly of believers (Acts 20:28,29; 1 Pet 5:2,3). It is so like our God to give without reluctance and without limit. As a form of address, "Fear not, little flock" is found nowhere else in the NT. The uniqueness of this expression helps us to appreciate its value. As a "little flock" they are dear to the heart of the tender Shepherd, and dear to the heart of the Father who takes pleasure in giving them the kingdom as a gift. This is a very important statement in NT kingdom teaching. The kingdom is not attained by any human effort, but received as a gift.

33-34   *Anakleiptos* ("that faileth not") is used only here in the NT as an adjective. A verb form (*ekleipō*) without the negative is used in 16:9 of the failing of life; in 22:32 in the Lord's prayer for Peter: "But I have prayed for thee that thy faith fail not"; and in 23:45 of the cause of the darkness that descended when the Lord of Glory hung on the cross: "And the sun was darkened (the sun failed)". What a contrast there is between the failing sun as the Saviour suffered and the unfailing treasures of heaven!

This is a summary of the Lord's teaching about earthly possessions. They are never to control the believer, or to be allowed to reign in the heart. The believer is cheerfully to give of his possessions to meet the needs of others, that is, "give alms"; his chief aim in life is to lay up treasure above, for unlike all the corruptible treasures of earth, heaven's treasure will never lose its value. Our true treasure is the Lord Jesus (Col 2:3) and He is now in heaven; therefore we are to set our affection on things above (Col 3:1). We also have the treasure in earthen vessels, for we have Christ and all the precious truths that relate to Him to enjoy and proclaim to others (2 Cor 4:5-7).

18.   *Men that Wait for their Lord*
12:35-40

v.35   "Let your loins be girded about, and *your* lights burning;
v.36   And ye yourselves like unto men that wait for their lord, when he will return from the wedding; that when he cometh and knocketh, they may open unto him immediately.
v.37   Blessed are those servants, whom the lord when he cometh shall find watching: verily I say unto you, that he shall gird himself, and make them to sit down to meat, and will come forth and serve them.

> v.38 And if he shall come in the second watch, or come in the third watch, and find *them* so, blessed are those servants.
> v.39 And this know, that if the goodman of the house had known what hour the thief would come, he would have watched, and not have suffered his house to be broken through.
> v.40 Be ye therefore ready also: for the Son of man cometh at an hour when ye think not."

35   The picture is of the Passover night in Egypt. The lamb has been slain and, in the houses sheltered by blood, each Hebrew stands with his loins girded, waiting for marching orders. This should be the attitude of all who wait for their Lord (v.36).

The Lord Jesus Himself, as the girded Servant of Jehovah, is the supreme example, " And righteousness shall be the girdle of his loins, and faithfulness the girdle of his reins" (Isa 11:5). As the girded Christ in John 13 He stooped in wondrous grace to wash the feet of His disciples. Perhaps the first principle in girded loins is readiness (1 Pet 1:13), but there is also the evidence of fitness, lowliness (girded with humility, 1 Pet 5:5), and willingness for service. This will be the attitude of the remnant in the coming day of tribulation. These things ought also to be true of us as we wait for our Lord.

"Burning lamps" tell of a dark night and the longing for the dawning of a blessed day: "And he shall be as the light of the morning, when the sun riseth, even a morning without clouds" (2 Sam 23:4). Lamps speak of testimony, trimmed and burning brightly, even though the night is so dark and hearts cry, "Lord, how long?". "Hold the fort for I am coming, Jesus signals still, Send the answer back to heaven, By thy grace we will.'?

36   This coming is to earth and in judgment, but even so the waiting is not for an event, no matter how glorious it will be; nor even for a kingdom of perfect righteousness, which will satisfy every need for perfect rule that has been absent from all human government; nor even for a blessed rest after weary toil; the anticipation is "their lord"; He is the Object of the longing of every heart. A treasure draws them (v.34), truth girds them (v.35), testimony occupies them (v.35), but the transport that awaits them is "the Lord himself". The two epistles that deal most fully with the truth of the coming of the Lord to the air speak about waiting. 1 Corinthians speaks of saints who wait expectantly (1:7), an attitude that results in godly conduct. 1 Thessalonians speaks of saints who wait with patience (1:9-10), an attitude that results in courage against the foe.

37   It has been suggested in the comments on v.35 that the girded Christ is a reference to the OT, where He is the faithful and righteous Servant of Jehovah (Isa 11:23; 42:1-7). In the days of His humiliation He "took upon him the form of a servant?" (Phil 2:7) and manifested true servant character, but even in the day of His glory He will not have ceased to be the true Servant. To those who are found watching when He comes will the great honour be granted to sit down at His table and He Himself will serve them, even as He served them that day on the shore of the sea, meeting all their need (John 21:13). This eternal character as the perfect Servant explains for us the use of *morphē* in Phil 2:7, for this word is always the display of essential nature, not a display of temporal features. In the incarnation the Lord Jesus became what He forever will be.

38   The Romans divided the night into four watches and in such passages as Matt 14:25 and Mark 6:48 the Roman reckoning is used. Here the entire night is divided into the three watches familiar to Jews (Jud 7:19). The force of the Lord's statement is that the servant is blessed who is found watching, no matter how soon his Lord comes or how long He may tarry. The hour of His coming is not known and watchfulness is to characterise those who wait. The subject in this passage is the return of the Son of man. As believers of the church age we wait for the Lord from heaven (1 Thess 1: 10) who will come to the air for His own (1 Thess 4:16,17), but the truth of imminence applies to both phases of His return. The great need to be ready has an urgent application to both saint and sinner, to Israel and the church.

39   This is a very brief parable and must be understood in the light of its context. No householder would have his house broken into if he knew when the thief was coming. The chief thought is that the thief comes at an unexpected hour. It cannot be correct to interpret that the Lord will come to His own as a thief in the night when Paul, Peter and John say that it is in judgment on the ungodly that He will so come (1 Thess 5:2; 2 Pet 3: 10; Rev 16:15). The good man is the master of the house, and the word does not imply any sense of godly goodness. Paul teaches that the day of the Lord will come as a thief in the night, "But ye, brethren, are not in darkness, that that day should overtake you as a thief" (1 Thess 5:4), so the Lord does not come as a thief to His own. This warning by the Lord is general, teaching the suddenness of His return, and the great necessity of being ready. It is not really necessary to make a positive identification of the householder.

40   The reason for interpreting the parable as a general warning to be ready is seen in this verse, for the Lord applies the principle of being ready (prepared) to His own disciples. Indeed, the entire section has had this as its major theme. The rich man was well prepared for time but totally unprepared for eternity, so "Be ye therefore ready also" must be understood in this context. Applications to a believer's heart and life are certainly appropriate, but the main teaching is to be prepared for a day of judgment. Throughout the passage there is on the one hand those who are "cast into hell" (v.5) and on the other, those who seek the kingdom of God (v.31), wait for the coming of their Lord (v.36), and will be blessed in their watching for Him (v.37).

19.   *The Parable of the Steward*
        12:41-48

> v.41 "Then Peter said unto him, Lord, speakest thou this parable unto us, or even to all?
> v.42 And the Lord said, Who then is that faithful and wise steward, whom *his* lord shall make ruler over his household, to give *them their* portion of meat in due season?
> v.43 Blessed *is* that servant, whom his lord when he cometh shall find so doing.
> v.44 Of a truth I say unto you, that he will make him ruler over all that he hath.
> v.45 But and if that servant say in his heart, My lord delayeth his coming; and shall begin to beat the menservants and maidens, and to eat and drink, and to be drunken;
> v.46 The lord of that servant will come in a day when he looketh not for *him*, and at an hour when he is not aware, and will cut him in sunder, and will appoint him his portion with the unbelievers.
> v.47 And that servant, which knew his lord's will, and prepared not *himself*, neither did according to his will, shall be beaten with many *stripes*.
> v.48 But he that knew not, and did commit things worthy of stripes, shall be beaten with few *stripes*. For unto whomsoever much is given, of him shall be much required: and to whom men have committed much, of him they will ask the more."

41   About which parable is Peter asking? The parable of the rich man was spoken to all (v.16), but at v.22 the Lord addressed the disciples specifically, and v.32 leaves us in no doubt that He is speaking to the little band of faithful disciples. There is a mini-parable in v.39, but the answer of the Lord to Peter's question makes it clear that He understood Peter to be referring to the watchful servants (vv35-38). In these four verses parabolic language is employed even though much of it can be understood literally. The Lord's answer also indicates that the warning of being watchful applies to all, even to the disciples.

42-44   The parable of "that faithful and wise steward" contains very valuable teaching about stewardship. It is paralleled by Paul's teaching in 1 Cor 4:1-5. Both passages contain four great principles of stewardship, and in both the Lord is absent but His return is expected at any moment.

1.   Authority   Luke 12 "his lord"
                          1 Cor 4 "he that judgeth me is the Lord"

2.   Reliability   Luke 12 "faithful and wise"
                          1 Cor 4 "that a man be found faithful"

3.   Responsibility   Luke 12 "give them their portion of meat"
                          1 Cor 4 "the mysteries of God"

4.   Accountability Luke 12 "when he cometh shall find"
                             1 Cor 4 "be found".

This bond servant is appointed over the household, not to lord it over the other servants (1 Pet 5:2-4) but to provide for the needs of each one "in due season". This latter phrase normally is used to convey the thought of God's full provision for man's need (Rom 5:6; 1 Tim 2:6; Titus 1:3). Into the bond servant's hands has been entrusted the goods of his Lord to be dispensed according to his Lord's will. God has committed to men the care and feeding of His people in every age. The overseers, shepherds and teachers of assemblies have a God-given responsibility "to feed the church of God" (Acts 20:28). It is tragic when God's people are not fed. There will be a day of accounting, and we will be found out regarding the reasons for our failure.

Faithfulness in stewards is a major theme of the pastoral letters. Paul writes to Timothy about his own stewardship (1 Tim 1:11) and charges Timothy to be faithful to the stewardship that has been entrusted to him (v.18). As a steward Timothy is exhorted to be faithful with himself (6:14), with the household (4:6), with the truth (6:20) and to His Lord (6:14). "It is required in stewards, that a man be found faithful" (1 Cor 4:2), and this is in view of the day when we will be found (out). Many a lowly steward who laboured for God without much recognition from man (1 Cor 4:3) in the day of accounting will be given high honour by his Lord.

45   "But and if" that opens this sentence marks a great contrast. Again we are reminded of the general application of these principles to those who are faithful servants of the Lord on the one hand and to false servants on the other. This part of the parable is most important teaching. It shows that God's punishment of evil is in accordance with the light and knowledge of the evildoer. Two sinners may commit the same act, yet one may have a greater measure of guilt than the other, and this is measured according to the knowledge of each one. The Lord Jesus taught this principle to Pilate (John 19:11).

46   The servant had begun his evil ways, but they were cut short by the unexpected arrival of the Lord. The expression "will cut him in sunder" is a translation of *dichotomeō* which is used in the LXX for the dividing of the ram at the consecration of the priests (Exod 29:17; see W.E. Vine). Those who want to make this the punishment of a genuine believer who has been unfaithful apply the word figuratively to the cutting with a scourge. "There is no example of the word being used of scourging" (A. Plummer). Even if we could use a figurative meaning here, the problem would remain about the meaning of the words, "appoint him his portion with the unbelievers", which refers to punishment after death. To be cut in sunder is a violent death (1 Chron 20:3), and to be with the unbelievers forever is the correct portion for this false servant.

47-48   These two verses fully explain that in the day of judgment the Lord will judge men according to their evil works (Eccles 12:14), but it will be righteous judgment. Although ignorance does not exempt a sinner from judgment (note the "few stripes"), yet light and knowledge make a sinner much more responsible when he sins against that light. From all we are told in the NT, there do not seem to be degrees of punishment in hell (*hadēs*), the present prison house of the lost, unless the remorse of memory is considered as added torment (16:25), but in the lake of fire there will be degrees of punishment according to works and the light that has been given (Rev 20:11-15).

This principle that light given results in increased responsibility has a broad application to saint and sinner. The latter part of v.48 makes this clear. We must answer to God for our obedience to the truth that He has given to us. Some have far higher privilege than others.

20.   *Christ as the Divider of Men*
 12:49-53

v.49 "I am come to send fire on the earth; and what will I, if it be a I ready kindled?
v.50 But I have a baptism to be baptized with; and how am I straitened till it be accomplished!
v.51 Suppose ye that I am come to give peace on earth? I tell you, Nay; but rather division:
v.52 For from henceforth there shall be five in one house divided, three against two, and two against three.
v.53 The father shall be divided against the son, and the son against the father; the mother against the daughter, and the daughter against the mother; the mother in law against her daughter in law, and the daughter in law against her mother in law."

49   Many interpretations have been given to the fire that has already been kindled. Some believe that He is referring to the wrath of God which the sin of mankind has already kindled. However, the Lord is referring to His own coming: "I am come" in grace as a Man among men. The first incarnation was not a coming to judge the world, "For God sent not his Son into the world to condemn the world" (John 3:17). In the light of this we suggest that the fire is the division that He speaks of in v.5 1. His coming caused "a division among the people" (John 7:43). The Lord desires the fire, not because it would be easy to endure, but because it would have good results. It would bring persecution to Him and those who love Him, but it would divide between His true followers and those who were opposed to Him. When He comes in judgment, a subject that has often been mentioned in the preceding verses, He will bring the fires of judgment upon His enemies, but at the baptism of which He speaks in v.50, the judgment will fall upon Him.

50   The Lord spoke of baptism as a violent death when He foretold the martyrdom of His disciples (Mark 10: 38), but His own baptism was unique and could be only His own. Immersion should never be divorced from baptism. The Lord is teaching that His death will be an immersion in divine judgment. In Ps 69 He speaks of coming into "deep waters", of "the floods" overflowing Him, and of the waters that came in unto His soul (vv.1,2). In Jeremiah's question, "how wilt thou do in the swelling of Jordan?" (Jer 12:5) Israel was given a picture of the overwhelming floods of death. The death of the Lord Jesus was to be a mighty accomplishment and toward it His spirit pressed.

Some have interpreted *sunechō* ("straitened") as meaning oppressed, troubled or suffering pain. They have suggested that "the prospect of His sufferings was a perpetual Gethsemane" (Plummer) to Christ. The use of *sunechō*, to seize or lay hold of, in 8:37 and in 22:63, where it is used for the Jews who held the Lord Jesus while they mocked and smote Him, may suggest these meanings. Although he does not want to take away the thought of the terrible weight of the coming events that pressed upon the spirit of our Lord, yet it seems to this writer that the meaning is best understood by seeing the way it is used in 8:45, " the multitude throng thee"; Acts 18:5, "Paul was pressed in the spirit"; 2 Cor 5:14, "the love of Christ constraineth us"; and Phil 1:23, " For I am in a strait betwixt two". The meaning seems to be that the spirit of the Lord Jesus with a great desire pressed toward the accomplishing of the will of the Father, even though it meant for Him the sufferings of the cross.

51-53   The promise of Isaiah was that the coming Immanuel would be the Prince of Peace (Isa 9:6), and for the fulfilling of this promise the disciples yearned, but the Lord must prepare them for the persecution that lay before them, so He warned them of the division that He brought. The word *diamerismos* ("division"), which is used only here, is in great contrast to peace, for it means to put asunder by dissension that which had formerly been joined. In many a household this division has been felt very keenly. Many have learned that they have a far closer link to fellow-believers than they have to their own natural kin who are outside of Christ. No suffering on the part of believers for the Lord's sake will ever go unrewarded (8:21).

21.   *Discerning the Time*
   12:54-57

> v.54 "And he said also to the people, When ye see a cloud rise out of the west, straightway ye say, There cometh a shower; and so it is.
> v.55 And when *ye* see the south wind blow, ye say, There will be heat; and it cometh to pass.
> v.56 *Ye* hypocrites, ye can discern the face of the sky and of the earth; but how is it that ye do not discern this time?
> v.57 Yea, and why even of yourselves judge ye not what is right?"

54-56   It is important to see that the Lord addresses the people. The cloud rises out of the west, coming from the Mediterranean Sea from which the land could expect rain. The wind from the southern desert normally brought scorching heat. They had ability to read these signs accurately, but the sign of John the Baptist and the signs of the Messiah were not discerned. They are charged with hypocrisy, so the question arises about wilful ignorance. It is not only that they did not discern the time but that they would not. Isaiah had accurately written, "when we shall see him, there is no beauty that we should desire him. He is despised and rejected of men" (53:2,3). They would have accepted a military conqueror, but they rejected a lowly, suffering Saviour.

57 This is a difficult verse, but this writer suggests that the Lord has just appealed to the evident signs of His Messiahship that could be read as easily as "the face of the sky" for those who were willing to see. However there were other powerful evidences of His claims: the moral beauty of His Person, words and works. "What is right" is literally "what is righteous", and the people to whom these words were spoken had witnessed the grace and beauty of the pathway of the perfect Man. The righteousness of His ways had condemned them, but His moral perfections should also have convinced them without any other signs. There has been but One perfectly righteous Man who walked upon the face of the earth, and they would be held accountable for having seen and heard Him.

22.   *The Last Mite Paid*
   12:58-59

> v.58 "When thou goest with thine adversary to the magistrate, *as thou art* in the way,
> give diligence that thou mayest be delivered from him; lest he hale thee to the
> judge, and the judge deliver thee to the officer, and the officer cast thee into
> prison.
> v.59 I tell thee, thou shalt not depart thence, till thou hast paid the very last mite."

58-59 There have been extreme interpretations of the terms adversary, magistrate, judge and officer in v.58, but in their application each of them has reference to God's judgment. The whole force of the teaching is that the sinner must be certain to settle out of court, for in the coming day of God's judgment the only terms that will be offered will be inflexible righteousness and holiness. There is a serious disagreement between sinners and God (Isa 55:7-9). God is not the adversary of sinners, but His judgment is against the sinner's sin and Luke has already stated this when he wrote, "the Pharisees and lawyers rejected the counsel of God against themselves" (7:30). Repentance is when a sinner is brought to agree with God (Matt 5:25) in His judgment. The subject of debt is not introduced until v.59, but this matter of a debt of sin has also been explained by Luke (7:41,42). To have the matter settled out of court brings the grace of forgiveness and the complete removal of every charge of guilt, but to rush on to the day of judgment with the debt unsettled can only mean eternal judgment.

The word for "officer" (*praktōr*), used twice in v.58 and nowhere else in the NT, exactly fits the thought of a debt owing. It literally means one who does, or accomplishes, and appears in the papyri frequently of a public accountant, a legal officer whose business it is to collect debts, an "exactor" (RV margin). The words of v.59, " till thou hast paid" are the translation of *apodidōmi* ("to pay"), meaning to pay back in full. *Lepton* ("mite") comes from a verb (lepo) which means to peel off the bark. Because it describes something that is small, thin and light in weight, it came to be used for the smallest Jewish copper coin. W.E. Vine says it was worth 1/128th part of a denarius.

There is another word, *katasuro* ("hale", v.58) that is found only here in the NT. *Surō*means "to drag or haul to trial or punishment" and is so used of the persecution of Saul of Tarsus against the believers when "he made havoc of the church, entering into every house, and haling men and women committed them to prison" (Acts 8:3). *Katasuro* is an intensive form and means to drag away to a judge or to prison.

23.   *Except Ye Repent*
   13:1-5

> v.1   "There were present at that season some that told him of the Galilaeans, whose blood Pilate had mingled with their sacrifices.
> v.2   And Jesus answering said unto them, Suppose ye that these Galilaeans were sinners above all the Galilaeans, because they suffered such things?
> v.3   I tell you, Nay: but, except ye repent, ye shall all likewise perish.
> v.4   Or those eighteen, upon whom the tower in Siloam fell, and slew them, think ye that they were sinners above all men that dwelt in Jerusalem?
> v.5   I tell you, Nay: but, except ye repent, ye shall all likewise perish."

1   The slaughter by Pilate of these Galileans evidently took place within the precincts of the temple, for their blood was mingled with the blood of their sacrifices. It was a recent event, or the telling of it would not be significant. It has been suggested that this was the time of the arrest of Barabbas, but this is mere conjecture. These desperate men may have fled to take hold of the horns of the altar for protection, as Adonijah did in 1 Kings 1:50-53. Solomon spared Adonijah that day but Pilate did not spare these people. Galileans were notable among the Jews as a problem to their Roman masters. Pilate had a long history of intolerance and cruelty in his procuratorship over the Jews.

2   This terrible atrocity has been "allowed to happen" to the Galileans. We know that the Jews believed that all such disasters were judgments from God, but behind the Lord's words is the reminder that God is on the throne and nothing gets out of His control even when the authority in the land is in the hands of a cruel Roman governor. The phrase, "sinners above all the Galileans "employs the preposition *para* ("beside") but used with the accusative, it means beyond or above (A.T. Robertson).

3   The Galileans who perished were sinners, but all have sinned and all deserve to suffer for their sins and "except ye repent, ye shall all likewise perish" applied to each one. The "likewise" does not mean by the same method, but with the same certainty. The last two verses of the preceding chapter belong to this subject of repentance. The justice of the law, not God, is the sinner's adversary. Justifying God in His judgment on me as a guilty sinner is a necessity before I can enter into the good of "being justified freely by his grace" (Rom 3:4,24). Repentance is when a sinner endorses the righteous condemnation under which he finds himself. In the language of the Law, "they then accept of the punishment of their iniquity" (Lev 26:41,43), acknowledging that God's judgment is righteous and, in the language of John Dickie learn:

> "When I took my place as sinner,
> And at mercy's footstool lay;
> Jesus took His place as Saviour
> And at once put sin away."

4-5   This tragic accident, as men would call it, did not overtake lowly Galileans, but eighteen inhabitants of Jerusalem who, as far as we know, were not threatening insurrection as Pilate seemed to think the Galileans were. Yet these eighteen perished suddenly, and stand as a warning to all of the need of immediate repentance. We learn from the Lord that it is effective to use local disasters to speak to hearts. The tense of the verb "repent" is changed from v.3, where it is a present subjunctive, suggesting a continuous attitude, to an aorist subjunctive (v.5), to stress the great necessity of immediate repentance to be ready for whatever may come. The men in v.2 are called sinners, but these eighteen men are called debtors (*opheiletēs*), and again we have a strong link with the debt of 12:59. As has been suggested in ch. 12, Luke frequently views sin as a vast debt which must be settled (7:41,42).

We should not hold a limited meaning of repentance, for it does not stand alone in the NT. Genuine repentance will always bring the penitent one to Christ. Therefore repentance often is used to describe a complete experience of personal salvation (Luke 5:32; 24:47; Acts 11:18; Rom 2:4; 2 Pet 3:9).

24.   *The Parable of the Fig Tree in the Vineyard*
13:13-9

v.6   "He spake also this parable; A certain *man* had a fig tree planted in his vineyard; and he came and sought fruit thereon, and found none.

v.7   Then said he unto the dresser of his vineyard, Behold, these three years I come seeking fruit on this fig tree, and find none: cut it down; why cumbereth it the ground?

v.8   And he answering said unto him, Lord, let it alone this year also, till I shall dig about it, and dung *it*:

v.9   And if it bear fruit, *well*: and if not, *then* after that thou shalt cut it down."

6 "The vineyard of the Lord of hosts is the house of Israel, and the men of Judah his pleasant plant" (Isa 5:7) is the great key to understanding the parables about vineyards. The fig tree was not in the vineyard by accident but had been planted there with definite purpose by the owner. Because of its location it had advantages, including fertile soil and careful protection, and we learn that it was the object of the special interest of both the owner and the dresser of the vineyard (v.7). All this could be said of Israel, yet the fact that there was only one fig tree in this vineyard makes the warning very personal. Later in this Gospel there is one lost sheep; one lost piece of silver; one lost son; one man who lifts up his eyes in hell and one man in Jericho who gets saved. The context here is personal repentance, or the lack of it, so we do well to make personal application of this warning in gospel preaching, even though we are aware that the vineyard has special reference to Israel as a nation.

God had lavished upon Israel His bountiful blessings, "What could have been done more to my vineyard, that I have not done in it?" (Isa 5:4); yet when He sought fruit He found none.

7 We are allowed to look in on a heavenly scene, a conference in heaven about a fig tree in a vineyard on earth. God has a secret (wonderful) Counsellor (Isa 9:6), and in eternal counsels plans of wondrous grace were devised (2 Sam 14:14). The elect of Israel (Matt 24:3 1) were part of those counsels, but we also, of this day of grace, were chosen "in him before the foundation of the world" (Eph 1:4). However, the counsel of this verse is about showing mercy to a barren fig tree. We must keep in mind that this is a parable, so to attempt an interpretation of every part of the story is a mistake. "Vinedresser" (*ampelourgos*) is used only here in the NT, and we can rightly speak of the Lord Jesus as the One who enters into the discourse with the owner of the vineyard over the barren fig tree, but to interpret the three years as the time of His public ministry to Israel stretches the meaning too far. The three years are counted from the time when the fig tree would normally be expected to bear fruit, not from the time of its planting and it just means that patience and longsuffering mercy were shown before the owner said "cut it down". *Ekkoptō* ("cut down") is literally "cut out", that is, out of the vineyard.

In the three years that the owner comes seeking fruit on the fig tree, and in contrast to Pilate's sudden wrath (v.1), there is a display of the longsuffering patience of God who is "merciful and gracious, slow to anger, and plenteous in mercy" (Ps 103:8). But there is a limit to the day of mercy, so the judgment is righteous and the command is to "cut it down". It is taking precious moisture, occupying the time of the keeper of the vineyard and taking up space that might well be used by a fruitful plant.

8 The vinedresser who has taken such tender care of the barren fig tree pleads for more mercy. He does not say a word about all his past labour. The words "this year also" suggest a retrospect, for there had been former years of tender care, and they remind us of the mercy that has spared it so long, but they also proclaim a limit. Let us remember that we are looking at an unrepentant sinner and "this year also" means another year of sin, yet another year of mercy, warnings and entreaties. As if not enough had been done in the past, the vinedresser will "dig about it" and fertilise it even more to give it every advantage. It will not be left to pursue indifferently its barren way, but great mercy from God will reach it. No wonder we find such pathos in the tragic statement "after that" (v.9). The word for "dig" (*skaptō*) is used only by Luke (6:48; 13:8; 16:3) and means to hollow out as with a spade (*skapanē*). It suggests hard labour, but in this case it is all in vain.

9   There is no word in the original to correspond to "well" in the AV, but even the Revisers have left it there. Darby translates, "and if it shall bear fruit-but if not, after that thou shalt cut it down". The Lord is indicating that words are not sufficient to describe the blessedness of the sinner who is brought to repentance. In ch. 16 language fails to describe the horrors of a lost soul (v.26). Many of us have seen the "after that" in the lives of people who, like the fig tree, had every advantage and then were cut down in their sins.

25.   *The Woman Healed on the Sabbath*
13:10-17

> v.10 "And he was teaching in one of the synagogues on the sabbath.
> v.11 And, behold, there was a woman which had a spirit of infirmity eighteen years, and was bowed together, and could in no wise lift up *herself*.
> v.12 And when Jesus saw her, he called *her to him*, and said unto her, Woman, thou art loosed from thine infirmity.
> v.13 And he laid *his* hands on her: and immediately she was made straight, and glorified God.
> v.14 And the ruler of the synagogue answered with indignation, because that Jesus had healed on the sabbath day, and said unto the people, There are six days in which men ought to work: in them therefore come and be healed, and not on the sabbath day.
> v.15 The Lord then answered him, and said, *Thou* hypocrite, cloth not each one of you on the sabbath loose his ox or *his* ass from the stall, and lead *him* away to watering?
> v.16 And ought not this woman, being a daughter of Abraham, whom Satan hath bound, lo, these eighteen years, be loosed from this bond on the sabbath day?
> v.17 And when he had said these things, all his adversaries were ashamed: and all the people rejoiced for all the glorious things that were done by him."

10   Luke tells us that the Lord was teaching in a synagogue without informing us of its location, and only defines the time as being a sabbath day. Yet there is a great significance in these two facts. This was the last recorded time that the Lord taught in a synagogue or even was found in one. The controversy between the Lord and the Pharisees about the proper use of the sabbath day is the issue.

11   Luke gives us such a vivid portrait of this woman that we can almost see her. After eighteen years in such a condition all hope that she could ever be better must have died. Every tragic feature of her deformity would draw pity. She was bowed together and the negative emphasises her total helplessness to lift up herself. "She was bent together and wholly unable to lift her head up" (JND). A more graphic picture of the helplessness of sinners to save themselves would be difficult to find. It was "when we were yet without strength, in due time Christ died for the ungodly" (Rom 5:6). "Without strength" (*asthenēs*) implies impotence, the absence of strength. Again Luke uses a unique word *sunkuptō* ("bowed together"), which can best be illustrated as being the posture of an animal, ever toward the ground and not "upright" (Eccl 7:29) as God made man in the beginning so that he can look up to his Creator.

12   This poor woman aptly expresses the truth of Isa 65:1, "I am found of them that sought me not". Her only commendation was her utter helplessness. She made no movement toward the Lord Jesus, but "he called her to him". It is said that she had "a spirit of helplessness". Into her trembling heart wondrous words of grace were spoken, "thou art loosed (away) from thine infirmity". She was set free from bondage just as every sinner who truly comes to Christ as Saviour and Lord is set free from sin and the fear of coming wrath. The Lord dealt with her spiritual need first.

13   He now deals with her physical needs. Prof. A. Rendle Short believed that he could rightly diagnose this woman as having a disease that had fused together the bones of her spine until they were one solid mass. Upon that twisted form were laid the gentle hands of the Lord from heaven and there was immediate healing. "Made straight" is the translation of the word *anorthoō* , that is used only three times in the NT (13:13; Acts 15:16; Heb 12:12), and is very possibly a medical term. It means to " to make straight again", returning her to the health that she knew before the eighteen years of her misery began. Immediate healing brought instant worship as she gave God the glory. The instantaneous effect of the Lord's hands is important in two ways. As a physical healing, there was not a gradual improvement until she was straight; as an illustration of salvation, there was an immediate result from the contact with the Lord Jesus.

14   The ruler of the synagogue "answered" even though he had not been addressed or questioned. The way Luke uses the verb *apokritheis* indicates that to an act of compassion and tender mercy the ruler responded with anger. Religion as a mere form can do some terrible things to people, making them forget love, kindness, mercy and compassion. He addressed his answer to the people. According to his reasoning healing should take place on the other six days of the week not on the sabbath. He was there to lead the sabbath service and this healing was an event in which his leadership was meaningless. It is said about Pilate at the trial, "he knew that the chief priests had delivered him for envy" (Mark 15:10). Envy was behind much of the opposition to the Lord.

15-17   The Lord used a plural when He said "Hypocrites!" (JND). Knowing the hearts of all men He knew how many were present who agreed with the ruler. The Lord was able to refute powerfully the objections to the healing on the sabbath and at the same time to expose the sham of the Jew's religion that could show pity to a thirsty animal and display callous indifference to the plight of a "daughter of Abraham". He said that the woman "must" (*edei*) be loosed, for Satan had bound her for eighteen years, and He had come to destroy the works of the devil (1 John 3:8). His adversaries were put to shame and the people rejoiced, not only over this miracle but over "all the glorious things that were done by him". The ox released from the stall was very little changed after it had been led away for watering, but this woman released from her bondage was brought back to God's original purpose and with adoration and worship she did what she could never do in her bondage, she looked up and worshipped (v.13). The adversaries were put to shame and the people rejoiced, not only over this miracle, but over "all the glorious things that were done by Him".

26.   *Parables of the Mustard Seed and the Leaven*
13:18-21

v.18   "Then said he, Unto what is the kingdom of God like? and whereunto shall I resemble it?

v.19   It is like a grain of mustard seed, which a man took, and cast into his garden; and it grew, and waxed a great tree; and the fowls of the air lodged in the branches of it.

v.20   And again he said, Whereunto shall I liken the kingdom of God?

v.21   It is like leaven, which a woman took and hid in three measures of meal, till the whole was leavened."

These two parables go together in Matthew as well as here. The key from Matt 13:31-33 that these parables are fulfilled in the mystery aspect of the kingdom, is of great help. There are two opposing ways of interpreting these parables. How we view the plan of God for the future is the issue. Those who believe that, by preaching and teaching, the kingdom will expand until it is universal and a christian world is produced, teach that these two parables describe the great progress of the kingdom. Those who believe that wickedness will increase (2 Tim 3:12,13) and human government will fail, bringing in anarchy and chaos and, in the end time, the universal kingdom of the beast (Rev 13:2-8), teach that these two parables describe the introduction of evil into the professing kingdom. These contrary views have a very strong effect on the attitude of christians toward the world. If we believe the former interpretation, then we should make every sacrifice within the range of possibility to improve the world by better laws, politics, social programs, education, a better moral climate, and true christian diplomacy to produce lasting peace between nations. However, if we believe the latter, that the world is like a sinking ship soon to founder beneath the waves of lawlessness (2 Thess 2:7), then we should do all we can to see souls saved from the wreck, and not waste our time trying to improve that upon which God has pronounced judgment.

18-19   The kingdom of God is like a mustard seed that a man cast into his garden. Luke says nothing about the smallness of the seed, but both Matthew and Luke emphasise the contrast between a tiny seed and a great tree. The "fowls of the air" are not interpreted here, but in the parable of the sower in 8:12, Matt 13:19 and Mark 4: 15, the coming of the birds to take away the seed is interpreted, "then cometh the devil and taketh away the word out of their hearts" (8:12). Seeing that in both Matthew and Mark the parable of the sower almost immediately precedes that of the mustard seed and is the only parable which is fully interpreted, it is not likely that the birds have suddenly changed their character. They represent evil men and systems that are attracted to christendom and find lodging in its branches. Mustard seeds do not normally produce trees, but this seed has produced "a great tree" which is used in Scripture as a symbol of a kingdom (Ezek 17:23,24). Since the days of Constantine, the Pergamos period of the church, christendom has developed into a mighty imperial power to the point where it at least influences and sometimes dictates the decisions of nations. Eventually the apostate church will control the beast (Rev 17:3-7).

20-21   What has been said about the parable of the mustard seed applies ten-fold to this parable. It is very poor interpretation to suppose that leaven can have a good meaning here when throughout all the rest of Scripture it stands as a symbol of evil. It was forbidden to Israel to have leaven in their houses for the seven days of Passover and the Feast of unleavened bread (Exod 12:19). Paul speaks of the "old leaven", a symbol of the former immoral lives of the now converted Corinthians, of "the leaven of malice and wickedness" (1 Cor 5:8), and of the leaven of evil doctrine (Gal 5:9). Some may argue that the Lord used leaven in a unique sense here, and He would have the prerogative to do this. But the Lord Jesus consistently used leaven in an evil sense. He warned against the leaven of the Pharisees (12:1), the leaven of the Sadducees (Matt 16:6) and of the leaven of Herod (Mark 8:15). See note on 12:1. This is a very strong background for interpreting leaven as an evil principle in this parable. This is particularly so when we remember that no other symbol of evil had been so impressed on the Jewish consciousness.

A woman hid this leaven. It was by "the woman" that sin came in at Eden (1 Tim 2:14). The leaven came in secretly and began to work unnoticed until the great bloat began that swelled the mass without increasing its weight or worth. The Lord has already warned against hidden things (12:2), and Paul warned the Ephesian elders about grievous wolves entering in among them (Acts 20:29). The creeping in of evil is a figure employed in Scripture (2 Tim 16; Jude 4).

This particular evil caused phenomenal growth. In the days of Constantine, when the favour of the emperor was lavished upon the once persecuted christians, the number of converts was truly phenomenal until christians in Rome outnumbered pagans. Religious priests were paid out of the imperial coffers, so to retain support the pagans became christians. This growth was the result of leaven, an evil principle. Both before and since the Reformation millions of children have been sprinkled and catechised, becoming christians nominally without being born of the Spirit. The Lord is warning against this mass growth brought about by nominal assent, ritual, form and light profession. A careful reader will ask at this point, If this is the true interpretation, why did the Lord teach it here? The answer is found in v. 17, "all the people rejoiced". It was a very brief interval until "they cried out all at once, saying, Away with this man" (23:18). In the fickle crowd the Lord saw the evidence for " the great tree" and the lump that was wholly leavened.

27.   *Are There Few that be Saved?*
        13:22-30

v.22 "And he went through the cities and villages, teaching, and journeying toward Jerusalem.

v.23 Then said one unto him, Lord, are there few that be saved? And he said unto them,

v.24 Strive to enter in at the strait gate: for many, I say unto you, will seek to enter in, and shall not be able.

v.25 When once the master of the house is risen up, and hath shut to the door, and ye begin to stand without, and to knock at the door, saying, Lord, Lord, open unto us; and he shall answer and say unto you, I know you not whence ye are:

v.26 Then shall ye begin to say, We have eaten and drunk in thy presence, and thou hast taught in our streets.

v.27 But he shall say, I tell you, I know you not whence ye are; depart from me, all ye workers of iniquity.

v.28 There shall be weeping and gnashing of teeth, when ye shall see Abraham, and Isaac, and Jacob, and all the prophets, in the kingdom of God, and you yourselves thrust out.

v.29 And they shall come from the east, and *from* the west, and from the north, and *from* the south, and shall sit down in the kingdom of God.

v.30 And, behold, there are last which shall be first, and there are first which shall be last."

22 Throughout these chapters, 9:51 to 19:41, the face of the Lord Jesus is set toward Jerusalem and His cross. Along the final journey of heaven's gentle Nobleman He teaches as He journeys. Every step in His pathway was a delight to the eye of God. A.T. Robertson points to the importance of the verb tenses of continued action in this verse. "He went through one city and village after another, teaching and journeying toward Jerusalem" is the way J.N. Darby translates *diaporeuomai* ("he journeyed through"), followed by *kata* (" throughout"). On the way, He stopped to teach in every city and village.

23   There is a spiritual order in these narratives. If the lawyers and the Pharisees do not believe on Him (11:45-54), and salvation is only for those who repent (vv.2-5), and the rulers of the synagogues are opposed to Him (v.14), how many do believe on Him? And is this not evidence that His claims are false? The question was not directly answered here, but the Lord had plainly said, "few there be that find it" (Matt 7:14). Scripture has much to say about the fewness of the saved. In Noah's day eight souls were saved and a world was destroyed. In Lot's day three were saved from the overthrow of Sodom. Elisha' saw two Gentiles reached. In the days of Isaiah the fewness of the saved are likened to the grapes left after the vintage (Isa 24:13). Behind this question was the scepticism suggested above, but the answer of the Lord also suggests that a general question is much more comfortable than a personal one.

All can be saved, but many are not saved and often the question has been asked, "Lord, are there few that be saved?" It is asked by the curious, as in this case. It is asked by many an earnest christian and gospel labourer. After visiting an entire city from door to door and talking to thousands of people, many of them religious, many professing to be christians, the worker has fallen on his knees before his God and asked, "Lord, are there few that be saved?" Millions will be in heaven through the blood of the Lamb of Calvary, but in comparison to the numbers who are outside the door, there are truly few saved.

24   The man had asked a general question about the number of the saved; the Lord's answer was personal. Although "strive" is plural the Lord's answer could be paraphrased, "Whether there are many or few, be sure that you are among them". In spite of the apathy of the questioner, the Lord directed a great appeal to him and to all who heard Him that day. The word "strive" is the source of our word agonise. It pictures a runner who will not be distracted or hindered. This is a major thought in striving. There must be earnestness, but there are many obstacles and they can hinder the sinner who is seeking salvation. Isaiah foretold that John's message would be to prepare the way of the Lord. A chief ingredient in his preaching was, Remove the obstructions, which is a brief summary of Isa 40:4. To "strive" does not mean that salvation is of works or the result of human effort, but it does mean that a sinner must put it first, allowing nothing to hinder or turn him aside from seeking it. People are never saved until they want it more than anything else. Oliver Smith, a much used evangelist, used to say, "Salvation is simple, but it isn't easy".

The door (gate) is the way into salvation and it is strait, that is, it is narrow. This must be preached in the gospel. The one entering this narrow door will find that there is not room to take his pride, pleasures or self-goodness with him. Many profess to enter the gate who afterward are unchanged in their lives. They have never entered the strait gate, for their former practices of sin and pleasure seeking could never have been taken through it.

The many who seek and are not able to enter are those who come too late. The verb "strive" is a present tense, but "seek" is future, literally, "will seek". They allowed themselves to be hindered when the door was open and will come after it is closed to discover that it is too late. Sadly, the many are not seeking now; it is only the few, but many will seek when the door is shut.

25 "The master of the house" cannot be taken as parabolic language. This is not a parable. The language is descriptive and literal. In 15:11-24 the house has a father, and he yearns over his prodigal son and waits to receive him home again. In 14:21 the house has a lord, and he directs his servant to invite the guests; but in this verse the house has a master, for it is his authority that is stressed (W.E. Vine). In 14:21 it is the master of the house who is angry at the refusal of the invited guests. Here, he rises up with the purpose of shutting the door. Mark closes his Gospel with the great fact that the Lord Jesus was "received up into heaven, and sat on the right hand of God" (Mark 16:19). The One who sat down in token of His finished work at the cross now arises in judgment. No eye on earth will see Him when He arises, but at the time "when once" He shuts the door they will "begin to stand without". It will be with a nail-printed hand that He reluctantly shuts the door. Only Luke uses *apokleiō* ("hath shut to"). It means to shut fast with no possibility of entering it after it is closed.

There was no need to knock before the Master rose up, for the door was open and the invitation was to come, but now that the door is shut, " the many", who would not come before, "stand without" and "knock at the door". "Knock, and it shall be opened unto you" (Matt 7:7) was spoken to spiritual children who are invited to ask the Father (v.11), not to sinners who have missed the day of salvation. "Ye begin to stand without" suggests the start of an effort that continues for a long time. How long will sinners knock and cry for admittance? It will continue until God's judgment falls upon them and they are swept away in the coming storm of wrath.

The double cry "Lord, Lord" certainly shows their deep anxiety, but it is also indicative of those who have a mere lip allegiance (6:46). The Lord Jesus knows His own (John 10:27; 2 Tim 2:19), but He does not "know" these seekers. More precisely, He does not know, or acknowledge "whence ye are". When He taught that He was sent from God (John 8:42), He also told the scribes and Pharisees, "ye are not of God" (v.47).

26 Those who began to stand without now "begin to say", and will continue to say it until judgment's doom shall end their cries. It is tragic for these lost souls to see how the tables have been turned. When the Lord ate with sinners in this Gospel, they mocked Him as "a friend of publicans and sinners" (7:34), but now they claim to have eaten in His presence. It is true that they heard His teaching, but their hearts and lives were not changed by it, which was what they so sorely needed. In the day of judgment many will make similar claims, some even saying that they often took the communion, observed the Lord's supper, and listened to preaching and teaching about Him.

27   It is not what they say when the door is shut that is the basis of their judgment. They were never "of God", that is, never born of God (John 1:12,13). John wrote, "ye know that everyone that doeth righteousness is born of him" (1 John 2:29). They came from Adam and are unregenerate; even worse, they are of the devil "and the lusts of your father ye will do" (John 8:44). This is the meaning of "workers of iniquity", the only time that this exact phrase is used in the NT. Their works showed their origin and character as " the sons of disobedience" (Eph 2:2 RV). As a result, the One who has so graciously welcomed sinners in the day of grace, in that day of judgment will say, "depart from me". This expression, literally, "stand away from me", is significant, for He did not say, Stand away from the door, or, Depart from heaven or from the kingdom, but, "depart from me". The simple answer is that the Lord Jesus Himself is every blessing, and to be compelled to depart from Him is every misery.

28   We have simply taken the door to be the door of salvation, and know of no reason why it should not be so understood. However, to be outside that door when it is closed will mean to be "thrust out" of the millennial kingdom of God and forever. The Lord moves on in His teaching to events that will take place after the door is shut, and this is what we would expect. In studying the earthly teaching of the Lord there is a tendency to attribute to the Lord the limited understanding of the disciples at that time, whereas the whole plan of God lay open to Him. All that we call eschatology was an open book before His eyes. He is outlining for us what we know to be the course of events in their order.

   Abraham, Isaac and Jacob were men with a heavenly hope (Heb 11:16). Their seed looked for an earthly kingdom, but the patriarchs themselves looked for a heavenly city. Even in the millennium they will not be on earth, but in the heavenly Jerusalem reigning over the earth (Rev 21:10-27). So, very simply, the gospel preacher can declare that the patriarchs will be in heaven and these sinners will be in hell. We should never allow too great a desire to be precise and exact in our dispensational thinking to blunt the edge of plain gospel truth. The "weeping and gnashing of teeth" will take place in the day of judgment and will continue forever in "the everlasting fire" where the wicked are consigned by the Judge (Matt 24:5 1; 25:30,41). The day of judgment will be "when ye shall see", for they will surely not "see" the saved from their place of eternal loss.

29-30   This is the final ingathering of the elect of God (Matt 24:31). Its first interpretation may be to the elect of Israel, but in the Gospel, in which the salvation of the lost, outcasts, publicans and Gentiles is stressed, it also includes all the saved of a coming day, the fruit of the work of the Jewish witnesses. They comprise two companies: those who are spared during the great tribulation (Matt 25:31-40); and those who are martyred (Rev 7:13-17).

The rejected Lord stood in the midst of the few who believed on Him, mostly unlearned men from Galilee, while around Him gathered the many who rejected Him, highly esteemed, religious leaders and their followers, and He dared to say, "they shall come". This is a thrilling prophecy, seemingly unlikely to be fulfilled when spoken, yet it has been, and will be, blessedly true. As a solemn warning to those who held place and influence then, in contrast to Christ and His disciples, He taught that "there are first which shall be last". We should never judge by mere appearance and should never follow the crowd. Always, in a day of evil, the crowd is wrong.

28.   *Herod, that Fox*
13:31-33

> v.31 "The same day there came certain of the Pharisees, saying unto him. Get thee out, and depart hence: for Herod will kill thee.
> v.32 And he said unto them, Go ye, and tell that fox, Behold, I cast out devils, and I do cures today and to morrow, and the third *day* I shall be perfected.
> v.33 Nevertheless I must walk to day, and to morrow, and the *day* following: for it cannot be that a prophet perish out of Jerusalem."

31   These Pharisees had not changed their attitude toward the Lord Jesus. They had for a long time sought opportunities to silence Him and to destroy Him. This was not a compassionate warning but a taunt. It may have been a scheme between Herod and the Pharisees to get the Lord Jesus out of any region of Galilee and into Judaea where the power of the Pharisees was far greater. The evils of Herod Antipas were well known to the Lord (3:19,20). He ruled over Galilee and Perea from BC 4 until AD 39 (see on 3:1).

32   In calling Herod "that fox" the Lord Jesus described his character. He was sly, crafty, deceitful and without honour. It was not name-calling, which was far beneath the dignity of our Lord.

Luke alone of the NT writers uses the word *iasis* ("cures"), only here in the Gospel and twice in Acts 4:22,30. *Iasis* is akin to *iatros* ("physician"). The words "I shall be perfected" (*teleioumai*) speak of the end of His work. He would truly die, but it would be in God's appointed time and not Herod's. The Lord did not explain the days, but we suggest that "to day" refers to His present ministry, "to morrow" to His death, and "the third day" reaches beyond the day of redemption on the cross to the day of resurrection. We bring in the resurrection not because of some strained meaning for the third day, but because "be perfected" is elsewhere used of the resurrection of the Lord and His saints (Phil 3:12; Heb 5:9; 11:40; 12:23).

33 The "Nevertheless" that opens this statement suggests that He is not merely repeating the former statement. He will not die at the hand of Herod; He will continue His ministry until it is completely accomplished, for He yet has today, tomorrow and the day following to continue His journey. That journey will take Him to Jerusalem where the finishing of His work will involve His death. "It cannot be" is the translation of *endechomai* ("to admit, allow") which is only here in the NT. With the negative it means, "it is not admissible" (W.E. Vine). It was Jerusalem where the authority of the chief priests and the Sanhedrin were centred and it was there where Jesus would be charged falsely, condemned and crucified. At the end of the NT, John wrote "the great city, which spiritually is called Sodom and Egypt, where also our Lord was crucified" (Rev 11:8).

29. *O Jerusalem, Jerusalem*
13:34-35

v.34 "O Jerusalem, Jerusalem, which killest the prophets, and stonest them that are sent unto thee; how often would I have gathered thy children together, as a hen *doth gather* her brood under *her* wings, and ye would not!
v.35 Behold, your house is left unto you desolate: and verily I say unto you, Ye shall not see me, until *the time* come when ye shall say, Blessed *is* he that cometh in the name of the Lord."

34 It is possible that Luke records this touching cry of the Saviour at this point because it links with His death at Jerusalem that has been mentioned in the previous verses. Matthew says it was when the Lord was in Jerusalem within the temple courts that He said these words (Matt 23:37; 24:1). Luke tells of the Lord drawing near and looking over the city in 19:41. The Lord may have uttered this lament on more than one occasion, or as in other instances, Luke may be following a spiritual order rather than a rigid chronological one.

When the Lord Jesus drew near to the city, He wept (19:41). We are not told of tears in this narrative, but the very language gives us the right to refer to it as a tearful reminder. It is evident that the heart of the Saviour was moved for He had a tender regard for Jerusalem although it was the place of a terrible rejection. This was a reminder of past sins, past mercies and past rejections. The past history of Jerusalem was one of warnings refused and God's witnesses slain. The present city was as wicked as in the days of the fathers and wrath was about to fall upon them. "How often would I" goes back before the days when the Lord Jesus stood in its streets; it tells of the mercy and grace of Jehovah to them throughout all their history. The picture is vivid: the mother hen gathers her chicks beneath her wings for shelter and protection; she is willing to face the danger while she shelters her brood. How perfectly these words were fulfilled! The storm of divine wrath fell on the Saviour and He became the "hiding place from the wind, and a covert from the tempest" (Isa 32:2). He would have "gathered" because they had gone astray, turning their back on God, His prophets and their message: I would ... but ye would not. "As a hen doth gather her brood" reminds us that the Lord will not force any under His wings, they must come in response to His call. Even at this late date, there is tender entreaty in His words. It is still an invitation to come. Those who do come find shelter, comfort and joy. David wrote, "Therefore in the shadow of thy wings will I rejoice" (Ps 63:7). The disciples, like the chicks, had fled to Him for shelter under His wings; the majority of the people refused the refuge.

35 "Your house" refers to the temple or, more exactly, to all that the temple represents of the presence of God among His people. The house is forsaken, as the Lord once forsook Shiloh (Ps 78:60) and as Jeremiah had prophesied long before that He would forsake Solomon's temple and leave it desolate (7:10-14; 12:7; 22:5). Their rejection of the Lord of the temple left them with nothing but an empty shell.

The city will not see Him until He comes in the name of the Lord (Ps 118:26). This was not fulfilled in His triumphal entry into Jerusalem on the colt (Matt 21: 1-11), for this had already taken place when the Lord said these words (Matt 23:39). These words rather refer to the day when the Lord "shall suddenly come to his temple" (Mal 3:1) in the day when "the Sun of righteousness (will) arise with healing in his wings" (Mal 4:2).

30.   *The Challenge to Pharisees and Scribes*
    14:1-6

> v.1   "And it came to pass, as he went into the house of one of the chief Pharisees to eat bread on the sabbath day, that they watched him.
> v.2   And, behold, there was a certain man before him which had the dropsy.
> v.3   And Jesus answering spake unto the lawyers and Pharisees, saying, Is it lawful to heal on the sabbath day?
> v.4   And they held their peace. And he took *him,* and healed him, and let him go;
> v.5   And answered them, saying, Which of, you shall have an ass or an ox fallen into a pit, and will not straightway pull him out on the sabbath day?
> v.6   And they could not answer him again to these things."

1 We know nothing of the motives behind the chief Pharisee's invitation to the Lord to eat in his house on a sabbath day. "They watched him" also involves the man who invited Him. He was *archōn*, a chief ruler, and may have been a member of the Sanhedrin. Under the closest scrutiny by clever men who sought opportunities to accuse Him, the Lord Jesus proved to be blameless. Luke records three times when they so watched Him (6:7; 14:1; 20:20). Mark also tells us that they watched Him to see if He would heal the man with the withered hand on the Sabbath day (3:2), and uses the same word for "watch" (*paratēreō*) as an active verb. Here it is used as a periphrastic imperfect tense, in the middle voice (A.T. Robertson). "They were watching him" (JND) for themselves; that is, insidiously, with evil intent to catch Him. Later, when the soldiers had crucified Him, "sitting down they watched him there" (Matt 27:36); the verb that is used, *tēreō* ("to keep") means that they guarded Him against any attempt at rescue, and Luke tells us that as they sat around the cross they also mocked Him (23:36).

2-3 It was well within the treachery of the Pharisees that the invitation to the Lord on the sabbath, coinciding with the presence of the man with the dropsy, was a preconceived scheme to entrap the Lord, "him that endured such contradiction of sinners against himself" (Heb 12:3). This is seen in the use of the verb "answering". No one had spoken to the Lord, so He was answering an action or hidden thought.

According to the rabbinical rules, it was not lawful to treat the sick or injured on the sabbath unless postponing treatment until its close would eventuate in death. Dropsy is not a disease in itself, but is a symptom of kidney or heart disease. The man was not likely to die that day, or so the Pharisees would have judged.

The Lord asked, "Is it lawful to heal on the sabbath?" The difficulty in the question for the Pharisees was that there was nothing in the Scriptures to forbid such healing. To plead the teachings of the rabbinical schools left them open to the charge of adding to the law, a charge which the Lord had laid against them very plainly (Mark 7:7; Luke 11:38-41).

4 Their silence was a confession of their inability to answer Him, but their opposition was fuelled by the incident, for it challenged their leadership in matters of the law where they were the experts and the authority. The man was healed and dismissed, indicating that he was present for healing and as a test for the Lord, not as a guest at the supper. This is the only time in the NT that *epilambanō* ("he took him") is used in a case of healing. Luke uses this word about the child that the Lord " took ... and set him by him" (9:47), but its other uses give its usual meaning "that they might take hold of his words" (20:20,26), and " they laid hold upon one Simon" (23:26). In Acts 16:19, "they caught Paul and Silas" suggests a sudden, violent arrest. Perhaps the meaning in connection with this victim of dropsy relates to his far advance in the disease and utter helplessness to come to the Lord of his own volition, so the Lord "took him" and then "healed him".

5-6 It was the normal Jewish custom that if an animal fell into a pit on a sabbath it would be pulled out on the same day. This was not so much out of pity for the hapless beast, but out of an unwillingness to suffer material loss. The point, pressed home, must have pierced deeply. They had a care for their material gain, but no real feeling for a man suffering from dropsy. Stephen's words not long after cut the Jewish leaders to the heart, but their response was to gnash on him with their teeth and condemn him to be stoned.

The word for "he will pull him out" (*anaspaō*) is only used elsewhere in the NT in Peter's description of the vision of the great sheet let down from heaven; "all *were drawn up* again into heaven" (Acts 11:10). The Lord Jesus chose a word that graphically pictures the labour involved, even on a Sabbath day, in drawing up out of a pit a large animal. In the case of the woman "whom Satan had bound" (13:16), the Lord used an illustration suitable to her need: an ox or ass bound in a stall that was unable to go to drink. In this case He used the figure of an animal in a pit because He was speaking of a man who was literally drowning in his own fluids. He was a master in the use of apt illustrations.

31.   *Taking the Lowest Room*
14:7-14

v.7   "And he put forth a parable to those which were bidden, when he marked how they chose out the chief rooms; saying unto them,

v.8   When thou art bidden of any *man* to a wedding, sit not down in the highest room; lest a more honourable man than thou be bidden of him;

v.9   And he that bade thee and him come and say to thee, Give this man place; and thou begin with shame to take the lowest room.

v.10 But when thou art bidden, go and sit down in the lowest room; that when he that bade thee cometh, he may say unto thee, Friend, go up higher: then shalt thou have worship in the presence of them that sit at meat with thee.

v.11 For whosoever exalteth himself shall be abased; and he that humbleth himself shall be exalted.

v.12 Then said he also to him that bade him, When thou makest a dinner or a supper, call not thy friends, nor thy brethren, neither thy kinsmen, nor *thy* rich neighbours; lest they also bid thee again, and a recompence be made thee.

v.13 But when thou makest a feast, call the poor, the maimed, the lame, the blind:

v.14 And thou shalt be blessed; for they cannot recompense thee: for thou shalt be recompensed at the resurrection of the just."

7   The feast mentioned in v.1 must have been a large gathering to which many had been invited, and the Lord watched how the chief seats were chosen. It has been suggested that there was "an undignified scramble" (Morris) as each guest struggled for the place of highest honour for himself. This selfish conduct gave to the Lord an object lesson. The choice of the "chief rooms" suggests to our minds a large house with many rooms in which the guests were seated. Actually *prōtoklisia* ("chief rooms") means the chief place of reclining at a table. It is used five times in the NT: Matt 23:6, "love the uppermost rooms at feasts"; Mark 12:39, "the uppermost rooms at feasts"; twice here (vv.7,8) and finally in 20:46 which is Luke's record of the same teaching of the Lord as given by Matthew and Mark. It is always used of a feast and the position of guests at the table; "chief room" meaning a place of honour such as being on the right or left of the host or

at least a near place. "The room of the unlearned" (1 Cor 14:16) is *topos* "place" or seat, and is used in v.9 in this passage.

8-9 The Lord extends the teaching to include an invitation to a wedding and exhorts guests not to presume on the chief seat on the immediate right of the host. A more honourable man may have been invited and the host will be obliged to tell the pretender to take a lower place. By this time the other seats of any honour will have been occupied and the man, now ashamed, must take the lowest place.

10 How much more comely to take the lowest place by personal choice than to be put there by the host, so that the host, aware of the low place taken by the guest, invites him to go up higher! It is only this man who is called "Friend". There is a clear gospel application in this teaching. All who are saved have taken the lowest room, acknowledging their guilt as sinners and have been lifted to the highest heights. Paul rejoiced that "Christ Jesus came into the world to save sinners, of whom I am chief" (1 Tim 1:15). Those who attempt to seat themselves in the lofty seat of self-righteousness will one day have to go down to the lowest room of hell. *Prosanabainō* ("go up") is used only here in the NT, and can be translated "come up higher" for the call is from up higher and *pros* ("towards") supports this thought.

11 From this simple example the Lord now teaches lessons which He exemplified as no man on earth has ever done. It has been said, "Go as low as e'er you will, the Highest has been lower still". The lofty One became the lowly One, and to believers He is the altogether lovely One. How perfectly He "knew what was in man" (John 2:25)! The desire for prominence, greatness, eminence, renown, prestige, honour, place, or whatever we may call it, is one of the most pronounced features of fallen humanity. It is a chief cause of assembly problems. This desire to put forward self can assume many disguises and take many forms, but human pride is hateful to God in whatever form it takes (Prov 16:5). None is immune from this fearful disease of selfish pride, but let us ever judge it as sin, and never adopt the spirit of this age that glorifies it.

A lack of self-esteem may be crippling to some people, but it is possible to be over-occupied with self even if that occupation is pity for our own inadequacy. The person who is always saying that he is of little worth may be taken up with self, for he is talking about self. There is a perfect balance in Scripture, "For I say ... to every man ... not to think of himself more highly than he ought to think; but to think soberly, according as God has dealt to every man the measure of faith" (Rom 12:3). We should never think of ourselves as worthless. The ultimate pattern is the lowly mind of the Lord Jesus: "Let this mind be in you, which was also in Christ Jesus" (Phil 2:5).

12   Now the Lord addresses the host of this feast. It is a mistake to think that He is condemning a gathering together of relatives or friends, but on the other hand we should never think that such social gatherings are devoted service to the Lord. He is condemning a selfishness which lives only to please self and seeks recompense for whatever is done for others. The phrase "also bid thee again" (*antikaleō*) is only here in the NT. The prefix *anti* tells us that one action is replaced with another, so it aptly describes "one good turn deserves another" which far too frequently passes as righteousness in the world. The right actions taught by the Lord go far beyond this human goodness.

13-14   True service to the Lord forbids the servant to insulate himself from the needs of others. "The poor, the maimed, the lame, the blind" cannot reciprocate, but this should never be a reason to exclude them from a feast or from other deeds of kindness. Although we acknowledge much failure through many years, we have seen this kind of love and service performed by many believers in their homes. The reward for such selfless service will not be in this world, but will be seen at "the resurrection of the just". The "maimed" (*anapēros*) which is found only here and in v.2 1 in the NT means to be "disabled in a limb" (W.E. Vine), or "lame all the way up" (A.T. Robertson). It can be seen that it means more than to be lame (*chōlos*, halt) for they also are listed.

32.   *The Great Gospel Supper*
14:15-24

v.15 "And when one of them that sat at meat with him heard these things, he said unto him, Blessed *is* he that shall eat bread in the kingdom of God.

v.16 Then said he unto him, A certain man made a great supper, and bade many:

v.17 And sent his servant at supper time to say to them that were bidden, Come; for all things are now ready.

v.18 And they all with one *consent* began to make excuse. The first said unto him, I have bought a piece of ground, and I must needs go and see it: I pray thee have me excused.

v.19 And another said, I have bought five yoke of oxen, and I go to prove them: I pray thee have me excused.

v.20 And another said, I have married a wife, and therefore I cannot come.

v.21 So that servant came, and shewed his lord these things. Then the master of the house being angry said to his servant, Go out quickly into the Streets and lanes of the city, and bring in hither the poor, and the maimed, and the halt, and the blind.

v.22 And the servant said, Lord, it is done as thou hast commanded, and yet there is room.

v.23 And the lord said unto the servant, Go out into the highways and hedges, and compel *them* to come in, that my house may be filled.

v.24 For I say unto you, That none of those men which were bidden shall taste of my supper."

This parable, unique to Luke, is one of the best, yet one of the most solemn in all the Gospels, and has provided the material for many a gospel message. We should not let its application to the future celebration of the marriage supper of the lamb hinder us from seeing a very real application to our day. The great supper is a beautiful picture of God's "so great salvation". The likeness can be seen in the nature of it, for eating is an illustration of personal acceptance or appropriation (John 6:53,54). The invitation was to the many and the provision was abundant (Isa 53:12). A free offer was made to the outcasts and they were compelled lovingly to come in (Luke 5:32). However, it is also like God's "so great salvation" in the excuses that were made and the final refusal of those who never tasted of the supper. We learn that those who are forever lost are fully responsible for their own damnation. Full provision was made for them, and they needed only to accept the invitation. Here, as throughout Luke, the highly favoured and religious miss the blessing while the poor and needy are richly blessed. Undoubtedly, there is a dispensational interpretation in keeping with Rom 11:7-25: the faithless of Israel, the natural branches, are broken off and the branches from the wild olive tree are grafted in.

15   It is not possible to judge a man's thoughts, but the Lord's answer indicates much more than was in the mind of the man who made the comment. It was a common figure among the Jews to speak of the bliss (*makarios*, blessed) of heaven as partaking of a feast. The man who spoke of this blessedness (6:20-22) undoubtedly thought of himself as being an honoured guest.

16   We are not told the occasion for the supper, but it was "great" and many were invited. There is no indication that they refused the invitations. It was not until the supper-hour that they began to make excuse. There are as many similarities as differences between the "great supper" here and the supper of Matt 22:2-14, which was "a certain king, which made a marriage for his son" (v.2). In both cases, the invitation was sent ahead of the time for the supper (Matt 22:3), and at the supper hour, there was refusal. Matthew says, "they made light of it and went their ways, one to his farm, another to his merchandise" which is paralleled in Luke by the excuses. In both cases, the refusal of those who were originally invited led to the invitation being extended to others. The differences are: Matthew describes a wedding supper for a king's son; Luke says, "A certain man made a great supper". Matthew tells of the spiteful treatment of the servants who were slain by the guests who had refused the invitation; the murderers and their city were then destroyed. Matthew's account of the guest without the wedding garment is not in Luke. These two parables were told at different times. The one in Matthew was told because of an attempt to arrest Jesus (21:46), but Luke's parable resulted from a self-righteous comment at a feast.

17   There is a double invitation here, or at least an invitation and then an announcement. An illustration may help the reader. A christian attended a breaking of bread meeting in an assembly in the Middle East. At the close of the meeting, a well-dressed Arab invited him to dinner. When the invitation was accepted the host walked away without giving instructions about how to get to his home or the time of the meal. Worried, the christian asked for information from others, and was told to go to his hotel and await developments. In a short time a servant came and asked the christian to follow him. He was taken to the home of the gracious host and the dinner was ready. The same custom prevailed in NT times.

The word "servant" in this parable is singular, not plural as in that of the wedding supper for the king's son (Matt 22:1-14). This is an important distinction. It was at the "supper-hour" that the servant was sent to those who were invited. In travelling to other lands we have learned that dinner can be in the middle of the day or in the evening, and at times have made a mistake when invited for dinner, but there is no mistaking the "supper-hour". It is always at the close of the day. We live at the close of the day of grace and the invitation now being heard is the "supper-hour" announcement. The time of salvation is called a day (2 Cor 6:2) but the time of invitation is called an hour, and it is the closing of the day.

The fulness of the provision thrills our hearts. All the great cost of the feast had been fully met, the supper was fully prepared. All was ready and those who were invited just needed to come. Over the cross where the Saviour suffered, bled and died the words could be emblazoned, "Come; for all things are now ready".

18 With one mind, or by mutual consent, or all together, they begged to be excused. The Greek text does not provide a word after "one", but the AV makes good sense and the RV agrees. Perhaps, "without exception" (JND) captures the sense even better. "To make excuse" and "I pray thee have me excused" are two forms of the verb *paraiteomai*, which is translated "refuse" (Acts 25:11; 1 Tim 4:7; 5:11) and "reject" (Titus 3:10). As most translations of this passage show, it was a polite refusal. In fact, "I pray thee have me excused" is very clearly its meaning, and we are reminded that God does hear sinners, for in some sense this is a prayer. It was answered and these people were excused from the supper, just as sinners are excused from heaven for the same reasons.

The reasons were trifling; merely polite ways of saying that they did not want to come. The first man had purchased a farm, but accepting the invitation to the supper would not effect the land. It would have remained unchanged in his brief absence.

19 The second man was going to test ten oxen that he had already purchased. Surely he would not have bought them without knowing their worth and there was no urgency for the test now that they belonged to him. They would not run away while he was at the feast, and were not likely to be stolen. The word for "yoke" (*zeugos*) meaning a pair of animals is only here and in 2:24 in the NT. It was a large purchase and must have occupied his attention to such a degree that the "supper" became unimportant to him. This attitude is behind all the excuses which actually were outright refusals.

20   The law exempted a man from military service during the first year of his marriage, but, as has often been suggested, his new wife should have been brought to the supper with him. It would have been a strange host who would have refused her admittance. Like the other excuses, this was another way of rejecting the invitation. It is interesting that Luke 13, 14 and 15 contain teaching about coming into the blessings of salvation: in 15:28 there is a tender entreaty from the father to come in; in 14:18-20 there are trifling excuses from sinners; and in 13:25 there is a tragic exclusion of those who came too late. The pride of the elder brother made him choose to remain outside; the pursuits of the invited guests made them excuse themselves; the closed door made the seekers unable to go in. It is so tragic that those who would not go in discovered later that they could not go in.

21   The one servant, who is a picture of the Holy Spirit, came and told his lord of the refusal of those who had been invited. The excuses are transparent to the Master of the house and His anger is kindled. When it is the sinner's folly that is prominent the house has a Master (13:25; 14:21), but when it is the forgiveness of a sinner that is prominent the house has a Father (15:21).

In this verse and the two that follow there are three very significant statements. "Go out quickly" tells of the need for urgency. "Yet there is room" tells of the extent of opportunity. "Compel them to come in" tells of the sovereignty of the Master and His Servant.

The fourfold description of those who are to be found in "the streets and lanes of the city" is a complete picture of all sinners. They were poor, without the ability to buy the supper; they were maimed, without attractiveness to make them desired guests; they were halt, without strength to do anything for themselves; they were blind, without sight to see their way. This fourfold description is from v.13. It pictures to us the desperate need and the utter helplessness of all sinners to save themselves.

22   The Servant accomplishes the will of the Master without fail. There is a contrast between this Servant and the servants of many other parables. They require examination as to their faithfulness (12:42-48) but this Servant is unfailing. There are four unnamed servants in the Bible that picture to us various activities of the Holy Spirit: in this passage He compels guests to come to the supper; in Gen 24 He seeks a bride for Isaac; in Mark 14:12-16 He leads to the large upper room (Matt 18:20); in Ruth 2:4-7 He is the Servant set over the reapers.

"Yet there is room" has lessons for us. Heaven (here it is the kingdom of God, v. 15) is a prepared place for a prepared people. It has limits, many mansions (John 14:2), even a seat (Luke 13:29), and here, it is likened to a house where there is room, or an allotted place. The house will be filled (v.23), and "yet there is room", but how long the word "yet" will remain true, none can say.

23   The Servant is sent out once more. The city was a place where many could be found easily, but "the highways and hedges", that is, the main roads in the country and the hedges that lined them would present a far greater problem in finding people, and suggests a more intensive search. This is an apt picture of the close of the day when it has become much more difficult to find guests for the supper, as many who labour in the gospel will agree. Easy profession is no more difficult than ever it was, but to see a genuine work of God in hearts is becoming more rare.

The reader will now see why we have insisted on the distinction between the many servants and the one Servant. Servants can warn, entreat, persuade, win, point to the Saviour and urge men to accept Him, but they cannot compel a sinner to come to Christ. It is very possible to use coercion to compel people to do things against their will, but it is not possible for men to compel their fellows to come to Christ against their will. But does the Holy Spirit compel sinners to come against their will? No, but by His awakening and convicting power He makes them willing and anxious to flee from the wrath to come (John 16:8-11).

We must never read into the word "compel" (*anankazō*) the thought of "irresistible grace". The Spirit does not use force, but He does constrain sinners to come, in spite of their reluctance, urging them by His patient strivings. However the ultimate responsibility for rejection lies at the door of the sinner; he can still refuse the invitation, and perish in his folly. The NT use of *anankazō* in all of its nine occurrences (Matt 14:22; Mark 6:45; Luke 14:23; Acts 26:11; 28:19; 2 Cor 12:11; Gal 2:3,14; 6:12) show that it means "to put constraint upon (from *anankē*, necessity), to constrain by threat, entreaty, force or persuasion" (W.E. Vine, *NT Words*, p.219).

24   Those who made excuse find that their plea has been heard and answered. They are excused and are outside of the blessings of the kingdom of God forever, and will never even taste of the supper. The rejection of the Lord Jesus and His teaching by the leaders of Israel is without question the point of the parable. They refused Him, but the poor and outcasts of the Gentiles will receive the invitation (Acts 13:46). The invitation to the supper was given by the Lord Himself as He preached the gospel (4:18,44; 8:1,39). The supper was made ready when He died and rose again and sent the Holy Spirit (the servant). When the Jews of Jerusalem continued to reject Him, the outlying areas of Judaea were visited and when no more could be found who were willing to come in, the gospel went out to the Gentiles.

33.   *Bearing the Cross*
14:25-27

v.25 "And there went great multitudes with him: and he turned, and said unto them,
v.26 If any *man* come to me, and hate not his father, and mother, and wife, and children, and brethren, and sisters, yea, and his own life also, he cannot be my disciple.
v.27 And whosoever doth not bear his cross, and come after me, cannot be my disciple."

25-26   Turning to the great multitude who were gathered to listen to Him, the Lord tested them as to their reality. The influence of a crowd may turn false disciples one way or another, but the genuine are able to stand alone. The Lord Jesus taught His disciples to love even their enemies (6:27), and caring for the needs of others was a major part of His practice and teaching. We cannot accept any interpretation of these verses about discipleship that would contradict that teaching. The true test of discipleship is such a whole-hearted devotion to the Lord Jesus that all other natural loves are as hatred in comparison. We are most fortunate when our natural loves for parents, wife, children, brethren and sisters in no way hinder full love to Him. There are many believers who must, not at the cost of loving but at the cost of showing love to their nearest on earth, prove loyal to the Lord. Many of us have loved ones who also love the Lord Jesus and it would displease them sorely if we put them before Him. When we are tested as to our devotion every earthly tie must be given a lesser place, with the Lord Jesus having preeminence. This is the "blood test" and for many it is very difficult to take sides with the Lord when it is against ties of blood, but it is the real test of true devotion to Him.

27   To "bear his cross" has popularly come to mean the carrying of a burden, but although a cross is a burden preeminently it was an instrument of death. To bear his cross means death to self and self-interests. Self-denial was at the very heart of the Lord's teaching about discipleship. To follow the Lord Jesus means not to please self. The major features of true discipleship are devotion to the Lord Jesus, the denial of self even to the point of death, and bearing his cross as we manifest likeness to His faithful obedience.

Only the Lord Jesus could bear the cross on which He suffered. There is not one case in the Lord's teaching about cross-bearing (Matt 16:24; Mark 8:34; 10:21; Luke 9:23; 14:27) where it is suggested that we can bear His cross. In fact, the phrase here is "bear his (own) cross" (*ton stauron heautou*). The believer's own cross is whatever it costs him in self-denial and opposition from others to follow the Lord Jesus. The phrase "bear his cross" uses *bastazō* ("to bear") which is a common verb in the NT, but is used only here for cross-bearing by a disciple. It is used in John 19:17, "And he (Jesus) bearing his cross went forth". In the other instances, Matthew, Mark and even Luke (9:23) use *airō* ("to take up").

34. Parables of the Tower, the King and the Tasteless Salt
14:28-35

> v.28 "For which of you, intending to build a tower, sitteth not down first, and counteth the cost, whether he have *sufficient* to finish *it?*
> v.29 Lest haply, after he hath laid the foundation, and is not able to finish *it*, all that behold *it* begin to mock him,
> v.30 Saying, This man began to build, and was not able to finish.
> v.31 Or what king, going to make war against another king, sitteth not down first, and consulteth whether he be able with ten thousand to meet him that cometh against him with twenty thousand?
> v.32 Or else, while the other is yet a great way off, he sendeth an ambassage, and desireth conditions of peace.
> v.33 So likewise, whosoever he be of you that forsaketh not all that he hath, he cannot be my disciple.
> v.34 Salt *is* good: but if the salt have lost his savour, wherewith shall it be seasoned?
> v.35 It is neither fit for the land, nor yet for the dunghill; *but* men cast it out. He that hath ears to hear, let him hear."

28-30 Discipleship can never be practised without personal cost. The degree of devotion can be measured only by the cost. In much modern evangelism people are told that the Lord wants them to give up nothing, just to receive Christ and have the blessings of salvation added to their worldly pleasures and amusements. These supposed conversions do not last because there has been no Spirit-wrought conviction about being utterly lost, no awakening and, therefore, no repentance. The true terms of discipleship are kept hidden until "a decision to accept Jesus into the heart" is made. The Lord Jesus told people to sit down and carefully count the cost. This is the opposite of the high pressure method employed in so many campaigns. Often profession is made in conditions similar to those in which a person is coerced into buying some piece of merchandise that is neither needed nor wanted. Good salesmanship is no asset in soul-winning. The message of the Lord is to count the cost first of all.

In v.28, *apartismos* ("to finish it") means "unto a completion" and is only in this verse in the NT. The verb "to finish" (*ekteleō*, vv.29,30) is also not used elsewhere in this form. It is an intensive form of *teleō*, and means to fully finish. These two words intensify the meaning of not only having sufficient means to make a start, but to be certain that there will be ability to completely finish what has been started. Many are able to follow the Lord along a flower-strewn pathway which seems at first to be popular, with many happy companions, but when asked to walk alone amid the cruel rocks of adversity or the spears of persecution, they soon discover that they are unable to continue.

31-32 This second parable reinforces the teaching of the previous one, but there are distinctions. The man who builds a tower can choose to do it or not, but the king who is under threat of invasion must act. Both must make a careful assessment of what it will cost to meet the need, but in the first case the man who builds the tower may discover that he cannot afford to finish it. In the second case, the king under attack, after careful assessment, may discover that he cannot afford to resist the king who is coming to him with far superior forces. The king who comes against him should be interpreted as being the claims of the Saviour and Lord. True disciples have sat down and considered the whole issue and have discovered that they cannot afford to resist the claims of the Lord and have made peace with Him.

Two of Luke's unique words are also found in these two verses. The phrase "to make war" uses *sumballō* ("to make"). Luke uses the same verb in 2:19: "But Mary kept all these things, and pondered (*sumballō*) them in her heart"; also in Acts 4:15, "conferred"; 17:18, "encountered"; 18:27, "helped"; and 20:14, "met with" as the result of a prearranged plan. In these five other occurrences, we learn that it conveys the thought of careful contemplation and planning. So the disciple who continues to follow his Lord has well considered the costs and has determined that he can and will pay the price. The other word is *presbeia* ("ambassage") and means elder in age or rank like the word *presbeuō* ("ambassador", 2 Cor 5:20; Eph 6:20). Although unrelated to the present context, the following is of interest. "There is a suggestion that to be an "ambassador" for Christ involves the experience suggested by the word "elder" (W.E. Vine).

33   The "likewise" confirms the interpretation that has been given above. The overwhelming claims of the Man who bears the wounds of Calvary have made the true believer forsake all else for Him. There is a very interesting word in the clause, "whosoever he be of you that forsaketh not all". *Apostassō* ("to forsake") literally means to say farewell and is used in this way in 9:6 1: "let me first go bid them farewell, which are at home". In Acts 18:18,21 there are similar expressions about "taking leave" (v.18) and "bidding farewell" (v.21). Such a leave-taking involves turning the back on that which has been dear or formerly has been loved and this is the exact meaning of the Lord's teaching. The heart that yields its affection to the Lord must be fully devoted. Halfhearted devotion meets with the strong language, "he cannot be my disciple". True discipleship has this high standard, and we must remember that this is the Lord's own definition.

34-35   When we think of the salt that we buy with our groceries, it is very difficult to imagine how it could remain a substance at all and lose its savour. However, the salt of which the Lord speaks was vastly different, and could by exposure have all its pure salt leached out of it. When this happened it no longer had any value even as a nutrient for plants in the field or as an additive to compost; it was cast out as useless.

There was ample reason for the Lord to use salt in the teaching about discipleship. God made a covenant of salt with David (2 Chron 13:5). The salt tells of its enduring character. Genuine discipleship will never be temporary or spasmodic. It will be lasting. Salt was to be used in all the sacrifices of the levitical system (Lev 2:13). It speaks of the eternal value of the cross-work of Christ. The sacrifices that became the food of the priests were seasoned with this salt, which speaks of the enjoyment and appreciation that the believing heart finds in Christ. In contrast, "have lost his savour" is akin to the word "foolishness" used in 1 Cor 1:18, "the preaching (word) of the cross is to them that perish foolishness". "Foolishness" is the thought of being without savour or tasteless. To the false disciple there is no real heart-appreciation of the Lord Jesus. Moreover salt is a purifier and stops the spread of decay. The Lord taught, "Have salt in yourselves" (Mark 9:49,50). Salted words (Col 4:5,6) are words free from, and that preserve from, moral defilement and corruption.

35.   *The Great Trilogy*
15:1-32

a. The Lost Sheep (vv.1-7)

v.1 "Then drew near unto him all the publicans and sinners for to hear him.
v.2 And the Pharisees and scribes murmured, saying, This man receiveth sinners, and eateth with them.
v.3 And he spake this parable unto them, saying,
v.4 What man of you, having an hundred sheep, if he lose one of them, doth not leave the ninety and nine in the wilderness, and go after that which is lost, until he find it?
v.5 And when he hath found *it*, he layeth *it* on his shoulders, rejoicing.
v.6 And when he cometh home, he calleth together *his* friends and neighbours, saying unto them, Rejoice with me; for I have found my sheep which was lost.
v.7 I say unto you, that likewise joy shall be in heaven over one sinner that repenteth, more than over ninety and nine just persons, which need no repentance."

It is not possible to approach this great chapter of the Bible without a sense of awe and wonder and yet of joy at the richness of its precious gospel truths. Often, and we have seen this in Luke, the Lord tells two parables to press home one truth, but here He tells three to impress on every heart the great truth of how the lost are found. The golden text of Luke's Gospel is fully depicted here, "the Son of man is come to seek and to save that which was lost" (19:10). The subject is the salvation of the lost, not the recovery of a straying believer, but the best we can do is to let the words speak their full wealth of meaning and depend on the Holy Spirit to apply it to each reader.

The old Puritan writers described this section of Luke as:

Ch.14-A Feast	Earth with all its madness	A Great supper.
Ch.15-A Famine	Heaven with all its gladness	A Great compassion.
Ch.16-A Fire	Hell with all its sadness	A Great gulf.

The parable is one story even though it has three parts, for it takes all three to give the true picture of being lost. The sheep was helplessly lost and it took painful toil to find it. The silver was unconsciously lost and it took diligent search to find it, but the son was wilfully lost and it took the yearning love of the Father's heart to find him. The first was an object of pity, the second was an object of value and the third was an object of love. There is no blame attached to the first two for being lost, but the third was responsible for his condition. The triune God is at work in saving the lost. The sheep was in danger and to find it took the sufferings of the Lord Jesus, the good Shepherd. The silver was in darkness and it took the striving of the Holy Spirit to find it. The son was in distress and it took the Father's tender love to recover him. The first two parts of the story have been rightly called the parables of the lost sheep and the lost coin, but the third part should rightly be called, "The Parable of the Father's Heart".

1-2   These two verses need to be considered together, for they describe the company to whom the Lord spoke the threefold parable. The great contrast in the crowd explains the same contrast in the parable. All are sinners and all are lost in sin, but the contrast is between those who knew that they were lost and those who did not. The publicans who collected taxes for the hated Roman rulers, and were regarded as traitors among the Jews, are ranked with the sinners who were the outcasts of Jewish society. The Pharisees were the highly religious, and the scribes were the experts in all the intricacies of rabbinical teaching that was professedly based on the law of Moses. The Lord Jesus did not come "to call the righteous, but sinners to repentance" (5:32). It is not just a simplistic statement from gospel preachers, but a great verity that He did not come to call the righteous because there were none (Rom 3:10). The Pharisees and scribes had "a righteousness" which they paraded before the eyes of men, but in God's sight it was nothing but filthy rags (Isa 64:6). We must keep in mind the contrast between the sinners and the self-righteous who heard the Lord on this occasion. There is only one gospel in the NT. Differences in the way it is presented can be traced to the need of the hearers (compare Acts 13:16-41 and 17:22 -31), and so it is here.

The sinners came near to hear the Lord. "The Pharisees and scribes murmured" and there is no suggestion that they had drawn near to hear Him. Ch.14 closed with the words, "He that hath ears to hear, let him hear" (v.35). The charge, "This man receiveth sinners", was spoken by those who hated the Lord Jesus, but, as in the case of other such charges (Matt 27:37,42), it was blessedly true. The murmuring was intended to affect the crowd. Only Luke uses *diagonguzō* ("to murmur"), here and in 19:7: "they all murmured, saying, That he was gone to be a guest with a man that is a sinner". It literally means to send a malignant murmur through the whole crowd.

3   The three stories are called one parable, for they are one, telling about the way lost sinners are saved. The lessons of the story of the lost sheep can be summarised very simply. All are sinners; all are lost in sin; only one knew he was lost; the cost of saving the lost is immeasurable, and only the painful toil of the Shepherd's search can find the lost. The shepherd of the story is the good Shepherd who laid down His life for the sheep. Seeing we are attempting to interpret the story, we will not write about a shepherd, but *the* Shepherd. It is important to understand that all of those who are described as being lost in this chapter were saved, so they represent those who have found out they are lost.

4   The hundred sheep are divided into the ninety-nine and the one. Elizabeth Frye wrote, "There were ninety and nine that safely lay in the shelter of the fold", but this otherwise excellent hymn has missed the entire point of the parable. The ninety-nine sheep were the Pharisees and scribes who did not know that they were lost. They were in the Jewish fold but not in the safe keeping of the Shepherd, so they are left in the wilderness and he goes "after that which is lost, until he find it". This statement teaches heaven's attitude toward the lost. How far will the Shepherd go? How long will He search? The blessed answer is "until he find it". We are also taught the worth of one soul. With God there are no common people; each individual is a precious, priceless soul, the object of the personal love and earnest search of the Shepherd.

The sheep has foolishly strayed away until it is made aware that it is lost. The entire world of Jews, Gentiles, Pharisees and sinners, highly religious and irreligious, is summed up in two statements, "that which is lost" and "my sheep which was lost" (v.6). The first statement describes all mankind who have not as yet been found; the second describes all who are saved. Those who are now saved were once lost, and unless a person has discovered that he is lost, and has been found by the Shepherd, he is still lost, no matter what he may profess in the way of faith, goodness or religion. The person who was never lost has never been saved.

There are some who claim that the ninety-nine were saved, not lost, and they appeal to the statement of v.7, that there are those who "need no repentance". Such an appeal charges the Lord with contradicting His own teaching, for in 13:3,5 He taught that all need repentance. Also, to interpret this story other than as we have done creates the even greater problem that it makes the Pharisees and scribes saved, when Luke says that they were rejectors of Christ and His teaching (11:52-54).

The search of the Shepherd was long and cost Him the pain and agony of Calvary's cross. Dear Elizabeth Frye was wrong in the opening of her hymn, but none has grasped the search so well as she when she wrote:

> "None of the ransomed ever knew
> How deep were the waters crossed,
> Nor how dark the night the Lord passed through,
> Ere He found His sheep that was lost.
> Out on the mountain, He heard its cry,
> Sick and helpless and ready to die."

5-6   "And when he hath found it" tells the touching story of the long search that cost the Saviour so much in toil and pain. When He finds it it is not left to wander home, but with great joy it is carried home on the omnipotent shoulders of the Shepherd (Isa 40:11). It is only after He has found it that He calls it "my sheep". In v.4 it is only "that which is lost", but once it is found, it is "my sheep which was lost". Only those who have been found by Him are truly His sheep. "Home" is likely not the thought of coming home to heaven at the end of the christian life, but of coming home to God while we still live in this world, which is the blessed portion of all the saved. This is the teaching of 1 Pet 3:18, " Christ also hath once suffered for sins, the just for the unjust, that he might bring us to God". However, the ultimate destination will be heaven, where the believer is now seated in Christ (Eph 2:6).

7   As there was joy among the friends and neighbours, "likewise joy shall be in heaven over one sinner that repenteth". This is why we noted that this one lost sheep is the object of all the interest of heaven, and the finding of it is the joy of heaven. Those who are said to "need no repentance" are those, like the Pharisees and scribes, who have never known their need and have never been brought to repentance. In his companion book the writer of this Gospel wrote that "God ... commandeth all men every where to repent" (Acts 17:30).

b. The Lost Silver (vv.8-10)

v.8   "Either what woman having ten pieces of silver, if she lose one piece, doth not light a candle, and sweep the house, and seek diligently till she find *it*?
v.9   And when she hath found *it*, she calleth *her* friends and *her* neighbours together, saying, Rejoice with me; for I have found the piece which I had lost.
v.10   Likewise, I say unto you, there is joy in the presence of the angels of God over one sinner that repenteth."

8-10   The full story of "lostness" is not satisfied only by the story of the lost sheep. Even the most foolish sheep might find its way to a shelter or return to its fold by itself, though this is most unlikely, but a lost piece of silver presents a picture of utter helplessness. It cannot find itself.

The main point of the parable is that the lost one is found. After we have established the primary meaning we can see other aspects of gospel truth in the details of the story. It is a woman that has lost the coin, lights a candle, sweeps the house, and searches diligently until she finds it. In our outline of this chapter we have linked these activities with the work of the Holy Spirit. The coin is a drachma, equivalent in value to the silver denarius that was minted by Rome and bore the inscription of the Caesar (Matt 18:28; Mark 12:15). It was about the amount paid for a day of labour. Whatever the commercial value of the piece of silver it had great value to the woman who lost it, for its loss made her a diligent seeker who did not give up the quest until she had found it. The finding caused great joy. All of this portrays to us the activities of the Holy Spirit who, when we were lost, sought us, in fact, set us apart as objects of His special attention (1 Pet 1:2; 2 Thess 2:13). The lighting of the lamp is a clear picture of the word of God which as a light penetrates the darkness of the lost sinner's heart. The sweeping suggests His searching activity, reaching into every corner to expose our sin, for the sinner is both lost and guilty and must be brought to a realisation of personal need through the convicting word and the Holy Spirit's striving. The word for "diligently" (*epimelōs*) is found only here in the NT. This adverb is formed from *melei*, the third person singular of *melō* ("to care"), with *epi* which intensifies its meaning. The woman swept and searched with great carefulness until she found the lost coin.

There is "joy in heaven" over the lost sheep found (v.7), but when the lost silver is found the joy is "in the presence of the angels of God" (v.10). There is not a significant difference between the two verses. Plummer points out that "in the presence of" means "in the estimation of" the angels of God; so we can be certain that all heaven places the highest estimate on the worth of one soul, and so should we, and rejoice with heaven in the lost one found. We are often asked if this means that redeemed souls already in heaven rejoice when loved ones are saved on earth. The simple answer seems to be that all heaven rejoices when any soul is found.

c. The Lost Son (vv.11-32)

v.11 "And he said, A certain man had two sons:

v.12 And the younger of them said to *his* father, Father, give me the portion of goods that falleth *to me*. And he divided unto them *his* living.

v.13 And not many days after the younger son gathered altogether, and took his journey into afar country, and there wasted his substance with riotous living.

v.14 And when he had spent all, there arose a mighty famine in that land; and he began to be in want.

v.15 And he went and joined himself to a citizen of that country; and he sent him into his fields to feed swine.

v.16 And he would fain have filled his belly with the husks that the swine did eat: and no man gave unto him.

v.17 And when he came to himself, he said, How many hired servants of my father's have bread enough and to spare, and I perish with hunger!

v.18 I will arise and go to my father, and will say unto him, Father, I have sinned against heaven, and before thee,

v.19 And am no more worthy to be called thy son: make me as one of thy hired servants.

v.20 And he arose, and came to his father. But when he was yet a great way off, his father saw him, and had compassion, and ran, and fell on his neck, and kissed him.

v.21 And the son said unto him, Father, I have sinned against heaven, and in thy sight, and am no more worthy to be called thy son.

v.22 But the father said to his servants, Bring forth the best robe, and put *it* on him; and put a ring on his hand, and shoes on his feet:

v.23 And bring hither the fatted calf, and kill *it*; and let us eat, and be merry:

v.24 For this my son was dead, and is alive again; he was lost, and is found. And they began to be merry.
v.25 Now his elder son was in the field: and as he came and drew nigh to the house, he heard musick and dancing.
v.26 And he called one of the servants, and asked what these things meant.
v.27 And he said unto him, Thy brother is come; and thy father hath killed the fatted calf, because he hath received him safe and sound.
v.28 And he was angry, and would not go in: therefore came his father out, and intreated him.
v.29 And he answering said to *his* father, Lo, these many years do I serve thee, neither transgressed I at any time thy commandment: and yet thou never gavest me a kid, that I might make merry with my friends:
v.30 But as soon as this thy son was come, which hath devoured thy living with harlots, thou hast killed for him the fatted calf.
v.31 And he said unto him, Son, thou art ever with me, and all that I have is thine.
v.32 It was meet that we should make merry, and be glad: for this thy brother was dead, and is alive again; and was lost, and is found."

The literary beauty of this story has touched hearts through the centuries, but far more important is the gospel truth it portrays, and the way it has been used to the salvation of many a prodigal. The story of the lost son is really "The Parable of the Father's Heart". He is mentioned twelve times, and it is His heart of love that is revealed in the events. It is touching to recall that the One who narrated it was the Son who never once grieved His Father, but ever brought joy and delight to His heart.

There is a clear distinction between the third part of the trilogy and the first two parts. There was no awakening nor recognition of guilt and distance in the stories of the lost sheep and silver. The love of God in seeking the lost is the whole story, but in the prodigal there is "the rise and growth of repentance in the heart" (A. Plummet). Once again we can see that all three parts of the parable are necessary to describe the ruin of lost sinners.

11   In the two sons we again see the two classes of sinners to whom the Lord was speaking (vv.1,2). "If I made up my mind to perish, I would probably choose the way of the prodigal over the elder brother because it would be less of a shock at the close" (Graham Scroggie). There are writers who have carefully traced in these two sons a story of backsliding believers being restored. We are sure that the Holy Spirit is able to use Scripture in His sovereign wisdom as He sees fit, and without question, He has so used this passage to reach the hearts of true believers away from God, but as will be seen, the teaching that follows interprets it as a wilfully lost sinner being found.

12   While the two sons remained at home all the father's provision was available to them. The younger son chose not to be any longer under his father's authority and demanded the inheritance that he would have received at a later time. The father divided his property between them both. According to Deut 21:17 the firstborn would receive double the inheritance of his younger brother. The inheritance could be divided before the death of the parents, but the heirs were required fully to provide for them. The sin of the younger son was primarily his profligacy, but he was also guilty of not honouring his father.

Many have contended that, because there is a father and two sons at the beginning of the story, it is to be interpreted not as a sinner being saved, but as a backslider being restored, thus isolating this parable from its context. Certainly God is not the Father of any unconverted soul, but He does have a Father's heart of love, which is enough to explain the aptness of the parable. After having spent over forty years of his life as an evangelist, the writer finds the recovery of a straying believer very difficult to fit into the story. The context of this chapter is the salvation of lost sinners. Matt 18:12 very carefully avoids using the word "lost" of a professed believer who has gone astray, nor is "lost" ever used anywhere except as the opposite of saved (Luke 19:10; John 17:12; 2 Cor 4:3). When the prodigal was found the Father said twice that he "was dead, and is alive again". This language is used only twice of those who were dead in sins and have "passed from death unto life" (John 5:24). A parable is used to illustrate one or several points that express great spiritual reality. The reality here is that all are lost, whether they learn it as the prodigal did, or never learn it in time, like the elder brother.

13   When the younger son departed from his father's house "he gathered all together", leaving nothing of interest there and cutting every tie. The best comment we know on this act is Isa 53:6: "All we like sheep have gone astray; we have turned every one to his own way". We are creatures of choice and God cannot remove the consequences of a wrong choice unless the full penalty is paid, either by the sinner or his Substitute.

He travelled to a remote country, as far from the father's house as he could go, where he would not be observed nor censured; there he squandered his property with prodigal living. We do not know if the elder brother's judgment was fair, but he said to the father: he "hath devoured thy living with harlots" (v.30). "Wasted" and "riotous" should be understood as a scattering of resources recklessly. It is from this word "riotous" (*asōtōs*) that the word "prodigal' has been attached to this young man. As W.E. Vine has written, "the word does not necessarily signify 'dissolutely' ", but it does denote wild and disorderly living without a thought for tomorrow (Kittel, Vol I, p.507).

14   The recklessness of his career can be measured by the fact that he was not brought to the end of it until "he had spent all". When he was bankrupt, a mighty famine hit that country and "he began to be in want". A more vivid description of the desperate plight of a sinner cannot be found. At the end of his resources, he discovers that he is in a land where a mighty famine prevails. It is not difficult to recognise this "far country". It is a world of sin without God.

15   The famine is not the only want in that land, for in his dire need he finds he
has no friend. He must have had many good-time friends, but they were very
unlike the sinner's Friend (v.2). "He went and joined himself to a citizen of that
country" as a servant to a stranger. This in itself was a deep disgrace to a son of a
wealthy Jew, but the depth of his degradation was even lower as "he sent him
into his fields to feed swine". The pig was unclean: "Of their flesh shall ye not
eat, and their carcase shall ye not touch; they are unclean to you" (Lev 11:8).
Every day he was reminded that he was a law-breaker and under the judgment of
God.

16   So deep was his need that the pigs ate better than he. He longed for the
"husks", the pods of the carob tree, eaten by the swine. The ration given to
him by his new master was far from enough to satisfy his hunger. This is a
solemn reminder of the desperate poverty of those who serve sin and Satan.
In the eyes of his master the pigs were of greater worth than he. No man
pitied the half-starved foreigner who had sunk to the lowest level on the
social scale. But God, in infinite mercy and kindness, had allowed him to be
brought to this place of shame and need. *Keration* ("husks") means a little
horn, referring to the little horn-like pods of the carob tree that is still very
common in Mediterranean lands.

17   When a sinner comes "to himself" he is at the place where grace can "much
more abound" (Rom 5:20). It is suggested that previously he had been out of
touch with reality, literally "beside himself". In the far country he thought of his
father's house and of his father's "hired servants" who had "bread enough and
to spare". This facing of reality led him to the conclusion that he was perishing.
We are correct in calling this experience an awakening. It is a necessity for the
salvation of every sinner whether he has walked the road of the prodigal, who
illustrates the publicans and sinners, or the road of the Pharisees, who are pictured
in the elder brother.

18-19   The son who had grown sick of home and its restraints is now homesick
with longing. The rising up reminds us of the depth of shame and despair to
which he has sunk. He speaks of going to his father rather than of going home.
He forfeited that home by his sin. Under the law it was written, "If a man have a
stubborn and rebellious son, which will not obey the voice of his father ... then
shall his father and his mother ... bring him out unto the elders of his city ... and
they shall say ... This our son is stubborn and rebellious, he will not obey our
voice; he is a glutton, and a drunkard. And all the men of his city shall stone him
with stones, that he die ... and all Israel shall hear, and fear" (Deut 21:18-21).
   The prodigal is under the sentence of death. He had truly sinned against
heaven, against the righteous laws of God and against his father; he was verily
guilty (Lev 5:17).

20   Genuine repentance is much more than mere words: "he arose, and came". It was "his own father" (JND) to whom he returned. He had thought of the father's house in the far country, and now he is about to learn the love of the father's heart that had never ceased to yearn over him. "When he was yet a great way off" tells a wonderful story. There were eyes that had grown weary with watching. The waiting, grieving, yearning father is a powerful portrayal of the heart of God. God was the first Seeker in the Bible (Gen 3:8,9), and now in the Person of the Son still seeks the lost (19:10).

The recognition was of the heart rather than the eyes. There was no hesitation; gathering up his garments, the father, in the dignity of a deep compassion, unashamedly ran, reached him, embraced him and kissed him tenderly. At this point, the son has made no confession, but actions speak louder than words; he has returned and this is enough for the father's welcome to be given so freely.

21   His confession was full and free. There are no excuses offered, just frank acknowledgement of guilt. He did not say a word about forgiveness and made no suggestion about how the father should treat him. He did this in the far country in his suggestion about being made a hired servant, but he is now within the circle of the father's affection and he is content to leave his treatment to the father. This is a necessity in all true repentance and confession. A sinner or a believer when making confession of sin has no mitigating circumstances to plead. The "stopped mouth" (Rom 3:19) pleads no excuses; the sinner is cast on pure mercy and the grounds of forgiveness and its terms are dictated by Him who forgives. We can thank God that we have found what every penitent sinner learns; He forgives frankly, fully and forever.

22   The confession was between the father and the prodigal. It was a private business and it was heart-work. When they have arrived at the father's house, he addresses the servants: "Bring forth quickly the best robe" (RV). What a contrast to his rags was the best robe in the house, the best that could be provided! Both the OT (Isa 61:10) and the NT (Rev 7:14) use a garment as a symbol of salvation. The garment is an outward evidence of the blessing he now enjoyed, a blessing that can be seen by all, rather than a picture of imputed righteousness. Righteousness reckoned to a believer (Rom 3:22) is a judicial act and is inward and seen only by God.

Upon his hand is placed a ring. Many believe it was the signet-ring of authority and relate it to Gen 41:42, "Pharaoh took off his ring from his hand, and put it upon Joseph's hand". It signified an unending relationship to his father.

The shoes on his feet mark him as a freeman, not a slave or even a hired servant, but a son who is able to stand in the presence of his father in full forgiveness and acceptance.

The blessings of the prodigal upon his return home have been likened to the believer's blessings in Christ in the Ephesian letter. They at one time "were dead in trespasses and sins" (Eph 2:1), as the prodigal "was dead and is alive again, was lost and is found" (v.24). As he had the best robe put on him, so the believer is "to put on the new man" (Eph 4:24); the ring speaks of the dignity of (the adoption of sons" (Eph 1:5); the shoes correspond to a "walk worthy of the vocation wherewith ye are called" (Eph 4:1); the preparation of the fatted calf was done by the servants, so the gifts minister to the "increase of the body unto the edifying of itself in love" (Eph 4:16), and the music and dancing correspond to "singing and making melody in your heart to the Lord" (Eph 5:19).

23-24   The fatted calf was a prize animal reserved for a feast in honour of a very special guest. In the mind of the father there could not be a higher occasion than the lost one found and the dead one raised. The three chief elements in the story can be simply described as the father's *house*, the father's *heart* and the father's *happiness*. In a tender, touching way, God's heart is revealed in this full measure of forgiveness, acceptance and unending joy. "To be merry" is a present infinitive and refers to continuous joy, a deliberate reference to eternal salvation. There is a very similar expression in Rev 21:6, "And he said unto me, It is done". J.N. Darby suggests in a footnote that it should be translated: "They are fulfilled". The context indicates "It is begun" and it will never end. So it is here, "they began to be merry".

25-27   At the beginning of this chapter the Pharisees murmured against the Lord that He received sinners and ate with them. The trilogy has been directed to them. Particularly they are seen in the elder brother. He was "in the field", at work, and had taken no part in the joy and feasting that have welcomed home the penitent prodigal. Drawing near to the house he hears the sounds of rejoicing and inquires from a servant what it all means. The wise servant resists any temptation to interpret the events, merely reporting, "thy brother is come; and thy father hath killed the fatted calf, because he hath received him safe and sound" (v.27). The words "musick" (*sumphōnia*) and "dancing" (*choros*) are found only here, but both are familiar to English readers for they are the source of our words "symphony" and "chorus".

28   The brother is angry and refuses to go in. His refusal was communicated to the father, for he came out himself and entreated him to come in. The repetition of the figure of a house in Luke 13, 14 and 15 should not be overlooked. In 13:25 it is "the master of the house" who rises up and shuts the door. It is the lord of the house in 14:23 who says, "that my house may be filled". In this chapter the house has a father in keeping with the words of the Lord in John 14:2, "In my Father's house are many mansions". The descriptions fit each context; the father entreats, the lord commands and the master shuts the door. Coming into the house is likened to salvation. The elder brother is entreated to come in and refuses (15:28). The guests are invited and make excuses (14:18), but when the door is shut great throngs clamour to get in and cannot enter (13:25).

29-30   The entreaty of the father is contrasted with the refusal of the elder son. It was a tender love that brought the father out to urge him to come into the house. His refusal is based on an unwillingness to accept the forgiveness which has been so freely given to his younger brother, whom he refuses to own, calling him "this thy son", not "my brother". This attitude comes from an unrepentant spirit. He has never been aware of his own need for forgiveness. His lifelong bondage (*douleuo*) in subjection to his father is the ground of acceptance that he claims, so he displays the character of a Pharisee, unforgiven because the need for it has never been accepted. A self-righteous spirit is the framework on which a hypercritical attitude towards others is built, so he puts the very worst interpretation on his brother's behaviour: he has "devoured thy living with harlots". Personal interest is so evident in his words: "thou never gavest me a kid, that I might make merry with my friends", but there is also here the evidence that there is no joy in religious servitude; it is merely bondage. A solemn warning is sounded in our ears, for if we too are hypercritical and fail in forgiving the penitent sinner, we partake of the spirit of a Pharisee.

31-32   The response of the father shows a tenderness toward this elder son which gives us a vivid picture of the yearning of God over Israel. We are reminded of Hos 11:4,8: "I drew them with cords of a man, with bands of love ... How shall I give thee up, Ephraim? how shall I deliver thee, Israel?". Even toward the Pharisees the Lord Jesus expresses a tender love and concern.

36.   *How Much Owest Thou unto my Lord?*
   16:1-13

> v.1   "And he said also unto his disciples, There was a certain rich man, which had a steward; and the same was accused unto him that he had wasted his goods.
>
> v.2   And he called him, and said unto him, How is it that I hear this of thee? give an account of thy stewardship; for thou mayest be no longer steward.
>
> v.3   Then the steward said within himself, What shall I do? for my lord taketh away from me the stewardship: I cannot dig; to beg I am ashamed.
>
> v.4   I am resolved what to do, that, when I am put out of the stewardship, they may receive me into their houses.
>
> v.5   So he called every one of his lord's debtors *unto him*, and said unto the first, How much owest thou unto my lord?
>
> v.6   And he said, An hundred measures of oil. And he said unto him, Take thy bill, and sit down quickly, and write fifty.
>
> v.7   Then said he to another, And how much owest thou? And he said, An hundred measures of wheat. And he said unto him, Take thy bill and write fourscore.
>
> v.8   And the lord commended the unjust steward, because he had done wisely: for the children of this world are in their generation wiser than the children of light.
>
> v.9   And I say unto you, Make to yourselves friends of the mammon of

unrighteousness; that, when ye fail, they may receive you into everlasting
habitations.
v.10 He that is faithful in that which is least is faithful also in much: and he that is
unjust in the least is unjust also in much.
v.11 If therefore ye have not been faithful in the unrighteous mammon, who will
commit to your trust the true *riches*?
v.12 And if ye have not been faithful in that which is another man's, who shall give
you that which is your own?
v.13 No servant can serve two masters: for either he will hate the one, and love the
other; or else he will hold to the one, and despise the other. Ye cannot serve
God and mammon."

The parable of the unjust steward has ever been a problem to interpreters. A difficulty of our own making is to think that the Lord commended a man who was obviously less than honest. The Lord did not commend the unjust steward, but "the lord" of the steward did (v.8) and this distinction is necessary. We can be certain that the perfect Man, who in this world displayed God's holiness, cannot be charged with upholding dishonesty. It is the Lord Jesus who calls the steward "unjust" (v.8), and He is not suggesting that anyone follow the path of unrighteousness. He told the story to give us an example of prudence, not of methods. The wisdom of the steward was seen in the use he made of present opportunities to prepare for the future. Worldly stewards use their influence and wealth to promote their own interests and to better their position for a future in this world. This is our lesson, but we must apply it to heavenly things. "As good stewards of the manifold grace of God" (1 Pet 4:10), we have had the Lord's treasures entrusted to us. Even our material blessings are Another's (v.12); they are held in trust against a day to come. In view of that day, when we must give account, we should use present opportunities to lay up treasure in heaven (12:31-34).

This parable can teach us a lesson which we are very slow to learn. A parable is a story, an earthly story that contains many details that are necessary to round out the picture; if we attempt to interpret all these details we shall obscure the real meaning. This parable has many details but one dominant lesson: use present opportunities for future blessings.

1-2 The first clause of this verse shows a turning from the mixed company of 15:1,2 to address the disciples. The teaching about grasping opportunities in this world in view of being received into the eternal habitations is clearly truth for His own, not for Pharisees who need salvation, but they remained within hearing and derided Him for this teaching (v. 14).

"A certain rich man" need not be interpreted as a major part of the lesson of the parable. It is any rich man who has a steward. In this case the steward was accused of mismanagement of his master's goods and is called to account and told that he is to be removed from his stewardship. The accusation was made against him by an unnamed person (or persons), but *diaballō* ("to accuse") suggests that they were "thrown about" as a "verbal assault" from one to another, eventually coming to the ears of the rich man. This is the only NT use of *diaballō,* but it is from the same root as *diabolos* ("slanderer") which is used for the devil six times in Luke (4:2,3,5,6,13; 8:12), and frequently throughout the NT. *Diaballō* describes the manner in which the slander passed among (*dia,* "through") the people, not whether or not it was true. In this case the charges were true (v.2). The devil tells lies, "because there is no truth in him. When he speaketh a lie, he speaketh of his own: for he is a liar, and the father of it" (John 8:44). He tells lies to us, but perhaps he knows better than to tell lies when he accuses us to God. His accusations against Job are an example (Job 1:9-12). This "unjust steward" gave cause to his enemies to accuse him; we must strive not to give the devil cause to accuse us. When he is finally cast down from heaven, he is exposed as "the accuser of our brethren ... which accused them before our God day and night" (Rev 12:10).

3-4   The servant knew he was guilty of embezzling his master's funds, and in his words "my lord taketh away (middle voice) from me the stewardship", he is admitting that his lord has acted for himself in his own best interests. Left now without work or means of support, he says, "to dig, I am not able, to beg, I am ashamed" (A. Marshall). The digging probably stands for any kind of hard manual labour. *Aiteō* ("to ask") is a common verb: *epaiteō* ("to beg") is an intensive form and is only here in the NT. The notice that his employment was terminated would require a final accounting, so the steward used the available time to work out a plan for his own future. He contemplated various kinds of work that he might attempt, but abandoned these plans when a better one came to his mind. He decided to put his lord's debtors in his debt so that when he was put out of his stewardship they would receive him into their houses.

5-7   He called each debtor personally, asking, "How much owest thou unto my lord?". Some knowledge of the financial structure in Israel helps greatly in understanding the story. The Law forbade taking interest (usury) for loans to fellow Israelites (Lev 25:35,36), but clever Jewish businessmen found ways around the prohibition. They argued that the Law aimed to protect the poor from exploitation; so as long as the borrower had any means at all he was not poor, and a scheme was worked out whereby the creditor could charge interest while calling it profit-sharing. Often, such arrangements were discreetly made by stewards, supposedly without the knowledge of their masters. This steward called the debtors and cancelled the profit-sharing part of the debt. If the lord had complained about this reduction in the debts, he would be allowing public knowledge of the hidden usury he had been charging. It was better to remain quiet and gain the appearance of being righteous and law abiding (J.D.M. Derrett, *Law in the New Testament*; A. Edersheim, *Jesus the Messiah*, pages 395-397).

In the word *chreopheiletēs* ("debtor", v.5) two words are combined: *chreos* ("a loan") and *opheiletēs* ("a debtor"). Luke already used this word in the short parable of the two debtors (7:41). It is found nowhere else in the NT. W.E. Vine says that Luke is referring to "a system of credit ... in agriculture". Luke's words, names and titles have been proven to be carefully given, drawn from the practices and usages of the culture of his day. A very effective application of the question, "How much owest thou unto my lord?" can be made to the hearts of believers.

8   The master made the best of a bad situation by commending the steward for his cleverness. If the view of the situation has been rightly assessed, the steward did not endear himself to his master by his actions but he did enhance his own position with the debtors. This clever scheme won the grudging admiration of his lord. In "He had done wisely", *phronimōs* ("discreetly", "shrewdly") is an adverb and is only here in the NT, but the adjective *phronimos* is used fourteen times, and is here in the phrase "wiser than the children of light". Paul uses it in an evil sense in Rom 11:25, "wise in your own conceits" or simply "wise in yourselves". He was using irony to the Corinthians when he wrote, "We are fools for Christ's sake, but ye are wise..." (1 Cor 4:10); and "ye suffer fools gladly, seeing ye yourselves are wise" (2 Cor 11:19). There may be something of the sense of Rom 11:25 in its application to the unjust steward. He certainly did not have the kind of wisdom that the Lord attributes to the steward in 12:42, "Who then is that faithful and wise steward, whom his lord shall make ruler over his household?".

"The sons of this age" (RV marg) is a graphic description of the worldly wise, and they are contrasted with the "sons of the light" (RV) who should show the same measure of wisdom in view of their future. This means a looking ahead and using present time, talents and means for eternity, sending our treasure on ahead, for "where your treasure is, there will your heart be also" (12:34).

9   "Mammon" (*mamōnas*) is found only four times in the NT; in Matt 6:24 and three times in this chapter (vv.9,11,13). Moulton and Milligan say it was derived from a Hebrew word meaning "deposited". W.E. Vine gives "treasure" (Gen 43:23) as an example. In Matt 6 and here (v.13) it is personified as a master and stands in apposition to God. We cannot compare "the mammon of unrighteousness" with a similar expression anywhere in Scripture. Titus 1:11 speaks of "filthy lucre" as the gain of false teachers, but the context is different. *Mamōnas* is riches, wealth or money that does have value in this temporal scene but is certain to fail to provide for eternal needs. The Lord calls it "the mammon of unrighteousness" for it is so often linked to evil and the covetous heart of man is ever ensnared by it. However, it will fail, and "when it fails ye may be received into the eternal tabernacles" (JND); note the change from "when ye fail" (AV). This part is clear, but we have not explained "Make to yourselves friends". The context helps us: the unjust steward used his opportunities to prepare for what lay in his future. In application, our use of means to minister to the needy, feed the hungry, clothe the poor, nurse the sick, further the work of the Lord is a "making friends" of mammon that if merely spent in self indulgence would fail and leave us with nothing. The proper use of the mammon gives it eternal value through the people who have been blessed by it. "They may receive you" may refer, as many think, to those who have gone on before to heaven.

10   This maxim applies to every aspect of life. The person who can be trusted in small things where there is little accounting, can be trusted in larger responsibilities. It is also true that dishonest acts seldom begin with large thefts. Conscience is usually fed the opiate of small dishonesties until there is a graduation to greater crimes.

However, this is one of the most profound statements of Christ and greater wisdom for time and eternity cannot be found. The order in which the Lord spoke the two contrasting statements indicates that He is giving positive teaching. "He that is faithful" is comparable to "he that is spiritual" (1 Cor 2:15). When we are "faithful" we are yielded to God and His Spirit, with Christ as the pattern. It means that the most insignificant task that springs from a heart devoted to His will has utmost importance and eternal value. "Faithfulness in that which is least" was epitomised by Abraham in his words to the king of Sodom, "I will not take from a thread to a shoelatchet..." (Gen 14:23). On the positive side, this faithfulness would include voluntary work in the care of a building where the believers meet; a gospel tract given to a stranger; a kind deed done for a needy person in the Lord's name; a careful preparation in prayer and study before sitting down with a little Sunday school class and much more. "Mighty deeds as we had thought them, He may show us were but sin. Little deeds that we'd forgotten, He will tell us were for Him".

11-12   We have less trouble with the meaning of "the unrighteous mammon' in this verse than in v.9. Here it is contrasted with the true riches. The heavenly riches are not called mammon, merely "the true", in contrast to the false wealth and possessions of this world. There is a sense in which the mammon is entrusted now, to be carefully stewarded, and the measure in which it is faithfully handled will be the measure of the true riches that will be entrusted in the world to come. The principle that is taught here is comparable to the parable of the ten pounds (19:11-26). All that we have as earthly blessings are entrusted to us to be used faithfully for the glory of God and to be accounted for when we stand in His presence. Unfaithfulness in present responsibilities will rob us of reward at the judgment seat of Christ, to be displayed in the kingdom.

13   The choice is between God and mammon, and the latter is here personified as an owner of slaves. To be at the absolute disposal of two masters is impossible. Their demands would conflict one with the other and neither would be served. Our problem seems to be that, instead of being wholly yielded to God as His bondslaves of love, we serve God at times and serve self and self-interests at other times. The teaching of our Lord will not allow this. True service to God demands that all that we are and have be at His disposal at all times. A divided heart is a great evil in Scripture (James 1:8; 4:4,8). In this lovely Gospel of Luke, the Lord Jesus perfectly personified total, unfailing service to God, He "took upon him the form (*morphē*) of a servant" (Phil 2:7).

37.   *The Contrast between Divine and Human Estimation* 16:14-17

v.14 "And the Pharisees also, who were covetous, heard all these things: and they derided him.

v.15 And he said unto them, Ye are they which justify yourselves before men; but God knoweth your hearts: for that which is highly esteemed among men is abomination in the sight of God.

v.16 The law and the prophets *were* until John: since that time the kingdom of God is preached, and every man presseth into it.

v.17 And it is easier for heaven and earth to pass, than one tittle of the law to fail."

The Lord Jesus, as the great Teacher, gave great summaries of truth in statements of eternal meaning. Four such statements are found in these four verses:

1.   "God knoweth your hearts"

2.   "That which is highly esteemed among men is abomination in the sight of God ",

3.   "The law and the prophets were until John",

4.   "It is easier for heaven and earth to pass, than one tittle of the law to fail".

14   It is the comment of the Holy Spirit that the Pharisees were covetous. The Lord's statement that God and mammon cannot be served at the same time caused them to scoff, for Pharisees believed that their faithfulness to God could be measured by their material wealth. The poor were poor because they had failed carefully to keep the ritual of the Law. The Pharisees "derided him" (*ekmuktērizō*), a word that is only found here and in the statement, And the rulers also with them derided him, saying, He saved others..." (23:35). Words accompanied the derision at the cross, but a person may deride without saying a word, for *ekmuktērizo* means "to turn up the nose at one, to sneer, to scoff" (A.T. Robertson).

15   To "justify yourselves before men" literally means to declare your own righteousness. Justification by God means that He declares the sinner righteous on the ground of the propitiation offered by the Lord Jesus at the cross (Rom 3:24-26). This is the major difference between religion and salvation. It is the contrast between "do" and "done" that we preach in the gospel.

"But God knoweth your hearts" is a searching statement with sweeping application, for "the Lord seeth not as man seeth; for man looketh on the outward appearance, but the Lord looketh on the heart" (1 Sam 16:7). Yet even among the Pharisees there were honest men who believed that they were serving God. We know of cases such as Gamaliel and Saul of Tarsus; therefore the Lord did not make a blanket condemnation of all of them without distinction.

"That which is highly esteemed among men" takes in a wide scope that includes all of society's values, all that men place value upon in the world of commerce, pleasure and religion. The word "abomination" originally meant that which totally offends the sense of smell. This is one of the most sweeping condemnations of the present evil age (Gal 1:4) to be found in all of Scripture.

16   "The law and the prophets were until John" is the third great, summary statement of four that make up this short section. It is most important in our understanding of the relationship of the OT to the NT. "The law and the prophets" is the recognised designation for all the OT. John the Baptist was in the long line of prophets through whom God spoke to Israel (Heb 1:1), and stood the last in line. A new day dawned with the incarnation and John as the forerunner helped to bridge the gap between the old dispensation of law and the new dispensation of grace. This statement needs to be considered seriously by those who confuse Israel and the church and mix law deeds with grace.

17   Even though with the new dispensation a great change in the dealings of God with men had taken place, the OT Scriptures will never lose their value. The witness that they gave to the coming Saviour has greater meaning than ever, having been fulfilled and becoming the "more sure word of prophecy" (2 Pet 1: 19). The many Scriptures already fulfilled in the first advent are a guarantee that all their promises of the coming manifest kingdom of God at the second advent will not fail. This statement is set against the background of the utter failure of mammon and "that which is highly esteemed among men" ever to bring in righteousness and peace. The " tittle of the law", not one of which could fail until all was fulfilled, was a dot projecting like a tiny horn from certain Hebrew letters to distinguish them from others of similar appearance. How careful we ought to be in the handling of "every word" that has proceeded " out of the mouth of God" (Matt 4:4)!

38. *Divorce and Adultery*
16:18

v.18 "Whosoever putteth away his wife, and marrieth another, committeth adultery: and whosoever marrieth her that is put away from *her* husband committeth adultery."

18 From the beginning it was the plan of God that a man and woman joined together in marriage became "one flesh". This standard has never been revoked and is the standard by which christian couples must enter the marriage union. They enter into a covenant before the Lord (Prov 2:17; Mal 2:14) that is indissoluble except by death. The Lord is teaching here a principle that goes back to creation.

The rabbinical schools in Israel were at variance regarding allowable divorce and remarriage (Matt 19:3-9). The school of Hillel went so far as to interpret the Deut 24:1 exception to include such displeasure on the part of a husband as the way his wife cooked his food. The school of Shammai allowed divorce for unchastity only. There is a higher principle by which believers' lives are governed. Even when there has been infidelity on the part of one partner the order of the NT is repentance, forgiveness and recovery (Matt 18:21,22,35; Luke 17:3,4; Eph 4:32). God's word sets a very high standard of forgiveness, and true believers will be brought to repentance and will be recovered, otherwise we have no right to call them christians. We must impress the permanence of marriage in all our practice and teaching. The wide disagreement among believers does not lie in this area, but in the area of sin committed prior to coming under the searchlight of the gospel and being saved. This writer believes that in such cases 1 Cor 6:9-11 applies.

39. *Two Men in Time and in Eternity*
16:19-31

v.19 "There was a certain rich man which was clothed in purple and fine linen, and fared sumptuously every day:

v.20 And there was a certain beggar named Lazarus, which was laid at his gate, full of sores,

v.21 And desiring to be fed with the crumbs which fell from the rich man's table: moreover the dogs came and licked his sores.

v.22 And it came to pass, that the beggar died, and was carried by the angels into Abraham's bosom: the rich man also died, and was buried;

v.23 And in hell he lift up his eyes being in torments, and seeth Abraham afar off, and Lazarus in his bosom.

v.24 And he cried and said, Father Abraham, have mercy on me, and send Lazarus, that he may dip the tip of his finger in water, and cool my tongue; for I am tormented in this flame.

v.25 But Abraham said, Son, remember that thou in thy lifetime receivedst thy good things, and likewise Lazarus evil things: but now he is comforted, and thou art tormented.

v.26 And beside all this, between us and you there is a great gulf fixed: so that they which would pass from hence to you cannot; neither can they pass to us, that would come from thence.

v.27 Then he said, I pray thee therefore, father, that thou wouldest send him to my father's house:
v.28 For I have five brethren; that he may testify unto them, lest they also come into this place of torment.
v.29 Abraham saith unto him, They have Moses and the prophets; let them hear them.
v.30 And he said, Nay, father Abraham: but if one went unto them from the dead, they will repent.
v.31 And he said unto him, If they hear not Moses and the prophets, neither will they be persuaded, though one rose from the dead."

This is one of the most solemn passages in all the Bible. General confusion about hell, particularly among cults, makes a fuller introduction to these verses necessary. One of the greatest proofs of the love and mercy of God is His faithful warnings of coming judgment. In this passage there is an unwilling witness; a voice comes down the corridor of time giving testimony to a place where he is "tormented in this flame". There is also an unsent witness, Lazarus, but the unfailing Witness who gives us the history of these two men in life, death and eternity is the true Witness who "delivereth souls" (Prov 14:25). This is the tender Saviour who asked the Pharisees and scribes, "How can ye escape the damnation of hell (*geenna*)?" (Matt 23:33) and then wept over those who were perishing (v.37). His warning is not only true and faithful (Rev 3:14) but it is tender and timely, for we all are travellers to eternity, and we dare not trifle with it. Obscure teaching on this subject and half-hearted warnings are not kindness but cruelty. The Lord Jesus spoke very plainly.

Men have always had subjective tests of truth, and so-called "modern" man has not advanced very far beyond his predecessors in this matter. A subject may be believed or disbelieved depending on factors which actually have no bearing on its truth or falsehood. One of the greatest errors is to suppose that if a thing is true it must be fully comprehensible. But our minds are not the court of final appeal, for there are many things in the universe which are beyond the range of our personal experience and therefore beyond our full comprehension, even in the material realm. In the spiritual realm the triune God and His holy character transcend our highest thought. We do not comprehend the cross nor the depths of the infinite sufferings of our Saviour there. No, it is not how much men know, even in this day of knowledge-explosion, that makes them reject the Bible's warnings about hell; it is human pride and ignorance.

If I say that the test of truth is the measure in which I feel comfortable in believing it, then my error is compounded. I am not really using logic but subjective emotion that has never been a reliable guide. In this world of hunger, disease, tragedy, pain and grief, there is so very much about which we are most uncomfortable, so much that does "not seem right", and yet we dare not reject reality because it pains us. The unfathomed ocean of human sufferings in this world, caused by sin and impossible to deny, is as difficult to comprehend as any truth we know. So we approach these verses knowing that the reality of hell far exceeds our feeble senses and can never be comfortably believed. We must always make a difference between what is against reason and what is beyond it.

(A note on the words for hell, hell fire, the grave and the pit is at the end of this section.)

19   "There was a certain rich man" (v.1) can be the words by which the Lord introduces a parable, but in no parable is a proper name given as it is to Lazarus in this story. Therefore we prefer to accept this account as history rather than an illustrative parable. The Lord, who in His omniscience knows the history of every man, can give us the true story of two men in time and eternity.

The summing up of a life in such a brief sentence, particularly the life of such a rich man as this verse describes, shows the emptiness of a life without God. He dressed like a king and had a banquet every day. There is no reference to heinous crimes or open hostility to God or His word. The outer garment of purple, a very costly dye obtained from a shellfish (murex), and the inner garment of fine linen may be applied to the respect he commanded among his fellow-men and the righteous conduct of his personal life, but the Lord tells these details to give us the facts of his wealth. The sumptuous feast was not merely on some high days but "every day". He lived a life of elegance and ease. The Bible does not teach that wealth is evil, but to use it only for self-gratification without a genuine, practical concern for the needs of others is evil.

20   The contrast could scarcely be greater than that which the Lord draws between these two men: the richest of the rich and the poorest of the poor. *Pulōn* is the Greek word for a large gateway or portico, the grand entrance to a mansion or palace. At this gate lay the beggar covered with rags and sores. When there is little or no means of cleanliness open ulcers are not uncommon, but Lazarus was covered with sores. This expression, "full of sores", translates *helkoō*, only used here in the NT, but it is from the same root as *helkos* ("sores" or " ulcers") in v.21. The only other two uses of *helkos* are in Rev 16:2,11, verses which describe the terrible sores with which men are afflicted when the vials of God's wrath are poured out.

"Named Lazarus " is not coincidental. The Lord, in giving us his name, a name that had no meaning and held no interest for the rich man and his friends, "must have been reading from that book where He found the name of Lazarus written, but the name of the rich man was missing" (C.H. Spurgeon, from a Puritan writer). Lazarus is Greek for *Eliezer* which by general consent means "God is (my) help", a meaning which has great significance when we apply it to this poor diseased beggar. The fact that he "was laid" (past perfect passive of *ballō*) suggests that he had been flung there. Luke uses *ballō* ("to cast") in this sense (12:28,58; 14:35), "as if contemptuous roughness is implied" (A. Plummer).

21   To the beggar the rich man offered nothing but indifference. He has been given the credit of not driving the beggar from his gate, but this good is far outweighed by the fact that he made no effort to help him. Lazarus was there for the crumbs, so he must have been able to gather some of them. "Desiring to be filled" (JND) tells us that what he was able to get was not enough to alleviate his hunger. "Nay, even the dogs came and licked his sores" (Plummet) may be interpreted by many as a kindness, but this is because we picture the domestic creature that is the friend of man. These unclean dogs of the street added to his misery and either he was too weak or they were too persistent and too many for him to drive away. At the door of Cain lay sin (Gen 4:7) and at the gate of this much later son of Cain lay the opportunity to relieve suffering and misery; it became sin that he callously refused to help.

22   The death of Lazarus cannot be a surprise after the description of his rags, sores and hunger, but these are not titles to heaven and we must attribute his destination after death to salvation, not to misery on earth. It is heartbreaking reality that many who have had suffering here will have it forever. The words of so many, "All the hell I will ever have, I have had on earth", is a serious mistake: it is appointed unto men once to die, but after this the judgment" (Heb 9:27).

    The omissions of the Lord are greatly significant; He does not tell us that Lazarus was buried. Considering Levitical law about defilement from a dead body we should not suppose that his body lay in the street after his death was discovered, but his burial must have been in some "potter's field" without mourners or ceremony. However, it is not about his body that we are told. The Lord of eternity rolls back the curtain of time and allows us to look beyond death into that region to which "he was carried away" (JND) by angels to a place of perfect bliss. " Abraham's bosom" may be figurative language, but it recalls to our minds the upper room and the beloved disciple "leaning on Jesus' bosom" (John 13:23). Lazarus had love, rest and blessing such as earth had never been willing or able to give to him.

    "The rich man also died", so death, without respect of persons, the common leveller, entered uninvited and perhaps unannounced into the palace of the rich man. His friends were allowed to follow his remains to the grave with pomp and splendour such as would be appropriate to a man in his station in life.

23   The Lord Jesus allows us to follow his soul beyond the limits of worldly sight and sense as it plunges from the grandeur of earth to the utter poverty of hell. "Lifting up his eyes" (JND) is a vivid description of an awakening that takes place too late. He is made aware of the torments of hell as soon as he is conscious of his location. There is no thought of soul sleep, or even the loss of sight, or self-awareness, or faculties by which he feels pain and want. Whatever we can conjecture about the existence of a soul without a body, the Lord Jesus uses sensations related to the body to convey the condition of the soul. Some say, "Jesus does that so that we on earth can understand, and we are not to take the language too literally". Our answer is in the form of a question, "Understand what?" If this is a picture, and the Lord Jesus as the faithful and true Witness is describing it, of what is it a picture? A word picture has a limited dimension, but if it is a true picture, then that which it portrays has full dimensions. This is another way of saying that the reality cannot be less than the picture.

The great distance, "afar off", between the place of bliss and the place of comfort is the distance between paradise and hades, but I would go further and plainly say that it is the distance between heaven and hell. Spatial measurements of distance and time are not restrictions in that other world. In that far off place he sees Abraham and, what to him must have been an amazing sight, the former beggar in his bosom. If riches were a total bar to heaven then how could Abraham be there?, for "Abram was very rich" (Gen 13:2).

24   The crumb on earth was very small but by it the beggar attempted to sustain life. The drop of water in hell was even less by earthly standards, but values had drastically changed and it became infinitely valuable. "Send Lazarus" may not have been so much the old arrogance of earth as it was the cry of a desperate soul, "I am in anguish in this flame" (RV). The word "torment" (*basanos*) that is used in vv.23,28 is used in a slightly different form in Rev 9:5 of the torment inflicted by the scorpion-like creatures out of the pit. The anguish of remorse will be present, but this word also implies retributive judgment (Vine's *Dictionary of NT Words*). The rich man said, "that I may cool (*katapsuchō*, to cool down) my tongue", a word that is only here in the NT, but is common in medical books of the time, and is another example of Luke's words that indicate an interest in medical matters (Hobart, p.32).

25   The answer of Abraham, "Son, remember", tells us that in hell the memory of the mercies and privileges of the life on earth are not forgotten, indeed, cannot be forgotten. Personality and memory are not left behind in the grave. One of the greatest horrors of hell will be a good memory. Horatius Bonar's eloquent poem has expressed it well,

> "Memory like an adder stingeth,
> All the wasted past upbringeth,
> Could I but that viper strangle,
> Half my miseries would be o'er,
> But around my heart it coileth,
> Every frantic effort foileth
> 'Tis the worm that never dieth,
> Gnawing at my bosom's core,
> Will it quit me nevermore?
> Echo answers, nevermore."

The "good things" were more than mere material riches, for as the conversation continues, we learn that the man in hell had said "No" to the word of God. So his "good things" in life included offers of grace and calls to repentance, but the chief purpose in mentioning the "good things" is to show the great contrast before and after death between the rich man and Lazarus. The word "thou art tormented" (*odunaō*) in vv.24,25 means "to be in anguish" or "to be greatly distressed", "in great pain" (*odunē*). This word *odunaō*, " rare in prose writers, is used in the NT only by Luke" (Moulton and Milligan). Its other occurrences are 2:48, when Mary said to the twelve year old Child, "thy father and I have sought thee sorrowing" or "with anguish", and Acts 20:38 of the believers in Ephesus, "Sorrowing most of all ... that they should see his face no more".

26   "And beside all this" is heart rending, for it means, in addition to all this torment and misery, " there is a great gulf fixed". After all the preachers of all the centuries have told, with burdened hearts, all they know of the torments of the lost in hell, it would still have to be said, "And beside all this". The great gulf formed in Eden that separated man from God because of sin, and bridged at Calvary (1 Tim 2:5,6) is here eternally fixed so that it can never be bridged or crossed. The soul in hell is beyond salvation, beyond mercy; there is no second chance; no verse in the Bible makes this more clear.

27-28   We do not know what motivated the rich man to make this request for his brothers. It has been suggested that souls in hell have no desire for the company of others in equal torment. However, his words imply a charge against God: If Lazarus' return from the dead "that he may earnestly testify" (JND) to them would result in their escaping the torment, then had he been sufficiently warned neither would he have been there. "No one has come back to tell us what lies beyond death" is a poor excuse, for a witness making such a claim would have a credibility problem that would make his testimony meaningless. When the Lazarus of John 11 was restored to life, rather than the chief priests believing in the Lord Jesus, they plotted to kill Lazarus (John 12:10). When the Lord Jesus rose from the dead the same priests and leaders of the nation did their utmost to kill the witnesses (Acts 5:33).

29-31   The answer of Abraham is, in effect, simply "They have the word of God, let them hear it". "Moses and the prophets" encompasses all the Scriptures that stand written (Matt 4:4). No greater or more effective warning can be given. The "nay" in v.30 is a plain no to the word of God and is the final explanation of why the rich man died and went to hell. He had not believed the word of God about his need as a sinner and God's provision for sinners, and he did not practise the teaching of it in his life as is evident from his callous indifference to the beggar who died at his gate. In hell he is unchanged, unrepentant, and still insisting that he must be right and God is wrong for not having given better warnings. This is expressed in the solemn words "neither will they be persuaded, though one rose from the dead". Hell will be a terrible place where men blame one another and blaspheme God and blame Him for all their pains (Rev 16:9). In hell lost souls are not saying, "If only I had believed the warnings and accepted the Saviour while there was time". "If only I" is not in their vocabulary, rather it is "If only God had given me more warning, opportunity or evidence that all of this is true". Lost souls will never be persuaded. Their hostility to God is eternal; therefore their punishment is eternal.

Notes

Words Used in Scripture for Hell

a.   The Old Testament
   i   **Sheol**-*the place of those who have departed this life.*
       Sheol is an OT word that corresponds to *hades* in the NT.
       Sheol is translated "hell" thirty-one times; "grave" thirty-one times; "pit" three times.
   ii **Qeber**-*the grave where dead bodies are buried.*
       Qeber is the OT word for grave. It is used thirty-four times. It is the body that goes to *qeber* at death, not the soul. *Sheol* never means the grave in spite of the thirty-one OT readings. It is a general term, referring to the abode of departed spirits. *Sheol* allowed for misery or bliss, so we are able in the light of NT revelation to link it with hades.

b.   The New Testament
   i   **Hadēs**-*the unseen world, the place where the dead go.*
       Hadēs is translated "hell" eleven times, once "grave" (1 Cor 15:55). Although *hadēs* is a general term for the abode of departed spirits the Lord taught that there were two roads and two destinies (Matt 7:13); so in *hadēs* there were two very different destinies, one of comfort the other of torment. Lazarus went to the former, the rich man to the latter. We rightly interpret these destinies after the resurrection and ascension of the Lord Jesus to be heaven and hell. There seems to be some evidence that before the cross souls went down even to the place of comfort (Gen 37:35; 42:38; Ps 30:3; 16:10; Acts 2:27), or this is the way it was perceived. After the resurrection we have no doubt that Paul had to be "caught up" to be in paradise (2 Cor 12:2).

   ii **Geenna**-*the place of unquenchable fire.*
       Geenna is found twelve times, eleven of these in the synoptic Gospels. It is the place where both body and soul are ultimately cast (Matt 10:28; Luke 12:5); it is unquenchable flame (Matt 18:8; Mark 9:43-48) and is called the lake of fire (Rev 20:15).
   iii **Abussos**-*the bottomless pit.*
       Abussos is used nine times and is translated seven times "bottomless pit", or "the pit of the abyss" (JND), all in the Revelation. It is translated in Luke 8:31 and Rom 10:7 as the "deep".
   iv **Tartarus**-*a prison house where angels are in chains of darkness.*
       Tartarus, or *tartaroō*, is translated "hell" in 2 Pet 2:4. This is a particular punishment of angels that sinned and should not be confused with any of the words above.

40. *Trespass and Forgiveness*
17:1-4

v.1   "Then said he unto the disciples, It is impossible but that offences will come: but
woe *unto him*, through whom they come!

v.2   It were better for him that a millstone were hanged about his neck, and he cast
into the sea, than that he should offend one of these little ones.

v.3   Take heed to yourselves: If thy brother trespass against thee, rebuke him; and
if he repent, forgive him.

v.4   And if he trespass against thee seven times in a day, and seven times in a day
turn again to thee, saying, I repent; thou shalt forgive him."

1   The word "impossible" (*anendekton*, "it cannot be") is found only here in
the NT. "Offences" (*skandalon*) are certain to come. This noun is found only
here in Luke; the verbal form is also used once (7:23). It originally meant the
bait-stick that was placed in a trap. It came to mean any kind of a snare that trips
up the feet of the unwary. To set such a trap was the intention of Balaam (Rev
2:14) who "taught Balac to cast a stumblingblock (*skandalon*) before the children
of Israel". He succeeded all too well in entrapping Israel in the sin of Baal-peor.
No wonder that the Lord pronounces woe on such a cruel and deliberate snare.

Unbelieving Jews and philosophical Greeks turned the preaching of the cross
into an offence (Gal 5:11; 1 Pet 2:8). The same word is used in Paul's warning,
"judge this ... that no man put a stumblingblock (*proskomma*) or an occasion to
fall (*skandalon*) in his brother's way" (Rom 14:13), so the offence can be caused
through carelessness as well as by evil intent. The contrast is found in 1 John
2:10. "He that loveth his brother abideth in the light, and there is none occasion
of stumbling in him", that is, he will not cause others to sin.

2   The judgment that will fall on the person who stumbles a believer is very
severe, particularly if it is "one of these little ones", perhaps a young believer, for
spiritual babes are under the Father's care (10:21). A stone used for grinding in
a mill would be large and heavy. The offender would be fortunate to have a
millstone hung about his neck and be thrown into the sea, rather than to have to
meet God's judgment for ensnaring a little one. Careless offence is a terrible sin,
intentional offence is an even greater evil, but both will meet with just judgment.
The word in Matt 18:6 is "a great millstone" too heavy to be turned by one or two
slaves (RV margin, "a millstone turned by an ass"). A different word is used here
(*mulikos*, of a mill) for a great stone (*lithos*) used for grinding without defining
it as the upper stone that was turned or the lower one that was fixed.

3-4   The link between these verses and the two preceding ones is by contrast.
When the judgment is against us for sinning against others, it is very severe.
When, as here, the sinning is against us, we are to be very tender. We should
never cause others to sin, but if they do sin, we should rebuke them, and when
they repent, we should grant immediate forgiveness. It does not need to be

earned; it is a gift. Complete confidence must be earned, but according to this teaching of our Lord, we must be able to make a difference between the two, and never withhold forgiveness on the ground that the person may do the same thing again, even if the same sin is committed seven times in the same day. The Lord says, "if he repent, forgive him". We do not have ability to judge hearts, so when it is a matter of personal offence, whether repentance is real or not is not our business, but God's. If the brother says, "I repent", then we must forgive him. We should be looking for the opportunity to forgive rather than seeking an excuse not to forgive (see Eph 4:32).

41.   The Smallness of Faith
   17:5-6

v.5 "And the apostles said unto the Lord, Increase our faith.
v.6 And the Lord said, If ye had faith as a grain of mustard seed, ye might say unto this sycamine tree, Be thou plucked up by the root, and be thou planted in the sea; and it should obey you."

5   The desire for an increase in faith may be related to the teaching of vv.3,4 but the link is not obvious. Perhaps the disciples are confessing their difficulty in putting into practice such a high standard of forgiveness. They are not asking for initial faith in Christ but for a working faith in which to serve Him acceptably. Faith is a very small thing and the size of it is far less important than its object. It never stands alone and has value only in the degree that its object has value. Strong faith in an unreliable person produces nothing but disappointment. But faith in Christ and His promises can never lead to disappointment because He said: "Heaven and earth shall pass away, but my words shall not pass away" (Matt 24:35). Only twice did the Lord credit a person with "great faith". The first was when the Syrophenician woman took the lowest place (Matt 15:28), and the second was when the centurion gave to the Lord Jesus the highest place (Luke 7:9), so great faith cannot be determined by worldly standards of greatness.

6   The mustard seed was often used as a figure of the smallest of things. The sycamine tree is not familiar to us by this name, but it must have been well-known to the disciples. Zacchaeus climbed into a sycomore (19:4), and the Greek words are very similar. It was a large tree with well-established roots or the Lord would not have used it as an example of the power of faith. Small faith in a great God can immediately move both trees and mountains (Matt 17:20). On the use of the two words by Luke, *sukaminos* ("sycamine") and *sukomorea* (" sycomore ", 19:4), A.T. Robertson has an interesting comment: "Luke alone in the NT uses either word ... The distinction is not observed in the LXX, but it is observed in the late Greek medical writers for both trees have medicinal properties. Hence it may be assumed that Luke, as a physician, makes the distinction".

42.   *The Duty of Servants*
17:7-10

v.7   "But which of you, having a servant plowing or feeding cattle, will say unto him
       by and by, when he is come from the field, Go and sit down to meat?

v.8   And will not rather say unto him, Make ready wherewith I may sup, and gird
       thyself, and serve me, till I have eaten and drunken; and afterward thou shalt
       eat and drink?

v.9   Doth he thank that servant because he did the things that were commanded
       him? I trow not.

v.10   So likewise ye, when ye shall have done all those things which are commanded
       you, say, We are unprofitable servants: we have done that which was our duty
       to do."

7   It is not necessary to suppose that the Lord turned from the disciples at this point to address some wealthy land owners. Although the disciples may not have had the experience of being masters over servants, it is enough that they would be familiar with the practices of masters and servants. The servant (*doulos*, slave) has been engaged all day in the work of his master, but this is what is expected of him so that when he comes in from the field, he is still expected to be a servant, not an honoured guest in his master's house. The two occupations of "plowing or feeding cattle" have been likened to the work of evangelists and teachers. But the word for "feeding cattle" (*poimainō*), "shepherding" (JND), involves all the activities that make up the work of a shepherd, so this servant engages in a threefold activity of "ploughing" (an evangelist), "shepherding" (an overseeing shepherd) and as the story unfolds, he also serves tables (a teacher). There are times when evangelists teach and overseers preach the gospel, but God can and does give men more than one gift, and there are many examples of men in the NT with the gifts of evangelist, shepherd and teacher. Such work is genuine labour and all of it has great value.

8   The servant prepares food for his master then girds himself in a fitting way to stand at his master's table to wait on him. When all the necessary service for his master has been done then he may look after his own needs. There is a great contrast to this when, in the day of His glory, the Lord Jesus will serve His own servants, "he shall gird himself, and make them to sit down to meat, and will come forth and serve them" (12:37). However the description of this servant's activities indicates that he does no more than is absolutely demanded of him. Even his reasons for slavish obedience may be self-serving, for if he disobeys he may not eat, so he does it grudgingly.

9   The lesson to be learned in this illustration is the difference between duty and true devotion. The servant has only done his duty. It is expected of him and he is not thanked for his service. Obedience to commandments is emphasised: "he did the things that were commanded him". The spirit of his service is that he

acts out of necessity, not out of devotion to his master. Such service is not approved because it is always done with an eye that primarily looks out for self.

10   "So likewise ye" does not mean that the servant described in the previous three verses is an example to follow; rather, that his spirit of service is a contrast to God's true servants in the kingdom of God. Paul's words, "Not with eyeservice, as menpleasers" (Eph 6:6) describes the unprofitable servant, but the contrast is "as servants of Christ, doing the will of God from the heart" (Eph 6:6). The word *achreios* ("unprofitable") is used only twice in the NT, here and in the parable of the talents, "the unprofitable servant" (Matt 25:30), and means to be without usefulness (*chreia*, use). From all this we learn that the Lord is looking for more than an outward show of service, which may indicate usefulness to men, but true usefulness to God comes for a devoted heart.

"When ye shall have done all those things which are commanded you" reminds us of the commission, " teaching them to observe all things whatsoever I have commanded you" (Matt 28:20). What a joy it would be to be able to say that we had completely fulfilled all that He has commanded! But notice the contrast! Duty may be done without devotion; in fact, it can be a harsh and bitter service. If the highest motive we reach is "We know what we ought to do", we have not known anything of the real joy of serving the Lord. Devotion from the heart that has been captivated by love is a far higher motive than mere duty. Duty gives a plain call, but it cannot stand alone as the motive for service. An example of true devotion follows in the healing of the Samaritan leper.

43.   *Where are the Nine?*
17:11-19

v.11 "And it came to pass, as he went to Jerusalem, that he passed through the midst of Samaria and Galilee.
v.12 And as he entered into a certain village, there met him ten men that were lepers, which stood afar off:
v.13 And they lifted up *their* voices, and said, Jesus, Master, have mercy on us.
v.14 And when he saw *them*, he said unto them, Go shew yourselves unto the priests. And it came to pass, that, as they went, they were cleansed.
v.15 And one of them, when he saw that he was healed, turned back, and with a loud voice glorified God,
v.16 And fell down on *his* face at his feet, giving him thanks: and he was a Samaritan.
v.17 And Jesus answering said, Were there not ten cleansed? but where *are* the nine?
v.18 There are not found that returned to give glory to God, save this stranger.
v.19 And he said unto him, Arise, go thy way: thy faith hath made thee whole."

11   This is the third time that Luke reminds us of the long journey that the Lord was taking toward the cross (9:51-53; 13:22). In 10:38 the Lord was in Bethany, a short distance south-east of Jerusalem. In John 10:40-42 He left Judaea and went into Peraea, on the east side of the Jordan. It is very likely that He was there when we are told, He "abode two days still in the same place where he was" (John 11:6) after hearing that Lazarus was sick. After the raising of Lazarus He returned north with his disciples to "a city called Ephraim" (John 11:54) which was in the hill country about twenty miles due north of Jerusalem. From the location given in this verse, a border area between Samaria and Galilee, it is not improbable that He continued north before again turning His steps toward Jerusalem (A. Edersheim). Many believe that "certain disciples from Galilee" met Him about this time and continued with Him on the final stage of His journey toward Jerusalem (*The Journeys of Jesus Christ*, A.T. Schofield and G. Biddulph). As has been pointed out in 9:51 Luke traces the footsteps of the Man of sorrows as He is journeying to Calvary, even though the route was not in a straight line.

12-13   The ten lepers were neither in the village nor at the entrance to it, but "stood afar off", for Israel's law concerning lepers was "All the days wherein the plague shall be in him he shall be defiled; he is unclean: he shall dwell alone; without the camp shall his habitation be" (Lev 13:46). So these ten men approached as near as they dared and, because the distance was still great, "they lifted up their voices" and cried for mercy. The Lord Jesus is addressed as *epistatēs*, "master", literally, "superintendent" or "commander". (Only in Luke is *epistatēs* used: 5:5; 8:24,45; 9:33,49; 17:13.) It is of great interest that when Peter was overwhelmed with the glory of the mountain top experience he called the Lord *epistatēs* (9:49). These lepers have a lesson to teach to people of our day. They did not address the Lord as Jesus, but recognising His sovereign power and authority, they called Him, "Jesus, Master".

14   "He saw them" as no other eyes could ever see them. They were unattractive, their disease making them repulsive in the eyes of others, but to the Lord they were objects of the compassion of His tender heart. He did not tell them that they were healed, but He spoke to them the words that must have been uppermost in their minds from the day the priest had pronounced them unclean. Their greatest longing had been to have that judgment reversed. They responded in faith to the Lord's command, and as they went they were cleansed.

15-16   It is likely that the nine were Jews. Would the one Samaritan go to one of Israel's priests? The disease that commonly afflicted them had already broken down the religious scruples that separated Jews from Samaritans (John 4:9). "As they went" indicates that he too obeyed the Lord, which must have been more difficult for him than the others, but when he saw that he was cleansed he turned back and "with a loud voice glorified God". He fell at the feet of the Lord Jesus in thankfulness and worship. "And he was a Samaritan" was a terrible rebuke to the proud priests and Pharisees who with their scribes so dishonoured this Jesus of Nazareth. A lowly, despised Samaritan is cleansed and is the only one of the ten healed lepers who returns to give thanks. This voluntary act of gratitude and devotion is the exact opposite of the attitude of the "eyepleasing" servant in vv.7-10. To act spontaneously as the heart motivates the action brings glory to God (v.18). In v.18, he is called "this stranger" (*allogenēs*) or "one of another race", a word found only here in the NT. Moulton and Milligan in *The Vocabulary of the Greek Testament* suggest that it may have been coined by the Jews, for although it is "frequent in the LXX" it is "found nowhere in profane writers. But note should be taken of the famous inscription on the Temple barrier... 'let no foreigner (*allogenēs*) enter within the screen and enclosure surrounding the sanctuary' " (p.23). So this Samaritan would have been barred from the temple precincts, but was welcome at the feet of the Lord.

17-18 There are many indications in the Gospels that healing did not automatically mean salvation. When the blind man whose eyes were opened had been cast out of the temple he was asked if he believed on the Son of God. His answer was, "Who is he, Lord, that I might believe on him?" (John 9:36). Only then did the Lord graciously reveal Himself to him, "And he worshipped him". We do not know about the state of the souls of the nine, but we need not assume their salvation because of their healing. Every saved sinner has a thankful heart, even though we lament that we often suffer from slowness of heart (24:25). In His omniscience the Lord knew that the ten were cleansed without being with them when it happened, but He also knew their hearts, and none of them was thankful. The Samaritan was the one exception. It is one of the most solemn indictments against men that "when they knew God, they glorified him not as God, neither were thankful; but became vain in their imaginations, and their foolish heart was darkened" (Rom 1:21; see also 2 Tim 3:2).

19 In v.15 the Samaritan saw that he was healed, for *iaomai* means "to heal", but "thy faith hath made thee whole (*sōzō*)" goes far beyond the leprosy. It normally means "to save". Looking into his heart, the Lord saw a man who was not only ready to receive Christ as his Healer but as his Saviour and Lord as well.

44. *The Two Aspects of the Kingdom*
17:20-37

v.20 "And when he was demanded of the Pharisees, when the kingdom of God should come, he answered them and said, The kingdom of God cometh not with observation:

v.21 Neither shall they say, Lo here! or, lo there! for, behold, the kingdom of God is within you.

v.22 And he said unto the disciples, The days will come, when ye shall desire to see one of the days of the Son of man, and ye shall not see *it*.

v.23 And they shall say to you, See here; or, see there: go not after *them*, nor follow *them*.

v.24 For as the lightning, that lighteneth out of the one *part* under heaven, shineth unto the other part under heaven; so shall also the Son of man be in his day.

v.25 But first must he suffer many things, and be rejected of this generation.

v.26 And as it was in the days of Noe, so shall it be also in the days of the Son of man.

v.27 They did eat, they drank, they married wives, they were given in marriage, until the day that Noe entered into the ark, and the flood came, and destroyed them all.

v.28 Likewise also as it was in the days of Lot; they did eat, they drank, they bought, they sold, they planted, they builded;

v.29 But the same day that Lot went out of Sodom it rained fire and brimstone from heaven, and destroyed *them* all.

v.30 Even thus shall it be in the day when the Son of man is revealed.

v.31 In that day, he which shall be upon the housetop, and his stuff in the house, let him not come down to take it away: and he that is in the field, let him likewise not return back.

v.32 Remember Lot's wife.

v.33 Whosoever shall seek to save his life shall lose it; and whosoever shall lose his life shall preserve it.

v.34 I tell you, in that night there shall be two *men* in one bed; the one shall be taken, and the other shall be left.

v.35 Two *women* shall be grinding together; the one shall be taken, and the other left.

v.36 Two *men* shall be in the field; the one shall be taken, and the other left.

v.37 And they answered and said unto him, Where, Lord? And he said unto them, Wheresoever the body *is*, thither will the eagles be gathered together."

20   The Pharisees' question was in relation to the kingdom in manifestation. The Lord's answer was in relation to the kingdom in its spiritual or mystery form. "The kingdom of God cometh not with observation" means that there would be no great outward display of its coming, yet when the kingdom is manifested and the King appears in power to reign, the display will be evident in every corner of the earth (v.24; Matt 24:27), so there are two aspects of the kingdom. "Not with observation" (*paratērēsis*) is only here in the NT and suggests a physician who closely watches the observable symptoms of his patient. The approach of the kingdom could not be observed, no matter how skilled the observers, which the Pharisees thought themselves to be. In fact, the King stood among them and was unrecognised. It is a serious error to interpret the Lord's answer as intending to deceive, for "neither was guile found in his mouth" (1 Pet 2:22). He did not give a simple answer because He had told His disciples: "it is given unto you to know the mysteries of the kingdom of heaven, but to them it is not given" (Matt 13:11). His questioners were not sincere and were looking for words to come from His lips by which they might accuse Him to the Sanhedrin and the Romans. They were told all that they were willing to receive and much more. If they were not ready to receive the lowly Saviour they would not be ready for the kingdom, and in rejecting it in mystery form they were unfit to receive it in its manifestation.

There is no confusion about the two aspects of the kingdom in the Lord's teaching, but confusion reigned in the thinking of the Pharisees and even in the thinking of the disciples until after Pentecost. The King came and was rejected by His own people; however, each believer is a subject in the kingdom (John 3:5; Col 1:13), which is now in its mystery form (Matt 13:11). The King is now absent and will not return until the kingdom in manifestation will be revealed (Rev 19:11-16). Such expressions as "the kingdom of heaven" and "the kingdom of God" must be understood in their contexts. "The kingdom of God" may be wider than the "kingdom of heaven". The former expression is a reality without the creation of earth at all, but the latter is the rule of heaven over earth. It does not help interpretation to insist on a significant difference in these two terms, for they are often used interchangeably (see Matt 19:23,24).

21 There is no contradiction between this verse and v.23. They will say "Lo here! or, lo, there! " but without good reason. False reports of the presence of the King are related to the great deceptions of the tribulation days (Matt 24:23 God had drawn near and was among them, represented by Jesus of Nazareth in their midst and His lowly followers from Galilee.

There has been long debate on the use of *entos* ("within" AV), in the clause, "the kingdom of God is within you", which J.N. Darby, Dean Alford, A. Plummer, J. Weiss, the RSV, NEB, RV (margin) and many others translate as "among" or "in the midst". In their long note on *entos*, Moulton and Milligan begin, "We have no citation which throws any light on the much disputed meaning of *entos humōn* in Luke 17:21 ..." Many scholars favour "within", but from the quotation just given and from their general arguments, there is not overwhelming evidence for it. The context strongly favours "among" and seeing that grammatical use does not militate against it, we accept it. It is very difficult to believe that the kingdom of God was within the heart of Pharisees who at the same time were thickening their plot to kill the King. Those who admit there is a problem in believing that the Lord is saying the kingdom is within the Pharisees yet reject "among you", suggest it means "it is really present" (Godet) even though it is unseen, which of course is true of the spiritual kingdom, and is a way of bypassing the debate without actually settling the meaning of *entos* in this context.

22 Using the occasion of the Pharisees' question the Lord now turns to the disciples to speak to them of the kingdom that would come with power and great glory. The desire to see one of the days of the Son of man has both an immediate and future interpretation. The Lord was on His way to Calvary; His body was to be laid in the garden tomb; as a living Man He would ascend back to the Father and no longer would His own enjoy His physical presence (5:35); they would "desire to see one of the days of the Son of man". However, this cannot be its full meaning, for the title "Son of man" must be understood by its use in Dan 7:13,14. The teaching that immediately follows gives weight to this future interpretation. "The days of the Son of man" refer to the time when He will take universal and eternal dominion and, as a Man, reign in perfect righteousness and peace. The desire is an intense longing and has great significance. "Days are coming" (JND) in which a distressed people in the great tribulation (Rev 7:14) will lift their eyes to heaven in longing for the dawning of "the days of the Son of man".

23 The kingdom in its mystery form was not inaugurated by signs in heaven, but the manifest kingdom will be preceded by signs. The sign mentioned in this verse, the appearance of false prophets and false Christs, is dealt with much more fully in the other synoptic Gospels (Matt 24:23-26; Mark 13:21-23). The deception will be so persuasive that the very elect would be deceived, were this possible (Matt 24:24).

In v.21, " Lo here! or, lo there! " and in this verse, " See here; or, see there", the same word *idou* ("behold") is used for "lo" and "see", so the two verses are more alike than the AV indicates. The invitation to "behold" is false in both verses, but v.21 begins "Neither shall they say", and v.23 begins, "And they shall say", so although the two verses have similarities, the two opening statements are opposites. The difference can be understood by interpreting v.21, as we have done, to be the kingdom coming in its mystery form, a kingdom already present, yet unrecognised by the Pharisees, and understanding v.23 to be the kingdom in manifestation, coming with signs in heaven and earth.

24 The warning that closes v.23 militates against any thought that the appearance of the Son of man will be a secret thing. He will not be found in some hidden desert place or in an inner chamber (Matt 24:26), but will be manifested from heaven in such a way that "every eye shall see him" (Rev 1:7). This coming is as swift as lightning and as sudden as the flood or the judgment on Sodom. His coming will also be as a thief in the night (Matt 24:43; 1 Thess 5:2). Note that this figure is used to show that it will be unexpected by those who are not ready, but it is not secret in the sense that only a limited number see it. It is not possible to make the coming of the Son of man to earth in judgment, when He will display His great power and glory, the same event as the rapture when the Lord comes to the air for His church (1 Cor 15:51-58; 1 Thess 4:13-18). The former event is not a mystery that was hidden in ages past (Eph 3:3-6), for it was the substance of hundreds of prophecies, but the rapture and the changed bodies of living saints is a mystery never revealed previously (1 Cor 15:51).

There is a great contrast between the false witnesses who say that Christ will be found "here" or "there" (v.23) in some secret place known only to them, and the dazzling display of His glory which will accompany His return. It will be as the "lightning (*astrapē*) that lighteneth (*astraptō*) out of the one part.. .", a dazzling brightness that cannot be hid. Only Luke uses this latter word, here and in 24:4, where it is used to describe the dazzling light shining from the garments of the two men by the empty tomb. In 9:29, a strengthened form, *exastraptō* ("glistering") is used for the radiant brightness of the Lord's garments on the mount of transfiguration, for none will rival the radiant glory of the coming King.

At His coming, the light will be like lightning because "None will foresee it, and all will see it at once, so that no report respecting it can have any value" (A. Plummer). The measurement, "out of the one part under heaven ... unto the other part", should be understood as meaning that His coming will be universally visible, rather than a local phenomenon. In vv34-36, every part of earth, whether it is their morning, midday or night will know the time of His return.

25   Seven times in Luke the Lord foretells His suffering and rejection (5:35; 9:22; 9:44; 12:50; 13:33; 17:25; 18:31-33) and there is a progressive revelation from the first mention to the last. There is significance in the expression "this generation". It was a generation of great privilege and great guilt and prefigured the generation of Israel in the end time which will remain in unbelief until they look on Him whom they pierced (Zech 12:10).

26-27   The comparison of end-time days to the days of Noah is found at least five times in Scripture (Matt 24:37-39; 1 Pet 3:20; 2 Pet 2:5; 3:4-7; see Heb 11:7). The days of Noah were characterised by great evil, unbelief, and total indifference to the warnings from God. These things will again be prominent in the days just preceding the return of the Son of man. Noah was "warned of God" and was "moved with fear" at "things not seen as yet" (Heb 11:7), but the people of his generation were unmoved and showed rank unbelief and indifference to the warnings. It is this utter carelessness that the Lord is describing here. The activities, eating, drinking and marrying, are not of themselves evil, but they carelessly continued with their normal activities as if they had never been warned. They "knew not until the flood came" (Matt 24:39), for unbelief made them so deaf that they were taken with shock and surprise.

28-30   The Lord is speaking of sudden judgment that falls on those who refuse to be warned, but the two illustrations also emphasise the great evil and perversion of antediluvian days and liken it to the evil of the end times. The flood of iniquity that will break out (Matt 24:12), when the Holy Spirit as the Restrainer of evil and the evil one is removed (2 Thess 2:7) out of this scene, is already manifesting itself. Evil events still future are casting their shadows over the affairs of men. Sodom is now a more true picture of the world of our day than Egypt.

As with the days of Noah, the Lord describes the normal activities of living in Sodom, but when men live in rebellion against God, the very "plowing of the wicked, is sin" (Prov 21:4). It was the same day that Lot went out of Sodom that the judgment fell. The departure of the only righteous man (2 Pet 2:8) was the signal for the destruction. The Lord removes His own from the scene of judgment before punishing the wicked. This will be fulfilled when a place of refuge is provided for the remnant of Israel in the last three and a half years of great tribulation (Rev 12:14-16).

So long as we make clear that it is application, we can apply this to the church at the rapture. As Noah and his family went through the flood, so will the remnant of Israel go through the great tribulation; as Lot was taken out before the judgment fell, so the church will be at the rapture. However, we must be careful not to teach that when the church departs the judgment will immediately fall. The opposite is true, for the Lord is saying here that the lives of men will continue in their evil course undisturbed by any warning, "For when they shall say, Peace and safety; then sudden destruction cometh upon them" (1 Thess 5:3). Luke was acquainted with Paul's teaching about these events, and there is perfect agreement between the Lord Jesus and Paul who wrote of the conditions that will prevail prior to the coming of "the day of the Lord" (1 Thess 5:2).

31 "In that day" does not refer, then, to the rapture, reference to which cannot be found anywhere in the synoptic Gospels, but to the days that immediately precede the coming of the Son of man. It helps to remove some of the difficulty when we understand that the events that precede the descent of the Lord in judgment are a part of "the day of the Lord" (Jer 46:10; Joel 2:1-32; Amos 5:18-20; Zeph 1:7-18). Joel calls the actual day when the Lord suddenly appears, "the great and the terrible day of the Lord" (Joel 2:31; Acts 2:20). The flight described here will take place when the Roman prince breaks the covenant with Israel in the middle of the week (Dan 9:27). Matthew marks it as "When ye ... shall see the abomination of desolation ... stand in the holy place" (24:15). This event will be the signal of Israel's "time of trouble", the last three and a half years of the tribulation period. The faithful remnant will flee from the power of "the beast" (Rev 13:4-8) and not turn back as did Lot's wife.

32 We do not make a mistake when we apply the tragedy of Lot's wife to the need for sinners to flee from the wrath to come. She had so long been occupied with the goods of Sodom, its fellowship and its friendship, that at the crucial moment when she must turn her back on it all and flee, she was drawn back and perished. The pillar of salt on the plain of Sodom stands as an object lesson to all who treat the warning lightly and are held in the grip of the world's goods and pleasures. She almost escaped, was so near to safety, yet looked back and perished. There was an intention to flee but a reluctance to leave Sodom behind because it held a deadly attraction for her, and so the world holds sinners.

It is interesting to draw a contrast in the various looks toward Sodom. In Gen 13:10 Lot looked upon the plain of Jordan with *pleasure:* it was "like the land of Egypt", but Sodom was far further advanced in evil than Egypt. Abraham, and the messengers from God looked toward Sodom in pity (Gen 18:16) because of its impending judgment. Lot's wife looked upon it as her *master* and truly it did overcome her (Gen 19:26). Abraham looked upon it as it burned with fire (Gen 19:28). He had forsaken this in Gen 14:21-24, and had relinquished any claim to the goods of Sodom because he knew they were destined for the fire.

33   We can scarcely be wrong in our gospel application of these events when the Lord Himself so applied them. In 9:24 we interpreted this saving and losing of life as being eternal destiny. We now see that this is the way the Lord is using it. This is not sacrificing for the Lord's sake as a believer; it is a lost sinner, awakened to his need, aware that judgment is coming and counting all else as nothing compared to the eternal salvation of his soul. People do not get saved without this awakening that causes a sinner to desire salvation more than all the world; to receive Christ is to reject the world. It will be true of those who are saved in a coming day of impending wrath, and it is true of all who flee to Christ for salvation in this present time.

34-36   We have tried to lay a foundation in interpreting the preceding verses that will help us in this difficult section. Those who are taken away are the objects of judgment and those who are left are the objects of mercy. This division is comparable to the dividing of the sheep and the goats in Matt 25:31-46 but is certainly not the same thing, for there the sheep are the saved out of Gentile nations. The ones taken away in this passage are visited with immediate judgment. It involves their instant death and assures their future punishment. They are Jews (Matt 24:42), not Gentiles; Jews that are unprepared for the Lord's return, and to them the words must be applied, "be ye also ready, for in such an hour as ye think not the Son of man cometh" (Matt 24:44). This taking away has been interpreted by some to mean death at the hands of the beast (Rev 13:7), but if this be true, then they are not the Lord's faithful martyrs whose death is blessed (Rev 14:13). The ones who die in this verse are found not ready and come under the judgment of God. Those who are spared are saved to go into the millennial kingdom; they endure to the end (Matt 24:13).

There is an interesting point about the omission of v.36 from so many manuscripts. The judgment will fall suddenly, yet two are in one bed, for it is night; two women are grinding at the mill, for it is morning; and two are working in the field, for it is the middle of the day. Well might an early scribe have wondered how an event that happens so suddenly could happen at three very different times, and be tempted to omit the troublesome passage. Of course we know that such an instantaneous event can take place at night in one longitude and by day in another. Will there be Jews prepared and unprepared in every part of the world or only in the land of Israel? Only a remnant will return to the land, and many who are sealed as witnesses will surely be among the nations (Rev 7:3).

37   This verse adds much weight to the interpretation that those who are taken away are the objects of judgment and are taken away by death. These dead bodies are the remains of people who have died under judgment and they attract the "vultures" (RV margin) who feed on them. Eagles do not feed on dead bodies and *aetos* can mean either vulture or eagle. At the coming of the Lord from heaven in judgment He makes war and smites the armies of the beast, slaying them with the sword of His mouth. The corpses of the slain will provide food for the birds of the air at "the great supper of God" (Rev 19:17,18 JND). These Jews who have taken the mark of the beast and are apostate will share the fate of all who come under the judgment of that day.

45.   The Unjust Judge and the Justice of God
18:1-8

v.1   "And he spake a parable unto them *to this end*, that men ought always to pray, and not to faint;

v.2   Saying, There was in a city a judge, which feared not God, neither regarded man:

v.3   And there was a widow in that city; and she came unto him, saying, Avenge me of mine adversary.

v.4   And he would not for a while: but afterward he said within himself, Though I fear not God, nor regard man;

v.5   Yet because this widow troubleth me, I will avenge her, lest by her continual coming she weary me.

v.6   And the Lord saith, Hear what the unjust judge saith.

v.7   And shall not God avenge his own elect, which cry day and night unto him, though he bear long with them?

v.8   I tell you that he will avenge them speedily. Nevertheless when the Son of man cometh, shall he find faith on the earth?"

1   There is a clear link between this parable and the teaching about "the day of the Son of man" that closes the previous chapter. There is to be an interval, perhaps a long one, between the promise of His coming and its fulfilment. Those who are faithful to Him will be sorely tried, and they will be tempted to give up their faith and cease to pray with simple confidence that the day of their vindication will truly come. The principle of the delay or the tarrying can be seen throughout the parable, and the question that closes this section adds much weight to this interpretation. The writer to the Hebrews uses this encouragement for those who had suffered the loss of all their worldly goods for the Lord's sake, urging them, "Cast not away therefore your confidence, which hath great recompense of reward. For ye have need of patience, that, after ye have done the will of God, ye might receive the promise" (Heb 10:35,36). He then assures them that the Lord will surely come (v.37).

Although it is true that it was "to them" (*autois*) that had just heard the teaching about the coming of the Lord that this exhortation is given, yet we must understand that it has a general application to prayer. It has been translated, "that they should always pray and not lose heart" (W. Hendriksen), or "not to be fainthearted" (J. Rotherham), so we should pray at all times and particularly when we are tempted to lose heart. To "not faint" (*ekkakeō*) is used only here by Luke, but Paul used it the five other times in the NT. In 2 Cor 4:1,16, it is "we faint not"; in Eph 3:13, "I desire that ye faint not", and in Gal 6:9 (some manuscripts) and 2 Thess 3:13, it is translated "be not weary". A lack of courage in a time of deep need is a terrible tragedy. The Lord is presenting an antithesis between praying and fainting which means that prayer provides the needed courage and strength not to faint. Paul wrote, "I have strength for all things in him that gives me power" (Phil 4:13 JND). Some have taken the meaning further and have interpreted the fainting itself as a failure to pray. Although it is true that failing to pray is a form of fainting, yet the previous interpretation seems to fit the language better. Let us never neglect the great privilege and constant duty of prayer!

2-5   The judge is depicted as godless and unmoved by compassion toward men. He would have been moved by a bribe but the poor widow had none to offer. However, she persisted in her coming and pleaded for justice. Her continual coming annoyed him (JND) and figuratively gave him "a black eye", so to be rid of her he heard her plea and rendered justice in avenging her of her adversary. The poverty and desperate need of the widow is an apt description of the plight of God's elect in distress and need, particularly the faithful remnant in tribulation days. When she pleaded "avenge me" (*ekdikeō*), her language meant that her case was just and her need to be vindicated was very great. A.T. Robertson points out that two prepositions, *ek* ("out of") and *apo* ("from"), are used in v.3, for both are needed to rightly picture the widow's sore plight. The verb "avenge" (*ekdikeō*) is used twice (vv.3,5), and the cognate noun ("execute vengeance", "vindication") is in vv.7,8. Elsewhere the verb is used twice by Paul: "Dearly beloved, avenge not yourselves" (Rom 12:19), "And having in a readiness to revenge all disobedience" (2 Cor 10:6); and twice by John: " judge and avenge our blood" (Rev 6: 10) and "hath avenged the blood of his servants (Rev 19:2). In Rom 12:19, believers are exhorted to wait until the Lord metes out justice. In the latter three cases it literally means, "let justice be done".

6-7   If even an unjust judge is capable of doing justice, how much more will the God of love and tender mercy act to vindicate His own elect who persistently cry day and night unto Him. We should take note of the expressions that suggest a delay in the answer. The elect "cry day and night unto him" and He bears "long with them". God's delays are a major part of our schooling in grace, for by them He teaches us lessons of faith and patience. There is a second reason for delay. In dealing with God's time-clock Peter writes, God is "not willing that any should perish, but that all should come to repentance" (2 Pet 3:8-10). This is the context here. When the Son of man returns He will bring judgment to the wicked and God patiently waits for evil men to be brought to repentance; therefore the Lord tarries.

8   When the time of vindication arrives, according to the divine plan, the judgment will fall suddenly. This agrees fully with the warnings that the Lord has just given about the sudden judgment when the Son of man returns. In the

Hebrew passage already cited these two elements, patience at the delay (Heb 10:36), and yet the suddenness of the coming, for "he ... will not tarry" (v.37), exactly parallel the Lord's own teaching. There will be delay; perhaps a long one that will mean severe testing for the faithful, but "yet a little while, and he that shall come will come, and will not tarry". This is the principle of imminence which may seem to be a paradox to unbelievers but has wonderful meaning for believers. The Lord commended the assembly at Philadelphia "Because thou has kept the word of my patience", so again the principle of delay is introduced, but then He says, "Behold, I come quickly" (Rev 3:10,11).

That the persistence in prayer and the exhortation not to faint are in view of His coming is clear from the question that closes the parable. "Faith on the earth" must be interpreted in a personal way and applied to faithful ones who continue to wait on the Lord in prayer and do not give up the hope of His return. A faithful remnant will be waiting when the Son of man descends from heaven to earth. This is the interpretation that suits the context of this parable, but we must never forget the practical lesson that persistence in prayer will be rewarded with answers from heaven.

46.   *The Parable of the Pharisee and the Publican*
   18:9-14

> v.9 "And he spake this parable unto certain which trusted in themselves that they were righteous, and despised others:
> v.10 Two men went up into the temple to pray; the one a Pharisee, and the other a publican.
> v.11 The Pharisee stood and prayed thus with himself, God, I thank thee, that I am not as other men *are*, extortioners, unjust, adulterers, or even as this publican.
> v.12 I fast twice in the week, I give tithes of all that I possess.
> v.13 And the publican, standing afar off, would not lift up so much as *his* eyes unto heaven, but smote upon his breast, saying, God be merciful to me a sinner.
> v.14 I tell you, this man went down to his house justified *rather* than the other: for every one that exalteth himself shall be abased; and he that humbleth himself shall be exalted."

9   There is a link between this parable and the preceding one about the unjust judge. The lesson of that parable was trust in God; this parable was spoken to those who trusted in themselves. They believed in their own self-righteousness, and the corollary was contempt of others. These two characteristics were so obvious in the Pharisees. Luke uses the word *exoutheneō* ("to despise") of their attitude here and in 23:11, "set him at nought", referring to the treatment of Christ by Herod and his men of war; it is not found elsewhere in the Gospels. It is the word used by Peter as he charged the elders of Israel, "This is the stone that was set at nought by you builders" (Acts 4:11). In all its other nine occurrences it is used by Paul: "despise" (Rom 14:3); "set at nought" (Rom 14:10); "despised" (1 Cor 1:28); "least esteemed" (1 Cor 6:4); "despise" (1 Cor 16:11); "contemptible" (2 Cor 10:10) and "despise" (Gal 4:14; 1 Thess 5:20). It literally means to regard as nothing, to treat with contempt. When the Lord said "certain which trusted in themselves", he used *peithō* ("to trust", in the perfect tense; cf. 11:22), but it is also the word for "persuade" (16:3 1; 20:6; Acts 13:43; 14:19; 18:4; 26:28). The same kind of reasoning that convinced these people of their own self-righteousness, persuaded them that others were worthy of only their contempt. This is the ultimate double standard.

10   When men who feared God prayed to the Lord, they prayed in the temple courts if they were near it, and toward the temple if they were far removed from it, and God heard them, as Solomon had requested at its dedication (1 Kings 8:29-52). This was the practice of Daniel in Babylon (Dan 6:10). So these two men in going to "the house of prayer" (Isa 56:7; Matt 21:13) were obeying Scripture. As in Luke 15, the Lord Jesus used the two extremes of Jewish society to illustrate the gospel; the highly religious Pharisees, and the irreligious publicans who were noted for their dishonesty and for being traitors to the Jews by collecting taxes for Rome.

11   The normal posture for prayer was to stand (Mark 11:25), but there are cases of OT saints bowing their knees, as Daniel did three times each day (Dan 6:10). If the Pharisee had bowed his knees he would have been contradicting his own words, for their was nothing to indicate any humility in his prayer. He must have felt no need, for he asked God for nothing. He placed himself in a position as far from the publican as possible and he "prayed thus to himself" (JND), indicating that he was inaudible to others; in both the standing and the praying to himself the Lord is indicating the attitude of his heart. Much has been written about the words, "prayed thus with himself" (AV). Using a variant reading, some have contended that it means "he stood by himself", but there is excellent authority for the text as the AV translates it. We have suggested that it means his words were inaudible to others, but many go further than this and say that it was "a soliloquy with his own soul ... for his own satisfaction" (A.T. Robertson); "the man was actually talking to himself, congratulating himself" (W. Hendriksen). The prayer was inaudible to others, we believe, but it is also true that it never reached God, therefore was a prayer "to" or "with himself".
It is right and normal to begin a prayer with thanksgiving so the Pharisee thanked God that he was not as other men, and then went on to describe them in the worst of terms, just as the elder brother had spoken of the prodigal (15:30).

12   The only total fast that was required by the law was in preparation for the great day of atonement (Lev 16:31), even though there are numerous fastings accompanied by prayer in the OT, but this Pharisee fasted two days out of every week. A. Edersheim says it was likely Mondays and Thursdays because these were the market days when the towns were full of people from the country, and the fasts would attract more notice on such days (Matt 6:16-18). Rabbi Simeon ben Jochai wrote, "If there are only two righteous men in the world, I and my son are these; and if there is only one, it is I (A. Edersheim). The Pharisee also claimed that he exceeded the demands of the law in his tithes. The AV says that he paid tithes of all that he possessed, but the RV and JND correct this as, "I give tithes of all that I get". The law required tithes of the harvests (Deut 14:22), but it seems clear from Matt 23:23 that this did not include the herbs of their gardens. The boast of this Pharisee was that he paid tithes of all, and we have no reason to suppose that his boastful claims were untrue.

13 The publican stood "afar off", sensing his unworthiness to mingle with God's people, and would not lift up his eyes to heaven, for God's presence was a fearful place for him. He beat continuously on his breast as an evidence of the sin that he knew was in him. He said by his action, "Herein lies the problem; it is my sin that burdens me". He did not say "a sinner", but like Saul of Tarsus (1 Tim 1:15) he called himself "the sinner" (JND). His prayer was "Be propitiated (*hilasthēti*) to me the sinner" (cf. Rom 3:25; 1 John 2:2; 4:10). He pleaded no merit but cast himself wholly on the tender mercy of God. Many a gospel preacher has paraphrased his cry, " God be merciful to me on the ground of the sacrifice", and in the light of the full truth of the gospel this is good interpretation. Wherever there is such an attitude of heart this side of hell and the day of wrath there is abundant mercy available from God.

14 The sinful publican was declared righteous by the judge of all. He had stood at the judgment bar of God, been found guilty, and then was acquitted of every charge by the very judge who had declared his guilt. Justification is the great word of the Roman epistle, and the Lord used it in the same way that Paul used it. It does not mean to impute righteousness but that the Judge declares the sinner to be righteous and does so on just and holy grounds. This is possible because propitiation, that is, satisfaction to offended justice, has been given by the precious blood of the Lord Jesus. The publican was justified because that blood was going to be shed (Rom 3:25). Full propitiation was made at the cross.

The humbling that will come to those who exalt themselves is described in such passages as Phil 2:10,11, "every knee should bow". Those who are not humbled in the day of mercy will be brought to their knees in the day of judgment, whereas those who now are brought to repentance gladly bow to Him and in a coming day will fall at His feet to give Him glory and share in His righteous reign.

47.   *The Lesson from a Little Child*
   18:15-17

> v.15 "And they brought unto him also infants, that he would touch them: but when *his* disciples *saw it*, they rebuked them.

v.16 But Jesus called them *unto him*, and said, Suffer little children to come unto
     me, and forbid them not: for of such is the kingdom of God.
v.17 Verily I say unto you, Whosoever shall not receive the kingdom of God as a
     little child shall in no wise enter therein."

The material used by Luke from the beginning of the journey toward Jerusalem (9:51) has been mostly unique with some parallels in Matthew. At this point Luke uses material that is also found in Mark.

15 "They" is masculine so may refer to fathers and mothers who brought their infants to the Lord that He might touch them, that is, lay His hands on them in blessing. For reasons that are not given the disciples rebuked the parents. They may have thought that the Lord was too busy to he troubled with infants. Both Matt 19:13 and Mark 10: 13 use *paidion* ("little children"), but Luke uses *brephos* ("infant") which is used for an unborn child (1:41,44); for a newborn infant (2:12,16); for infants a little older (18:15; Acts 7:19; 2 Tim 3:15) and for spiritual infants (1 Pet 2:2). Of its eight occurrences in the NT, Luke uses it six times. It is characteristic of Luke's carefulness in physical descriptions to make a distinction between a young child and an infant, but in so doing he also portrays the tenderness of Christ in His request that these infants (in arms) be brought to Him.

16-17 It appears that the discouraged parents were departing when the Lord called to them, saying, "Suffer little children to come unto me, and forbid them not". The lesson is far greater than the blessing of infants. All who receive the kingdom of God must come to the Lord Jesus with the simplicity and humility of a little child. The unquestioning faith of a child and the total dependence of babes must characterise true conversion. Without being brought down to this level no one can enter the kingdom (Matt 18:3). The link with the confession of the publican of vv.9-14 is obvious, as well as with what follows. In Matthew it is the poor in spirit who inherit the kingdom of heaven (Matt 5:3); in Luke it is the lost sinners (19:10).

48.   *A Rich Young Ruler*
         18:18-30

v.18 "And a certain ruler asked him, saying, Good Master, what shall I do to inherit
     eternal life?
v.19 And Jesus said unto him, Why callest thou me good? none *is* good, save one,
     that is, God.
v.20 Thou knowest the commandments, Do not commit adultery, Do not kill, Do not
     steal, Do not bear false witness, Honour thy father and thy mother.
v.21 And he said, All these have I kept from my youth up.
v.22 Now when Jesus heard these things, he said unto him, Yet lackest thou one
     thing: sell all that thou hast, and distribute unto the poor, and thou shalt have
     treasure in heaven: and come, follow me.

v.23 And when he heard this, he was very sorrowful: for he was very rich.
v.24 And when Jesus saw that he was very sorrowful, he said, How hardly shall
      they that have riches enter into the kingdom of God!
v.25 For it is easier for a camel to go through a needle's eye, than for a rich man
      to enter into the kingdom of God.
v.26 And they that heard it said, Who then can be saved?
v.27 And he said, The things which are impossible with men are possible with
      God.
v.28 Then Peter said, Lo, we have left all, and followed thee.
v.29 And he said unto them, Verily I say unto you, There is no man that hath left
      house, or parents, or brethren, or wife, or children, for the kingdom of God's
      sake,
v.30 Who shall not receive manifold more in this present time, and in the world to
      come life everlasting.

18   Matthew tells us that this man was young; all the synoptics say he was rich;
only Luke tells us that he was a "ruler". His youthfulness discourages the thought
that he was the ruler of a synagogue, and if he was a priest or a scribe we would
have been told this, so he was likely a government official. He was very rich, so
such an official position would have been available to him. When he came running
to the Lord he kneeled down to Him (Mark 10:17) and addressed Him as "Good
Master". His actions and words indicated urgency and earnestness. A. Plummer
writes, "There is no instance in the whole Talmud of a rabbi being addressed as
'Good Master'; the title was absolutely unknown among the Jews". The law was
"good" and God is "good', but men are never called "good" in this sense. That
he ascribed to the Lord Jesus divine goodness cannot be doubted, and we doubt
if we can sit in judgment on his sincerity and claim that he spoke carelessly. His
very question indicates that he accepted the teaching of the Lord Jesus as having
authority from God. We should not be surprised at this for Nicodemus also gave
to the Lord this honour (John 3:2).

He did not seem far from the kingdom of heaven in his attitude toward the
Lord Jesus, but his attitude toward himself was very wrong. He imagined that
eternal life could be earned by his own effort. In his question there is a paradox,
for he spoke of an inheritance and yet wanted to know how to work for it. An
inheritance is normally obtained without working to receive it, although there
may be exceptions to the norm. When the inheritance was eternal life he was
totally wrong.

19   The Lord Jesus did not deny the goodness that the young ruler had
attributed to Him, and now gave him opportunity to consider the full
implications of his form of address, that the One who is "good" is God. We
do not conclude from this that he grasped the truth of the identity of the
Lord Jesus, but the implications are clear. There is, however, another truth
that is in the Lord's words. Only God is good in the absolute sense, therefore
the young ruler is sinful. The greatest of all soulwinners is showing a sinner
how far short he has come of the standard demanded by divine holiness

(Rom 3:9-23). The acknowledgment of his guilt as a sinner is the necessary requirement to receive eternal life, not as a reward for personal goodness but as a gift.

20-21   The Lord took the young ruler on the ground that he claimed for himself. He wanted to do good, so the Lord told him what he must do. The five commandments quoted are all manward. He answered with conviction, "All these have I kept from my youth". We are reminded of Paul's claim about his life as a Pharisee; "touching the righteousness which is in the law, blameless" (Phil 3:6). It was very likely that in all outward observances he had kept these commandments. Mark adds the tender note, "Then Jesus beholding him loved him" (10:21).

Paul describes a man in Rom 7:7-11 to whom conviction of sin came by the tenth commandment, "Thou shalt not covet" (Exod 20:17); "And the commandment, which was ordained to life, I found to be unto death" (Rom 7: 10). Saul of Tarsus (or the man of Rom 7) was condemned by it, and yet the Lord left this commandment unspoken when He was speaking to the young ruler. Many have wondered why. The answer may be that obedience to the five commandments named could be seen in actions, but obedience to "Thou shalt not covet" could be seen only in the heart. The young man did not know his own heart, and it has been suggested that leaving it unspoken was to allow the word of God to do its own work in him, for he knew the commandments (v.20). We have often been impressed that the Holy Spirit uses what is learned in childhood to bring about conviction and salvation in adulthood. This should be a great incentive to teach children to memorise Scripture.

22   His outward observance was excellent but his heart was very wrong. The requirements that the Lord set before him comprehended both tables of the law; they were Godward and manward. If he truly loved his neighbour as himself then he would sell his goods and give to the poor. If he truly loved God with all his heart then he would gladly turn his back on every worldly ambition and follow the Lord Jesus. A. Plummer remarks, "Peter, James and John were not told to sell their boats and nets and give the proceeds to the poor; because their hearts were not wedded to them".

It is not correct to suggest that the "one thing" he lacked was to show charity to the poor. The proud Pharisee said, "I give tithes of all that I gain" (v. 12 JND), which may have been true, but it did not justify him. When the Lord said, " One thing is lacking to thee yet" (JND), he was referring to his heart's love which had been captivated by his possessions. If his heart were to be changed, the evidence would be seen in selling all and giving it to the poor; but this would not be enough for "though I bestow all my goods to feed the poor, and though I give my body to be burned, and have not charity (*agapē*, love), it profiteth me nothing"

(1 Cor 13:3); so the Lord continued, "and come, follow me". The Lord Jesus lays claim to every heart that He cleanses. He does not merely claim a place, or even a prominent place, He claims preeminence in the heart of all who profess to love Him.

"Yet lackest thou one thing" uses *leipō* ("to lack") as an active verb. In its passive use, it means " destitute" or "to be in want" (James 2:15), but here it means the young ruler is still lacking or wanting in spite of his best efforts. He fits exactly into the category of the many who say, "I have done the best that I can do", but they still "come short" (Rom 3:23).

23   The young man had come face to face with the Revealer of men's hearts, who had given him complete evidence that he had not fulfilled the law. There was no virtue in the young man giving all his substance away; even this act would not cause him to inherit eternal life. He needed to know that he was a sinner. Self-righteousness, the same disease that afflicted the Pharisee who prayed in the temple, was his problem. Again, we are reminded of Paul's preaching so familiar to Luke: "by the deeds of the law there shall no flesh be justified in his sight: for by the law is the knowledge of sin" (Rom 3:20); "the law is holy, and the commandment holy, and just, and good" (7:12), but men are sinful and cannot be justified by law-keeping. Mark says, "He was sad at that saying, and went away grieved" (10:22). Luke tells us "he became very sorrowful, for he was very rich" (JND).

24-27   The Lord's comment concerned the extra difficulty in being saved that great riches bring. It is possible for a rich man to be saved but he has many hindrances, such as trusting in his riches, being made proud by his position in the world, failing to understand his own spiritual poverty and even being too self-sufficient to accept a salvation that cannot be bought, being a gift. Luke is the Gospel to the poor, the outcast, the lost, the publican and sinner. Riches are a great hindrance to receiving such a gospel. There is nothing to prove that "a needle's eye" is a small door for pedestrians in a much larger door for carriages. It is simply the eye of a needle used for sewing, and the saying expresses impossibility; however, "The things that are impossible with men are possible with God". Later Paul was to write, "not many wise men after the flesh, not many mighty, not many noble, are called" (1 Cor 1:26), but he did not say, Not any.

The question "Who then can be saved?" is based on a belief that a rich man was in the favour of God and if he, with all his advantages, could only be saved with difficulty, what hope could there be for others? The question is not, How can a rich man be saved? but, How can anyone be saved? The answer is that none can be saved unless God does it.

28-30   The application of the teachings of the Lord is very personal, so the disciples ask about their own future. They had left their homes to follow Him. The Lord made it clear that man cannot obligate God to bless him. There are many reasons for this, the first being that as sinners we rightly deserve His righteous judgment, so all God's actions toward us in grace are undeserved. Material blessing in the present time was prominent in the thinking of all Jews as a mark of God's favour. The Lord Jesus has taught that those who follow Him renounce the material things of the world, but what will they receive? Surely not material blessings; but God will be no man's debtor and whatever the cost of discipleship God will meet their need now (Phil 4:19) and there will be a full reward in a coming day. As the Ecuadorian martyr, Jim Elliott, wrote, "He is no fool who gives up that which he cannot hold to gain that which he can never lose".

49.   *A Prediction of Death and Resurrection*
     18:31-34

> v.31 "Then he took *unto him* the twelve, and said unto them, Behold, we go up to Jerusalem, and all things that are written by the prophets concerning the Son of man shall be accomplished.
> v.32 For he shall be delivered unto the Gentiles, and shall be mocked, and spitefully entreated, and spitted on:
> v.33 And they shall scourge *him*, and put him to death: and the third day he shall rise again.
> v.34 And they understood none of these things: and this saying was hid from them, neither knew they the things which were spoken."

31   In Luke this is the seventh time that the Lord has foretold His rejection and suffering. As on other occasions He addresses the disciples, and it immediately follows a selfish display on their part. Everything that is written of the Son of man is to be fulfilled. Luke wrote, "And when they had fulfilled all that was written of him, they took him down from the tree" (Acts 13:29). The Gospels do not record such things as the plucking of the hair from His face (Isa 50:6), nor the smiting with a rod upon the cheek (Micah 5:1), but we are assured that they did these things as well as the many other predictions that were so perfectly fulfilled in His rejection, suffering and crucifixion.

32   Matthew and Mark record the Lord's prediction that it would be the high priests and scribes who would hand Him over to the Romans. Luke says, "he shall be delivered" including in one statement that the Jews did it; yet that it was "by the determinate counsel and foreknowledge of God" (Acts 2:23). Only Luke says that He was "insulted" (*hubrizō*, "spitefully entreated" AV). Vine says it means "to treat insolently" which was in addition to the mockery and spittle. The description of His sufferings here, taken with the words of 22:37, "that this that is written must yet be accomplished in me, And he was reckoned among the transgressors", pictures the total submission of the "lamb led to the slaughter". When "delivered unto the Gentiles" He would offer no resistance, for it was also written, "I gave my back to the smiters, and my cheeks to them that plucked off the hair; I hid not my face from shame and spitting" (Isa 50:6). How difficult it must have been for the disciples to understand how He would submit to such abuse when they had seen such displays of His power over nature and disease and His authority over the spirit world!

33 The Lord reveals more details in this prediction than in any that have preceded it. He is going up to Jerusalem; the shadow of His cross is falling dark across His pathway. He does not disclose the means by which He will die, but in keeping with His words (v.31) they will pierce His hands and His feet, and on the way to that shameful death they will scourge His back; on "the third day he shall rise again". The Scriptures contain fourteen references to "the third day" (Matt 16:21; 17:23; 20:19; 27:64; Mark 9:31; 10:34; Luke 9:22; 13:32; 18:33; 24:7,21,46; Acts 10:40; 1 Cor 15:4). It is a mistake to interpret Matt 12:40, "so shall the Son of man be three days and three nights in the heart of the earth", in any way that is out of harmony with "the third day". It has been suggested that when Paul wrote, "that he rose again the third day according to the scriptures" (1 Cor 15:3); the "scriptures" to which he refers may be Matthew or Mark rather than an OT passage such as Lev 23:11 or it may refer to both.

34 All three statements of this verse emphasise that the disciples did not understand that the Lord would die and rise again: "They understood none of these things" because their own mind was set. They were so certain about the inauguration of a kingdom of glory that anything that contradicted it fell on deaf ears. The second statement contains the passive verb "was hid" from them, suggesting that their blindness was allowed for the time. In the third statement, the imperfect tense of "neither knew they" means that it was an ongoing ignorance even when the events themselves were happening before their eyes (9:45). It is not usual to commend ignorance, but their blindness at this time was used by God to add weight to their testimony to the risen Christ, for it could not be said that they believed in His resurrection because they looked for it. "Their dullness was providential, and it became a security to the church for the truth of the resurrection" (A. Plummet). We have often been amazed that the chief priests and Pharisees remembered the Lord's teaching– "we remember that that deceiver said, while he was yet alive, 'After three days I will rise again' " (Matt 27:63)- while the disciples, to whom He so often spoke the same words, never grasped their meaning. The answer is "this saying was hid from them". The words were remembered by those who denied their truth, for unbelief comes naturally to the heart of man, but faith is against nature and beyond it.

50.   *A Blind Man Near Jericho*
   18:35-43

> v.35 "And it came to pass, that as he was come nigh unto Jericho, a certain blind
>   man sat by the way side begging:
> v.36 And hearing the multitude pass by, he asked what it meant.
> v.37 And they told him, that Jesus of Nazareth passeth by.
> v.38 And he cried, saying, Jesus, *thou* son of David, have mercy on me.
> v.39 And they which went before rebuked him, that he should hold his peace: but he
>   cried so much the more, *Thou* son of David, have mercy on me.
> v.40 And Jesus stood, and commanded him to be brought unto him: and when he
>   was come near, he asked him,
> v.41 Saying, What wilt thou that I shall do unto thee? And he said, Lord, that I
>   may receive my sight.
> v.42 And Jesus said unto him, Receive thy sight: thy faith hath saved thee.
> v.43 And immediately he received his sight, and followed him, glorifying God: and
>   all the people, when they saw *it*, gave praise unto God."

Because we believe that the original autographs of Holy Scripture were without
error, there is a need to reconcile the seeming differences in the three accounts
of this miracle. If the NT writers had merely copied each other, or if, after they
had written their records, they had attempted to reconcile the differences, we
would never have had the problem, but we thank God that they knew better
than to tamper with the work of the Holy Spirit. There are reasons why Matthew
says there were two blind men healed as the Lord went out of Jericho (20:29-34).
This is not a contradiction, as Matthew has merely given information not found
in the other Gospels, and is using the principle of plural witnesses. Mark and
Luke do not deny that two were healed. Mark gives the name of one man,
Bartimaeus, whom the Lord healed "as he went out of Jericho" (10:46-52). Many
have thought that Luke says the healing happened when the Lord approached
Jericho, but all he does say is that the blind man cried out at that time, was
rebuked, and hindered by the crowd, yet continued to cry out until the Lord
stopped, commanded him to be brought to Him and healed him. Luke does not
say how long it took for these events to transpire, but in the meantime the Lord
had entered and passed through Jericho (19:1), a small city through which He
moved quickly. This is an explanation that goes back as far as Maldonatus and
was accepted by John Calvin. Others suggest that the healing took place between
the old Jericho and the new Roman Jericho (F. Godet, A.T. Robertson, Leon
Morris).

35-37 Mark and Luke tell us that the blind man begged. There was no other
recourse for him, and sightless eyes evoke pity. The one advantage he had
was that he sat in the place where the Lord would pass by. Sinners cannot
hope to save themselves, but they can put themselves in the place where the
Saviour is passing. "Asked" is the imperfect tense in the middle voice, so his
inquiry was persistent and pathetic, for at first he seemed to receive no

attention. For poor sinners in our day it is still true that "Jesus of Nazareth passeth by", waiting for the cry that expresses earnestness, need and helplessness.

38-39   "Son of David" is a Messianic title, so he cannot have been ignorant of the claims of the Lord Jesus. He really shouted (*eboēsen*, a loud expression of strong emotion), causing the crowd to rebuke him, but he would not be silent and cried a great deal more. He recognised a passing opportunity that would never be repeated, and he was correct, for the Saviour was moving toward the cross and would never pass that way again. Urgency and the recognition of a passing time of visitation are elements in the experience of all who receive salvation. "Have mercy on me" is the plea of an undeserving, needy sinner. It was the cry of the publican (v.13) who was aware that he was " a sinner", so we have good reason to believe that this blind man knew he had a deeper need than his physical blindness.

40   It has been suggested above that there was a time lapse between the inquiry of v.36 and the Saviour stopping and commanding the blind man to be brought to Him. There is often a wait in the experience of sinners. The Lord does not force Himself upon half-hearted seekers. This chapter begins and ends with a persistent cry: first a poor widow and then a blind beggar. The OT comment is "Seek ye the Lord while he may be found, call ye upon him while he is near" (Isa 55:6). The widow's plight was desperate (vv.2,3) and she had no recourse but to an unjust judge. The blind man in his pitiful darkness had recourse to the mercy of the "Son of David", who came as the Light of the world.

41   Many have been brought to the Saviour by others. This man was also brought and the cry for mercy is now interpreted in relation to his need. A vague understanding of need may be the start of stirring in the heart of a sinner, but definite need must he known before it is met. There can be no salvation for those who are unawakened to their true condition. In his response to the question about his need, he addressed Jesus as "Lord". The significance of this can be more fully appreciated by comparing the various forms of address to Christ. He was never addressed as Lord by Judas. He was often called *didaskalos* ("master" or "teacher"): by the lawyers (10:25; 11:45); by the man who disputed with his brother over the inheritance (12:13); by the rich young ruler, "Good Master" (v.18); by the Pharisees (19:39); by the chief priests (20:21); by the Sadducees (20:28); by the scribes (20:39); and by the disciples (21:7). The Lord called Himself *didaskalos* ("Master", 22:11; cf. John 13:13,14) and it is more frequently used in Luke than in the other Gospels; but the blind man said, "Lord, that I may receive my sight". He recognised that the "Son of David" was truly the Lord, so the man with blinded eyes had an enlightened heart by which he understood the words of David, "The Lord said unto my Lord..." (Ps 110:1).

42-43   Now there is no hesitation. The moment the man confesses his need, that moment the Saviour speaks words of power and blessing. We have used language throughout this miracle-story to indicate that a sinner was coming to the Saviour. The reason for this will be seen in the Lord's words to him, "Receive thy sight", referring to the healing of his body; "thy faith hath saved thee ", referring to the salvation of his soul. "Followed him", that is "continued to follow", is an imperfect active verb and explains why Mark and Luke give us the story of Bartimaeus, and only Matthew speaks of the other blind man. Bartimaeus continued to follow the Lord and was known to other believers in the day when Luke wrote.

This chapter contains illustrations of the various aspects of salvation. The publican's sin was a heavy burden and he needed mercy. He cried to a God of infinite mercy who was able and willing to fully forgive him. His sickness was sin and he received the mercy he craved. The young ruler also was afflicted by sin and needed life, but his disease had no obvious symptoms. His problem was fatal, for it was in his heart, but he was ignorant of it and did not receive the life that he requested. The blind man was in darkness and needed light. He cried out to the Lord and light opened his eyes, flooded his heart and shone out in his life as he followed the Lord.

51.   *The Lord Passes Through Jericho*
19:1-9

v.1   "And *Jesus* entered and passed through Jericho.

v.2   And, behold, *there* was a man named Zacchaeus, which was the chief among the publicans, and he was rich.

v.3   And he sought to see Jesus who he was; and could not for the press, because he was little of stature.

v.4   And he ran before, and climbed up into a sycomore tree to see him: for he was to pass that *way*.

v.5   And when Jesus came to the place, he looked up, and saw him, and said unto him, Zacchaeus, make haste, and come down; for to day I must abide at thy house.

v.6   And he made haste, and came down, and received him joyfully.

v.7   And when they saw *it*, they all murmured, saying, That he was gone to be guest with a man that is a sinner.

v.8   And Zacchaeus stood, and said unto the Lord; Behold, Lord, the half of my goods I give to the poor; and if I have taken any thing from any man by false accusation, I restore *him* fourfold.

v.9   And Jesus said unto him, This day is salvation come to this house, forsomuch as he also is a son of Abraham."

Jericho's archaeological history makes it one of the oldest sites in the Middle East. From earliest times it was famed for its excellent fresh water spring and the oasis which it fed. Deut 34:3 calls it "the city of the palm trees". Herod the Great built a winter palace with ornamental gardens and died there. The city lies 3 000 feet lower than Jerusalem although it is only seventeen miles to the north-east.

A. Edersheim gives a graphic picture of the scene that early spring day, as the Lord Jesus entered and passed through it: "It was already summer, for even in winter, it is so warm that the inhabitants only wear the lightest clothing. It is protected by walls, flanked by four forts ... All around wave groves of palms; stretch gardens of roses, and especially sweet-scented balsam plantations". Its roads and avenues were lined with gardens and beautiful trees with the wide-spreading sycamore fig tree found frequently among them. It was prized for its shade and often chosen as a wayside tree.

However, the city of Jericho, in spite of its pleasant location and sweet water, was a city old in sin. After its destruction by God in the days of Joshua a curse was pronounced on the man who would rebuild it (Josh 6:26). It was in the days of wicked king Ahab that Hiel, a worshipper of Baal, rebuilt the city, fulfilling the ancient prophecy, laying the foundation when his son, Abiram, was born and setting up the gates at the birth of his youngest son, Segub (1 Kings 16:34). It was an act of rebellion, and even in the naming of his sons, Hiel showed his pride, for both names mean lofty or exalted. So Jericho is a picture of the world under the curse, old in sin, a world of haughty pride and rebellion against God. Yet even ancient Jericho was a place where God had shown His mercy in the saving of Rahab, and now even greater mercy is displayed there.

1 As has been suggested in the previous paragraph, the Lord Jesus entering and passing through Jericho is a beautiful picture of "the tender mercy of our God" (1:78), the mercy of His heart, "whereby the dayspring from on high hath visited us". Because the verb "passed through" is in the imperfect tense in the middle voice it is correct to translate, "he was making his way through it".

In the last journey to Jerusalem, fully recorded only by Luke (9:51; 17:11; 19:28), the Lord and the company with Him must have crossed the Jordan at the upper fords, passing through Perea and recrossing the Jordan at the fords of Jericho. A.T. Schofield and G. Biddulph in *The Journeys of Jesus Christ* have pointed out that to avoid going through Samaria the caravan of men and women, going up from Galilee to the Passover in Jerusalem, followed this route and suggest that this caravan journeyed with the Lord. This would explain Mark 15:41, "many other women came up with him unto Jerusalem".

2 Zacchaeus (meaning "the just" or "pure") was a Jew who by his own confession did not live up to his name. *Architelōnēs*, "chief among the publicans", is used only here and may mean something like "Commissioner of Taxes", locally "the head of the tax and customs department" (Edersheim). Jericho was situated on the important trade route between Jerusalem and the east. Zacchaeus was rich with ill-gotten wealth, not popular in his own city and according to 18:25 an unlikely candidate for salvation. Each time Luke has mentioned publicans (3:12; 5:27; 7:29; 15:1; 18:10) he has described them as accepting the teaching of the Lord or actually being saved.

3 Again Luke uses an imperfect tense to tell us that Zacchaeus was a seeker. He had heard of Jesus; he knew that He had passed up the six miles of road from the fords of Jordan and had entered the city. Zacchaeus had never seen Him and wondered how he would ever get to see Him because of "a solid wall of onlookers" (Edersheim) and "because he was little of stature". These hindrances have a wide application to all who seek the Lord. It was not mere curiosity that drove him, nor was it just to see the Lord, but he wanted to "see who he was", suggesting that he had prior information about the Saviour. Unlike many others who sought the Lord, Zacchaeus was neither poor, sick, blind nor possessed with demons. He was "little" (*mikros*), which is twice translated "least" in Luke (7:28; 9:48), but he did not ask the Lord to increase his "stature" (2:52; 12:25).

4 Not letting his station in life hinder him, he ran ahead to the place where a wide-spreading sycomore tree stood at the side of the garden-road. The low branches made the climb easy, even for a little man, and he sat perched in the tree, hoping to catch at least a glimpse of the Lord as He passed along the road. It has been pointed out at 17:6 that Luke distinguishes between two trees with similar names, "sycamine" (17:6) and "sycomore", even though this distinction is not found in the LXX. It may be that Luke is displaying his interests as a physician for these trees were the sources for two different medicines (A.T. Robertson).

5 The moment came, eagerly anticipated by the little man in the tree, when the Lord "came to the place". Edersheim describes the scene with eloquence: "Those eyes, out of which heaven seemed to look upon earth, were upturned, and that face of infinite grace, never to be forgotten, beamed upon him the welcome of recognition, and He uttered the invitation in which the invited was the real Inviter, the guest the true Host". It is usually preached that the tree speaks of pride and self-righteousness, and this is applied to sinners who climb such trees. Adam hid among the trees, but Zacchaeus was not hiding but seeking. We can scarcely enter into the feelings of the heart of the little man when the Lord stopped, called his name, commanded him to descend, and informed him that He "must be" a guest at his house that very day.

6 He moved with great speed and "received him joyfully". Perhaps there is an extended meaning in this reception. It is the expression used of Martha welcoming the Lord to her home (10:38), so the reception was to his home, but was it not to his heart first? In such meetings with the Lord there is a story that only eternity will unfold. Much went on in the soul of Zacchaeus between the moment when he heard the Lord speak, came down from the tree and received Him to his home. An ancient story tells of the converted tax collector returning to that spot all the days of his life.

7 The growing opposition to the Lord Jesus now has new fuel to feed upon.

Zacchaeus was a sinner, not a pagan, not even a Samaritan; a true Jew, but a sinner among them and recognised to be one (15:2). This is the only time the Lord Jesus ever offered Himself as a Guest in a home. In "they all murmured", *diagonguzō* is used; it occurs only here and in 15:2. Luke used the same word without the prefix (*dia*) in 5:30 where the scribes and Pharisees "murmured" against the Lord and His disciples for eating with "publicans and sinners" in the home of Levi. The more intensive word that is used here means that the complaint went through the whole crowd. It is not difficult to picture the low-toned complaint passing from one to another with growing intensity and hostility.

This is the only time in the NT that *kataluō* is translated to be ' guest", but it is translated to "lodge" in 9:12. It means to unloose, so came to have the intransitive meaning "to lodge" because in such a lodging a weary traveller would unyoke his beasts of burden and unloose his pack. This is very possibly the last house in which the Lord slept before the cross, unless we speculate that He slept in the home at Bethany at some time during the final week. Zacchaeus was the last convert of the Lord Jesus before He went to the cross, but the thief was saved while the Saviour hung on the tree.

8 Overcome by the gentle grace of the Saviour, Zacchaeus stood before Him in his own home. His very form of address signifies that his longing had been fulfilled; he had "sought to see Jesus who he was"; now he knows He is "the Lord". Zacchaeus is not saying, as Godet suggests, that he had made it a habit to give to the poor in the past. The present tense indicates that for the first time he acknowledges his greed and extortion and pledges to make restitution. He will give the half of all his wealth to the poor, and in the cases where he has defrauded others in his business, and he knows that there have been such cases, he will restore fourfold. It has been suggested that the half of his wealth that he kept was to enable him to make this restitution. Under the law a voluntary confession of having taken another's goods unlawfully was corrected by restoring the amount taken and adding a fifth part to it (Lev 6:1-7), but Zacchaeus had discovered the true trespass Offering; his heart was won, and giving away his wealth was a joy. The very thing that was such a hindrance to the rich young ruler (18:23) was done voluntarily, showing us that riches do not need to be any hindrance to salvation. When love fills the heart, the pockets are opened.

When Zacchaeus said "if I have taken anything ... by false accusation", he used *sukophanteō* from which we get our English sycophant. It is used here and in 3:14 only, but is common in the LXX and means "to falsely accuse" or "exact wrongfully". "It is derived from *sukon*, a fig, and *phainō*, to show (W.E. Vine). A.T. Robertson says that to export figs from Attica was against the law, but it was a lucrative trade, so there were people whose business it was to inform the authorities about the illegal traffic and they were called *sukophantai*. Vine does not dispute this, but also traces its meaning from the practice of shaking a fig tree to make it give up its ripe fruit, so Zacchaeus and men like him were adept at shaking down rich men for their wealth. The very fact that the saved man used this word about his former life indicates how much he now abhorred his former practices.

9   Zacchaeus was not the recipient of salvation because he gave away half his wealth to the poor. Such a thought is completely swept away by the next verse, but what he did was evidence of the reality of his conversion, reality that must have impressed the murmuring crowd. The salvation that Zacchaeus enjoyed may have also reached his household, although nothing is said of them. The Lord's words "he also is a son of Abraham" have great significance (Rom 4:1-5) and show that the faith by which Abraham was justified was the faith of this despised publican in Jericho, in whose house the Lord Jesus spent the night, an honour Abraham never knew (Gen 18:16). Both Zacchaeus and Abraham met the Lord under a tree, for the same Lord, prior to His incarnation, passing by the tent of Abraham, was gladly received and entertained.

52.   *The Golden Text of Luke*
   19:10

v.10 "For the Son of man is come to seek and to save that which was lost."

10   These sixteen words in our AV (eleven in Greek) make up the golden text of Luke's Gospel and are as full of meaning as any gospel utterance ever given. The lofty title "Son of man" was often used by the Lord Jesus when speaking of Himself. It is a mistake to think of it as inferior to any other title that rightly belongs to Him, even to "Son of God". A careful look at the way Scripture and the Lord used it will quickly convince the reader that it is the title of His universal and eternal dominion as "the last Adam" (1 Cor 15:45; Dan 7:13; John 1:51; 3:13; Matt 24:30; Mark 14:62; Luke 22:69).

The lowly stoop of the Lord of all is given in the very simple aorist verb "came" (1 Tim 1:15): "He came from the brightest of glory". That coming is the central event of all salvation history, and therefore is the central point in time around which the ages revolve. Everything that was before looked forward to that event and all that follows will look back to it. He came not only to Bethlehem but He came to Calvary, and these words were uttered within a few short days of His cross.

The longing search is described by the words "to seek", an aorist infinitive referring to an actual event, teaching that wherever there is a lost sinner, at whatever point in time, there is a seeking Saviour, to seek that lost one. God was the first Seeker in the Bible (Gen 3:9) and still seeks the lost.

The loving act is that He came "to save", another aorist infinitive making clear that His saving work was a stupendous act. We know from Scripture that it was one act of grace, one act of righteousness, one act of obedience (Rom 5:18-21). There is a helplessness in those who can do nothing to save themselves, but there is an ability in Christ who did everything. Is it any wonder that we preach that it is total folly to attempt to add anything to His work?

"That which was lost" is a neuter, perfect active participle, which A.T. Robertson says indicates "the collective whole" of mankind. The lost is not a special group among the billions of mankind but a descriptive term for all men (ch.15). The simple facts about his lostness are that all are lost; no one can save himself; each one who is saved was once lost; Christ alone can save, and there is a time of seeking and saving that will soon be past forever. There are many similarities between the "lost" here and the lost in ch.15, but there is also a contrast because in ch. 15 the lost are those who are saved, and only the lost were saved, but here the "lost" are all mankind and many of them will never be saved even though the Son of man came that all men through Him might be saved (John 3:17).

53.   *The Parable of the Ten Pounds*
19:11-27

v.11 "And as they heard these things, he added and spake a parable, because he was nigh to Jerusalem, and because they thought that the kingdom of God should immediately appear.

v.12 He said therefore, A certain nobleman went into a far country to receive for himself a kingdom, and to return.

v.13 And he called his ten servants, and delivered them ten pounds, and said unto them, Occupy till I come.

v.14 But his citizens hated him; and sent a message after him saying, We will not have this *man* to reign over us.

v.15 And it came to pass, that when he was returned, having received the kingdom, then he commanded these servants to be called unto him, to whom he had given the money, that he might know how much every man had gained by trading.

v.16 Then came the first, saying, Lord, thy pound hath gained ten pounds.

v.17 And he said unto him, Well, thou good servant: because thou hast been faithful in a very little, have thou authority over ten cities.

v.18 And the second came, saying, Lord, thy pound hath gained five pounds.

v.19 And he said likewise to him, Be thou also over five cities.

v.20 And another came, saying, Lord, behold, *here is* thy pound, which I have kept laid up in a napkin:

v.21 For I feared thee, because thou art an austere man: thou takest up that thou layedst not down, and reapest that thou didst not sow.

v.22 And he saith unto him, Out of thine own mouth will I judge thee, *thou* wicked servant. Thou knewest that I was an austere man, taking up that I laid not down, and reaping that I did not sow:

v.23 Wherefore then gavest not thou my money into the bank, that at my coming I might have required mine own with usury?

v.24 And he said unto them that stood by, Take from him the pound, and give *it* to him that hath ten pounds.

v.25 (And they said unto him, Lord, he hath ten pounds.)

v.26 For I say unto you, That unto every one which hath shall be given; and from him that hath not, even that he hath shall be taken away from him.

v.27 But those mine enemies, which would not that I should reign over them, bring
hither, and slay *them* before me."

The two similar parables of the talents (Matt 25:14-30) and the pounds have
often been compared and contrasted. The parable of the talents was addressed
to the disciples from the Mount of Olives; this parable was spoken to the people
at Jericho. The former was spoken after He had entered Jerusalem; this one
before He had reached the city. The different number of talents were given
according to the differing abilities of the servants; they are responsible to use
their abilities well that they may be ready for greater responsibilities in the future.
In the parable of the pounds each of the ten servants is given one pound to
show that all have one basic opportunity. In the absence of their Master they
must prove true to Him and occupy in His business until He returns.

An important aspect of almost all the parables is the absence of the Lord. At
the wedding feast (Matt 22:1-14) the king's son does not appear until the guests
are gathered; it is a night season and the virgins slumber and sleep while the
bridegroom is absent (Matt 25:1-13); when the wounded man is taken to the inn
(Luke 10:35), the good Samaritan departs promising that he will return; the
householder departs leaving meat for His household and promising to return
(12:41-48). The length of the absence is described differently. In Mark 13:33- 37
the Son of man takes a far journey. He may return by night or day so the servants
are to work by day and watch at night. In the parable of the talents it is "After a
long time the lord of those servants cometh" (Matt 25:19). The parable of the
pounds adds to all this information the reason for His absence- "to receive for
himself a kingdom".

11   In two of the parables of ch.18 the Lord gave the reason for telling them
(vv.1,9). In the parable of the pounds He gave two reasons; because "he was
nigh to Jerusalem"; and because "they thought that the kingdom of God should
immediately appear". Of course, these two things belong together. If the Son of
David it to take the throne it must happen in the city of David. The two personal
pronouns "they" must refer to the crowd who had murmured at the Lord's going
to the house of Zacchaeus. The word that Luke uses for "appear" (*anaphainō*) is
found only here and once in Acts. Vine suggests that it was originally a nautical
term. In that sense it is used in Acts 21:3, "having discovered" ("having sighted"
JND), meaning to appear suddenly on the horizon, for as Paul and his companions
sailed toward Tyre, Cyprus was sighted to the left of their ship. This word picture
vividly describes a waiting for the kingdom to suddenly appear.

12   Nowhere can a more fitting title be found for the gracious gentle Man who
moves through the pages of Luke's Gospel than "a certain nobleman". The title
involves a noble birth, name, home, character, position and wealth. He is the
incomparable, heavenly Nobleman, as Samuel Stennett wrote,

> "No mortal can with Him compare
> Among the sons of men;
> Fairer is He than all the fair
> That fill the heavenly train."

The country to which He has gone is "far" above the place of His lowliness, shame and suffering. Paul told the Ephesians He is "far above all" (1:21). But He has not gone away to stay. He who cannot lie and will never break a promise has said that He will return. He went away a Nobleman, but will return a King.

13   Ten is the number of responsibility, but since each servant is given an equal amount the emphasis is on their opportunity. Leon Morris concludes that they were not slaves because he does not believe a slave would have the necessary authority to transact business, but here, as in the parable of the talents, the servants were "his own slaves" (lit.). He may have had many more slaves, but these were counted as trustworthy to transact business in their lord's name and to account to him on his return. A pound, *mna*, was a Greek coin worth 100 drachmas, from which JND translates "minas". It was equivalent to about four English pounds (Plummet). With the pound they were to "trade" or "conduct business" or "Occupy till I come". It was a proving ground for them in view of larger responsibilities after his return. The AV translators chose well when they used "occupy" for *pragmateuomai*, for it grasps the fact that this "trading" is to be the occupation of the servants during all the time of the nobleman's absence. The root word is *pragma* ("business") and is used in Rom 16:2 of the activity of Phebe in Rome which seems to have been some service for the Lord on behalf of the assembly at Cenchrea. *Pragmateuomai* is only here in the NT; the compound *diapragmateuomai* ("had gained by trading") is only in v. 15.

Miss Ada Habershon in *The Study of the Parables* gives seven occupations of the servants in their Lord's absence; they are to be "bearing fruit; inviting others to the feast; tending the needy; keeping awake; caring for fellow-servants; trimming their lamps, and trading with what He has entrusted to them".

14   In the parable the reason for the absence of the nobleman was "to receive for himself a kingdom", and we now learn that the country he has left is to be the scene of his future reign. The interpretation is clear: the Lord Jesus is going to heaven, the "far country", but He will return to reign in this very world where He was rejected and despised. "His citizens hated him" corresponds to the words of the prophet, "They that hate me without a cause are more than the hairs of mine head" (Ps 69:4). The hatred against Him was as causeless as His love for sinners. The message they sent was unmistakable, "Away with this man" (23:18), they cried to Pilate, and the Lord is here interpreting the attitude of their hearts in rejecting Him as their rightful King. *Presbeia* ("a message") is only here and in 14:32 ("embassage") in the NT. The citizens delegated a group of representatives to speak for them. The whole world was represented in the people of that day who said, "We will not have this man to reign over us". In spite of changes in manner or method, the attitude of the world is unchanged toward Christ.

Similarities can be noted between this parable and the reign of Herod Archelaus who was ethnarch over Judaea after his father, Herod the Great, from BC 4 to AD 6. He went to Rome to receive a kingdom from the emperor and returned with the authority to rule, but he was so hated by the Jews that a deputation of the aristocracy went to Rome to warn Augustus that, unless Archelaus were removed, there would be a full-scale revolt. He was deposed and banished (I.B.D. Tyndale). His palace, according to Josephus, was at Jericho. He deserved the hatred of the Jews, for in the first year of his ascension to the throne of Judaea, he slaughtered about 3 000 of them at the Passover, and stands in great contrast to the heavenly Nobleman who, at the first preaching of the gospel after His ascension to the throne of heaven, saved 3 000 Jews (Acts 2:41).

15-19   The return of the nobleman was the day of accounting for the servants. The first two servants do not boast of diligence or skill as businessmen. The pound that had been left in their trust was still "thy pound" and they claimed none of it for themselves whether the gain was ten pound or five pounds more. A rare word *prosergazomai* ("hath gained") is used in v.16 to describe how that in addition to the nobleman's one pound, nine more have been added. It suggests that the pound, when given opportunity, or put into trade, had in itself this ability to make more. The "Well done" (JND) by the nobleman who is now the king of the realm was a very important part of the reward, because he said similar words to the second servant (v. 19). These who have been "faithful in a very little" are now given large responsibility, commensurate with the way in which they have handled their former opportunities.

Many dear believers seem to feel that reward for faithful stewardship on earth will be rest in heaven, but the actual reward is a sphere of service that so far exceeds our opportunities here that it can be compared to the difference between a pound and ten cities. "His servants shall serve him" (Rev 22:3) is one of the fruits of His suffering on the tree that we will enjoy in His everlasting kingdom. It will be perfect service without weariness, failure, or lack of ability. There will be administrative responsibilities given by the King to His faithful servants, but let us not suppose that saints of the church age will be given the rule over the earth. We will reign with the Lord Jesus from the heavenly city above the earth (Rev 5:10 JND; Rev 21:22-27).

20-23   We do not know the story of the other seven servants, for after telling of the two faithful ones, the Lord tells of the one who, motivated by fear, had laid up the pound in "a towel' (JND). It is usually taken that he was afraid that the pound would be lost, so he carefully hid it, but his hiding place would likely be the first searching place of any robber who entered his house. His own words tell what he feared, not the loss of the pound, but that the nobleman would receive gain from the servant's labour. This is the meaning of the charge that the nobleman was an exacting man and could profit from the labour of others, "Thou takest up that thou layedst not down": to paraphrase his words, "I know you have profited from the labour of others, but you are not going to profit from me". It is this attitude that explains, "thou wicked servant...". In heart he belonged to that company who cried, "We will not have this man to reign over us". He had no love for the nobleman and no desire for his honour. The very least he could have done was to put the money on the moneychanger's table where it would have been for lending, and the principal and interest would have returned to the owner. In the exchange between the returned king and the "wicked servant", the word *austēros* ("austere") is used twice (vv.21,22), its only occurrences in the NT. Vine says it means to be "dry, stringent to the taste, like new wine not matured ... harsh, severe". This was the attitude of the servant toward the king, not only his opinion of his methods. Many have speculated about whether this man was saved or lost, but there seems to be evidence that he was among the "wicked" who refused the reign of the king. However, we are not distinctly told, as in the case of the man who hid the talent in the earth who was cast into outer darkness (Matt 25:25,30).

24-26   The pound is taken away from the unfaithful servant and given to the servant who has gained ten pounds, not as a reward, but because he would use it well. It still belonged to the King. The principle is that those who are faithful in little will be given greater opportunity to serve their Lord. It is impossible to take away from a person who has nothing, but this is not what the Lord said. The one who "hath not", that is, has not manifested a faithful stewardship, from him will be taken even the small responsibility that had been entrusted to him. What a solemn warning to us who have had the great responsibility of being made "stewards of the mysteries of God" (1 Cor 4:1)! It is in this context that Paul wrote, "Moreover, it is required in stewards, that a man be found faithful".

27   A contrast is drawn between the faithful servants and the enemies. The word *katasphazō* is not found anywhere else in the NT, but from its use in the LXX it means "hew them down, slay them utterly" (Plummet). The severity of the judgment on His enemies is in keeping with their sin of utter rejection. There is a difference of interpretation in this verse as to whether the speaker is still the nobleman-king in the parable or whether the Lord is giving interpretation. It is not an important difference, for if the speaker is the nobleman of the parable, he represents the coming Son of man in judgment. The ones described here as "those mine enemies" are again mentioned in 20:43: "Till I make thine enemies thy footstool".

V. The Ministry of the Lord Jesus in Jerusalem (19:28-23:25)

1.   The Lord Enters Jerusalem on a Colt
19:28-40

v.28 "And when he had thus spoken, he went before, ascending up to Jerusalem.

v.29 And it came to pass, when he was come nigh to Bethphage and Bethany, at the mount called *the mount* of Olives, he sent two of his disciples,

v.30 Saying, Go ye into the village over against *you*; in the which at your entering ye shall find a colt tied, whereon yet never man sat: loose him, and bring *him hither.*

v.31 And if any man ask you, Why do ye loose *him?* thus shall ye say unto him, Because the Lord hath need of him.

v.32 And they that were sent went their way, and found even as he had said unto them.

v.33 And as they were loosing the colt, the owners thereof said unto them, Why loose ye the colt?

v.34 And they said, The Lord hath need of him.

v.35 And they brought him to Jesus: and they cast their garments upon the colt, and they set Jesus thereon,

v.36 And as he went, they spread their clothes in the way.

v.37 And when he was come nigh, even now at the descent of the mount of Olives, the whole multitude of the disciples began to rejoice and praise God with a loud voice for all the mighty works that they had seen;

v.38 Saying, Blessed *be* the King that cometh in the name of the Lord: peace in heaven, and glory in the highest.

v.39 And some of the Pharisees from among the multitude said unto him, Master, rebuke thy disciples.

v.40 And he answered and said unto them, I tell you that, if these should hold their peace, the stones would immediately cry out."

The triumphal entry into Jerusalem is the terminus of the journey that began at 9:51. It was literally a journey that had begun at the highest pinnacle of heavenly glory and had brought the Lord of all to Bethlehem, Nazareth and now to Jerusalem to fulfil the purpose of His coming. Sir Robert Anderson in The Coming Prince has calculated the years of the great time prophecy of Dan 9:24-27, from "the going forth of the commandment to restore and to build Jerusalem unto the Messiah, the Prince"; the 69 weeks, or 483 years, culminated on the day that the Lord Jesus rode into Jerusalem on the colt. Anderson's calculations were amazingly accurate and have stood up under close scrutiny, but information not available to him has caused some changes. For further information, the student should consult a work such as H. Hohner, *Chronological Aspects of the Life of Christ* (pp.137,138). Daniel wrote, "And after ... shall Messiah be put to death; but not for His own sake" (v.26, H. Spurrell).

At this point in Luke the final week has arrived, the days of which are easier to trace in Mark than in Luke. The triumphal entry took place on the first day (19:29-40); He cleansed the temple on the second (19:45-48); the third was the long day of questioning from scribes, priests, Pharisees and Sadducees (20:1-47); the day when He was anointed was the fourth day (Mark 14:3-9); and the fifth day was the institution of the supper, the day of Judas' betrayal, and the warning to Peter about his denial (22:1-38); on the evening of that day He went out to Gethsemane, where He was arrested, tried that night in the high priest's palace, and the following morning in the court of Pilate, and on that sixth day taken out to Calvary to be crucified (22:39-23:56). All will not agree with this chronology but it is an attempt to show the sequence of events. We know from 21:37 that the Lord went to the temple during the days but went out of the city each night.

28   The Holy Spirit through Luke has traced the footsteps of Jesus of Nazareth, beautiful in His holiness, tender grace and moral perfections, from Galilee, where He had spent the most of the days of His public ministry, until now He climbs the final miles from Jericho to Jerusalem and enters the city in triumph. "He went before" and His disciples followed, accompanied as we believe by a large crowd, many of whom had journeyed from Galilee to be in Jerusalem at the Passover.

"Ascending up" to Jerusalem is the way the journey was described no matter from which direction the traveller came. From Jericho it was a physical climb of 3 000 feet. Luke can be divided into five periods in the life of our Lord by similar expressions. He was *growing up* (chs.2,3); *raising up* in the miracles of chs.4 to 9; *going up* to Jerusalem in chs.10 to 19; *offered up* in chs.20 to 23, and *raised up* in ch.24.

29   Bethany was a village two miles from Jerusalem, along the road to Jericho on the eastern slopes of the Mount of Olives. It may be that the Lord and His disciples arrived there at the beginning of the sabbath, or were so close to it when the sabbath day arrived that the distance was not greater than was allowed for the sabbath. It is likely that the crowd went on into the city when the Lord turned aside to Bethany, the home of Martha, and her sister and Lazarus, and of Simon the leper, in whose house he was anointed (Mark 14:3-9). Bethphage must have lain close by. Its location is not known today, some believe it was the name given to the region between Bethany and Jerusalem.

Various attempts have been made to correlate the sequence of events in John 12:1-15 to the synoptic Gospels. John says, "Then Jesus six days before the passover came to Bethany" (12:1), but he does not say that the supper was made on the day when He arrived. Mark 14:1 says, "After two days was the feast of the passover" and in v.3 tells of the supper when the Lord was anointed. If the days given at the introduction to this section are the correct sequence, then the Lord came to Bethany several days before the supper was held. A greater problem to many is John's statement, "On the next day much people that were come to the feast" (12:12) which is his introduction to the triumphal entry into Jerusalem, putting it after the anointing. Luke does not mention the anointing, but Matthew and Mark place the triumphal entry before the anointing (Matt 21:1-9; Mark

11:1-10). One explanation of John 12:12 is that "On the next day" refers back to 12:1, "Then Jesus six days before the passover", placing the triumphal entry on the exact day that agrees with Mark and Matthew.

The phrase "when he was come nigh" is found in all the synoptic Gospels, but more frequently in Luke, where it is used eighteen times. It has often been debated where the Lord spent the nights of His final week in Jerusalem. Some suggest that he stayed at Bethany in the home of Lazarus and the two sisters. We know He would have been welcome there, but if He did stay with His friends in Bethany, why would He have been hungry (Matt 21:18) in the morning as He came into the city? Perhaps this verse helps us. He came "nigh to Bethphage and Bethany", but may have spent the nights, at least some of them, on the mountainside rather than in the home, and from His solitary vigil came hungry into the city.

30-34   He sent two of His disciples to the opposite village, the name of which we are not given, instructing them that as they entered it they would find an unbroken colt tied, which they were to bring to Him. He could perfectly describe the place, the colt, and the reaction of the owners because He is the omniscient Lord, not because He had prearranged the use of the colt, or only "knew" these things from Zech 9:9 as Godet suggests. He knew the owners (plural) would challenge the action of two strange men as they loosed the colt to lead it away, and told them to reply; "the Lord hath need of him". Seldom did the Lord Jesus use the title Lord, when speaking about Himself, but He did on this occasion, suggesting that the owners of the colt recognised the title in the light of such Scriptures as Ps 110:1.

Plummer compares the unbroken colt to the virgin's womb and Joseph's new tomb, and this is excellent, for the Lord Jesus was unique in His birth, life, words, works, suffering, death and resurrection. Finding the colt, as afterward they found the upper room, not only met the need of the Lord but at the same time strengthened their faith. These two disciples were Galilean fishermen, more trained in handling boats than beasts, so to handle an unbroken colt was a new experience for them. He who was able to control the wild beasts in the wilderness and calm the waves of the sea found no problem in controlling an untamed colt.

35   They brought the colt to the Lord. Jewish leaders, religious and political, rejected Him, but just as the sea and storm (8:22-25) recognised the Lord of all, so the little creature was subject under His hand. Although never broken to carry a rider nothing is said of bit or bridle (Ps 32:9). His gentle voice and hand were all the guidance it needed. The disciples set the Lord upon the colt, first having placed their garments on it. Matt 2 1:7 says, "they set him thereon", that is, on the garments. That they did not spare the very best garments they owned is suggested by the wording, "Throwing on of them the garments" (A. Marshall). A colt is not a warhorse, but "an animal which was the symbol of peace" (Farrar). It is not an attractive creature and the garments of the disciples added nothing to its appearance. Therefore, we read with wonder the amazing prophecy, "Rejoice greatly, O daughter of Zion; shout, O daughter of Jerusalem: behold, thy King cometh unto thee: he is just, and having salvation; lowly, and riding upon an ass, and upon a colt the foal of an ass" (Zech 9:9).

The triumphal entry into Jerusalem is not only the culmination of the journey that began at 9:5 1, and the fulfilment of the prophecy by Zechariah, it is one of the most important events in the life and ministry of the Lord. It is recorded in all four Gospels which is not true of His birth, temptation, transfiguration nor the Gethsemane experience. If He had not ridden on the colt in fulfilment of Zechariah's prophecy, they the nation would have had some excuse for not knowing Him. At the time of this entry He proclaimed His kingship publicly and officially, so that in the language of the parable, the nation said, "this is the heir, come let us kill him"; they knew the claims of the One they were killing. The leaders of the nation rejected His claims, believing that they possessed superior wisdom; "Have any of the rulers or of the Pharisees believed on him?" (John 7:48). The ignorant people who cried, "Blessed be the King that cometh in the name of the Lord" were described by them as "this people who knoweth not the law (and) are cursed" (John 7:49). But Paul describes the leaders as "the princes of this world" whose "wisdom" came "to nought" (1 Cor 2:6). Referring to "the hidden wisdom, which God ordained before the world unto our glory", Paul wrote, "Which none of the princes of this world knew: for had they known it, they would not have crucified the Lord of glory" (1 Cor 2:7,8).

Application is most appropriate here. The tied colt is a picture of a sinner, held by sin and Satan. The colt, hidden by the garments, under the Lord's hand and holding Him up is a beautiful picture of a believer, honoured to lift up Christ before others. Only Luke uses the word *epibibazō* ("to set on") in this verse; in 10:34, "set him on his own beast"; and in Acts 23:24, "provide them beasts ... set Paul on". It was likely the twelve who set the Lord on the colt, and Luke says "they spread their clothes in the way" (v.36) which seems to refer to the disciples, but Matthew tells us "a great multitude spread their garments in the way" (21:8). Luke uses a different word for "spread" (*hupostrōnnuō*) which is found only here in the NT and means "to spread under" (W.E. Vine); JND renders it "they strewed".

36-38 Luke omits the branches that were strewn in the way (Matt 21:8; Mark 11:8), but does tell of the garments that the people spread before Him. "The whole multitude of the disciples" identifies in a general way those who had followed Him, many of them all the way from Galilee. Luke speaks of "a loud voice". Matthew describes a shout that increased in fervour (21:9). Ellicott (*Lectures on the Life of Christ*, p.287) estimates that the crowd gathered for the Passover represented not much less than half of the entire population of Judaea and Galilee. This great outburst was entirely spontaneous, fuelled by the thought that, at long last, Jesus of Nazareth was declaring His kingship and about to take His throne. The expressions that they used came from such Psalms as 45 and 118, describing His glory, and they thought that the time had come. How very wrong they were, for the streets that rang with the loud "Hosanna" of this great throng were soon to ring with the cry, "Crucify, crucify". The excited people were sincere and their praise was for the mighty miracles that they had seen performed by the One who now fulfils the prophecy of Zechariah, written five centuries earlier.

39-40 Fearful of a mob scene the Pharisees tried to rebuke the people through the Lord. None of the excitement reached to them. Standing aloof from it all they looked on with displeasure. The Lord Jesus speaks of stones crying out, and we think that they have no voice, but we are wrong. The crying out of inanimate nature for the day of the enthroning of the King is not fanciful, but literal, for "the whole creation groaneth and travaileth in pain together until now" (Rom 8:22). When at last "the King of righteousness, and ... King of peace" (Heb 7:2) takes to Himself His great power and reigns over a redeemed earth, all nature will be subdued under His hand (1 Cor 15:27,28). The crowd had rightly identified the King, but it was not the time for His reign.

2.   *The Lord Weeps over Jerusalem*
     19:41-44

> v.41 "And when he was come near, he beheld the city, and wept over it,
> v.42 Saying, If thou hadst known, even thou, at least in this thy day, the things which belong unto thy peace! but now they are hid from thine eyes.
> v.43 For the days shall come upon thee, that thine enemies shall cast a trench about thee, and compass thee round, and keep thee in on every side,
> v.44 And shall lay thee even with the ground, and thy children within thee; and they shall not leave in thee one stone upon another; because thou knewest not the time of thy visitation.

41   Many, familiar with the topography of the ascent to Jerusalem from the east, believe they can pinpoint the actual spot where the Lord stood and viewed the city. In v.37, Luke took great care to point out the very spot where the people "began to rejoice". He said it was "at the descent of the mount of Olives", using *katabasis* ("descent"), its only occurrence in the NT. The expression here "when he was come near" can be found in 18:35,40 and in vv.29,37 of this chapter, but in ch.21, the same word is used for "the time draweth near" (v.8); "the desolation (of Jerusalem) is nigh" (v.20) and "your redemption draweth nigh" (v.28). Luke is giving us a location on the road, "he was come near" to portray that the Lord is drawing near to the cross which was the very purpose of His coming into the world.

The Lord may have wept as an infant but it is not recorded. From Heb 5:7 we know that in "the days of his flesh" there were "strong crying and tears". At the grave of Lazarus Mary looked up into a blessed face wet with tears, and here, looking upon the favoured city, the Man of sorrows wept. He had already expressed His deep grief at the rejection of the people of Jerusalem (13:34,35); we are not told that He wept then, although He likely did.

42   Jerusalem was a city of great past glory, "the city of David" (1 Kings 2:10) in whose streets had stood so many of God's great messengers, but now the great grace of the past is to be enlarged in manifold measure as in its midst stands not one of the many servants but the unique Son of God; "I will send my beloved son" (20:13). In their rejection of Him they became the city of the great crime. This tragic story is in the heart of the Saviour as He mourns their terrible blindness. Their "day" was the presentation of the King; "thy King cometh unto thee" (Zech 9:9). Their "peace" would have been fully enjoyed by the reception of the Prince of Peace, but "thou knewest not the time of thy visitation". He speaks in language indicating that the choice has already been made and their judgment is certain.

Into this dark scene bursts the light of a blessed promise. The city so great in grace, guilt and grief will yet be great in glory and in that new Jerusalem there will be no sin, no Satan and not even the need of the sun (Rev 21:22-27).

43-44   In this description there is again powerful evidence of the omniscience of the Lord. He gave an accurate and graphic description of the actual siege of Jerusalem by Titus and the Roman legions in AD 70, some forty years before the event. The Jewish revolt against the Romans began in AD 66, the siege was long and bitter. The Romans built a defensive palisade to protect themselves as they encircled the city. The Jews burned it and the Romans constructed a wall. The defence was a story of human courage and religious fanaticism almost unparalleled in history, but eventually the walls were breached and the city fell at the sacrifice of one million lives (Unger). The anger of Titus and the Roman legions was not only displayed against the hapless inhabitants who were slain, but on the very stones of the city and temple which were torn down so that the very site would be abandoned, and the source of the rebellion destroyed (F.F. Bruce, *The Spreading Flame*, pp.154-157). The Romans later rebuilt it as a Gentile city.

"The time of thy visitation" is a frequent OT phrase. In all its occurrences in the Prophets it is a day of calamity or a day of judgment (Isa 10:3; Jer 8:12; 10: 15; 11:23; 23:12; 46:21; 48:44; 50:27; 51:18; Hos 9:7; Micah 7:4). He who came in grace used it of a visitation of the grace of God. Although there is a difference of mind about 1 Pet 2:12, it seems that Peter also uses it of a visitation in grace rather than judgment. "And *shall lay* (thee) *even* with the ground" (v.44) is the translation of one word *edaphizō* that is found only here in the NT. It means "to beat even with the earth" (W.E. Vine); "shall dash you to the ground, you and your children within you" (RSV); "and will level thee with the ground, and thy children within thee" (J. Rotherham). The walls, towers and houses of Jerusalem were to be beaten as level as a threshing floor, and this was literally fulfilled.

The Jews had rejected the testimony of their own Scriptures to the Lord Jesus. They had refused the powerful testimony of His own miracles, the moral perfection of His life, and the power and authority of His words which all felt. Wilfully they had shut their eyes until, as Paul wrote, "the wrath is come upon them to the uttermost" (1 Thess 2:16). The destruction of Jerusalem was a direct result of their rejection of Messiah. What a solemn warning to Christ rejectors!

3.   The Lord Enters and Purifies the Temple
19:45-48

> v.45 "And he went into the temple, and began to cast out them that sold therein, and them that bought;
> v.46 Saying unto them, It is written, My house is the house of prayer: but ye have made it a den of thieves.
> v.47 And he taught daily in the temple. But the chief priests and the scribes and the chief of the people sought to destroy him,
> v.48 And could not find what they might do: for all the people were very attentive to hear him."

45-46   There were two cleansings of the temple (John 2:13-22; Mark 11:15-18; Matt 21:12-16). Luke's account is brief in comparison to the others. Only Tyrian coins were acceptable as a temple offering for they had a high level of silver purity, better than the standard Roman coinage. When offerers came to the temple the money-changers, for a surcharge, sold Tyrian coins for other kinds. The practice gave room for dishonesty and at the Passover time the trade was unusually brisk, so the Lord upset the business of the money-changers at the busiest time of the year (I.B.D. Tyndale). The Lord quoted from Isa 56:7, referring to the temple as "an house of prayer for all people". The moneychanging may have been a necessary fact of life, but the Lord did not approve of its operation within the temple. He also charged them with dishonesty in their exchange. It is probable that some of these same men had been cast out of the temple at the first cleansing, but that first lesson had not been heeded. At that first cleansing, He had charged them with making His "Father's house an house of merchandise" (John 2:16), but here He charged them, "ye have made it a den of thieves" (AV); "den of robbers" (JND, RV); "a cave for robbers" (C.B. Williams). These words infer that the practices had deteriorated to an even lower level of fraudulence.

47-48   He taught daily in the temple, hated by the chief priests and scribes, and "the principal men of the people sought to destroy him" (RV), but were hindered in their evil purpose by the common people in the crowded city who hung upon His words. During these days of temple teaching He did not remain in the city at night but "remained abroad on the mountain called the mount of Olives" (21:37 JND). When Luke tells us "all the people were very attentive to hear him" he uses *ekkremannumi* ("to hang from"). It is the only time it is found in the NT and paints a graphic picture of the listening crowds, "all the people hung on him to hear" (JND); "for the people, to a man, were hanging on his words" (E.V. Rieu). This is the key to the strange behaviour of the leaders of the Jews. They wanted to utterly "destroy" (*apollumi*) Jesus, but they "did not find what they could do" (JND); "they found they were helpless" (NEB).

4.   *Who Gave Thee this Authority?*
20:1-8

v.1   "And it came to pass, *that* on one of those days, as he taught the people in the temple, and preached the gospel, the chief priests and the scribes came upon *him* with the elders,

v.2   And spake unto him, saying, Tell us, by what authority doest thou these things? or who is he that gave thee this authority?

v.3   And he answered and said unto them, I will also ask you one thing; and answer me:

v.4   The baptism of John, was it from heaven, or of men?

v.5   And they reasoned with themselves, saying, If we shall say, From heaven; he will say, Why then believed ye him not?

v.6   But and if we say, Of men; all the people will stone us: for they be persuaded that John was a prophet.

v.7   And they answered, that they could not tell whence *it was*.

v.8   And Jesus said unto them, Neither tell I you by what authority I do these things.

1   When we remember that the words we are pondering were given by the Holy Spirit and that no word of His was ever redundant, we must take notice that the Lord " taught the people in the temple, and preached the gospel". He is the pattern for both teachers and preachers but we should be able to distinguish the two distinct functions. We are inclined to forget, or neglect, in our day the very old and scriptural practice of preaching, heralding the message of salvation. Quiet talks on a personal level are very necessary groundwork for gospel blessing, but it is "preaching" that has been chosen by God as a divine method of salvation (1 Cor 1:21). "Preached the gospel" is only one word (*euangelizō*) and describes the function of a gifted evangelist. Upon this gracious activity of the Lord came chief priests and scribes.

2   The cleverly-worded questions designed to discredit the Lord before the people must have been devised in the council, so it was likely an informal delegation from the Sanhedrin which accosted Him. The two questions about His authority were a demand that He produce the credentials that would tell that His teaching had the authority of the rabbinical schools. A teacher was known by the teachers under whom he had been taught (Acts 22:3); the more renowned the teacher the more authority was ascribed to the teaching, much in the way that a degree from a prestigious university has greater value than the same degree from an unknown college (Edersheim, Vol.2, p.384). If He had claimed to be Messiah and that His authority was from God, they would have charged Him with blasphemy to the Sanhedrin and with insurrection to the Romans. "These things" refer to the triumphal entry into Jerusalem and the cleansing of the temple.

3-8   The Lord knew that His questioners were acting a part. They neither wanted to hear about His schools of learning nor the authority of His acts, but they did want to discredit Him in the eyes of the people who were listening so attentively to Him. Knowing their hearts He asked them a question that was also of great importance in the court of public opinion. Was John commissioned by God or was he only a messenger from men? If they admitted, as the people believed, that John was a prophet from God, then their rejection of him was rank unbelief against the messenger of God. If they said that John did not have authority from God, they feared the people who believed in him. They were caught on the horns of a dilemma and refused to answer, which caused the Lord to reply: "Neither tell I you by what authority I do these things". The difficulty with the Lord's question is greater because John had given such clear witness to Christ. The conversation between the chief priests, scribes and elders is faithfully recorded by the Holy Spirit, for it is most unlikely that any from outside their meeting heard the debate. When they said, "all the people will stone us", they used an intensive form of *lithazō* ("to stone"), and this word, *katalithazō*, is found only here in the NT. It expresses the potential violence of the crowd, for these religious leaders genuinely feared the people who had been "very attentive to hear" Christ (19:48) and a large company waited to hear their answer.

There is a very touching lesson in this exchange. The Lord knew He would soon be condemned by these chief priests and scribes; yet He gave them no material by which they could charge Him. He did nothing to seek their opposition, but in grace and dignity endured it when it broke out in all its hatred and cruelty.

5.   *I Will Send My Beloved Son*
20:9-18

v.9 "Then began he to speak to the people this parable; A certain man planted a vineyard, and let it forth to husbandmen, and went into a far country for a long time.

v.10 And at the season he sent a servant to the husbandmen, that they should give him of the fruit of the vineyard: but the husbandmen beat him, and sent *him* away empty.

v.11 And again he sent another servant: and they beat him also, and entreated *him* shamefully, and sent *him* away empty.

v.12 And again he sent a third: and they wounded him also, and cast *him* out.

v.13 Then said the lord of the vineyard, What shall I do? I will send my beloved son: it may be they will reverence *him* when they see him.

v.14 But when the husbandmen saw him, they reasoned among themselves, saying, This is the heir: come, let us kill him, that the inheritance may be ours.

v.15 So they cast him out of the vineyard, and killed *him*. What therefore shall the lord of the vineyard do unto them?

v.16 He shall come and destroy these husbandmen, and shall give the vineyard to others. And when they heard *it*, they said, God forbid.

v.17 And he beheld them, and said, What is this then that is written, The stone which the builders rejected, the same is become the head of the corner?

v.18 Whosoever shall fall upon that stone shall be broken; but on whomsoever it shall fall, it will grind him to powder."

The key to the meaning of the vineyard, its care and the fruit produced in it must be understood in the light of the OT, particularly of such passages as Ps

80:8-16; Isa 5:1-7 and Jer 2:21. The key is "the vineyard of the Lord of hosts is the house of Israel" (Isa 5:7). After planting it with the choicest vine and caring for it so diligently the Lord laments, "What could have been done more to my vineyard, that I have not done in it? wherefore, when I looked that it should bring forth grapes, brought it forth wild grapes? " (v.4). The tragic result was "I will lay it waste". In Ps 80:8-16 Asaph gives a beautiful description of the vine that was brought out of Egypt, planted in the land of Israel, that grew until it filled the land, but eventually was burned with fire and cut down at the rebuke of the Lord.

9   God had said, Israel is "my vineyard", so we can identify the Owner, and the planting of the vineyard is very similar to the prototype of Isa 5, but the letting of it out to husbandmen and the departure "into a far country for a long time" are unique to the Lord's teaching. Matthew adds that the owner "hedged it round about, digged a winepress in it, and built a tower", which were all signs of his care and the investment he made in it (21:33). In this verse, as in 8:27 and 23:18, *hikanos* (" long" or " sufficient") is used with *chronos* ("time", "season"). This "long time" or interval between the going away and the return were sufficient to have produced much fruit. This is the normal use of *chronos* which "denotes a space of time, whether short or long" (W.E. Vine). It is *chronos* that is used in the phrases, "since the world began" (Rom 16:25), "times of the ages" (JND), and "before the world began" (2 Tim 1:9), "times eternal" (RV). Luke uses *kairos* ("at the season") in v.10 to describe that it was a definite period that had been allowed, probably fixed ahead of time, and the season for fruit had arrived. This has direct application to Israel, for after their many opportunities and blessings and God's long patience with them, He waited for the fruit and the season for it had arrived.

10   We are not told what amount was agreed upon as rent, but we know that it was fruit from the vineyard to the owner. When the time of fruit was near a servant was sent to collect the revenue, but he was beaten and sent away empty. The husbandmen may have concluded that the owner was far away and his authority over them was unenforceable, so they acted with arrogance in rejecting his claims. They may even have argued that their possession of the vineyard was evidence enough that it belonged to them and they were not accountable to an absent owner. The prophets of God who were sent to Israel brought home to the people the demands of God for the many blessings He had lavished on His vineyard and His expectations from it. The prophets were God's rental agents.

11-12   There is great patience evident in the sending of the second servant, but they not only beat him, but "cast insult upon him, (and) sent him away empty" (JND). "And again, he sent a third" must mean that the first and second returned to him after the abuse and insult. Yet once more he sent this one who is wounded and cast out. This treatment of the servants was an exposure of Israel's treatment of God's prophets. Stephen charged them: "Which of the prophets have not your fathers persecuted? and they have slain them which showed before of the coming of the Just One; of whom ye have been now the betrayers and murderers" (Acts 7:52). The word that is used for "wounded" (*traumatizō*) is only found here and in Acts 19:16 in NT and may be another of the words that Luke used because of his training as a physician. To traumatise in English means to inflict a wound with violence.

13 According to v.16 the owner of the vineyard had the authority and ability all this time to come and destroy these wicked men, but instead he said, "I will send my beloved son". This was a display of grace and mercy unexpected and undeserved. "But last of all he sent them his son" (Matt 21:37). Even the blind, arrogant chief priests and scribes knew the meaning of the parable. The One who is telling it is "the beloved son" sent from the Father in heaven. All the sources of heavenly love are drawn upon and displayed fully: He sent unto them His Son, and it may be that they will reverence Him when they see Him. He is unique among all the servants; He bears such a majesty and dignity in His Person that surely they will give Him respect.

The Holy Spirit through Luke has put great pathos into this little word *isōs* ("it may be") or "perhaps". It is the only time it is found in the NT and a more appropriate use for it would be very difficult to find. The adjective *isos* ("equal") may at first thought seem far removed from "perhaps", but the association is that the action of sending his "beloved son" would have prompted a proper (equal) reaction of acceptance and "reverence". That it did not is the whole point of the parable. A certain action should "equal" a certain reaction. "Reverence" (*entrepō*) literally means "to turn upon one oneself" or "to be put to shame"; Matt 21:37 and Mark 12:6 are the parallel passages and both use the same word. Luke used it twice in 18:2,4 "regard". When it is used in the passive voice, as it is here, it means "to be shamed into respect" (W. Hendriksen).

14 He surely did have the bearing of the Father's Son. The likeness was unmistakable. They saw in Him that He was truly the worthy heir, but they envied and hated Him without a cause and were determined to kill Him that the inheritance might belong to them alone with no other claimant. The phrase, "they reasoned among themselves" uses *dialogizomai* (" reasoned"). It " is used in the NT chiefly of thoughts and considerations which are more or less objectionable" (W. E. Vine). The "reasoning" reveals hearts that were full of envy, hatred, covetousness and murder, "come, let us kill him, that the inheritance may be ours". The impact of these words must have been like a physical blow to the chief priests and scribes who "perceived that he had spoken this parable against them" (v.19).

15   The casting out was done before they killed Him. Parable and reality draw very close together here. A dead body in a vineyard would so defile it that buyers would not purchase wine from it. It was the time of the Passover in Jerusalem and the city must not be defiled, so they cast Him out and slew Him. "What ... shall the lord of the vineyard do?". When patience, mercy and matchless grace have produced hatred and rejection what can he do? God's tender mercy to the Jew had been responded to by man's terrible cruelty.

16   The final result will be God's fearful wrath, but He adds that He "shall give the vineyard to others". Matthew adds that He "will let out his vineyard unto other husbandmen, which shall render him the fruits in their seasons" (21:41). Who are the "others"? To the amillennialist who interprets all of Israel's future blessings as spiritual blessings for the church, and allows no future for Israel, the answer is simple: the "others" are saved Gentiles who replace Israel as the Lord's vineyard. We may accept this is an application but not the interpretation. We know that God has set aside His chosen people. Paul preached in Antioch of Pisidia, "It was necessary that the word of God should first have been spoken to you: but seeing ye put it from you, and judge yourselves unworthy of everlasting life, lo, we turn to the Gentiles" (Acts 13:46). But "God hath not cast away his people which he foreknew" (Rom 11:2,25). In keeping with the fact that the vineyard is the house of Israel (Isa 5:1-7), even though the generation that rejected Messiah produced no fruit and were judged, God will again place in the land a redeemed Israel which will accept their Messiah (Zech 12:10). It may be that the people who exclaimed, "God forbid" were thinking of God turning from Israel to Gentiles.

17   The Lord turned a piercing glance upon the people and quoted Ps 118:22, one of the Hallel Psalms, sung at the Passover as well as at other festivals of Israel. The point was exceptionally piercing. He is saying, If My rejection is a sign that I am not the Messiah, explain this Psalm: "The stone which the builders rejected". Even the Rabbis recognised that this was a Messianic Psalm. "The head of the corner" can mean the stone at the top of the wall that unites and holds the two walls together, or the foundation-stone at the bottom of the corner that forms the two walls. Either stone is the key to the two walls. In Eph 2:20 Paul is dealing with the uniting of the two walls, Jew and Gentile, in Christ so he speaks of Him as "chief corner stone". 1 Pet 2:6 quotes Isa 28:16, "Behold, I lay in Zion for a foundation a stone, a tried stone, a precious corner stone, a sure foundation".

18   Isa 8:14 speaks of Messiah as "a stone of stumbling and ... a rock of offence to both the houses of Israel", and is the passage to which the Lord makes reference. Israel stumbled over the lowly One who had come among them. Looking for the might and majesty of the great Deliverer they failed to accept

Jesus of Nazareth as the Saviour and ultimate Deliverer. The rest of the statement makes reference to "the stone … cut out without hands" that falls on the feet of the great image in Dan 2:34,35 and breaks in pieces and grinds to powder all the might of Gentile empires. Israel stumbled at the lowly Stone; Gentiles will be crushed by the descending Stone.

We have frequently heard gospel preachers apply this verse to repentance, contrasting those who fall upon the stone and are broken before God with all those who do not repent and will know the grinding judgment of the stone that shall fall on sinners. If a preacher chooses to use such an application, it is wise to explain the meaning of the verse first. Those who "fall upon that stone" are broken to pieces. *Sunthlaō*("to break") is used only here and in Matt 21:44 with the meaning "to dash to pieces". It is not a word that can be rightly interpreted as repentance. The contrast is not between repentance and judgment, but between those who stumbled at the "stumbling stone" and rejected Christ at His first advent and those who will be here to experience His judgment in the second advent. It is also only here and in Matt 21:44 that *likmaō*("it will grind him to powder") is used.

6.   *Show Me a Penny*
   ## 20:19-26

v.19 "And the chief priests and the scribes the same hour sought to lay hands on him; and they feared the people: for they perceived that he had spoken this parable against them.

v.20 And they watched *him*, and sent forth spies, which should feign themselves just men, that they might take hold of his words, that so they might deliver him unto the power and authority of the governor.

v.21 And they asked him, saying, Master, we known that thou sayest and teachest rightly, neither acceptest thou the person *of any*, but teachest the way of God truly:

v.22 Is it lawful for us to give tribute unto Caesar, or no?

v.23 But he perceived their craftiness, and said unto them, Why tempt ye me?

v.24 Shew me a penny, Whose image and superscription hath it? They answered and said, Caesar's.

v.25 And he said unto them, Render therefore unto Caesar the things which be Caesar's, and unto God the things which be God's.

v.26 And they could not take hold of his words before the people: and they marvelled at his answer, and held their peace."

19   Following the chronology of this final week we believe that the long day of questioning began at this point. The previous day closed with the chief priests and scribes seeking to lay their hands on Him. They well understood the meaning of the parable of the vineyard. They were ready to seize Him "the same hour", but the people who crowded the city at the Passover were still ready to listen to the Teacher from Galilee, and might oppose the arrest, so the leaders bided their time.

20   But they watched Him with evil intent and sent spies from the Sanhedrin, pretending to be just men, to listen to His words so that they might have a charge to lay against Him before Pilate, the Roman governor. Their plans are already laid, they have discussed the problem of stoning Christ in the city at the Passover. The alternative left to them is to turn Him over to the authority of Rome and have the governor crucify Him. The spies were both Pharisees and Herodians sent from the chief priests, scribes and elders according to Mark 11:27 and 12:13.

There are two words in this verse that are not found anywhere else in the NT. In the clause, "they ... sent forth spies", the word "spies" (*enkathetos*) is an adjective but is used as a noun. It literally means has been "let down into" for the purpose of spying (W. Hendriksen). The phrase, "which should feign" (*hupokrinomai*) "primarily denotes to give an answer; then, to answer on the stage, play a part and so... to feign, pretend" (W.E. Vine). These deceitful men had set their own stage and were playing their part. We are truly staggered when we consider that the One who was the object of their perfidy saw their hearts and knew their motives and purpose.

21 They flattered Him that He had integrity and was not guided by human opinion but taught the way of God without partiality. Satan and the world have lost none of their cunning and still use flattery as a weapon to snare our feet. The danger is that we might lend an ear to flattering remarks and be put off our guard. The Lord practised His own preaching, "Woe unto you when all men shall speak well of you! " (6:26). This is a warning that we need to heed in a day when evangelical preaching seems to be accepted by so many who are still rank worldlings.

22 Paying tribute was a highly charged, political and religious issue far exceeding the amount of the tax. The Zealots, where possible, refused to pay any taxes; the Pharisees paid them resentfully; the Herodians supported the payments; none would have suggested that it was "lawful" according to the law of Moses or the teachings of the Rabbis. An affirmative answer would discredit Him to the people who regarded the tax as a shameful proof of their subjection to Rome. A negative answer would be just cause to accuse Him to the Roman authorities, so the question was designed cleverly to do Him harm in whatever way it was answered. It is not a far fetched suggestion that the council may have worked late the night before to come up with this and the other questions of that day.

23 "He perceived their craftiness" is a statement, not so much of His ability to read hearts, but of His awareness of the political and social issues that were involved in their deceit; He also knew that they were ready to do anything to trap Him. JND includes the words, "Why tempt ye me?" as does the AV. The text on which the RV is based does not include it. Mark 12:15 has the question, which can be read, "Why are you putting me to the test?". In throwing the question back at them, the Lord exposed the intent of their hearts. The reason why they ask it was of far greater importance than any answer that might be given. "He perceived" (*katanoeō*) is used fourteen times in the NT and eight of its occurrences are found in Luke's writings. It is used of the man who beheld the mote in a brother's eye, but failed "to perceive" the beam in his own eye, and means "to carefully consider" with the mind. The Lord used it in teaching the disciples, "Consider the ravens" (12:24); "Consider the lilies" (12:27). The Lord carefully considered and rightly assessed the enemies who surrounded Him.

24   Jewish copper coins would not carry the image of any person or living thing, and even Roman copper coins used among the Jews probably did not have an image. The silver penny, a denarius, the only coin acceptable as tax money, bore the image of Tiberias. The inscription on one side said, "Tiberias Caesar Augustus, son of the divine Augustus", and the obverse side read, "Pontifex Maximus" and had the head of a woman holding a branch and sceptre (I.B.D. Tyndale). The British "d" as an abbreviation for the old penny is taken from the Roman denarius.

It is very unlikely that either Christ or His disciples possessed a denarius, but then it is also unlikely that the Pharisees carried such coins because of the effrontery of their inscriptions. When the coin was brought the Lord Jesus asked whose image and superscription it bore, and they had to answer " Caesar's".

25   The Lord Jesus is the true" wisdom" that is from above (James 3:17),and He surely displayed it in His answer in which there are three lessons for all. First, He recognised civil authority, which we also are taught to do (Rom 13:1-7). Secondly, He denied that He had come to set up a political kingdom in opposition to imperial Rome. Thirdly, He made a distinct difference between God and Caesar, for this distinction was utterly blurred by the imperial cult. So His answer not only showed the claims of Caesar, but of far greater importance, the claims of God, and the two claims should never be confused. "The things of God" that are to be rendered to God certainly include recognition by His creatures of the bounties of His creation, but there is more in these words. They were addressed to professed representatives of His covenant people, so "the things of God" encompass all that He has revealed in His Word and covenants and require from them the appropriate response of love, honour, reverence, faith and obedience. It is in the light of this that we should see the words, " it may be they will reverence him when they see him" (v.13). If they had truly honoured the Father, they would have honoured His Son (John 5:23).

26   His answer amazed them in its wisdom and brought them to silence. The majesty and dignity that were displayed by the Lord on this occasion remind us of the fact that all who are brought before Him are eventually reduced to silence (Job 40:4; Rom 3:19), and in the day when He sits as judge there will be no excuse (Rom 1:20).

7.   *The God of the Living*
     20:27-40

v.27 "Then came to *him* certain of the Sadducees, which deny that there is any resurrection; and they asked him,

v.28 Saying, Master, Moses wrote unto us, If any man's brother die, having a wife, and he die without children, that his brother should take his wife, and raise up seed unto his brother.

v.29 There were therefore seven brethren: and the first took a wife, and died without children.

v.30 And the second took her to wife, and he died childless.

v.31 And the third took her; and in like manner the seven also: and they left no children, and died.

v.32 Last of ail the woman died also.

v.33 Therefore in the resurrection whose wife of them is she? for seven had her to wife.

v.34 And Jesus answering said unto them, The children of this world marry, and are given in marriage:

v.35 But they which shall be accounted worthy to obtain that world, and the resurrection from the dead, neither marry, nor are given in marriage:

v.36 Neither can they die any more: for they are equal unto the angels; and are the children of God, being the children of the resurrection.

v.37 Now that the dead are raised, even Moses shewed at the bush, when he calleth the Lord the God of Abraham, and the God of Isaac, and the God of Jacob.

v.38 For he is not a God of the dead, but of the living: for all live unto him.

v.39 Then certain of the scribes answering said, Master, thou hast well said.

v.40 And after that they durst not ask him any *question at all.*"

27   Luke gives more information about the influence and beliefs of the Sadducees in the book of Acts than any other NT writer (4:1; 5:17; 23:6-8) but this is the only time he mentions them in his Gospel. There is not a lot of reliable information about Sadducees, and it is normally pointed out that sources such as the Mishnah or Josephus were antagonistic to them. The information given in the NT links them to the high priest's family and other powerful priestly families of Judaea (Acts 5:17). In NT days they probably predominated in the Sanhedrin, but because the people favoured the Pharisees their influence was limited. Many if not all the priests were Sadducees, but it seems that all Sadducees were priests. Luke tells "the Sadducees say that there is no resurrection, neither angel, nor spirit" (Acts 23:8). They believed that only what Moses wrote was valid law, rejecting the oral tradition so important to the Pharisees. Did they believe in annihilation? It is likely; at least Josephus says they did. Although he came from an aristocratic priestly family, at nineteen Josephus joined the Pharisees. In view of their confidence in the Law of Moses it is interesting that in debating with them the Lord used the Pentateuch.

It is serious to think that the priests who were to be keepers and teachers of the law and were charged with the judgment of those who broke it were at this time Sadducees. This is a reminder to us that in religious high places are to be found men who question almost every vital truth of Scripture. It is from the highest levels of religious hierarchy that have come the most critical attacks against inspiration and inerrancy. Seminaries are hotbeds of unbelief. Earlier in this century, it was very common to call this "modernism", but it is as modern as the Sadducees.

28-33   The method of confrontation used in this exchange followed a standard procedure. Scripture is appealed to and an illustrative story is told. They referred to the law of a brother raising up seed to his dead brother and calling the child by the dead man's name, so "that his name be not put out of Israel" (Deut 25:5-10). They repeated an extreme story of a widowed woman and seven brothers each taking her for his wife and dying, with the woman remaining childless. At the end they asked the question: "Therefore in the resurrection whose wife of them is she?". It may have been an argument often used with great success against their foes to make the resurrection look ridiculous.

34-38   In His infinite wisdom, the Lord Jesus corrected four errors of the Sadducees. They were wrong in their interpretation of the resurrection life, for although in this world the married state is common it is not continued in the resurrection life, for they "neither marry, nor are given in marriage". He corrected them about their unbelief in the power of God to raise the dead. He corrected them in their unbelief about angels, saying of those who are raised from the dead: "neither can they die any more: for they are equal unto the angels; and are children of God, being the children of the resurrection". He is referring only to those who died in faith, and so to "the resurrection from among the dead" (JND), not "of the dead", that is, of the wicked dead. As an aside in His teaching they were shown that angels are real, are deathless, and do not marry. There is nothing in this to indicate that heaven will see a break-up or a breakdown of family relationships. In fact only in heaven will unmarred relationships of true devotion last forever.

Then, He correctly interpreted the meaning of one of the OT passages most commonly read in the synagogues: "Moreover he said, I am the God of thy father, the God of Abraham, the God of Isaac, and the God of Jacob" (Exod 3:6). The words spoken to Moses at the burning bush were uttered hundreds of years later after the death of the three patriarchs, yet God does not say, "I was the God of Abraham", for He is revealing to Moses the meaning of the infinite "I am". Dead things can have a Creator but only living men can know the living God. "I am the God of Abraham" means "I am his God today", so Abraham still lives, not in his body, but as the spirit of a just man; he lives with God, awaiting the day when "the spirits of just men" will be "made perfect" (Heb 12:23) in resurrection. Only Luke adds "for all live for him" (JND), that is, they are alive for God's sake. They are dead in our realm of death but are alive in God's realm of life.

39-40   The general unpopularity of the Sadducees may account for the pleasure of the scribes, likely of the Pharisees, when they were put to silence. But the

Lord Jesus truly had answered in a way befitting His Sonship, but totally unsuspected from a carpenter raised in Nazareth. The phrase Luke uses of the Sadducees, "they durst not ask", uses *tolmaō* ("to dare") with a negative, "they did not dare to ask" (JND). Matthew and Mark used it in the parallel passages (Matt 22:46; Mark 12:34). Luke used it in Acts 5:13, "And of the rest durst no man join himself to them", and in Stephen's address, "Moses trembled and durst not behold" when the Lord appeared "in a flame of fire in a bush" (Acts 7:32).

8. The Question About the Son of David
20:41-47

v.41 "And he said unto them, How say they that Christ is David's son?
v.42 And David himself saith in the book of Psalms, The LORD said unto my Lord, Sit thou on my right hand,
v.43 Till I make thine enemies thy footstool.
v.44 David therefore calleth him Lord, how is he then his son?
v.45 Then in the audience of all the people he said unto his disciples,
v.46 Beware of the scribes, which desire to walk in long robes, arid love greetings in the markets, and the highest seats in the synagogues, and the chief rooms at feasts;
v.47 Which devour widows' houses, and for a shew make long prayers: the same shall receive greater damnation."

41 The last section closes with the Sadducees not daring to ask Him any more questions, but now He asks a question. We are not told by Luke to whom this question was directed but a comparison with Matt 22:34-40 and Mark 12:28- shows that, after the Sadducees had been put to silence, a proud lawyer of the Pharisees asked another question about the greatest of the commandments. It was after His response to this question that the Lord "said unto them", that is, to Pharisees and scribes: "How do they say that the Christ is David's son?" (JND).

42-44 The Holy Spirit made a plain statement in 3:4 that the book of Isaiah consisted of the words written by Isaiah the prophet. The Lord Jesus says that "David himself" wrote Ps 110. Thus we have the greatest of authority for our humble belief in the authors of these portions of the OT, so the contrary opinions of liberal scholars can be safely rejected.

"Son of David" was a common title given to the long expected Messiah (1:32; 18:38,39). Can He be both David's Son and yet David's personal Lord? not just a mighty conqueror like David, but so high that even Israel's greatest king will acknowledge His Lordship? This strikes at the very heart of Israel's rejection. The Messiah is not merely another king in David's line. He is the Root as well as the Offspring of David (Rev 22:16). He is David's own Lord, the lesser always giving honour to the One who is greater.

45 After long discourses with Pharisees, scribes, Sadducees and Herodians, the Lord now turns back to that little company of faithful men who hung on His words, the disciples, but now He speaks to them in such a way that all the people could hear Him. This is another display of the gentleness, yet the faithfulness of the Lord. He did not speak to the scribes to rebuke them publicly but warned the disciples not to follow their wicked hypocrisy.

46-47   They desired to wear special, distinctive robes to set them apart from ordinary men. They liked to be noticed, to attract attention to themselves in the market, in the synagogues and at feasts. Seeing beyond the facade the Lord charges them with devouring widows' houses. Scribes were forbidden by law to take money for teaching, but many of them were supported by gifts. This was a legitimate means of their livelihood and the Lord does not condemn it, but being unscrupulous they worked defenceless widows to get from them more than they could afford to give, thus impoverishing them. This was a secret aspect of their conduct. A more public aspect was their prayer life, performed before as many witnesses as possible so as to receive the praise of men. The faithful Lord warns that for such conduct "the same shall receive greater damnation". Perhaps the comparative goes back to the Sadducees who were heterodox in their beliefs. The scribes were orthodox but their practice was wicked. A solemn warning against holding truth with which life is in disagreement.

9.   The Widow's Two Mites
       21:1-4

v.1   "And he looked up, and saw the rich men casting their gifts into the treasury.
v.2   And he saw also a certain poor widow casting in thither two mites.
v.3   And he said, Of a truth 1 say unto you, that this poor widow hath cast in more than they all:
v.4   For all these have of their abundance cast in unto the offerings of God: but she of her penury hath cast in all the living that she had."

There is a link between the widow's two mites and the abuse of wealth and privilege that has occupied a large place in this Gospel. The practices of the scribes who devour widows' houses are further rebuked by the sacrifice of this poor widow. She has been likened to the godly Hannah (1 Sam 1,2) who gave her best to God in spite of the failure of Eli and his sons. If the widow had wanted an excuse for not giving she could easily have reasoned that those who were using it were unworthy and even corrupt. She gives us a similar lesson as the one that the aged John gave to the godly Gaius, "Beloved, thou doest faithfully whatsoever thou doest" (3 John 5), and this was in spite of the intolerable behaviour of Diotrephes. The failure of others should never be used as an excuse to hold back that which rightly belongs to God. This story of the widow illustrates the truth of the Lord's words in the previous chapter, "Render therefore ... unto God the things which be God's" (20:25).

1   Mark records that the Lord sat in the temple area watching the people casting money into the temple treasury (Mark 12:41). Luke tells us that it was "the rich" who cast in money out of "their abundance". Edersheim speaks of "boxes with trumpet-shaped mouths that were placed in the Court of the Women", adding that each box had a label which intimated the use for which the offerings would be used.

2   It was one pauper widow whom He observed as she came alone, separate from the crowd, very likely dressed in garments that marked her as a mourner and desolate, casting in her "two mites". This was the smallest offering that it was legal to give, but it represented much more than the least amount to her. The word "poor" (*penichros*) is used only here in the NT but it is frequent in the papyri and is found in the LXX in Exod 22:25; Prov 28:15 and 29:7, "The righteous considereth the cause of the poor", but in contrast, the scribes who profess to be righteous "devour widows' houses" (20:47).

3   The Lord said, "Of a truth I say unto you", indicating that only He saw the amount and knew that she had given her all. The two mites were so small that they would be unnoticed by other watchers, and none but the Lord knew her heart and her true poverty. Luke uses a different word for "poor" from that in the previous verse. "Poor" (*ptōchos*) has the meaning given to it here but is used as a noun in 4:18; 7:22; 14:13,21. it is also the word translated "beggar" of Lazarus (16:20,22). it comes from *ptōsso* "to cower down or hide oneself for fear" (W.E. Vine). It occurs again as an adjective in Gal 4:9 "beggarly". James used it to give us an excellent commentary that likely applies to this "poor widow", " Hath not God chosen the poor of this world, rich in faith, and heirs of the kingdom which he hath promised to them that love him?" (James 2:5).

4   It was "all the living that she had", that is, all that she possessed, with nothing left for herself. A true view of eternity always calls for total commitment. The widow was not looking at the great structures of the temple with all the grandeur that Herod had added to them, or she would have concluded that her two Jewish copper coins, with a total value of about two-tenths of a British penny, could have no meaning in the presence of such splendour. She did not give to the temple but to God who could value rightly her sacrifice, and He who came from God saw it and knew the cost to her. Paul wrote about the assemblies of Macedonia, "the abundance of... their deep poverty abounded unto the riches of their liberality" (2 Cor 8:2). In the same context Paul wrote, "For ye know the grace of our Lord Jesus Christ, that, though he was rich, yet for your sakes he became poor" (v.9). He was the merchant man who sold all that he had to purchase one pearl of great price (Matt 13:45,46). Again, Paul's comment suits the widow's case exactly, "if there be first a willing mind, it is accepted according to that a man hath, and not according to that he hath not" (v.12). Our giving is rightly valued by God, and He "is not unrighteous to forget" (Heb 6:10).

10. *When Shall These Things Be?*
   ## 21:5-36

v.5   "And as some spake of the temple, how it was adorned with goodly stones and gifts, he said,

v.6   As *for* these things which ye behold, the days will come, in the which there shall not be left one stone upon another, that shall not be thrown down.

v.7   And they asked him, saying, Master, but when shall these things be? and what sign *will there be* when these things shall come to pass?

v.8   And he said, Take heed that ye be not deceived: for many shall come in my name, saying, I am *Christ*; and the time draweth near: go ye not therefore after them.

v.9   But when ye shall hear of wars and commotions, be not terrified: for these things must first come to pass; but the end *is* not by and by.

v.10 Then said he unto them, Nation shall rise against nation, and kingdom against kingdom:

v.11 And great earthquakes shall be in divers places, and famines, and pestilences; and fearful sights and great signs shall there be from heaven.

v.12 But before all these, they shall lay their hands on you, and persecute *you*, delivering *you* up to the synagogues, and into prisons, being brought before kings and rulers for my name's sake.

v.13 And it shall turn to you for a testimony.

v.14 Settle *it* therefore in your hearts, not to meditate before what ye shall answer:

v.15 For I will give you a mouth and wisdom, which all your adversaries shall not be able to gainsay nor resist.

v.16 And ye shall be betrayed both by parents, and brethren, and kinsfolks, and friends; and *some* of you shall they cause to be put to death.

v.17 And ye shall be hated of all *men* for my name's sake.

v.18 But there shall not an hair of your head perish.

v.19 In your patience possess ye your souls.

v.20 And when ye shall see Jerusalem compassed with armies, then know that the desolation thereof is nigh.

v.21 Then let them which are in Judaea flee to the mountains; and let them which are in the midst of it depart out; and let not them that are in the countries enter thereinto.

v.22 For these be the days of vengeance, that all things which are written may be fulfilled.

v.23 But woe unto them that are with child, and to them that give suck, in those days! for there shall be great distress in the land, and wrath upon this people.

v.24 And they shall fall by the edge of the sword, and shall be led away captive into all nations: and Jerusalem shall be trodden down of the Gentiles, until the times of the Gentiles be fulfilled.

v.25 And there shall be signs in the sun, and in the moon, and in the stars; and upon the earth distress of nations, with perplexity; the sea and the waves roaring;

v.26 Men's hearts failing them for fear, and for looking after those things which are coming on the earth: for the powers of heaven shall be shaken.

v.27 And then shall they see the Son of man coming in a cloud with power and great glory.

v.28 And when these things begin to come to pass, then look up, and lift up your heads; for your redemption draweth nigh.

v.29 And he spake to them a parable; Behold the fig tree, and all the trees;

v.30 When they now shoot forth, ye see and know of your own selves that summer is now nigh at hand.

v.31 So likewise ye, when ye see these things come to pass, know ye that the kingdom of God is nigh at hand.

v.32 Verily I say unto you, This generation shall not pass away, till all be fulfilled.

v.33 Heaven and earth shall pass away: but my words shall not pass away.
v.34 And take heed to yourselves, lest at any time your hearts be overcharged with surfeiting, and drunkenness, and cares of this life, and so that day come upon you unawares.
v.35 For as a snare shall it come on all them that dwell on the face of the whole earth.
v.36 Watch ye therefore, and pray always, that ye may be accounted worthy to escape all these things that shall come to pass, and to stand before the Son of man."

5 Both Matthew (24:1) and Mark (13:1) tell us that it was the disciples who drew the Lord's attention to the magnificent temple structure. Josephus has given a full description of this great reconstructed temple, designed by a master-builder, Herod, and not yet completed. It stood on a massive base of masonry in which some of the stones were enormous, and had marble columns standing more than forty feet high. It was adorned with many costly gifts from princes and wealthy private individuals. Josephus tells of one such gift from Herod the Great, a golden vine with bunches of grapes as high as a man's head. Herod had boasted that the temple was built for permanence and would outlast the pyramids, but he could not have been more wrong. The word used for "gifts" (*anathēma*) is literally "consecrated offerings" (JND) and is found only here in the NT. It is of interest to see that the word for "curse" (*anathema*) which has only one vowel different, means "a thing devoted to God" whether it is for His service or its destruction. In 1 Cor 16:22, the Greek word is transliterated "anathema" and means devoted to judgment. "Accursed" (anathema) in Gal 1:8,9 is used in condemnation of those who "preach any other gospel".

6 The Lord's prediction of the destruction of the temple fell on shocked ears. They believed that Jesus was the Messiah, and that His kingdom would have Jerusalem as its centre and the temple as the place to which all nations would come. The prediction of 19:43,44 had not penetrated their conscious thought. The Lord's prophecy of the destruction of the temple was fulfilled with great violence in AD 70 under Titus and the Roman legions.

7 There is some indication in Matthew and Mark that the puzzled disciples had discussed among themselves the meaning of the Lord's prediction that the temple would be destroyed. As they left the temple and walked with the Lord through the Valley of Kidron and up the slopes of the Mount of Olives, they asked the double question, "when shall these things be?" and "what sign will there be ... ?". Mark tells us that it was Peter, James, John and Andrew who asked these questions. It is necessary to understand that it was the Lord's statement about the destruction of the temple in Jerusalem that triggered the two questions, so there is an association between these predictions and the destruction of the temple and city in AD 70. The two aspects of near and far prophecy are very frequently found in the OT, and the Lord follows this same method, but as has been stated in the following comments, much that the Lord foretold is not exhausted by the "near" fulfilment. In His knowledge of all coming events, He was able to view simultaneously the destruction of Jerusalem in AD 70 and its future destruction and use the events that were near at hand as prefiguring the future events at the "end time".

Jewish teaching centred around two distinct ages: the present age when Israel waited for Messiah to be revealed, an age that would end in judgment; a future age when Messiah would come and set up the kingdom, preceded by judgments that included the siege of Jerusalem and the city falling to the invader (Zech 14:1 -3). It is vital to see that, in the mind of the disciples, these events would be followed immediately by Messiah's rule. Matthew informs us that the questions were, "when shall these things be? and what shall be the sign of thy coming, and of the end of the world (age)?". These questions are the key to understanding the Lord's answer. He was not describing the future of His church, but the future of Israel, Jerusalem and the land. The events that follow are not to be seen as in the church age, but are related to "the time of the end" (Dan 12:4,9), and the time of "Jacob's trouble" (Jer 30:7) so fully described by Israel's prophets.

8-11   Many commentators see the predictions of vv.8-19 as being completely fulfilled in this present age. It is true that persecution against believers, wars among nations, and, in the natural realm, earthquakes, famines and pestilences have marked the course of this age, but this is not the context of the questions nor of their answers. The Lord is not speaking of natural catastrophes but of supernatural events that usher in the day of the Lord, the coming of which is accompanied by "fearful sights and great signs ... from heaven" (v.11). In our day heaven is silent and sin goes on unhindered; in the natural course of events, "whatsoever a man soweth, that shall he also reap" (Gal 6:7), yet God is not intervening in human affairs. A comparison of Luke, Mark and Matthew will show that in the end time such disasters are to be much increased over what has occurred in the course of history, and these coming events cast their shadows upon our day.

The disciples are told that when they see these "signs" of false Christs, wars and tumults, "the end is not by and by"; that is, the coming of the Son of man is not immediately to follow, for other events will happen before He comes. Believers today wait for the rapture which is not preceded by signs and can take place at any moment without any preceding event (1 Thess 4:13-18).

12   It is helpful to see that in the synoptic Gospels the Lord addressed the disciples as a remnant that prefigured the believing remnant of Israel in the great tribulation (Matt 24:4-26; Mark 13:5-23; Luke 21:28-36). In John He addressed them as a remnant that prefigured the remnant church testimony throughout this present time (John 13:31-16:33). We know this because of the content of the teaching and the contrast between the synoptists and John. At this point in His teaching He described the suffering "for my name's sake" (vv. 12,17) that would befall the remnant during tribulation days. There would be violent arrests, bitter persecution and hatred against them by their fellow Jews, and they would be delivered up to the authorities, including kings and rulers of the land.

13 The day would be dark and evil, yet out of the bitterest persecution God would bring light. The faithfulness of the suffering saints would be a testimony to God's glory and to the condemnation of their persecutors. Describing the effect of the patience of suffering believers on their persecutors Paul wrote, "which is to them a demonstration of destruction" (Phil 1:28 JND). Even though we have interpreted the complete fulfilment of these predictions in the days of the future remnant of tribulation days, we must not miss the immediate application to the disciples who as a remnant for God in days of bitter persecution, as outlined in the book of Acts, needed to be prepared. The Lord had said to them, "be not terrified" (v.9, *ptoeō*) which is found only here and in 24:37.

14-15 When they were delivered up to their foes they were not to rehearse words that they would use in their own defence, for the Lord would take over the very operation of their speech, enabling them to answer with such wisdom that their "opposers shall not be able to reply to or resist" (JND).

"To meditate" (*promeletaō*) is found only here and means " to meditate before hand". Mark uses *meletaō* ("premeditate") in the corresponding passage (13:11) with the same meaning as Luke. *Meletaō* is found in only two other places in the NT. "Meditate upon these things" (1 Tim 4:15) is translated "Occupy thyself with these things" (JND) or "Be diligent in these things" (RV) or perhaps even closer to its meaning, "Make these things thy care" (Alford) because *meletaō* "primarily means, to care for" (W.E. Vine). Its other occurrence is Acts 4:25, "imagine" in the sense of "meditated vain things" (JND). It is very difficult to understand how anyone can suppose that this applies to preparation for teaching or preaching. Such preparation requires "diligence" and much "meditation".

"To gainsay" (*anteipon*) is the aorist of *antilegō* ("to contradict"), Luke uses this latter word in 2:34, "a sign which shall be spoken against", and in 20:27 of the denial of the resurrection by the Sadducees. Paul used it to describe the rejection by Israel of the word of God, "a disobedient and gainsaying people" (Rom 10:21), "a people disobeying and opposing" (JND). The early believers and the saints of the "end time" would face many adversaries and bitter opposition, but the antidote is "I will give you a mouth and wisdom", words that have been proven to be true by persecuted saints from that day until now.

16 Even the nearest of their earthly relations would turn against them (Matt 10:36), betraying them to the emissaries of the kingdom of the beast; some of them would be put to death, for "it was given unto him to make war with the saints, and to overcome them" (Rev 13:7). As can be seen in many of these statements, they have application to days of persecution whenever they occur. The very men to whom the Lord spoke would experience rejection with their rejected Lord and to them He said, "Ye shall drink indeed of my cup, and be baptized with the baptism that I am baptized with" (Matt 20:33). The verb thanatoo ("to put to death") which is only here in Luke is used of the putting to death of Christ in Matt 26:59; 27:1.

17   These witnesses in tribulation days will face the hatred of an evil age that will be opposed to God and all that is holy. It is most touching that the Lord Jesus should be describing such hatred against His own when He who was "hated ... without a cause" was only a few final steps from the cross with all its hatred and shame heaped upon His blessed Person. He taught His own, "If the world hate you, ye know that it hated me before it hated you" (John 15:18). The world that hated Him was the world of religion, of human pride and self-righteousness. There is a serious danger of supposing that the world that is supremely opposed to God is the world of immorality, drunkenness, violence and crime. All know that this aspect of the world is evil, but it was not this "Sodom world", but the religious world that stood opposed to Christ.

18   The Lord is describing a remnant in a coming day who will be sealed in their foreheads as a mark of their preservation in the midst of hatred and cruelty (Rev 7:3). These sealed ones are spared through the time of terrible trouble, and at the close of it they stand with the Lamb on mount Zion (Rev 14:1). Although a great multitude of saints redeemed out of the nations will be delivered up to death (Rev 7:9-17), yet these who are numbered as the 144 000 will be miraculously spared during the entire period of persecution and will "endure unto the end" (Matt 24:13).

We have given the future interpretation first to show that no contradiction exists between the two statements "and some of you they will cause to be put to death' , and " there shall not an hair of your head perish", but again, there was an immediate meaning to the Lord's words. Not even the hairs of our heads are excluded from the tender care of God for "the very hairs of your head are numbered" (Matt 10:30), so whatever believers suffer for Christ's sake, nothing can be out of the control of our Father.

19   This difficult verse has received some very unsatisfactory treatment. It does not teach that the salvation of the soul depends on faithfulness in the face of persecution. We have just seen how the endurance of the remnant in trial affects their enemies. This verse tells us how this steadfastness will affect themselves. The Lord will come as their Deliverer. It is this assurance that enables them to endure and manifest the reality of their salvation. They are assured that even if they are called to die they will "possess", that is "gain", their own souls in a glorious resurrection life. The Lord had already taught them not to fear those who could kill only the body (12:4).

20   "Jerusalem compassed with armies" is one of the great events of prophecy which allows us to link the teachings of Daniel, Zechariah and Revelation with the chronology of the Lord's teaching in the Synoptic Gospels. The siege of Jerusalem under Titus in AD 70 is the "near fulfilment", but what happened then was a portent of another great siege of the city in the time of the end, just preceding the coming of the Son of man (Zech 14:1-3). Those who limit the teaching of the Lord to the event of AD 70, must, when they reach vv.25-27, move on to the coming of the Son of man. Some have used Luke's account of the Lord's teaching to interpret Matt 24, but there is nothing in Matthew that can rightly be given a "near" interpretation. Luke does combine the " near" and the "far", but much of this material is yet future. The events of verses 8 to 19 are what Matthew has called, "the beginning of sorrows" (24:8).

The breaking of the covenant made by the Roman prince with Israel at the beginning of the seventieth week (Dan 9:27) takes place in the middle of the week and marks the beginning of the "great tribulation". When the protection of the beast is withdrawn the armies of Israel's foes are free to move against Israel and Jerusalem. It is at this time that "he (the beast) shall cause the sacrifice and the oblation to cease". Daniel says that from this event there will be 1290 days (Dan 12:11) remaining until the end of the period, approximately three and one half years. Also, "the abomination of desolation" (Matt 24:15) is set up in the temple at this time, an event not recorded by Luke but found in Dan 11:31 and pointed out by Matthew as the answer to the question, "when shall these things be?". So there are two events, the breaking of the covenant, and the placing of "the abomination of desolation" in the temple, that are crucial to the understanding of the chronology of these times. These are the events that will result in the final siege of Jerusalem.

21   The saints are to flee from the city before it is completely surrounded. The expression "compassed with armies" means that they were closing in around the city but as yet had not made the encirclement complete. All in Judaea were to flee to the surrounding mountains, while those in the city were to depart out of the midst of it; people in the country were not to attempt to enter the walled city for protection. When Luke described the surrounding series, he used *stratopedon* (v.20, "armies"). This is its only occurrence in the NT. Vine says "it denotes an army encamped" and literally means "encampments". For the people of the city under siege, the directives are very plain, "let them ... depart out", "let not them ... enter thereinto". These imperatives help to emphasise the crisis.

22   "Days of vengeance" have application to the AD 70 destruction of Jerusalem, but we would have a serious problem in limiting this expression to the historical event. "The days of vengeance" is an OT expression used frequently to describe the coming time of "Jacob's trouble" (Isa 34:8; 35:4; 61:2; 63:4; Dan 12:1; Hosea 9:5-7; Micah 5:15; Zech 12:1-3), and the vengeance that God will bring upon Israel's enemies. Then there is the Lord's sweeping statement, "all the things that are written may be accomplished" (JND). All that is written will not be accomplished until David's greater Son, who is truly David's Lord (20:41-44) will sit upon His own throne of glory (Matt 25:31), righting every wrong and establishing a kingdom of righteousness and peace that cannot be shaken (Heb 12:28).

23   The distress of the remnant in the time of trouble will not be limited to the evangelists who carry the message of salvation to the nations (Matt 24:14), but will affect every home and life, including mothers and their infants. Matthew adds that "except those days should be shortened, there should no flesh be saved" (24:22). The Jews have seen many dark days, such as their fearful experiences at the hands of Hitler and his henchmen. Can anything be worse than what they have already experienced? Yes, for it was in one land and several surrounding lands that the Jew was so treated, while in other lands he was safe; but the time that is coming will involve every Jewish home and family throughout the world, and "shall be a time of trouble, such as never was since there was a nation even to that same time" (Dan 12:1).

24   Terrible atrocities and sufferings accompanied the Roman siege of Jerusalem. Many commentators have pointed out that those who obeyed the commands of Christ to flee and not return again to the city (v.21) saved their lives. We should remember that a large number of believers lived in Jerusalem when the siege began. In his Jewish Wars, which is not totally reliable, Josephus claimed that over a million Jews were slain in the fall of the city. So many captives were taken to be sold as slaves that the market was glutted and they were literally "led away captive into all nations" as the Lord predicted.

In the future siege, Zechariah tells us "The city shall be taken, and the houses rifled, and the women ravished; and half of the city shall go forth into captivity" (14:2), language that exactly fits the Lord's teaching. Zechariah tells us that it will happen when the "day of the Lord" comes (14:1).

The expression "shall be trodden down" refers to a continuing condition. It has the force: "will be, being trodden down by nations". Certainly this has been the long history of Jerusalem after the days when Gentile dominion over the land began under Nebuchadnezzar even though in the present time Israel has greater control over it than for many centuries. However, some of the darkest days Jerusalem has ever known still lie ahead. The armies that surround it will take the city and slay many of its inhabitants. Gentile dominion over Jerusalem will continue "until the times of the Gentiles be fulfilled". We know this terminus, for Gentile dominion over Jerusalem will cease when the "mighty ... Man of war",

He who "doth judge and make war", comes from heaven to destroy the beast and his armies and deliver Jerusalem and Israel (Zech 14:3; Rev 19:11-21). This is "the Stone ... cut out without hands, which smote the image upon his feet that were of iron and clay, and brake them to pieces" (Dan 2:34). The great empire, destroyed by the Lord at His coming, will be the final expression of "the times of the Gentiles".

25-26   The signs in the sun, moon and stars will be evident to all the nations. They are not minor disturbances of the course of nature, but major cataclysms involving the darkening of the sun and the failure of the moon to give light, with stars falling (Matt 24:29). On the earth, corresponding physical disturbances cause great upheavals on land and sea so that distressed nations are perplexed, and men's hearts fail for fear; judgment follows judgment, increasing in intensity, until the very powers of the heavens are shaken. These are the events described in great detail in Rev 8 to 16 when the trumpets of judgment sound and the bowls full of the wrath of God are poured out. So fearful will be the judgments that "in those days shall men seek death, and shall not find it; and shall desire to die, and death shall flee from them" (Rev 9:6).

These verses contain five words that are unique to Luke's writings in the NT. "With perplexity" (v.25, *aporia*) is derived from *poros* ("a way") and literally means "without a way", "in the sense of being at one's wit's end" (W.E. Vine), "not knowing which way to turn" (NEB). *Salos* (v.25, "waves") means "to toss", particularly the swelling and tossing of the waves or "billows" (RV) of the sea. The "roaring" (v.25, *ēchos*) of these tossing billows adds to the chaos leaving people completely confused without escape and nowhere to turn. *Apopsuchō* (v.26, "hearts failing") means "to breathe out life" (W.E. Vine). Darby renders this verse, "Men ready to die through fear and expectation of what is coming on the habitable earth, for the powers of the heavens shall be shaken". *Prosdokia* (v. 26, "looking after") is a noun with a corresponding verb, *prosdokaō* which is used in 2 Pet 3:12,13,14 where it means " to await" (JND) or "to expect" (RV). However, the noun in Luke is used to describe an apprehensive dread at the things that are coming.

27   It is when the chaos has reached its climax that into this scene will descend the Son of man. It will not be a secret coming but will be as the sudden lightning that streaks across the heavens (17:24). He will not come in lowliness to be rejected and despised but "with power and great glory". This is the event that was foretold in hundreds of OT prophecies. It is to this event that every believing son of Abraham has looked through the centuries. This is the coming of the Son of man, the last Adam, the second Man, the Victor of Calvary and the Conqueror of death and hell. His feet will stand upon the Mount of Olives (Zech 14:4) whence He had once ascended from amidst the little band of wondering disciples. He will come to destroy the beast and his armies, to put an end to Gentile rule and dominion over Israel and Jerusalem, to deliver the oppressed and set the captives free. He will come at the crucial hour for the deliverance of His earthly people, and with Him will be "the armies in heaven" following Him. "Out of his mouth goeth a sharp sword, that with it he should smite the nations: and he shall rule them with a rod of iron: and he treadeth the winepress of the fierceness and wrath of Almighty God. And he hath on his vesture and on his thigh a name written, KING OF KINGS, AND LORD OF LORDS" (Rev 19:15,16).

28   With these stirring events to move their hearts it is no wonder that He said to the little band from Galilee, "look up, and lift up your heads; for your redemption draweth nigh". Yet His own beloved head would soon be laid on His breast in death, for He was going to Calvary to lay down His life as a ransom to purchase their redemption.

The "look up" (*anakuptō*) and "lift up" (*epairō*) are both imperatives. E.V. Rieu has translated, "straighten your backs and look up". Moulton and Milligan give an illustration from the papyri in which is found the sentence, "it is not possible ever to show face (*anakuptō*) again in Tricomia for very shame" (page 35, Vocab). In spite of the shame of the cross and being hated and persecuted, the disciples were "to stand erect and lift up the heads" (A. Marshall). *Apolutrō sis* ("redemption") has here its only occurrence in the Gospels. It is the strengthened form of the word *lutrōsis* and looks back to the ransom paid at the cross and forward to the complete deliverance at the coming of the Lord. "Not accepting deliverance" (Heb 11:35) uses redemption (*apolutrōsis*) as deliverance from physical torture and this aspect of it may be included in v.28.

29-31   Closely related to the Lord's teaching of coming events is this section in which He warns His own to watch and be prepared. The illustration from nature was simple and familiar. After the bare and barren state of the fig tree throughout winter, the first green shoots of spring tell that the summer is at hand. "These things" (v.31) refer to the signs of vv.9-28. Even the beginning of these events is to be a signal to the remnant (v.28). The kingdom of God that is "nigh at hand" is the manifest kingdom that will be brought in by the coming of the Son of man.

These verses are said to be a parable. As we have suggested, "the fig tree" represents the nation of Israel, "and all the trees" likely refers to conditions among other nations. The suddenness of the appearance of the manifest kingdom is graphically expressed by Luke's use of the expression "they now shoot forth" (*proballō*). The only other occurrence of this word in the NT is in Acts 19:33, "putting him forward". Vine give its meaning as "to throw before" and links it to trees suddenly putting forth leaves, "they already sprout" (JND). Before the leaves burst forth, much activity has been going on unseen in the trees and this is the picture here. Events have been leading up to the manifestation of the kingdom, but at the predetermined time in the counsels of God (Acts 1:7) it will burst forth.

32 "This generation shall not pass away" is difficult and has been interpreted in different ways. Those who limit the entire teaching to the historical destruction of Jerusalem (AD 70) insist that it means that the generation then living would be alive when the city was destroyed. The problem this creates is that the Lord said "all" would be fulfilled. It is not possible to suppose that vv.25-27 were fulfilled then. Even if we could accept this meaning, the difficulty of Matt 24:34 and Mark 13:30 would remain.

Thirty or forty years is considered to be a generation. It is not always agreed if this means all the people living at one time or all the people who are born within the time span. Are the children of parents in their early twenties of the same generation as their parents or are they two separate generations? The duration of the wilderness experience of Israel is called a generation, and this is the approximate time from the cross to the destruction of Jerusalem. However, "generation" (*genea*) is also used to mean those who are successively born into a particular family (Matt 1:17), a particular nation or people (Matt 11:16), or a group of people who have similar attitudes or characteristics (Matt 17:17; Mark 9:19). This is how it is used in Phil 2:15 "a crooked and perverse nation", and perhaps is the meaning of our verse. There is a likeness between the generation by whom the Lord Jesus was rejected and the future generation who will remain in unbelief.

There is another explanation which many accept. "This generation" refers to the generation that lives while the signs are being observed. The events described in the Lord's teaching will all take place during the life of one generation. We know this time as the great tribulation or the seventieth week in Dan 9:24-27. One generation will see the beginnings of sorrows and will be here when the Son of man descends in glory and power.

33 No sane man can read these words of Christ without facing tremendous issues. Many speak of Christ as being "a good man", a "great teacher with the highest ethical system ever presented", but at the same time they say that He is "not God", not "deity in a Man". If v.33 is not true then any man who makes this statement is neither good nor holy; he is one of the world's greatest madmen. But our Lord is all that He claimed to be. Looking out on a universe of blazing suns and swirling galaxies He said that they would all pass away, but in contrast to dying suns and exploding star systems His words will stand for ever. How can puny man resist such claims? We, like Thomas, fall at His blessed feet and cry, "My Lord and my God".

34 The solemn warning in this verse is to guard against a heart that gets burdened with cares and overcome by pleasures of this world, for this departure in heart will soon become evident in behaviour. The AV, RV and JND use "surfeiting" as the translation of *kraipalē*. Vine agrees with A. Plummer that it refers to the drunken nausea that follows a debauch of drinking. *Methe* means strong drink and was used for habitual intoxication (W.E. Vine). The word "cares" is the translation of *merimna* and means to be pulled in two directions at one time. Any of these three things would render a believer unfit to be ready for the return of the Lord.

35   Unprepared sinners will be ensnared unexpectedly in the terrible judgments that have just been described. From the previous verse it is learned that even one who professes to be ready can be overburdened with other things. In the case of unbelievers they are totally unprepared; in fact the word translated "dwell" means "to sit at ease", as people sat in the palace of Belshazzar on the night of unexpected judgment. It is at this point that Matthew gives the solemn warning; "Therefore be ye also ready: for in such an hour as ye think not the Son of man cometh" (24:44; cf. Luke 12:40).

36   Slothfulness or even carelessness is not the characteristic of a genuine believer, yet the warning of this verse covers the professed believer of v.34 and the unbeliever of v.35. An attitude of watchfulness and prayer is evidence of being ready. To be "accounted worthy" does not infer self-worth, because this is a divine accounting; God counts believers worthy of their calling (2 Thess 1:11). Nor does it mean to make worthy but to *account* worthy. An identical expression is used in 20:35 where believers are "accounted worthy to obtain that world" referring to heaven, yet none can make themselves worthy of heaven; it is a divine estimation of true believers and has nothing to do with self- effort or working for salvation. Those who "stand before the Son of man" will be searched to the very depth of their beings. This is a clarion call for reality in all who profess to be waiting for His coming.

11.   A Summary of Days Spent in Jerusalem
21:37-38

> v.37 "And in the daytime he was teaching in the temple; and at night he went out, and abode in the mount that is called *the mount* of Olives.
> v.38 And all the people came early in the morning to him in the temple, for to hear him."

37   These days were so very full that we must be reminded of the dark shadow of the cross that stretched across the path of the Saviour. During these days of the final week, He taught in the temple each day where the people gathered. He did not stay in the city overnight, but went out to the Mount of Olives. Plummer suggests that He "camped out" or made "a bivouac" on the mountain side, "and by night, going out, he remained abroad on the mountain called the mount of Olives" (JND). There were villages on the slopes of Olivet, and one of them was

Bethany, the home of Martha, Mary and Lazarus, and it may be that He spent some of these nights, His last nights before the cross, in the company of His beloved friends, but we have no statement that confirms it. The fact that He came into the city hungry (Matt 21:17-18), even when we are told He was at Bethany, scarcely fits with the love and care He would have known in the home.

38 In the mornings the people rose early and gathered to hear Him. Edersheim suggests that the hills around Jerusalem would be covered with tents, and every available corner of the city occupied by the vast number of Jews who, from every part of the land of Israel and from many far-flung places in the Roman empire, had come to Jerusalem for the Passover. The crowds were very large and the interest of the people in His teaching was still very great.

12. *Judas Conspires with the High Priests*
22:1-6

> v.1 "Now the feast of unleavened bread drew nigh, which is called the Passover.
> v.2 And the chief priests and scribes sought how they might kill him; for they feared the people.
> v.3 Then entered Satan into Judas surnamed Iscariot, being of the number of the twelve.
> v.4 And he went his way, and communed with the chief priests and captains, how he might betray him unto them.
> v.5 And they were glad, and covenanted to give him money.
> v.6 And he promised, and sought opportunity to betray him unto them in the absence of the multitude."

1 Two of the seven feasts of Lev 23 are linked so closely in this verse that they are described as being one event. This is not difficult to understand when we consider that the Feast of Unleavened Bread typifies the moral condition demanded of those who would observe the Passover. They are spiritually linked in 1 Cor 5:7: "Christ our passover is sacrificed for us", which is followed by the exhortation, "Therefore let us keep the feast, not with old leaven, neither with the leaven of malice and wickedness; but with the unleavened bread of sincerity and truth" (v.8). This keeping of the feast is not a reference to the Lord's supper, but is an exhortation to those who have been cleansed by the blood of the Lamb to fulfil in their lives the separation from sin that the Feast of Unleavened Bread typifies.

In Israel's feasts, leaven was not allowed in their houses at Passover (Exod 12:8,15), so v.7 says, "Then came the day of unleavened bread when the passover must be killed", and Matt 26:17 agrees with this, "Now the first day of the feast of unleavened bread the disciples came to Jesus, saying unto him, Where wilt thou that we prepare to eat the passover?" According to Lev 23:5, the Passover was observed on the fourteenth of Nisan (formerly called Abib) and in preparation for it, leaven was removed from their houses. The lamb was slain "between the two evenings" (Exod 12:6, RV margin, Lev 23:5; Num 9:3,5,11), "between 3 p.m. and sunset" (Edersheim). The Feast of Unleavened Bread began on the fifteenth day (Lev 23:6), but because no leaven was allowed at the Passover Feast, the Jews linked together the two feasts. The second feast that continued for seven days typified a continual separation from sin.

2 Throughout the Gospel records, opposition to the Lord Jesus came chiefly from the Pharisees and their scribes, but as the intention to kill Him became their main purpose, the chief priests, who held the political power and were motivated by envy (Mark 15:10), took charge. However, their power was limited by the people on one hand, whom they feared, and the Roman authority on the other, which made it unlawful for them "to put any man to death" (John 18:31); only the Roman governor had this power (20:20; John 19:10). The many pilgrims who were present in Jerusalem for the Passover were still ready to listen to the Lord, and the crafty priests were not willing to risk an uprising of the people.

3 Luke and John record that Satan entered into Judas (John 13:27). The vague suggestion that Judas was overcome by an evil influence does not satisfy these statements. Satan did not leave such an important task to any of his emissaries. In a coming day, Satan will so energise the beast that he will speak Satan's words and do his deeds (Rev 13:1-7). It is significant that only two men in all of history are called "the son of perdition", Judas in John 17:12, and "that man of sin" in 2 Thess 2:3. Luke's comment that Judas was "of the number of the twelve" is a tremendous contrast to "Then entered Satan into Judas". Although Satan and his demons were able to identify Christ, it does not naturally follow that they understood the Scriptures relating to His suffering and death. Satan's hostility moved him to attempt to destroy anyone in whom God had pleasure, and in His beloved Son the Father had His greatest delight.

4-6 Judas knew to whom he could go with his offer of betrayal for money. It is not necessary to find in Judas a deeper motive than the money, but Satan, who used him as an instrument, had deeper motives. The chief priests and captains of the temple were glad of the defector from within the close ranks of the twelve. Only Matthew tells us that the agreed price was thirty pieces of silver (26:15). Peter tells us that Judas was "guide to them that took Jesus" (Acts 1:16). The question arises why they needed a guide. After the days that He taught in the temple, was He not easy to identify? The answer is that Judas knew how to find Christ when the multitude, who might have started a tumult at His arrest, were absent. "In the absence" (*ater*) is used by Luke in v.35, "without" purse, but is found nowhere else in the NT. The RV margin reads, "without tumult".

The Synoptic Gospels, when listing the twelve, place Judas Iscariot last; only Luke adds, "which also was the traitor" (6:16), which was Luke's only previous mention of his name. He may have been the only non-Galilean among the disciples. When the Lord called him, He knew that Judas would betray Him. Many have a problem regarding the Lord's choice. As finite creatures, we find it very difficult to understand infinite foreknowledge in relation to choices made about events in time. Any attempt, in our present state to being together divine prerogatives and temporal choice is doomed to failure. We may never be in a condition when we will fully understand this relationship, even in a glorified state. We can be confident that God will reveal to us all that we are able to understand, but we will never have the infinite wisdom and knowledge that belong only to God. A little humility of mind in the present will keep us from stumbling over truth that transcends our thought.

13.   *The Large Upper Room*
22:7-13

> v.7 "Then came the day of unleavened bread, when the passover must be killed.
> v.8 And he sent Peter and John, saying, go and prepare us the passover, that we may eat.
> v.9 And they said unto him, Where wilt thou that we prepare?
> v.10 And he said unto them, Behold, when ye are entered into the city, there shall a man meet you, bearing a pitcher of water; follow him into the house where he entereth in.
> v.11 And ye shall say unto the goodman of the house, The Master saith unto thee, Where is the guestchamber, where I shall eat the passover with my disciples?
> v.12 And he shall shew you a large upper room furnished: there make ready.
> v.13 And they went, and found as he had said unto them: and they made ready the passover."

It is at this point in the narrative that John gives us the upper room ministry of the Lord (John 13-14). Luke gives a much shorter account, yet his record has more details than either Matthew's or Mark's.

7   The "day of unleavened bread" probably refers to the first day of the feast when all leaven was removed from the houses. It was on this first day that the passover was killed. The difference between John's record of these days and the other Gospels may be that he used a different calendar; there is evidence for this suggestion. Variant views of these final days of our Lord's sojourn on earth can easily be found. The order followed in this commentary is known as "a traditional view" but has not been accepted on any traditional ground, but rather because it seems best to suit the Gospel records. If there were no difficulties, there would not be so many different views, so dogmatism is to be avoided. In understanding v.7, please note the comments at v.1.

8-9   Only Luke names the two who were sent to make the necessary arrangements for the Lord and His disciples to eat the Passover. It was not only unfamiliarity with the city on the part of the Galilean disciples that made them ask where to make ready. Jerusalem was crowded with people who had come to the Feast, and even a corner to themselves would have been difficult to find.

Some of the disciples are most familiar to us; others are scarcely mentioned. The disciples are usually listed in three groups of four. The first tetrad were Peter, James, John and Andrew, two sets of brothers. The first three were often chosen by the Lord from among the twelve to be nearer to Him at times of special revelation, as on the mount (9:27-36), or at times of deep grief, as in the garden (Matt 26:36-46). In this case, it was Peter and John who were sent to prepare the Passover. This experience strengthened their faith to prepare them for the critical days that lay just before them.

10   The man bearing the pitcher of water did not need to be found. He found the two disciples by coming to meet them. Then he led them to the house. This unnamed man is a beautiful picture of the gathering ministry of the Holy Spirit who will ever refresh the spirits of saints, such refreshment being seen in the water, and lead them to the place where they can meet with their Lord, like the upper room. We need not speculate about previous arrangements made between the Lord and this man. It is more important to see that he knew the need and had a place reserved for the Lord. Comparisons can be made between this unnamed man and the unnamed servant of 14:17 who brought guests to the supper. These are pictures of two of the activities of the Holy Spirit in the present dispensation.

11   The "goodman of the house" expected the disciples and had the guestchamber prepared. Mark tells us that the Lord called it "my guestchamber" (JND, RV) for it had features that will ever characterise a gathering around the Lord Jesus. The word for guestchamber (*kataluma*) is used frequently for a place where there is rest on a journey, such as an inn or a place of lodging. This is the sense in which it is used in 2:7 (Kittel, Vol.4, p.338). But the *kataluma* in this verse was a room in a private residence, as Vine has pointed out in his excellent treatment of this word (W.E. Vine, p.184). *Pandocheion* (10:34) is the word normally used for a public inn providing overnight shelter, food and a place to care for animals at a recognised charge.

12-13   The large room suggests to us that in it there was room for the Lord Himself and His own. In an assembly there is room for Him, His Spirit and His word, and all His people who are willing to submit to its authority and be lead by the Holy Spirit. There is room for the NT priesthood to function in all its liberty, and room for the gifts in all their variety. The word used for "upper room" (*anagaion*), usually signified a room "over a porch or connected with a roof, where meals were taken and privacy obtained" (W.E. Vine, p.304). It was a place raised above the world and its ways that are so contrary to God's ways. The world and the flesh are not to invade this private "upper room". Like Eden, it is elevated above the natural plain with blessing flowing out from it to all around (Gen 2:8-10). It is tragic when a local testimony comes down to the level of the world and fleshly activity is displayed in it.

Even though the room was completely furnished and prepared, the disciples also had to "make ready". The bitter herbs and other necessary things for the supper must be prepared. Spiritually, the preparation by the disciples, even the bitter herbs, suggests to us the searching of heart and preparation of spirit, accompanied by confession and humility, that are so necessary if we are to meet with the Lord (1 Cor 11:28).

14.   *The Lord Keeps the Passover*
22:14-18

> v.14 "And when the hour was come, he sat down, and the twelve apostles with him.
> v.15 And he said unto them, With desire I have desired to eat this passover with you before I suffer:
> v.16 For I say unto you, I will not any more eat thereof, until it be fulfilled in the kingdom of God.
> v.17 And he took the cup, and gave thanks, and said, Take this, and divide it among yourselves:
> v.18 For I say unto you, I will not drink of the fruit of the vine, until the kingdom of God shall come."

14   "The hour" refers to the appointed hour between the Lord and His disciples when He sat down or "reclined", "placed himself at table" (JND), in a position in which the feet were not put under the table, as is our custom, but pointed away from it, so that the body reclined. The significant facts are that it was the Lord and His apostles, and it was at the time of His appointment. The hour of eating was in the evening and was likely at the very commencement of the fourteenth day. The reclining position was also the normal practice, for according to the teachings of the rabbis, not only were the participants to view the Passover as a celebration of deliverance and joy and be dressed in their most festive garments, but they were to be at rest. "The left elbow was placed on the table, the head resting on the hand" (*Unger's Bible Dictionary*, p.354.).

The Passover supper consisted of unleavened bread, bitter herbs, the roasted lamb and four cups. There were frequent ritual hand-washings. Each paschal lamb was to serve a company of not less than ten nor more then twenty, so there is significance to the statement, "he sat down and the twelve apostles with him".

15   The repetition in "With desire I have desired to eat this passover with you" reveals a yearning from the heart of the Lord Jesus. It is in this Gospel that He revealed His being pressed in His spirit toward the accomplishment of the work of redemption (12:50). The meaning of the first paschal lamb sacrificed in Egypt so long before was about to be fulfilled in its Antitype. This Passover with His disciples was to be the last that could point forward to the accomplishment of redemption. "Before I suffer" tells us that His heart was filled with thoughts of all that the suffering would mean to His holy soul. The Psalmist had written, "while I suffer thy terrors I am distracted" (Ps 88:15). Luke was to write later on, "he presented himself living, after he had suffered, with many proofs" (Acts 1:3 JND). At this point the suffering lay before Him and well He knew the true meaning of the Passover.

16   That He did eat the Passover with His disciples, but would not again partake of it until it would be fulfilled in the kingdom of God, seems to be the meaning of this verse. To say that it means that He longed to eat of it, but would not, inserts a problem into His words that is not there. His last meal before Calvary was this Passover supper. He did not say, "I will not eat", but "I will not . . . eat thereof" i.e. of the Passover; for after He had risen, He ate a broiled piece of fish and a piece of honeycomb as powerful evidence to His disciples that He was truly alive (24:42). The next time that He will partake of it will be with a redeemed Israel when the kingdom of God is manifested. The Passover will be observed in the millennial kingdom (Ezek 45:21).

17   "And having received a cup" (JND) refers to a Passover cup, of which there were four. Alfred Edersheim, in *Jesus the Messiah*, gives a very full account of the ritual practised at Passover time in a Jewish household. The head of the company took the first cup, which seems to be the cup mentioned here. He spoke over it the thanksgiving, which was first of all a thinks for the contents of the cup, and then thanks for the return of another Passover supper and for their being preserved to observe it. Although the prayer for the wine was a simple thanks, the further thanksgiving was traditionally an expression of Israel's national pride and their righteousness as a nation. We cannot believe that the Lord would have uttered such words, seeing that the leaders of that very nation were at this moment conspiring how they might kill Him.

18   We have already commented on a similar statement in v.16. In Matthew and Luke, the Lord made this statement after He had instituted the Lord's supper. The partaking of "the fruit of the vine" is given a spiritual meaning by the Lord; He uses it as a symbol of the joy and blessing of the coming manifest kingdom. This prospect must be the reason for this second statement, the first about not eating until the kingdom would come and this one about not drinking. When Paul gave the order of the Lord's supper that he had received from the Lord, the words are added, "ye do shew the Lord's death till he come" (1 Cor 11:26). These words are not found in the Gospel accounts of the institution of the supper, but the statements by the Lord about the coming kingdom, which Luke places before the institution of the supper and Matthew and Mark place afterward, show that two events filled the heart and mind of the Lord, His cross work and His coming again in glory. The supper, which was instituted in the following verses, points back to His suffering and forward to His coming.

15. The Institution of the Lord's Supper
22:19-20

v.19 "And he took bread, and gave thanks, and brake *it*, and gave unto them, saying, This is my body which is given for you: this do in remembrance of me.
v.20 Likewise also the sup after supper, saying, This cup *is* the new testament in my blood, which is shed for you."

19 Bread (*artos*) means a loaf, usually small and having an oval or round shape, made of flour and water and about "as thick as the thumb" (W.E. Vine). Recounting this event, and writing prior to Luke's account, Paul recorded, "the Lord Jesus the same night in which he was betrayed took bread" (1 Cor 11:23). There is good evidence from the imperfect tense used by Paul, and from the account in John 13:26-30, that Judas went out immediately after receiving the Passover morsel from the Lord's hand, so was not present when the Lord Jesus took the loaf and gave thanks, breaking it and giving it to His own.

This tender scene is vividly described by Luke. The hands that lifted the loaf were soon to be pierced with the nails and the thanks given to the Father was thanksgiving for His own body soon to be hung on the tree. He knew the true meaning of the bread as no other could, and yet He thanked God for it. This is the evidence of total submission to the will of God and the willing offering of Himself as the sacrifice acceptable to God.

"This is my body" has produced such teachings as transubstantiation, by which it is claimed that the bread is changed into His literal body, and the lesser teaching of consubstantiation, by which the bread though still bread yet is also His body. However, the Lord had one physical body, not two, and He was present there in His body, so the disciples could not have thought that He meant that the bread was His literal body. The bread is the emblem, symbol, or token of His body, given for them. The broken bread did not suffer for them, but Christ was soon to suffer in His own body. Even after the thanks was given it was still bread (1 Cor 11:26-28).

The institution of the Lord's supper was accompanied by the blessed injunction, "this do in remembrance of me". There is authority here to remember Him throughout the centuries in the breaking of bread. This holy yet simple remembrance has been preserved to us until this very day. We remember Him as we ponder His pre-existence, deity, downstooping into lowly humanity, the grace of His gentle life, the impeccability of His nature, the delight He brought to the Father in His obedience and faithfulness, His blood-like sweat in the garden, His majesty as shame and contempt were heaped upon Him, His total submission to suffering, agony and death, His triumph over sin, death and hell, His resurrection and ascension, and His present and coming glory. This, and more than tongue can tell, is the remembrance of Him.

20 "After supper" is important. This was not a part of the Passover celebration, but took place afterward. He had just taken the bread, given thanks for it, broken it and given it to His own; "In like manner" (JND) He did with the cup. Paul received his understanding of the events in the upper room from the Lord, not from other disciples, and he gives the same details. The Lord thanked the Father for the cup and in so doing gave thanks for the shedding of His own blood. This precious blood of Christ was the basis for the establishment of a new testament of grace by which sinners would be brought near to God to enjoy all the blessings that have been purchased by it. The terms of this testament are described in the entire NT rather than in Jer 31:31-34 which gives only aspects of a new covenant that will affect Israel as a nation. The blood is the foundation of a new relationship and communion with God and is mentioned first in 1 Cor 10:16 for this reason.

The institution of the supper was the essence of simplicity. Of all the material things that were on the Passover table, only two remain for us, the bread and the cup. In this dispensation of the Holy Spirit, only the minimum of material things has a place amongst the saints when we come together.

The two statements: "This is my body which is given for you" (v.19) and "my blood, which is shed for you" are the first very clear statements to His own that not only would he suffer and die, but He was to die in their stead as their Substitute. This caused great wonder in our hearts at the moment we were saved and the wonder increases as we learn more of the infinite value of His sacrifice. When we remember Him, as He commanded, we say, "He died for me", which is symbolically expressed as each one partakes of the one loaf and drinks of the one cup. Paul wrote about this act, "you proclaim the Lord's death until he come" (RSV). This word "proclaim" (*katangellō*) is used ten times by Luke in the Acts for the public declaration of the gospel. We are familiar with the NT statements: "Jesus died" (1 Thess 4:14) which brings to mind His pathway of shame and suffering that led to the cross; "Christ died" (Rom 5:6) which expresses the divine purpose in sending Him from heaven to die on the cross, but in the supper, it is "the Lord's death" and "the blood of the Lord" (1 Cor 11:27,27), which tells of the triumph of the crucified Lord.

> " 'Tis in Thy cross, Lord, that we learn
> What Thou in all Thy fulness art;
> There, through the darkening cloud discern
> The love of Thy devoted heart".
>
> Edward Denny

16.   *Who Shall be Accounted the Greatest?*
     22:21-30

v.21 "But, behold, the hand of him that betrayeth me *is* with me on the table.
v.22 And truly the Son of man goeth, as it was determined: but woe unto that man by whom he is betrayed!
v.23 And they began to inquire among themselves, which of them it was that should do this thing.
v.24 And there was also a strife among them, which of them should be accounted the greatest.
v.25 And he said unto them, The kings of the Gentiles exercise lordship over them; and they that exercise authority upon them are called benefactors.
v.26 But ye *shall* not *be* so: but he that is greatest among you, let him be as the younger; and he that is chief, as he that doth serve.
v.27 For whether *is* greater, he that sitteth at meat, or he that serveth? *is* not he that sitteth at meat? but I am among you as he that serveth.
v.28 Ye are they which have continued with me in my temptations.
v.29 And I appoint unto you a kingdom, as my Father hath appointed unto me;
v.30 That ye may eat and drink at my table in my kingdom, and sit on thrones judging the twelve tribes of Israel."

21   "Behold, the hand of him that delivers me up (is) with me on the table" (JND). The form of this sentence does not require the presence of Judas when it was spoken. It is a statement about the nearness of Judas to the Lord at the Passover. Matthew and Mark put these words before the institution of the supper rather than afterward and their order may be correct. By placing them here, Luke links them with the strife over who would be the greatest (v.24), thus showing the great contrast between the perfect Man and His very imperfect followers.

22   The Lord taught that every man is responsible to God for his own sin. We are greatly helped by this to understand the relationship between the predetermined counsel of God and man's guilt in crucifying the Saviour. Peter uses this language in the same context in Acts 2:23. "The determinate counsel and foreknowledge of God" do not in any way diminish the guilt of man's lawlessness in taking Him and "by wicked hands" crucifying Him. Judas' guilt was his own and was without excuse. The other great truth of this verse bows our hearts in worship at the grace of God, for it was determined in divine counsels before the world began that Christ should be taken by men and nailed to the tree. Even at this time, the woe pronounced on Judas is more of a lament than a condemnation. It means "Alas to that man" and is an expression of grief from the heart of the Man of sorrows. We know from John 13:21 that the betrayal caused the Lord to be deeply troubled in His spirit.

23-24   There is such a contrast between these two verses that we have difficulty in linking them together. The very men who question among themselves about which of them would betray Him are disputing over who will have the greatest place in the kingdom. It is not necessary to suppose that any of them claimed the highest place, but that they were greatly interested in who would have it. The cross was so near and the soul of the Saviour was heavy with the suffering that lay before Him. How tragic to find the disciples disputing over place and position at such a time! It is no wonder that from men who were so far removed from His spirit the sorrowing Saviour could find no comfort (Ps 69:20). Flesh is ever seeking place, and displays itself at the most inappropriate times. "Strife" (*philoneikia*) literally means "a love of strife", and "signifies eagerness to contend".

25-27   The Lord Jesus taught the greatest lessons in humility that the ears of men ever heard, but the lessons went to hearts through eyes as well as ears, for He was the great example of true lowliness. Paul echoed this teaching when he wrote: "Let this mind be in you, which was also in Christ Jesus" (Phil 2:5). He who held the highest place in heaven took the lowest place on earth. Puny lords of men lord it over those who are under their authority, but He who held the highest authority in the universe "took upon him the form of a servant" (Phil 2:7). He said, "I am among you as he that serveth" which is a translation of *diakonōn* and refers to a waiter on tables. What a rebuke to those who desired authority over their fellows! Let us take the lesson to heart!

28   The words of rebuke must have hit home very hard, for the tender Saviour now encourages those who have remained faithful to Him when so many have turned away. They truly loved Him and in their hearts was a willingness to suffer or even die for Him, if necessary (v.33). It touches our hearts to know that when the Lord spoke those words of approval and cheer He knew that these very men who "forsook all and followed him" (5:11) would forsake Him and flee (Matt 26:56). However, there is a vast difference between weak men who failed in their courage and the evil Judas who for greed betrayed Him. Judas was absent when the supper was instituted and was certainly absent when v.28 was spoken. Reference has already been made (v.29) to Paul's use of the imperfect tense in 1 Cor 11:23, "in the night in which he was being delivered up" (J. Rotherham), indicating that Judas was engaged in carrying out his plot while the Lord gave the bread and cup to His own.

29-30   There is a reminder in these words that it is not yet the time to reign. He must suffer and these dear men will suffer too, but He has appointed to them a kingdom and they will sit down at His table and enter with Him into the joy of that day of His glory. Not only the joy will be shared, but they will also share with Him in His glorious reign. Judging is here used as it is in Acts 17:31, namely as "ruling" rather than sitting to condemn as a judge would a criminal. Many have expressed a difficulty in picturing the apostles of the church age as judges over the twelve tribes. The difficulty should be solved when we remember that the millennial reign of Christ will be a rule from the heavenly city over the nations on earth including a redeemed Israel (Rev 5:9; 21:21-27). The apostles will be in the heavenly city with the Lamb who is its Centre and Light (Rev 21:14,22,23).

17. *The Lord Foretells Peter's Denial*
22:31-34

> v.31 "And the Lord said, Simon, Simon, behold, Satan hath desired *to have* you, that he may sift *you* as wheat:
> v.32 But I have prayed for thee, that thy faith fail not: and when thou art converted, strengthen thy brethren.
> v.33 And he said unto him, Lord, I am ready to go with thee, both into prison, and to death.
> v.34 And he said, I tell thee, Peter, the cock shall not crow this day, before that thou shalt thrice deny that thou knowest me."

31 The repetition of the name "Simon, Simon" tells us something of the anguish of the heart of the Saviour as He foretold Peter's denial. He who never spoke a redundant word is deeply moved. Satan's hand in Peter's threefold denial is recorded only in Luke. Although the address is to Peter, through him the others are being addressed, for the "you" is plural and includes all the disciples. It was all of them who would be sifted as wheat. Again we believe Judas was absent, for he was not wheat, but all of these, failing as they were, were not chaff; they were His genuine wheat. The sifting by Satan himself, not by one of his emissaries, is an experience that few believers have encountered. Let us remember this when we concentrate on Peter's failure! when the Lord said, "Satan hath desired to have you" He used *exaiteō*, its only occurrence in the NT; it is an intensified form of *aiteō* ("to ask") and has been translated "begged earnestly for" (Marshall). A number of translators have rendered it as a demand, "Satan has demanded to have you" (JND) or as a right that belongs to him in virtue of the fall, "has claimed the right to sift you" (Mft). Sift (*siniazō*) is a unique word, with the thought of figuratively winnowing disciples as wheat is winnowed to separate it from chaff.

32 "Thee" is now singular and indicates a special trial for Peter. Many think it was a young woman that Peter met, and that he denied his Lord because of her question. In reality it was Satan he met, with all the forces of darkness mustered at his call. We do well to remember this lest we become too free in our condemnation of dear Peter. The prayer of the Lord for him was a perfect plea before God that was answered. Peter did face Satan, and he did not escape the trial. His faith did not fail, and he was turned again and used mightily of God to strengthen his brethren. We have the blessed assurance that the intercession of the Lord on behalf of His own still prevails before the throne of God. To every believer, faced with trial and temptation, the Lord said: "But I have prayed for thee". How good to know that this is personal (Rom 8:27)! For a believer who has sinned, He is still the perfect Advocate before God (1 John 2:1,3).

33 Peter's words began "Lord, with thee I am ready . . ." (JND). We have no doubt that he was "ready to go . . . both into prison, and to death". There was nothing wrong with Peter's affection for his Lord, but he just did not fully know his own heart nor the kind of temptation with which he would be confronted. He said, "with thee I am ready" but he found that, when alone, he was not ready (1 Pet 3:15). It is important to see that Peter's courage failed, but neither his faith nor his affection. The Lord had just said, "I have prayed for thee (*sou*, singular) that thy faith fail not". "Fail" (*ekleipō*) occurs four times in the NT and three of these are in Luke. It is used of the failure of natural life (16:9); of the light of the sun (23:45), and of the unfailing years of Christ (Heb 1:12). The Lord prayed that Peter's faith would not be eclipsed, and the prayer was answered. The association between *ekleipō* and the English word "eclipse" is not ground for supposing that the darkness at the cross was caused by the phenomenon of an eclipse of the sun.

34 It is seldom in the Gospels that we are given the feelings of the Lord; they give the facts of the Lord's sufferings, while it is in the Psalms that we learn His feelings. Not one word is said of Peter's feelings at the Lord's words. They did register, however, and they came back to him with great force and conviction in the high priest's palace (v.61). Rarely did the Lord call him Peter, but He did so here, perhaps as a reminder that he should stand as a rock. Peter will deny Him, not once, but three times, and this will be before the cock will crow which is the same thing as giving the time on a clock in our day. Before He ever left the throne in heaven to stoop down in grace for our salvation, the Lord knew all that would happen to Him and the sufferings that awaited Him.

18. *Behold, Here are Two Swords*
22:35-38

v.35 "And he said unto them, When I sent you without purse, and scrip, and shoes, lacked ye any thing? And they said, Nothing.

v.36 Then said he unto them, But now, he that hath a purse, let him take *it,* and likewise *his* scrip: and he that hath no sword, let him sell his garment, and buy one.

v.37 For I say unto you, that this that is written must yet be accomplished in me, And he was reckoned among the transgressors: for the things concerning me have an end.

v.38 And they said, Lord, behold, here *are* two swords. And he said unto them, It is enough."

35   The Lord, nearing the cross, looks back on the days when He first sent His disciples to the towns and cities as His witnesses. He reminds them of His full provision for all their needs then, so, although He will soon leave them, He will not leave them destitute. In fact, as the ascended Lord above, He will meet their needs by His word and Spirit, just as fully as He did when physically present with them. This teaching is only hinted at by Luke but was fully given by John (14:14-30).

36   However, it is for the immediate future that He wants to prepare them. Knowing that wicked hands will tear Him from them and that they will be made to fear for their lives, He prepares them with words that they could not mistake. When we consider how often His warnings about His rejection and death had failed to reach them, we can understand why He now used terms that they would easily understand. They were facing peril and real physical danger, so He speaks to prepare them to meet foes who hated them and would kill them if they could. From what follows it is plain that the Lord never intended them to smite anyone with a sword.

37   He then quoted from Isa 53:12: "and he was numbered with the transgressors". This is most significant when we think that this is the Gospel of the Man of sorrows. He who was separate from sinners (Heb 7:26) was numbered with the transgressors, for all that was written of Him must be fulfilled and the time of their fulfilment had come. No words from the lips of the Lord more fully reveal who He is and why He was in the world. He is the perfect Servant of Jehovah who came to be marred, bruised and crushed as the sin offering, suffering as the perfect Substitute for the sins of many.

38   Only Luke gives us the account of the two swords. As we have suggested above, the Lord wanted the disciples to be warned thoroughly and prepared for personal assault. He was soon to be taken by the hands of wicked men, beaten, abused, scourged, spat upon and nailed to the cross. In speaking of the actual swords, He has made them understand that their peril is immediate and in the physical realm. It would be ridiculous to think that the Lord meant that two swords were enough to stand against the garrison of imperial Rome in Jerusalem. His words mean "Enough of this kind of talk!". "By saying, 'It is enough', the Lord did not mean that two swords were enough, but the subject had been discussed enough" (J. Heading). The disciples took literally what the Lord had meant figuratively. The chief purpose of His instruction was to prepare them for the change they were to experience when He left them.

19.   *The Agony in the Garden*
22:39-46

v.39 "And he came out, and went, as he was wont, to the mount of Olives; and his disciples also followed him.

> v.40 And when he was at the place, he said unto them, Pray that ye enter not into temptation.
> v.41 And he was withdrawn from them about a stone's cast, and kneeled down, and prayed,
> v.42 Saying, Father, if thou be willing, remove this cup from me: nevertheless not my will, but thine, be done.
> v.43 And there appeared an angel unto them from heaven, strengthening him.
> v.44 And being in an agony he prayed more earnestly: and his sweat was as it were great drops of blood falling down to the ground.
> v.45 And when he rose up from prayer, and was come to his disciples, he found them sleeping for sorrow,
> v.46 And said unto them, Why sleep ye? rise and pray, lest ye enter into temptation."

39 Luke's account of the agony in the garden is not as detailed as Matthew's and Mark's. He omits the fact that a garden called Gethsemane was there; nor does he mention three prayers, nor tell about Peter, James and John being taken aside to go further with their Lord, but he does give a unique description of the agony of the soul of the Saviour, and it is most often to this account that we turn when we remember the Lord's sufferings in the garden. The Lord frequently had climbed this western side of the Mount of Olives to get away from the crowds, to be alone in communion with His Father. Luke says, "he . . . went, as he was wont"; John says, "Jesus ofttimes resorted thither with his disciples" (John 18:2), and adds, "Judas also, which betrayed him, knew the place". The appropriateness of its name is not a coincidence. Gethsemane, so called only in Matt 26:36 and Mark 14:32, means oil-press. It may well be that at the time of its naming, as in many cases in Scripture when people or places were named, their was a divine superintendence. "The olives when pressed yield their oil which is used for healing and light. It is believed the garden was located in an olive orchard on the western side of the mount of Olives" (H. Paisley, *What the Bible Teaches*, Mark p.563).

The Lord Jesus had frequently prayed in this garden, but the circumstances of this night are unique in all the events of time. Luke only says, "the disciples followed him", but Matt 26:36 tells us that when He came to the place (*chorion*), a garden that was enclosed by a wall and had a gate in it, he said to the disciples, "Sit ye here, while I go and pray yonder", leaving them at the gate. Then taking with Him Peter, James and John, He went further and "began to be sorrowful and very heavy" (Matt 26:37), and leaving them, "he went a little further". "In Gethsemane, the 'little further' implies typically that the Lord was within the vail" (J. Heading, *What the Bible Teaches*, Matthew, p.368). Using the tabernacle as the illustration, eight disciples were left at the gate, three drew near to the vail, but only One stepped inside, and it was truly a holy place where none but the eye and heart of God could fathom the depth of sorrow and agony that the holy soul of His Son must endure.

Genesis 22 illustrates this scene beautifully. It was when Abraham "beheld the place" that he "said unto his young men, Abide ye here with the ass, and I and the lad will go yonder and worship, and come again to you" (v.5). From that point, Abraham and Isaac went on alone, "so they went both of them together" (v.8); only after the young men were left behind did Isaac speak about the fire and the wood and asked about the lamb. This is a lovely picture of Gethsemane.

40 The place to which Luke refers was the garden, and it is likely that at its gate He turned to His disciples and exhorted them to pray. In Matthew and Mark these words to the disciples are spoken between His first and second prayer. "Pray that ye enter not into temptation" may refer to prayer for deliverance from severe trial, but it may also imply prayer for deliverance from sins of the flesh, to which they and we are so prone. Because of our fallen natures, sin is often present in our response to trials. The Lord Jesus showed His moral beauty in His trials. As the meal offering of Lev 2, no amount of external pressure nor the heat of the oven could reveal one coarse grain or one flaw in the perfections of His nature.

41 "He was withdrawn from them", or "He was drawn away from them", by the intensity of His sorrow. It was "too great to tolerate the sympathy of even the closest" to Him (A. Plummer). He was alone, separated from the main body of disciples as well as from the three whom He had chosen to go further with Him. The position of prayer was often to stand with uplifted eyes, but the Lord bowed down, His soul "exceeding sorrowful unto death" (Mark 14:34). The verb "prayed" is the imperfect tense which describes repeated action.

Only Luke tells us that the distance to which He withdrew was "about a stone's cast" (*bolē*), akin to *ballō* ("to throw"), used only here in the NT. The true significance of the distance was stated above, the scene was too intimate and holy to be intruded upon by the nearest to Him on earth, but this scene also illustrates how perfectly the Lord Jesus took our place. Under the law (Deut 21:18-21), "a stubborn and rebellious son" which would not "obey the voice of his father, or the voice of his mother", was brought "unto the elders of his city, and unto the gate of his place", the testimony of his father and mother was used against him and he was condemned, placed at a distance of "a stone's cast" and stoned to death. At this holy scene in the garden, we are allowed to see the Son who could say "the Father hath not left me alone; for I do always those things that please him" (John 8:29), removing Himself the distance of "a stone's cast" from those He loved as if He were disobedient, even though He was the son whose obedience was impeccable. This identification of Himself with our guilt was so complete that although He could never be defiled by sin, yet "he hath made him to be sin for us, who knew no sin" (2 Cor 4:21). The verses that follow in Deut 21:22-24 describe a man "worthy of death"; "if . . . he be put to death and thou hang him on a tree; his body shall not remain all night upon the tree . . . (for he that is hanged is accursed of God)". These closing words are quoted and applied to Christ in Gal 3:13, so we have good authority for applying them to Him. The disobedient son is a great contrast to the obedient son, and the man who was worthy of death stands in contrast to the One who is altogether worthy to be adored.

42   He asks that, if the Father is willing, this cup should be removed from Him. The OT uses a full cup as a metaphor of guilt that has reached the height where it demands the wrath of God to be poured out. The first mention of such an illustration is in Gen 15:16 when God told Abram: "the iniquity of the Amorites is not yet full", which tells us that, although God in mercy had spared them up to this point, there was a limit beyond which He would not hold back His wrath. Ps 11:6 speaks of "the portion of (the) cup" of the wicked, and Ps 75:8 says that such a cup of righteous indignation and wrath is in the hand of Jehovah. (See Isa 51:17; Jer 25:15; 49:12.) The cup referred to by the Lord Jesus was in the hand of God (John 18:11) and, from many references, we learn that it was full of bitter wrath and righteous judgment against our sins. That He "should taste death for every man" (Heb 2:9) means that on the cross He drank every drop of the bitter cup until He had drained it dry.

The will of the Father is His chief desire even though that will means that He should be the sin offering and drink the cup of wrath to its last dregs. "Not my will" is not a suggestion that His will was opposed to the Father's will, but is the expression of His heart that the Father's will should be done. This willing submission sets the Antitype apart from every OT type of His sacrifice. They were unwilling victims; He "gave himself".

43   Angelic ministry is normally physical, not spiritual, preservation. Ps 91:11 is quoted in Matt 4:6 and suits this pattern of physical aid. The Lord never ministered to His own bodily needs, as can be seen from the temptation (Matt 4:2-4), so this kind of ministry was put into the hands of angels. By this angel's ministry the Lord was strengthened, and we suggest it was strength ministered to Him physically, even though His body never knew the effects of sin. Some manuscripts omit vv.43,44.

44   The word agony (*agōnia*) is found only here in the NT. Vine links it to the intense physical and emotional strain that accompanied the efforts of a participant in the Greek athletic contests. The agony of the Lord was so great that "his sweat became as great drops of blood, falling down upon the earth" (JND). Surely this is most holy ground. How can we, whose senses have been numbed by sin, ever enter into the holy anguish of the soul of the Man of sorrows? The physical evidence of His agony is given that we might have some understanding of it. Human eyes were not allowed to look on that sight. The Holy Spirit has recorded it for our learning. We are well aware of the simile word "as", but the AV "drops" (*thrombos*), is a medical term, which means "thick clots" of coagulated blood. Vine interprets *thrombos* as "large, thick drops of clotted blood". The appearance of the Saviour as One whose "visage was so marred more than any man" must be understood in the light of this suffering as much as the result of what men did to Him.

There is yet another unique word in this verse, beside the two already mentioned. "Sweat" (*hidrōs*) is only here, but is used in the LXX in Gen 3:19.

Adam was told to dress and keep the garden, but not until he had sinned do we read "in the sweat of thy face shalt thou eat bread". In the garden the sinless Man is sweating; in contrast to Adam, He was submitting to the will of God, not rebelling against it. The Lord had often prayed in this very place, but never before had prayed with such a burden on His heart, and never had any man sweat as He did. It is meaningless to attempt to draw medical parallels.

45-46   Rising up from prayer, fully aware that He went to do the Father's will and knowing all that His will involved, He came to sleeping disciples. They had been overcome by grief and for them there was the oblivion of sleep, but it was not a time for sleeping. Even for them peril was at hand, and again He exhorted them to pray to be preserved in trial and temptation.

The sleeping disciples remind us of how much sleep Christ lost during these days of rejection and grief. From the time of His triumphal entry into the city, He had spent long days enduring hateful opposition and questioning, and very likely nights of prayer and lonely vigil. On Thursday, the preparation was made for the Passover which He kept with His disciples, and from there He went to the garden. The arrest followed, with a night of abuse at the hands of wicked men; the trials before the high priests and Pilate came next, and on Friday He was led out to be crucified; there had been no break for sleep or rest.

20.   *This is Your Hour*
22:47-53

> v.47 "And while he yet spake, behold a multitude, and he that was called Judas, one of the twelve, went before them, and drew near unto Jesus to kiss him.
> v.48 But Jesus said unto him, Judas, betrayest thou the Son of man with a kiss?
> v.49 When they which were about him saw what would follow, they said unto him, Lord, shall we smite with the sword?
> v.50 And one of them smote the servant of the high priest, and cut off his right ear.
> v.51 And Jesus answered and said, Suffer ye thus far. And he touched his ear, and healed him.
> v.52 Then Jesus said unto the chief priests, and captains of the temple, and the elders, which were come to him, be ye come out, as against a thief, with swords and staves?
> v.53 When I was daily with you in the temple, ye stretched forth no hands against me: but this is your hour, and the power of darkness."

47   He was still speaking to the disciples when the multitude came to arrest Him. Judas led them and approached the Lord Jesus to mark Him out by a kiss to the officers of the high priest and the Roman guard who accompanied them. Luke's words are full of pathos: "Judas, one of the twelve". Luke does not record that the kiss was ever given, but Matthew and Mark both say that he "covered him with kisses" (JND). No man could be closer to heaven and still end in hell. To this account Matthew adds, "Now he that betrayed him gave them a sign" (26:48). The *sēmeion* ("sign") was chosen by Judas, and perhaps no fact in the complete story of his treachery so thoroughly displays his wickedness. Knowing full well the meaning of the "sign", and the falsity behind the greeting "Hail" (*chairō*, to rejoice), even then, the tender Saviour responded with gentle words.

48   We would say that Judas was past recovery, yet the Lord's words to him were spoken in grace that he might know the heinousness of his crime and to draw him back from it. It was betrayal of which the heart of man is capable, yet behind it was the malicious will of Satan who had entered into Judas (John 13:27).

49-50   The Lord had spoken to them about having swords (v.36) and they had told Him that they had two (v.38), so now they asked if they should use them. It ill becomes us to berate these dear men for an act of extreme courage that in itself was so hopeless. They did what they could, but it was far removed from the spirit of Him "who was brought as a lamb to the slaughter". The question was asked, but Peter displayed his impetuous nature by not waiting for a reply. From John 18:10, we know it was Peter who struck with sudden violence. Fishermen had little training in swordplay, so instead of cutting off a head or inflicting a serious wound, he only succeeded in cutting off the ear of one of the servants of the high priest. Luke uses a unique means to give us the suddenness of the actions in these two verses. In the clause, "they (disciples) . . . saw what would follow" there is a construction that is only here in the NT and literally means "the thing going to be" either said or done. Peter's sudden act was his response to Judas' sudden kiss.

   The phrase, "they which were about him", referring to the little band of loyal men whose hearts had been won, stands in great contrast to them "which were come to him" or "who were come against him" (v.52, JND). The Lord Jesus was the centre of each group, but the one was drawn by love, the other by hate. In these two groups all men are portrayed, for around the Lord Jesus there can be no neutrality. In all that follows, these two representative groups "around him" can be recognised (vv.52,63,66; 23:1,35,47-49; 24:36).

51   The Lord repudiated this use of the sword, but His words, "Suffer ye thus far", have been translated in many different ways. Their literal meaning is "Allow you until this". JND and the RV stay with the AV, and this seems as clear as any translation. It is a rebuke to Peter personally, telling him that he must allow these men to make their arrest. The ear was cut off and the healing created a new one. There is no evidence of the Lord stooping down to lift the piece that was cut off. It was an act of the Creator (John 1:3).

   This is the only healing by the Lord of an injury inflicted upon another person with intent to do harm. Only Luke tells us that he "cut off his right ear" and only John says that it was Peter who did it and that the servant's name was Malchus (John 18:10). This impulsive act contributed to Peter's denial of his Lord, for one of the accusers by the fire was "his kinsman whose ear Peter cut off" (John 18:26).

The "ear" (*ōtion*, in most manuscripts) that is used in the four Gospels in speaking of the ear of Malchus is not the same word that is used by Luke in other passages. Six times he uses *ous* ("ear") metaphorically, in the sense of understanding and knowing (1:44; 4:21; 8:8; 9:44; 12:3; 14:35). Both words can mean a physical ear, and are used equivalently in vv.50 (*ous*) and 51 (*ōtion*), but *ous* is almost always used by the Holy Spirit to infer a hearing with understanding. This lends support to the application that is so often made, that in seeking to defend truth we should not cut off ears. The tragedy is that we do cut off ears; as in the case of Malchus who was perfectly healed, some whose ears were cut off are not permanently injured, but again, like Malchus, they never forget the wound that was struck.

52   The arrest by night was done clandestinely, but it was not left to subordinates to perform. Present with the officers of the temple guard were elders of the Sanhedrin and chief priests. They came with swords and staves which were weapons that would wound and bruise, fully intending to do battle if resistance were offered. When He stood before Pilate, the Lord Jesus said: "if my kingdom were of this world, then would my servants fight, that I should not be delivered to the Jews" (John 18:36). By these words we must judge Peter's act. He was as wrong that night in the garden as he had been when he attempted to restrain the Lord Jesus going to the cross (Matt 16:22,23).

53   The secrecy connected with the arrest was to keep an uprising from taking place among the people (22:2), so in the temple, where so many were gathered for the Feast of the Passover, no attempt had been made to take Him. "This is your hour" may be related to the darkness and the night that clothed their evil deed, but the Lord is saying much more than this. It was the hour when men were allowed to stretch out their puny hands against the Lord of all. They could not have done this if divine sovereignty had not allowed it (Acts 2:23). It was His hour that had fully come (John 13:1), but it was also the hour of "the power of darkness". This goes beyond the evil conspiracy of the Jewish leaders and sees behind it the scheme of Satan. The forces of the unseen world of darkness had been mustered to array themselves with all their fearful power against the Lord of Light (John 14:30). Like David, He met the foe all alone with nothing in His hand, and proved Himself to be the "King of glory . . . The Lord strong and mighty, the Lord mighty in battle" (Ps 24:7,8). It was the battle of the ages and Satan met a defeat that annulled his power, determined his eternal destiny, and delivered us from his grasp (Heb 2:14,15).

21.   *The High Priest's Palace and Peter's Denial* 22:54-65

v.54 "Then took they him, and led *him*, and brought him into the high priest's house. And Peter followed afar off.

> v.55 And when they had kindled a fire in the midst of the hall, and were set down together, Peter sat down among them.
> v.56 But a certain maid beheld him as he sat by the fire, and earnestly looked upon him, and said, This man was also with him.
> v.57 And he denied him, saying, Woman, I know him not.
> v.58 And after a little while another saw him, and said, Thou art also of them. And Peter said, Man, I am not.
> v.59 And about the space of one hour after another confidently affirmed, saying, Of a truth this *fellow* also was with him: for he is a Galilaean.
> v.60 And Peter said, Man, I know not what thou sayest. And immediately, while he yet spake, the cock crew.
> v.61 And the Lord turned, and looked upon Peter. And Peter remembered the word of the Lord, how he had said unto him, Before the cock crow, thou shalt deny me thrice.
> v.62 And Peter went out, and wept bitterly.
> v.63 And the men that held Jesus mocked him, and smote *him.*
> v.64 And when they had blindfolded him, they struck him on the face, and asked him, saying, Prophesy, who is it that smote thee?
> v.65 And many other things blasphemously spake they against him."

54   According to John 18:3,12, a cohort of Roman soldiers was present at the arrest, but the chief actors were the rulers of the Jews, so Christ was taken to the house of the high priest. He who created the stars, who calls them by their names and leads them in their courses (Isa 40:26), was led by His creatures to be tried by a human tribunal. Peter followed, but it was at a great distance, and of the rest of the disciples Luke says nothing; both Matthew and Mark give this moment as the time when they all forsook Him and fled (Matt 26:56); Mark 14:50).

55   The house of the high priest was built as a rectangle around an open court. Into it Peter entered, introduced by John (John 18:15-17), and when a fire was kindled in the middle of the court they sat down around it, and Peter sat down among them. It is very possible that the rooms of the house were so arranged around this open court that it was visible from any of them. The Lord stood in one of the rooms; Peter sat among the officers who had made the arrest and the servants of the house. Mark calls them *huperetes* (Mark 14:54), that is, attendants to whom specific tasks were assigned in the service of the high priest. During this night, "Peter sat down among" the enemies of his Lord. Throughout Scripture saints are found in unlikely places, such as Lot in Sodom, or David in the court of the Philistines, but none could be more strange than Peter at this fire, particularly when we remember that he had so recently sat at the table in the upper room with the Lord. The fire had been "kindled" (*periaptō*), a word used only here, picturing the lighting of the fire "in the midst" of the large court. At this fire Peter denied his Lord, but at another "fire of coals" Peter was restored (John 21:9).

56   All the Gospels tell us that the first question addressed to Peter came from a young maid. John tells us that she also kept the door and had allowed Peter to come in; but it was by the fire, with its light cast upon him, that she looked at him intently and made the confident statement: "This man was also with him". She was just a serving girl and her statement could not hold much terror for Peter, but let us not forget that it was Satan who was sifting him (22:31).

57   The denial must have been spawned by terror. Peter, in unfamiliar surroundings, a fisherman from Galilee in the court of the house of the high priest, with enemies on every side, was not prepared for the challenge. We can understand why, many years later, he wrote; "be ready always to give an answer to every man that asketh you a reason for the hope that is in you with meekness and fear" (1 Pet 3:15). Peter was not ready and he denied the Lord. We are staggered to think that the same man who had made the great confession, "Thou art the Christ, the Son of the living God" (Matt 16:16), said "I know him not". But in reading of Peter's shameful denial, let us not forget that there are times when we shrink from confessing what we know, and while not putting our denial into words, as Peter did, yet we fail because of what it might cost us to be open and frank.

58   Luke says it was "after a little while" that another saw him. Into this interval John inserts an examination of the Lord before Annas, the father-in-law of Caiaphas the high priest. There should be no problem with the various accounts for they dovetail into one another. There were several questioners, and a question asked by one would be taken up by others who also wished to voice their suspicions. Luke writes, "another" (*heteros*, that is a different person) asked the second question, which charged Peter with being "of them", that is, of the little band around the Lord. Dear Peter said, "Man I am not".

59   It was an hour later that "another" (*allos*, of the same kind as the second questioner) "stoutly maintained it, saying, In truth this (man) was also with him, for also he is a Galilean" (JND). The speech of Galilee was easily recognisable. All who read the Gospels carefully are aware that there are significant differences in the accounts of the accusations against Peter and his answers. Dr. Heading has given an excellent comparison in his commentary on Matthew in this series of NT commentaries (pages 378-379) that shows there are no irreconcilable facts in the records. In his commentary on John in this series, he wrote, "The differences arise because Peter was surrounded by hostile people, and several were accusing him at the same time; the differences in his answers on each occasion arise because he was seeking to deny his connection with the Lord to all the various speakers" (p.293).

60-62   Peter's third denial was immediately followed by the crowing of the cock, "And the Lord turned, and looked upon Peter". This is the reason for suggesting that in whatever area of the house the Lord stood waiting to be examined, the court where the fire was kindled was visible from it. "Peter remembered"; a flood of memory swept over him, engulfing him in grief and sorrow. The first denial may have been made on the impulse of the moment, but the two that followed were the result of the first. As he wept alone in an outside place Peter's memories of that buffeted face must have wrung his heart. He wrote after many years: "the face of the Lord is against them that do evil" (1 Pet 3:12).

Throughout the training of Peter, he was given many lessons from the animal kingdom. The draught of fish taught him that he would catch men (5:9); the piece of money in the mouth of the fish taught him that the Lord is able to provide for all need (Matt 17:27); the crowing cock taught him his pride (vv.60-62), and the sheet let down from heaven, full of beasts, taught him the oneness of Jews and Gentiles (Acts 10:9-16). Events such as these are "pegs" on which memories are hung. Memory played a great part in the torment of the rich man in hell (16:25) and in the recovery of Peter, a believer away from God. To the fallen church at Ephesus, the risen Christ said, "Remember therefore from whence thou art fallen" (Rev 2:5). Peter's epistles are the memories of his lessons so that his memories have become our lessons too.

63-65   The officers (*hupēretēs*, Mark 14:65) who were commanded to guard the Lord Jesus used the time interval for their own sadistic pleasure. These servants of the high priest and officers of the temple began to mock, but their mockery degenerated into beating Him. He who came "to preach . . . recovering of sight to the blind" (4:18) was blindfolded and struck repeatedly while they taunted Him with cries, "who . . . smote thee?" The blows of their fists were accompanied by words that were like blows to Him who was the "tender plant". He felt, as no mere man could, every cruel taunt and blasphemy that these wicked men hurled at Him. We have no clear statement to prove how the chief priests, elders and scribes were occupied in the part of the night that remained until they assembled the council at daybreak (v.66), but there is good reason to believe that they went to their beds, while the Lord endured the abuse and contempt of the household servants. There was no moment of ease for Jesus that night.

22.   *The Lord Jesus before the Council*
22:66-71

v.66 "And as soon as it was day, the elders of the people and the chief priests and the scribes came together, and let him into their council, saying,

v.67 Art thou the Christ? tell us, And he said unto them, If I tell you, ye will not believe:

v.68 And if I also ask *you*, ye will not answer me, nor let *me* go.

v.69 Hereafter shall the Son of man sit on the right hand of the power of God.

v.70 Then said they all, Art thou then the Son of God? And he said unto them, Ye say that I am.

v.71 And they said, What need we any further witness? for we ourselves have heard of his own mouth."

66 The whole body of the elders of the Sanhedrin gathered together at the break of day and led Him away into their council. Luke says that the elders were divided into two companies, both chief priests and scribes. Many, if not all, of these priests were Sadducees and the scribes were mostly, if not all, Pharisees. The origin of the Sanhedrin is traced to the seventy elders chosen to assist Moses (Num 11:16,17), but nothing is said about it in the OT, so it likely had its beginning in the days of the Maccabees. It was the high court of the Jews in NT days and had power over both religious and civil matters, so far as the Roman occupation of the land would allow. Herod and the Romans, at this time, allowed them complete civil authority, limiting them only in the matter of capital punishment (John 18:31), a restriction they ignored in stoning Stephen to death (Acts 6:12-15; 7:58-60). The death of the Lord Jesus could not be by stoning (John 12:31-33), for God was working out His predetermined plan even when the circumstances seemed completely out of control.

67 This was a formal trial and should have followed a standard procedure, but it did not. No charge was read or formal statement made. Instead, they asked Him if He was the Messiah and He answered, "If I tell you, ye will not believe". The truth about His Messiahship was so far removed from their thoughts about it that it was pointless even to discuss it with them. Telling them the truth would have been followed by their denial of His claims, for they believed in a Messiah of power and majesty who, when He came, would break the Roman yoke and restore the royal kingdom of David to Israel.

68 How many questions He could have asked them that would have exposed their utter ignorance of the sufferings through which Messiah would procure the glory of the coming kingdom! But no amount of questions would have enlightened them. Jeremiah had written about the "foolish people . . . without understanding, which have eyes, and see not; which have ears, and hear not" (Jer 5:21).

69 "Hereafter" in the AV conveys the meaning of the Lord's statement. "Henceforth" (RV, JND), or after what we call now, they would see "the Son of man . . . seated at the right hand of the power of God" (RV). The highest place of honour in the universe would be given to Him because of the work He was about to accomplish by suffering and dying.

It is correct to understand "hereafter" in an eschatological sense, and this is the emphasis in Matt 26:64 and Mark 14:62, where Christ tells them that they will see Him "sitting on the right hand of power, and coming in the clouds of heaven". Luke omits the fact that they will see Him and the statement about the future coming. A possible reason for Luke's omission is that he is linking the present rejection and shame of the Lord to the immediate glory into which He will enter as a result of His suffering, a glory that these men will not see, but is none the less immediate, and they will see it in the future. This is the force of Luke's "hereafter" (*apo tou nun* - "from now").

70   The Sanhedrin rightly understood this claim to highest glory, even though they were totally dark about the road that He must take to it, and utterly rejected the claim. The words of the Lord Jesus caused them all to say, "Art thou then the Son of God?". The form of the question is important, not "sons of God" which was used of angels (Job 38:7), and of men (Hos 1:10), but "the Son of God". Only the Lord Jesus in all of Scripture is called the Son of God with the definite article and in the singular. The answer of the Lord Jesus was a positive affirmative. He simply said, Yes. It is impossible to make anything else of His answer. No greater evidence can be found for this than the answer of Christ to Judas, "Then Judas, which betrayed him, answered and said, Master, is it I? He said unto him, Thou hast said" (Matt 26:25).

71   The Sanhedrin, sitting in official capacity as the governing body of the Jews, understood that He was claiming to be the Son of God, and on this they condemned Him, needing no other witness against Him. How strange that some modern thinkers, though not present at that event, attempt to make His testimony mean something very different! So far as we know, not one man in that judicial body misunderstood His words. He said that He was the Son of God and they accepted this claim as blasphemy which made Him to be worthy of death.

Many studies have been made by men trained in law and the history of law of the trials of Christ before Annas (John 18:13-24) and before Caiaphas and the Sanhedrin, and they point to many breaches of procedure. In these religious trials some of the violations of Talmudic law cited are (1) a night session of the court, (2) conducting a trial on a holy day, (3) failing to allow a second session to take place on a following day, (4) a wrong definition of blasphemy, (5) holding the trial away from the official chambers, (6) suborned testimony, (7) the absence of any defence witnesses in a capital case, (8) a predetermination of guilt, (9) a sentence decided in council before the trial. Jewish scholars in our day have felt that it was demanded of them to defend the conduct of the Sanhedrin by whom Christ was condemned. For the most part, they have done so by attempting to discredit the Gospel records. As the record stands, and it does stand, the judges of Christ were extremely culpable.

23.   *The Lord Jesus before Pilate*
23:1-5

v.1   "And the whole multitude of them arose, and led him unto Pilate.
v.2   And they began to accuse him, saying, We found this *fellow* perverting the nation, and forbidding to give tribute to Caesar, saying that he himself is Christ a King.

> v.3   And Pilate asked him, saying, Art thou the King of the Jews? And he answered
>   him and said, Thou sayest *it*.
> v.4   Then said Pilate to the chief priests and *to* the people, I find no fault in this man.
> v.5   And they were the more fierce, saying, He stirreth up the people, teaching
>   throughout all Jewry, beginning from Galilee to this place."

1   Pontius Pilate was the procurator of Palestine from AD 26 to 35. He made
Jerusalem the headquarters of the Roman military garrison rather than Caesarea.
His disdain for the Jews and their religion was displayed by hanging in the
governor's palace gilt shields with the names of pagan gods on them. So many
were the complaints lodged at Rome by the Jews that Tiberius ordered their
removal. He used the sacred temple funds to build an aqueduct for the benefit
of the people, but this caused an insurrection which he violently crushed. We
know from this Gospel (13:1) that he had slaughtered some Galilaeans inside
the temple precincts, mingling their blood with the blood of their sacrifices. He
was far from being a Jewish favourite, so when the whole company of the
Sanhedrin brought the Lord Jesus to him to be tried, they only did so because
the power of life and death was his to dispense, and they wanted Christ put to
death.

2   The threefold formal charge against Christ before Pilate was of a very
different nature from the charge of being the Son of God by which the
Sanhedrin had condemned Him. Such a theological issue would have had
little meaning to Pilate. The three-count indictment by the Jews charged the
Lord Jesus with "perverting our nation" (JND), which probably meant that
He had incited the common people, notably Galilaeans, to revolt against the
rulers. The second and third charges were to impress Pilate, "forbidding to
give tribute to Caesar" and saying that "he himself is Christ a King". These
were political issues and would surely have brought upon a guilty person the
most severe judgment of Rome.

3   Pilate looked at the gentle Man who now stood at his judgment throne. The
Jews had described a reactionary, a rebel and rabble rouser, a leader in resistance
to the powers that be, and Pilate must have looked with amazement on the face
of heaven's Nobleman. Pilate's incredulity is best understood by the great contrast
between the charges laid and the appearance of the accused. Each Gospel records
that Pilate burst out with an emphatic "Thou". Perhaps English would be best
served by translating, "Thou? Art thou the King of the Jews?". Although the Lord
knew well how much misunderstanding was in the question and how wrongly
His answer would be construed, He could not deny the claim and agreed that
He was the King of the Jews. John 18:37 supplies the much fuller answer, "To this
end was I born, and for this cause came I into the world, that I should bear
witness unto the truth". Pilate's question did not contain much truth, but the
answer contained full truth.

4   We also know from John's record that the leaders and the multitude remained outside the judgment hall, because entering it would have made them ceremonially unclean, and unfit to observe the Passover, so Pilate went out to speak to them several times and each time went again into the judgment hall further to question the Lord. His words, "I find no fault in this man", were not well received by the rulers and the people. The issue now is not just between Christ and the Jews, but between the Romans and the Jews. The chief priests, in their craftiness, well knew that this would incline the people toward them. Pilate was giving a legal judgment when he said, "I find no crime in this Man". The real crime in the eyes of the leaders of the Jews was that the common people listened to Christ's teachings. Envy stirred their hearts, and Pilate knew it (Matt 27:18; Mark 15:10).

5   Pilate's refusal to indict the Lord of any crime made the Jewish leaders even more insistent. They charged the Lord with stirring up the people, that is, with inciting them to revolt and riot. "All Jewry" is literally "all Judaea", but the AV had rightly grasped the usage, for Galilee was not part of Judaea, and the expression probably means, "all the land of the Jews". In contrast to this charge of stirring up the people is Mark's statement about Pilate, "willing to content the people" (15:15). Pilate was more influenced by the people's choice than any righteous judge should have been.

24.   *The Lord before Herod*
   23:6-12

> v.6   "When Pilate heard of Galilee, he asked whether the man were a Galilaean.
> v.7   And as soon as he knew that he belonged unto Herod's jurisdiction, he sent him to Herod, who himself also was at Jerusalem at that time.
> v.8   And when Herod saw Jesus, he was exceeding glad: for he was desirous to see him of a long *season*, because he had heard many things of him; and he hoped to have seen some miracle done by him.
> v.9   Then he questioned with him in many words; but he answered him nothing.
> v.10 And the chief priests and scribes stood and vehemently accused him.
> v.11 And Herod with his men of war set him at nought, and mocked *him*, and arrayed him in a gorgeous robe, and sent him again to Pilate.
> v.12 And the same day Pilate and Herod were made friends together: for before they were at enmity between themselves."

6-7   Looking for a way out of a dilemma, Pilate grasped at the thought that if Christ was from Galilee, then the entire problem came under the jurisdiction of Herod. Under Roman law, a trial was held in the province where the crime was committed, but it could be referred to the home province of the person who was charged.

Herod Antipas was in Jerusalem at the Passover time. Although the Herods were Idumaeans, they were crafty politicians and observed Jewish festivals because it pleased the Jews. This son of Herod the Great had been called "that fox" by the

Lord. He had heard John the Baptist "gladly", yet through the evil scheme of Herodias, his half-brother Philip's wife, whom Herod had stolen away from her husband, he had put John to death. He was ruler of Galilee and Peraea under the title of tetrarch, and never had the official title of king even though he later tried hard to obtain it when Caligula was the Roman emperor.

8   As early as 9:9, we are told that Herod "desired to see him". At this point, Luke provides us with the reason that lay behind the desire; he had heard of Christ's miracles and wanted to see some "sign" (JND) done by Him. In the synoptic Gospels the word used to refer to Christ's miracles is usually *dunamis*, a mighty work. In John, where Christ's miracles are distinct "signs" of His power as the Son of God, John uses *sēmeion*. However *sēmeion* is the word used here, indicating that Herod was interested only in a display of what to him would be some form of magic. Although the miracles of Christ were a powerful evidence of His deity, He never used them for display, nor for the satisfaction of the curious.

9   The shallow interest of Herod is exposed by the silence of Christ before him. He answered Pilate's questions and before him "witnessed a good confession" (1 Tim 6:13), even though He was silent to the charges of the Jews, "insomuch that the governor marvelled greatly" (Matt 27:14); but before Herod He was completely silent. There are comparisons between Pilate and Herod, but there are also contrasts. Of the two men, Herod was far better acquainted with Jewish politics and religion, but his character was more shallow than the Roman governor's and his malicious nature was well known to the Lord, which accounts for Christ's complete silence before him.

10   The vehement charges hurled at the Lord by the chief priests and scribes in Herod's hearing were lest Herod should release Him uncondemned. To every charge there was silence, as "he is brought as a lamb to the slaughter, and as a sheep before her shearers is dumb, so he openeth not his mouth" (Isa 53:7). The word that Luke uses for "vehement" (*eutonōs*) is found only here and in Acts 18:28 where it is used of Apollos who "mightily (*eutonōs*) convinced the Jews . . . showing by the scriptures that Jesus was Christ". Vine gives an illustration from LXX in Josh 6:7 where Moses commanded the priests with the trumpets before Jericho, "Let seven priests having sacred trumpets proceed thus before the Lord, and let them sound loudly" (*eutonōs*, LXX, Bagster translation). We can well believe that these rulers of the Jews "sounded loudly" in their accusations. They "accused him violently" (JND), and Herod did not need much convincing.

11   Herod's contempt for the Saviour had been thinly veiled by his curiosity, but when this went unsatisfied, he displayed his true attitude. Around him were gathered a detachment of soldiers, possibly his personal bodyguard. With their willing help, Herod set at nought the gentle Saviour. This is the epitome of contempt and means "to count as nothing", utterly to despise Him. How little the Jewish leaders knew that previously Isaiah had described them perfectly, "he was despised, and we esteemed him not" (53:3). The mockery was both by word and action. Among the vehement charges of the Jews was that He had claimed to be king, a position and rank lusted after in Herod's heart. The mockery was fed by that unfulfilled desire, and Christ was arrayed in a gorgeous robe, which normally would have been worn by a candidate for a high office, and sent back to Pilate. It was meant to be a cruel jest, but if their eyes had not been blinded, they would have seen before them "the King of glory", majestic in His royalty.

12   The cause of the enmity between Pilate and Herod is now known, but officials of subjugated lands fell in and out of favour with Roman authorities with regularity. The intrigues and jealousies of such men fed many such quarrels. It is a sad commentary on these two men that their friendship was cemented by a common rejection of Christ. In describing the former enmity, Luke uses one of his unique words, *prouparchō* ("for before they were"). The only other NT occurrence of this word is in Acts 8:9, in reference to Simon the sorcerer, "which beforehand in the same city used sorcery". Vine gives a LXX reference to Job 42:18 which is not found in our OT, but is part of an additional note about Job in the LXX where it is written, "and his name before (*prouparchō*) was Jobab". The examples of the use of this word indicate that it refers to a former condition of long standing which is likely true of the enmity between Pilate and Herod.

25.   *Christ or Barabbas?*
23:13-25

v.13 "And Pilate, when he had called together the chief priests and the rulers and the people,
v.14 Said unto them, Ye have brought this man unto me, as one that perverteth the people: and, behold, I, having examined *him* before you, have found no fault in this man touching those things whereof ye accuse him:
v.15 No, nor yet Herod: for I sent you to him; and, lo, nothing worthy of death is done unto him.
v.16 I will therefore chastise him, and release *him*.
v.17 (For of necessity he must release one unto them at the feast.)
v.18 And they cried out all at once, saying, Away with this *man*, and release unto us Barabbas:
v.19 (Who for a certain sedition made in the city, and for murder, was cast into prison.)
v.20 Pilate therefore, willing to release Jesus, spake again to them.
v.21 But they cried, saying, Crucify *him*, crucify him.
v.22 And he said unto them the third time, Why, what evil hath he done? I have found no cause of death in him: I will therefore chastise him, and let *him* go.
v.23 And they were instant with loud voices, requiring that he might be crucified. And the voices of them and of the chief priests prevailed.
v.24 And Pilate gave sentence that it should be as they required.
v.25 And he released unto them him that for sedition and murder was cast into prison, whom they had desired; but he delivered Jesus to their will."

13-14   The hope of Pilate that Herod might decide the thorny issue of the trial of Christ had been dashed. Receiving Him back again, Pilate summoned the chief priests, the rulers and the people of the Jews together to deliver a not-guilty verdict. This was an official decision of the judge, for under Roman law there was no evidence by which he could condemn Him to die. He repeated their charge that the Lord was guilty of "seducing people from their allegiance" (A. Plummer) to Rome. The chief priests actually believed that allegiance to them had suffered under the teachings of the Lord. These verses should be understood in the light of Peter's words: "whom ye delivered up, and denied him in the presence of Pilate, when he was determined to let him go. But ye denied the Holy One and the Just, and desired a murdered to be granted unto you" (Acts 3:13,14). Pilate's dilemma was between the desire of the Jews and Roman law. He was certainly determined to release Christ and declared four times in this chapter that He was not guilty (vv.4,14,15,22).

15-17   These verses fairly well summarise Pilate's efforts not to condemn Christ to die. He first tried to get the Jews to judge the case themselves, but the most serious sentence by the Sanhedrin must stop short of the death penalty. He sent Christ to Herod and no sentence of death was pronounced by the tetrarch. He then offered to assuage their enmity against Christ by publicly scourging Him, and finally, he offered to release Him, as the custom of the feast required that a criminal should be set free in honour of the Passover (Mark 15:6). But all these efforts were doomed to failure, for the chief priests and leaders of the Jews would accept only one verdict, the death sentence. Because we know the plan of redemption as it is revealed in Scripture, we are rather untouched by Pilate's efforts, but they were genuine. He was not motivated by compassion for the innocent Christ nearly so much as by the fear of reprisal from Rome if he failed to act in complete accord with Roman law. Experts in imperial law tell us that Luke gives us "technically correct" procedure in all these aspects of the trial.

18-19   The response from the throats of the crowd, goaded by the terrible enmity of their leaders, was a spontaneous outburst, "Away with this man". It is true that the word "man" is not in the text, and although it is common enough to use the masculine demonstrative pronoun without a noun, yet it may be significant here. In the parable of the nobleman, the cry was almost identical (19:14). The phrase "rejected of men" (Isa 53:3) may be accurately translated, "rejected from amongst men". He who was hated "without a cause" (Ps 69:4) was so thoroughly rejected by His own people that they refused to own Him as one of their fellow men.

Barabbas was guilty of having "committed murder in (an) insurrection" (Mark 15:7). He had his supporters, for the insurrection in which he was involved had taken place in the city of Jerusalem. At least some of the Jews, particularly the Zealots, would have looked upon him as a hero and a martyr, rather than a criminal. Christ had none to support Him or even to pity Him. The verb "(take) away" is a present imperative, meaning that the crowd were impatient to see the action done and Barabbas released to them without further delay. Pilate noted this impatience that began to border on mob violence. These words of Pilate were addressed to "the chief priests and the rulers and the people" (v.13). The priests and rulers had sought to incite the people and had succeeded so well that Luke tells us, "they cried out all at once" (*panplēthei*). This unique word is made up of *pan* ("all") and *plēthos* ("multitude"). The latter word is frequently found in this Gospel even in the first verse of this chapter, "the whole multitude".

20-21	In his next statement, still attempting to release Christ, Pilate called out to them; this suggests to us the growing tumult and the size of the crowd. The next voice is the shout of the crowd, with the chilling cry heard now for the first time, "Crucify, crucify him" (JND). In each of the Gospels, the demand that He should be crucified was not voiced until Pilate's suggestion that he should release the Lord as a favour on the feast day, but it was crucifixion that was in the plan of the priests and leaders from the very beginning. "But they cried" is literally, "but they roared" (Mft). *Epiphōneō* ("to cry") is used here and in only two other places in the NT: Acts 12:22, "and the people gave a shout", and Acts 22:24, "they cried so against him", referring to the outcry against Paul in the temple court. Luke is using metaphorical language that compares the tide of opposition rising against Christ to the rising of a mighty storm at sea (v.23).

22	Luke tells us that this was the third time that Pilate proclaimed Christ's innocence. Four times are recorded by Luke from the lips of Pilate, but one of them was when he was repeating the judgment of Herod (v.15). In this statement that he will release Christ, he is actually speaking with all the dignity and authority that his position as governor and judge would demand. He made the positive statement, "I will therefore chastise him, and let him go", but this was not to be.

23-24	The word *epikeimai*, translated "were instant", was used for the "rush and swirl of a tempest". It is used here as an imperfect tense in the middle voice, showing how persistently they cried and how emotional the crowd had become as they were swept by the intense desire to destroy Jesus. The mob prevailed over Pilate's determination to let Him go and he made the sudden decision to carry out their request. The fact, known to us in Scripture, that He was "delivered by the determinate counsel and foreknowledge of God" (Acts 2:23) does not diminish by one iota the guilt of Pilate and the people, with their leaders. In v.24, Pilate "gave sentence" (*epikrinō*), a word that is found only here in the NT. In Acts 15:19, in the council at Jerusalem, James said, "Wherefore my sentence is . . ." (*krinō*). The prefix *epi* adds the meaning, "to give", but we should understand that Luke uses this language because he is recording the final legal decision of

Rome at the hands of its representative in Judea. "Thus all the world combined to bring to death God's only Son; there Jew and Gentile, priest and king for once were truly one".

25 Luke's rather full description of Barabbas' guilt points out the people's guilt. They chose a murderer, who had wantonly taken life, in preference to the One who was willing to give His life to save guilty men. To these very people, Peter preached, "I wot that through ignorance ye did it, as did also your rulers" (Acts 3:17). Yet, when He was raised from the dead and the Holy Spirit came down in power to open their eyes, many of these same priests and people sealed their doom by rejecting Him despite many infallible proofs. On this day of infamy, Pilate "delivered Jesus to their will".

This was the decision of the highest court in the land of Judea, a court that had the power of life and death. All are agreed that a terrible miscarriage of justice took place. Authority to dispense judgment carries with it solemn responsibility. It has been suggested that an application can be made to the elders of an assembly, who are the supreme court on earth for settling wrongs among the believers of that assembly. Every godly leader desires to avoid these judgments so there are lessons to learn from Pilate. In fact, in all matters of judgment, the following principles apply.

The mistakes can be enumerated as follows: (1) those who demanded the extreme penalty and would accept nothing less were wrong; (2) the witnesses changed their charges to have maximum effect on the judges; altering the charge is a weakness in any case; (3) as Pilate tried to pass the case to Herod, so it is wrong for leaders to try to evade giving judgment, passing the case to someone else; (4) even though Pilate knew the evil motives of the accusers, he still allowed their charges to be heard; (5) he was unduly influenced by the crowd, but the majority might be, and often are, wrong; (6) he gave his verdict against his own conscience, which is a terrible evil; (7) the dread of the consequences of offending a superior is no excuse for unjust judgment.

VI. The Crucifixion of the Lord Jesus (23:26-49)

1. The Place Called Calvary
23:26-38

> v.26 "And as they led him away, they laid hold upon one Simon, a Cyrenian, coming out of the country, and on him they laid the cross, that he might bear *it* after Jesus.
> v.27 And there followed him a great company of people, and of women, which also bewailed and lamented him.
> v.28 But Jesus turning unto them said, Daughters of Jerusalem, weep not for me, but weep for yourselves, and for your children.
> v.29 For, behold, the days are coming, in the which they shall say, Blessed *are* the barren, and the wombs that never bare, and the paps which never gave suck.

v.30 Then shall they begin to say to the mountains, Fall on us; and to the hills, Cover us.
v.31 For if they do these things in a green tree, what shall be done in the dry?
v.32 And there were also two other, malefactors, led with him to be put to death.
v.33 And when they were come to the place, which is called Calvary, there they crucified him, and the malefactors, one on the right hand, and the other on the left.
v.34 Then said Jesus, Father, forgive them; for they know not what they do. And they parted his raiment, and cast lots.
v.35 And the people stood beholding. And the rulers also with them derided *him*, saying, He saved others; let him save himself, if he be Christ, the chosen of God.
v.36 And the soldiers also mocked him, coming to him, and offering him vinegar.
v.37 And saying, If thou be the king of the Jews, save thyself.
v.38 And a superscription also was written over him in letters of Greek, and Latin, and Hebrew, THIS IS THE KING OF THE JEWS."

26   We have linked Isaiah's description of the Man of sorrows with Luke's account of all the things that the Lord experienced during His last days in Jerusalem. Being led away brings to mind, again, the vivid language of the prophet, "he is brought as a lamb to the slaughter, and as a sheep before her shearers is dumb, so he openeth not his mouth" (53:7). Unresisting, the gentle Saviour was led by His creatures and nailed to the cross.

Many views are currently held about how and why Simon bore the cross. He was coming out of the country, that is, "from the field" (JND), when he was accosted by the soldiers and commanded to bear the cross. He bore it "behind Jesus" (JND). Does this mean that he lifted the upright as it dragged on the ground behind the Lord Jesus? or as some believe, was the upright piece already at the place of execution, and did Simon bear the crossbeam, the *patibulum*? The Lord did bear His own cross (John 19:17), and a comparison of the accounts by Matthew and Mark along with John's testimony indicate that it was the entire cross that was carried. Without dogmatism, I suggest that Luke has given the key to the difficulty. Simon lifted the end of the cross that dragged on the ground and carried it behind the Lord. As to why Simon was recruited, the usual view that Christ was too weak to carry His own cross is not supported by a single line of Scripture.

27   One of the unique features of Luke's Gospel is his description of women and their ministry. In the Gospels, not once did a woman abuse the Lord, or take part in open opposition to Him, but only Luke records the tears of this company of women who were among the great throng that followed the procession to the place of crucifixion. The verses that follow, vv.28-31, give us all the recorded words of Christ from the time of His sentence until He uttered the seven sayings from the cross.

28-29   "Daughters of Jerusalem" identifies these women as being distinct from the women who ministered to Him in Galilee and throughout His journey to Jerusalem (8:3). Turning to them the tender heart of Christ went out to them, for He knew the disaster that would befall Jerusalem and its inhabitants in AD70, a destruction that would be a judgment from God, directly linked to their rejection of Himself. He desired from them tears of true repentance rather than tears of sympathy. It touches our hearts that at such a moment He thought of the plight of others. However, we do not limit "the days (that) are coming" to the siege of AD70, for they go far beyond it, to the eternal loss of those who reject Him. It would have been better never to have had children born to them than to see them engulfed in the coming judgment.

30   This verse confirms that the judgment of which the Lord speaks will fall upon Jerusalem and Israel in the coming day of wrath. When "the great day of his wrath is come" (Rev 6:17), men will pray to the mountains to fall on them and to the hills to cover them. They "shall desire to die, and death shall flee from them" (Rev 9:6). The sorrow of these words is multiplied when we remember that the day of vengeance will reveal "the wrath of the Lamb" (Rev 6:16), for they were spoken by God's Lamb as He was on His way to bear that very wrath as a Substitute to provide a way of escape from it for guilty men. As we have noted in the teaching of the Lord in 21:6-26, the destruction of Jerusalem under Titus is prominent in His predictions in Luke. The mountains and hills were the only refuge for the people in that terrible destruction of the city, but as has been suggested above (vv.28,29), the judgment at that time was to be followed by far greater judgment at the end time. The word for "hills" (*bounos*) is used in NT only by Luke, here and in 3:5. It means "a mound" so that some have suggested that these "mounds" might be mounds of rubble left from the destruction of the city. *Oros* is the usual word for a natural mountain (19:29,37; 22:39).

31   The most common explanation of this difficult verse is that if the righteous Lord Jesus was suffering as He was, what would be the fate of guilty sinners? but it leaves difficulties. The Lord Jesus was to suffer more than any man has or could suffer, therefore the explanation must be wrong that suggests that His sufferings as the innocent One were less than their sufferings as guilty ones will be. In fact, the real contrast is between the reaction of Israel "in the green tree" from their reaction "in the dry", so our problem is to determine the meaning of these two statement. The "green tree" can be identified as the Lord Himself, "I am like a green olive tree in the house of God" (Ps 52:8; see J. Heading, Luke's Life of Christ, p.268). The "dry tree" has been likened to the unfruitful nation in their rejection of Messiah, and this may be correct. But there is a man coming in his own name (John 5:43) to "consume and to destroy" (Dan 7:26). A paraphrase of the Lord's words therefore might be, "If the Jews deal thus with One who has come to save them, how will they react in the presence of one who comes to destroy them?". The "dry tree' has also been interpreted as being Jerusalem in the day of its judgment in AD 70. In support of this alternative interpretation, the personal pronoun "they" refers to the soldiers of Rome who are leading Christ out to be crucified; "they", Roman soldiers, will come and destroy the city in a day not far distant. The word *hugros* ("green") is found nowhere else in the NT. It means a living, moist tree, the opposite of *xēros* ("dry").

32   The Lord Jesus quoted from Isa 53:12, "And he was reckoned among the transgressors" (22:37). So thoroughly was this to be fulfilled that two criminals, malefactors, were crucified with Him, one on either side, Jesus in the midst. No legal charge had been proven against Him, but He was crucified between thieves as the worst of the three. Wherever Christ moved among men, He presented a contrast to the company around Him for He alone was a sinless Man, absolutely impeccable, but never was the contrast greater than at His death. "Malefactor" (*kakourgos*) is made up of the two words "evil" (*kakos*) and "to work" (*ergon*). These two men were workers of evil, their deeds were bad. The works of Christ were full of love, mercy and grace. Luke says "two other" (*heteros*), of a different kind, and never has *heteros* been employed with more meaning.

33   *Calvary* is a Latin word, and it means "the skull"; *Golgotha* in Hebrew. This event at Calvary is the climax of the ages; the hinge of the vast forever. All the ages preceding it looked forward to it, all eternity will look back to it. As Erich Sauer wrote, in "The Triumph of the Crucified" "Of all times, it is the turning point; of all love it is the highest point, and of all salvation it is the starting point, of all worship it is the central point". The words "Calvary" and "eternity" are found only once in the AV, and this is important to us, for Calvary has changed eternity for every believing soul. It should be noted that most translations do not use the name "Calvary" but "the Skull".

Three words, "they crucified him", are found in the AV in each of the four Gospels. No further description of hammer or nails or the weight of a body hanging on torn wounds is given. No mention is made of the curse connected to hanging on a tree (Deut 21:23; Gal 3:13) or the horrors of such a death. The Gospels give the facts of the crucifixion with an economy of words that more vividly describe the scene than detailed explanations could.

34   "Then said Jesus", that is, at the moment when man's sin in rejecting Him and crucifying Him reached its highest tide of evil. "Where sin abounded, grace did much more abound" (Rom 5:20); where sin reached its high water mark, grace overflowed. The imperfect tense of "said" means that He kept on saying it. When they nailed Him to the tree, He said, "Father, forgive them"; when they mocked Him and scoffed at His claims, He said, "Father, forgive them"; when they shouted for Him to come down from the cross, He said, "Father, forgive them". Stephen did pray for his tormentors, after praying for himself (Acts 7:60). The Saviour who yielded Himself to wicked men to be crucified, prayed first for the very ones who crucified Him.

"Forgive" means simply to forgive one who has wronged the sufferer, but *aphiēmi* also has the meaning "to lay aside, to leave, to let be, to allow, to hold back". To this writer, this suits this context. He asked God to let be, that is, to hold back the wrath that His tormentors deserved. It bows redeemed spirits in worship that He who prayed that wrath should be restrained from falling on them, yet bared His own soul to the full weight of wrath divine.

This prayer was not a special forgiveness for those who did the crime, as if their act were virtuous, but a distinction is made between the ignorant and the knowing. Paul said, "I did it ignorantly in unbelief" (1 Tim 1:13), not that this entitled him to forgiveness; rather he obtained mercy, for he did it in blind ignorance. Without this prayer, would divine judgment from heaven have fallen on Christ's tormentors? I believe it would.

The last sentence of this verse tells of the direct fulfilment of prophecy by men who were totally ignorant of it ever having been written. Luke gives a much briefer statement than the other Gospels about the parting of the Lord's garments. John gives it full treatment (19:23-24), quoting the prophecy (Ps 22:18); Matthew gives the parting and the gambling and also quotes the prophecy (27:35); and Mark gives a shorter statement (15:24). All the Gospels, even Luke, give the distinction between the garments that were divided among the soldiers and the one seamless garment for which they cast lots. In the judgment hall, they removed His garments as they mocked Him, but they put them on Him again before taking Him away to crucify Him. At the cross, they stripped Him, taking away from the Saviour all that He possessed on earth, leaving a little pile of garments (*himation*) on the ground, to be divided among themselves. When they removed the one inner, seamless garment (*chitōn*, John 19:23) they said, "Let us not rend it, but cast lots for it whose it shall be" (John 19:24). One man left the cross that day who wore the garment of Christ. Many in their spiritual experience have been to the cross and ever since they have worn something of the beauty of the Saviour as they reproduce His character by the grace of God.

35 "The people stood beholding", while the rulers scoffed in their comments one to another. Their identification of Jesus as "Christ, the chosen of God" shows that they well understood the words of Christ and had rejected Him and all His claims. He was truly the chosen One to suffer, to shed His blood and die an atoning death for His guilty creatures. He did save others, for the scorn heaped on Christ often contained much truth, but He would not save Himself. His substitution was voluntary and with full knowledge of the cost in shame and suffering. In the people, and particularly the rulers around His cross, we are reminded of the Psalm of the perfect Sin Offering. Prophetically, He cried, "Many bulls have compassed me" (Ps 22:12), a description of these very leaders as they encircled Him. In the next clause, "strong bulls of Bashan have beset me round", the verb is stronger and means that the encircling enemies were closing in upon Him, to throw their words like blows. David wrote, "They gaped upon me with their mouths, as a ravening and roaring lion", desiring to roar, rend and tear their unresisting victim. To describe this cruel derision, Luke uses *ekmuktērizō* ("to deride out and out", W.E. Vine). Its only other occurrence in the NT is 16:14 where comment has been made on it.

36 On three occasions the Lord was offered drink. He was offered "drugged wine" before His crucifixion which He refused (Matt 27:34; Mark 15:23). Again,

He was offered vinegar, a cheap wine when He cried "I thirst", just before He died (John 19:29). Luke tells us that the soldiers (of the governor) mocked Him, offering Him vinegar. It has been suggested that one way of mocking Him would be to hold the desperately needed moisture just out of reach of His mouth. The terrible thirst connected with His crucifixion cannot be more vividly described than in the words: "My strength is dried up like a potsherd; and my tongue cleaveth to my jaws; and thou hast brought me into the dust of death" (Ps 22:15).

37   The scoffing of the soldiers was in keeping with their knowledge of the events and the inscription above His head. They knew little or nothing of the "Christ . . . of God", but their scorn at Him and the Jews is obvious in their taunt, "king of the Jews". They looked on the crucified One with His thorny crown, torn back, spittle-covered face that was battered and bruised, pierced hands and feet, and all that they saw added to their mockery, "This is the Jew's king". As the leaders had fulfilled Ps 22 in their derision (v.35), so unwittingly did the soldiers, for David also wrote, "Surely dogs have encompassed me, a company of the malignant surrounded me; They pierced my hands and feet" (Ps 22:16, H. Spurrell). The two verbs in this verse, as in v.12, express degrees of encompassing Him, forming a circle and then drawing closer as their vicious taunts drew no response from the silent Sufferer.

38   Above His head is the writing that fuelled their derision. All four Gospel writers tell us of the superscription, written in Greek, Latin and Hebrew. The entire writing was, "This is Jesus of Nazareth, the King of the Jews". We can well understand why the Jews demanded a change in this inscription (John 19:19-22). The different wordings in the Gospels of the inscription can be explained by the fact that three languages were used. It may be, considering each of the accounts, that the entire title was, "THIS IS JESUS OF NAZARETH, THE KING OF THE JEWS" (Matt 27:37; Mark 15:26; John 19:19). The "superscription was written over" (*epi*), and Matthew wrote, "And set up over (*epanō*) his head" (27:37), telling us that the cross was so formed that a piece of it extended "up over" His head on which the title was written. Evidence points to an actual cross with a crossbeam, and from this inscription we understand that the crossbeam crossed the upright somewhere below the top, as a traditional cross.

2.   *Two Malefactors*
23:39-43

> v.39 "And one of the malefactors which were hanged railed on him, saying, If thou be Christ, save thyself and us.
> v.40 But the other answering rebuked him, saying, Dost not thou fear God, seeing thou art in the same condemnation?
> v.41 And we indeed justly; for we receive the due reward of our deeds: but this man hath done nothing amiss.
> v.42 And he aid unto Jesus, Lord, remember me when thou comest into thy kingdom.

> v.43 And Jesus said unto him, Verily I say unto thee, To day shalt thou be with me in paradise."

39 Matthew tells us that both thieves cast on the Saviour the same reproaches as did the soldiers and the rulers. There is no reason to support that there was any difference in the past life of these two criminals. Both were common thieves, greedy for gain at the cost of their victims. The man who was saved that day had no moral life before his conversion and no christian life afterward. He was saved without merit of any kind, and this is a pattern for all who are saved, so far as the grounds of forgiveness are concerned. The evidence of forgiveness is a transformed life. Artists have painted one man with evil countenance and the other appearing as an angel. This is far from the truth, but Luke tells us of the particular insults of the one thief, hurled at the Saviour, "Art not thou the Christ? save thyself and us" (JND).

40 The cross of Christ was not only in the midst of these two men, physically; it was a division that was spiritual and eternal. The other man watched the Sufferer on the middle cross as He endured the abuses of the crowd. He saw the gentleness and dignity of the Man of sorrows, and his heart was deeply moved, and the work of repentance was begun in his soul. There is no place that so exposes sin as the presence of perfect righteousness. An old Puritan wrote: "It pleased God to show the truth of salvation by saving a man at the time that Christ died that all men might be saved. So it must have pleased Satan to see a man die and lose his soul from the very side of the Saviour". The awakening of the dying thief had made him realise that he must meet God and the fear of God had entered his heart. This is not in a man unless God puts it there (Rom 3:18). His words, "seeing thou art in the same condemnation", may refer to all three of the crucified, adding force to the words of Isa 53:12 that Christ was "numbered with the transgressors".

41 The admission of his guilt and the agreement with his condemnation is the powerful evidence of true repentance. A right view of himself and his sin was the precursor to a right view of Christ and His work. We know nothing of his background, but he may well have been among the publicans and sinners who had heard the Saviour speak. "This man hath done nothing amiss" should not be limited to the verdict of Pilate that Christ had done nothing deserving of the death penalty. The thief has been speaking of fearing God and receiving from Him the due reward of his deeds, which goes far beyond the Roman law and its penalties.

42 Turning to the Saviour, he addressed Him as Lord. This mighty change in his attitude to Christ came before the hours of darkness, the earthquake, the rent earth and the mighty cry. He took a bleeding, suffering Man on a cross as his Saviour and Lord. His understanding is a wonder to us. The disciples thought it was the end (Matt 26:58). Their hopes of Messiah's kingdom were dashed by the rejection and crucifixion of their Lord. Here is a dying thief who sees every visible evidence that it is the end, yet does not accept the testimony of his eyes but by faith speaks of a glorious future when this rejected and despised Saviour will come into His kingdom of glory and power. Faith is not limited by sight and circumstances.

43 The "verily" was gentle grace on the part of the crucified Lord, spoken to assure a dying man. The answer was very different from what the thief had expected. He looked to a future day of kingdom glory, but the Lord gave him an immediate response with assurance that on that very day he would be with Him in paradise. Cults make a confusion of this verse, so it is necessary to point out that "to day" is linked to "thou shalt be with me", not to "I say unto thee", as if He had said, "I say unto thee today". This strange reading enables those who deny the separation of the soul from the body at death to deceive themselves into thinking that the Lord did not make the promise that the saved thief would be with his Lord in paradise on that very day; but the Lord's promise is unmistakable, "Today thou shalt be with me".

"Paradise" is a Persian word that means a park, or an enclosed garden. It was used by Jews to describe the place where the redeemed go between death and the resurrection. From Ps 16:9-11 and Acts 2:26-28, we believe that the place to which the Lord and the thief went was hades, not the hell of torment, but the place of comfort (16:22), a temporary abode of rest until the Lord was raised from the dead. If Eden was paradise, it was not innocent man that made it, but because the Lord God was there. The presence of the Lord made the place of comfort paradise. Paradise is now above, for He is there (2 Cor 12:1-4). The Puritans said, " 'Today', what promptitude! 'Thou shalt be', what assurance! 'With Me', what company!".

3.   *Noonday Darkness*
      23:44-45

> v.44 "And it was about the sixth hour, and there was a darkness over all the earth until the ninth hour.
> v.45 And the sun was darkened, and the veil of the temple was rent in the midst."

44 If this verse said "the darkness", it would mean the darkness that is known, the darkness of night, or, at the very least, the darkness that was previously mentioned. Luke does not say "the darkness", for it was not an ordinary darkness, nor a darkness ever known by men in the past. We should not rationalise it by talking about an eclipse of the sun, for although the sun was darkened (v.45), it was not naturally, but supernaturally. Darkness results when light is withdrawn, and God chose to withdraw the light from that dreadful scene when God-incarnate hung nailed to a cross. The sixth hour was noon, and the period of the darkness was three hours. It was as the Sin Offering that Christ suffered when there was "darkness over the whole land" (JND). It was impenetrable by angels and men, not because the scene was unholy, but because it was too holy for human eye to behold: "In the place where the burnt offering is killed shall the sin offering be killed before the Lord: it is most holy" (Lev 6:25). All eternity will not exhaust the story of what the holy soul of the Lord Jesus endured in those dark hours on Calvary's cross. Edward Denny wrote:

> "There through Thine hour of deepest woe,
>   Thy suffering Spirit passed;
> Grace there its wondrous victory gained,
>   And Love endured its last."

45   We need not speculate about the extent of the darkness, for the sun failed to give its light, and over "all the land" where it would normally shine there was a darkness.

The rending of the veil that hung between the holy place and the holiest of all in the temple was a tremendous event. It did not merely suffer a tear, but was "rent in the midst". Matthew says it "was rent in twain from the top to the bottom" (27:51). Many descriptions have been given of its weight, strength and thickness, but the truth that was symbolised by the veil is far greater than a physical curtain. The tabernacle and the temple were patterned after a heavenly reality (Heb 9:24). Let us not mistake the earthly picture for that of which it speaks. Sin had shut man out from God, but the suffering of the Saviour in His flesh has opened the way into the very presence of God (Heb 10:20-22). He who suffered on the tree has entered heaven itself and because He is there, we have confidence to draw near within the veil, not the one in the earthly temple, but the heavenly veil.

4.   *The Lord Dismisses His Spirit*
   23:46

v.46   "And when Jesus had cried with a loud voice, he said, Father, into thy hands I commend my spirit: and having said thus, he gave up the ghost."

46   The rending of the veil is preceded in Matthew and Luke by the cry of the Saviour, "My God, my God, why hast thou forsaken me?" (Matt 27:46; Mark 15:34). Luke does not record these words, but tells us that there was a loud cry before He commended (*paratithēmi*) His spirit to the Father and expired (*ekpneō*). The latter one is used also by Mark (15:37) and may best be described as a word of gentle submission. John uses *paradidōmi* which is a word of willing sacrifice; He delivered up His spirit. It is in John that the Son of God said: "No man taketh it from me, but I lay it down of myself" (10:18). Matthew uses *aphiēmi* which is a kingly gesture; He dismissed His spirit. Each Gospel uses language appropriate to its theme.

5.   *Witnesses*
   23:47-49

> v.47 "Now when the centurion saw what was done, he glorified God, saying, Certainly this was a righteous man.
> v.48 And all the people that came together to that sight, beholding the things which were done, smote their breasts, and returned.
> v.49 And all his acquaintance, and the women that followed him from Galilee, stood afar off, beholding these things."

47   Luke sums up in this section the reaction of some of the witnesses. The centurion gave glory to God, not because an innocent man was dying, but because he saw in Christ true righteousness. We must await the day when the saved will be all joined in the Father's house to know with certainty if this man was saved, but it may well be that he saw in Christ his Saviour God. "He glorified (doxazo) God" is an expression that can be traced through this Gospel, but it only once in Mark and four times in Matthew. The nine occurrences in Luke are 2:20; 4:15; 5:25,26; 7:16; 13:13; 17:15; 18:43; 23:47. It occurs twenty-two times in John, but often in John the glory is ascribed to the Son; in Luke, the glory is to God in heaven. The change in the centurion can be compared to the conversion of the thief, both men are demonstrations at the place where the Lord was crucified of the fruit of His work. The thief was a Jew and the centurion a Gentile, giving an example of blessing reaching out to all men from the cross.

   Matthew tells us that he was "watching Jesus" and adds, "and those things which were done" (27:54). He saw a sight that day that he had never seen before and would never see again. It was customary for four soldiers to crucify a victim (John 19:23) because not only did victims curse with rage, but the cruelty of being nailed often made it necessary to forcibly wrestle with a victim and by brute strength hold the arms and legs while another soldier with a hammer drove in the nails. Such sights must have been common, but on this day, the victim offered no resistance; when His hands were held against the wood to be nailed there was no struggle, no drawing back of the hand, but He was "as a lamb led to the slaughter". No wonder the centurion said, "Certainly this was a righteous man" (v.47), "Truly this was the Son of God" (Matt 27:54).

48   The crucifixion was a spectacle that drew a great crowd. This is the meaning of "sight" (*theōria*) that is found only here in the NT. Vine relates it to *theōreo* ("to gaze, to behold"). Luke uses *sumparaginomai* ("that came together") to describe how the people were "standing" to watch the "spectacle". Many of them returned to their homes deeply moved by the submission and gentleness of the silent Sufferer on the middle cross. It would be common for crucifixion victims to curse and revile their executioners and the people who gathered to watch, but this Man suffered in dignity and silence. In a little more than fifty days, they were going to hear the preaching of Peter that the Christ who died had risen from the dead, and 3 000 of them would believe it and be saved. Many have thought that these who beat upon their breasts after having viewed the scene at Calvary were beginning to be convicted and prepared for the preaching they would later hear. To Agrippa, Paul said: "this thing was not done in a corner" (Acts 26:26). How could the witnesses fail to be impressed?

49   The woman from Galilee were there, "beholding these things". There is a difficulty about this in the language of Christ prophetically in Ps 69:20; "I looked for some to take pity, but there was none; and for comforters, but found none". Would these women from Galilee not pity Him, or at the very least desire to comfort Him? The answer to this mystery can be found in the Psalm. The Lord is speaking about the inner sufferings of His holy soul that no human eye could trace and no mind of man could comprehend. Pity and comfort must be based on a knowledge of the nature of the suffering, and none could enter into the depths of His heart sorrow and pain.

VII. The Burial, Resurrection and Ascension of the Lord (23:50-24:53).

1.   *The Burial of the Lord Jesus*
   23:50-56

> v.50 "And, behold, *there* was a man named Joseph, a counsellor; *and he was* a good man, and a just:
> v.51 (The same had not consented to the counsel and deed of them;) *he was* of Arimathaea, a city of the Jews: who also himself waited for the kingdom of God.
> v.52 This *man* went unto Pilate, and begged the body of Jesus.
> v.53 And he took it down, and wrapped it in linen, and laid it in a sepulchre that was hewn in stone, wherein never man before was laid.
> v.54 And that day was the preparation, and the sabbath drew on.
> v.55 and the women also, which came with him from Galilee, followed after, and beheld the sepulchre, and how his body was laid.
> v.56 And they returned, and prepared spices and ointments; and rested the sabbath day according to the commandment."

Luke has contributed his unique part to the story of the burial of Christ. There is great significance in this event. The burial proved that His death was real, and that a physical body was laid in a tomb, and a physical but glorified body arose from the tomb. It fulfilled Scripture with amazing detail and exactness (Ps 16:10; Isa 53:9). It is a picture to believers of our death, burial and resurrection with Him (Rom 6:3). Once we have understood the grave of Christ, the grave of every believer is lit with blessed hope.

50-51   Joseph was a "counsellor", a member of the Sanhedrin, but had not cast his vote with the "all" who had condemned Christ (Luke 22:70); Mark 14:64). The comprehensiveness of the "all" means that he was absent when the vote was taken. Luke is emphatic that the Sanhedrin was guilty of a wrong deed as well as a wrong choice. We know only what we are told there about the place Arimathaea, but Joseph, with his companion, Nicodemus, were described by Isaiah eight centuries earlier (Isa 53:9). He was a believer and a man of great wealth. Luke does not mention the weight of the spices and ointments, but "a mixture of myrrh and aloes, about an hundred pound weight" (John 10:39) would have been sufficient riches for the burial of a king, and only men of great wealth would have been able to provide it.

52   Mark tells us that he "went in boldly unto Pilate" to beg "the body of Jesus" (15:43). It took courage to come out publicly as a supporter of the rejected and crucified Christ. The death of the Saviour caused the disciples to forsake Him, but it caused Joseph to show his love and loyalty.

Stepping in at this moment of great need, Joseph affectionately upset the plans of the Jewish leaders for "they made his grave with the wicked" (Isa 53:9). This implies that all three were to have been buried in a common grave, but no unclean hands were allowed to tamper with the body of the Lord. God, in His infinite wisdom, had man prepared and an undefiled tomb ready. It makes us glad to know that the chief priests, elders and scribes did not have these events in their hands after all. They had used treachery and a traitor at His arrest; they used slander to charge Him; lies to condemn Him; mockery to deny His claim; derision and contempt in rejecting Him, and they used bribery to deny His resurrection, but God had rich men prepared and His enemies did not bury Him.

Joseph requested Pilate to give him the body (*sōma*), but Mark 15:45 tells us that "he gave the corpse (*ptōma*) to Joseph". Some have denied that these two words are significantly different, but *ptōma* is linked to *piptō* ("to fall"), and literally means a thing that has fallen (W.E. Vine), but mary anointed His "body" (*sōma*) for the burial (Matt 26:12). Moulton and Milligan give an illustration from the papyri of *heteron ptōma* being used for the corpse of a stranger. *Ptōma* occurs in Matt 24:28, "For wheresoever the carcase (*ptōma*) is, there will the eagles be gathered together", which is likely a good illustration of its meaning. It is good to see that to Joseph, the body of the Lord Jesus was precious, and not a mere corpse as it was to Pilate.

53   First century nails were long and sharp with rough heads made by hand, each distinct from each other. We are not told how it was done, but in some way the body was taken from the cross, either the nails pulled from the wood or the hands and feet pulled over the heads of the nails. We can be certain that it was done tenderly and with love.

He gently wound the body in a linen cloth, and John adds, "with the spices, as the manner of the Jews is to bury" (John 19:40). The body was not tampered with, or mutilated in any way, as Romans or Greeks would have done, and that fragrant winding was never to know a taint of the decay of death.

The attendants at the funeral numbered about four; no hymn was sung and no sermon preached yet not even king Asa, whose body was laid in a bed "filled with sweet odours and divers kinds of spices prepared by the apothecaries' art" (2 Chron 16:14) had a richer burial. Only by planning beforehand and preparing the materials could Joseph and Nicodemus (John 19:39) have done so much within an hour or two. This is the entire record of the service of Joseph for the Lord, but how needed and appropriate it was, for he was the right man at the right time, and is an example to all who seek to serve the Lord Jesus. It could be said of Mary who beforehand anointed His body for the burial, "she hath done what she could". No greater commendation can ever be earned. Some serve God in a life of seventy years or more and others have a very short service, but if each has fulfilled his course, this is all that matters. Luke begins, "she . . . laid him in a manger" (2:7) and closes, he "laid him in a tomb" (RV). What a story lies between these two statements!

Joseph's tomb was new, "wherein never man before was laid", and it was as much a virgin tomb when the Lord arose as before His body was laid in it. It was rock-hewn, and was Joseph's own tomb (Matt 27:60). The garden tomb was sealed with a great stone and its violation protected by a great seal: "make it as sure as ye can" (Matt 27:65). No aspect of that unique tomb can ever be so important as the fact that it was emptied on the third day.

54-56   There was a need to make haste and complete the burial, for the Sabbath day began at sunset.

These faithful women had followed the Lord and ministered to Him in Galilee and all along that last journey to Jerusalem which takes up such a large portion of Luke's Gospel. They are faithful to the last, following, likely at a distance, the activities of Joseph as he prepared the body and laid it in the tomb. Whether they were aware of the precious ointments that had been wrapped with the windings about the body we do not know, but they returned to their place of abode while in Jerusalem, and "prepared spices and ointments; and rested the sabbath day" intending to use them as soon as the Sabbath had ended. Their intentions were good, and they arrived early on the first day of the week, bringing "the spices which they had prepared" (24:1), but the Lord had risen.

2. *He is Not Here, But is Risen*
   24:1-12

v.1 "Now upon the first *day* of the week, very early in the morning, they came unto the sepulchre, bringing the spices which they had prepared, and certain *others* with them.
v.2 And they found the stone rolled away from the sepulchre.
v.3 And they entered in, and found not the body of the Lord Jesus.
v.4 And it came to pass, as they were much perplexed thereabout, behold, two men stood by them in shining garments:

v.5　And as they were afraid, and bowed down *their* faces to the earth, they said unto them, Why seek ye the living among the dead?

v.6　He is not here, but is risen: remember how he spake unto you when he was yet in Galilee,

v.7　Saying, The Son of man must be delivered into the hands of sinful men, and be crucified, and the third day rise again.

v.8　And they remembered his words,

v.9　And returned from the sepulchre, and told all of these things unto the eleven, and to all the rest.

v.10　It was mary Magdalene, and Joanna, and Mary *the mother* of James, and other *women that were* with them, which told these things unto the apostles.

v.11　And their words seemed to them as idle tales, and they believed them not.

v.12　Then arose Peter, and ran unto the sepulchre; and stooping down, he beheld the linen clothes laid by themselves, and departed, wondering in himself at that which was come to pass."

Each gospel gives its own unique account of the resurrection of the Lord Jesus; we would have missed much without this great chapter in Luke's. The account of the walk to Emmaus is one of the most precious treasures of all that has been recorded.

The resurrection is the most significant event in all the annals of history. Its authenticity rests on facts so convincing that vast numbers of tough-minded sceptics have been brought from unbelief to faith through examination of the evidence. The witnesses were willing to suffer for the truth of their testimony and many endured lashings, dungeons and death. It transformed their lives, brought frightened, discouraged, thoroughly-beaten men from dark doubt to powerful conviction. It caused them to preach with such power that "The Lord is risen indeed" (v.34) that they "turned the world upside down" (Acts 17:6) and pointed many thousands to the living Christ.

No truth of the Bible has greater meaning. Paul wrote, "if Christ be not risen, then is our preaching vain, and your faith is also vain. Yea, and we are found false witnesses of God . . . ye are yet in your sins . . . they also which are fallen asleep in Christ are perished . . . we are of all men most miserable. But now is Christ risen from the dead" (1 Cor 15:14-20).

Luke 24 has often been described as the chapter of opened things:

1. The opened tomb　　　　　　v.2　Resurrection
2. The opened Scriptures　　　　v.27 Communication
3. The opened eyes　　　　　　v.31 Illumination
4. The opened wounds　　　　　v.39 Revelation
5. The opened understanding　　v.45 Comprehension
6. The opened heaven　　　　　v.51 Ascension
7. The opened mouths　　　　　v.53 Appreciation.

1　The writers of the four gospels have given individual, unique testimony to the empty tomb and the risen Lord. A careful comparison of the accounts will show significant distinctions, but nothing contradictory. There is important evidence in this that the writers made no attempt to copy each other or even to harmonise their records. All agree that the women came first to the tomb, very early in the morning on the first day of week. They brought "the spices which they had prepared", intending to apply them to the body in the tomb. The devotion and faithfulness of these dear women was honoured by God in that the Lord appeared first to them. The earlier anointing of His body by Mary of Bethany, recorded by Matthew, Mark and John, is now seen in a greater light than ever. The Lord said, "she did it for my burial" (Matt 26:12), and she was in time to do it, whereas these dear women, in spite of a right heart, came at the wrong time.

The time of their coming is carefully accounted: "Very early in the morning" is the translation of *orthrou batheōs*, literally "at deep dawn". Deep dawn conveys the thought of "the first signs of dawn" (Phps), or "in the dim light of dawn (E.V. Rieu). This very early hour is important when we consider all of the events of this most blessed "first day of the week". John says, Mary Magdalene came "early, when it was yet dark, unto the sepulchre" and these women came at the earliest signs of the dawn.

2   Mark tells us that on the way to the tomb the women were perplexed about how they could anoint His body, for the stone was so great that they could not move it (16:1-4). We learn that it must be "rolled away" (Mark 16:4), "taken away" (John 20:1) and "rolled back" (Matt 28:2). The usual practice was to prepare the tomb so that the door could be covered by rolling a great stone down a slope to be locked in place in a slot prepared for it. Once in place its removal would be very difficult. When the women arrived at the site the stone had already been rolled away. Matthew tells us, "the angel of the Lord descended from heaven, and came and rolled back the stone from the door" (28:2). All the Gospels tell of the stone rolled away, but only Matthew says that the angel "sat upon it", a position that denotes victory over death and authority that supersedes the authority of Rome by which the tomb was sealed.

3   The unanimous testimony of these women, along with John, Peter and Mary Magdalene was that the tomb was empty: they "found not the body of the Lord Jesus"; note "the body of the Lord Jesus" rather than "the body of Jesus" (23:52), for "God hath made that same Jesus, whom ye have crucified, both Lord and Christ" (Acts 2:36). Throughout his Gospel, Luke has carefully described "physical reality" (W. Liefield). He alone tells us that the Spirit descended "in bodily form" (*sōmatikos*) upon Jesus at His baptism, and he alone says they "found not the body (*sōma*) of the Lord Jesus".

4-5   The empty tomb produced perplexity, for the thought of a risen Christ did not dawn on their minds. The sudden appearance of the two men (angels) in shining garments terrified them and caused them to bow down their faces to the earth in fear and wonder. In the question, "Why seek ye the loving one among the dead?" (JND), we are reminded of the words of the glorified Christ to John, "I am . . . the living one: and I became dead, and behold, I am living to the ages of ages" (Rev 1:18 JND). The cause of the fear of the women is not difficult to find. Luke uses *astraptō* "(shining") as he did in 17:24. It means "lightning", and Matthew, who mentions one angel, says, "And for fear of him the keepers did shake and became as dead men". The expression "bowed down" (*klino*) is used by Luke in the statement "the Son of man hath not where to lay his head" (9:58). In this chapter, it is used again in v.29, "the day is far spent". The complete statement "bowed down their faces to the earth" is to be taken literally. The "keepers" became as dead men, and the women lay with their faces on the ground and were in terror (*emphobos*) which is here translated "afraid" and in v.37, "affrighted" (see comment).

6   "He is not here, but is risen" is a foundation truth upon which all our hope rests. Some of the results of His resurrection are: the declaration of His Sonship, "declared to be the Son of God with power . . . by the resurrection from the dead" (Rom 1:4); the verification of prophecy, "he rose again the third day according to the scriptures" (1 Cor 15:4); the proof of Christ's victory over Satan, "that through death he might destroy him that had the power of death, that is, the devil" (Heb 2:14); the evidence of the power of God, "according to the working of his mighty power, which he wrought in Christ, when he raised him from the dead" (Eph 1:19,20); the ratification of our justification, "who was delivered for our offences, and was raised again for our justification" (Rom 4:25); the guarantee of the resurrection of believers, "But now is Christ risen from the dead, and become the firstfruits (actually the word is singular) of them that slept" (1 Cor 15:20), and the assurance that none of His promises will fail, "remember how he spake unto you".

7-8   The verb that is here translated "delivered" (*paradidōmi*, to deliver over) is used in 22:4,6,21,22 and 48 for the betrayal of Judas. In predicting His death, the Lord said, "the Son of man shall be delivered into the hands of men" (9:44), and "delivered unto the Gentiles" (18:32), and Pilate "delivered Jesus to their will" (23:25), but this statement of the angels contains the added truth, "The Son of man must be delivered into the hands of sinful men". Luke frequently records these statements of necessity and their study is a rich source of truth. As a boy, Jesus said, "I must be about my Father's business" (2:49); in His ministry, He said, "I must preach the kingdom of God" (4:43); regarding His death, He said, "I must preach the kingdom of God" (4:43); regarding His death, He said, "The Son of man must suffer" (9:22; 17:25); referring to the prophecies of the suffering Servant in Isaiah, He said, "this that is written must (yet) be accomplished in me" (22:37), and in ch.24, "Ought not Christ to have suffered" (v.46). Acts 17:3 uses similar language, "Christ must needs have suffered". These necessities were decided in the counsels that took place before the world began (1 Pet 1:20), so the angels' statement is a summary of the divine plan of redemption. All of this was necessary to accomplish the will of God, to fulfil the prophecies of the OT and the predictions of Christ in the NT, and to provide salvation for fallen sinners such as we.

Related to His rising on the third day is the Feast of Firstfruits (Lev 23:9-14), when the sheaf was waved before the Lord on "the morrow after the sabbath" (v.11). The Lord had spoken clearly about the third day (Matt 16:21; 17:23; 20:19; Mark 9:31; Luke 18:33; John 2:19), "And they remembered his words".

9-11   The news of the empty tomb and the message of the angels was faithfully carried by those faithful women. They may have found the eleven together, or they may have come together as a result of the message of Mary Magdalene and the other women (John 20:19). The message seemed to them as "an idle tale" (JND) and met with total unbelief. They were not prepared for such an event in spite of all that the Lord had said about it. This is not admirable, but it adds value to their later testimony to a living Lord.

In Mark's record of this event, he wrote, Mary Magdalene "went and told them that had been with him" but they "believed not" (Mark 16:10,11). The Holy Spirit has recorded the names of these noble women, giving them due honour, for they were trustworthy, so the unbelief of the apostolic band stands out sharply in contrast. It is only here that "idle talk" (*lēros*) occurs, so we cannot compare it with any other passage. "Medical writers used it for the wild talk of those in delirium or hysteria" (A.T. Robertson). Multon and Milligan draw examples from the papyri to show that it means, "talking nonsense". Seeing the first witnesses to the resurrection met such a response from those who had walked and talked with the Lord, we should not be too surprised that as Paul preached the resurrection, Fergus said "with a loud voice, Thou art mad, Paul" (Acts 26:24 JND), nor should we be surprised at the response of unbelievers, for they are spiritually blind. These women gave personal testimony to the resurrection, but when it was a matter of public testimony, Paul lists the witnesses beginning with Peter (1 Cor 15:5). The witnesses here were all women even though in the phrase "other women that were with them" there is no word for "women", but *loipai sun autais* ("the rest with them") are feminine words and do mean "women".

12   John gives a much fuller account of Peter's run to the tomb and the miracle of the wrappings from which the body had risen. Peter had great cause for wonder in what he saw (John 20:3-10), for nothing but a mighty miracle from God could have left the grave clothes wrapped as they had been around His body, untorn and yet empty. The "stooping down" (*parakuptō*) is a beautiful expression and is used in an identical way in John 20:5,11. This word has drawn such attention because it is used by James for the man who "looketh into the perfect law of liberty" (1:25), meaning that he stoops down to look in. Just as touching is its use by Peter as he writes of our salvation, "which things the angels desire (stoop down and) look into" (1 Pet 1:12).

This verse is omitted from the Nestle text, because it was rejected by Westcott and Hort, relying so dominantly on the so-called "Western text", so it is not found in the RSV nor NEB translations, but Darby includes it without a comment and it is in the RV with a note. It should be accepted as authentic; it is fully verified by John 20:6-7. A student who wishes to pursue this kind of investigation will find a conservative and well balanced treatment in such works as *The Byzantine Text-type and New Testament Criticism* by H.A. Sturz, Thomas Nelson Pub. 1984.

Notes

Resurrection Appearances

1. Mary Magdalene is closely related to the resurrection and was the first to see the risen Lord (Mark 16:9; John 20:11-18).
2. The other women, who were went to carry the message to the eleven, saw Him as they went (Matt 28:9).
3. He appeared to the two travellers bound for Emmaus (vv.13-32).
4. Peter saw Him in a private appearing (v.34; 1 Cor 15:5).
5. He stood in the midst of the eleven in the upper room (vv.36-49; John 20:19-23).
6. After eight days He again appeared in the midst of the disciples when Thomas was present (John 20:26-29).
7. He appeared to the disciples by the sea of Tiberias (John 21:1-25).
8. He appeared to 500 brethren at one time (1 Cor 15:6).
9. Paul records an appearance to James (1 Cor 15:7).
10. Matthew and Mark tell of His appearance to the eleven in a mountain in Galilee (Matt 28:16-20; Mark 16:15-18) when He gave them the great commission.
11. There was another appearance in Jerusalem at the close of the forty days, when He led them out as far as Bethany and ascended from their midst (24:50-53; Acts 1:3-12).
12. He appeared to Saul on the Damascus Road (Acts 9:3-8).

This does not exhaust the number of His appearances to the witnesses of His resurrection, but these are given in an order that seems to be in accordance with the accounts.

3.   The Road to Emmaus
24:13-35

v.13 "And, behold, two of them went that same day to a village called Emmaus, which was from Jerusalem *about* threescore furlongs.

v.14 And they talked together of all these things which had happened.

v.15 And it came to pass, that, while they communed *together* and reasoned, Jesus himself drew near, and went with them.

v.16 But their eyes were holden that they should not know him.

v.17 And he said unto them, What manner of communications *are* these that ye have one to another, as ye walk, and are sad?

v.18 And the one of them, whose name was Cleopas, answering said unto him, Art thou only a stranger in Jerusalem, and hast not known the things which are come to pass there in these days?

v.19 And he said unto them, What things? And they said unto him, Concerning Jesus of Nazareth, which was a prophet mighty in deed and word before God and all the people:

v.20 And how the chief priests and our rulers delivered him to be condemned to death, and have crucified him.

v.21 But we trusted that it had been he which should have redeemed Israel: and beside all this, to day is the third day since these things were done.

v.22 Yea, and certain women also of our company made us astonished, which were early at the sepulchre;

v.23 And when they found not his body, they came, saying, that they had also seen a vision of angels, which said that he was alive.

v.24 And certain of them which were with us went to the sepulchre, and found it even so as the women had said: but him they saw not.

v.25 Then he said unto them, O fools, and slow of heart to believe all that the prophets have spoken:

v.26 Ought not Christ to have suffered these things, and eo enter into his glory?

v.27 And beginning at Moses and all the prophets, he expounded unto them in all the scriptures the things concerning himself.

v.28 And they drew nigh unto the village, whither they went: and he made as though he would have gone further.

v.29 But they constrained him, saying, Abide with us: for it is toward evening, and the day is far spent. And he went in to tarry with them.

v.30 And it came to pass, as he sat at meat with them, he took bread, and blessed it, and brake, and gave to them.

v.31 And their eyes were opened, and they knew him; and he vanished out of their sight.

v.32 And they said one to another, Did not our heart burn within us, while he talked with us by the way, and while he opened to us the scriptures?

v.33 And they rose up the same hour, and returned to Jerusalem, and found the eleven gathered together, and them that were with them,

v.34 Saying, The Lord is risen indeed, and hath appeared to Simon.

v.35 And they told what things were done in the way, and how he was known of them in breaking of bread."

This tender account allows us to feel with the disciples some of the dismay that clouded their minds and the sorrow that filled their hearts at what, to them, was the terrible tragedy of the crucifixion. No other account could be more convincing, and no experience so assuring.

13   The first two words of this verse, "And, behold" (*kai idou*) are used to introduce a completely new phase of the narrative. It is not a new subject, for "that same day" ties it into all the events of the resurrection day. The number "two" is also significant, for a twofold witness was necessary in Jewish law (Deut 17:6; 19:15) and the NT also calls for two witnesses (Matt 18:16; Luke 10:1; 2 Cor 13:1; Acts 19:22; 1 Tim 5:19). Two witnesses, Simeon and Anna had borne witness to His birth (2:25 and 36) and these two travellers are to bear witness to His resurrection. It is not until we get to v.18 that any name is given and then it is Cleopas (Kleopas), a name unknown to us from any other part of the NT. It is not likely that he is the same man as the Cleophas (Klōpa) of John 19:25.

"Two of them" refers back to v.11, where the company of the disciples were unbelieving, so we know they belonged to the company who followed the Lord, but were not of the eleven. Their statements indicate a very close association with the events and the hopes of the believing remnant. They said, "We trusted that it had been he which should have redeemed Israel" (v.21), and "certain women of our company . . ." (v.22), "And certain of them which were with us . . ." (v.24). It has often been suggested that this was a man and his wife, mainly from the statement, "Did not our heart burn within us . . ." It is good to think of a man and his wife having one heart, but this is not conclusive, for regarding the Lord Jesus all true believers have one heart. One thing we do know, this journey took place on the very day of the resurrection. Emmaus was sixty stadia from Jerusalem, approximately seven and a half English miles.

14   Their conversation was about the Lord Jesus, His rejection, suffering, death, burial and the report of the women that contended that He was alive. In this verse and the next one "talked together" and "communed together" are the translation of *homileō* which is used only by Luke in the NT and occurs four times. Vine says it "signifies to be in company, as associate". At Troas, Paul "talked a long while, even till break of day" (Acts 20:11) and Felix often sent for Paul "and communed with him" (Acts 24:26). The LXX uses this word in Dan 1:19, "And the king communed with them", describing the conversations between Nebuchadnezzar and the wise men of Babylon among whom Daniel and his companions excelled. Moulton and Milligan say the original meaning is "to assemble together". In 1 Cor 15:33, Paul writes, "Evil communications (*homilia*) corrupt good manners", a word only used in this verse that is akin to *homileō* The two disciples had holy communications, a conversation into which the Lord Jesus could enter and change its outlook, but not its subject. A solemn word of warning is suitable to our hearts. What are the subjects of our frequent and long conversations?

15   The discussion occupied them fully as they conversed with each other, when a fellow Traveller joined them on the road. "Jesus himself drew near, and went with them" has been the blessed experience of many weary and heart-sore travellers. "Drew near" probably signifies that He overtook them on the way. In Matt 28:9, the women departed quickly from the sepulchre while in their hearts mingled "fear and joy" and "behold, Jesus met them"; *apantaō* ("to meet") in its seven occurrences in the NT and is usually used for a gradual approach such as would be the case when one walker overtakes another. To have risen Lord as a Companion of the road is a blessing beyond human language.

16   God's purpose in withholding them from recognising Him at this point was that they might have a greater recognition of Him later. Unbelief blinds eyes and it must have been an ingredient of their inability to recognise Him; yet their experience was according to divine grace and mercy. The verb *krateo* ("to be holden") normally means "to be strong" or "to prevail" and frequently is rendered "to take hold" (W.E. Vine). In this case it is used in the sense of "restraint". It is used in this way in Rev 7:1 where four angels restrain "the four winds of the earth". It is used in Acts 2:24 by Peter as he preached the resurrection, "whom God raised up, having loosed the pains of death; because if is not possible that he should be holden (*krateô*) of it". The eyes of these two disciples were "holden" so that they failed to recognise Him, but the power that held them is not named. Mary Magdalene had a similar experience (John 20:14); "the disciples knew not that it was Jesus" (John 21:4); and in this chapter, "while they believed not for joy, and wondered . . ." (v.41). We should be careful not to think that these are equal events because the causes of the failure may have been different. Whatever the cause in this case, God used this present blindness to enhance the joy of the moment when their eyes were opened. In this need to wait we have one of the greatest mysteries of life from our viewpoint, but we have often learned that when it is required that we wait, the blessing is all the greater when it is given.

17   The question of the Lord, "What discourses are these which pass between you?" (JND) stopped them. "They stood still, looking sad" (RV). Luke used *antiballô* to describe the exchange of words between the two travellers. This is the only occurrence of this word in the NT. It literally means "to throw back and forth".

They were "sad"; *skuthropos* is only here and in Matt 6:16 of the "sad countenance" through which hypocrites sought to deceive others. The sadness of these two was most genuine, and the question so surprised them that they stood still. The word in the text is *estathêsan*, the aorist passive of *histêmi*, but it is not translated in the AV. Other readings are: "they stood still, looking sad" (NASB); "they stopped, looking downcast" (Mft); "they halted, their faces full of gloom" (NEB), and "they stopped, their faces drawn with misery" (Phps).

18   This is the only mention of Cleopas by name in the NT. These two disciples were unknown so far as the records go; yet their doubts and perplexity were fully known to the Lord Jesus and He was able and ready to meet their hearts' deepest needs. The word "stranger" in the question is "sojourner", one who has a temporary dwelling, or a visitor to Jerusalem. Surely if He lived there, He would know all that had happened in these recent days.

19   Without answering the question about His residence in Jerusalem or giving any information, He asked them to explain what things they were talking about. They called the Lord Jesus a prophet, but One whose deeds and words were "mighty" before both God and the people. They had seen His deeds and heard His words, and were giving personal witness to their power. In the expression "a prophet mighty in deed and word before God and all the people", there is the language of Deut 18:18-22 where the coming Prophet was to be "raised up among their brethren" who truly would be mighty in word and deed. In this statement they used a word that is only found in Luke's writings, *enantion* ("before") is made up of *en* ("in") and *anti* ("against"). It has the meaning here and in its three other occurrences, "in the presence of" or "in the sight of" (Luke 20:26). God gave Abraham "favour and wisdom in the sight of Pharaoh" (Acts 7:10) and it is used of Christ, "like a lamb dumb before his shearer" (Acts 8:32). It is touching that in their misery, the two are stating their faith that Christ was not only mighty before men, but "before" God. Like Peter, they had lost the joy of their hope, but not their faith.

20   It is important that they did not charge the Romans with His crucifixion, but directly placed the blame on "the chief priests and our rulers" who "delivered him to be condemned to death, and have crucified him". The guilt of the leaders of Israel added much grief to the sorrow of the disciples. It is true that crucifixion was an act of the Romans, but they placed the greatest blame on those who had the greatest light, which is where God places it. In some sense, they too felt the shame of the guilt, for they said, "our rulers".

21   "We trusted" is better translated "we were hoping" (literally). This use of the imperfect tense with a verb of wishing indicates hopelessness because the desire can never be realised. The death of the Lord Jesus had shattered their hopes that the Kinsman Redeemer had come to buy back Israel's lost inheritance. They knew a price must be paid for such a redemption, but they had no understanding that the shame and suffering of the cross was that price. The mention by them that "to day is the third day since these things were done" is the introduction to the explanation of their perplexity over the empty tomb.

Some have tried to interpret this verse as if the two speakers fully understood redemption and their hope was that Christ was the One who would deliver Israel by paying the ransom with His life's blood. It is true that the word "redeem" (*lutroō*) is the same beautiful word that occurs in Titus 2:14 and 1 Pet 1:18, but it is a mistake to suppose that these disciples understood it in this way. They used it for a natural and temporal deliverance from the bondage of Israel under the Roman yoke, whereas Titus and 1 Peter view it as a spiritual and eternal deliverance from the thraldom of sin.

22-24   The experience of the women at the tomb, the message of the angels and the inspection of the tomb by Peter and John are all recounted. Earlier Luke had spoken only of Peter going to the tomb (v.12), but here they tell of at least two who went, "but him they saw not". These two disciples left Jerusalem after having heard the report of Peter and John that the tomb was empty, so the Lord's appearances to the women and Peter were unknown to them.

Luke employs *orthrinos* ("early") which is akin to *orthros* that was combined with *bathus* in v.1 to mean, "at early dawn". Vine comments that *orthrinai* is literally "early ones". Peter and John left the empty tomb pondering on its meaning and returned to Jerusalem. By the time the two disciples on the road to Emmaus had returned to Jerusalem, Peter had seen the Lord (v.34). When, where and how we are not told, but this silence manifests the grace of the Lord to Peter. There are experiences with the Lord that are completely intimate and are not to be told in detail in public testimony. At the private meeting with the Lord he had denied, we have no doubt that Peter shed many more of the tears that must have blinded his eyes when he left the high priest's palace (22:62).

25 The rebuke of the Lord was spoken with tender love and compassion. He chided them for slowness of heart to believe all that the prophets had spoken. "O foolish *men*", as the RV reads, is not as conclusive as some think. Such a form of address would also have been made if the couple were a man and his wife. We can identify only Cleopas as a man, not his companion. They should have known the necessity of the sufferings of Christ from the great utterances of Isaiah, David and other prophets. Slow hearts are a spiritual malady; these need radical treatment that only the Lord Himself can administer. How well He treated these slow hearts!

26 "Ought not the Christ to have suffered" (JND) means, was it not necessary? Paul used this language in Thessalonica, "Christ must needs have suffered, and risen again from the dead" (Acts 17:3) and to Agrippa, "that Christ should suffer, and that he should be the first that should rise from the dead" (Acts 26:23). The words of the Lord contain in summary the great truth that the way to the glory was by the cross. It had not penetrated the minds and hearts of His disciples. Peter surely learned it, and it became the theme of his Epistle, "the sufferings of Christ, and the glory that should follow" (1 Pet 1:11). To trace Luke's frequent use of the things that "must" happen, refer to the Scriptures that are part of the comment on vv.7-8. We should not miss the point that the first communication made to the hearts of these disciples was the meaning of His suffering. Unless the cross is rightly understood, nothing else can be clear.

27 "Moses and all the prophets" can mean the entire OT, but when this phrase is accompanied by "all the scriptures" then we know that Moses was the starting place of a systematic searching of all the Scriptures of "the things concerning himself". There has never been a believer who has read these words who has not found in his heart a great yearning to have been present at such an unfolding. Yet, we have the Holy Spirit, who "shall take of mine, and show it unto you" (John 16:15). This verse gives us authority to believe that in all the Scriptures there are prophecies, promises, types, shadows and illustrations of the Lord Jesus.

In Pisidian Antioch, Paul preached, "And though they found no cause of death in him, yet desired they Pilate that he should be slain. And when they had fulfilled all that was written of him, they took him down from the tree, and laid him in a sepulchre. But God raised him from the dead: And he was seen many days of them which came up with him from Galilee to Jerusalem" (Acts 13:28-31). There is a link between the two expressions, "in all the Scriptures the things concerning himself" and "all that was written of him". The second clause is limited by its context, but the first is unlimited. In great summaries of truth, such as Paul's preaching and in a far greater degree in the discourse of the Lord from "all the scriptures" there is truth to nourish the heart and fill the mind for many days. As an example, consider the words "in him . . . took him . . . laid him . . . raised him . . . with him" in the three verses from Acts 13, and there are at least three parties referred to by the pronoun "they" in these verses. How many precious things must have been spoken to the two travellers!

28-29   Emmaus was at hand. How quickly the time must have passed as the blessed Lord Jesus revealed to these sorrowing hearts the wonder of the word of God that gave so much testimony to Himself! He would have gone on and left them at this point, for He acted as if He was about to continue the journey. They strongly prevailed on Him to remain with them that evening, for the day was already "far spent". Perhaps this is an indication of a man and his wife, for this was their home and the Lord went in to remain with them.

These verses contain three of Luke's rare words. "He made as though" (*prospoieomai*) is only here in the NT, but two examples from the LXX are given by Vine, 1 Sam 21:13 "feigned", and Job 19:14, "not acknowledged". When the Lord Jesus did not acknowledge their invitation to spend the night, their urging was very strong. To express it, Luke uses *parabiazomai* ("to constrain"). It is only used elsewhere in Acts 16:15 to describe the entreaty to Paul and his companions by Lydia to come into her house after she was saved. Vine says it means "to employ force contrary to nature and right". Moulton and Milligan give the meaning "to urge or press against nature or law". The other uncommon word is *hespera*, "evening", which occurs only three times and is translated "eventide" in Acts 4:3, and is in the phrase "from morning until evening" (Acts 28:23). The English "vesper" is derived from it. These paint a vivid picture: it was late in the evening, the Companion of the way who had caused their hearts to burn is about to leave them, and they exceed the bounds of any ordinary invitation to urge Him to stay. We can well understand their fervour.

30   It would be normal for the host to give thanks and break the bread at the commencement of a meal. On this occasion, the Guest took the bread into His hands and broke it and handed it to them. Luke again uses *kataklinō* ("sat at meat") which is also found in 7:36 (some texts); 9:14,15 and 14:8 and although it means "to recline" is only used in connection with meals and only by Luke. He also uses *anapiptō* ("to fall backward, to recline for a meal") in 14:10; 17:7, and

22:14. Another word, *anaklino* ("to lay, to sit") is used in 2:7 for the action of Mary in laying the infant Christ in the manger, also in 12:37; 13:39. These three words are fairly close synonyms, but have different shades of meaning. To recline was the usual position taken at a meal, as was stated in the comment on the Passover (22:14), with one elbow on the table and the head resting on the hand.

31 Nail-pierced hands broke the bread, but the opening of their eyes was a divine act. Up to then they "were holden", but now "they were opened", and they looked with wonder on the face of the Lord. There can be no doubt that the print of the nails served to identify Him further as the crucified and risen One. Perhaps it is significant that we are not told that he departed, but became invisible (*aphantos*) to their sight. The verb, "to render unseen" (*aphanizo*) is found in such verses as James 4:14, "vanisheth away". The adjective, *aphantos*, is used here, and this is its only occurrence in the NT. Vine says that Luke used it "with *ginomai*, (to become) and followed it with *apo* (from)" so "he became invisible from them". How blessed to see Him! How infinitely blessed when He is revealed to us and how good to know that even when we cannot see Him with our natural eyes, He is still present at the breaking of bread or whenever two or three are gathered in His name (Matt 18:20)!

32 Their "heart" (singular) burned within them when He talked with them and opened to them the meaning of the Scriptures. The Expositor was Himself the Key to the Scriptures (2 Cor 3:12-14), so the truth opened to them was the most precious that is contained in the word of God, "the things concerning himself". The verb that is used in the passive voice in v.31, *dianoigo* ("to open"), is used in this verse in the active voice ("he opened"). Except for Mark 7:34,35, this verb is only found in Luke and Acts. Vine gives its meaning as "to open up completely". The other occurrences are 2:23; when Stephen saw "the heavens opened" (Acts 7:56); the opening of Lydia's heart (Acts 16:14); the opening of the Scriptures (Acts 17:3), and v.45 of this chapter when the risen Lord "opened . . . their understanding".

33 All thoughts of weariness and a night's sleep have left them. They "rose up the same hour" and returned to Jerusalem. The breaking of the bread was only the commencement of a meal, so it appears that they did not finish it. Their thoughts were on the same One who had filled their minds before the Lord drew near on the journey out, but how different were their thoughts on the return. They found the eleven gathered together with other disciples present. Each time we read of the eleven we are reminded of the twelfth, who had been a traitor.

The perfect passive participle of *athroizo* ("to gather, to collect") is used to describe the gathering together of the eleven. This is the only occurrence of this verb in the NT. It can be compared to Luke's use of *sunathroizo* in the active

voice ("to gather together"), or "gathered together" (Acts 19:25 AV), and the use
of the same verb in the passive voice in Acts 12:12, "were gathered together". It
is only used in these two passages, but *epathroizō* ("to assemble besides", W.E.
Vine) is found one time in 11:29. The use of the same root here, in the passive
voice, is of great interest. We are not told what agent or power assembled them
together. Without question, the testimony of the women and Peter, who had
already seen the risen Christ were factors in their being "gathered together", but
whatever physical elements were involved, we are very certain that there was
also the superintendence of the Holy Spirit. A comparison should be made with
Matt 18:20 where *sunagō* ("gathered together") is used, but it is also in the passive
voice, "having been assembled".

34   Unbelief on the part of the gathered disciples has been replaced with joy
and wonder. The Lord's appearing to Peter is recorded only here and in 1 Cor
15:5, where he is the first public witness to the resurrection. After the three
denials, the bitter weeping and the conversion of which the Lord had spoken,
we can be certain that what transpired in His appearing to Peter was between
Peter and his Lord. Peter could speak the words of David from blessed experience,
"He restoreth my soul". The silence about this meeting manifests the grace of
the Lord to him. There are experiences with the Lord that are completely intimate
and are not to be told in detail in public testimony. It is enough to know that
Peter had the private meeting and all was right between him and the Lord he had
denied.

35   The testimony of the two travellers was about their experience by the way,
and "how he was known of them in breaking of bread". We cannot have their
experience of His visible presence until we see Him in glory, but we surely can
know the spiritual power of their experience when we break bread in
remembrance of Him. How many times He has drawn near and made Himself
known to us as we have sat around Himself at the breaking of bread! It has been
the nearest place to heaven we have ever known in the world. We cannot be
accused of over applying this experience when it is considered that only in this
verse and in Acts 2:42 is *klasis* ("a breaking") found in the NT.

4.   *The Lord in the Midst of His Own*
24:36-45

v.36 "And as they thus spake, Jesus himself stood in the midst of them, and saith
unto them, Peace *be* unto you.

v.37 But they were terrified and affrighted, and supposed that they had seen a spirit.

v.38 And he said unto them, Why are ye troubled? and why do thoughts arise in your
hearts?

v.39 Behold my hands and my feet, that it is I myself: handle me, and see; for a spirit
hath not flesh and bones, as ye see me have.

> v.40 And when he had thus spoken, he shewed them *his* hands and *his* feet.
> v.41 And while they yet believed not for joy, and wondered, he said unto them, Have ye here any meat?
> v.42 And they gave him a piece of a broiled fish, and of an honeycomb.
> v.43 And he took *it*, and did eat before them.
> v.44 And he said unto them, These are the words which I spake unto you, while I was yet with you, that all things must be fulfilled, which were written in the law of Moses, and *in* the prophets, and *in* the psalms, concerning me.
> v.45 Then opened he their understanding, that they might understand the scriptures,"

36-38 The two were still speaking when "Jesus himself stood in the midst of them". Knowing their hearts, He spoke words of peace to them. Such words were needed for they were afraid at His presence, supposing "that they had seen a spirit". They had just testified, "The Lord is risen indeed", but as yet only Peter of the eleven had actually seen Him. He stepped into the midst of them, appearing suddenly, so their fear can be understood. They had become comfortable in the presence of the lowly Jesus, but let us not forget that now He stands in a glorified body. He had not yet manifested His radiance, or like Saul they would have been blind (Acts 22:11), or like John they would have fallen before Him as dead ones (Rev 1:17); but glory was displayed in Him, and they were made to know "the terror of the Lord". He knew their fear, for they must have shown it, but He also knew the thoughts of their hearts.

The two words of v.37, "terrified" (*ptoeō*) and "affrighted" (*emphobos*) are rare words in the NT. *Ptoeō* is found only here and in the Lord's words to the disciples: "But when ye shall hear of wars and commotions, be not terrified" (21:9). *Emphobos* ("affrighted") is used five times: in Luke 24:5,37 and Acts 10:4; 22:9; 24:25. There is one other occurrence in Rev 11:13, where it is used to describe the fear that accompanied the great earthquake that slew 7000 people in Jerusalem. It is not easy to find authoritative statements about the distinction between the two words, but *ptoeō* seems to mean to be suddenly startled or "astonished" (24:22) and *emphobos* to continue in a state of fear.

39-40 These verses reveal much about the resurrection body of the Lord Jesus. His hands and feet still showed the print of the nails, and He was more than spirit, so much more than the vision they supposed they were seeing. He had a body of flesh and bones. The absence of blood in this description is significant; it was shed fully on the cross. Showing them His hands and His feet through Galilee and to Calvary. John mentions His hands and His side (20:20) in the gospel that emphasises the love of His tender heart and was written by the man who rested on His breast at supper. They were invited to handle Him, for He is real. His resurrection body of glory is tangible and touchable.

41 Such a revelation of Himself filled their hearts with wonder and joy so intense that they were still hindered in fully grasping the truth that He was the same blessed Lord whom they had known and loved, and had followed for so long. This wonder and failure to grasp the truth of the resurrection completely does away with the strange lie of the unbeliever that the disciples imagined that Christ would fulfil their will and rise from the dead. They had never even thought of His coming back to them from the dead in a body of flesh and bones, and their incredulity is the powerful proof of it.

42-43 The evidence was already in the category of "infallible proofs", but in grace He gives them more, asking for a piece of broiled fish and a piece of honeycomb and eating before their eyes. Nothing could be more plain or more common than a living man eating a piece of fish. It was for their sakes, not to meet any need of His, but a greater evidence of being alive from the dead could not be conceived. This is the only occurrence of *brōsimos* ("meat", v.41) in the NT. It simply means "edible food", "anything to eat" (JND). It is also only in v.42 that *optos* ("broiled") occurs. It "is said of food that is prepared by fire" (W.E. Vine). These plain words about edible food that has been roasted with fire help us to understand the reality of the body of the risen Christ.

44 He referred to His life on earth as a past event, "while I was yet with you", and then reminded them that all that had happened to Him He had told them beforehand. The cross and His sufferings were not a hindrance to His work, but the very means by which it had been accomplished. He then directed them to the Scriptures which would be their stay during all the time of His absence until He returned. What gentle grace from the living Lord to point them to Moses, the Prophets and the Psalms that "must be fulfilled" in His life, death, burial and resurrection. This is the only place in the NT where this threefold division of the OT is specifically mentioned.

45 This opening of their understanding must have been a flood of light into the darkness of their minds. Training from childhood had to be corrected, for their teachers' interpretations of the coming of Messiah had been in error. Such misconceptions die slowly, but in the end it took a divine revelation to give them understanding of the correct meaning of the Scriptures concerning Him.

The verb that is used in the passive voice in v.31, *dianoigō* ("were opened"), and in v.32 in the active voice ("he opened") is again used here as a present infinitive. Its meaning "to open up completely" is well exemplified in this chapter (see introduction to chapter). "Understand" (*suniēmi*) originally meant "to bring together". Vine writes of "uniting (*sun*) . . . the perception with what is perceived". Even eyewitnesses to events may not be accurate in describing what they saw. Accompanying the sight must be an intelligent understanding of what is happening. In the case of the disciples, there was the added problem that their minds were closed to the true purpose of the first advent. To open their understanding at this point was not to give them a single flash of light, but a constant beam that opened their minds to so many Scriptures which previously had been dark to them. This illumination continued and is a present activity of the Holy Spirit, for "we have received . . . the spirit which is of God; that we might know the . . . words . . . which the Holy Ghost teacheth, comparing spiritual things with spiritual" (1 Cor 1:12-13). Christ Himself was the Key to understanding Scripture.

5.   *Ye are Witnesses*
24:46-48

> v.46 "And said unto them, Thus it is written, and thus it behoved Christ to suffer, and to rise from the dead the third day:
> v.47 And that repentance and remission of sins should be preached in his name among all nations, beginning at Jerusalem.
> v.48 And ye are witnesses of these things."

46-47   The suffering and death of Christ were a great necessity if repentance was to be granted to men and forgiveness offered. The resurrection the third day is the evidence of the value of the work accomplished by the suffering and death of the Saviour. Those who have claimed that Luke does not preach the value of the atonement have obviously missed this plain statement. It is true that in the Gospels the Holy Spirit gives facts, and in the epistles we are given meanings, particularly in Romans, 1 Corinthians, Galatians and 1 Timothy; but Luke contains many precious gospel statements such as this one. The universal call of the gospel to "all nations, beginning at Jerusalem" is paralleled in Matt 28:19; Mark 16:15; Acts 1:8; 2:39; 10:43; Rom 3:29-31 and 1 John 2:2. It is touching that in the place where He was despised, rejected and crucified, the blessed news of forgiveness and salvation is to be first preached.

48   "Ye are witnesses" is directly related to the resurrection, but in a wider sense it includes all that He said and did. The word martyr comes from the word translated "witness". All but one of the eleven, it is claimed, were to be called to lay down their lives for their witness. In Luke's continuation of the story of the spread of the gospel, he enlarges on the theme of "Ye shall be witnesses unto me" which were the words by which they were commissioned (Acts 1:8); their witness that began at Jerusalem was "unto the uttermost part of the earth". Perhaps even closer to the truth expressed in v.48 is the statement of Acts 1:22 regarding the choice of Matthias, "ordained to be a witness with us of his resurrection".

6.   *The Ascension of the Lord Jesus*
24:49-53

> v.49 "And, behold, I send the promise of my Father upon you: but tarry ye in the city of Jerusalem, until ye be endued with power from on high.
> v.50 And he led them out as far as to Bethany, and he lifted up his hands, and blessed them.

> v.51 And it came to pass, while he blessed them, he was parted from them, and carried up into heaven.
> v.52 And they worshipped him, and returned to Jerusalem with great joy:
> v.53 And were continually in the temple, praising and blessing God. Amen."

49   At this point in the narrative we are given the link between Luke and Acts. It is at this point that Acts begins and more fully develops this great subject of the Lord Jesus ascending to heaven and sending the Holy Spirit. The coming of the Spirit would enable them to be witnesses. Any attempts at evangelism apart from this being "clothed with power from on high" (JND) is merely human activity that can never produce results for eternity.

50   This is a final scene. Bethany was the place of the home to which He had resorted from the clamour and rejection of the city. It was the location of the Mount of Olives where He had prayed in "an agony" and calmly accepted the Father's will. Now He stands with the little band on the mountain. He has been the Leader of His own to this outside place which, throughout the Gospels, is a beautiful picture of an assembly of His own gathered around their Lord. Lifting up holy, nail-printed hands, He blesses them.

51   In the act of blessing He is lifted from the midst of His disciples, parted from them, ascending into heaven, not just a heaven of clouds or stars, but into the very presence of God. Mark says, "he was received up into heaven, and sat on the right hand of God" (Mark 16:19). Peter said, "who is gone into heaven, and is on the right hand of God; angels and authorities and powers being made subject unto him" (1 Pet 3:22). It was a far different event than when He disappeared while breaking bread with the two at Emmaus. This is one of the greatest events of all that ever happened on earth and in heaven. He took His glorified Manhood to the throne above. There is a real Man in heaven.

52-53   Slow hearts have been quickened; closed eyes have been opened; ignorance of Scripture has been exchanged for understanding; weeping, sorrowing men have been filled with joy and worship, and closed mouths have been opened in praise. We thank God that this worship will continue for eternity.

Appendix 1
Links Between Luke and Acts

The Book of Acts was written to be the continuation of "all that Jesus began both to do and teach, until the day that he was taken up . . ." (Acts 1:1,2). Both books were addressed to the same man and intended to be two parts of the same subject. Luke describes His earthly ministry and Acts describes His ministry continued, directed from heaven by the ascended Lord through His servants who are indwelt and empowered by the Holy Spirit (Acts 1:8). Luke closes with the perfect accomplishment of His finished work on earth. Acts continues with an unfinished work, perfectly performed in heaven, while imperfect servants are His witnesses on earth.

Luke gives thirty-three years of the life and testimony of the Lord Jesus, in the localities of Galilee and Judaea. Acts gives thirty years of the life and testimony of believers who are gathered in local churches, spreading throughout the known world. Luke describes Christ as the meal offering of Lev 2 in which there was no leaven. Acts describes Jews and Gentiles who are saved and are the new meal offering of Lev 23 that was baked with leaven. In the gospel, the opposition of Satan reveals the perfections of the perfect Man and, in His sufferings, He triumphs over every foe. In Acts, the opposition of Satan reveals the weakness of persecuted saints, but in their suffering, by the power of the Spirit, they triumph over their foes.

Luke begins with the incarnation; Acts with the ascension of Christ. Luke gives the birth of Christ; Acts the birth of the Church. The birth of each is attributed to the power of the Holy Spirit (Luke 1:35; Acts 1:8). In the gospel, John is filled with the Spirit and baptises in water. In Acts, believers are baptised in water and filled with the Spirit. Luke demonstrates the power of the Holy Spirit in the birth, life and ministry of the Lord Jesus and promises the baptism of the Spirit to those who believe on Him. Acts records the fulfilment of the promise and gives the evidence of the Spirit's power in the disciples. In Luke, the Lord Jesus takes a body, and in perfect humanity reveals the heart of God. In Acts, Christ is revealed in His body, the church. Luke describes the footsteps of the Shepherd (1 Pet 2:21-25); Acts describes "the footsteps of the flock" (Songs 1:8).

In Luke, "the good tidings of great joy" (2:10) are declared by an angel from heaven to shepherds in an open field. In Acts, the good news of the gospel is declared to all nations and many hearts are opened to receive it. The Lord had foretold that the message of repentance would be preached in His name in all nations (Luke 24:47). Acts gives the account of how this was accomplished, and lays emphasis on all being done "in his name". In the Gospel, prayer is the constant recourse of the perfect Man. In the Acts, prayer is the recourse of imperfect servants in almost every chapter; therefore the Gospel pictures the Lord on His knees and, in Acts 4:31; 7:60; 12:5 and throughout the records of the early days of testimony, the saints were on their knees.

The Lord's supper is instituted in Luke 22:14-20 and consistently practised by the disciples after Pentecost (Acts 2:42). In Luke 24:35, the two disciples told the eleven in Jerusalem how the Lord "was known of them in breaking of bread". In Acts 2:42, the same word, "breaking" (*klasis*) is used. The teaching of the Lord at the institution of the supper continued into the night. In Acts 20:7, "On the first day of the week, when the disciples came together to break bread, Paul preached unto them . . . and continued his speech until midnight".

A major subject of the gospel is the journey of Christ to Jerusalem and what would befall Him there is foretold. From Acts 21, the main subject is the journey of Paul to Jerusalem and what would befall him there is foretold. Luke tells of Christ's agony in the garden and how he was "strengthened" (*enischuo*). The only other time that this word is used in the NT is about Paul in Acts 9:19. Of Christ, it was foretold, "reproach hath broken my heart" (Ps 69:20), and He prayed in the garden, "not my will, but thine be done" (Luke 22:42). Acts 21:13 tells of Paul's heart being broken, and the believers said, "The will of the Lord be done" (v.14).

Christ performed His last miracle on an injured man in the garden who was among the company who came to arrest Him (Luke 22:51). Paul performed his last miracle on a man after he had been arrested and was on his way to trial (Acts 28:8). The Lord foretold the future to His disciples to prepare them for persecution by wicked men (Luke 21). Paul foretold the future to the disciples to prepare them for the infiltration of wicked men (Acts 20:28-38). The Lord was first tried before religious leaders in Jerusalem and condemned by them before being sent to Herod and Pilate, Rome's governor in Judaea. Paul was condemned by religious leaders in Jerusalem before being sent to Herod Agrippa and Caesar, the emperor in Rome. Christ was charged with three counts in Luke and Paul was charged with three counts in Acts. Luke 24 records the last words of the Lord to His own; Acts 28 records Paul's last words to the Jews at Rome; in both cases the message of the Gospel would reach the nations of the world.

Appendix 2

Words in Luke

The following are a list of words that help to give to Luke a unique character among the Synoptic gospels and among the books of the NT. All of these words are peculiar to Luke's writings and are not found elsewhere in any NT writer except in a few cases where another reference is noted. Many of these words are dealt with in the commentary. The figure in brackets after the verse number indicates the number of times the word occurs in Luke or Luke-Acts. Many of these words are found frequently in the LXX and the papyri.

Chapter 1
"forasmuch" (*epeidēper*) v.1 (2)
"taken in hand" (*epicheireō*) v.1 (3)
"to set forth in order" (*anatassomai*) v.1 (1)
"declaration" (*diēgesis*) v.1 (1)
"eyewitness" (*autoptēs*) v.2 (1)
"in order" (*kathexēs*) v.3 (5)
"certainty" (*asphaleia*) v.4 (2); also in 1 Thess 5:3
"course" (*ephēmeria*) vv.5,8 (2)
"executed the priest's office" (*hierateuō*) v.8 (1)
"to burn incense" (*thumiaō*) v.9 (1)
"strong drink" (*sikera*) v.15 (1)
"beckoned" (*dianeuō*) v.22 (1)
"hid" (*perikruptō*) v.24 (1)
"reproach" (*oneidos*) v.25 (1)
"was troubled" (*diatarassō*) v.29 (1)
"cousin" (*sungenis*) v.36 (1)
"old age" (*gēras*) v.36 (1)
"hill country" (*oreinos*) v.39 (2)
"leaped" (*skirtaō*) v.41 (3)
"she spake out" (*anaphōneō*) v.42 (1)
"neighbours" (*perioikos*) v.58 (1)
"made signs" (*enneuō*) v.62 (1)
"writing table" (*pinakidion*) v.63 (1)
"dwelt round about" (*perioikeō*) v.65 (1)
"were noised abroad" (*dialaleō*) v.65 (2)
"shewing" (*anadeixis*) v.80 (1).

Chapter 2
"governor" (*hēgemoneuō*) v.2 (3)
"being great with child" (*enkuos*) v.5 (1)
"manger" (*phatne*) v.7 (3)

"abiding in the field" (*agrauleō*) v.8 (1)
"a pair" (*zeugos*) v.24 (2)
"turtledove" (*trugōn*) v.24 (1)
"young" (*nossos*) v.24 (1)
"custom" (ethizō) v.27 (1)
"virginity" (*parthenia*) v.36 (1)
"gave thanks" (*anthomologeomai*) v.38 (1)
"company" (*sunodia*) v.44 (1)

Chapter 3
"being tetrarch" (*tetrarcheō*) v.1 (1)
"smooth" (*leois*) v.5 (1)
"accuse falsely" (*sukophanteō*) v.14 (2)
"do violence" (*diaseiō*) v.14 (1)
"will through purge" (*diakathairō*) v.17 (1)
"tetrarch" (*tetrarchēs*) v.19 (3); also in Matt 14:1

Chapter 4
"moment" (*stigmē*) v.5 (1)
"to keep" (*diaphulassō*) v.10 (1)
"captive" (*aichmalōtos*) v.18 (1)
"recovering of sight" (*anablepsis*) v.10 (1)
"are bruised" (*thrauō*) v.18 (1)
"closed" (*ptussō*) v.20 (1)
"cast down" (*katakremnizō*) v.29 (1)
"brow" (*ophrus*) v.29 (1)
"amazed" (*thambos*) v.36 (3)

Chapter 5
"draught" (*agra*) vv.4,9 (2)
"beckoned" (*kataneuō*) v.7 (1)
"began to sink" (*buthizō*) v.7 (1); also in 1 Tim 6:9
"to have round" (*periechō*) v.9; also in 1 Pet 2:6
"shalt catch" (*zōgreō*) v.10 (1); also in 2 Tim 2:26
"withdrew" (*huperchōreō*) v.16 (2)
"tiling" (*keramos*) v.19 (1)
"strange things" (*paradoxos*) v.26 (1)
"feast" (*dochē*) v.29 (2)
"must be put" (*blēteos*) v.38 (1)

Chapter 6
"rubbing" (*psōchō*) v.1 (1)
"communed" (*dialaleō*) v.11 (2)

"continued all night" (*dianuktereuō*) v.12 (1)
"plain" (*pedinos*) v.17 (1)
"sea coast" (*paralios*) v.17 (1)
"laugh" (*gelaō*) vv.21,25 (2)
"leap" (*skirtaō*) v.23 (3)
"hoping for nothing again" (*apelizō*) v.35 (1)
"pressed down" (*plezō*) v.38 (1)
"running over (*huperekchunnō*) v.38 (1)
"measured in return" (*antimetreō*) v.38 (1)
"bringeth forth" (*propherō*) v.45 (twice), (2)
"digged" (*skaptō*) v.48 (3)
"deep" (*bathunō*) v.48 (1)
"flood" (*plēmurra*) v.48 (1)
"ruin" (*rhēgma*) v.49 (1)

Chapter 7
'trouble" (*skullō*) v.6 (2); also in Matt 9:36; Mark 5:35
"was being carried out" (*ekkomizō*) v.12 (1)
"bier" (*soros*) v.14 (1)
"creditor" (*danistēs*) v.41 (1)
"ceased" (*dialeipō*) v.45 (1)

Chapter 8
"went throughout" (*diadeuō*) v1 (2)
"were gathered together" (*suneimi*) v.4 (3)
"were come to him" (*epiporeuomai*) v.4 (1)
"fell" (*katapiptō*) v.6 (3)
"sprang up with" (*sumphuo*) v.7 (1)
"bring to perfection" (*telesphoreō*) v.14 (1)
"to come at" (*suntunchanō*) v.19 (1)
"he fell asleep" (*aphupnoō*) v.23 (1)
"were filled with water" (*sumpleroō*) v.23 (3)
"over against" (*antipera*) v.26 (1)
"had caught" (*sunarpazō*) v.29 (4); cf. Acts 27:15
"gladly received" (*apodechomai*) v.40 (6)
"press' (*apothlibō*) v.45 (1)

Chapter 9
"shake off" (*apotinassō*) v.5 (2); cf. Acts 28:5
"was much perplexed" (*diaporeō*) v.7 (4)
"went aside" (*huperchōreō*) v.10 (2)
"received" (*apodechomai*) v.11 (6); cf. 8:40
"victuals" (*episitismos*) v.12 (1)

"companies" (*klisia*) v.14 (1)
"with him" (*suneimi*) v.18 (3); cf. 8:4
"glistering" (*exastraptō*) v.29 (1)
"when they were awake" (*diagrēgoreō*) v.32 (1)
"departed from" (*diachōrizō*) v.33 (1)
"next day" (*hexēs*) v.37 (5)
"foam" (*aphros*) v.39 (1)
"perceived" (*aisthanomai*) v.45 (1)
"hid" (*parakaluptō*) v.45 (1)
"time was come" (*sumpleroō*) v.51 (3); cf. 8:23
"received up" (*analēmpsis*) v.51 (1)
"master" (*epistatēs*) v.49 (6)
"plough" (*arotron*) v.62 (1)

Chapter 10
"appointed" (*anadeiknumi*) v.1 (2)
"lambs" (*arēn*) v.3 (1)
"wipe off" (*apomassō*) v.11 (1)
"half dead" (*hēmithanēs*) v.30 (1)
"by chance" (*sunkuria*) v.31 (1)
"passed by on the other side" (*antiparerchomai*) vv.31,32 (2)
"as he journeyed" (*hodeuō*) v.33 (1)
"bound up (*katadeō*) v.34 (1)
"wounds" (*trauma*) v.34 (1)
"pouring in" (*epicheō*) v.34 (1)
"inn" (*pandocheion*) v.34 (1)
"host" (*pandocheus*) v.35 (1)
"when I come again" (*epanerchomai*) v.35 (2); cf. 19:15
"thou spendest more" (*prosdapanaō*) v.35 (1)
"sat at" (*parakathezomai*) v.39 (1)
"was cumbered" (*perispaō*) v.40 (1)
"troubled" (*thorubazō*) v.41 (1)

Chapter 11
"lend" (*chraō*) v.5 (1)
"importunity" (*anaidia*) v.8 (1)
"thoughts" (*dianoēma*) v.17 (1)
"armed" (*kathoplizō*) v.21 (1)
"spoils" (*skulon*) v.22 91)
"were gathered thick together" (*epathroizō*) v.29 (1)
"grievous to be borne" (*dusbastaktos*) v.46 (1)
"touch" (*prospsauō*) v.46 (1)
"provoke" (*apostomatizō*) v.53 (1)

"catch" (*thēreuō*) v.54 (1)
"laying wait" (*enedreuō*) v.54 (2); cf. Acts 23:21

Chapter 12
"covered" (*sunkaluptō*) v.2 (1)
"to cast into" (*emballō*) v.5 (1)
"divider" (*meristēs*) v.14 (1)
"brought forth plentifully" (*euphoreō*) v.16 (1)
"clothe" (*amphiennumi*) v.28 (2); also in Matt 6:30; 11:8
"shall be required" (*apaiteō*) v.20 (2); cf. 6:30
"ravens" (*korax*) v.24 (1)
"spin" (*nēthō*) v.27 (1); also in Matt 6:28
"of doubtful mind" (*meteorizō*) v.29 (1)
"that faileth not" (*anekleiptos*) v.33 (1)
"portion of meat" (*sitometrion*) v.42 (1)
"division" (*diamerismos*) v.51 (1)
"shower" (*ombros*) v.54 91)
"hale" (to the judge) (*katasurō*) v.58 (1)
"officer" (*praktōr*) v.58 (2)

Chapter 13
"dresser of his vineyard" (*ampelourgos*) v.7 (1)
"dung" (*koprion*) v.8 (1)
"dig" (*skaptō*) v.8 (3)
"bowed together" (*sunkuptō*) v.11 (1)
"was made straight" (*anorthoō*) v.13 (2); also in Heb 12:12
"stall" (*phatnē*) v.15 (4)
"hath shut to" (*apokleiō*) v.25 91)
"do cures" (*iasis*) v.32 (3)
"brood" (*nossia*) v.34 (1)

Chapter 14
"watch" (*paratēreō*) v.1 (4); also in Mark 3:2; Gal 4:10
"dropsy" (*hudrōpikos*) v.2 (1)
"will pull out" (*anaspaō*) v.5 (2)
"chief rooms" (*prōtoklisia*) vv.7,8 (3); also in Matt 23:6; Mark 12:39
"go up" (*prosanabainō*) v.10 (1)
"bid thee again" (*antikaleō*) v.12 (1)
"maimed" (*anapēros*) vv.13,21 (2)
"feast" (*dochē*) vv.13,29 (3)
"yoke" (*zeugos*) v.19 (2)
"to finish" (*apartismos*) v.28 (1)
"to finish" (*ekteleō*) vv.29,30 (2)

"to make" (war) (*sumballō*) v.31 (6)
"embassage" (*presbeia*) v.32 (2)
"dunghill" (*kopria*) v.35 (1)

Chapter 15
"murmured" (*diagonuzō*) v.2 (2); cf. 19:7
"diligently" (*epimelos*) v.8 (1)
"goods", substance (*ouisia*) vv.12,13 (2)
"riotous" (*asōtōs*) v.13 (1)
"husks" (*keration*) v.16 (1)
"hired servants" (*misthios*) vv.17,19 (2)
"ring" (*daktulios*) v.22 (1)
"fatted" (*siteutos*) vv.15,27,30 (3)
"music" (*sumphōnia*) v.25 (1)
"dancing" (*choros*) v.25 (1)

Chapter 16
"was accused" (*diaballō*) v.1 (1)
"steward" (*oikonomeō*) v.2 (1)
"dig" (*skaptō*) v.3 (3)
"to beg" (*epaiteō*) v.3 (1)
"debtors" (*chreōpheiletēs*) v.5 (2); cf. 7:41
"measure" (*batos*) v.6 (1)
"scoffed" (*ekmuktērizō*) v.14 (2); cf. 23:35
"sumptuously" (*lamprōs*) v.19 (1)
"fine linen" (*bussos*) v.19 (1)
"sores" (*helkos*) v.21 (1); also in Rev 16:2,11
"licked" (*epileichō*) v.21 (1)
"cool" (*katapsuchō*) v.24 (1)
"great gulf" (*chasma*) v.26 (1)
"tormented" (*odunaō*) vv.24,25 (4); cf. 2:48; Acts 20:38

Chapter 17
"impossible" (*anendektos*) v.1 (1)
"millstone" (*mulikos*) v.2 (1)
"sycamine" (*sukaminos*) v.6 (1); cf. 19:4
"unprofitable" (*achreios*) v.10 (1); also in Matt 25:30
"stranger" (*allogenēs*) v.18 (1)
"observation" (*paratērēsis*) v.20 (1)
"lighteneth" (*astraptō*) v.24 (2); cf.24:4

Chapter 18
"avenge" (*ekdikeō*) vv.3,5 (2); also in Rom 12:19; 2 Cor 10:6; Rev 6:10; 19:2
"tithes" (*apodekateuō*) v.12 (1); cf. 11:42; Matt 23:23; Heb 7:5
"needle" (*belonē*) v.25 (1)
"manifold more" (*pollaplasiōn*) v.30 (1)
"beggar" (*prosaitēs*) v.35 (1); also in John 9:8

Chapter 19
"chief tax-collector" (*architelōnēs*) v.2 (1)
"murmured" (*diagonguzō*) v.7 (2); cf. 15:2
"false accusation" (*sukophanteō*) v.8 (2); cf. 3:14
"fourfold" (*anaphainō*) v.11 (2); cf. Acts 21:3
"a message" (*presbeia*) v.14 (2); cf. 14:32
"gained by trading" (*diapragmateuomai*) v.15 (1)
"gain" (*prosergazomai*) v.16 (1)
"austere" (*austerōs*) vv.21,22 (2)
"slay" (*katasphazō*) v.27 (1)
"olive" (*elaiōn*) v.29 (3); cf. 21:37; Acts 1:12
"spread" (*hupostrōnnuō*) v.36 (1)
"descent" (*katabasis*) v.37 (1)
"trench" (*charax*) v.43 (1)
"compass round" (*perikukloō*) v.43 (1)
"shall dash to the ground" (*edaphizō*) v.44 (1)
"attentive", to hang upon (*ekkremannumi*) v.48 (1)

Chapter 20
"stone" (*katalithazō*) v.6 (1)
"wounded" (*traumatizō*) v.12 (2); cf. Acts 19:16
"it may be" (*isōs*) v.13 (1)
"spy" (*enkathetos*) v.20 (1)
"childless" (*ateknos*) vv.28-30 (3)
"marriage" (*gamiskō*) vv.34,35 (2); also in Mark 12:25
"equal to angels" (*isangelos*) v.36 (1)

Chapter 21
"poor" (*penichros*) v.2 (1)
"gifts" (*anathēma*) v.5 (1)
"terrified" (*ptoeō*) v.9 (2); cf. 24:37
"pestilence" (*laimos*) v.11 (2); cf. Acts 24:5
"to meditate before" (*promeletaō*) v.14 (1)
"gainsay" (*anteipon*) v.15 (2); cf. Acts 4:14
"encompassed" (*kukloō*) v.20 (2)
"perplexity" (*aporia*) v.25 (1)

"waves" (*salos*) v.25 (1)
"roaring" (*ēchos*) v.25 (1)
"failing" (*apopsuchō*) v.26 (1)
"looking after" (*prosdokia*) v.26 (2); cf. 12:11
"shoot forth" (*proballō*) v.30 (2); cf. Acts 19:33
"surfeiting" (*kraipalē*) v.34 (1)
"olive" (*elaiōn*) v.37 (3); cf. 19:29; Acts 1:12
"came early in the morning" (*orthrizō*) v.38 (1)

Chapter 22
"captains" (*stratēgos*) v.4 (10)
"in the absence" (*ater*) v.6 (2); cf. v.35, "without purse"
"strife" (*philoneikia*) v.24 (1)
"desired" (*exaiteomai*) v.31 (1)
"strengthening" (*enischuō*) v.43 (2); cf. Acts 9:19
"agony" (*agōnia*) v.44 (1)
"drop" (*thrombos*) v.44 (1)
"sweat" (*hidrōs*) v.44 (1)
"kindled" (*periaptō*) v.55 (1)

Chapter 23
"vehemently" (*eutonōs*) v.10 (1)
"before" (*prouparchō*) v.12 (2); cf. Acts 8:9
"all at once" (*pamplēthei*) v.18 (1)
"cried" (*epiphōneō*) v.21 (4)
"gave sentence" (*epikrinō*) v.24 (1)
"hills" (*bounos*) v.30 (2); cf. 3:5
"green" (*hugros*) v.31 (1)
"sight" (*theōria*) v.48 (1)
"not consented with" (*sunkatatithēmi*) v.51 (1)
"hewn in stone" (*laxeutos*) v.53 (1)
"following after" (*katakoloutheō*) v.55 (2); cf. Acts 16:17

Chapter 24
"early" (*orthros*) v.1 (2); also in John 8:2
"shining" (*astraptō*) v.4 (2); cf. 17:24
"idle tales" (*lēros*) v.11 (1)
"talked together", "communed together" (*homileō*) vv.14,15 (4)
"one to another", "exchange thoughts" (*antiballō*) v.17 (1)
"before" (*enantion*) v.19 (4)
"early" (*orthrinos*) v.22 (1); cf. v.1 (*orthros*)
"constrained" (*parabiazomai*) v.29 (2); cf. Acts 16:15
"evening" (*hespera*) v.29 (3)

"made as though" (*prospoieō*) v.28 (1)
"sat at meat" (*kataklinō*) v.30 (5)
"vanished" (*aphantos*) v.31 (1)
"gathered together" (*athroizō*) v.33 (1)
"breaking" (*klasis*) v.35 (2); cf. Acts 2:42
"terrified" (*ptoeō*) v.37 (2); cf. 21:9
"meat" (*brōsimos*) v.41 (1)
"broiled" (*optos*) v.42 (1)
"parted" (*diistēmi*) v.51 (4)